IFIP Advances in Information and Communication Technology 626

Editor-in-Chief

Kai Rannenberg, Goethe University Frankfurt, Germany

Editorial Board Members

TC 1 – Foundations of Computer Science
Luís Soares Barbosa, University of Minho, Braga, Portugal

TC 2 – Software: Theory and Practice
Michael Goedicke, University of Duisburg-Essen, Germany

TC 3 – Education
Arthur Tatnall, Victoria University, Melbourne, Australia

TC 5 – Information Technology Applications
Erich J. Neuhold, University of Vienna, Austria

TC 6 – Communication Systems
Burkhard Stiller, University of Zurich, Zürich, Switzerland

TC 7 – System Modeling and Optimization
Fredi Tröltzsch, TU Berlin, Germany

TC 8 – Information Systems
Jan Pries-Heje, Roskilde University, Denmark

TC 9 – ICT and Society
David Kreps, National University of Ireland, Galway, Ireland

TC 10 – Computer Systems Technology
Ricardo Reis, Federal University of Rio Grande do Sul, Porto Alegre, Brazil

TC 11 – Security and Privacy Protection in Information Processing Systems
Steven Furnell, Plymouth University, UK

TC 12 – Artificial Intelligence
Eunika Mercier-Laurent, University of Reims Champagne-Ardenne, Reims, France

TC 13 – Human-Computer Interaction
Marco Winckler, University of Nice Sophia Antipolis, France

TC 14 – Entertainment Computing
Rainer Malaka, University of Bremen, Germany

IFIP – The International Federation for Information Processing

IFIP was founded in 1960 under the auspices of UNESCO, following the first World Computer Congress held in Paris the previous year. A federation for societies working in information processing, IFIP's aim is two-fold: to support information processing in the countries of its members and to encourage technology transfer to developing nations. As its mission statement clearly states:

> *IFIP is the global non-profit federation of societies of ICT professionals that aims at achieving a worldwide professional and socially responsible development and application of information and communication technologies.*

IFIP is a non-profit-making organization, run almost solely by 2500 volunteers. It operates through a number of technical committees and working groups, which organize events and publications. IFIP's events range from large international open conferences to working conferences and local seminars.

The flagship event is the IFIP World Computer Congress, at which both invited and contributed papers are presented. Contributed papers are rigorously refereed and the rejection rate is high.

As with the Congress, participation in the open conferences is open to all and papers may be invited or submitted. Again, submitted papers are stringently refereed.

The working conferences are structured differently. They are usually run by a working group and attendance is generally smaller and occasionally by invitation only. Their purpose is to create an atmosphere conducive to innovation and development. Refereeing is also rigorous and papers are subjected to extensive group discussion.

Publications arising from IFIP events vary. The papers presented at the IFIP World Computer Congress and at open conferences are published as conference proceedings, while the results of the working conferences are often published as collections of selected and edited papers.

IFIP distinguishes three types of institutional membership: Country Representative Members, Members at Large, and Associate Members. The type of organization that can apply for membership is a wide variety and includes national or international societies of individual computer scientists/ICT professionals, associations or federations of such societies, government institutions/government related organizations, national or international research institutes or consortia, universities, academies of sciences, companies, national or international associations or federations of companies.

More information about this series at http://www.springer.com/series/6102

Luis M. Camarinha-Matos ·
Pedro Ferreira · Guilherme Brito (Eds.)

Technological Innovation for Applied AI Systems

12th IFIP WG 5.5/SOCOLNET
Advanced Doctoral Conference on Computing,
Electrical and Industrial Systems, DoCEIS 2021
Costa de Caparica, Portugal, July 7–9, 2021
Proceedings

Springer

Editors
Luis M. Camarinha-Matos
NOVA University of Lisbon
Monte Caparica, Portugal

Pedro Ferreira
NOVA University of Lisbon
Monte Caparica, Portugal

Guilherme Brito
NOVA University of Lisbon
Monte Caparica, Portugal

ISSN 1868-4238 ISSN 1868-422X (electronic)
IFIP Advances in Information and Communication Technology
ISBN 978-3-030-78290-0 ISBN 978-3-030-78288-7 (eBook)
https://doi.org/10.1007/978-3-030-78288-7

© IFIP International Federation for Information Processing 2021, corrected publication 2022
Chapters “Characteristics of Adaptable Control of Production Systems and the Role of Self-organization Towards Smart Manufacturing” and “Predictive Manufacturing: Enabling Technologies, Frameworks and Applications” are licensed under the terms of the Creative Commons Attribution 4.0 International License (http://creativecommons.org/licenses/by/4.0/). For further details see license information in the chapter.
This work is subject to copyright. All rights are reserved by the Publisher, whether the whole or part of the material is concerned, specifically the rights of translation, reprinting, reuse of illustrations, recitation, broadcasting, reproduction on microfilms or in any other physical way, and transmission or information storage and retrieval, electronic adaptation, computer software, or by similar or dissimilar methodology now known or hereafter developed.
The use of general descriptive names, registered names, trademarks, service marks, etc. in this publication does not imply, even in the absence of a specific statement, that such names are exempt from the relevant protective laws and regulations and therefore free for general use.
The publisher, the authors and the editors are safe to assume that the advice and information in this book are believed to be true and accurate at the date of publication. Neither the publisher nor the authors or the editors give a warranty, expressed or implied, with respect to the material contained herein or for any errors or omissions that may have been made. The publisher remains neutral with regard to jurisdictional claims in published maps and institutional affiliations.

This Springer imprint is published by the registered company Springer Nature Switzerland AG
The registered company address is: Gewerbestrasse 11, 6330 Cham, Switzerland

Preface

This proceedings, which collects selected results produced in engineering doctoral programs, focuses on research and development in technological innovation for applied Artificial Intelligence systems. Artificial Intelligence (AI) is a branch of computer science for which purpose is to replicate human intelligence based on computational means. AI is shaping and rebuilding society's basic constructs - such as the economy, health, education, and lifestyle - and having an impact on people's lives through the implementation of intelligent algorithms in everyday applications, and promoting technological advancements that allow for a better and more sustainable quality of life. AI is expected to become an important vehicle for large-scale economic and technological growth, like previous revolutionary technologies such as the steam engine, electricity, and the internet. AI techniques (e.g., machine learning and deep learning, automated reasoning, and planning) can be applied to several knowledge areas, from electronics and energy to the biomedical field and industrial collaborative networks, providing impactful technological developments that can result in the enhancement of healthcare, the environment, manufacturing, transportation, and communication systems across the globe. AI is forecasted to have a substantial influence across all sectors of industry and services, and is therefore of paramount importance for both industrial and research innovation.

The 12th Advanced Doctoral Conference on Computing, Electrical and Industrial Systems (DoCEIS 2021) aimed to provide a venue for the exchange and discussion of ideas and results from doctoral research in various inter-related areas of engineering, while promoting a strong multi-disciplinary dialog. Furthermore, the conference aimed to create collaborative opportunities for young researchers as well as an effective way of collecting valuable feedback from colleagues in a welcoming environment. As such, participants were challenged to look beyond the specific technical aspects of their research question and relate their work to the selected theme of the conference, namely, to identify in which ways their research topics can contribute to the technological innovation in applied AI systems. Furthermore, current trends in strategic research programs point to the fundamental role of multi-disciplinary and interdisciplinary approaches in innovation. More and more funding agencies are including this element as a key requirement in their research agendas. In this context, the challenge proposed by DoCEIS 2021 contributed to the process of acquiring such skills, which are becoming essential in the research profession [1].

DoCEIS 2021, which was sponsored by SOCOLNET, IFIP, and IEEE IES, attracted a good number of paper submissions from a good number of PhD students and their supervisors from 16 countries. This book comprises the works selected by the International Program Committee for inclusion in the main program and covers a wide spectrum of application domains. As such, research results and on-going work are presented, illustrated, and discussed in areas such as

- Collaborative Networks
- Smart Manufacturing
- Cyber-Physical Systems and Digital Twins
- Intelligent Decision Making
- Smart Energy Management
- Communications and Electronics
- Classification Systems
- Smart Healthcare Systems
- Medical Devices

We hope that this collection of papers will provide readers with an inspiring set of new ideas and challenges, presented in a multi-disciplinary context, and that by their diversity these results can trigger and motivate richer research and development directions.

We would like to thank all the authors for their contributions. We also appreciate the efforts and dedication of the DoCEIS International Program Committee members, who both helped with the selection of articles and contributed valuable comments to improve the quality of papers.

April 2021

Luis M. Camarinha-Matos
Pedro Ferreira
Guilherme Brito

Reference

1. L. M. Camarinha-Matos, J. Goes, L. Gomes, P. Pereira (2020). Soft and Transferable Skills Acquisition through Organizing a Doctoral Conference. *Education Sciences* 10(9), 235. DOI: https://doi.org/10.3390/educsci10090235

Organization

12th IFIP/SOCOLNET Advanced Doctoral Conference on Computing, Electrical and Industrial Systems
Costa de Caparica, Portugal, July 7–9, 2021

Conference and Program Chair

Luis M. Camarinha-Matos	NOVA University of Lisbon, Portugal

Organizing Committee Co-chairs

Luis Gomes	NOVA University of Lisbon, Portugal
João Goes	NOVA University of Lisbon, Portugal
João Martins	NOVA University of Lisbon, Portugal

International Program Committee

Antonio Abreu, Portugal
Vanja Ambrozic, Slovenia
Frederick Bénaben, France
Luis Bernardo, Portugal
Xavier Boucher, France
Giuseppe Buja, Italy
Luis M. Camarinha-Matos, Portugal
Ricardo Carelli, Argentina
Laura Carnevali, Italy
Wojciech Cellary, Poland
Noelia Correia, Portugal
Jose de la Rosa, Spain
Filipa Ferrada, Portugal
Florin G. Filip, Romania
Maria Helena Fino, Portugal
Adrian Florea, Romania
José M. Fonseca, Portugal
Rosanna Fornasiero, Italy
Paulo Gil, Portugal
João Goes, Portugal
Luis Gomes, Portugal
Juanqiong Gou, China
Paul Grefen, Netherlands
Michael Huebner, Germany
Ricardo Jardim-Gonçalves, Portugal
Tomasz Janowski, Poland
Vladimir Katic, Serbia
Asal Kiazadeh, Portugal
Evgeny Kuzmin, Russia
Matthieu Lauras, France
Marin Lujak, France
João Martins, Portugal
Rui Melicio, Portugal
Paulo Miyagi, Brazil
Filipe Moutinho, Portugal
Horacio Neto, Portugal
Paulo Novais, Portugal
Luis Oliveira, Portugal
Rodolfo Oliveira, Portugal
Angel Ortiz, Spain
Peter Palensky, Austria
Luis Palma, Portugal

Nuno Paulino, Portugal
Pedro Pereira, Portugal
Paulo Pinto, Portugal
Armando Pires, Portugal
Ricardo J. Rabelo, Brazil
Luis Ribeiro, Sweden
Juan Rodriguez-Andina, Spain
Enrique Romero-Cadaval, Spain
Carlos Roncero, Spain
Imre Rudas, Hungary
Roberto Sabatini, Australia
Ioan Sacala, Romania
Eduard Shevtshenko, Estonia
Thomas Strasser, Austria
Zoltán Ádám Tamus, Hungary
Kleanthis Thramboulidis, Greece
Damien Trentesaux, France
Manuela Vieira, Portugal
Ramon Vilanova, Spain
Valery Vyatkin, Sweeden
Lai Xu, UK
Soufi Youcef, France

Local Organizing Committee (PhD Students)

Guilherme Brito, Portugal
Pedro Ferreira, Portugal
Daniel Dias, Portugal
Ali Gashtasbi, Portugal/Iran
Carlos Marques, Portugal
Ricardo Martins, Portugal
João Pires, Portugal
Omid Nasrollahi, Portugal/Iran
Dyar Fadhil, Portugal/Iraq
Ayman Abu Sabah, Portugal/Jordan
Luis Estrada, Portugal/Ecuador

Medical Devices Special Session Organizers

Hugo Gamboa, Portugal
Mauro Guerra, Portugal
Alda Moreno, Portugal
Carla Pereira, Portugal
Cláudia Quaresma, Portugal
José Paulo Santos, Portugal
Valentina Vassilenko, Portugal
Ricardo Vigário, Portugal

Technical Sponsors

Society of Collaborative Networks

Project

IFIP WG 5.5 COVE
Co-Operation infrastructure for Virtual Enterprises
and electronic business

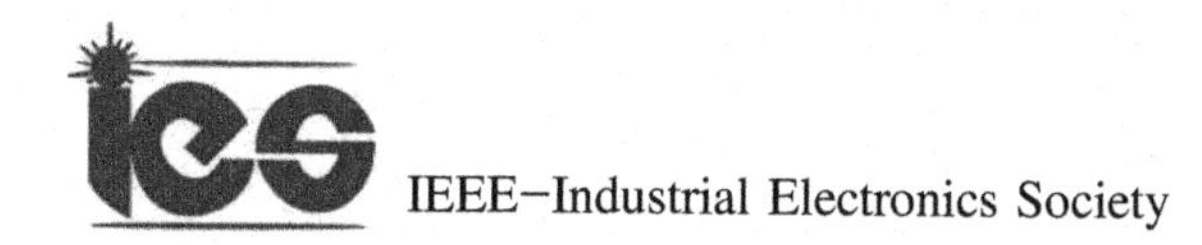

IEEE−Industrial Electronics Society

Organizational Sponsors

Organized by:

PhD Program in Electrical and Computer Engineering,
in collaboration with PhD Program in Biomedical Engineering
School of Science and Technology - NOVA University of Lisbon

Contents

Collaborative Networks

Smart Manufacturing

Cyber-Physical Systems and Digital Twins

Communications and Electronics

Classification Systems

Smart Healthcare Systems

Medical Devices

Collaborative Networks

AI and Simulation for Performance Assessment in Collaborative Business Ecosystems

Paula Graça[1,2](✉) and Luís M. Camarinha-Matos[1](✉)

[1] School of Science and Technology and Uninova CTS, NOVA University of Lisbon, Campus de Caparica, 2829-516 Caparica, Portugal
paula.graca@isel.pt, cam@uninova.pt

[2] Instituto Superior de Engenharia de Lisboa, Instituto Politécnico de Lisboa, Rua Conselheiro Emídio Navarro 1, 1959-007 Lisbon, Portugal

Abstract. Artificial Intelligence advances have enabled smarter systems, which in the business world, particularly in Collaborative Business Ecosystems, can lead to more streamlined, effective, and sustainable processes. Moreover, the use of well-defined performance indicators to assess the organisations' collaboration level can influence their behaviour, expecting to improve their performance and that of the ecosystem. This paper presents a case study using a simulation and agent-based model to represent the organisations' behaviour. True data gathered from three IT industry organisations running in the same business ecosystem allowed to shape the model with three classes of agents with different collaboration willingness levels. As such, some scenarios are simulated and discussed, considering a CBE populated with a given combination of organisations and a variation of the weighted adopted performance indicators.

Keywords: Collaborative networks · Business ecosystem · Performance indicators · Simulation · Agent-based modelling · Reinforcement learning

1 Introduction

Artificial Intelligence (AI) progress have enabled smarter systems, which in the business world, particularly in Collaborative Business Ecosystems (CBEs), can streamline collaborative processes among organisations, promoting its sustainability and resilience [1]. We adopted the name CBE [2] according to Moore's view [3], who was the first to introduce the term Business Ecosystem inspired by biological ecosystems, and according to Camarinha-Matos and Afsarmanesh's taxonomy of a Collaborative Network (CN) [4, 5], to highlight the collaboration aspect of our view of a business ecosystem.

An essential facet in this context is evaluating the collaboration performance between organisations in an ecosystem to identify potential earnings. On the one hand, many studies can be found in the literature at the network level, supporting broad theories on inter-organisational networks, many of them highlighting the capabilities that come with it [6]. However, just a few studies on business networks can be found [7] and more particularly on evaluating their collaboration, despite some performance assessment attempts.

© IFIP International Federation for Information Processing 2021

Published by Springer Nature Switzerland AG 2021
L. M. Camarinha-Matos et al. (Eds.): DoCEIS 2021, IFIP AICT 626, pp. 3–15, 2021.
https://doi.org/10.1007/978-3-030-78288-7_1

Some examples of such attempts include: (i) A proposal of indicators of collaboration and for relationship and assets analysis in CNs [8, 9]; (ii) Suggestions of using balanced scorecards in CNs [10, 11] and supply chain management [12–14]; (iii) various methods and metrics to measure the performance of supply chain collaboration [15–18]; and (iv) Structural analysis of the relationships that link actors in social network analysis as an essential input for the design of performance indicators [19].

The identification of this need motivated our work, driven by the following research question:

What can be a suitable approach to assess collaboration performance and promote collaboration sustainability in a collaborative business ecosystem?

Collaboration is a key element of sustainability, deriving its benefits from differences in perspectives, knowledge and approaches. It also solves problems while offering benefits to all the participants in the process [20]. Some frequent benefits include optimising human and financial capital, access to the markets and knowledge, the emergence of creativity by utilising diversity of participants' backgrounds, more efficient use of resources, and shorter time to reach objectives [20]. As such, we argue that promoting collaboration in a CBE is an incentive towards its sustainability.

This paper presents a case study using a CBE simulation model, previously proposed in [21], populated with agents representing the organisations whose behaviour is modelled using true data gathered during the year 2019 from companies running in the same ecosystem in the IT industry. The organisations have different profiles classified into classes of collaboration willingness that characterize their collaborative behaviour and their response when assessed by a Performance Assessment framework proposed in [22]. Similar to individuals, when organisations know how they are measured, it is expected that they adjust their behaviour in order to increase their evaluation results. Thus, this study aims to show that the organisations' collaboration performance and that of the ecosystem can be improved by the CBE Manager, using the Influence Mechanism proposed in [23].

The remaining sections are organised as follows: section two presents the relationship with innovation in Artificial Intelligence systems; section three presents the simulation model, describes the true data used to configure the agents' behaviour, briefly explains the performance assessment and the influence mechanism, details the internal behaviour of an agent and finally presents and discusses the simulation results of different scenarios; the last section contains a summary of the study, refers the ongoing work and identifies future work.

2 Relationship with Innovation in Artificial Intelligence Systems

Facing today's challenges and supporting the digital transition encourages organizations to apply Artificial Intelligence (AI) to their business areas to improve sustainability and quality of life. Efforts have been made in AI to build rational agents capable of perceiving the world and taking actions to advance specified goals [24]. In our case, a CBE can be modelled with reasoning agents that simulate companies' behaviour as a mean to understand the pattern of decisions that produce value.

This work presents a CBE simulation model to assess the influence of collaboration among organisations. The CBE is seen as a community of agents that interact, creating relationships to accomplish business opportunities. A particular emphasis is put on modelling the behaviour and reasoning mechanisms of the various agents. The work also focuses on understanding how a chosen set of performance indicators can influence the behaviour of those agents and the global performance of the CBE.

The use of Reinforcement Learning (RL), as illustrated in Fig. 1, a field of AI increasingly applicable to real-life problems [25], can lead to optimized decisions in the CBE. Applied to the performance assessment of a CBE, RL can play a role by training some agents, i.e. some organisations (O_1, O_2, O_3, ..., O_n) in the CBE simulation model, to learn the best collaboration decisions to optimise their performance, and consequently, that of the CBE. This aspect corresponds to a planned extension to the performed work described in this paper.

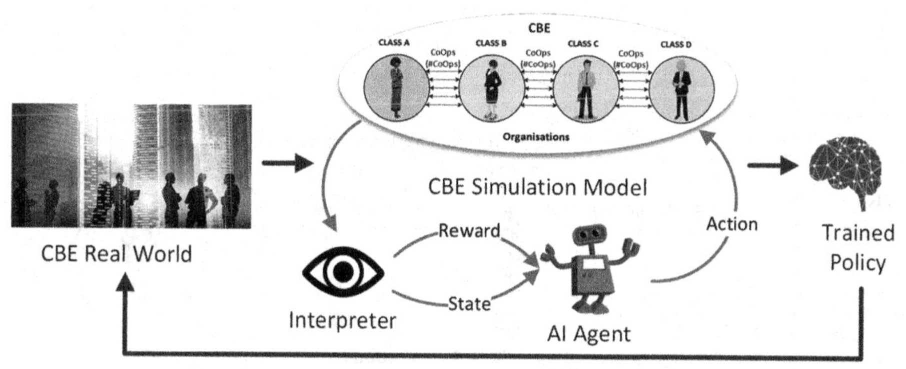

Fig. 1. Reinforcement Learning applied to a CBE simulation model for performance assessment and optimization

3 The Simulation Model

Considering the simulation objectives of this study in evaluating the performance of CBEs, we adopted the Performance Assessment and Adjustment Model (PAAM) [21], illustrated in Fig. 2, which is designed using AnyLogic tools [26]. A CBE model can be represented as a business environment composed of organisations collaborating in response to market opportunities. These collaborations are relationships between the organisations expressed in collaboration opportunities (*CoOps*), represented in the model of Fig. 2 by links, which, in turn, have a weight that corresponds to the number of times the organisations collaborate (*#CoOps*).

Organisations are of different profiles classified into Classes of Collaboration Willingness, which characterize their collaborative behaviour when realizing market opportunities. Each profile is made up of a set of attributes, namely *Contact rate*, *Accept rate*, and *New products rate*, whose decimal values between 0 and 1, expresses a collaboration intensity factor, i.e., the propensity to collaborate by sending invites to other organisations, the inclination to accept the invitations, and in particular those that are associated to innovation. Table 1 describes a CBE in terms of its structural organisation and collaborative behaviour. It is possible to instantiate the CBE model with any number of organisations of different profiles, characterized by classes of collaboration willingness generically designated by Class A, B, C, …, Z.

The PAAM of Fig. 2 also includes a Performance Assessment to measure the collaborative behaviour of the CBE by using performance indicators: Contribution Indicator (CI), Prestige Indicator (PI), and Innovation Indicator (II). The CBE Manager can adopt some or all of the indicators with a given weight (*wCI*, *wPI* and *wII*), which acts as an Influencing Mechanism in organisations, hoping to influence a change in their behaviour, since, in the same way as individuals, organisations also adapt to the way they are assessed. The CI influences the organisations' accomplished capacity, PI is more related to reputation, and II influences innovation creativity.

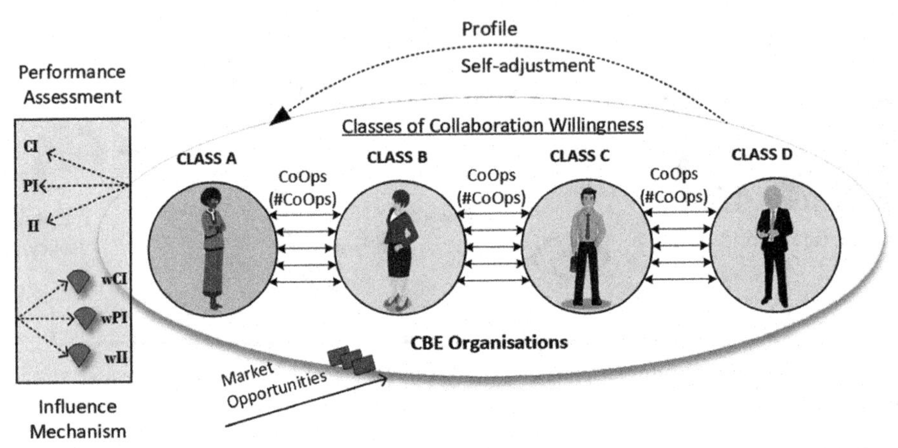

Fig. 2. Conceptual view of the PAAM (Performance Assessment and Adjustment Model) for a CBE

3.1 Characterisation of the Data

An implemented experiment using the PAAM model instantiates five organisations for each of the three classes of collaboration willingness, shown in Fig. 3, according to Table 1 namely Class A, Class B and Class C, which are characterized in Table 2 by radar charts.

Each class uses true data collected during 2019 from three organisations operating in the IT sector in the same business ecosystem. As such, it is possible to configure the different organisations' behaviour (the agents in the model) to perform more realistically. These data, consolidated in Table 3, allow estimating the classes of collaboration willingness (*Contact rate*, *Accept rate* and *New products rate*). The data also includes the total number of human resources (expressed in quantity and days/person) and percentage of allocation by main activity (consulting, research & development and inner

Table 1. A framework to understand and model a CBE.

Model of a CBE		
Description	A CBE is a network of organisations, connected by relationships that mean the market opportunities they share collaborating, called collaboration opportunities, to accomplish business opportunities.	
Structural Organisation	**Name**	**Model**
	Collaborative Business Ecosystem (CBE)	Network of nodes
	Organisations (O_n)	Nodes
	Collaboration opportunities (CoOps)	Ties between nodes
	Number of shared CoOps (#CoOps)	Ties' strength
Collaborative Behaviour	**Classes of Collaboration Willingness**	**Profiles of Organisations**
	Contact rate [0..1] Willingness to invite other organisations to collaborate.	Contact rate; 1,0; 0,8; 0,6; 0,4; 0,2; 0,0; Class A; Class B; Class C; Class D; Class Z
	Accept rate [0..1] Readiness to accept invitations from other organisations.	Accept rate
	New products rate [0..1] Tendency to accept opportunities related to innovation.	New products rate

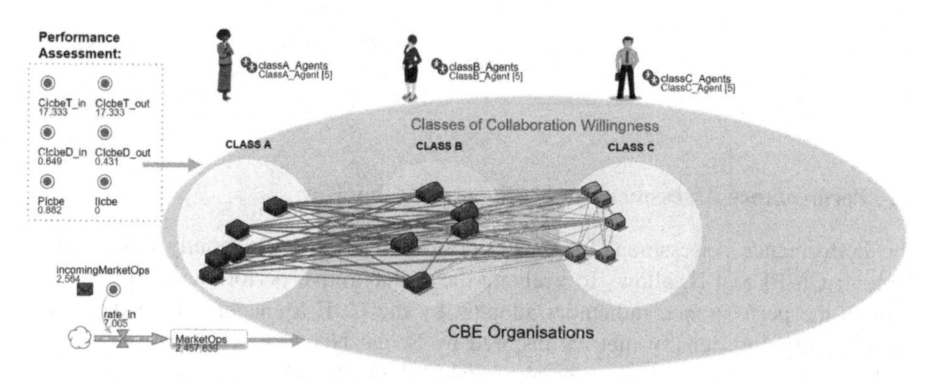

Fig. 3. A view of the PAAM (Performance Assessment and Adjustment Model) for a CBE instantiated with five organisations for each of the three different classes of collaboration willingness

tasks), the number of market opportunities sent and received, expressed in days/person (min, max and mode, i.e. the typical duration), and the percentage (min and max) of the opportunity involved in the collaboration, i.e. the units to distribute in a collaboration opportunity (*CoOp*).

Table 2. Profile of the organisations, instantiated in the CBE, classified in different classes of collaboration willingness (Class A, B, and C).

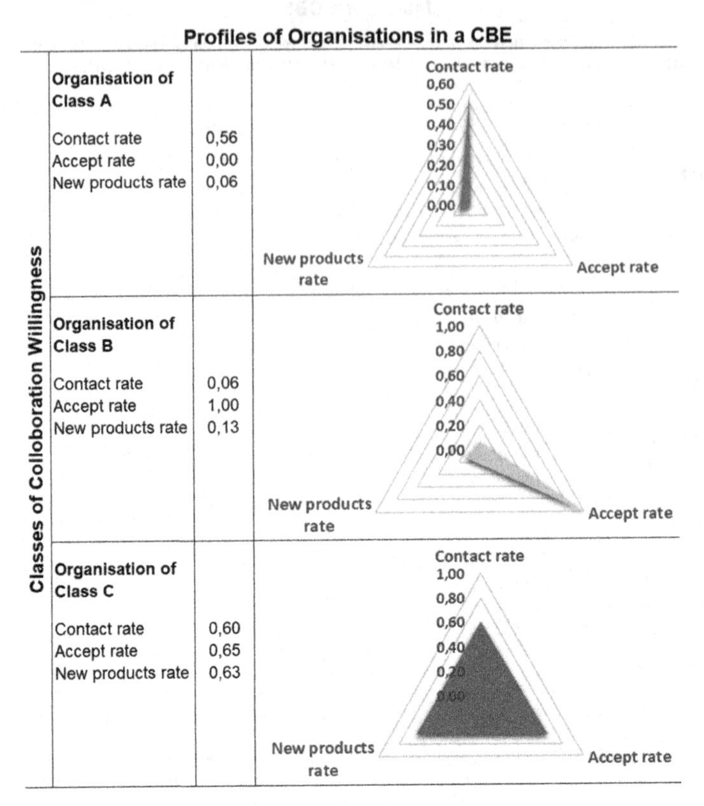

Profiles of Organisations in a CBE

Classes of Colloboration Willingness		
Organisation of Class A		
Contact rate	0,56	
Accept rate	0,00	
New products rate	0,06	
Organisation of Class B		
Contact rate	0,06	
Accept rate	1,00	
New products rate	0,13	
Organisation of Class C		
Contact rate	0,60	
Accept rate	0,65	
New products rate	0,63	

3.2 Performance Assessment and Influence Mechanism

The Performance Assessment for CBEs introduced in [23] and briefly described in Table 4: CI, PI and II, allows to evaluate the collaborative performance of the CBE through the performance indicators adopted by the CBE Manager. These indicators use centrality and density metrics inspired by Social Network Analysis, whose network structures are described as social capital [27]. On the other hand, applied to inter-organisational research, the network structure and strength of the links among organisations influence their behaviour and performance [6]. Moreover, findings suggest that strong links among organisations increase trust, which, in turn, increases benefits and lowers transaction costs [6]. The organisations' high degree centrality is positively related to their performance, and structural holes and closure generate social capital [6]. The exposed performance indicators take these concerns into account: CI measures the value creation in terms of new collaboration opportunities created in the CBE, PI measures how collaboration among organisations spreads, highlighting those that are most influential, and finally, the II measures the new products, services or patents created in collaboration.

Table 3. Consolidated real data from the organisations, considered as Class A, B, and C.

	Organisation of Class A		Organisation of Class B		Organisation of Class C	
Resources	**value**		**value**		**value**	
Total (persons)	62		16		33	
Total (days/person)	13640		3520		7260	
Consulting	74%		87%		85%	
R&D	2%		0%		6%	
Inner Tasks	24%		13%		9%	
Market Opportunities	**min**		**mode**		**max**	
Duration (days/person)	0		20		100	
Classes of Co. Willingness	**value**		**value**		**value**	
Contact rate	0,56		0,06		0,60	
Accept rate	0,00		1,00		0,65	
New products rate	0,06		0,13		0,63	
Units to Distribute	**min**	**max**	**min**	**max**	**min**	**max**
	4,0%	7,2%	0%	16,7%	0,4%	4,5%

Based on each indicator's objective, organisations are expected to react differently, according to their profiles' characteristics, as a response to a set of influence factors, the Influence Mechanism introduced in [23] and summarized in Table 5. Each indicator has an associated weight (defined by the CBE Manager) to allow a more meaningful influence on the direction that the CBE Manager intends to enhance: the *Contact rate is* related to CI (the more the contacts, the more likely to create *CoOps* in the CBE), the *Accept rate* related to PI (the more the accept of *CoOps*, the more likely to be influent in the CBE), and the *New products rate* related to II. As such, given a factor of influence (FI%), the organisations' class of collaboration willingness is increased by a percentage calculated by formulas FI_{wCI}, FI_{wPI}, and FI_{wII}. Formulas consider an influencing factor ($\pm Fe$) to add a positive or negative exogenous/random influence.

3.3 Model of the Agents

In the PAAM model, organisations are modelled as agents (ABM) that use statecharts, system dynamics (SD), and distribution functions [26] to simulate their behaviour, as shown in Fig. 4. The statechart is responsible for an agent's state transitions. On the other hand, the SD provides stocks for human resources: *Consulting, Research & Development,* and *Inner Tasks.* Finally, when an organisation receives a new *CoOp* (*InviteReceived*) or invites others to collaborate (*InviteToCollaborate*), it uses probabilistic functions parametrized with the classes of collaboration willingness: *Contact rate, Accept rate* and *New Products rate*). The resultant formulas (1), (2), (3) use the Bernoulli distribution, where the higher the parameters, the higher the probability of having a positive outcome if resources are available. Formula (4) uses a Triangular distribution to generate the number of business units to give to other organisations when collaborating.

$$invite_{toCollaborate} = bernoulli(contactRate) \quad (1)$$

Table 4. Summary of the Performance Indicators to evaluate collaboration in a CBE.

Performance Indicators	
Contribution Indicator of an Organisation (CI_i) and the CBE (CI_{CBE})	
$CI_i in/out = \frac{C_D(O_i) in/out}{C_D(O^*) in/out} = \frac{\sum_j O_{ij} \#CoOp_{ij} in/out}{\max \sum_j O_{ij} \#CoOp_{ij} in/out}$	Assesses the contribution of organisation O_i in terms of the number of accepted/created (in/out) collaboration opportunities (#CoOp).
$CI_{CBE} in/out = \frac{\sum_i [C_D(O^*) in/out - C_D(O_i) in/out]}{C_D(O^*) in/out * (\#O - 1)}$	Assesses the degree to which the most popular/active organisation [max degree centrality $C_D(O^*)$ in/out] exceeds the contribution of the others.
$CI_{CBE} t = \frac{\sum_i \#CoOp_i}{\#O}$	Ratio of the total number of collaboration opportunities (#CoOp) created/accepted in the CBE by the total number of organisations (#O).
Prestige Indicator of an Organisation (PI_i) and the CBE (PI_{CBE})	
$PI_i = \frac{C_B(O_i)}{C_B(O^*)} = \frac{\sum_k \sum_j O_{kj}(O_i)}{\max \sum_k \sum_j O_{kj}(O_i)}$	Assesses the prominence/influence of organisation O_i in terms of the number of collaboration opportunities (#CoOp).
$PI_{CBE} = \frac{C_B(CBE)}{maxC_B(CBE)} = \frac{\sum_i [C_B(O^*) - C_B(O_i)]}{C_B(O^*) * (\#O - 1)}$	Assesses the degree to which the most prominent/influent organisation [max betweenness centrality $C_D(O^*)$] exceeds the contribution of the others.
Innovation Indicator of an Organisation (II_i) and the CBE (II_{CBE})	
$II_i = \frac{\#NewPd_i}{\#PortPd_i}$	Measures the ratio of the number of new products/services/patentes ($NewPd_i$) of the organisation O_i by the total portfolio ($PortPd_i$) created.
$II_{CBE} = \frac{\sum \#NewPd_i}{\sum \#PortPd_i} * r(\#VO, \#NewPd)$	Calculates the ratio of innovation of the organisations in the CBE, weighted by the correlation between the collaboration (participation in Vos) and new products/ services/patents [r(#VO, #NewPd)].

Note: The values of the indicators are normalised between [0..1].

$$accept_{collaboration} = bernoulli(acceptRate) \quad (2)$$

$$accept_{collaboration} = bernoulli(newProductsRate) \quad (3)$$

$$businessUnits_{toDistribute} = triangular(minUnits, maxUnits) \quad (4)$$

The CBE Manager may vary the weights of the adopted performance indicators to influence the agents' behaviour, resulting in the simulation model, in an increment of the corresponding parameters: *Contact rate*, *Accept rate* and *New products rate*. This influence causes a change in the organisations' behaviour in the desired direction, the same way as individuals, when they know they are measured, their behaviour is adjusted to perform towards that goal.

Table 5. Summary of the Influence Mechanism of the organisations in a CBE.

Influence Mechanism				
Classes of Collaboration Willingness	**Related to**	**Perf. Indicator**	**Weight**	**Factor of Influence (FI %)**
Contact rate	It is related to activity	*CI*	*wCI*	$FI_{wCI} = wCI * \frac{FI}{wCI + wPI + wII} \pm F_e$
Accept rate	It is related to prominence/influence	*PI*	*wPI*	$FI_{wPI} = wPI * \frac{FI}{wCI + wPI + wII} \pm F_e$
New products rate	It is related to innovation	*II*	*wII*	$FI_{wII} = wII * \frac{FI}{wCI + wPI + wII} \pm F_e$

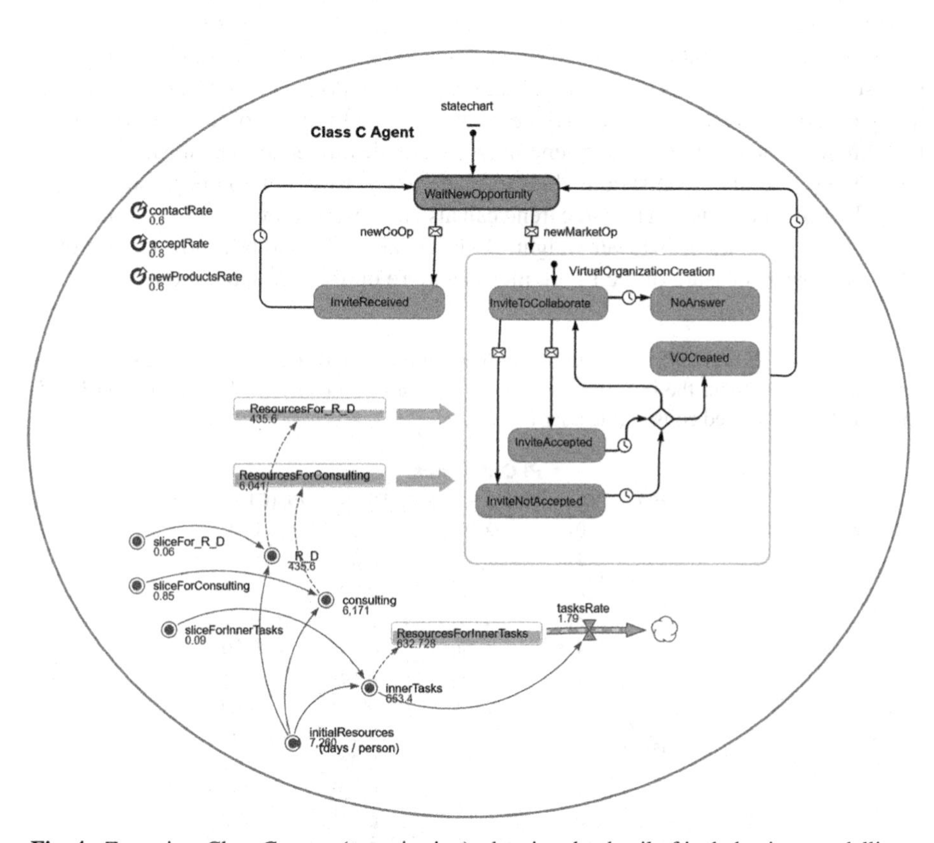

Fig. 4. Zoom in a Class C agent (organisation), showing the detail of its behaviour modelling

On the other hand, reinforcement learning in the simulation model can help the CBE Manager understand how to achieve an assessment goal for an individual organisation or the whole ecosystem. The environment (CBE environment in this case) is typically stated in the form of a Markov decision process (MDP) [28], and the AI agents, based on the environment's status, ought to take actions in order to maximise the notion of cumulative reward.

3.4 Simulation Results

Considering the PAAM model configured with three IT organisations' true data, as shown in Fig. 3, the outcomes can be attained using the Performance Assessment and Influence Mechanism summarized in Tables 4 and 5. The model ran one year (virtual time) in the simulation environment using Poisson's distribution [26], assuming 2 thousand market opportunities, plus 20% of opportunities with innovation.

This experiment analyses the PI outcome in three scenarios: (A) measures without influence; (B) measures with a $FI = 20\%$ and the weights $wCI = 2$, $wPI = 5$, and $wII = 1$; and (C) measures with a $FI = 20\%$ and the weights $wCI = 5$, $wPI = 2$, and $wII = 1$.

Analysing the results of the three simulation's scenarios in Table 6 and the graphical representation (Gephi tool [29]) in Fig. 5 and Fig. 6, we can observe that due to the profile of organisations of Class A have an *Accept rate* = 0, the PI indicator that is more related to prominence is equal to zero and remains zero after de influence mechanism. However, we can perceive the organisations' bias in scenario (B) to acquire more prestige due to the influence mechanism. The same trend can also be observed in scenario (C) but not as pronounced given the PI's lower weight. Both scenarios (B) and (C) show an improved CBE as a lower measure of the PI_{CBE} means a more uniform collaboration.

Table 6. Shows PI normalized measures for organisations and the CBE, using three scenarios of simulation: (A) without the influence mechanism; (B) after influenced considering a $wPI = 5$; and (C) after influenced considering a $wPI = 2$.

		PI Outcomes		
Profile	**O_i**	**PI_i (A)**	**PI_i (B)**	**PI_i (C)**
Organisations of Class A	0	0,00	0,00	0,00
	1	0,00	0,00	0,00
	2	0,00	0,00	0,00
	3	0,00	0,00	0,00
	4	0,00	0,00	0,00
Organisations of Class B	5	0,00	0,08	0,07
	6	0,00	0,00	0,00
	7	0,13	0,00	0,03
	8	0,00	0,00	0,13
	9	0,00	0,00	0,00
Organisations of Class C	10	0,06	0,31	1,00
	11	0,32	0,77	0,67
	12	1,00	0,48	0,49
	13	0,08	1,00	0,90
	14	0,18	0,25	0,72
	PI_{CBE}	**0,88**	**0,81**	**0,73**

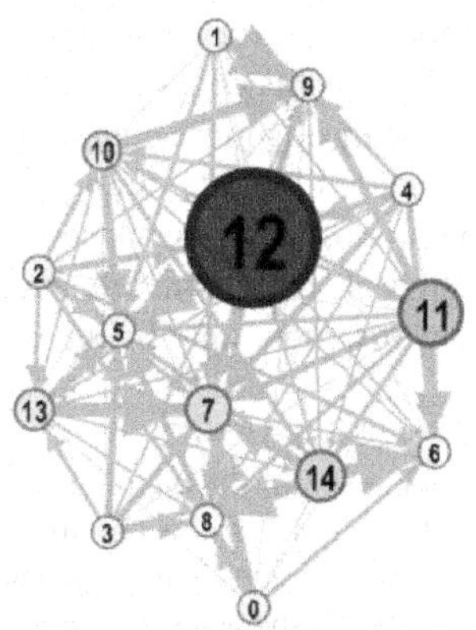

(A) PI measures before the influence.

Fig. 5. Graphical view of PI measures before the CBE's influence; the nodes' size is related to the PI value. i.e., the bigger the nodes, the greater the indicators' values; the connections' strength is weighted by the number of collaboration opportunities in the organisations.

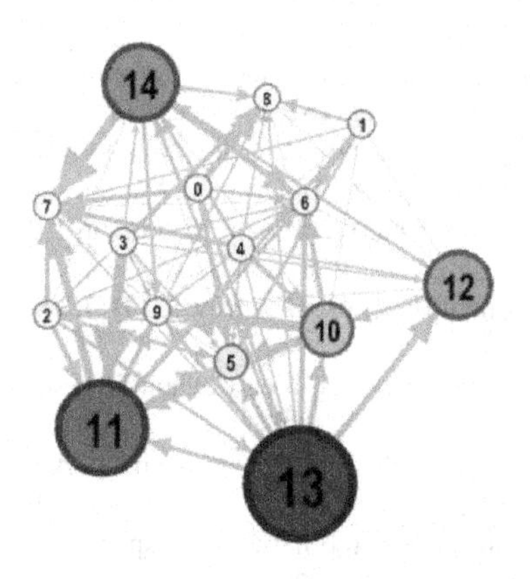

(B) PI measures after the influence.

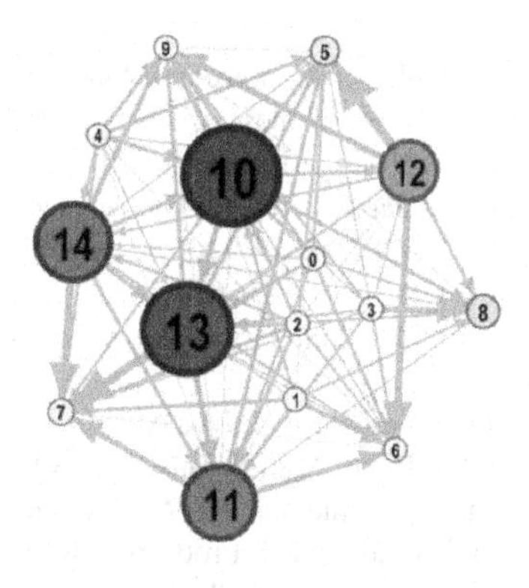

(C) PI measures after the influence varying the indicatorss' weights.

Fig. 6. Graphical view of PI measures before the CBE's influence considering (B) $wPI = 5$ and (C) $wPI = 2$; the nodes' size is related to the PI value. i.e., the bigger the nodes, the greater the indicators' values; connections' strength is weighted by the number of collaboration opportunities in the organisations.

4 Conclusions and Further Work

The simulation results showed that it is possible to configure the PAAM model using real data from organisations to obtain realistic scenarios. The PI indicator's simulation outcomes using the Performance Assessment and Influence Mechanism showed that the CBE collaboration can be measured and influenced by varying the weights of the performance indicators adopted by the CBE Manager. In this way, organisations can be influenced to improve their collaboration performance, thereby improving collaboration sustainability in the CBE, due to the benefits collaboration can bring, as argued in [20].

The ongoing work is related to analysing more comprehensive simulation scenarios, using the same actual data to configure different combinations of organisations' profile and different combinations of the proposed performance indicators.

Future work includes the design of more complete and reasoning agents to model the organisations' behaviour towards more intelligent decisions promoting a more sustainable CBE.

Acknowledgements. This work benefited from the ongoing research within the CoDIS (Collaborative Networks and Distributed Industrial Systems Group), which is part of both the Nova University of Lisbon (UNL) - School of Science and Technology and the UNINOVA - CTS (Center of Technology and Systems). Partial support also comes from Fundação para a Ciência e Tecnologia through the program UIDB/00066/2020 and European Commission (project DiGiFoF (Project Nr. 601089-EPP-1–2018-1-RO-EPPKA2-KA).

References

1. Ramezani, J., Camarinha-Matos, L.M.: Approaches for resilience and antifragility in collaborative business ecosystems. Technol. Forecast. Soc. Chang. **151**, 119846 (2020)
2. Graça, P., Camarinha-Matos, L.M.: The need of performance indicators for collaborative business ecosystems. In: Camarinha-Matos, L.M., Baldissera, T.A., Di Orio, G., Marques, F. (eds.) DoCEIS 2015. IAICT, vol. 450, pp. 22–30. Springer, Cham (2015). https://doi.org/10.1007/978-3-319-16766-4_3
3. Moore, J.F.: Predators and prey: a new ecology of competition. Harv. Bus. Rev. **71**(3), 75–86 (1993)
4. Camarinha-Matos, L.M., Afsarmanesh, H.: Collaborative networks: a new scientific discipline. J. Intell. Manuf. **16**(4–5), 439–452 (2005)
5. Camarinha-Matos, L.M., Afsarmanesh, H.: On reference models for collaborative networked organizations. Int. J. Prod. Res. **46**(9), 2453–2469 (2008)
6. Zaheer, A., Gözübüyük, R., Milanov, H.: It's the connections: the network perspective in interorganizsational research. Acad. Manag. Perspect. **24**(1), 62–77 (2010)
7. Provan, K.G., Fish, A., Sydow, J.: Interorganizational networks at the network level: a review of the empirical literature on whole networks. J. Manag. **33**(3), 479–516 (2007)
8. Camarinha-Matos, L.M., Abreu, A.: Performance indicators for collaborative networks based on collaboration benefits. Prod. Plann. Control **18**(7), 592–609 (2007)
9. Abreu, A., Camarinha-Matos, L.M.: An approach to measure social capital in collaborative networks. In: Camarinha-Matos, L.M., Pereira-Klen, A., Afsarmanesh, H. (eds.) PRO-VE 2011. IAICT, vol. 362, pp. 29–40. Springer, Heidelberg (2011). https://doi.org/10.1007/978-3-642-23330-2_4
10. Duan, L.N., Park, K.H.: Applying the balanced scorecard to collaborative networks. In: 2010 6th International Conference on Advanced Information Management and Service (IMS), pp. 131–134. IEEE (2010)
11. Schmitt, J., Trang, T.N., Kolbe, M.: Steering information technology in collaborative networks. In: First International Conference on Resource Efficiency in Interorganizational Networks-ResEff 2013, p. 180 (2013)
12. Bhagwat, R., Sharma, M.K.: Performance measurement of supply chain management: A balanced scorecard approach. Comput. Indus. Eng. **53**(1), 43–62 (2007)

13. Motadel, M.R., Amiran, H., Etemad, S.H.: Presenting a mathematical model for evaluation of the (effectiveness of) supply chain management through balanced scorecard approach (a case study of isaco corporation). Not (2012)
14. Chang, H.H., Hung, C.-J., Wong, K.H., Lee, C.-H.: Using the balanced scorecard on supply chain integration performance - a case study of service businesses. Serv. Bus. **7**(4), 539–561 (2013)
15. Ramanathan, U.: Performance of supply chain collaboration - a simulation study. Expert Syst. Appl. **41**(1), 210–220 (2014). 21st Century Logistics and Supply Chain Management
16. Vereecke, A., Muylle, S.: Performance improvement through supply chain collaboration in europe. Int. J. Oper. Prod. Manag. **26**(11), 1176–1198 (2006)
17. Ramanathan, U., Gunasekaran, A., Subramanian, N.: Supply chain collaboration performance metrics: a conceptual framework. Benchmark. Int. J. **18**(6), 856–872 (2011)
18. Ramanathan, U., Gunasekaran, A.: Supply chain collaboration: impact of success in long-term partnerships. Int. J. Prod. Econ. **147**, 252–259 (2014)
19. Jackson, M.O.: Social and economic networks, vol. 3. Princeton University Press, Princeton (2008)
20. Lozano, R.: Collaboration as a pathway for sustainability. Sustain. Dev. **15**(6), 370–381 (2007)
21. Graça, P., Camarinha-Matos, L.M.: Evolution of a collaborative business ecosystem in response to performance indicators. In: Camarinha-Matos, L.M., Afsarmanesh, H., Fornasiero, R. (eds.) Collaboration in a Data-Rich World: 18th IFIP WG 5.5 Working Conference on Virtual Enterprises, PRO-VE 2017, Vicenza, Italy, September 18-20, 2017, Proceedings, pp. 629–640. Springer , Cham (2017). https://doi.org/10.1007/978-3-319-65151-4_55
22. Graça, P., Camarinha-Matos, L.M.: A proposal of performance indicators for collaborative business ecosystems. In: Afsarmanesh, H., Camarinha-Matos, L.M., Soares, A.L. (eds.) PRO-VE 2016. IAICT, vol. 480, pp. 253–264. Springer, Cham (2016). https://doi.org/10.1007/978-3-319-45390-3_22
23. Graça, P., Camarinha-Matos, L.M.: Evaluating and influencing the performance of a collaborative business ecosystem – a simulation study. In: Camarinha-Matos, L.M., Afsarmanesh, H., Ortiz, A. (eds.) PRO-VE 2020. IAICT, vol. 598, pp. 3–18. Springer, Cham (2020). https://doi.org/10.1007/978-3-030-62412-5_1
24. Parkes, D.C., Wellman, M.P.: Economic reasoning and artificial intelligence. Science **349**(6245), 267–272 (2015)
25. Yu, C., Liu, J., Nemati, S.: Reinforcement learning in healthcare: a survey (2020)
26. Borshchev, A.: The Big Book of Simulation Modeling: Multimethod Modeling with AnyLogic 6. AnyLogic North America, Chicago (2013)
27. Burt, R.S.: The network structure of social capital. Res. Organ. Behav. **22**, 345–423 (2000)
28. van Otterlo, M., Wiering, M.: Reinforcement learning and Markov decision processes. In: Wiering, M., van Otterlo, M. (eds.) Reinforcement Learning, pp. 3–42. Springer, Berlin, Heidelberg (2012). https://doi.org/10.1007/978-3-642-27645-3_1
29. Bastian, M., Heymann, S., Jacomy, M.: Gephi: an open source software for exploring and manipulating networks (2009)

The Benefits of Applying Social Network Analysis to Identify Collaborative Risks

Marco Nunes[1](✉) and António Abreu[2,3](✉)

[1] Department of Industrial Engineering, University of Beira Interior, 6201-001 Covilhã, Portugal
marco.nunes@ubi.pt

[2] Department of Mechanical Engineering, Polytechnic Institute of Lisbon, 1959-007 Lisbon, Portugal
ajfa@dem.isel.ipl.pt

[3] CTS Uninova, 2829-516 Caparica, Portugal

Abstract. It is often argued that efficient collaboration is the key for successful organizations. However, achieving efficient collaboration still represents a challenge for most organizations. Often, hidden involuntary behaviors (also known as behavioral risks), threat efficient collaboration in a blink of an eye. Either by the lack of supportive models to manage sscollaboration or due to misunderstandings of what the different dimensions of collaboration are and represent, most organizations fear the engagement in collaborative approaches due the high chances of failure. In this work is proposed a heuristic model to identify organizational collaborative risks by applying social network analysis . This work aims to illustrate how organizations can benefit from the application of social network analysis in the efficient identification and management of collaborative risks. A case study illustrates the application of the proposed model in this work.

Keywords: Collaborative risks · Social network analysis · Organizational performance · Organizational business intelligence architecture · Case study

1 Introduction

It is often said that efficient collaboration is the key for success [1, 3]. According to literature, to organizations succeed in the actual complex and unpredictable market landscape they should engage in collaborative partnerships with other organizations such as universities, institutes or even their competitors [1, 3, 4]. By doing so organizations access resources, such as technologies, expertise, financial support, access new markets, just to name a few, which they alone would never have access to [1, 3, 4]. However, defining collaboration is far from being fully understood [1, 4, 5]. Research shows that there is no consensus regarding to what collaboration really means, as well as its dimensions [5, 6]. This fact represents a challenge for organizations regarding the management collaborative initiatives. Adding to this, research shows that there is a lack of efficient models to support the management of collaborative initiatives [4–6]. Both facts together

© IFIP International Federation for Information Processing 2021
Published by Springer Nature Switzerland AG 2021
L. M. Camarinha-Matos et al. (Eds.): DoCEIS 2021, IFIP AICT 626, pp. 16–23, 2021.
https://doi.org/10.1007/978-3-030-78288-7_2

hinder organizations from profiting the advantages that collaborative partnerships may offer. To help organizations to overcome such obstacles is proposed a heuristic model developed based on three key pillars ((1) collaborative risks, (2) social network analysis, and (3) business intelligence), that will help to identify collaborative risks, by analysing how different dynamic collaborative behaviors (also called as collaborative risks) may impact organizational outcomes. The research question can be as follows stated: *to which extent can project outcomes be impacted by the different dynamic behavioral patterns that emerge across a project lifecycle?* This analysis will be done by the application of social network analysis (SNA), that quantitatively measures data collected in several interaction tools, such as emails, chats, messages, virtual-meetings, or virtual surveys. The model was developed to be integrated into an organizational business intelligence architecture. In this work, it will be illustrated the benefits of applying SNA analysis in organizations to identify collaborative risks, and how organizations can profit from the incorporation of the model into a business intelligence architecture, transforming the integration into an artificial intelligent system that automatically collects, transforms and analysis organizational dynamic behavioral data, giving unique, meaningful, and actionable insights. This will help improve decision making activities by turning it more data informed. The proposed model acts as a supervised machine learning type, whereby the application of SNA centrality metrics algorithms, identifies, measures, and correlates organizational outcomes, with specific identified behaviors. Both aspects, give the model a novelty characteristic regarding the management of collaborative risks. Risk is translated by the different dynamic behaviors (DB) of actors in each project phase, where such different repeatable DB can be correlated to project outcomes. Collaborative risks lay in the interactions between project entities (people, organizations, or others), and not in the entities themselves. In this work, business intelligence is related to the network architecture that enables the treatment of behavioral data that contains such DBs that occurred across a phase of a given project. More concretely, it acts as a tool to accurately, precisely, and in a timely manner accomplish all the necessary steps to take insights out of dynamic data that is being created as project entities deliver a project. The indicators that will enable to quantitatively measure such DBs are SNA centrality metrics (in, out, and average degree), which are supported by strategic surveys or observations that conducts the assessment to a particular collaborative risk type that is aimed to be identified and mapped. For example, the answer provided to the question; *whom do one trusts to discuss project related matters without being afraid of retaliation*, would be a trust indicator, that quantitatively measures (individual and collective) the trust level within a project social network. This work is divided into five chapters. In Sect. 1 is done an introduction to the proposed model highlighting the motivation and importance in the organizational context. In Sect. 2 are introduced the three key pillars that support the development of the model (state of the art). In Sect. 3 is illustrated the model development and application in a typical organizational business intelligence architecture context. In Sect. 4 is presented a small case study showing the application and interpretation of results of the proposed model. In Sect. 5, are presented the conclusions and further research recommendations. The model presents a novel approach to manage collaborative risks, resulting of a multidisciplinary approach by connecting the three mentioned key pillars. This way the model adds unique value to the process of identification of organizational collaborative risks.

2 Literature Review

2.1 Collaborative Risks

Collaborative risks can be defined as risks that emerge from the several dimensions that can be found in the several definitions of collaboration [1, 4]. However, according to research, collaborative risks can be divided into four major types [6]. They are: (1) risk of critical enterprise, (2) risk in allocation of resources, (3) managerial risks, and (4) behavioral risks. Risk of critical enterprise comprises risks related to collaborative network members (people, groups, or organizations) who hold exclusive resources or competencies needed to the accomplishment of work-related tasks or activities. Risk in allocation of resources comprises risks related to how work-related tasks or activities are distributed across the different collaborative network partners, which can result in delay or bottlenecking's and thus compromise the success of an organization. Managerial risks are risks related to the structure and degree of communication and authority across all members of a given collaborative network. Finally, behavioral risks, are risks related with the different types of dynamic relationships that emerge across the several participants in a given collaborative network. In this work, the focus will be directed to behavioral risks, which by the application of social network analysis centrality metrics, will be quantitatively measured and further correlated with organizational outcomes [1, 4].

2.2 Social Network Analysis (SNA)

SNA is the process of analysing and studying social structures, by applying metrics developed based on the graph theory [1, 7]. The purpose of such analysis is to understand and explain how different social structures emerge and evolve in the environment where they do exits across time [8]. In SNA analysis, entities (people, organizations or other) are represented as dots, and the relationships between any two entities is represented by lines connecting such dots. This is the underlying basics of the graph theory. The application of SNA in organizations essentially supports the decision-making processes [1, 3]. This happens, as the process analysis how employees' behaviors may be correlated with organizational outcomes [1, 3]. The application of SNA in organizations has been exponentially growing in popularity within the latest years [1, 3–5], and can be applied in several different dimensions, such as the analysis of employee turnover and retention, individual and collective performance levels, different organizational cultures, dynamic behaviors, well-being, fraud, social cohesion, information diffusion, innovation performance, and may others [1, 4, 6, 9]. In this work, the application of social network analysis centrality metrics, such as in-degree, out-degree, density, average in-degree, closeness, betweenness, just to name a few [1, 3], are used to quantitively measure dynamic collaborative behaviors that may emerge as people carry work related tasks or activities. SNA is considered as a unique approach to measure human dynamic behavior accurately and undoubtedly, by opposition to traditional approaches essentially supported by human resources theories which introduce a huge amount of bias [1, 3, 4]. More concretely in this work, it will be used the in-degree, out-degree, and the average in-degree metrics.

2.3 Organizational Business Intelligence Architecture (BI)

Organizational busines intelligence (BI) can be defined as set of technologies and strategies to analyze business data in an efficient and data-driven way [10]. A traditional BI architecture comprises a variety of tools, methodologies, frameworks, and systematic processes, that collect, store, transform, and analyze business data, uncovering hidden, unique, and meaningful actionable information. Such information is the used by organizations essentially to understand past trends, see in real time actual trends, and predict future business trends, such as consumer behavioral patterns. Furthermore, such information is very often used by organizations to support their strategical decision-making processes [10, 11]. An efficient BI architecture comprises a dynamic organizational interconnected communication network, where information from several departments, is accessed, acquired, both, internal and external, and can be easily accessed and readable [10]. In this work, is illustrated the incorporation of the propose model into a typical organizational BI architecture, and how organizations benefit from it in the efficient identification of collaborative risks.

3 Model Development and Application

The implementation of the proposed model in this work is illustrated in Fig. 1.

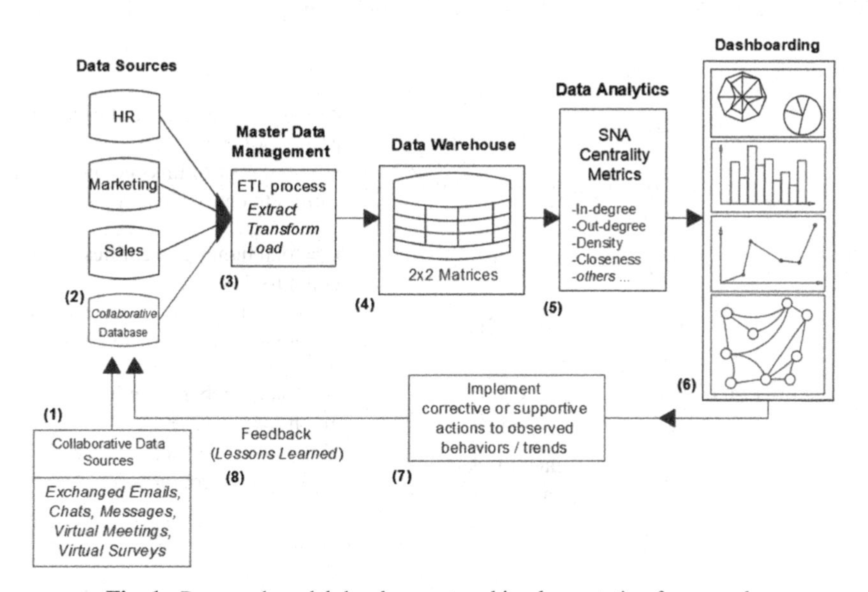

Fig. 1. Proposed model development and implementation framework.

In Fig. 1 is illustrated the integration of the proposed model into a typical organizational business intelligence architecture. According to Fig. 1, first (1), organizational behavioral data is collected through several methods, such as exchanged emails, chats conversations, chats messages, virtual meetings, or virtual surveys. Then, (2) collected data will be stored in a dedicated organizational behavioral database to further processing. Then, (3), data undergoes a ETL process (extract, transform and load), where is essentially is checked if any data is missing, if data was correctly collected, and if collected data can be used in the further step. Then, (4) data is placed in a 2 × 2 matrix form, where the relationships (interactions) between entities can be quantitatively visible, which represent the centrality degree of each entity present in network. Then, (5) SNA centrality metrics, such as in-degree, out-degree, total-degree, density, closeness, just to name a few, are applied to data stored in the 2 × 2 matrix form, to quantitatively measure organizational behavioral data across a finite period. Then, (6) the results of the quantitative analysis will be illustrated (usually dashboarded) in several forms, such as chart bars, circular graphs, trend lines, or even graphs, to provide actionable and meaningful help in decision making processes. Then, (7) according to the results obtained from the analysis to the organizational behaviors, corrective or supportive actions may be implemented. Finally, (8) after the implementation of corrective or supportive measures to quantitatively identified organizational behaviors, feedback must be given in the form of lessons learned to continuously improve the way that organizational behaviors impact organizational outputs and outcomes (continuously improvement cycle). To quantitatively measure organizational behaviors captured in collected data, a set of SNA centrality metrics can be applied as illustrated in Table 1 [12].

Table 1. Some SNA centrality metrics that can be used in the proposed model in this work.

SNA Metric	Equation	Brief description
In-degree	$C_{ID}(n_i) = \sum_j x_{ji} (1)$ C_{ID}= in degree of an entity within a graph	n = total number of entities within a graph for i = 1…, n xji = number of links coming from entity j to entity i, where i ≠ j,
Out-degree	$C_{OD}(n_i) = \sum_j x_{ji} (2)$ C_{ID}= out degree of an entity within a graph	n = total number of entities within a graph for i = 1…, n xji = number of links going from entity j to entity i, where i ≠ j,
Average In-Degree	$C_{AID}(n_i) = \frac{\sum_j x_{ji}}{n} (3)$ C_{AID}= Average In- degree of an entity within a graph	n = total number of entities within a graph for i = 1…, n xji = number of links from entity j to entity i, where i ≠ j,

4 Application Case of the Proposed Model

The following application case of the proposed model is a small extract of a larger case study conducted by an international market leader in the food and energy organization in mid-Europe in 2020. This organization (denominated Organization A) conducted a case study in his engineering department to understand the extent to which dynamic behaviors were correlated with outcomes. In Fig. 2 is illustrated part of the case study conducted by Organization A.

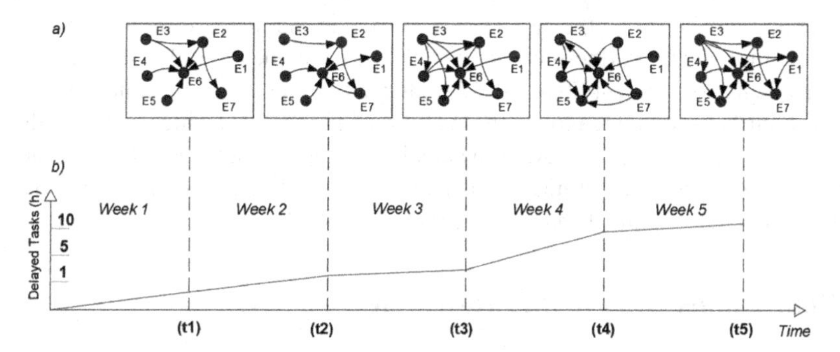

Fig. 2. Application case of the proposed model in this work (dashboarding results).

In Fig. 2 is illustrated the evolution of the organizational dynamic behaviors across five different weeks (a), and the evolution of several tasks accomplishment delays for the same period (b). Figure 2 represents point 6 of Fig. 1 (dashboarding). To understand how dynamic behaviors could impact the execution of tasks organization A conducted a study in the engineering department, (which is comprised by 7 engineers E1, E2, E7) across 5 weeks. As it can be seen in Fig. 2 a) the resulting 5 networks (for different five times – t1, t2, t3, t4, and t5) were built with data collected in virtual surveys addressed to all 7 engineers. To map the five networks in a), the following question was directed to the 7 engineers: *to whom did you turn in this last week with high frequency to ask for help or discuss any work-related matters?* This question was addressed five different times (close at the end of each week). The results obtained in the networks illustrated in a), show the answers to the respective questions. For example, applying (1) for the network of t1, engineer E6 has a degree of 5, which means that he was named by five other engineers as a resource for help and discussion regarding work related matters. For the same network applying (2), for E6, he has a degree of 0. This means that in week 1, E6 did not ask for help to any other colleagues in the engineering department. When analysing other networks, it can be seen (applying (1)), that E6 is a fundamental central piece in the engineering department because its degree, as the time moves along, goes from 5 to 5 to 6 to 6 and to 6 for t1, t2, t3, t4, and t5, respectively. This trend clearly indicates a strong dependency from the engineering team on element E6. This may represent a behavioral collaborative risk, in the sense that may introduce information bottlenecking, and ultimately the emergence of over central and extreme peripherical people in the engineering network. In fact, it can be clearly seen a certain correlation between the evolution of the different dynamic behavioral networks in Fig. 2 a), and the work-related tasks cumulative delay in Fig. 2 b). This effect can be better explained (correlated) when applying other SNA centrality metrics such as density or average in-degree. Applying (3) there is a positive evolution across time, moving from 1 to 1, 14 to 1,6 to 1,7 to 1,9 for t1, t2, t3, t4, and t5, respectively. This means that there has been an increase of dynamic interactions across the analyzed period. Simultaneously, when analysing Fig. 2b, where is illustrated the cumulative delay in hours of all work-related tasks relative to what was ahead planned, as the number of dynamic interactions increased across time, so did the cumulative delays of work-related tasks, from 1 up to almost 10 h in the engineering department. In this case, it can be concluded a strong correlation between increase in dynamic interactions of the engineering team, and the increase in the work-related tasks execution delay. Furthermore, it can also be concluded that the disproportionate centrality degree of element E6 in the different dynamic networks illustrated in Fig. 2 a), may have further contributed to the trend observed in Fig. 2 b), which clearly indicates a collaborative behavioral risk. After the conducted analysis supported by the proposed model, follow up assessment need to be undertaken to identify the underlying reasons for the uncovered dynamic behaviors illustrated in Fig. 2.

5 Conclusions and Further Research

In this work is presented a model to identify collaborative risks developed based on three key pillars ((1) collaborative risks, (2) social network analysis, and (3) business intelligence). The model applies SNA centrality metrics to quantitatively measure dynamic behaviors that emerge as organizations engage in collaborative networks. It is demonstrated the importance of SNA centrality metrics as a unique and meaningful approach to accurately measure human dynamic behavior by opposition to traditional approaches essentially supported by human resources theories which introduce a considerable amount of bias. Furthermore, it is illustrated how organizations can incorporate the model into a BI architecture, which enables organizations to collect, treat, transform, and analyze behavioral data automatically and accurately. The model can be used by organizations to identify behavioral risks and simultaneously critical success factors as it correlates identified behavioral patterns with organizational outcomes. In a managerial perspective, the model enables organizations to shift their decision-making processes from a more traditional approach based on intuition and opinions of influent people, towards a more decision-informed decision-making process. This enhances the chances of success of an organization and contributes to the achievement of sustainable competitive advantages. The model helps organizations to overcome the two main mentioned obstacles regarding collaborative initiatives (misunderstanding of what collaboration is and its dimensions, and the lack of proper models to support collaborative initiatives). This contributes to enable organizations to profit from the advantages of collaborative partnerships. In a research perspective, the model in highlights the importance of the application of SNA in organizations which may contribute to the development of further SNA centrality metrics to better map the myriad of hidden organizational collaborative behaviors. It still sheds light into the collaborative risks dimension, by enabling a deeper understand of how such collaborative risks emerge and evolve across time, which in tur may help to generate new theories regarding the development and importance of behavioral risk sin organizational outcomes. As for future research, it is recommended the use of more existing SNA centrality metrics, but not only centrality, to in a 360°-degree perspective, map the existing dynamic interactions within a group or organization as they execute work-related tasks or activities. Finally, further research should be undertaken in new methods of data collection to capture information that flows across other communication tools, such as telephone conversations, while coping with the regulatory GDPR (General Data Protection Regulation) norms and ethical aspects.

References

1. Nunes, M., Abreu, A.: Applying social network analysis to identify project critical success factors. Sustainability **12**, 1503 (2020)
2. Abreu, A., Nunes, M.: Model to estimate the project outcome's likelihood based on social networks analysis. KnE Eng. **5**(6), 299–313 (2020)
3. Nunes, M., Abreu, A.: Managing open innovation project risks based on a social network analysis perspective. Sustainability **12**, 31–32 (2020)
4. Nunes, M., Abreu, A.: A model to support OI collaborative risks applying social network analysis. In: Camarinha-Matos, L.M., Afsarmanesh, H., Ortiz, A. (eds.) Boosting Collaborative Networks 4.0: 21st IFIP WG 5.5 Working Conference on Virtual Enterprises, PRO-VE 2020, Valencia, Spain, November 23–25, 2020, Proceedings, pp. 324–335. Springer International Publishing, Cham (2020). https://doi.org/10.1007/978-3-030-62412-5_27
5. Nunes, M., Dias, A., Abreu, A., Martins, J.D.M.: A predictive risk model based on social network analysis. In: Modelling and Simulation 2020-The European Simulation and Modelling Conference, ESM 2020, pp. 82–88 (2020)
6. Abreu, A., Moleiro, M., Duarte, J., Calado, J.M.F.: Fuzzy logic model to support risk assessment in innovation ecosystems. In: 2018 13th APCA International Conference on Automatic Control and Soft Computing, Ponta Delgada, pp. 104–109 (2018)
7. Borgatti, S.: Introduction to Social Network Analysis Stephen. University of Kentucky (2016). https://statisticalhorizons.com/wp-content/uploads/SNA-Sample-Materials.pdf. Accessed 15 Sep 2019
8. Cross, R., Parker, A.: The Hidden Power of Social Networks: Understanding How Work Really Gets Done in Organizations; HBS Press: Boston. MA, USA (2004)
9. Liaquat, H., Wu, A., Choi, B.: Measuring coordination through social networks. In: Proceedings ICIS 2006, Milwaukee, Wisconsin, USA, 10–13 December 2006
10. Saeed, R., Sara, A., Vahid, M.: Review Study: Business Intelligence Concepts and Approaches. Am. J. Sci. Res. **50**, 62–75 (2012)
11. Rad, R.: Microsoft SQL Server 2014 Business Intelligence Development Beginner's Guide. Packt Publishing, Livery Place, 35 Livery Street Birmingham B3 2PB, UK (2014)
12. Wasserman, S., Faust, K.: Social network analysis in the social and behavioral sciences. In: Social Network Analysis: Methods and Applications, pp. 1–27. Cambridge University Press; Cambridge, USA (1994). ISBN 9780521387071

A Mixed Method for Assessing the Reliability of Shared Knowledge in Mass Collaborative Learning Community

Majid Zamiri(✉) and Luis M. Camarinha-Matos

NOVA School of Science and Technology and UNINOVA - CTS, NOVA University of Lisbon, 2829-516 Caparica, Portugal
zamiri_majid@yahoo.com, cam@uninova.pt

Abstract. The recent trends in open, informal, and collective education have gradually been shaping an innovative approach to learning called "mass collaborative learning" where large and limitless number of scattered but interested people (with different backgrounds and levels of knowledge) join a networked community aiming to learn new things interactively. Even though the potential benefits of mass collaborative learning for learners are enormous, the process is by nature prone to be harmed by sharing unhealthy materials within the community. In order to minimize the dissemination of disinformation and promote the quality of shared contents in mass collaborative learning communities, this study, as a contribution in this context, proposes a mixed method that can help involved learners to assess the reliability and quality of shared knowledge or information through a multi-user and multilevel evaluation approach. Preliminary findings of this research work are discussed.

Keywords: Mass Collaborative Learning (MCL) · Mixed method · Assessment · Reliability · Content · Knowledge · Information

1 Introduction

Education ecosystems are rapidly developing, facilitated by emerging technological trends that open diverse opportunities for innovative and more interactive learning approaches. These trends lead to blurring the lines between digital and physical arenas, being expected that this constructive movement proliferates worldwide. In this context, Mass Collaborative Learning (MCL), as an example of novel opportunity, by focusing on lifelong learning, facilitates the way that even general public can engage in collaborative learning practice outside the conventional organizational structures and traditional education system. In other words, interested learners from around the world can jointly and continually create, share, and acquire new knowledge through transforming and exchanging their experiences and information by means of ICT platforms in an informal way. Opposed to traditional learning methods and bureaucracies i.e., formal learning that is hierarchically structured, explicitly controlled, chronologically graded,

© IFIP International Federation for Information Processing 2021
Published by Springer Nature Switzerland AG 2021
L. M. Camarinha-Matos et al. (Eds.): DoCEIS 2021, IFIP AICT 626, pp. 24–36, 2021.
https://doi.org/10.1007/978-3-030-78288-7_3

and delivered by an instructor in a systematic intentional way, MCL defies many hierarchical practices, goes outside of a traditional formal learning environment and is not necessarily intentional [1–4].

MCL communities are mostly self-directed, non-hierarchical, heterogeneous, and support dynamic initiatives that bring together diverse sets of autonomous learners (with various levels of expertise and performance) aiming to reap the power of collaboration and the advantages of diverse minds toward learning of favorite subjects. There are several potential and substantial benefits of this promising complementary approach of learning which include but not limited to: creating a dynamic environment of involved, simplified, and exploratory learning; increasing the access to general and specific knowledge and information; solving some complex problems by using collective intelligence and crowdsourcing; enhancing global interactions with peers and experts; fostering self-management and self-learning skills; stimulating critical thinking and assisting learners to develop ideas through community discussion; promoting alternate content assessment; and encouraging an atmosphere of positive collaboration. Finally, the provided synchronous or near real-time communication through ICT platforms enables MCL communities to maneuver with great agility and speed [1, 2].

Despite the positive and promising features of MCL, and the opportunities that it can open for the societies, communities, and learners, MCL (as a type of social network) faces with a huge number of problems, challenges, and limitations. For example, MCL must deal with the challenge of determining and controlling the quality and reliability of shared materials within the community. In fact, mass collaboration is regarded as a double-edged sword when it comes to learning. From one side, it is relatively low cost, accessible, and it can potentially facilitate knowledge sharing and increase public awareness. On the other side, the size (big) and environment (online) of the community can potentially put it at risk of encountering, involving, abusing, and damaging with unreliable knowledge or information. On top of that, the anonymity of community participants can likely intensify the problem. Since MCL is typically supported by a public platform, any participant can post anything with various degrees of truthfulness. The dissemination of such unhealthy contents throughout the community, without doubt, can negatively influence its members (e.g., to be misinformed or mislead) [1, 5, 6]. Thus, it is left to community members to recognize whether the content is true or not. Unfortunately, this is a dark side to MCL.

On that account, it has raised MCL community's concerns about not only the accuracy of the shared knowledge or information, but also in which way the community can properly gauge the quality of those materials. To contribute to solving this problem, this study proposes a potential mechanism that can assist MCL community members to assess the reliability and trustworthiness of shared knowledge or information in a systematic way. Therefore, the main objective of this work is to raise our level of consciousness about the impact of sharing unreliable contents (knowledge and/or information) in a MCL community and more concretely propose a mixed method that can help the MCL community members to assess the reliability and quality of shared contents through a multi-user and multilevel evaluation approach. Thus, the key research question that emerges is:

What could be a suitable assessment method to help minimize the problems related to the reliability of shared contents through mass collaboration within a community?

The following hypothesis is then set for this research question:

The problems related to the reliability of shared contents through mass collaboration could be minimized if the community benefits not only from the combination and application of a set of appraisal rules, criteria, and methods, but also the content materials are critically assessed through a collective effort.

It is noteworthy that despite great achievements in this specific area, there are still several ambiguities about the mass collaboration and learning process. Furthermore, the related concepts and associated mechanism are still evolving. In particular, the process of detection and evaluation of unreliable contents is not easy to be accomplished since it certainly requires adapting and deploying advanced technologies and comprehensive methodologies [1].

It should be also pointed out that in the early stage of our research we first conducted a systematic literature review to provide an exhaustive summary in connection with MCL and also to gain better understating about the main concepts, opportunities, challenges, and influential factors in this context [1, 2]. In next stage of research, we reviewed and analyzed the organizational structures of 14 real examples of mass collaboration and their most suitable features to be then able to propose a general organizational structure for mass collaborative learning purpose [3]. Afterward, a reference model for MCL was developed, aiming to highlight the main internal and external components of the community [4]. To complete our research and develop the proposed organizational and governance structure, the current study concentrates on specific management issues associated to content quality.

The remaining of this paper is organized as follow: Sect. 2 presents the relationships of this study with technological innovation for applied artificial intelligence systems. In Sect. 3, the literature and related work are reviewed. Section 4 explains the proposed mixed method for assessing the reliability of shared knowledge or information. Section 5 discusses the importance of proposed mixed method in assessment of shared materials in MCL community. Finally, the conclusion is given in Sect. 6.

2 Relationship to Technological Innovation for Applied Artificial Intelligence Systems

Assessment is an integral part of learning, and technology has long been one of the main contributing instruments in the assessment process. The most common types of assessment technologies in use nowadays are, in many ways, the tools that were once innovative, such as automated scoring. Indeed, the Information Communication Technologies have been providing the possibility to evaluate what learners are studying, learning, and sharing at very fine levels of detail (from distant locations) by means of vivid simulations of real-world situations. Such technologies have extensive potential to not only provoke radical changes in learning ecosystems at all levels, but also can bring greater sophistication, timeliness, and efficiency to different aspects of assessment method design and implementation. "*ThinkerTools, for example, is a computer-enhanced middle school science curriculum that promotes metacognitive skills by encouraging students to evaluate their own and each other's work using a set of well-considered criteria*" [7].

Artificial Intelligence (AI) technologies have proved the potential to be adopted in teaching and learning. That is, AI can open a wide range of opportunities for learning through providing a deep and fine-grained understanding of how and when learning really occurs. There are various types of AI techniques (e.g., semantic analysis, speech recognition, natural language processing) that can each be used to assess learning processes [8]. More specifically, AI can: (a) evaluate massive amounts of contents (knowledge, information, and data), (b) enable learners to conduct objective and consistent assessments of contents at a much earlier stage, (c) aid MCL communities to eliminate conscious and unconscious bias, (d) compared with practices of human raters, the process of assessment by AL is a more transparent, open to challenge, and legally-defensible approach, and (e) potentially accelerate, optimize, and promote the process of assessment. In addition, AI scoring and grading systems can create multiple-choice test questions (for different purposes like voting) and then truly leverage adaptive scoring [9]. Even though, AI can simultaneously perform several types of evaluations (even far more than any human), we do believe that, in the context of MCL, the assessment of shared knowledge or information requires interaction between human and computer and their effective contributions. However, in this paper, the focus is given more to human part and highlighting the power of "mass collaboration".

3 Related Work

In the era of knowledge economy, it is highly significant to form strategic alliances through properly sharing reliable and valid knowledge or information across the collaborative networks. Such community networks can open new doors for participants to easily and freely access, use, share, create, and develop a variety of knowledge or information around different topics, and then leverage their knowledge and expertise for creating value. Furthermore, they can or should tackle the spread and impact of unhealthy contents, enhance the security and reliability of the shared knowledge or information, and build and promote the community resilience to disinformation. In this respect, identification of healthy knowledge or information (that stands on proper evaluation method) for reuse and exploitation in different contexts is one of the most crucial parts of knowledge sharing and enrichment in MCL. As such, it is considered as a hallmark of high-performing organizations [1, 10, 11].

Unreliable knowledge and inaccurate information, in this study, are considered verifiably false contents that might be created, and/or disseminated by one or some MCL community participants who most probably intend to inform, but are unaware that the materials are false or incorrect (e.g., a wrong interpretation, a false connection, a misconception), or in rare case(s) (knowingly) intend to deceive and mislead other participants (e.g., misleading information, fabricated or manipulated contents), either for the purposes of causing harm, or for political, personal, or financial gain [12, 13]. Such deleterious materials are dangerous and can act like a destructive weapon with damaging effects on both community and members. Sometimes this might have far-reaching consequences including but not limited to, destroying the reputation of the community and its members, driving participants to cut out their collaborative and social relationships with other peers or even drop out the community, and to simply create and/or consume less (reliable) knowledge and information overall [1, 2].

To combat the creation and distribution of unreliable contents, build resilience in the learning ecosystem, reduce the community members' vulnerability, improve the accuracy in judging the suspicious contents, and consequently develop proper collaborative learning, the literature recommends different strategies (e.g., providing appropriate training, guiding information, or tips for learners) [1, 14], approaches (e.g., deep learning [15]), or technologies (e.g., smart systems and software) [2, 16, 17] to be adopted. In this context, several research works have also attempted to introduce or develop useful learning procedures and evaluation methods. In [18], for example, the authors introduce a multilevel method for building organizational learning in three integrated levels namely, micro (individual), meso (network), and macro (systems). The study in [19] also focuses on a method of multilevel organizational learning as a systems approach to connect the individual, team, and organizational levels. In another study [20], the validity of content is assessed by using a mixed method approach. The authors use of a Table of Specifications (ToS) for estimating content validity. The ToS stands upon triangulating multiple data sources, expert debriefing, and using peer review.

Even though there are several references for evaluating the validity of shared knowledge in the literature [21, 22], there is relatively little comprehensive discussion about knowledge sharing in MCL [1, 2]. The existing literature, furthermore, lacks sufficient evidence and results on the way according to which the learners can assess the reliability and quality of shared knowledge in MCL communities. To fill part of these gaps, this study proposes a potential complementary assessment approach to equip MCL community participants with the basic information and needed analysis skills (e.g., ability to assess both content and sources) and evaluation techniques (e.g., thinking critically, logical reasoning, investigation, evidence-based reasoning, sharing views, community discussion, checklist approach, and voting) to determine the validity of what other contributing members deliver. Thereupon, a mixed method (that uses the above-mentioned qualitative and quantitative techniques) is introduced to, from one side, help making the results of knowledge assessment broader, deeper, and/or more precise. From another side, the application of this mixed method in different levels of the MCL community (individual and network) also assists reaping the advantages of diverse community members inclusion. However, content evaluation is an extremely complicated process, and it remains as one of the major concerns in this realm. In fact, there are still no universally agreed ways for assessing the reliability of contents, or the set of corresponding measurement technologies.

To successfully deal with the issue of content unreliability, one possible alternative for MCL is focusing on the prevention and reducing the risk of creating and sharing unreliable contents within the community, before involving with reliability assessment. In this respect, MCL could for example adapt the Failure Mode and Effects Analysis (FMEA). FMEA as a structured approach helps identifying potential unreliable contents and their major causes and effects on the community. The major causes could be related to human errors, procedural problems, management oversight, training deficiency, etc. In this process, the community can take needed actions to reduce the chance of potential unreliability occurrence. Unreliable contents can be also prioritized according to how easily they can be detected, how serious their consequences are, and how frequently they occur. Furthermore, a list of recommendations for reliability improvement can be then provided. The aim of applying FMEA is to take actions to eliminate or reduce unreliable contents. In case a piece of unreliable content is created and shared, despite utilizing FMEA, the community can then proceed to utilizing MAM-MCL.

4 Proposed Mixed Method for Assessing the Reliability of Shared Knowledge or Information (MAM-MCL)

In MCL, a huge amount of knowledge and/or information can be shared within the community. It is note taking that not all need quality and reliability assessment because a number of them can be readily, logically, and/or reasonably realized as a true content (e.g., facts, verified contents). However, there might be some contents that give the impression of being untrue or suspicious (e.g., completely false contents, fabricated contents, manipulated contents, misleading contents). In such cases, the MCL participants can use the proposed MAM-MCL to assess and gauge the reliability and quality of shared knowledge or information. In this framework, MAM-MCL can benefit from different innovative technologies such as digital fingerprints to for example, facilitate the identification of community participants, reduce their anonymity, and better track their contributions particularly in the case that they might share unreliable contents. MAM-MCL comprises of 5 main steps (see Fig. 1).

These steps are briefly explained in following.

- *Step 0 – preliminary assessment (by technology)*: in this step the shared knowledge or information (that are marked for assessment by community contributors) will be initially checked and then filtered by means of technology (e.g., AI software filtering system). The contents that are not deleted or rejected in this step (those that the technology marks for further evaluation), will be referred to the next step.
- *Step 1 – assessment by moderators* and content controllers: in this step the received contents (e.g., suspicious contents, controversial cases) from step 0 will be first checked by moderator(s) to prioritize them (based on predefined importance) for reliability assessment. The checked contents will be then classified based on the preset fields, classes, and topics. The classified contents shall be then codified based on predetermined codes (e.g., controversial, not controversial, scientific and professional, and not scientific and professional). Then after, they will be sent to the respective assessment level (Step 1.1). If the checked contents "are not controversial", they will be sent to the individual level. If the checked contents "are controversial" (e.g., ethical, cultural, critical issues), they will be sent to the community level. The assumption here is that compared with individuals, the community can better assess and make decisions about the controversial contents.
- *Step 1.1 – referring to individual or community level*: in this step the checked contents will be referred by moderator(s) either to individual or community level:

  > <u>Individual level:</u> indicates that the reliability and quality of "not controversial contents" should be evaluated individually. If the considered contents "are scientific and

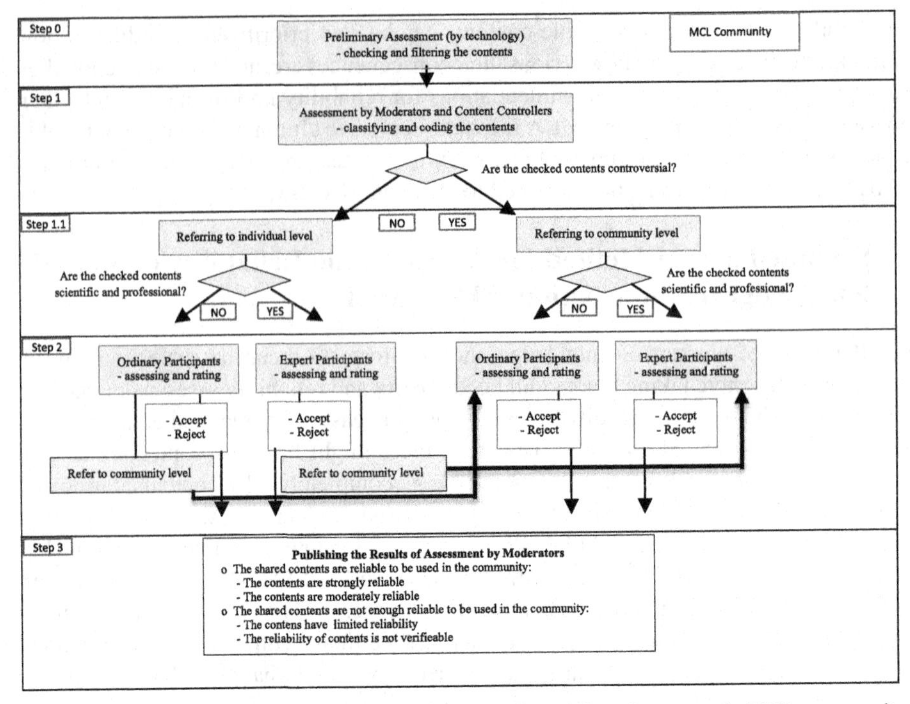

Fig. 1. Proposed MAM-MCL for assessing the reliability of shared contents in MCL community

professional", they will be sent to expert participants (at individual level). If the considered contents "are not scientific and professional", they will be sent to ordinary participants (at individual level).
> Community level: shows that the reliability and quality of "controversial contents" should be evaluated collaboratively. If the considered contents "are scientific and professional", they will be sent to expert participants (at community level). If the considered contents "are not scientific and professional", they will be sent to ordinary participants (at community level).

- *Step 2 –assessment by ordinary members and expert participants (in individual and/or community levels)*: the last stage of assessment. In this step the considered contents will be assessed either by ordinary or expert participants in both levels, individual and community:

> Ordinary participants (at individual level): they assess the knowledge or information that "are not controversial, scientific, and professional". There are 5 defined questions (addressed in Table 1) to which the ordinary participants will give a rate (based on 5-point Likert Scale) to determine the reliability and quality of considered contents. In this personal evaluation, if the sum of given rates to all 5 questions is lower than the mid-point (2.5 point), the evaluator notes the contents as "rejected" or "unreliable". If the sum of the given rates to all 5 questions is above the mid-point, the participant

notes the contents as "accepted" or "reliable". In cases that the contents seem needing further/deeper evaluation, the evaluator marks them. When the number of marked contents reaches a certain percentage, the moderator(s) will send them to "ordinary participants at the community level".
> Expert participants (at individual level): they assess the knowledge or information that "are not controversial but are scientific and professional". Similarly, by responding to 5 questions, they will give a rate (based on 5-point Likert Scale) in order to individually and professionally determine the reliability and quality of considered contents. In this personal evaluation, if the sum of given rates to all 5 questions is lower than the mid-point (2.5 point), the evaluator notes the contents as "rejected" or "unreliable". If the sum of the given rates to all 5 questions is above the mid-point, the evaluator notes the contents as "accepted" or "reliable". In cases that the contents seem needing further/deeper evaluation, the expert participant marks them. When the number of marked contents reaches a certain percentage, the moderators will send them to "expert participants at the community level".
> Ordinary participants (at community level): the process of assessment and rating by ordinary participants at the community level follows the same process as for ordinary participants at individual level. Even though, in this step and level, the ordinary participants first by collaborative efforts (e.g., group discussion, sharing ideas and viewpoints) exchange their opinion and findings about the considered contents that "are controversial, but not scientific, and professional". Considering the raised points in the community, the ordinary participants then go through a personal rating.
> Expert participants (at community level): the process of assessment and rating by expert participants in community level is similar to the process for expert participants at individual level. Although, in this step and level, the expert participants first by collaborative efforts (e.g., group discussion, sharing ideas and viewpoints, peer review, Delphi method) exchange their opinions and findings about the considered contents that "are controversial, scientific, and professional". Taking into account the raised points in the community, the expert participants then go through a personal rating.

- *Step 3 – publishing the results of assessment by moderators:* having received the results of assessment from step 2, the moderators will proceed to the last phase of assessment. They first analyze the received results and then publish their final decisions about the reliability of the shared contents.

The frequently updated results of assessment from step 2 are visible to all community participants. They can, however, individually analyze and judge the reliability and quality of assessed knowledge or information.

The 5 defined questions, 5-point Likert Scale, and proposed formula for calculation of the given rates (in both levels) are presented in Table 1 and Table 2. It is note taking that every Likert question addressed in Table 1 corresponds to one quality indicator, but the same weight (1) is adopted for the 5 addressed questions, because they all are closely correlated and also considered equally important in the assessment.

Table 1. Examples of questions and 5-point Likert Scale for assessing the reliability and quality of shared knowledge or information in MCL community.

Questions (checklist approach)	5-point Likert Scale				
1. How much the content is worthy for consideration?	1	2	3	4	5
2. How well the content is written and understandable?	1	2	3	4	5
3. How much the content is accurate and factual?	1	2	3	4	5
4. How much the content is verifiable?	1	2	3	4	5
5. How much is the expertise and reputation of the author/publisher (of content)?	1	2	3	4	5

Table 2. Proposed formula for calculation of given rates at individual and community levels

Proposed formula for calculation of given rates in both levels (individual and community)

$$\mathbf{Z} = \frac{\sum_{i=1}^{n} \boldsymbol{E_i} \times \boldsymbol{R_i}}{\boldsymbol{n}} \times \boldsymbol{L}$$

$$\mathbf{Z} > \mathbf{Mid} \rightarrow \forall_{accept} : \left(\sum_{i=1}^{n} \boldsymbol{E_i} \times \boldsymbol{R_i}\right) > \left(\sum_{i=1}^{n} 12.5 \times \boldsymbol{R_i}\right)$$

- **Z** = content quality/value
- $\boldsymbol{E_i}$ = evaluation result (is an integer in a Likert Scale between 1 to 5 which shows the final opinion of the evaluator)
- $\boldsymbol{R_i}$ = personal ranking*
- $\boldsymbol{L}$ = rate of acceptance (in individual level = (1), and in community level = (2)
- $\boldsymbol{n}$ = number of evaluators

*** E.g. Personal rankings:**

- Diploma = **1**
- Degree student = **2**
- Degree graduated = **3**
- Master student = **4**
- Master graduate = **5**
- PhD = **6**
- Post-doc = **7**
- Assistant, Prof = **8**
- Associate, Prof = **9**
- Full, Prof = **10**

5 Discussion

MCL is an emerging learning mechanism relying on a ubiquitous source of jointly created, shared, and developed knowledge and information for interested learners. However, the quality of shared contents in a MCL community is highly variable. As MCL is indeed (by nature) a self-governed community, it is significant that all community participants spontaneously and responsibly take part in the process of content reliability assessment, although the managerial group members (e.g., moderators and content controllers) have active roles in managing this process [3].

Determining the reliability and quality of contents is an extremely complicated process. This complication might arise for several reasons, for example:

a) When the number of contents (to be assessed in a short time frame) increases to a large number. This case would require more computer-human interaction particularly the applications of AI in order to facilitate and speed of the process of assessment.
b) When the knowledge (to be assessed) is complex in terms of, for example, structure, or grammar. In this case strong human contribution and intervention is indispensable. The idea is thus that by leveraging of multiple and diverse minds, expertise, and experiences in MCL community, the complexity could be minimized.

Determining the reliability and quality of such contents is an extremely complicated matter, and it often involves sophisticated technologies, experimental investigation, and extensive background knowledge. There is a variety of proposed solutions for evaluating the reliability of shared materials in virtual learning environments [23]. The review of content quality assessment methods under diverse collaborative learning scenarios can provide a basic understanding on the state-of-the-art on false content detection methods.

It should be added that the assessment of content reliability and quality in MCL is still in the early stage of development, and there are several unsolved and challenging issues that still require further consideration, clarification, and research contributions. Furthermore, MAM-MCL is here introduced for the first time and at this stage it is proposed theoretically (although taking inspiration from some successful examples of mass collaboration such as Wikipedia that utilizes fact-checking approach). Without doubt, MAM-MCL needs to be applied to a wider range of real case studies (in future works) to not only focus on its possible challenges (e.g., how can we encouragingly involve a large number of participants in the task of content assessment, and how can we appropriately direct the series of steps addressed above), but also provide more practical solutions. From this perspective, this study attempts to (a) raise the concern about the dissemination of unhealthy contents in learning environments like MCL, (b) underline the importance of developing needed skills at the community level and providing supportive technologies for content assessment, (c) highlight the role of social involvement and power of collaboration, and (d) increase the awareness about the potential solutions in dealing with such cases in the real world. Therefore, it is expected that the proposed MAM-MCL, by taking the advantages of human and technology inclusion, could assist learners to minimize the effect of false and unreliable contents in MCL communities.

In a previous stage of our research, we focused on the organizational structure and governance principles of MCL [4], towards the elaboration of a reference model for such communities. Current work assumes the existence of such MCL organizational structure and focus on specific management issues related to handling false and unreliable contents. Therefore, MAM-MCL, which is still an ongoing work, will contribute to a more robust governance of such collaborative communities.

In the current stage of development, the focus is on the validation of the proposed MAM-MCL, a process that will comprise several steps:

1. Define the purpose and scope of the proposed method (as presented in previous sections);
2. Conduct a survey to gather feedback from some experts (focus group) regarding MAM-MCL (ongoing);
3. Analyze collected feedback and make adjustments to the method (if needed);
4. Consolidate the method towards optimization;
5. Integrate the MAM-MCL in the MCL governance model.

This process is summarized in Fig. 2.

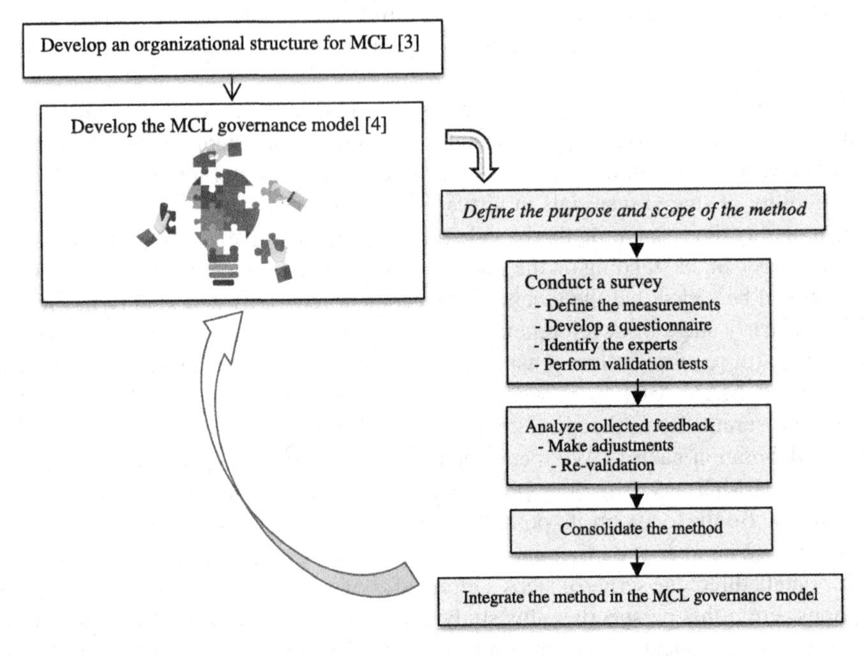

Fig. 2. Plan for the development and validation of MAM-MCL

6 Conclusion

The rapid development of collaborative activities, and informal lifelong learning, coupled with technological advances, led to emerging and developing innovative and useful approaches for social learning. MCL, as an example, bring diverse contributions from a pool of minds, talents, experiences, and skill sets to come up with productive learning practices. However, the quality of exchanged knowledge or information by contributing members in the MCL community is extremely variable. Thus, there is a need for the application of an appropriate assessment system. Given that, this study, by proposing the MAM-MCL, attempts to introduce an assessment method to help evaluating the reliability of shared contents through simultaneously bringing into service a) various technological support tools (e.g., ICT platforms, AI, and digital fingerprints), b) community involvement and collaborative evaluation, and c) combination of different evaluation strategies and techniques (e.g., brainstorming, critical thinking, group discussions, debates, peer evaluations, inquiry-based learning, rating, and expert consult).Validation of MAM-MCL is the ongoing step of development.

Acknowledgements. This work has been funded in part by the Center of Technology and Systems and the Portuguese FCT program UIDB/00066/2020.

References

1. Zamiri, M., Camarinha-Matos, L.M.: Mass collaboration and learning: opportunities, challenges, and influential factors. Appl. Sci. **9**(13), 2620 (2019). https://doi.org/10.3390/app9132620
2. Zamiri, M., Camarinha-Matos, L.M.: Learning through mass collaboration - issues and challenges. In: Camarinha-Matos, L.M., Adu-Kankam, K.O., Julashokri, M. (eds.) DoCEIS 2018. IAICT, vol. 521, pp. 3–17. Springer, Cham (2018). https://doi.org/10.1007/978-3-319-78574-5_1
3. Zamiri, M., Camarinha-Matos, L.M.: Organizational Structure for Mass Collaboration and Learning. In: Camarinha-Matos, L.M., Almeida, R., Oliveira, J. (eds.) DoCEIS 2019. IAICT, vol. 553, pp. 14–23. Springer, Cham (2019). https://doi.org/10.1007/978-3-030-17771-3_2
4. Zamiri, M., Camarinha-Matos, L.M.: Towards a reference model for mass collaborative learning. In: Camarinha-Matos, L.M., Farhadi, N., Lopes, F., Pereira, H. (eds.) DoCEIS 2020. IAICT, vol. 577, pp. 18–30. Springer, Cham (2020). https://doi.org/10.1007/978-3-030-45124-0_2
5. Liang, W., Morstatter, F., Carley, K.M., Liu, H.: Misinformation in social media definition manipulation and detection. ACM SIGKDD Explor. Newsl. **21**(2), 80–90 (2019). https://doi.org/10.1145/3373464.3373475
6. Islam, M.R., Liu, S., Wang, X., Xu, G.: Deep learning for misinformation detection on online social networks: a survey and new perspectives. Soc. Netw. Anal. Min. **10**(1), 1–20 (2020). https://doi.org/10.1007/s13278-020-00696-x
7. National Research Council: Information Technologies: Opportunities for Advancing Educational Assessment. Chapter, In: Knowing What Students Know: The Science and Design of Educational Assessment. The National Academies Press, Washington, DC (2001). https://doi.org/10.17226/10019
8. Luckin, R.: Towards artificial intelligence-based assessment systems. J. Nat. Hum. Behav. **1**(3), 0028 (2017). https://doi.org/10.1038/s41562-016-0028
9. Cope, B., Kalantzis, M., Searsmith, D.: Artificial intelligence for education: knowledge and its assessment in AI-enabled learning ecologies. J. Educ. Philos. Theory (2020). https://doi.org/10.1080/00131857.2020.1728732
10. Choudhary, A.K., Harding, J., Camarinha-Matos, L.M., Lenny Koh, S.C., Tiwari, M.K.: Knowledge management and supporting tools for collaborative networks. J. Prod. Res. **51**(7), 1953–1957 (2013)
11. Evans, S., Roth, N.: Collaborative knowledge networks. In: Camarinha-Matos, L.M., Afsarmanesh, H. (eds.) Collaborative Networked Organizations, pp. 139–146. Kluwer Academic Publishers, Boston (2004). https://doi.org/10.1007/1-4020-7833-1_17
12. Talwara, S., Dhirb, A., Kaurc, P., Zafare, N., Alrasheedy, M.: Why do people share fake news? Associations between the dark side of socialmedia use and fake news sharing behavior. J. Retail. Consum. Serv. **51**, 72–82 (2019). https://doi.org/10.1016/j.jretconser.2019.05.026

13. Kendeou, P., Robinson, D.H., McCrudden, M.T.: Misinformation and Fake News in Education. Information Age Publishing, Inc., Charlotte, North Carolina (2019)
14. Keshavarz, H.: How credible is information on the web: reflections on misinformation and disinformation. J. Infopreneurship **1**(2), 1–17 (2014)
15. Thota, A., Tilak, P., Ahluwalia, S., Lohia, N.: Fake news detection: a deep learning approach. J. SMU Data Sci. Rev. **1**(3), 10 (2018)
16. Zhang, Y., Sun, Y., Xie, B.: Quality of health information for consumers on the web: a systematic review of indicators, criteria, tools, and evaluation results. J. Am. Soc. Inf. Sci. **66**(10), 2071–2084 (2015)
17. Jain, A., Shakya, A., Khatter, H., Gupta, A.K.: A smart system for fake news detection using machine learning. In: International Conference on Issues and Challenges in Intelligent Computing Techniques (ICICT), Ghaziabad, India, pp: 1–4, (2019). https://doi.org/10.1109/ICICT46931.2019.8977659.
18. Hannah, S.T., Lester, P.B.: A multilevel approach to building and leading learning organizations. J. Elsevier Leadersh. Q. **20**(1), 34–48 (2009). https://doi.org/10.1016/j.leaqua.2008.11.003
19. Wiewiora, A., Smidt, M., Chang, A.: The 'How' of multilevel learning dynamics: a systematic literature review exploring how mechanisms bridge learning between individuals, teams/projects and the organization. J. Eur. Manage. Rev. **16**(1), 93–115 (2018). https://doi.org/10.1111/emre.12179
20. Newman, I., Lim, J., Pineda, F.: Content validity using a mixed methods approach: its application and development through the use of a table of specifications methodology. J. Mixed Methods Res. **7**(3), 243–260 (2013). https://doi.org/10.1177/1558689813476922
21. Noble, D.F.: Assessing the reliability of open source information. In: Svensson, P., Schubert, J., (eds.) Proceedings of the Seventh International Conference on Information Fusion, vol. 2, pp. 1172–1178. International Society of Information Fusion, Mountain View, CA (2004)
22. Pierce, R.: Evaluating information: validity, reliability, accuracy, triangulation. Chapter, In: Research Methods in Politics. SAGE Publications Ltd. (2008). https://doi.org/10.4135/9780857024589.d12
23. van Zyl, A., Turpin, M., Matthee, M.C.: How can critical thinking be used to assess the credibility of online information? In: Hattingh, M., Matthee, M., Smuts, H., Pappas, I., Dwivedi, Y., Mäntymäki, M. (eds.) Responsible Design, Implementation and Use of Information and Communication Technology I3E 2020. Lecture Notes in Computer Science, vol. 12067, pp. 199–210. Springer, Cham (2020). https://doi.org/10.1007/978-3-030-45002-1_17

Smart Manufacturing

Characteristics of Adaptable Control of Production Systems and the Role of Self-organization Towards Smart Manufacturing

Luis Alberto Estrada-Jimenez[1,2](✉), Sanaz Nikghadam-Hojjati[1], and Jose Barata[1,2]

[1] Centre of Technology and Systems, UNINOVA Instituto Desenvolvimento de Novas Tecnologias, 2829-516 Caparica, Portugal
{lestrada,Sanaznik,jab}@uninova.pt

[2] Department of Electrical and Computer Engineering, School of Science and Technology, NOVA University of Lisbon, 2829-516 Caparica, Portugal

Abstract. Self-adaptive control of production systems has attracted a lot of research during last years. Nevertheless, most of these approaches are still unable to tackle current manufacturing expectations, they are very particular for the case study, are in an initial stage of research or do not apply the concept of self-organization and their properties in its strong sense. Thus, leaving the systems without enough robustness, adaptability, or emergence that are highly desirable considering current market requirements. Therefore, the purpose of this work to identify some of the important characteristics that have been applied in past studies and that can be considered together as a baseline to build future manufacturing frameworks.

Keywords: Self-organization · Smart manufacturing · Cyber-physical production systems · Manufacturing requirements

1 Introduction

In past decades, the high dynamicity of markets and high rate of personalization of products has brought the need for companies to change their internal business and manufacturing structure to stay competitive. This situation entails the proposition of novel production strategies where resources have to be ready to change, in such a way that no delays can be allowed, operations have to be continuous and opportunities to increase performance should be part of a constant manufacturing evolution [1]. This new level of agility is envisioned by the 4th industrial revolution that applies current emerging technologies offering a more efficient and adaptable manufacturing scenario [2]. This level of adaptability introduces the need of having systems that can dynamically self-organize, with agents that have no global vision of the system and with a global awareness that is the result of a high interaction and cooperation.

The original version of this chapter was revised: this chapter was previously published non-open access. The correction to this chapter is available at
https://doi.org/10.1007/978-3-030-78288-7_35

© The Author(s) 2021, corrected publication 2022
L. M. Camarinha-Matos et al. (Eds.): DoCEIS 2021, IFIP AICT 626, pp. 39–50, 2021.
https://doi.org/10.1007/978-3-030-78288-7_4

However, such level of self-organization is not simple to implement [3]. Several design constrains and safety issues have to be considered due to the high level of decentralization required. Thus, making the self-organization process as a field of continuous research considering manufacturing expectations [4].

Self-organization in the strong sense does not mean just the dynamic organization of manufacturing resources, functionalities, or services. Considering its basic definition in biology or software engineering, there are several characteristics that support this concept e.g. emergence, learning, robustness, etc. [5]. However, most studies rarely apply all these characteristics together due to the difficulty of its formalization in control architectures and due to the high level of abstraction that these concepts have. Therefore, it is main interest of this work to discuss some of these characteristics from the literature in such a way that can contribute to build future manufacturing solutions. It is also envisaged that the research findings can build a solid foundation for better developing in the research phase of the PhD dissertation, which is generically guided by the following research question.

Q. *What could be a suitable set of interaction patterns, methods, and tools to promote adaptability and evolvability in cyber-physical production systems, namely the self-organization of manufacturing resources and the introduction of experienced based knowledge and control principles to assist this adaptability in the context of smart manufacturing?*

The rest of this paper is organized as follows: Sect. 1 described the objective of the work. Section 2 links the content of this paper with applied artificial systems. Section 3 provides a brief overview of Smart manufacturing and of the concept of self-organization. Section 4 presents and integrated vision of current requirements and characteristics; and Sect. 5 concludes summarizing main findings and future works.

2 Relation to Applied Artificial Intelligence Systems

Smart manufacturing is the result of a digital transformation accompanied with the design and implementations of more complex and sophisticated production systems, highly needed to overcome current manufacturing expectations. Thus, new technologies are influencing the introduction of smart and autonomous Cyber-Physical Production Systems (CPPS).

In order to support this smartness and autonomy, Artificial Intelligence (AI) and more specifically distributed AI solutions have paved the way towards the introduction of tools and technologies that are reshaping traditional production design principles for several reasons. First, by providing a highly distributed infrastructure. While traditional production environments are mostly centralized, such level of centralization implies rigidity in the decision making and poor levels of adaptability [6]. Additionally, centralized systems are failure-prone due to the high dependency in one central decisional element. If this element fails, the whole system automatically crashes. While in distributed systems, elements can make individual decisions.

Thus, novel solutions should be decoupled and decentralized. Distributed AI and more specifically multi-agent systems (MAS) have been highly applied in last decades to overcome such challenge. These distributed computerized systems can support the instantiation of adaptable and distributed solutions and thus create intelligent entities to facilitate the emergence of a global behavior [6]. Additionally, current data availability, as well as the high number of sensors and Information and communication infrastructures inside and outside the shop floor, improve the integration with the supply chain and provide necessary information to adapt and optimize processes in real time. Finally, AI provides the necessary methods and tools to promote experience-based knowledge, reasoning, and learning. Novel AI solutions are attracting a considerable set of applications and undoubtedly will pursue the development and optimization of adaptable production systems. Furthermore, a preliminary research in these fields has shown an increasing attention in the application of bio-inspired AI. Indeed, several manufacturing paradigms towards agile manufacturing such as Bionic Manufacturing Systems (BMS), Holonic Manufacturing Systems (HMS) [7], or Evolvable Production Systems (EPS) [8] have found inspiration in the patterns provided by natural systems. Those have been an interesting source of research to provide novel mechanisms to fulfill current smart manufacturing vision taking advantage of information and enabling high flexibility and connectivity in the physical process.

3 Smart Manufacturing and Cyber-Physical Production Systems

Traditional manufacturing plants following the mass production paradigm have relied to a large extend into dedicated production lines. These production systems even though highly capable of generating standardization and fast and cost-effective solutions were not able to manage the new era of high product personalization. The need of a higher product variety and its high heterogeneous requirements introduced a new conception of production development [9]. Thus, the emergence of new production paradigms i.e. Flexible Manufacturing Systems (FMS) and Reconfigurable Manufacturing Systems (RMS) to increase flexibility, agility and reconfigurability [9]. Such approaches, aimed to provide rapid adaptation to market changes, increasing usability of hardware, personalization, decentralization and decreasing engineering effort and time [10]. In addition to this, novel solutions took advantage of enabling technologies like AI, robotics, high sensor availability and high levels of computation and networking to introduce digitalization in factories with the aim of make them smarter. Thus, generating the concept of smart manufacturing where CPPS are main enablers. CPPS have high capabilities of computation and communication [11]. Their main expectations include self-x properties i.e. self-adaptation, self-organization, self-learning [12] and are therefore a focus of continuous research. Even though there is narrow applicability of self-organization, it is highlighted here because of the tremendous number of benefits for future industries e.g. to achieve the idea of lights-out manufacturing philosophy where processes and machines are fully automated and require no human intervention.

3.1 Self-organization in Smart Manufacturing

The self-organization plays a very important role in current production systems. Self-organization can be described as the set of structural or behavioral changes that arise in response to an external input, or variations in the conditions of a system. This continuous variations and evolution can cause instability due to the inappropriate process synchronization with the decentralized units [13]. Due to this reason, self-organizing systems should maintain an adequate level stabilization and equilibrium. While classical systems have normally an external control, self-organization occurs spontaneously [14]. In this case "*...spontaneous means that no internal or external agent is in control of the process: for a large enough system, any individual agent can be eliminated or replaced without damaging the resulting structure...*" [14]. This makes self-organization a truly collective process characterized by robustness and adaptability.

Although all units in a self-organizing system should have only local vision and be able to communicate just with their closer neighbors, such interactions can be propagated to distant regions of the system [14].

In self-organizing systems, the whole is the result of the sum of their parts. Such interaction brings several emerging behaviors i.e. behaviors that were not directly preprogrammed. In manufacturing, this is translated to the no need to specify a production sequence or flow. Thus, a manufacturing system can automatically self-organize without previous models or rules. A high level of robustness and adaptability because of self-organization is still a continuous research endeavor. Therefore, it is worth examining some of previous works to understand how manufacturing paradigms and enterprises can enhance or adopt common characteristics, integrating new technologies and thus being ready to change generating more benefit to companies, increasing quality, and reducing cost of production.

4 Characteristics of Adaptable Production Systems Towards Smart Manufacturing

In the control of self-adaptable manufacturing systems, there are different characteristics that allow the system to run efficiently. While there have been approaches that asses this objective successfully, such implementations are highly constrained by knowledge-based models that somehow neglects the idea of adaptability in the system at least in its strong sense. A collection of works mainly from popular databases (Web of science, Scopus, and Google scholar) has been included in this study, considering key words like self-adapt, evolve, organize and manufacturing, being main interest of such research effort to extract and discuss main characteristics and requirements as will be shown in Sect. 4.1. A summary of the works considered is presented in Table 1.

4.1 Characteristics Description

In smart manufacturing, the control of adaptable production systems should be highly **decentralized**. Even though centralized systems can be considered as essential for data collection, logging or interfacing the benefits from distributed systems pushes more agility and reactivity in presence of environmental changes and disturbances. The decision-making should not rely on centralized control units with a global vision [6]. Instead, single units should be independent and should have the ability to make autonomous decisions. Nevertheless, high levels of decentralization imply also high levels of myopia and perhaps non-optimal behavior. Myopia refers to the efficiency in decision making considering the close environmental vision of individual entities; it can cause global degradation due to the lack of a central supervisory element.

Therefore, an equilibrium between adequate levels of centralization and decentralization are necessary as shown by some examples in the literature where hybrid control architectures report and adequate performance. In addition, adaptability implies the existence of **modularization** of resources.

Modularization promotes reconfigurability and granularity in terms of hardware and software [15]. The finer the **granularity**, the finer the level of engineering design and abstraction. Coarser levels of granularity advocate entire shop floors, while finer granularity levels represent sensors or grippers. This results in higher levels of **complexity** in the control of a production plant, higher levels of **composability** and possibly communication delays. Factories need to be highly **scalable** and their constituent elements **pluggables**. Such elements should have minimal cost of reconfiguration and if possible null re-engineering effort. Aforementioned levels of scalability are achieved by compatible modules in terms of mechanical and software design [16]. This results in systems that are highly **adaptable or robust** i.e. that can maintain certain conditions regarding external changes or modifications [17]. Adaptability is normally applied in runtime to provide a set of alternative strategies, structural changes and behaviors that allow continuous work of the system.

Despite the decentralization needed, manufacturers require a certain level of **optimization**. The optimization process might have different visions. It might refer to the capability components, machines or devices to change their behavior with the aim of improving the overall process efficiency [32]. Also, it might refer to a reconfiguration process with the objective of maximizing resource utilization [33] and to the needed strategies that can improve the overall process performance [34]. This means the reduction of due times, energy consumption, etc. considering also the avoidance of queues or bottlenecks. It is possible to find optimization strategies in dispatching and scheduling operations [35]. Dispatching decisions might improve the sequential resource operation i.e., routing a product to the most suitable resource. It is not easy no find fully optimized systems in self-organizing control architectures since this means the need for having global vision. Thus, it is important to introduce **hybrid architectures** that allow hierarchies or supervisory entities to have control of the overall performance of the process.

Emergence plays an important role in self-organizing control architectures. In engineering, emergence brings the chance of finding novel structural self-organizing patterns. Such emerging patterns are not pre-defined; thus, giving the system the ability to autonomously find alternatives of organization to unexpected situations. This is one of the most important differences with classical knowledge-based approaches, where most of the behavior is predefined and makes systems unable to cope with unexpected situations. The myopia caused by the high level of decentralization of individual units can result in instability. The result of this instability is consequence of very unpredictable environments and sometimes uncontrolled emerging properties [17]. In engineering systems, this is caused by conflicting policies or rules due to the lack of a centralized unit. With such possibility of system degradation, it is essential to provide a **stability** mechanism that can guide the whole adaptability process and provide the necessary evolution and

Table 1. Selected works in the context of self-adaptable production systems.

Reference, year	Adaptation driver and description
Frei et al. [18], 2011	Self-organization of tasks in creation time (chemical reaction basis) and adaptation in runtime. Automatic layout generation according to available modules and ontological based decision-making
Onori et al. [19], 2012	Presents the concept of EPS and more specifically the concept of plug & produce. A multi agent architecture allows the communication between resources, products and transport systems
Leitao et al. [20], 2012	Routing of a product (dynamic task allocation) according to product availability through a mechanism of potential fields
Rocha et al. [21], 2014	Plug and produce of components using and agent based data model. It supports monitoring, data analysis and human machine interaction
Barbosa et al. [22], 2015	2-dimensional self-organization: structural and behavioral. Composed of hybrid architecture: (hierarchical and heterarchical) and modules for learning (behaviors) and nervousness stabilizer
Ribeiro et al. [23], 2015	Agent based architecture for focused on runtime topological changes in the routing of products. Measurement of transport cost and path computation. Transport cost is used to quantify stability
Ferreira et al. [24], 2016	Fully bio-inspired architecture. Self-organization based on the firefly algorithm. Resources attract mobile parts based on an attraction mechanism (each resource has a template of available operations)
Wang et al.[25], 2016	Self-organization of a conveying route based on agent based negotiation and rules. Self-organization is supported by big-data analysis using a coordinating entity that has global vision of the system. There are mechanisms that prevent deadlocks
Zhang et al. [26], 2017	Self-organization consists on optimal task matching of services of resources and tasks. Self-adaptation is implemented in run time. Mechanisms presented are conflict resolution and optimal configuration model (based on metrics evaluation)
Jimenez et al. [27], 2017	Dynamic hybrid control system that integrates a switching mechanism to alter between hierarchical and heterarchical architectures according to a governance parameter

(*continued*)

Table 1. (*continued*)

Reference, year	Adaptation driver and description
Zhang et al. [28], 2018	Cooperation between production and logistics. Tasks and resources are virtualized as services and a self-organizing configuration layer based on an intelligent task and logistics decomposition process based on a ATC model
Sanderson et al. [29], 2019	This approach is based on the design of an ontological modelling of the system based on a function-behavior-structure methodology. The product development relies on a recipe that formalizes its design features
Ding et al. [30], 2020	Autonomous manufacturing task orchestration. Based on a Hidden Markov model to determine the most optimal machine sequence after a production task has been launched. Based on probabilities to perform an adequate autonomous work in progress
Guo et al. [31], 2021	The work proposes a collaborative control for adaptive and smart production logistics. It uses the hybrid automata to model the relation of physical components and data processing and adaptive strategies to deal with production exceptions

support in presence of dynamic changes [13]. Natural systems are continuously changing because of continuous **learning** from external and internal modifications. In control architectures, the role of learning might depend on the level of granularity to which it is referred. P. Neves et al. [36] define three learning levels in a multi-agent architecture considering module (finer granularity), group (coalitions) and global learning level. Because of such mechanisms, parameters, logical behavior, and structural modifications can be improved e.g., regulation of the speed of conveyor, self-organization of the functionalities of components and even structural changes. Naturally, all these mechanisms need to be in constant evaluation and adjustment, by the operator or by predefined goals or experience so that learning mechanisms can take effect. Additionally, manufacturing systems can take advantage of **data driven approaches** and high availability of data to reinforce their production adaptability. Under this continuous evaluation, it is important to note the **measurement of various metrics** examining variables that have strong influence in the manufacturing process. Few works consider such evaluation as part of the adaptation, and therefore, keep their adaptability tied to very general drivers. Some examples are: cost of production, quality, time and flexibility [37]. The reduction time for self-organizing processes is highly desirable. Such minimization can typically be done by reducing the setup, processing, transport and waiting times [38].

4.2 Self-adapting and Self-organizing Manufacturing Applications

Despite the manufacturing industry having a wide scope of subfields, a considerable number of works make use cases in the assembly line. Most likely due to the simplicity of abstracting modules or engineering steps and because it makes simpler the engineer reductionist process in this type of applications. Different types of adaptation applications have been recognized from this overview. First, the manufacturing **scheduling and planning** influences the utilization of resources and clearly provides an optimal or near optimal manufacturing task sequence to fulfill plan specifications. This is highly related to the **autonomous task allocation** of resources, which describes which machines' services are available to fulfill specific jobs. In run time, this generally results in transportation from one resource to another from shipment to final production. The **transportation** e.g., in conveyors, automated guided vehicles (AGVs) or cranes provides the means of **routing** a product to the adequate resource or **re-routing** it in case of disruptions or when trying to optimize the process (reducing transportation time, distributing weight, etc.).

During the run time operation, different modules can be added or replaced without extra engineer effort (**plug and produce**) which includes not just hardware adaptation but also the dynamic organization of the digital entities. This clearly increases hardware re-usability, facilitating also process customization. In terms of hardware composability, and more precisely fine granularity modules, the **composability of skills** or the adequate functionalities re-arrangement (self-organization) provide a variety of different compound services from very simple ones, adding more complex capabilities to the system. Figure 1 presents a summary of characteristics and applications of self-adapting and self-organizing manufacturing applications and characteristics.

4.3 The Role of Self-organization Towards Smart Manufacturing

Main challenges and requirements in the context of CPPS converge in the inappropriate assumption that a strong predefined knowledge should be available about the system behavior, which is not always feasible considering the high dynamism of markets and high level of unexpected situations.

In this context, the adaptability of manufacturing process should not rely on the application of model-driven approaches since they are mostly static and therefore not able to overcome unanticipated events.

Several approaches have introduced self-organization mechanisms to increase adaptability in manufacturing. Nevertheless, the term is sometimes misused, considering its original roots in software engineering and natural and biological systems. Thus, most current implementations lose the real essence of self-organization and end up developing traditional systems with hard-coded knowledge or modelling-based techniques and relying into some extend to having external control. Consequently, the consideration of main self-organization emerging requirements can assist in overcoming the pitfall of making CPPS highly adaptable and at the same time bringing a set of necessary engineering considerations. However, despite such assumptions and benefits, a high-distributed system in the strong sense of self-organization has many drawbacks, too. The high level of myopia may cause a chaotic behavior and even process inefficiency. This is of course not desired by industrial practitioners and consequently can cause aversion to its industrial adoption. In such case, it is unavoidable the consideration of hybrid architectures as shown for example by implementations of the holonic paradigm, which by the way does not contradicts the main definition of self-organization [5].

Thus, we believe that the future of self-organizing manufacturing systems should be a holistic and interdisciplinary process. Clearly, it does not mean the creation of new frameworks or architectures from scratch; but the convergence of a set of architectural patterns and methodologies from different fields and works i.e. biological self-organizing patterns, control and stability of distributed architectures, machine learning and a strong baseline of concepts especially from EPS, HMS and CPPS. Additionally, we believe that the consideration of the studied requirements and characteristics would push this research endeavor for future implementations.

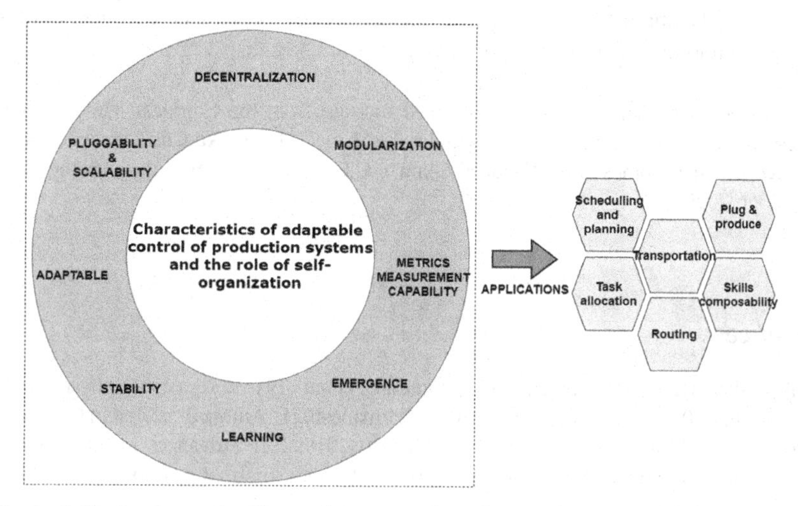

Fig. 1. Self-adapting and self-organizing manufacturing applications and characteristics.

5 Conclusions and Further Work

This paper conducts a short review of characteristics of self-adaptable production systems that may be consider together to develop a generic framework. Most of works are specific for the case study and therefore neglect the consideration of a high scope of requirements. Thus, some challenges emerge because of the lack of a fully extensive solution. In addition, the concept of self-organization even though introduced to some extent in few works, does not seem to be fully exploited; for example, with biological or software foundation. This does not mean to develop fully distributed solutions, but to take advantage of such patterns and adapt them to the production context and their needs.

Within such ideas, we believe that novel solutions should take advantage of current research, methodologies, and technologies to provide a holistic and robust approach. Of course, a benchmarking of such concepts and ideas is important before implementing them. This becomes critical nowadays to fulfill current manufacturing expectations, taking advantage also of fully digitalized factories and high data availability.

Future works need to consider these ideas and connect them. Additionally, it is important to note how self-organizing patterns can improve the process adaptability and how holistic solutions based on these characteristics can be implemented. For example, considering the work proposed in [24] where a fully distributed bio-inspired solution is presented. It would be interesting to include in this approach learning techniques for dynamic adaptation or the inclusion of control-based models or metrics evaluation for an enhanced self-organized process. In addition, it is important to consider and analyze managerial implications of this research. This will push the industrial adoption of self-organizing systems. Future work of this research will also include practical applications in use cases like material handling, transporting and routing where concepts of self-organization and emergence are easy to analyze.

Acknowledgements. This project has received funding from the European Union's Horizon 2020 research and innovation programme under the Marie Skłodowska-Curie grant No. 814078. Partial support also comes from Fundação para a Ciência e Tecnologia through the program UIDB/00066/2020.

References

1. Nikghadam-Hojjati, S., Barata, J.: Computational creativity to design cyber-physical systems in industry 4.0. In: Camarinha-Matos, L., Afsarmanesh, H., Antonelli, D. (eds.) Collaborative Networks and Digital Transformation, PRO-VE 2019, IFIP Advances in Information and Communication Technology, vol. 568. Springer, Cham (2019). https://doi.org/10.1007/978-3-030-28464-0_4
2. Lasi, H., Fettke, P., Kemper, H.-G., Feld, T., Hoffmann, M.: Industry 4.0. Bus. Inf. Syst. Eng. **6**(4), 239–242 (2014). https://doi.org/10.1007/s12599-014-0334-4
3. Leitão, P., Karnouskos, S., Ribeiro, L., Lee, J., Strasser, T., Colombo, A.W.: Smart agents in industrial cyber-physical systems. Proc. IEEE **104**, 1086–1101 (2016). https://doi.org/10.1109/JPROC.2016.2521931
4. Napoleone, A., Macchi, M., Pozzetti, A.: A review on the characteristics of cyber-physical systems for the future smart factories. J. Manuf. Syst. **54**, 305–335 (2020). https://doi.org/10.1016/j.jmsy.2020.01.007
5. Di Marzo Serugendo, G., Gleizes, M.P., Karageorgos, A.: Self-organization in multi-agent systems. Knowl. Eng. Rev. 20, 165–189 (2005). https://doi.org/10.1017/S0269888905000494
6. Trentesaux, D.: Distributed control of production systems. Eng. Appl. Artif. Intell. **22**, 971–978 (2009). https://doi.org/10.1016/j.engappai.2009.05.001
7. Van Brussel, H., Wyns, J., Valckenaers, P., Bongaerts, L., Peeters, P.: Reference architecture for holonic manufacturing systems: PROSA. Comput. Ind. **37**, 255–274 (1998). https://doi.org/10.1016/S0166-3615(98)00102-X
8. Frei, R., Barata, J., Onori, M.: Evolvable production systems context and implications. In: IEEE International Symposium on Industrial Electronics, pp. 3233–3238 (2007). https://doi.org/10.1109/ISIE.2007.4375132
9. Mourtzis, D., Doukas, M.: Decentralized manufacturing systems review: challenges and outlook. Logist. Res. **5**(3–4), 113–121 (2012). https://doi.org/10.1007/s12159-012-0085-x
10. Zhang, D.Z.: Towards theory building in agile manufacturing strategies - case studies of an agility taxonomy. Int. J. Prod. Econ. **131**, 303–312 (2011). https://doi.org/10.1016/j.ijpe.2010.08.010

11. Monostori, L., et al.: Cyber-physical systems in manufacturing. CIRP Ann. **65**, 621–641 (2016). https://doi.org/10.1016/j.cirp.2016.06.005
12. Leitão, P., Colombo, A.W., Karnouskos, S.: Industrial automation based on cyber-physical systems technologies: prototype implementations and challenges. Comput. Ind. **81**, 11–25 (2016). https://doi.org/10.1016/j.compind.2015.08.004
13. Leitão, P.: Self-organization in manufacturing systems: challenges and opportunities. In: Proceedings - 2nd IEEE International Conference on Self-Adaptive and Self-Organizing Systems Workshops, SASOW 2008, pp. 174–179 (2008). https://doi.org/10.1109/SASOW.2008.40
14. Heylighen, F.: Complexity and Self-organization. CRC Press, Boca Raton (2008)
15. Scholz-Reiter, B., Freitag, M.: Autonomous processes in assembly systems. CIRP Ann. - Manuf. Technol. 56, 712–729 (2007). https://doi.org/10.1016/j.cirp.2007.10.002
16. Putnik, G., et al.: Scalability in manufacturing systems design and operation: state-of-the-art and future developments roadmap. CIRP Ann. - Manuf. Technol. **62**, 751–774 (2013). https://doi.org/10.1016/j.cirp.2013.05.002
17. Di Marzo Serugendo, G., Gleizes, M.P., Karageorgos, A.: Self-organising software: from natural to artificial adaptation (2011). https://doi.org/10.1007/978-3-642-17348-6
18. Frei, R., Di, G., Serugendo, M.: Self-organizing assembly systems. IEEE Trans. Syst. Man. Cybern. **41**, 885–897 (2011)
19. Onori, M., Lohse, N., Barata, J., Hanisch, C.: The IDEAS project: plug and produce at shop-floor level. Assem. Autom. **32**, 124–134 (2012). https://doi.org/10.1108/01445151211212280
20. Leitão, P., Barbosa, J., Trentesaux, D.: Bio-inspired multi-agent systems for reconfigurable manufacturing systems. Eng. Appl. Artif. Intell. **25**, 934–944 (2012). https://doi.org/10.1016/j.engappai.2011.09.025
21. Rocha, A., et al.: An agent based framework to support plug and produce. In: Proceedings of 2014 12th IEEE International Conference on Industrial Informatics, INDIN 2014, pp. 504–510 (2014). https://doi.org/10.1109/INDIN.2014.6945565
22. Barbosa, J., Leitão, P., Adam, E., Trentesaux, D.: Dynamic self-organization in holonic multi-agent manufacturing systems: the ADACOR evolution. Comput. Ind. **66**, 99–111 (2015). https://doi.org/10.1016/j.compind.2014.10.011
23. Ribeiro, L., Rocha, A., Veiga, A., Barata, J.: Collaborative routing of products using a self-organizing mechatronic agent framework - a simulation study. Comput. Ind. **68**, 27–39 (2015). https://doi.org/10.1016/j.compind.2014.12.003
24. Dias-Ferreira, J., Ribeiro, L., Akillioglu, H., Neves, P., Onori, M.: BIOSOARM: a bio-inspired self-organising architecture for manufacturing cyber-physical shopfloors. J. Intell. Manuf. **29**(7), 1659–1682 (2016). https://doi.org/10.1007/s10845-016-1258-2
25. Wang, S., Wan, J., Zhang, D., Li, D., Zhang, C.: Towards smart factory for industry 4.0: a self-organized multi-agent system with big data based feedback and coordination. Comput. Netw. **101**, 158–168 (2016). https://doi.org/10.1016/j.comnet.2015.12.017
26. Zhang, Y., Qian, C., Lv, J., Liu, Y.: Agent and cyber-physical system based self-organizing and self-adaptive intelligent shopfloor. IEEE Trans. Ind. Inform. **13**, 737–747 (2017). https://doi.org/10.1109/TII.2016.2618892
27. Jimenez, J.F., Bekrar, A., Zambrano-Rey, G., Trentesaux, D., Leitão, P.: Pollux: a dynamic hybrid control architecture for flexible job shop systems. Int. J. Prod. Res. 55, 4229–4247 (2017). https://doi.org/10.1080/00207543.2016.1218087
28. Zhang, Y., Guo, Z., Lv, J., Liu, Y.: A framework for smart production-logistics systems based on CPS and industrial IoT. IEEE Trans. Ind. Inform. **14**, 4019–4032 (2018). https://doi.org/10.1109/TII.2018.2845683
29. Sanderson, D., Chaplin, J.C., Ratchev, S.: A function-behaviour-structure design methodology for adaptive production systems. Int. J. Adv. Manuf. Technol. **105**(9), 3731–3742 (2019). https://doi.org/10.1007/s00170-019-03823-x

30. Ding, K., Lei, J., Chan, F.T.S., Hui, J., Zhang, F., Wang, Y.: Hidden Markov model-based autonomous manufacturing task orchestration in smart shop floors. Robot. Comput. Integr. Manuf. **61**, 1–9 (2020). https://doi.org/10.1016/j.rcim.2019.101845
31. Guo, Z., Zhang, Y., Zhao, X., Song, X.: CPS-based self-adaptive collaborative control for smart production-logistics systems. IEEE Trans. Cybern. **51**, 188–198 (2021)
32. Kephart, J.O., Chess, D.M.: The vision of autonomic computing. Computer (Long. Beach. Calif). 36 (2003). https://doi.org/10.1109/MC.2003.1160055
33. Frei, R., McWilliam, R., Derrick, B., Purvis, A., Tiwari, A., Di Marzo Serugendo, G.: Self-healing and self-repairing technologies. Int. J. Adv. Manuf. Technol. 69, 1033–1061 (2013). https://doi.org/10.1007/s00170-013-5070-2
34. Lee, J., Bagheri, B., Kao, H.A.: A cyber-physical systems architecture for industry 4.0-based manufacturing systems. Manuf. Lett. **3**, 18–23 (2015). https://doi.org/10.1016/j.mfglet.2014.12.001
35. Baker, A.D.: A survey of factory control algorithms that can be implemented in a multi-agent heterarchy: dispatching, scheduling, and pull. J. Manuf. Syst. **17**, 297–320 (1998). https://doi.org/10.1016/S0278-6125(98)80077-0
36. Neves, P., Ferreira, J., Onori, M., Barata, J.: Context and implications of learning in evolvable production systems. In: IECON Proceedings (Industrial Electronics Conference, pp. 2740–2745 (2011). https://doi.org/10.1109/IECON.2011.6119745
37. Hon, K.K.B.: Performance and evaluation of manufacturing systems. CIRP Ann. - Manuf. Technol. **54**, 139–154 (2005). https://doi.org/10.1016/s0007-8506(07)60023-7
38. Johnson, D.J.: A framework for reducing manufacturing throughput time. J. Manuf. Syst. **22**, 283–298 (2003). https://doi.org/10.1016/S0278-6125(03)80009-2

Open Access This chapter is licensed under the terms of the Creative Commons Attribution 4.0 International License (http://creativecommons.org/licenses/by/4.0/), which permits use, sharing, adaptation, distribution and reproduction in any medium or format, as long as you give appropriate credit to the original author(s) and the source, provide a link to the Creative Commons licence and indicate if changes were made.

The images or other third party material in this chapter are included in the chapter's Creative Commons licence, unless indicated otherwise in a credit line to the material. If material is not included in the chapter's Creative Commons licence and your intended use is not permitted by statutory regulation or exceeds the permitted use, you will need to obtain permission directly from the copyright holder.

Predictive Manufacturing: Enabling Technologies, Frameworks and Applications

Terrin Pulikottil[1,2](✉), Luis Alberto Estrada-Jimenez[1,2], Sanaz Nikghadam-Hojjati[1], and Jose Barata[1,2]

[1] Centre of Technology and Systems, UNINOVA Instituto Desenvolvimento de Novas Tecnologias, 2829-516 Caparica, Portugal
{tpulikottil,lestrada,jab}@uninova.pt, s.nikghadam@fct.unl.pt
[2] Department of Electrical and Computer Engineering, School of Science and Technology, NOVA University of Lisbon, 2829-516 Caparica, Portugal

Abstract. The impact of globalization and the recent advancements in Information and Communication Technologies has pushed the manufacturing sector towards a new transformation. Current manufacturers with the help of recent advances in Cloud Computing, Artificial Intelligence, and Internet of Things are moving towards a new intelligent system called Predictive Manufacturing Systems (PMS). These systems can be used in a wide array of applications, including proactive maintenance, improved quality control and higher performance. This paper provides an overview of the current trends in Predictive Manufacturing Systems in recent years. The paper discusses the developed frameworks, enabling technologies and various applications of Predictive Manufacturing Systems.

Keywords: Predictive manufacturing systems · Smart manufacturing · Artificial intelligence · Cloud computing · Internet of Things · Data analytics

1 Introduction

Smart Manufacturing

The need for mass customization and competition from emerging markets has pushed the manufacturers to shift towards a new manufacturing paradigm by utilizing the emerging technologies in computer engineering. This new manufacturing paradigm is called Smart Manufacturing. Smart manufacturing can be defined as "A set of manufacturing practices that use networked data and Information & Communication Technologies (ICTs) for governing manufacturing operations" [1].

Predictive Manufacturing Systems

In smart manufacturing, to have a competitive advantage in the market, many manufacturers have started to utilize the data generated from sensors and converted them into

The original version of this chapter was revised: this chapter was previously published non-open access. The correction to this chapter is available at
https://doi.org/10.1007/978-3-030-78288-7_36

© The Author(s) 2021, corrected publication 2022
L. M. Camarinha-Matos et al. (Eds.): DoCEIS 2021, IFIP AICT 626, pp. 51–61, 2021.
https://doi.org/10.1007/978-3-030-78288-7_5

useful information. This has led to the development of intelligent systems called "Predictive Manufacturing Systems (PMS)" which gives self-x capabilities (self-predicting, self-maintaining & self-learning) for manufacturers.

Need for this Work
In the last half decade, there were very limited reviews which gives a general overview of the current frameworks, technologies, and applications of a PMS. Nikolic et al. [2] presents the current trends in predictive manufacturing system but mainly focuses on the benefits and challenges. The authors provided very little information on the developed frameworks or applications of PMS. Other authors have tried to explain in detail specific areas which fall under PMS. Lee et al. [3] reviewed predictive manufacturing with focuses on maintenance. Peres et al. [4] focused on industrial artificial intelligence in industry 4.0. Few other reviews [5, 6] focuses on the application of big data for predictive manufacturing. Hence, there is a need for a review which focuses on the developed frameworks, enabling technologies and current application of PMS.

Aim of the Work
This work will act as the starting point in formulating the hypothesis for the PhD Dissertation of the first author whose tentative research question is, *"Which is an effective generic framework for the realization of a Predictive Manufacturing System (PMS) to improve the overall equipment effectiveness (OEE) in a smart manufacturing environment?"*.

We hope that our work helps in giving new researchers a brief overview of the current trends in predictive manufacturing. More specifically, with this work, we aim to give a concise view for researchers to understand the current frameworks, technologies, and applications of PMS. We also would like this work to act as a guide for manufacturers in implementing PMS for their specific requirements.

2 Relation to Applied Artificial Intelligence Systems

PMS utilizes the emerging technologies in computer engineering to provide an intelligent system for current manufacturing needs. In these emerging technologies Artificial Intelligence stand out as a promising technology for predictive manufacturing. As we will explain in later sections, many researchers have preferred to use Applied Artificial Intelligence System for predictive applications. These applications include Quality Control [7], performance [8], parameter estimation [9, 10], Planning & Scheduling [11, 12] and Maintenance [13]. According to our analyzes, around 40% of the publications in the last 5 years use machine learning techniques for predictive manufacturing. We believe that this trend will steadily increase in the coming years with more manufacturers implementing advance technologies like Internet of Things and Data Analysis for achieving competitive advantage. Hence, Applied Artificial Intelligence Systems will act as a very relevant and effective tool for the realization of PMS.

3 Adopted Methodology

To understand the current trends in PMS a structured literature review was carried out (Fig. 1). The first and the most important step is to identifies relevant research questions (RQ) which would satisfy the requirements of the review. The 3 Research Questions identified for this review paper are mentioned below,

RQ1: What are the various frameworks developed in recent years for the realization of PMS?
RQ2: What are the different technologies used for the development of PMS in recent years?
RQ3: What are the different areas of application of PMS in recent years?

Our review will answer these three research questions and analyze & Discuss their results.

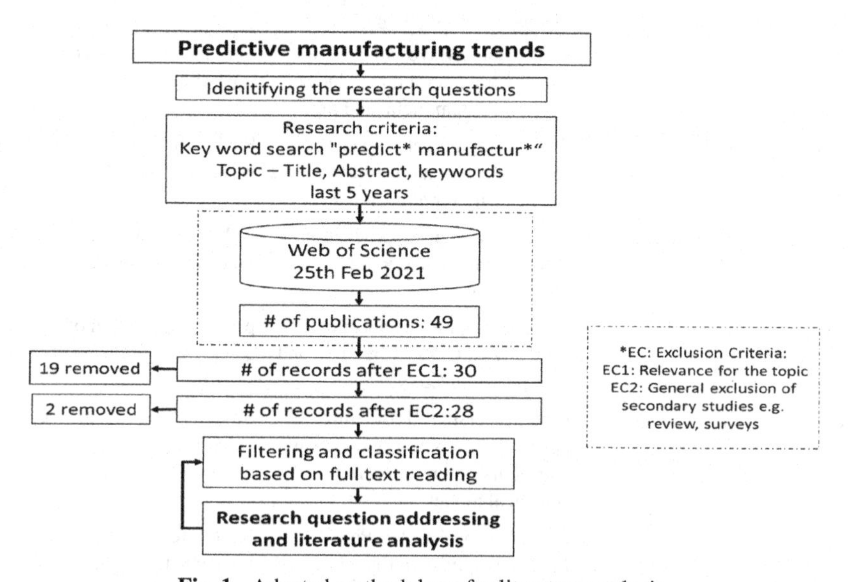

Fig. 1. Adapted methodology for literature analysis.

4 Results and Discussions

RQ1: What are the various frameworks developed in recent years for the realization of PMS?

The term "framework" is the context of this paper is a broad term which defines the basic structure or model underlying a system or concept. In the literature works presented here this is mentioned using different terminologies like architecture, structure, methodology, model etc. From the 28 research papers we reviewed, we found only 13 papers which describes a framework. Others are experimental work based on previously established framework. The brief overview of these papers is mentioned in Table 1. One paper (by Luter et al. [14]) was excluded from the table as the paper gives insight on a methodology to predict the manufacturer's viability to succeed. This paper does not fit the criteria of providing a solution for PMS.

Finding a common ground among these wide variety of frameworks is a tedious task, which show a greater challenge in creating a generic framework for PMS. We also

Table 1. Frameworks for realization of PMS.

Article	Framework	Significance
Majiwala, Parmar and Gandhi [6]	Data classification into different level of management Data optimized using lean principle	Decision trigger from different levels of management
Gyulai et al. [15]	Closed loop controller Data from MES* and ERP* to a Machine Learning engine	Real time prediction of lead time
Park et al. [16]	Multi- Entity Bayesian Networks model with at least three kinds of entities: System, item, and time	Introduce self-awareness capabilities
Cai, Guo and Lui [17]	Considering trajectory patterns and dataset equations followed by synthesizing for a result list	Predict the next location of the work-in-process
Kostolani, Murin and Kozak [18]	Node layer - sensor, production system, Augmented Reality Fog and Cloud layer	Rule based intelligent predictive maintenance control
Jin et al. [19]	5C Architecture - Connection, Conversion, Cyber, Cognition and Configuration Level	predict degradation of critical assets
Takada et al. [20]	Data Processing - formatting, analysis, enrichment and viewing Hybrid modeling - experience & statistical model	Solution for maintenance, enhanced efficiency, and quality
Peres et al. [21]	3 components - Cyber Physical Production System, Real time Data Analysis & Knowledge Management	Real time supervision for maintenance and quality control
Yang et al. [9]	Super-meta model - a composition of weighted individual models (like kriging, ANN*, polynomial regression)	Improve prediction accuracy without need for additional data
Fang et al. [11]	IoT based data collection, data pre-processing, input and output sequence generation, Parallel gated recurrent units model development	Near, mid and long-future bottleneck prediction and its shifting trends
Fang, Guo, Liao, Ramani et al. [12]	Stacking multiple symmetrical Neural Network with dropout and batch normalization layer to make outer layer as linear regression	Robust and accurate prediction of jobs remaining time

(continued)

Table 1. (*continued*)

Article	Framework	Significance
Kwon and Kim [22]	Control unit - sensor, equipment, actuator; Wireless/Wired sensor node & gateway; PC based measurement system	Real time production data acquisition for quality analysis

*Acronyms: ANN – Artificial Neural Network, MES – Manufacturing Execution System, ERP – Enterprise Resource Planning

noticed that only very few frameworks provide real-time prediction which show a need for greater focus on this area. Data collection, storage and analysis plays a vital role in all the frameworks and almost all frameworks require the need for the collection of historical data.

RQ2: What are the different technologies used for the development of PMS in recent years?

We categorize enabling technologies for Predictive Manufacturing applications into twelve dimensions, as shown in Fig. 2. Results of this question do not aim to provide a very strict statistical analysis but to offer a general vision of what scope of technologies and with what strength are supporting predictive manufacturing.

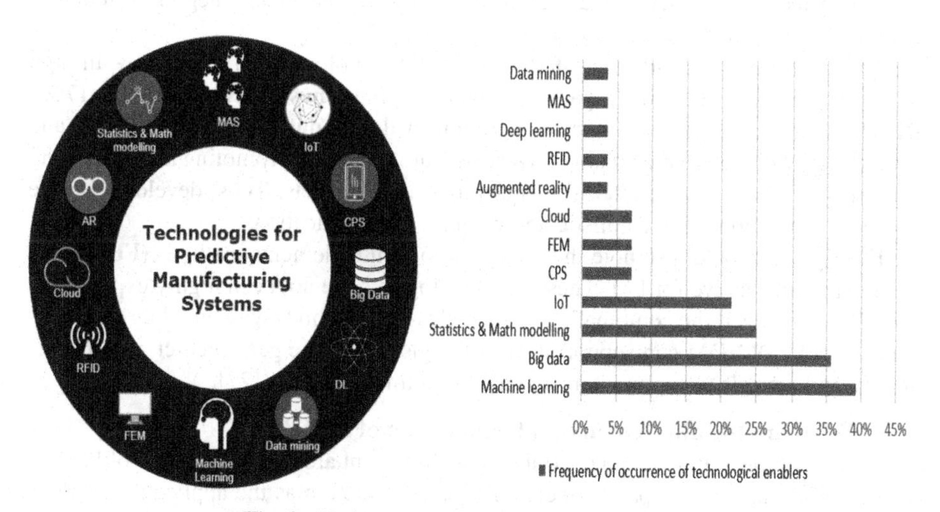

Fig. 2. Various technologies that support PMS.

No surprisingly, we found that **Machine Learning (ML)** algorithms are used more frequently (39%). ML provides mechanisms that utilize experience-based knowledge i.e., supervised and non-supervised techniques like lineal regression. Based on a pre-trained data set, ML allows production monitoring in non-linear environments in which historical data sets are used as a prediction input [23]. **Deep learning (DL)** as part of ML algorithms is less exploited (4%). We argue that such result implies the lack of computational efficiency and complexity of model representation [24]. Similarly, and to a lesser extent, **Data mining (DM)** (4%) promotes the extraction of useful knowledge from data sets. In general, DM is used to discover new patterns and for machine forecasting in presence of huge and raw data sets [25].

We should also highlight the presence of tools related to **statistics and mathematical modelling formulation** (25%). The model representation aims to develop mechanisms that can predict environmental variables on a prospective timeline and therefore recognize what variables may need assistance [26]. Despite promising ideas, it is our opinion that such approaches are less adopted due to high complexity in mathematical formulation. Conversely, ML and DL techniques hide all this complexity and thus promote a more straightforward methodology for manufacturing prediction.

Moving towards scalability and decentralization of manufacturing processes [4], **big data (35%)** and **cloud technologies (7%)** provide the necessary infrastructure for data storage, analysis, security and interoperability [12]. These technologies also act like data lakes or data warehouses to be used by ML and DL. Big Data predominantly uses either database like NoSQL or NewSQL or cloud storage (ex. cloud services from Amazon, Microsoft or Google). We state that the low percentage of cloud applications reflects the needed research effort for such technological integration especially due to the lack of real time communication and interoperability. At the same time, **multi-agent systems (MAS) (3%)** and despite not being highly considered in the set of papers, are a recognized technology for distributed applications. Agents can abstract resources which are distributed over the network and at the same time manage them, negotiate, monitor, predict and adapt to unforeseen events in real time [21].

The introduction of **internet of things (IoT)** technologies (21%) along with high interconnectivity, networking capability, sensors, **Cyber-physical systems (CPS)** (7%), **RFID** identifiers (3%) and human integration in the manufacturing supervision and control e.g., with augmented reality (**AR**) (3%), are gradually promoting manufacturing digitalization and creating intelligent machines and products. Thus, developing more awareness and supporting a holistic approach for PM applications.

Finally, we should also note the utilization of finite elements methods (**FEM**) as a mechanical alternative for PM. These methodologies have not been highly exploited in PM (7%). However, the combination of such classical methods with enabling technologies i.e., ML, DL, DM can support novel strategies for PM e.g. to predict and analyze quality of materials to capture defect behavior in finalized parts [27].

RQ3: What are the different areas of application of PMS?
This research question gives an overview of the different areas of application of PMS in the reviewed papers. The papers mentioning cost reduction as the application of PMS was ignored from this analysis as all applications directly or indirectly aims at cost reduction for the manufacturers. Figure 3 presents percentage distribution of each application compared to the number of publications. Others mentioned in Fig. 3 represents applications which are addressed in less than 5% of total publications. Some articles address more than one application. These articles are added more than once in different applications. The results shows that 70% of all application of PMS are in Quality Control, Planning & Scheduling and Maintenance. This shows strong focus of PMS research

in the lower level of ISA 95 levels (International Society of Automation levels) and on real time predictions.

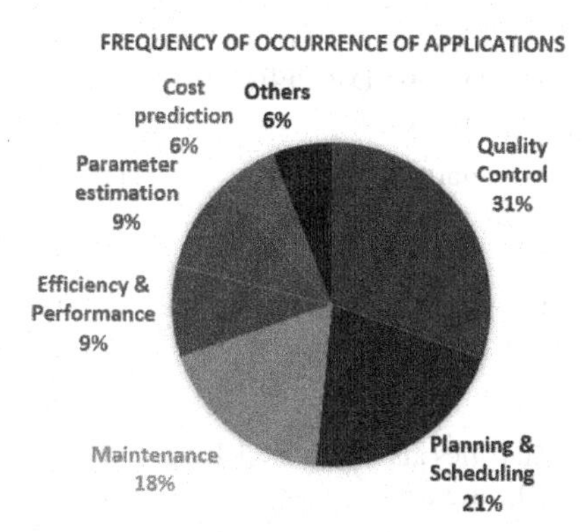

Fig. 3. Application of PMS in manufacturing.

Further Discussions – Towards a Generic Framework for PMS

When we combine the answers of individual research questions, we obtain further interesting results. We believe that these results can guide future researchers in developing a generic framework for PMS. Table 2 list the various technologies used for different manufacturing applications. We could notice that big data and machine learning techniques have been used for all the applications with just one exception (machine learning techniques were not used in cost prediction). This shows that a system developed with the combination of these two technologies might help in giving a solution for the realization of a generic framework. Further analyzing these technologies shows Neural Network as the most promising tool used compared to other machine learning tools.

Implementing the developed framework in multiple applications validates the claim of developing a generic framework for PMS. We found that, from the 13 frameworks described for the realization of a PMS only three frameworks have been utilized in more than one application. These three frameworks (See Table 1 for more details of the framework) and their applications are explained below,

1. Park et al. [16] developed a predictive situation awareness system using Multi- Entity Bayesian Networks model for production scheduling and quality control.
2. Peres et al. [21] used multi-agent system and machine learning for realizing a flexible and pluggable data analysis and real time supervision framework. The framework was used for predictive maintenance and Quality Assurance.
3. Monozukuri Navigation System [20] is the only framework in our analysis which applied it's framework in three different scenarios – Predictive Maintenance, Quality Control and efficiency. The System is developed using Big Data Analysis and Internet of Things.

Even if Parenti et al. [33] has applied their graphical method in three different applications namely, process planning, performance and cost prediction, they dint present a

Table 2. Technologies used for various application of PMS.

Application	Technologies used	References
Quality control	Statistics and Math modelling, ML, DL, Big Data, FEM, IoT, CPS, MAS	[7, 16, 20, 21, 22, 27, 28, 29, 30, 31]
Planning & Scheduling	ML, Statistics and Math modelling, RFID, IoT, Big data, DL, ML	[11, 12, 15, 16, 17, 32, 33]
Maintenance	IoT, AR, Cloud, IoT, Big data, MAS, ML, DL	[13, 18, 19, 20, 21, 34]
Efficiency & Performance	DL, IoT, Big data	[8, 20, 33]
Parameter estimation	Statistics and Math modelling, DL, Big data	[9, 10, 26]
Cost prediction	Statistics and Math modelling, Big data	[33, 35]

Acronyms: DL - Deep Learning, ML - Machine Learning, FEM - Finite Element Methods, IoT - Internet of Things, RFID - Radio frequency Identification, MAS - Multi-Agent Systems, CPS - Cyber Physical Systems.

novel framework for PMS. These results show that there are very few publications which have developed a framework for the full realization of PMS.

5 Conclusion

Some of the key takeaways from this review article are listed below,

- In recent years, only very few articles have developed a generic framework for the realization of a PMS. Only three works have validated their framework in more than one application.
- PMS technologies are highly constrained by real-time manufacturing expectations. Thus, most approaches rely on using AI technologies locally. We evidence this by the lack of adoption of cloud infrastructures. Therefore, it is not feasible to create interoperability that involve PMS with the manufacturing supply chain and that can integrate and optimize the process holistically. Further research should be conducted into increasing such technological real-time applicability.
- 70% of the applications of PMS are in Quality Control, Maintenance and Production Planning & Scheduling.
- Many researchers have used Neural Network models for wide variety of applications. This indicates that Neural Network techniques might be a promising tool for achieving an effective PMS.

Future research direction would focus on the use of AI technologies for the development of a generic PMS and validating them on various manufacturing applications.

Another research direction would be to use IoT and Edge-Fog-Cloud architecture for real time prediction - which lacks in current research works.

Acknowledgements. This project has received funding from the European Union's Horizon 2020 research and innovation programme under the Marie Skłodowska-Curie grant No. 814078. Partial support also comes from Fundação para a Ciência e Tecnologia through the program UIDB/00066/2020 (CTS- Center of Technology and Systems).

References

1. Mittal, S., Khan, M.A., Romero, D., Wuest, T.: Smart manufacturing: characteristics, technologies and enabling factors. Proc. Inst. Mech. Eng. Part B J. Eng. Manuf. **233**(5), 1342–1361 (2019). https://doi.org/10.1177/0954405417736547
2. Nikolic, B., Ignjatic, J., Suzic, N., Stevanov, B., Rikalovic, A.: Predictive manufacturing systems in industry 4.0: trends, benefits and challenges. In: International DAAAM Symposium, pp. 796–802 (2017). Ann. DAAAM Proc. https://doi.org/10.2507/28th.daaam.proceedings.112
3. Lee, J.: Intelligent Maintenance Systems and Predictive Manufacturing, November 2020. https://doi.org/10.1115/1.4047856
4. Peres, R.S., Jia, X., Lee, J., Sun, K., Colombo, A.W., Barata, J.: Industrial artificial intelligence in industry 4.0 -systematic review, challenges and outlook. IEEE Access **4**, 1–21 (2020). https://doi.org/10.1109/ACCESS.2020.3042874
5. Guha, S., Kumar, S.: Emergence of big data research in operations management, information systems, and healthcare: past contributions and future roadmap. Prod. Oper. Manag. **27**(9), 1724–1735 (2018). https://doi.org/10.1111/poms.12833
6. Majiwala, H., Parmar, D., Gandhi, P.: Leeway of lean concept to optimize big data in manufacturing industry: an exploratory review. In: Mishra, D., Yang, X.S., Unal, A. (eds.) Data Science and Big Data Analytics, Lecture Notes on Data Engineering and Communications Technologies, vol. 16. Springer, Singapore (2019). https://doi.org/10.1007/978-981-10-7641-1_16
7. Bai, Y., Sun, Z., Deng, J., Li, L., Long, J., Li, C.: Manufacturing quality prediction using intelligent learning approaches: a comparative study. Sustainability 10(1) (2017). https://doi.org/10.3390/su10010085
8. Tan, L.P., Wong, K.Y.: A neural network approach for predicting manufacturing performance using knowledge management metrics. Cybern. Syst. **48**(4), 348–364 (2017). https://doi.org/10.1080/01969722.2017.1285161
9. Yang, Z., Eddy, D., Krishnamurty, S., Grosse, I., Lu, Y.: A super-metamodeling framework to optimize system predictability, August 2018. https://doi.org/10.1115/detc2018-86055
10. Adesanya, A., Abdulkareem, A., Adesina, L.M.: Predicting extrusion process parameters in Nigeria cable manufacturing industry using artificial neural network. Heliyon **6**(7), e04289 (2020). https://doi.org/10.1016/j.heliyon.2020.e04289
11. Fang, W., Guo, Y., Liao, W., Huang, S., Yang, N., Liu, J.: A Parallel Gated Recurrent Units (P-GRUs) network for the shifting lateness bottleneck prediction in make-to-order production system. Comput. Ind. Eng. **140**, 106246 (2020). https://doi.org/10.1016/j.cie.2019.106246
12. Fang, W., Guo, Y., Liao, W., Ramani, K., Huang, S.: Big data driven jobs remaining time prediction in discrete manufacturing system: a deep learning-based approach. Int. J. Prod. Res. **58**(9), 2751–2766 (2020). https://doi.org/10.1080/00207543.2019.1602744

13. Ang, E.C.: Smart manufacturing with an artificial neural network to predict manufacturing healthiness. In: 2019 IEEE 15th International Colloquium on Signal Process, pp. 120–123 (2019)
14. Luter, N., et al.: An updated methodology to review developing-country vaccine manufacturer viability. Vaccine **35**(31), 3897–3903 (2017). https://doi.org/10.1016/j.vaccine.2017.04.087
15. Gyulai, D., Pfeiffer, A., Bergmann, J., Gallina, V.: Online lead time prediction supporting situation-aware production control. Procedia CIRP **78**, 190–195 (2018). https://doi.org/10.1016/j.procir.2018.09.071
16. Park, C.Y., Laskey, K.B., Salim, S., Lee, J.Y.: Predictive situation awareness model for smart manufacturing. In: 20th International Conference on Information Fusion, Fusion 2017 - Proceedings (2017). https://doi.org/10.23919/ICIF.2017.8009849
17. Cai, H., Guo, Y., Lu, K.: A location prediction method for work-in-process based on frequent trajectory patterns. Proc. Inst. Mech. Eng. Part B J. Eng. Manuf. **233**(1), 306–320 (2019). https://doi.org/10.1177/0954405417708222
18. Kostolani, M., Murin, J., Kozak, S.: Intelligent predictive maintenance control using augmented reality. In: Proceedings of 2019 22nd International Conference on Process Control, PC 2019, pp. 131–135 (2019). https://doi.org/10.1109/PC.2019.8815042
19. Jin, W., Liu, Z., Shi, Z., Jin, C., Lee, J.: CPS-enabled worry-free industrial applications. In: 2017 Prognostics and System Health Management Conference, PHM-Harbin 2017 - Proceedings, November 2017. https://doi.org/10.1109/PHM.2017.8079208
20. Takada, E., Kobayashi, T., Matsuoka, H., Soeda, T., Maida, M.: Monozukuri navigation system to deliver outstanding quality and efficiency. Fujitsu Sci. Tech. J. **53**(4), 70–76 (2017)
21. Peres, R.S., Dionisio Rocha, A., Leitao, P., Barata, J.: IDARTS – Towards intelligent data analysis and real-time supervision for industry 4.0. Comput. Ind. 101, 138–146 (2018). https://doi.org/10.1016/j.compind.2018.07.004
22. Kwon, Y.J., Kim, D.H.: IoT-based defect predictive manufacturing systems. In: 2017 International Conference on Information and Communication Technology Convergence, pp. 1067–1069 (2017). https://doi.org/10.1109/ICTC.2017.8190856
23. Liu, Y., Wang, L., Wang, Y., Wang, X.V., Zhang, L.: Multi-agent-based scheduling in cloud manufacturing with dynamic task arrivals. Procedia CIRP **72**, 953–960 (2018). https://doi.org/10.1016/j.procir.2018.03.138
24. Angelov, P., Sperduti, A.: Challenges in deep learning. In: ESANN 2016 - 24th European Symposium on Artificial Neural Networks, pp. 489–496 (2016)
25. Widmer, T., Klein, A., Wachter, P., Meyl, S.: Predicting material requirements in the automotive industry using data mining. In: Abramowicz, W., Corchuelo, R. (eds.) Business Information Systems, BIS 2019, Lecture Notes in Business Information Processing, vol. 354. Springer, Cham (2019). https://doi.org/10.1007/978-3-030-20482-2_13
26. Kumari, M., Kulkarni, M.S.: Single-measure and multi-measure approach of predictive manufacturing control: a comparative study. Comput. Ind. Eng. **127**, 182–195 (2019). https://doi.org/10.1016/j.cie.2018.12.018
27. Stavropoulos, P., Michail, C., Papacharalampopoulos, A.: Towards predicting manufacturing effect on hybrid part efficiency: An automotive case. Procedia CIRP **85**, 156–161 (2020). https://doi.org/10.1016/j.procir.2019.09.044
28. Dalia, F., Rauf, A., Schiøler, H., Kulahci, M., Zaki, M., Westermann-rasmussen, P.: Cost-sensitive learning classification strategy for predicting product failures. Expert Syst. Appl. **161**, 113653 (2020). https://doi.org/10.1016/j.eswa.2020.113653
29. Lin, H.K., Hsieh, C.H., Wei, N.C., Peng, Y.C.: Association rules mining in R for product performance management in industry 4.0. Procedia CIRP **83**, 699–704 (2019). https://doi.org/10.1016/j.procir.2019.04.099

30. Peres, R.S., Barata, J., Leitao, P., Garcia, G.: Multistage quality control using machine learning in the automotive industry. IEEE Access **7**, 79908–79916 (2019). https://doi.org/10.1109/ACCESS.2019.2923405
31. Dörr, D., et al.: A benchmark study of finite element codes for forming simulation of thermoplastic UD-tapes. Procedia CIRP **66**, 101–106 (2017). https://doi.org/10.1016/j.procir.2017.03.223
32. Gan, W., Lin, J.C.W., Chao, H.C., Vasilakos, A.V., Yu, P.S.: Utility-driven data analytics on uncertain data. IEEE Syst. J. **14**(3), 4442–4453 (2020). https://doi.org/10.1109/JSYST.2020.2979279
33. Parenti, P., Cacciatore, F., Ratti, A., Annoni, M.: A graphical method for performance mapping of machines and milling tools. Procedia Manuf. **26**, 1500–1508 (2018). https://doi.org/10.1016/j.promfg.2018.07.089
34. Rastegari, A., Archenti, A., Mobin, M.: Condition based maintenance of machine tools: vibration monitoring of spindle units. In: Proceedings of Annual Reliability and Maintainability Symposium, January 2017. https://doi.org/10.1109/RAM.2017.7889683
35. D'Urso, G., Quarto, M., Ravasio, C.: A model to predict manufacturing cost for micro-EDM drilling. Int. J. Adv. Manuf. Technol. **91**(5–8), 2843–2853 (2017). https://doi.org/10.1007/s00170-016-9950-0

Open Access This chapter is licensed under the terms of the Creative Commons Attribution 4.0 International License (http://creativecommons.org/licenses/by/4.0/), which permits use, sharing, adaptation, distribution and reproduction in any medium or format, as long as you give appropriate credit to the original author(s) and the source, provide a link to the Creative Commons license and indicate if changes were made.

The images or other third party material in this chapter are included in the chapter's Creative Commons license, unless indicated otherwise in a credit line to the material. If material is not included in the chapter's Creative Commons license and your intended use is not permitted by statutory regulation or exceeds the permitted use, you will need to obtain permission directly from the copyright holder.

Control of Manufacturing Systems by HMS/EPS Paradigms Orchestrating I4.0 Components Based on Capabilities

Jackson T. Veiga(✉), Marcosiris A. O. Pessoa(✉), Fabrício Junqueira(✉), Paulo E. Miyagi(✉), and Diolino J. dos Santos Filho(✉)

University of São Paulo (USP), São Paulo, Brazil
{jackson.veiga,marcosiris,fabri,pemiyagi,diolinos}@usp.br

Abstract. The fourth industrial revolution has driven initiatives worldwide following the Industry 4.0 (I4.0) context, requiring better integration and relationship between elements. This work was applied the Reference Architecture Model Industry 4.0 (RAMI 4.0) to present new models for standardizing entities in the I4.0 context to migrate legacy systems and standardize assets based on I4.0 Components (I4.0C). The management and orchestration of I4.0C can be achieved by attaching Artificial Intelligence (AI) concepts through intelligent entities describing the behavior and resources relationship, applying Multi-Agent systems (MAS), and adding self-organization, reconfiguration, plug ability, adaptation, and reasoning. Therefore, a manufacturing systems control framework is proposed based on capabilities and HMS/EPS application to orchestrate I4.0C.

Keywords: Industry 4.0 (I4.0) · Holonic Manufacturing Systems (HMS) · Evolvable Production Systems (EPS) · I4.0 Component (I4.0C) · Digital transformation · Artificial Intelligence (AI) · Manufacturing systems control

1 Introduction

In the traditional industry, engineering tasks are systematized, depending on the application domain where tools define the project's functionality, establish necessary resources, formalize the process, and finally determine each real asset's functionalities "skills" throughout its entire life cycle. However, when putting the system into operation, unpredictable behaviors can be identified, such as resource unavailability or new product insertion. In the current concept, service orders link competencies to real resources but, these models no longer respond to the context of I4.0. Therefore new paradigms that better meet the concept of "Intelligent Manufacturing" must be applied [1].

The digital industry transformation requires new approaches related to the virtualization of the physical systems. In [2], the digital transformation can understand the digitization of all processes, operations, supply, production, and logistics, through intensely digital models and ontology. I4.0 platform introduced I4.0C [3] utilizing methods to standardize and systematize the information and communication of assets and be a

© IFIP International Federation for Information Processing 2021
Published by Springer Nature Switzerland AG 2021
L. M. Camarinha-Matos et al. (Eds.): DoCEIS 2021, IFIP AICT 626, pp. 62–70, 2021.
https://doi.org/10.1007/978-3-030-78288-7_6

library that comprises different meta-models capable of presenting its semantics and the development of new models that enable applications for Intelligent Manufacturing [4].

This work intends to minimize the gap between emerging manufacturing solutions and intelligent manufacturing concepts. The RAMI 4.0 guidelines are used, and the digital models are described by Asset Administration Shells (AAS), according to the I4.0C context based on "capabilities" [1, 4]. Therefore, concepts of multi-agent systems (MAS) were introduced, based on Holonic Manufacturing Systems (HMS)/Evolvable Production Systems (EPS) paradigms.

It was also foreseen here agents specification, seen as "holons," which internally have knowledge and capacity for self-learning, evolution to seek new capabilities and negotiation. The aspects described deal with artificial intelligence systems (AIs) requirements [1, 7, 8].

This work focuses on designing a framework for controlling and optimizing resources (skills) coalition [1, 3, 8, 14]. Still, in these works, there are no specific control approaches that meet the I4.0 guidelines. Therefore, the scientific gain presented in this work was the conception of agent models based on the EPS/HMS paradigm to orchestrates services through resources "skills" that are reflected in the "Administration Shell" as a point of access and communication between virtual parties, which present their "capabilities" [1, 5–7].

2 Relationship to Applied Artificial Intelligence Systems

Intelligent agents are fundamental components for system control to optimize, improve and organize manufacturing processes. With the objective of modeling iterations between intelligent entities, those are responsible for attributing to the system characteristics such as cooperation, coexistence, or competition, by attaching concepts of Artificial Intelligence (AI) and "Distributed Processing" [6]. Multi-Agent Systems (MAS) are widely studied in the literature [10], i.e.: (i) Tools for intelligent decisions apply MAS to distribute control and automation to components, providing autonomy, flexibility, robustness, or reconfigurability on traditional systems [5, 6, 8–10]; (ii) MAS uses advanced data analysis combined with AI for self-awareness, data mining, processing, calculation of health forecast, or valuable life estimate in manufacturing systems [11, 12]; (iii) In [13] uses a generic data-oriented architecture to interconnect different legacy systems; (iv) An architecture that describes the control of fault-tolerant manufacturing systems based on HMS was proposed [8]; (v) A formalism for EPS was presented, based on the description of models, to create an environment for developing evolutionary systems [9].

However, MAS exposes functionality through services transparently, without clarifying the ontology used from representation, integration, and relationship between assets models.

3 Literature Review

This paper has analyzed the works in Table 1 and combining some prominent features to generate the framework proposal.

In [1, 3], an ontological description represents resource abilities using capacities concepts and standard models in the I4.0 context. This work contributed to an architectural guideline for virtual resources representation by AAS. The works [5, 7] are state-of-art for specific architectural control applications based in HMS and MAS. In [8] has been validated an architectural engineering method using the features described in [5, 7], adding aspects of service based on internal components structure. These works inspire the agents modeled to attend I4.0 (capacities-based and object interactions) described in this paper.

Lastly, in [9, 10, 14], the EPS paradigm has HMS and MAS characteristics for integrated legacy systems based on modules. The disadvantage of these last references was that they presented embedded tools to support applications without clarifying the modeling and mechanisms to add such evolvable aspects. The second point was about society applications that do not deal with I4.0 guidelines architecture.

Therefore, this paper has extracted the means characteristics discussed in this section to generate the framework proposal. That treats a reconfigurable and evolvable application based in HMS/EPS to orchestrate functionalities described in AAS dealing with I4.0 standard.

Asset Administration Shell (AAS) standardizes information and other resources through descriptions in virtual models [4]. The concept of "Capabilities" composing ontological bases for AAS is described; however, different application domains must validate it, such as intelligent systems coordinating resources through "Capabilities" described in AAS [1].

3.1 Architectures to Orchestrate "Capabilities"

It was combined the following architectures to model the intelligent application based on "capacity engineering":

a) Holonic Manufacturing Systems (HMS) - inspired in [8] based on PROSA (Architecture for Holonic Manufacturing Systems [7]) assigns "self-organization" capacity and "coalition" through temporary resource, also provides the system a description for agents specifications in the proposed architecture [5].
b) Evolvable Production Systems (EPS) - apply characteristics of "reconfiguration", "modularity", and "adaptation", inspired in [9] descriptions that present the IADE (IDEAS Agent Development Environment) [14].

3.2 Ontology and Modeling's Approaches for Virtual Representation Using "Component I4.0"

In [1, 3], the I4.0C is detailed, solving the introduction gap and allowing intelligent models to be implemented, such as "capabilities", self-organization of resources, or evolution based on the asset condition.

In addition to described architectures in the previous item, the I4.0 context requires virtual resources guidelines [5]. A three-dimensional model, divided into layers for the treatment of information (including the life cycle and hierarchical levels of traditional systems), was introduced by RAMI4.0 [4]. This reference architecture standardizes and

Table 1. Comparison of characteristics of the reference projects studied in this article

Reference(L)/Features(C)	Project	Paradigm	Mains aspects
1 - Bayha	RAMI4.0/AAS	I4.0/ SOA	Guidelines for virtual entities in I4.0 context, Capability-based engineering, and pluggability
3 - Bedenbender			Granularity abstraction to functionalities and resources representation, I4.0, DIN SPEC 91345
5 - Barbosa	ADACOR2	MAS	Self-organization components, generic architecture with a model for self-organization, and pheromone in entities
7 - Van Brussel	PROSA	HMS	Guidelines for developing a generic control layer, collaboration, changes and disturbances, adaptation, flexibility, a reference architecture for self-configuration, and plug-in plug out
8 - Da Silva	Hybrid	RMCS/ HMAS	A reconfigurable manufacturing control system, flexibility, safety in fault occurrence, architecture for optimizing reengineering
9 - Onori	FP6 EUPASS	HMS/ EPS	Integrate legacy subsystems, evolutive production systems, reconfigurability, distributed control, intelligence, and dynamic control
10 - Dias	PERFoRM	MAS/ SOA	Generic architecture, reconfiguration, legacy systems, distributed-service based layer, modularity
14 - Ribeiro	FP7 IDEAS	MAS/ EPS	Self-organization, plug-ability, tolerance to disturbance, and mechatronic MAS architecture

systematizes virtual resources through technical descriptions in I4.0C. To better describe the techniques and functions of I4.0Cs, [4] presents the "Asset Administration Shell" (AAS), containing a set of sub-models, allowing the "Assets" to perform a specific function through the "Administration Shell".

A sub-model is responsible for defining technical descriptions to support applications, as resources "Tasks" representation, "Events", and "Capabilities". A meta-model

"Capabilities" allows mapping the asset's abilities from systematic descriptions of skills. In this context, the need for intelligent solutions through mechanisms connected to submodels is evident (for example, "Events" sensing new functionalities, new resource composition, or even monitoring conditions). Besides that, intelligent control for coalition or reconfiguration of resources through the sub-model "Capacities" can be implemented using "Administration Shell".

4 Work Purpose

This work's proposal represented by the "framework" in (Fig. 1) generates a systematic standardization for I4.0 through I4.0C to express an intelligent manufacturing process applying the ontology descriptions in Sect. 3. In Fig. 2 is illustrated a model for "Administration Shell Resources", described in this example as "Distribution Work Station". The resource "capabilities" were represented by two "Task" submodels. In each "Task", the submodel was described specific operations (for example, "removing the base from buffer", "transporting material").

It is noted that "Capacities" are described depends on the "project granularity" in "Product Administration Shell". It implies a certain "Administration Shell Resource" that has knowledge about its assignment but needs an "intelligent entity" to combine "Capabilities" between AAS and to form the production plan described in "Administration Shell Product".

This work purpose determines three "Administration Shell" types to support the representation of components in a manufacturing process: (i) "Administration Shell Production Plan" - represents the standardized knowledge of recipes to design each product; (ii) "Product Administration Shell" - in charge of providing the "Tasks" descriptions needed to manufacture a given product chosen from process steps; and (iii) "Administration Shell Resource" - represents the "functionality" attributes of real "resources", which can choose based on their "ability".

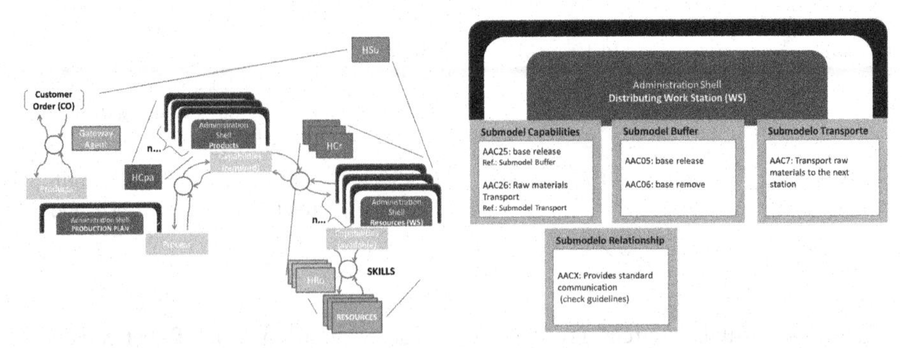

Fig. 1. Proposal framework orchestrating AAS.

Fig. 2. Administration shells resource example.

When the traditional system introduces a CO, an "Administration Shell Production Plan" is standardizing, and processes are externalized by the MAS control and links “Product Administration Shell - PaS”. The PaS describes the process with specific “capabilities” of “resources” contained in the respective “Administration Shell Resource”.

The control aspects (Fig. 1) in this proposal deal with the intelligent application, chosen through HMS/EPS, that attributes to the I4.0C capacity of relationship, communication, coalition, reasoning, and decision making. A set of “holons” are assigned in this proposal: Holon Product Capacity (HCpa) is programmed to invoke and externalize the “capabilities” described in “Product Administration Shell”. Holon Resource Capabilities (HCr) manages and negotiates with operational holons (HRo) and externalizes resource “capabilities”. Holon Operational Resource (HRo) represents the physical resources, perceives the abilities of the resources, has the sequence of operational events, and executes service orders from (HCr), implements conditions, and updates data of “Administration Shell Resources”. Holon Supervisor (HSu) coordinates operations and evolution, adds new components, verifies system behavior, and manages coalition and reconfiguration presented in proposal results.

5 Results

In this work, some propositions are made; - Coalition: means the possibility of grouping services described in “Administration Shell” by capacities; - Reconfiguration: means the system’s ability to organize itself in case of resources change or if the equipment conditions are different compared with “original plan”; - Skill: defines an agent able to deliver value to an application, considering EPS paradigms [6]. Also, in [1], this term is described in Administration Shell “Tasks” sub-models. Therefore, this section presents two intelligent agents designed to meet these criteria. The integration between these systems PFS (Production Flow Schema) was chosen for modeling, as it is widely known in the engineering area (Figs. 3 and 4).

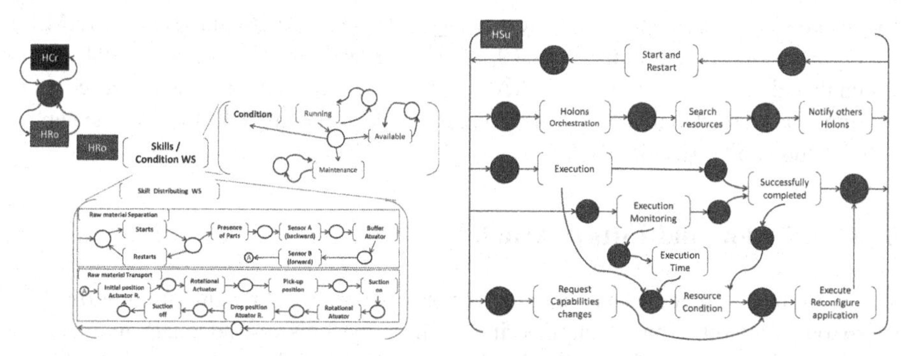

Fig. 3. Modeling intelligent agents “HRo” – Skill and condition monitoring.

Fig. 4. Modeling “HSu” for supervision of capacities and reconfiguration.

The definition in [1] shows standardized descriptions in sub-models “tasks” of Administration Shell, which meets the requirements in the I4.0 context. However, this information provides a process operations domain, and a superior intelligent entity must access these. For this, this work used the descriptions contained in "HRo" (Holon Operational Resource) inspired in [8], which was revised and modeled to deal with AAS and evolution characteristics observed in [9].

Holon resources (Hro): implements two main routines: (i) Realize the capabilities of the resources (Skills) -Through the agent's knowledge, the Hro externalize "resource skills", as well, negotiate the "service orders" linked by the "HCpa" (Holon Capabilities). HCpa demands "skills" utilizing operation knowledge. An example of this system is dealt with in the PFS in Fig. 3 [8]; (ii) Condition monitoring (Events) - in addition to the knowledge about "skills", to meet the requirements of reconfiguration, plug-and-produce, and evolution of "capacities", the ability to express "events" about resource "condition" was modeled on the "HRo". These events are treated, processed, and then externalized to the respective "AAS-Resource" through the "Hsu".

Holon Supervisor (HSu): This agent is in charge of informing about changes in "capacities", reconfiguring the system by calling other projected holons, as well as adding or removing new agents (Fig. 4). The main characteristics implemented in these agents: (i) Execution Monitoring - this function involves the coordination of "relationships" between holons, monitoring the operations in execution, the tasks related to each interface between holons and AAS in addition to orchestrating the individual strategies of the holons [8]; (ii) Holons orchestration - perform entities coalition by an internal mechanism that determines the sequencing of holons capable of answering a call [8]; (iii) Execution Time - utilizing "events", sending messages within a specified time interval; (iv) Capabilities changes (evolution) - occurs when a CO has finalized the HSu external messages through "Events" to the participants if there was a success or not in the execution, if not a reconfigurable mechanism, must update the information contained in "Administration Shell of Resources".

The advantage achieved by this structure is to enable the coalition of resources by "engineering capacities based". This proposal makes it possible to change the traditional systems. The resources are standardized in the virtual environment (AAS), reducing programming efforts. The manufacturing life cycle is optimized to meet the connected world's demands, characterized by distributed equipment. The EPS/HMS is widely discussed in academia [5, 7–10, 14]. There are few use cases with real data in which they do not apply to the I4.0 (AAS) context. The concept of capacity-based engineering is addressed in this proposal through a framework that seeks to solve the gap for orchestration and coalition of I4.0C.

6 Conclusion and Future Work

This work proposal describes a method for orchestration and reconfiguration of I4.0C based on "Capability-based engineering". These systems are adequate to meet the intelligent control system specification based on HMS/EPS paradigms. A framework containing a multi-agent system (MAS) proposes to add intelligence requirements on AAS.

An application that improves the relationship between virtual entities by adding the characteristics described above establishes its ontology. It requires MAS-based tools to be integrated with the submodels and specifications according to the I4.0 paradigm. It was possible to observe the functional modeling for implementing EPS agents and an elementary domain for holonic systems specification.

The system's behavior presents PFS diagrams, respecting both the MAS project's characteristics and the guidelines for I4.0C through standardized meta-models. That results in preliminary data showing that the proposal is viable and achieves engineering based on capabilities by adding an intelligent framework to control the coalition and reconfigure the resource's abilities (skill). However, more experiments are needed to validate the proposal as a whole.

In the future, can be unified these projects, i.e., can be integrated MAS ontological specifications in different areas of knowledge with the respective AAS through intelligent submodels providing all the necessary characteristics for implementing these paradigms.

Acknowledgments. The authors would like to thank the Brazilian governmental agencies CAPES, CNPq, PET, and FAPESP for their partial support.

References

1. Bayha, A., Bock, J., Boss, B., Diedrich, C., Malakuti, S.: Describing capabilities of industrie 4.0 components. In: German Electrical and Electronics Manufacturers Association, Frankfurt am Main, Germany (2020). http://www.plattform-i40.de/
2. Borangiu, T., Trentesaux, D., Thomas, A., Leitão, P., Barata, J.: Digital transformation of manufacturing through cloud services and resource virtualization. Comput. Ind. **108**, 150–162 (2019)
3. Bedenbender, H., et al.: Relationships between I4. 0 Components–Composite components and smart production. In: Federal Ministry for Economic Affairs and Energy (BMWi), Berlin (2017). www.bmwi.de
4. Bader, S., et al.: Details of the asset administration shell part 1 - the exchange of information between partners in the value chain of industrie 4.0 (Version 3.0RC01). In: German Electrical and Electronics Manufacturers Association, Frankfurt am Main, Germany (2020). http://www.plattform-i40.de/
5. Barbosa, J., Leitão, P., Adam, E., Trentesaux, D.: Dynamic self-organization in holonic multi-agent manufacturing systems: the ADACOR evolution. Comput. Ind. **66**, 99–111 (2015)
6. Frei, R., Barata, J., Serugendo, G.: A complexity theory approach to evolvable production systems. In: Proceedings of 3rd International Workshop on Multi-Agent Robotic Systems in Conjunction with ICINCO, pp. 44–53 (2007)
7. Van Brussel, H., Wyns, J., Valckenaers, P., Bongaerts, L., Peeters, P.: Reference architecture for holonic manufacturing systems: PROSA. Comput. Ind. **37**(3), 255–274 (1998)
8. Da Silva, R.M., Junqueira, F., Santos Filho, D.J., Miyagi, P.E.: Control architecture and design method of reconfigurable manufacturing systems. Control Eng. Pract. 49, 87–100 (2016)
9. Onori, M., Barata, J.: Evolvable production systems: mechatronic production equipment with process-based distributed control. IFAC Proc. Vol. **42**(16), 80–85 (2009)
10. Dias, J., Vallhagen, J., Barbosa, J., Leitão, P.: Agent-based reconfiguration in a micro-flow production cell. In: 2017 IEEE 15th International Conference on Industrial Informatics (INDIN), Emden, pp. 1123–1128 (2017)
11. Shalini, R., Kumaravel, A.: Production harmonized reconfiguration of flexible robots and machinery using manufacturing industry 4.0. J. Comput. Theor. Nanosci. **15**(11–12), 3558–3564 (2018)

12. Chakravorti, N., Rahman, M.M., Sidoumou, M.R., Weinert, N., Gosewehr, F., Wermann, J.: Validation of PERFoRM reference architecture demonstrating an application of data mining for predicting machine failure. Procedia CIRP **72**, 1339–1344 (2018)
13. Trunzer, E., et al.: System architectures for industrie 4.0 applications. Prod. Eng. **13**(3–4), 247–257 (2019). https://doi.org/10.1007/s11740-019-00902-6
14. Ribeiro, L., Barata, J., Onori, M., Hanisch, C., Hoos, J., Rosa, R.: Self-organization in automation-the IDEAS pre-demonstrator. In: IECON 2011–37th Annual Conference of the IEEE Industrial Electronics Society, pp. 2752–2757 (2011)

A Framework for Self-configuration in Manufacturing Production Systems

Hamood Ur Rehman[1,2](✉), Jack C. Chaplin[1], Leszek Zarzycki[2], and Svetan Ratchev[1]

[1] University of Nottingham, Nottingham, UK
{Hamood.Rehman,Jack.Chaplin,svetan.ratchev}@nottingham.ac.uk
[2] TQC Ltd., Nottingham, UK
leszek.zarzycki@tqc.co.uk

Abstract. Intelligence in manufacturing enables the optimization and configuration of processes, and a goal of future smart manufacturing is to enable processes to configure themselves – called self-configuration. This paper describes a framework for utilising data to make decisions for the self-configuration of a production system device in a smart production environment. A data pipeline is proposed that connects the production system via a gateway to a cloud computing platform for machine learning and data analytics. Agent technology is used to implement the framework for this data pipeline. This is illustrated by a data oriented self-configuration solution for an industrial use-case based on a device used at a testing station in a production system. This research presents possible direction towards realising self-configuration in production systems.

Keywords: Data analytics · Smart manufacturing · Agent technology · Configuration

1 Introduction

Dynamic manufacturing solutions are required to satisfy the demands of part customisation, facility optimisation and equipment efficiency. A newer direction being explored in this domain is intelligent production systems [1]. The majority of research that targets intelligent systems has dealt with the study and modelling of whole systems and often makes assumptions about the constituent elements of the system (machines, instruments, and components) including assumptions on machine integration, capabilities and performance.

Different types of products with differing features and characteristics may require operations with different configuration settings in a production system. These changes in configuration may be due to changes in physical parameters or calibrations, or due to system settings like data logging, or communication settings. The configuration change may also be due to a change in physical infrastructure, therefore there can be different configurations on the same machine. Significant work has been done that deals with change in configuration at the infrastructure level [2–4]. In contrast, the self-management

© IFIP International Federation for Information Processing 2021
Published by Springer Nature Switzerland AG 2021
L. M. Camarinha-Matos et al. (Eds.): DoCEIS 2021, IFIP AICT 626, pp. 71–79, 2021.
https://doi.org/10.1007/978-3-030-78288-7_7

of the internal configuration of the machine by the machine itself is explored in fields like computer science and telecommunications, but there remain significant gaps in manufacturing.

The research outlined in this paper aims to close this gap in knowledge. It presents a framework with data models that establish a self-configuration mechanism for existing manufacturing equipment. Initially, the research focuses on an industrial use-case production system device and equipment used in testing processes in a manufacturing setup, that later could be used to address self-configuration in all production systems in the setup. In the remainder of the paper Sect. 2 gives a short literature review on the topic followed by an introduction to the developed framework for self-configuration in Sect. 3. Section 4 discusses a use-case implementation and Sect. 5 concludes the paper.

Research Question: Can artificial intelligence be used for internal configuration of a production system, allowing it to be managed by the production system itself (self-configuration)? What are the data model and technologies for it?

2 Literature Review

2.1 Artificial Intelligence for Smart Production Systems

Industry 4.0 is a shift towards smart digital manufacturing utilising concepts such as internet of things (IoT), cloud computing and cyber physical systems [1] to enhance manufacturing productivity. Conceptually, a smart manufacturing system should be able to gather information, parameters, and perceptions about itself for production and monitoring purposes and use it to make intelligent decisions.

Meyer et al. [5] described intelligence in procurement, manufacturing and transport as a way for the systems to influence operations. The criteria for an intelligent production system is based on five base characteristics: a component that can uniquely identify itself, communicate with other devices, retain data, deploy language to display features and is capable of participating in or making decisions [6].

Zhong et al. [7] defines intelligent production systems as technologies that embed and utilise informatics and advanced manufacturing techniques to address the dynamic and customised nature of products by achieving flexibility, re-configurability and scalability. Artificial Intelligence (AI) is a means to introduce such aspects of intelligence in production systems [5, 7, 9].

2.2 Self-concept in Manufacturing

The UK Government presented its new data strategy policy that addresses the move towards establishing a 'data-ecosystem' along with the potential use of data driven technologies in industry [8]. In manufacturing environments, there exists a general lack of homogeneity between different platforms and sources, which inhibits the implementation of smart production systems [9]. This heterogeneity necessitates a collaborative framework for device interaction. The collaborative framework must address the environment in a multi-level format. For the manufacturing environment these levels are

Table 1. Value extraction levels for intelligent systems [10]

Level	Description	Consideration
Level I – smart connection level	The effective acquisition of data from a source. Includes a platform that accepts data from a source and communication protocol for data transfer	This level relies heavily on data transparency and accessibility [11]
Level II – data-to-information level	Converting data to information. Capability should be present for data accumulation from multiple sources [12]	Data should be consistent and structured [13]
Level III – cyber level	Extracting meaning from gathered information for smart decision making	The gathered information may follow a trend in values [14]. This helps in developing knowledge base for smart decisions
Level IV – cognition level	Algorithms that are used to make approximations for objective functions	The possible solutions developed by this level should complement the goals of process/system [10]
Level V – configuration level	This level deals with acting on cognitive inferences	This level should make the system robust and resilient against loss and capable of making smart decision by itself

the smart connection-level, data-to-information level, cyber level, cognition level and configuration level [10] (see Table 1).

The Configuration level (V) deals with developing systems where each machine has the capability to decide its own parameters and operations, hence acting on 'cognition' - the generation of insight by AI algorithms based on useful information extracted from data. This is a new domain witnessing significant growth, where applications are capable of automatically adjusting and adapting themselves to varying scalability, complexity, and insight needs. The properties which make a system capable of such adaptability are referred to as self-* properties [15] and include self-management [3], self-stabilisation [2], self-healing, self-organisation [16], self-protection [17], self-optimisation, self-configuration, self-scaling, self-awareness, self-immunity and self-containment. For the purpose of this research, the concept of self-configuration is defined as:

- *The property that deals with response. It is the ability of system to change its configuration (i.e., the connection between different system modules, parameters, and calibration) in order to improve or restore system functionality in response to actions.*

2.3 Enabling Technologies for Self-configuration

Manufacturing is being transformed by data acquisition technologies (like smart sensors), data management systems, data processing techniques (such as cloud computing, big data, artificial intelligence and machine learning), information and communication management methods, and digital twins. Embedding and utilising these technologies on manufacturing objects (like machines, tools, and products) bridges the gap between physical and cyber, enabling smart equipment [18].

Technologies such as multi-agent systems, grid computing, control theory (distributed resources connected through information technology network [16]) and component-based development show promise towards enabling the self-configuration objective. The dominant approaches that are currently being researched to address the issue are multi-agent systems [4] and component-based development [19]. Multi-agent system approach will be taken for this implementation of self-configuration capability in production system. It will be deployed on an industrial use-case and validated for readiness in introducing self-capabilities for industrial adoption.

3 Framework for Self-configuration in Production Systems

In general, a production system comprises numerous pieces of equipment and processing stations or stages. Initially, this concept of a framework for self-configuration is limited to a single (configurable) device or stage, and is presented here in the context of a production testing process. Current approaches require expert knowledge for configuration, and show clear need for self-configuration processes.

Table 2. Agent description in the context of a testing system

Agent	Description
Geometrical Agent (GA)	Agent responsible for part feature identification and feature comparison with cloud-based feature libraries. Based on features identified it also identifies the part that is being tested
Criterion Agent (CA)	Searches and implements potential testing configurations that satisfy the testing criteria. Interacts with the Function Agent (FA) to select the best configuration possible during iteration loops
Function Agent (FA)	Responsible for functionality execution and comparison with objective function. It interacts with CA to select best possible configuration during iteration loops. It is also responsible for communicating the selected configuration to the user

The framework involves seven actors; the *user*, the testing production *system device*, *Geometric Agents* (GA), *Criterion Agents* (CA), *Function Agents* (FA) (see Table 2), a *database/Machine Learning* (ML) *pipeline*, and a *cloud platform*. The cloud platform is a group of services hosted in a cloud environment that forms the part of data pipeline for self-configuration. The services along with formation of a general data pipeline for self-configuration is elaborated in the next subsection. The developed framework is outlined in Fig. 1. The self-configuration framework and the sequence of operations is explained in Fig. 2.

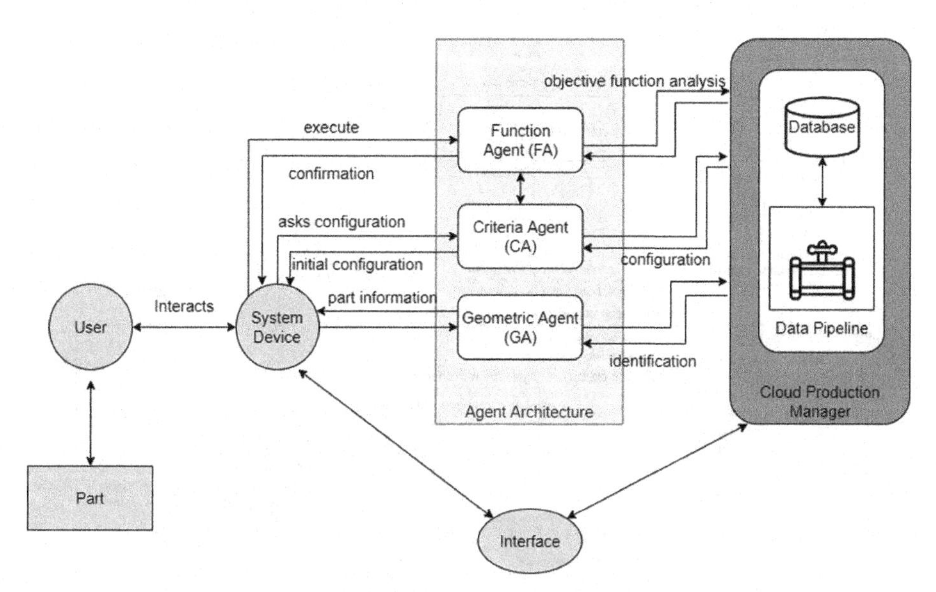

Fig. 1. Architecture of the framework for self-configured production system

3.1 Sequence of Proposed Self-configuration Strategy

The process parameters, communication/connectivity settings, and calibration data are the main constituents of a configuration in production testing systems. The movement of data in the operation loop is managed by agent technology that oversees, monitors, initiates, and terminates the operations happening during execution as needed. These agents interact and communicate with the equipment in conjunction with the cloud platform to perform self-configuration. The chain of interactions between agents, systems, and users is shown in the sequence diagram (Fig. 2).

- **Part Introduction:** The sequence commences with the user introducing the part to the system device (e.g., the production test equipment). This event triggers a response from the Geometric Agent (GA) that extracts information about features from the system device and sends them for a look-up to the cloud platform. The cloud platform is aided by ML pipelines that refer to features stored in a database. The ML pipeline looks up the features and confirms to the cloud platform of features recognised. The set of the features are compared with known parts having those features. The part that has maximum feature mapping is recognised as the part submitted for testing by the user. This information is sent to the system device to be displayed to the user by the GA.

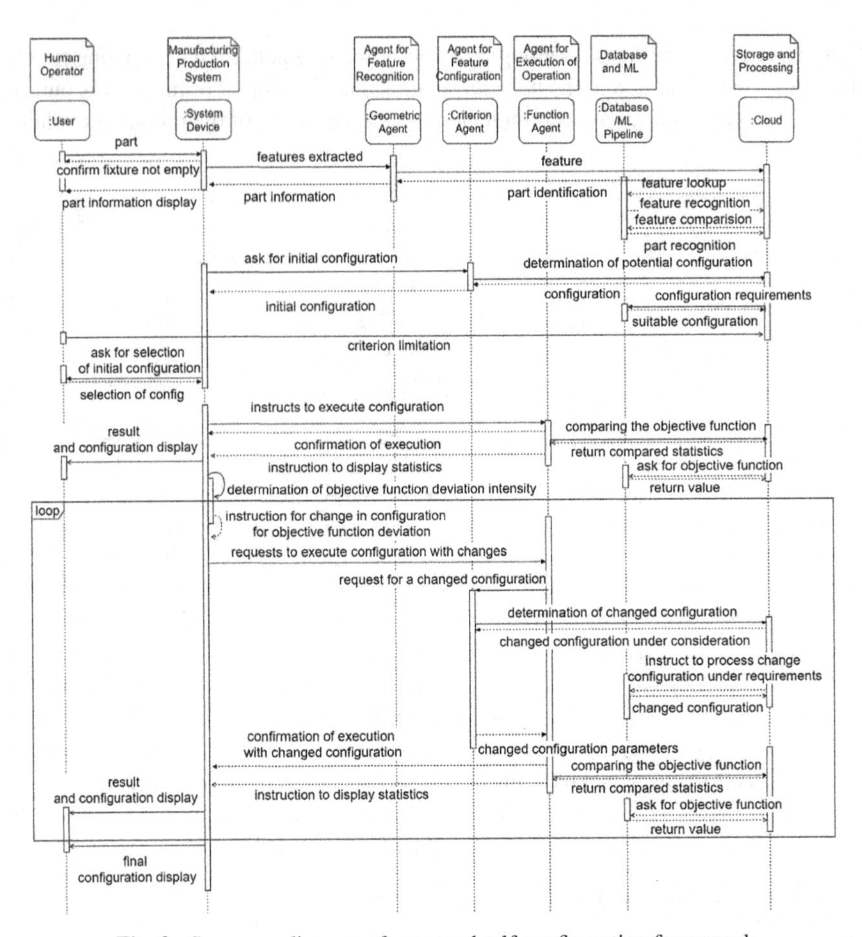

Fig. 2. Sequence diagram of proposed self-configuration framework

- **Look for Configuration:** The next step for the system is to look for a suitable configuration. The system uses the Criterion Agent (CA) to accomplish this. The CA sends an inquiry to the cloud platform that utilises the help of the database to look for a previous or a similar configuration for the part or similar parts. The database returns the testing configuration as a standard schema to the system device through the CA. Any limitations specified by the user is incorporated in the configuration file at this stage.
- **Operation Execution:** The device executes the configuration guided by the Function Agent (FA). The FA logs the execution start and confirms the finish. The results obtained from the operation are sent to the cloud platform by the FA.
- **Result Analysis and Comparison:** The cloud platform uses a ML pipeline to provide a comparison between the result and a suitable objective function. The objective function selected depends on the operation being performed, outcome desired and operation specifics. The comparison is returned by the cloud platform and relevant statistics displayed to the user. If there is no unacceptable deviations from the threshold

then the initial configuration is selected as the final configuration and displayed to user. This deviation in testing is the effectiveness of the pass/fail criteria based on current parameters and calibration settings in system configuration.

- **Reiteration of Operation:** If significant deviation is present then the process is repeated by the system. The function agent (FA) requests the criterion agent (CA) for a new/changed configuration. The CA forwards this request to cloud platform ML pipeline and database for changed configuration values. This lookup to new values is dependent on the instruction obtained from the system device for change in configuration as per objective function deviation. The changed configuration is sent back to the FA from CA and through FA to the system device. Execution of the operation is carried out.
- **Operation Loop:** The results are again compared to objective function. The statistics are displayed to the user by the system as required. If the deviation is acceptably low then this becomes the final configuration else the process is looped till an optimum or a maximum iteration limit is reached.

4 Implementation and Deployment to an Industrial Use-Case

Validation of the framework can be carried out by demonstrating the data pipeline connected to a physical production device through a gateway to the cloud platform services (Fig. 3). The gateway device interfaces with the production equipment, sends the data to the cloud platform, and hosts the agents. Data transferred to storage is retrieved and loaded into a data warehouse service where the table and schema are defined. For the purpose of analysis, data is retrieved from the data warehouse into the coded ML model in the ML supported service on the cloud platform. The insights generated by the ML model is sent back to the warehouse service (to structure the data) and then to storage hosted in the cloud. The cloud storage sends the data to the gateway device from where the agents control the working of the equipment.

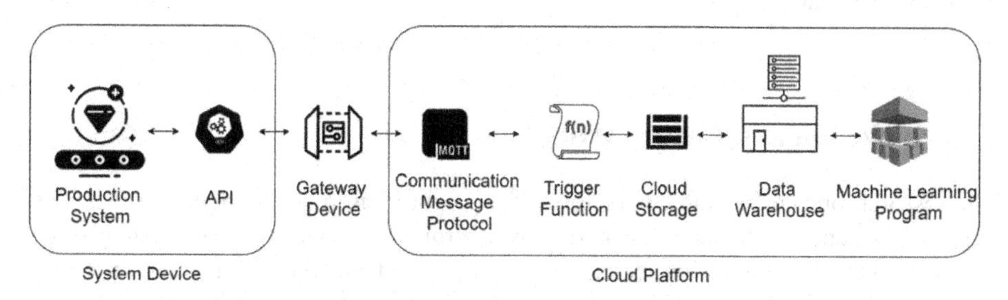

Fig. 3. Data pipeline deployment for self-configuration in production systems

Pipeline automation is achieved by an event-based service called a trigger function. In the cloud, single purpose functions are attached to events that happen in real-time. These functions are triggered as events being observed are executed. The gateway device that connects the system device to the IoT services via a communication message protocol can have regular set of events logged, and these events could trigger functions that co-ordinate the components of data pipeline for self-configuration. An Application Programming Interface (API) is also needed between the testing production system and the gateway device that makes the functionality of the testing system accessible to the rest of the pipeline.

A data pipeline (Fig. 4) was set up connecting an industrial (TQC Ltd.) leak testing rig TAMI (Test bench for leakage identification on aircraft fluid mechanical installations) and dry-air leak testing device MALT (Micro Application Leak Test) with a Raspberry Pi (the gateway device) through the API. The physical hardware was connected to Google Cloud Platform through MQTT Pub/Sub Protocols and an IoT gateway. The future work on self-configuration of production systems will involve this pipeline to optimise parameters (stabilisation time, test pressures and differential pressures) for pneumatic leak testing. Based on this setup the self-configuration framework is deployed and will be validated for testing applications.

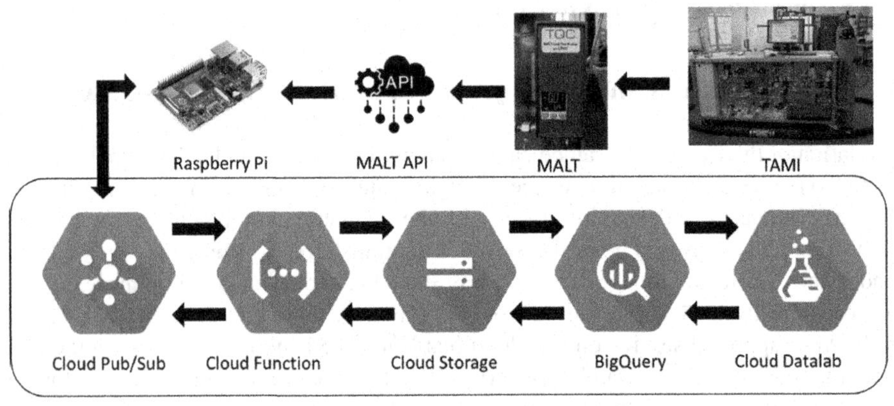

Fig. 4. Complete pipeline deployed for the use-case with API: an initial pipeline for self-configuration research

5 Conclusion and Future Work

The research presents a framework for self-configuration in production systems. This approach is beneficial in saving expert worker's time, costs and reducing management overheads for common testing scenarios. A cloud-based data pipeline is integrated with multi-agent system to support a machine learning process for self-configuring and executing testing processes. Future work involves the full implementation of this framework with state transition management under real-time constraints. The solution will be generalised with a common ontology and semantics developed to enable broader application. The industrial use-case will continue to be used as validation platform for the research, the solution will be iteratively developed and deployed on it.

Currently, this approach is limited to a single device or stage and is tailored for testing applications. It is envisaged that with further research it can encompass multiple interconnected devices and the production system as a whole and abstracted to other production applications. Another limitation observed in the research is related to interoperability and adaptation requirements of the production system. Enforcement of the necessary self-configuration capability is subject to a production system's interface with agents via gateway devices, and to maintain effective data transmission across the cloud pipeline.

References

1. Uhlmann, E., Hohwieler, E., Geisert, C.: Intelligent production systems in the era of industrie 4.0–changing mindsets and business models. J. Mach. Eng. **17** (2017)
2. Botygin, I., Tartakovsky, V.: The development and simulation research of load balancing algorithm in network infrastructures. In: 2014 International Conference on Mechanical Engineering, Automation and Control Systems (MEACS), pp. 1–5. IEEE (2014)
3. Antzoulatos, N.: Towards self-adaptable intelligent assembly systems. Ph.D. thesis, University of Nottingham (2017)
4. Barbosa, J., Leitão, P., Adam, E., Trentesaux, D.: Dynamic self-organization in holonic multi-agent manufacturing systems: the ADACOR evolution. Comput. Ind. **66**, 99–111 (2015)
5. Meyer, G.G., Framling, K., Holmström, J.: Intelligent products: a survey. Comput. Ind. **60**(3), 137–148 (2009)
6. McFarlane, D., Sarma, S., Chirn, J.L., Wong, C., Ashton, K.: The intelligent product in manufacturing control and management. IFAC Proc. Vol. **35**(1), 49–54 (2002)
7. Zhong, R.Y., Xu, X., Klotz, E., Newman, S.T.: Intelligent manufacturing in the context of industry 4.0: a review. Engineering **3**(5), 616–630 (2017)
8. GOV.UK: Policy paper UK National Data Strategy, pp. 1–73 (2020)
9. Sztipanovits, J., et al.: Toward a science of cyber–physical system integration. Proc. IEEE **100**(1), 29–44 (2011)
10. Kao, H.A., Jin, W., Siegel, D., Lee, J.: A cyber physical interface for automation systems—methodology and examples. Machines **3**(2), 93–106 (2015)
11. Aazam, M., Hung, P.P., Huh, E.: Smart gateway based communication for cloud of things. In: 2014 IEEE Ninth International Conference on Intelligent Sensors, Sensor Networks and Information Processing (ISSNIP), pp. 1–6 (2014)
12. García, C.G., Meana-Llorián, D., Lovelle, J.M.C., et al.: A review about smart objects, sensors, and actuators. Int. J. Interact. Multimedia Artif. Intell. **4**(3) (2017)
13. Mourtzis, D., Vlachou, E., Milas, N.: Industrial big data as a result of IoT adoption in manufacturing. Procedia CIRP **55**, 290–295 (2016)
14. Curcurú, G., Cocconcelli, M., Rubini, R., Galante, G.M., Miraglia, V.M.: Bayesian approach in the predictive maintenance policy. In: Proceedings of 9th International Conference Surveillance, pp. 22–24 (2017)
15. Sanchez, M., Exposito, E., Aguilar, J.: Implementing self-* autonomic properties in self-coordinated manufacturing processes for the industry 4.0 context. Comput. Ind. **121**, 103247 (2020)
16. Khalgui, M., Mosbahi, O.: Intelligent distributed control systems. Inf. Softw. Technol. **52**(12), 1259–1271 (2010)
17. Yan, J., Vyatkin, V.: Extension of reconfigurability provisions in IEC 61499. In: 2013 IEEE 18th Conference on Emerging Technologies and Factory Automation (ETFA), pp. 1–7. IEEE (2013)
18. Xu, G., Huang, G.Q., Fang, J.: Cloud asset for urban flood control. Adv. Eng. Inform. **29**(3), 355–365 (2015)
19. Jann, J., Browning, L.M., Burugula, R.S.: Dynamic reconfiguration: basic building blocks for autonomic computing on IBM pSeries servers. IBM Syst. J. **42**(1), 29–37 (2003)

Cyber-Physical Systems and Digital Twins

Verification of the Boundedness Property in a Petri Net-Based Specification of the Control Part of Cyber-Physical Systems

Marcin Wojnakowski(✉) and Remigiusz Wiśniewski

Institute of Control and Computation Engineering, University of Zielona Góra, 65-516 Zielona Góra, Poland
{M.Wojnakowski,R.Wisniewski}@issi.uz.zgora.pl

Abstract. A method of analysis of a control part of the cyber-physical system described by a Petri net is presented in the paper. In particular, boundedness of the system is examined. Contrary to other well-known techniques, the proposed idea does not require obtaining of all place invariants, nor computation of all reachable states in the net. Therefore, it is possible to check the boundedness of a net in a more effective and efficient way, compared to the traditional, well-known methods. Furthermore, the proposed algorithm has been examined experimentally with a set of 243 benchmarks (Petri nets). The research results show the high efficiency of the proposed method, since a solution was found even for such nets where popular techniques were not able to analyse boundedness of the system. Finally, the presented idea is illustrated by a case-study real-life example.

Keywords: Boundedness · Petri nets · Control part of cyber-physical systems · Invariants · Linear algebra

1 Introduction and Problem Formulation

Petri nets are popular state-transition systems that allow for comfortable and easy specification of concurrent systems [1–4]. They offer the possibility of graphical modelling, as well, as a wide opportunity of analysis techniques [3, 5, 6]. Recently, Petri nets have become particularly popular in the modelling of the control part of the cyber-physical systems [7–9]. A cyber-physical system (CPS) [7, 10] combines computation with physical routes. The behaviour of a CPS is defined by two parts: the cyber and the physical parts [11]. Such systems join physical processes, networks and the computational modules of the system. A CPS finds applications in various fields of human life, for instance medical systems [12], vehicular systems [13], power electronic converters [14] and smart homes [15].

This work focuses on the analysis of the control part of the cyber-physical systems, which plays the computational part of the system. A Petri net-based approach benefits the verification of the design even at the specification phase, allowing a reduction in time and costs of the design of CPS [3, 8]. A very important property of a Petri net-based

© IFIP International Federation for Information Processing 2021
Published by Springer Nature Switzerland AG 2021
L. M. Camarinha-Matos et al. (Eds.): DoCEIS 2021, IFIP AICT 626, pp. 83–91, 2021.
https://doi.org/10.1007/978-3-030-78288-7_8

system is boundedness [1, 2, 5]. Various design methods require this property in their inputs (cf. [6, 8, 9, 16, 17]). Furthermore, boundedness is an essential in case of systems that are oriented on the implementation in the hardware (for example within the field programmable gate arrays, FPGAs).

The two most popular methodologies for boundedness examination of a Petri net are one which applies linear algebra (place invariants computation [5, 18]), and another which involves reachability tree exploration [19]. However, they are seriously limited, since the number of invariants (or reachable states, respectively) can be exponential [2, 4, 5]. So-called *state explosion problem* may be a real challenge to the designer during the analysis of the system. Usually, in such a case the solution is not found within the assumed time due to the exponential computational complexity.

In the paper a technique for the boundedness verification of the Petri net-based CPS is proposed. The method does not involve computation of all invariants in the system, thus it is more efficient and effective compared to the most popular techniques. The idea of the presented solution is based on the computation of the reduced set of the place invariants. The main contributions are as follows:

- A method that allows for the boundedness verification of the control part of a Petri net-based CPS is proposed.
- The presented technique allows for the efficient boundedness verification of the system, which means that the solution is found in the assumed time.
- The idea has been validated and verified experimentally in order to confirm its efficiency and effectiveness.
- The algorithm is explained by a case-study real-life example of a CPS.

2 Petri Nets in Applied Artificial Intelligence Systems

Application of various Petri net-based aspects can be found in the artificial intelligence systems [23]. In particular, boundedness property may play important role in analysis and verification of such systems. Let us briefly present the possible applications that show relations between Petri nets and Applied AI.

Analysis and modelling aspects of multi-agent systems are considered in [20]. The paper studies several important properties of Petri net-based systems, including boundedness and liveness. As stated by the Authors, those features are applicable in the modelling of multi-agent systems. In particular, the system is verified against the deadlocks by analysis of boundedness and liveness properties.

Application of Petri nets for intelligent control and supervision is shown in [21]. The Authors propose a modelling tool called Continuous Fuzzy Petri Net (CFPN). Such a net can be used for the improvement of the performance and optimization of the system. Moreover, CFPNs are applicable in fault tolerance and diagnostics (e.g., to help the operator in the controlling and monitoring of thousands of actuators and sensors). The idea is explained by an example of a water treatment plant.

The overview of scheduling, planning and control of manufacturing systems with the application of AI-based search methods and Petri nets is presented in [22]. The paper focuses on the various aspects, starting with Petri nets and their utilization in the modelling of manufacturing systems. Then, scheduling techniques are presented, including combination of Petri nets and AI-based heuristic search methods.

3 Definitions and Notations

The presented definitions correspond to the notations shown in [2, 4, 5, 24, 25].

Definition 1. *A Petri net* N is a 4-tuple: $N = (P, T, F, M_0)$, where P is a set of places, T is a set of transitions, $F \subseteq (P \times T) \cup (T \times P)$ is a set of arcs, $M_0 : P \rightarrow \mathbb{N}$ is an initial marking.

Definition 2. *An incidence matrix* $A_{|T|\times|P|}$ of a Petri net $N = (P, T, F, M_0)$ is given by:

$$a_{ij} = \begin{cases} -1, \left(p_j, t_i\right) \in F \\ 1, \left(t_i, p_j\right) \in F \\ 0, \textit{otherwise} \end{cases},$$

where cell a_{ij} of matrix A refers to transition t_i and place p_j.

Definition 3. *A place invariant (p-invariant)* of a Petri net $N = (P, T, F, M_0)$ is an integer vector such that $A\vec{x} = 0$.

Definition 4. A Petri net $N = (P, T, F, M_0)$ is *covered* by place invariants if every place $p \in P$ belongs to at least one p-invariant.

Definition 5. A Petri net $N = (P, T, F, M_0)$ is said to be *bounded* if there is no marking (state) M_n such that any place $p \in P$ contains more than a finite number of tokens. A Petri net N bounded for any finite initial marking M_0 is said to be *structurally bounded.*

Theorem 1. A Petri net $N = (P, T, F, M_0)$ is structurally bounded if it is covered by p-invariants [19].

4 The Idea of the Proposed Method

This section presents the idea of the proposed technique. Firstly, we will show the main steps of the proposed method, supplemented by an adequate description. Next, the case study example of the boundedness verification of the real-life cyber-physical system is presented.

The proposed method includes the following steps:

1. Initialization:

   a) Read incidence matrix $A_{|T|\times|P|}$ of Petri net $N = (P, T, F, M_0)$ that describes the control part of the cyber-physical system.

b) Form the unit matrix $Q = [D_{|P|\times|P|}|A^{\mathrm{T}}_{|T|\times|P|}]$, where D is an identity matrix, and $A^{\mathrm{T}}_{|T|\times|P|}$ is the transposed incidence matrix of N.
c) Initialize the place invariants cover: $C = \emptyset$.

2. Searching for the place-invariants cover: for each column $t \in T$ in $A^{\mathrm{T}}_{|T|\times|P|}$:

a) Find all pair of rows that annul the j-th transition (column) of A^{T} and add them to the matrix Q.
b) Find all rows which the intersection with the j-th transition (column) is not equal to 0 and delete them from Q.
c) Find all rows that cover binary the other ones and delete them from Q.
d) Boundedness verification: for each row r of A^{T} such that all entries of r are equal to 0:

- add place invariant I that refer to the row r in D to the set C: $C = C \cup \{I\}$ (i.e., values of I refer directly to the row r in the matrix D),
- examine, whether C covers all places in the net:

  – break if C covers all places, the system is structurally bounded;
  – otherwise, execute the algorithm from step 2(a).

3. Boundedness verification:

- if the net is covered by place invariants, **the system is structurally bounded**,
- otherwise, its **boundedness of the system is not determined**.

The presented method involves linear algebra. It is based on the technique initially proposed in [18], however it does not require computation of all place invariants in the Petri net. The algorithm works as follows. Initially, the unit matrix Q of matrices D and A^{T} is formed. Matrix D is initially equal to the identity matrix, while A^{T} denotes the transposed incidence matrix of the Petri net. Next, the method searches for the invariants by transformations of the matrix Q. In particular, subsequent transitions are examined in order to zeros matrix A^{T}. Meanwhile, matrix D holds partially obtained invariants. If any row of A^{T} is completely zeroed (that is, all its entries are equal to 0), the proper invariant can be obtained from matrix D. The algorithm verifies existence of new invariants at each stage, add adds them to the set C. The method finishes, once the set C covers all the places.

Let us now explain the proposed algorithm with a real-life example. Figure 1 shows a Petri net-based control system responsible for managing a multi-robot, initially presented in [26]. There are nine places and six transitions in the net, denoted by $p_1, \ldots, p_9$ and $t_1, \ldots, t_6$, respectively. The system involves pick-and-place operations in order to transfer or obtain parts by two robot arms. Places $p_1, \ldots, p_3$, and transitions $t_1, \ldots, t_3$ refers to the activities of robot first arm. Similarly, places $p_4, \ldots, p_6$, and transitions $t_4, \ldots, t_6$ are related to the second arm. The presented example focuses on the collision-free movements. Therefore, only one robot arm is able to access the workspace at a time.

The activities in common workspace are represented by places p_3 and p_6. The collision-free movements are secured by the mutual exclusion technique, and involvement of place p_7 (places p_8 and p_9 are used as additional buffers).

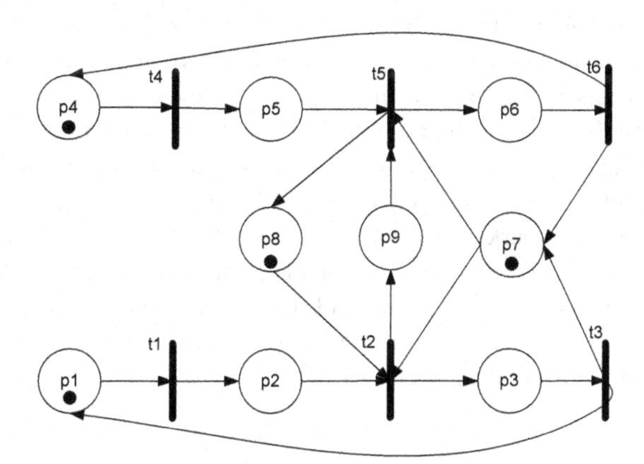

Fig. 1. A multi-robot controller specified by a Petri net.

Let us now examine the boundedness of the system with the proposed method. According to the algorithm, initially the unit matrix $Q = [D|A^T]$ is formed (Table 1, left). Next, the matrix is transformed, while the subsequent transitions are examined. In the presented example, only three transitions (out of six) are required to be processed to obtain the solution. Table 1 (right) shows the unit matrix after examination of the third transition. Note that four rows of A^T are already zeroed. They refer to the place invariants formed in the matrix D (marked by blue boxes). Clearly, those invariants cover all places in the net. The algorithm terminates its execution with the result that the system is bounded.

Table 1. Matrix $Q = [D|A^T]$ before the transformation (left) and after the transformation (right).

p_1	p_2	p_3	p_4	p_5	p_6	p_7	p_8	p_9	t_1	t_2	t_3	t_4	t_5	t_6
1	0	0	0	0	0	0	0	0	-1	0	0	0	1	0
0	1	0	0	0	0	0	0	0	1	-1	0	0	0	0
0	0	1	0	0	0	0	0	0	0	1	0	0	-1	0
0	0	0	1	0	0	0	0	0	0	0	-1	0	0	1
0	0	0	0	1	0	0	0	0	0	0	1	-1	0	0
0	0	0	0	0	1	0	0	0	0	0	0	1	0	-1
0	0	0	0	0	0	1	0	0	0	-1	0	-1	1	1
0	0	0	0	0	0	0	1	0	0	-1	0	1	0	0
0	0	0	0	0	0	0	0	1	0	1	0	-1	0	0

p_1	p_2	p_3	p_4	p_5	p_6	p_7	p_8	p_9	t_1	t_2	t_3	t_4	t_5	t_6
0	0	0	0	0	0	0	1	1	0	0	0	0	0	0
1	1	1	0	0	0	0	0	0	0	0	0	0	0	0
0	0	1	0	0	1	1	0	0	0	0	0	0	0	0
0	0	2	0	0	0	1	1	0	0	0	0	0	-1	1
1	1	0	0	0	1	0	0	1	0	0	0	0	1	-1
0	0	0	1	1	1	0	0	0	0	0	0	0	0	0
0	0	1	1	1	0	0	1	0	0	0	0	0	-1	1

5 Experiments

The proposed method was verified experimentally. Its effectiveness and efficiency was compared to the popular technique of place invariants computation (denoted as an *exact algorithm*), initially shown in [18]. Both methods were examined in terms of their runtime and obtained results (covering of the net by p-invariants). The set of benchmarks includes 243 Petri nets, modelling real and hypothetical cyber-physical systems and control systems. Their description can be found on the websites: http://gres.uninova.pt and http://hippo.iee.uz.zgora.pl. The experiments were perfor-med on the dedicated computational server: Intel® Xeon® Platinum 8160 @2.1 GHz processor, 16 GB of RAM. The results for selected benchmarks are shown in Table 2. The particular columns contain the following values: *Name of the system* – the name of the system described by a Petri net, |*P*| - the number of places, |*T*| - the number of transitions, *covered* – whether the system is covered by place invariants according to the algorithm, *runtime* – the execution time of the algorithm in milliseconds.

Table 2. Exemplary results of the experiments.

Name of the system (Petri net)	|*P*|	|*T*|	Exact method		Proposed method	
			Covered	Runtime [ms]	Covered	Runtime [ms]
traffic_light_v2	4	3	Yes	0.424	Yes	0.415
pn_silva_05e	4	4	No	0.439	No	0.635
esparza2	15	13	Yes	3.366	Yes	1.061
2pusher	15	18	No	10.743	No	6.536
silva5	16	8	Yes	2.660	Yes	1.496
hulgaard1	19	12	Yes	27.805	Yes	3.275
ConsistentExample	29	26	No	42986.800	No	5752.120
zuberek1	30	22	Yes	22.324	Yes	3.273
crossroadSM_FPGA	32	12	Yes	807879.000	Yes	183.985
zuberek5	41	31	n/a	Timeout	Yes	45.045
cn_crr7	56	15	n/a	Timeout	Yes	155.278
cn_crr25	200	51	n/a	Timeout	Yes	78954.828

It can be observed that for small systems, containing a few places and transitions, (such as *traffic_light_v2* or *pn_silva_05e*) both methods are efficient. It can be even noticed that the exact method computes the result faster than the proposed algorithm. However, in case of more complicated systems (such as *ConsistentExample*, *crossroadSM_FPGA*), the difference is notable. The proposed method was able to compute the solution within a few seconds, while the runtime of the exact method is much longer (even more than 13 min in case of *crossroadSM_FPGA*). Finally, a huge difference can be noticed in case of complex systems (*zuberek5*, *cn_crr7*, *cn_crr25*). For such systems, the exact method was not able to compute results due to the state explosion problem (the method was stopped after one hour, and denoted as "timeout" in the table). In contrast, the proposed method found the result for the worst case (*cn_crr25*) in less than one and a half minute. Finally, let us note that module *crosroadSM_FPGA* describes the real-life cyber-physical system (collision free crossroad for cars and pedestrians). It was implemented and partially reconfigured within the programmable device, thus the boundedness property was essential.

The performed experiments proved the effectiveness and efficiency of the proposed technique. The results obtained by both methods were the same for all examined benchmarks (for which the result for the exact method was obtained). This provides experimental validation of the correctness of the method. Furthermore, the runtime of the proposed method confirms its very high efficiency, since the result for the worst-case example was obtained in less than one and half a minute.

6 Conclusions

The design process of the control part of cyber-physical systems involves several aspects. One of them refers to the proper specification and further formal verification. In the paper an analysis technique of the boundedness property is proposed. The presented solution is based on the existing solutions and applies transformations of the incidence matrix of the system. Contrary to the other, most popular analysis techniques, the introduced method does not require computation of all place invariants in the system. The performed experiments proved its efficiency and effectiveness.

On the other hand, there is a limitation of the presented method. The boundedness of the Petri net is guaranteed only for those systems that are covered by place invariants. Otherwise, the system might be unbounded, but the final result remains unsolved. However, it should be underlined that such a situation (the net being bounded but not covered by place invariants) is rather rare (about 5.5% of the examined benchmarks). Nevertheless, this aspect is planned for further enhancement of the algorithm. Moreover, plans for future research include analysis of well-formed nets (safeness, liveness), which are the key properties of Petri net-based description of the control part of cyber-physical systems.

Acknowledgments. This work is supported by the National Science Centre, Poland, under Grant number 2019/35/B/ST6/01683.

References

1. Girault, C., Valk, R.: Petri Nets for Systems Engineering: A Guide to Modeling, Verification, and Applications. Springer, Heidelberg (2003). https://doi.org/10.1007/978-3-662-05324-9
2. Karatkevich, A.: Dynamic Analysis of Petri Net-Based Discrete Systems. Springer, Heidelberg (2007). https://doi.org/10.1007/978-3-540-71560-3
3. Zhou, M., Wu, N.: System Modeling and Control with Resource-Oriented Petri Nets, 1st edn. CRC Press, Boca Raton (2009)

4. Murata, T.: Petri nets: properties, analysis and applications. Proc. IEEE **77**(4), 541–580 (1989). https://doi.org/10.1109/5.24143
5. Wiśniewski, R.: Prototyping of Concurrent Control Systems Implemented in FPGA Devices. Springer, Switzerland (2017). https://doi.org/10.1007/978-3-319-45811-3
6. Wisniewski, R., Wisniewska, M., Jarnut, M.: C-exact hypergraphs in concurrency and sequentiality analyses of cyber-physical systems specified by safe Petri nets. IEEE Access **7**, 13510–13522 (2019). https://doi.org/10.1109/access.2019.2893284
7. Yu, Z., Zhou, L., Ma, Z., El-Meligy, M.A.: Trustworthiness modeling and analysis of cyber-physical manufacturing systems. IEEE Access **5**, 26076–26085 (2017)
8. Grobelna, I., Wiśniewski, R., Wojnakowski, M.: Specification of cyber-physical systems with the application of interpreted nets. In: Proceedings of the IECON'19 - 45th Annual Conference of the IEEE Industrial Electronics Society, Lisbon, Portugal, pp. 5887–5891 (2019)
9. Wiśniewski, R., Bazydło, G., Szcześniak, P., Wojnakowski, M.: Petri net-based specification of cyber-physical systems oriented to control direct matrix converters with space vector modulation. IEEE Access **7**, 23407–23420 (2019). https://doi.org/10.1109/access.2019.2899316
10. Lee, E.A.: Cyber physical systems: design challenges. In: 2008 11th IEEE International Symposium on Object and Component-Oriented Real-Time Distributed Computing (ISORC), May 2008, pp. 363–369 (2008). https://doi.org/10.1109/isorc.2008.25
11. Lee, E.A., Seshia, S.A.: Introduction to Embedded Systems: A Cyber-Physical Systems Approach, 2nd edn. The MIT Press, Cambridge (2016)
12. Dey, N., Ashour, A.S., Shi, F., Fong, S.J., Tavares, J.M.R.S.: Medical cyber-physical systems: a survey. J. Med. Syst. **42**(4), 74 (2018). https://doi.org/10.1007/s10916-018-0921-x
13. Jia, D., Lu, K., Wang, J., Zhang, X., Shen, X.: A Survey on platoon-based vehicular cyber-physical systems. IEEE Commun. Surv. Tutor. **18**(1), 263–284 (2016). https://doi.org/10.1109/comst.2015.2410831
14. Wiśniewski, R., Bazydło, G., Szcześniak, P.: Low-cost FPGA hardware implementation of matrix converter switch control. IEEE Trans. Circuits Syst. II Express Briefs **66**(7), 1177–1181 (2019). https://doi.org/10.1109/tcsii.2018.2875589
15. Wiśniewski, R., Karatkevich, A., Adamski, M., Costa, A., Gomes, L.: Prototyping of concurrent control systems with application of Petri nets and comparability graphs. IEEE Trans. Control Syst. Technol. **26**(2), 575–586 (2018). https://doi.org/10.1109/tcst.2017.2692204
16. Clempner, J.: An analytical method for well-formed workflow/Petri net verification of classical soundness. Int. J. Appl. Math. Comput. Sci. **24**(4), 931–939 (2014). https://doi.org/10.2478/amcs-2014-0068
17. Li, B., Khlif-Bouassida, M., Toguyéni, A.: On–the–fly diagnosability analysis of bounded and unbounded labeled Petri nets using verifier nets. Int. J. Appl. Math. Comput. Sci. **28**(2), 269–281 (2018). https://doi.org/10.2478/amcs-2018-0019
18. Martínez, J., Silva, M.: A simple and fast algorithm to obtain all invariants of a generalised Petri net. In: Girault, C., Reisig, W. (eds.) Application and Theory of Petri Nets. Informatik-Fachberichte, vol. 52, pp. 301–310. Springer, Heidelberg (1982). https://doi.org/10.1007/978-3-642-68353-4_47
19. Reisig, W.: Nets consisting of places and transistions. In: Reisig, W. (ed.) Petri Nets. EATCS Monographs on Theoretical Computer Science, vol 4, pp. 62–76. Springer, Heidelberg (1985). https://doi.org/10.1007/978-3-642-69968-9_6
20. Celaya, J.R., Desrochers, A.A., Graves, R.J.: Modeling and analysis of multi-agent systems using Petri nets. In: 2007 IEEE International Conference on Systems, Man and Cybernetics, pp. 1439–1444, October 2007. https://doi.org/10.1109/icsmc.2007.4413960

21. Pang, G.K.H., Tang, R., Woo, S.S.: Intelligent control and supervision based on fuzzy Petri nets. In: Tzafestas, S.G. (ed.) Methods and Applications of Intelligent Control. Microprocessor-Based and Intelligent Systems Engineering, vol. 16, pp. 217–243. Springer, Dordrecht (1997). https://doi.org/10.1007/978-94-011-5498-7_8
22. Cang, S., Yu, H.: Overview of modelling, scheduling, planning, and control using Petri net representation and AI search. In: Advanced Design and Manufacture to Gain a Competitive Edge, London, pp. 397–406 (2008). https://doi.org/10.1007/978-1-84800-241-8_41
23. Edelkamp, S., Jabbar, S.: Action planning for directed model checking of Petri nets. Electron. Notes Theor. Comput. Sci. **149**(2), 3–18 (2006). https://doi.org/10.1016/j.entcs.2005.07.023
24. Wisniewski, R., Wojnakowski, M., Stefanowicz, Ł.: Safety analysis of Petri nets based on the SM-cover computed with the linear algebra technique. In: AIP Conference Proceedings, vol. 2040, no. 1, p. 080008, November 2018. https://doi.org/10.1063/1.5079142
25. Wiśniewski, R., Karatkevich, A., Stefanowicz, Ł., Wojnakowski, M.: Decomposition of distributed edge systems based on the Petri nets and linear algebra technique. J. Syst. Archit. **96**, 20–31 (2019). https://doi.org/10.1016/j.sysarc.2019.01.015
26. Zurawski, R., Zhou, M.: Petri nets and industrial applications: a tutorial. IEEE Trans. Ind. Electron. **41**(6), 567–583 (1994). https://doi.org/10.1109/41.334574

Collaborative Cyber-Physical Systems Design Approach: Smart Home Use Case

Artem A. Nazarenko(✉) and Luis M. Camarinha-Matos

School of Science and Technology and UNINOVA-CTS, Nova University of Lisbon, 2829-516 Monte Caparica, Lisbon, Portugal
a.nazarenko@campus.fct.unl.pt, cam@uninova.pt

Abstract. The growing trend on moving from isolated services to dynamically integrated/composed ones in a context where the cyber and physical worlds are interlinked, led to emergence of the concept of Collaborative CPSs (CCPSs). These systems rely on collaboration among internal and external components. An important aspect, in this regard, is the establishment of a design methodology for those systems. To satisfy agility requirements, the design process should be accomplished in a modular way, so that the system can be updated by adding or replacing modules. In traditional ICT systems the design process can be split into two parts/phases: the computational model design, i.e., functionality modules, and the design of a shell or service layer, providing the auxiliary services to utilize the computational model, e.g., security, human-machine interface, etc. In the case of CCPS design, the process also must consider the collaborative aspects within the design workflow. In the proposed work, we provide a model and design pattern (framework and a set of steps) for building Collaborative CPSs. To illustrate the approach, a smart home use-case is used.

Keywords: Collaborative cyber-physical systems · Smart home · Design patterns · Collaborative services

1 Introduction

The concept of systems composed of integrated physical and digital elements is referred as Cyber Physical Systems (CPS) [1]. Along with Internet-of-Things (IoT), CPSs are considered as one of the pillars of Industry 4.0, being applied in many other areas of human activities, such as: smart home, smart city, healthcare, smart farming, etc. The concepts of IoT and CPS are often interchanged. Both concepts include cyber and physical parts, however, IoT is more focused on connectivity to Internet, while CPS is more concerned with integration [2]. In both cases, the underlying idea of the concept is that a physical layer composed of physical devices, such as sensors, actuators, or more complex machines, is integrated with software or virtual components. This integration adds intelligence to the physical components. The idea of virtual and physical space integration is also the basis of the notion of Digital Twins (DT), used to establish virtual

© IFIP International Federation for Information Processing 2021
Published by Springer Nature Switzerland AG 2021
L. M. Camarinha-Matos et al. (Eds.): DoCEIS 2021, IFIP AICT 626, pp. 92–101, 2021.
https://doi.org/10.1007/978-3-030-78288-7_9

replicas of physical entities through the modelling of the behaviour/processes occurring in the physical layer [3] and connecting to the physical counterparts.

An important element of advanced CPS is the collaborative aspect, as added value can be gained through the collaboration of system's components with each other, and even collaboration between those components and humans enabling the necessary abstraction level. This led to emergence of the concept of Collaborative CPS (CCPS), defined as systems "jointly acting and sharing information, resources and responsibilities in order to achieve a common goal" [2]. A common goal is, for instance, a collaborative or complex service that is delivered to the human-users of the system or the other components. The collaborative parties can originate from within the system (intelligent sub-systems) or be external entities. These ideas reflect an ongoing trend of moving from isolated services to rather interlinked ones [4].

CCPSs have to consider the collaborative aspect from the very beginning or the design phase. It is important to provide such a structure that can include technical components, "things", as well as users who can potentially collaborate and establish new services for mutual benefit. Most of the works devoted to design issues of CPS usually address the low-level design challenges. Some examples can be the timing requirements of CPS [5], model-based performance analysis [6] or use-case related design [7]. In this work we are focused on the CCPS design process, contemplating mechanisms to facilitate collaboration, and guided by the following research question:

What could be a suitable set of models and organizational structures to support the design of increasingly complex and evolving CCPSs?

Even though, the adopted design process is briefly addressed, we provide an example of such process applied to a Smart Home domain. Domestic environments have been identified as "typical application domain for CPS" [8]. A smart home contains different sensors, actuators and smart appliances controlling the physical environment, as well as humans interacting/collaborating with them. Thus, a smart home can be considered as suitable case for validating the proposed design process.

2 Contribution to Applied AI Systems

Due to growing intelligence interconnection, autonomy and collaboration readiness of devices and sub-systems, modern CPS can be described as Cyber Physical Systems of Systems with "unprecedented capabilities and opportunities" [9]. Moreover, the constituents of those systems have a heterogeneous nature and vary from cyber and physical artefacts to human members [3], including the integration of different levels of complex sub-systems. Thus, modern CPS, where collaboration is one of the corner stones, can be seen as collaborative ecosystems of smart components/sub-systems. However, even a system containing smart and intelligent components cannot be fully recognised as smart, as only collaborative mechanisms forcing components to interact and establish more complex units makes the systems really smart. Thus, conceiving a proper organisational structure, as well as the methodology to design Collaborative CPS is needed to contribute to further smartification of these complex systems.

One possible way for systems' smartification is the creation of collaborative services, in analogy with Business Services [10], where several parties come together to satisfy user's or customer's needs. In the case of CCPS, these parties can be the smart sub-systems or smart components within the systems that can collaborate to generate added value. The formation of such networks or consortia/coalitions is an interesting topic derived from the Collaborative Networks domain [11]. As defined in previous work [12], a coalition of Smart Components is formed from the pool of virtual agents/digital twins associated to Smart Environments. After the coalition is established, it can provide collaborative services targeting the users' needs, and considering conditions of a particular environment.

3 Research Approach

The research approach is based on the CCPS design framework proposed in [3], inspired in the Design Science Research method (Fig. 1). The core pillars of this framework are: (i) Application Domain, possessing information about the use-case and its requirements, (ii) CCPS Design, used to design and develop solutions, and (iii) Knowledge Base, that corresponds to a repository of models, taxonomies, and design rules. The idea is to focus on the design of the CCPS ecosystem, in which members, as smart entities, are able to build temporary alliances in order to provide collaborative services. One of the key advantages of the adopted framework is that it allows storing the knowledge generated during the iterative design process within the Knowledge Base. Thus, generated knowledge can be re-used during the next design iterations. Moreover, the system being designed is considered as a set of modules – modular approach, which after the design phase can evolve and be further updated during the operational phase.

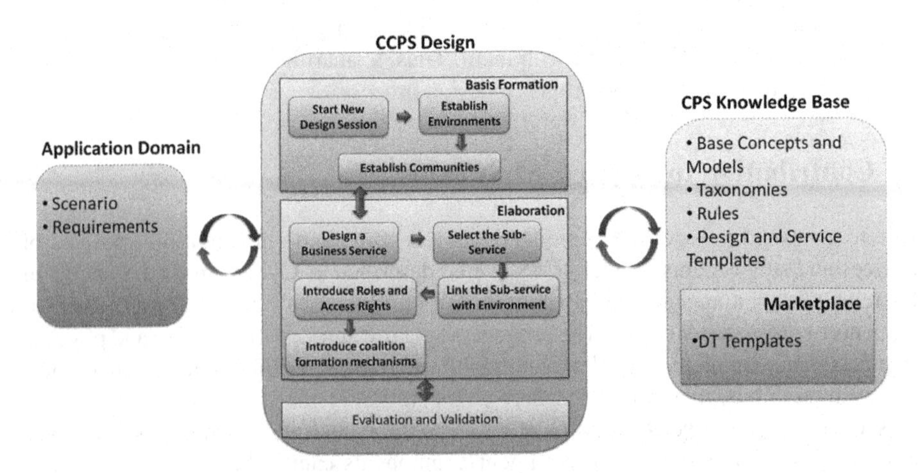

Fig. 1. Adopted CCPS design framework

After identifying/setting the requirements for the planned CCPS and acquiring the information about the domain, the CCPS design process starts. It includes some core steps: (i) new design session or establishment of the ecosystem, (ii) establishment of Smart Environments (SEs), (iii) establishment of Smart Communities (SCs), (iv) business service design, (v) sub-service selection, (vi) linking the sub-services with appropriate SE, (vii) access policy formulation and (viii) coalition formation mechanisms. The overall process is supported by the Knowledge Base. There is also the possibility, besides the models, taxonomies, and rules, to connect to an external Marketplace delivering DT building blocks.

One of the key models, part of the contribution from the Knowledge Base, is the high-level model (meta-model) of the complex CCPS. This model has three layers: (i) Ecosystem Layer, (ii) Organisational Layer, and (iii) Entities layer. The Ecosystem Layer gives the high-level view, while integrating both technical and social aspects of the system. The Organisational Layer relates to the social or human-related and technical entities, which are grouped into communities or Smart Communities and environments or Smart Environments, respectively. Thus, in general, the CCPS ecosystem can be considered as a set of Smart Environments and a set of Smart Communities. Moreover, the Organizational Layer is used to group/form/organize digital entities or digital representations of the physical objects (e.g., devices or human users) as digital twins. The model considers the existence of two types of DTs, the Asset and Human DTs that are used to reflect the real-world entities, such as devices/systems, and humans respectively. The Smart Environments are used to represent the logical partition of the Ecosystem that can match the physical partition, e.g., rooms in a home. In the case of the smart home, each environment stands for a certain room, such as bedroom, kitchen, etc. A typical SE consists of Asset DTs which are deployed in the environment at each moment. Please note that some smart devices/objects are mobile and can move among different SEs.

The Smart Community (SC) is an important element used as organizational entity for the human members of the ecosystem. Along with the SE, it belongs to the Organizational Layer. The human members of a SC are represented through Human DTs used to enable collaboration within the digital layer.

Human DTs are considered along with Asset DTs as a part of the Entities Layer. A typical Asset DT represents either a smart object, i.e., sensor or actuator, or a subsystem that might encapsulate several smart objects. The human DT, on one hand, is part of the system, providing some data about the owner, but on the other hand fulfilling social and administrative tasks [3]. The Entities layer can be considered as a bridge between virtual and physical entities. The DTs in the context of this work are used as data aggregators providing the necessary abstraction from the field level details. For instance, sensor sending the values every second, however, not every value triggers the change in condition/state of the DT. Thus, the Entities Layer containing Asset DTs and Human DTs aggregates data acquired from the field level, only focusing on the state/condition of the physical entity within the virtual layer. The high-level abstraction allows focusing on collaborative aspects, at the same time not ignoring the real-world events/processes. In this regard, behavioural changes are considered at design time through introduction of a set of rules or meta-rules determining the behavioural patterns of DTs. During the operational phase, the case-specific rules can be applied under the assumption that they are not violating the meta-rules, enabling customization and dynamic adjustment of services provided.

Further contribution is detailed elaboration of the design process steps introducing the order and logic of actions required to establish a CCPS. As the design is modular based, missing modules can be added during the next design sessions. The next section presents some domain-specific taxonomies that are utilized during the design process and used to populate the KB.

4 Smart Home Scenario

In this work, as mentioned above, the considered use-case is a Smart Home scenario. The models that are acquired from the KB are loaded into the design space in the form of taxonomies with interrelated concepts, attributes, and corresponding relations. At the end, the designed system can be represented as a complex graph composed of elements extracted from different models stored within the KB. However, the designer can enrich the KB, while updating the currently available taxonomies/models, so that the updates are available for other sessions. After the designed system will be in the operational stage, semantic relations can change due to dynamic nature of real-world systems [13], e.g. device changing the location. In this section we address the steps of the design process identified in the previous section (Fig. 2). The logic of every step, for the sake of explicitness, is represented in the form of simplified pseudo-code that can be converted into the Prolog and Python code.

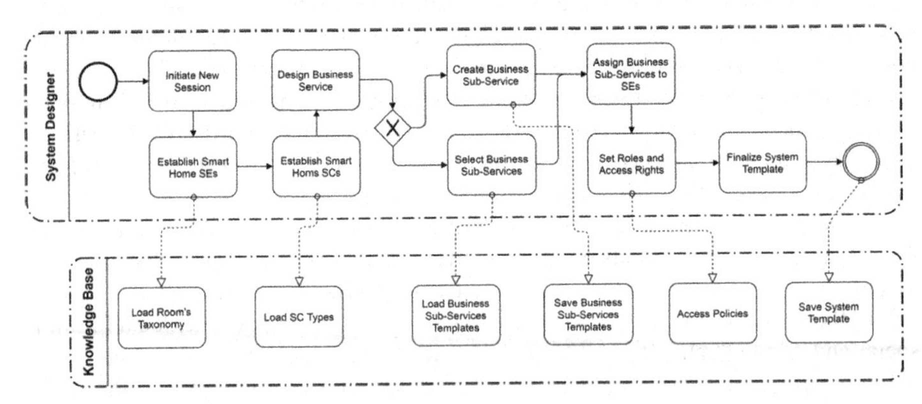

Fig. 2. CCPS design process

During the first step a new ecosystem entity is created, that belongs to a specific domain, in the example case a Smart Home. When the design process is launched, several options for the ecosystem type are offered to the designer acquired from the Knowledge Base. If no suitable options are available, the designer can update the currently available options and thus enrich the KB:

```
INPUT: ecosystem creation request, KB
for each ecosystem request do
    show available ecosystem types in KB
    if type required is available then
            set ecosystem type
    else
            enter new ecosystem type and save to KB
    end if
            return ecosystem instance of type
end for each
```

The second phase involves the creation of SEs that are immediately associated with the corresponding Ecosystem established during the previous step. Each SE is, as mentioned in the section above, an abstraction used for services/devices grouping. In the case of a Smart Home, SEs are associated with specific rooms/location types that can be imported from the KB.

```
INPUT: Ecosystem instance, KB
if ecosystem type is in KB then
    show available SE types from KB
    if SE type is available then
            set SE and assign to Ecosystem instance
    end if
else
    update KB
end if
```

Figure 3 shows a room's/space's taxonomy stored in the KB, where every room type like a "kitchen" is assigned to a more generic type, such as "utility spaces". Moreover, the taxonomy can be updated or extended, while importing new taxonomy and accomplishing appropriate mapping [14] or by integrating other atomic concepts into the common taxonomy.

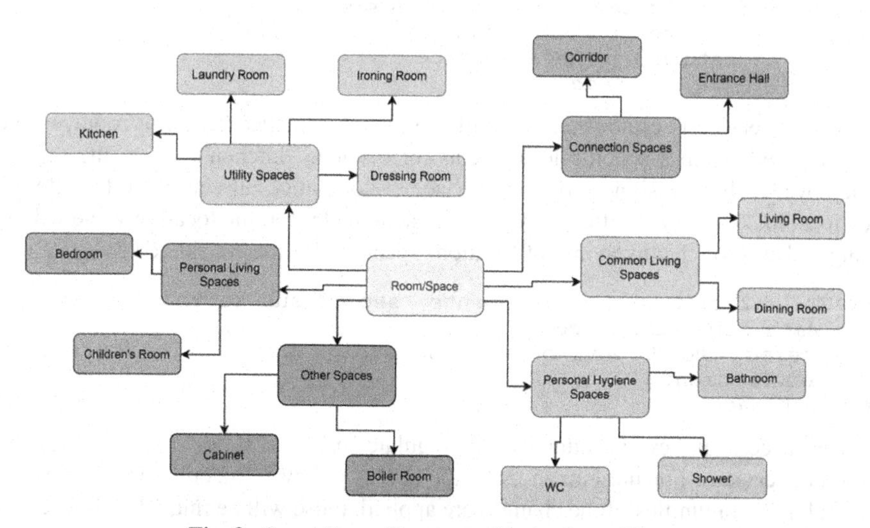

Fig. 3. Space/Room Taxonomy for the Smart Home

The third step involves the creation of SCs that are needed to reflect/represent different user's groups existing within the ecosystem. There can be also different types of communities that can be acquired from the KB. Some examples are: "family members", "visitors" and "service personnel". The type of community directly affects the priority and access rights to the resources. Similar to SEs, the SCs are assigned to a particular instance of the Ecosystem:

```
INPUT: Ecosystem instance, KB
if community type is in KB then
    show available SC types from KB
    if SC type is available then
        set SC and assign to Ecosystem instance
    end if
else
    update KB
end if
```

After SEs and SCs are established, the business services can be formed. Some service templates are also stored within the KB. The business services are of generic types, such as "comfort", "entertainment" or "care" services. Based on these generic types, sub-services can be formed that will directly target certain users' requirements and needs. The services might be complex, i.e., composed of some capillary/smaller ones. Important is to mention, the high-level entities that are designed hide the implementation information, such as protocols used to transmit payload, etc. Thus, we consider that sub-services are offered by the Asset DTs and Human DTs virtual entities:

```
INPUT: environment, Asset DT, Human DT, KB
select business service type
for each business service type
Create sub-services
    for each sub service
    Assign Asset DT or Human DT
    return sub service
return business service
end for each
```

After a service is established, it can be assigned to a specific SE or room, where it is available. Then a specific location, as for instance "kitchen", where the service is deployed will be assigned. If some service is not static, but can move to different locations, like the service offered by a smart vacuum cleaner, the location value will be changed, based on the taxonomy of locations specified for the considered ecosystem.

```
INPUT: set of smart environments, set of sub-service
for each sub-service do
    select smart environment and assign sub-service to smart
    environment
end for each
```

The access policy is intended to regulate the access of users to various resources/services. For the human-users the access policy is specified inside the corresponding communities; if the changes are applied, those will be immediately relevant for all the community members. The SCs have a set of roles, being intrinsic to the SC type that can be assigned to the community members defining the access to the services of the smart home. The access policy depends both on belonging to a certain community, as well as on having a certain role within this SC. All the entities getting access to a specific resource are restricted by the defined policy, unique for every community type. If the access policy residing in a different service is different from the SC one, first the access policy of the system (SC), in terms of priorities for the service access, will be applied and afterwards the access policy of external service. A possible solution for conflict resolution, if the access policy of a service is different from the access policy of a community for the same or compatible role, is to use the approach similar to logical conjunction. In other words, if both policies presume granting different access rights for the same role, e.g., the one defined by SC allows reading and writing, but the service one only allows reading, only reading option should be granted. Moreover, members of different SC can have different access rights, as well as members within the same SC also can have different access rights based on roles assigned.

The final step is the establishment or design of use-case specific reasoning rules. These rules should be generic enough, whereas setting the framework in which the ecosystem components can co-exist. To some extent this aim is similar to the invariant-based approach, relying on identification of basic situations that can appear during the algorithm execution [15] including the pre- and post-conditions. One simple example could be the case, when a fire alarm is raised (pre-condition), then all devices have to be switched off (post-condition). Moreover, additional reasoning rules are needed to back up the coalitions' formation and subsequently collaborative services.

The reasoning rules serve as the basis for coalition's formation (see Fig. 4) that is a complex process of combining various Asset and Human DTs in order to provide integrated collaborative services. The notion of the "coalition of smart components" corresponds to "*a temporary association of a set of cyber entities – digital twins, representing physical components, which can be dynamically configured and adjusted to a changing surroundings/demand in order to provide an integrated solution*" [12].

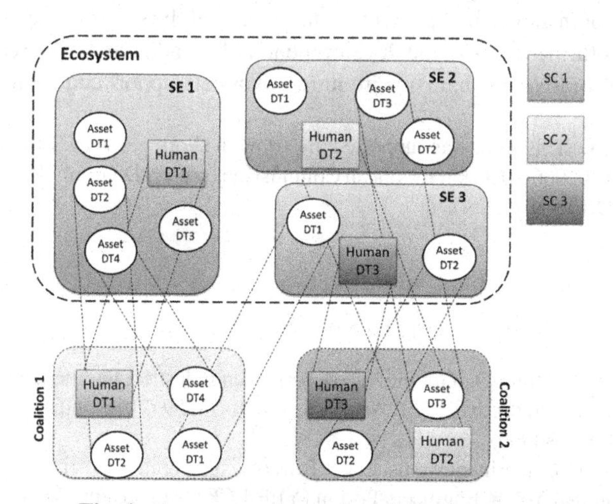

Fig. 4. Ecosystem view and coalition formation

The process of coalition formation consists of a set of stages, as for instance, partners' (i.e., DTs) suggestion [15]. An example of coalition's formation workflow presented in [12] contains the following stages: (i) ecosystem establishment, (ii) discovery/selection of components to be included into the coalition, (iii) negotiation, (iv) coalition launching. The full life cycle of a coalition also includes the operation stage (when the service is delivered) and the dissolution or evolution stages. These stages make a good match with the process of virtual organization creation in the context of a virtual organization breeding environment [10].

Figure 4 shows a simplified view of the coalition's formation process. The ecosystem and related components are already established in pool of virtual agents/digital twins. From this pool a set of ready-to-collaborate Asset and Human DTs are chosen to form the temporary alliances in order to generate collaborative services. After the service is no longer needed, we can consider a final stage of coalition's dissolution or evolution. The work on coalition formation mechanisms is still ongoing.

5 Conclusions

The main goal of this work is to have a design framework and a set of design steps/stages for complex Collaborative CPS. Advanced CCPS are viewed as systems composed of heterogeneous digital/virtual entities that tend to collaborate with each other, and thus able to generate added value. Two types of digital/virtual entities are considered: Asset digital twin and the Human digital twin. Foremost, the CCPSs are considered as intelligent systems taking into account the intelligence and autonomy of their components, as well as the collaborative focus of the systems. In this regard, the concept of coalitions of smart components formation is included in the work. The proposed framework is applied to a Smart Home use-case. Following a Design Science method, a knowledge base supports the design process through the provision of a CCPS meta-model and some domain taxonomies, as for instance the Space/room taxonomy of the smart home. A direction for the ongoing and further work is the development and broadening of the reasoning rules, setting the collaborative mechanisms, required to assist/support coalition's formation.

Acknowledgments. This work was supported in part by the Portuguese FCT foundation through the program UIDB/00066/2020 and European Commission (project DiGiFoF (Project Nr. 601089-EPP-1-2018-1-RO-EPPKA2-KA).

References

1. Xu, H., Yu, W., Griffith, D., Golmie, N.: A survey on industrial Internet of Things: a cyber-physical systems perspective. IEEE Access **6**, 78238–78259 (2018). https://doi.org/10.1109/ACCESS.2018.2884906
2. Nazarenko, A.A., Camarinha-Matos, L.M.: Towards collaborative cyber-physical systems. In: 2017 International Young Engineers Forum (YEF-ECE), Almada, pp. 12–17 (2017). https://doi.org/10.1109/YEF-ECE.2017.7935633

3. Nazarenko, A.A., Camarinha-Matos, L.M.: The role of digital twins in collaborative cyber-physical systems. In: Camarinha-Matos, L.M., Farhadi, N., Lopes, F., Pereira, H. (eds.) DoCEIS 2020. IAICT, vol. 577, pp. 191–205. Springer, Cham (2020). https://doi.org/10.1007/978-3-030-45124-0_18
4. Camarinha-Matos, L.M., Rosas, J., Oliveira, A.I., Ferrada, F.: A collaborative services ecosystem for ambient assisted living. In: Camarinha-Matos, L.M., Xu, L., Afsarmanesh, H. (eds.) PRO-VE 2012. IAICT, vol. 380, pp. 117–127. Springer, Heidelberg (2012). https://doi.org/10.1007/978-3-642-32775-9_12
5. García-Valls, M., Perez-Palacin, D., Mirandola, R.: Pragmatic cyber physical systems design based on parametric models. J. Syst. Softw. **144**, 559–572 (2018). https://doi.org/10.1016/j.jss.2018.06.044
6. Pagliari, L., Mirandola, R., Trubiani, C.: Engineering cyber-physical systems through performance-based modelling and analysis: a case study experience report. J. Softw. Evol. Process (2019). https://doi.org/10.1002/smr.2179
7. Bhuiyan, M.Z.A., Wu, J., Wang, G., Cao, J., Jiang, W., Atiquzzaman, M.: Towards cyber-physical systems design for structural health monitoring. ACM Trans. Cyber-Phys. Syst. **1**(4), 1–26 (2017). https://doi.org/10.1145/3086508
8. Seiger, R., Huber, S., Schlegel, T.: Toward an execution system for self-healing workflows in cyber-physical systems. Softw. Syst. Model. **17**, 551–572 (2018). https://doi.org/10.1007/s10270-016-0551-z
9. Törngren, M., Grogan, P.T.: How to deal with the complexity of future cyber-physical systems? Designs **2**, 40 (2018). https://doi.org/10.3390/designs2040040
10. Oliveira, A.I., Camarinha-Matos, L.M.: Negotiation environment and protocols for collaborative service design. In: Camarinha-Matos, L.M., Baldissera, T.A., Di Orio, G., Marques, F. (eds.) DoCEIS 2015. IAICT, vol. 450, pp. 31–41. Springer, Cham (2015). https://doi.org/10.1007/978-3-319-16766-4_4
11. Camarinha-Matos, L.M., Afsarmanesh, H.: Collaborative networks: a new scientific discipline. J. Intell. Manuf. **16**, 439–452 (2005). https://doi.org/10.1007/s10845-005-1656-3
12. Nazarenko, A.A., Camarinha-Matos, L.M.: Basis for an approach to design collaborative cyber-physical systems. In: Camarinha-Matos, L.M., Almeida, R., Oliveira, J. (eds.) DoCEIS 2019. IAICT, vol. 553, pp. 193–205. Springer, Cham (2019). https://doi.org/10.1007/978-3-030-17771-3_16
13. Wang, X., Dong, J.S., Chin, C.Y., Hettiarachchi, S., Zhang, D.: Semantic space: an infrastructure for smart spaces. IEEE Pervasive Comput. **03**(03), 32–39 (2004). https://doi.org/10.1109/mprv.2004.1321026
14. Nazarenko, A.A., Sarraipa, J., Camarinha-Matos, L.M., Garcia, O., Jardim-Goncalves, R.: Semantic data management for a virtual factory collaborative environment. Appl. Sci. **2019**(9), 4936 (2019). https://doi.org/10.3390/app9224936
15. Back, R.-J., Preoteasa, V.: Semantics and proof rules of invariant based programs. In: Proceedings of the 2011 ACM Symposium on Applied Computing - SAC 2011 (2011). https://doi.org/10.1145/1982185.1982532
16. Rosas, J., Camarinha-Matos, L.M.: An approach to assess collaboration readiness. Int. J. Prod. Res. **47**(17), 4711–4735 (2009). https://doi.org/10.1080/00207540902847298

Digital Twin for Supply Chain Master Planning in Zero-Defect Manufacturing

Julio C. Serrano(✉), Josefa Mula(✉), and Raúl Poler(✉)

Research Centre on Production Management and Engineering (CIGIP), Universitat Politècnica de València, C/ Alarcon 1, 03801 Alcoy, Alicante, Spain
{jserrano,fmula,rpoler}@cigip.upv.es

Abstract. Recently, many novel paradigms, concepts and technologies, which lay the foundation for the new revolution in manufacturing environments, have emerged and make it faster to address critical decisions today in supply chain 4.0 (SC4.0), with flexibility, resilience, sustainability and quality criteria. The current power of computational resources enables intelligent optimisation algorithms to process manufacturing data in such a way, that simulating supply chain (SC) planning performance in real time is now possible, which allows relevant information to be acquired so that SC nodes are digitally interconnected. This paper proposes a conceptual framework based on a digital twin (DT) to model, optimise and prescribe a SC's master production schedule (MPS) in a zero-defect environment. The proposed production technologies focus on the scientific development and resolution of new models and optimisation algorithms for the MPS problem in SC4.0.

Keywords: Supply chain 4.0 · Master production schedule · Digital twin · Reinforcement learning · Zero-defect manufacturing · Conceptual framework

1 Introduction

The effect of technological advances on industrial companies is remarkable and guides their development towards a production paradigm in which flexibility, robustness, resilience, responsiveness and sustainability emerge as decisive SC management elements, for not only the future occupation of better market positions, but also for survival purposes [1].

The flow of materials, products and information in the traditional SC goes through stages that are largely discrete and isolated from one another [2], and this problem pushes it towards digital transformation. The operations strategy needs to ensure that the acquisition of new digital technologies is perfectly aligned with the SC decision area, which implies making productive decisions to properly manage resources and acquiring the right competences to meet market requirements.

Critical decisions in addressing a SC4.0 strategy are mainly related to SC attributes: (1) digital; (2) smart; (3) visible; (4) interconnected; (5) labour-organised; and (6) sustainable. These attributes are particularly relevant for the planning area in SC4.0. At the

© IFIP International Federation for Information Processing 2021
Published by Springer Nature Switzerland AG 2021
L. M. Camarinha-Matos et al. (Eds.): DoCEIS 2021, IFIP AICT 626, pp. 102–111, 2021.
https://doi.org/10.1007/978-3-030-78288-7_10

tactical decision level, the procedures applied in the master production schedule (MPS) process differ significantly depending on which decisions are made to reinforce these SC attributes.

In order to react rapidly to unforeseen situations, production systems should be developed as autonomous systems with the ability to accomplish their assignments without human supervision, and by choosing from a set of alternative actions and orchestrated events in real time as a reaction to changes in relevant internal and external data [3]. In this context, the digital twin (DT) [4] potential to simulate, optimise, predict and share data in real time is noteworthy from not only the planning point of view, but also as a means by which the "*do things right at the first time*" idea, emphasised by the zero-defect manufacturing (ZDM) philosophy, becomes feasible [5].

This paper aims to present an overview of the addressed problem and proposes an initial DT-based framework for autonomous MPS management in an SC4.0 context with a zero-defect characteristic to answer a threefold research question: 1) what general conceptual framework characteristics can respond to the problem by a holistic approach considering the SC structure and its hierarchies, intervening actors, processes, resources, data, information and flows?; 2) how does this framework push the SC towards the zero-defect goal?; and 3) which mechanisms can endow DT with the ability to autonomously manage SC MPS?

The rest of the paper is organised as follows. Section 2 presents the contribution of this study to applied artificial intelligence (AAI) systems. Section 3 offers an overview of the related literature. Section 4 describes the proposal. Finally, Sect. 5 discusses the proposal implications, provides the main paper contributions and conclusions, and points out the lines towards which further research can be conducted.

2 Contribution to Applied Artificial Intelligence Systems

The potential of artificial intelligence is remarkable at any decision level of operations planning and control (OPC) [6], and its application possibilities are numerous. For the MPS at the tactical level, its emphasis is placed on time and spatial disintegration of cumulative planning targets and forecasts, along with the provision and forecast of required resources. This procedure eventually becomes difficult and slows down as the number of considered resources, products and time periods increases [7]. Most of the classic modelling approaches present limitations as the MPS dimension grows, particularly if the MPS is posed as a multi-objective issue. These limitations can lead to unacceptable computational times for a decision support system (DSS) when this is expected to facilitate real-time decision making, especially if it is intended to provide it with a certain level of autonomy.

For this reason, the addressed MPS issue is determined by its degree of complexity, its non-linear stochastic problem condition and by the feasibility of its formulation as a Markov decision process (MDP) [8]. All this generates an appropriate context for applying reinforcement learning (RL) techniques, in which the decision maker or agent, based on a reward policy, continually observes and learns from its environment until efficient levels of reliability and computational times are achieved.

Here the main contribution to AAI systems comes from using a deep RL (DRL) method for modelling a DSS with an optimising-prescriptive role, and in such a way that when unexpected events occur in the MPS, the DSS can meet rescheduling needs in real time.

3 Literature Review

Since the term SC4.0 [9] was coined halfway through the last decade, research on this topic abounds. This term has one main meaning, which usually refers to the SC emerging from the Industry 4.0 (I4.0) context [10], although some researchers also use it to refer to the digital SC [11]. In any case, the SC is a conceptual framework that has been approached from many different angles and has had more than 50,000 entries in Scopus in the past decade alone. In an attempt to identify each trend, Maryniak et al. [12] diagnose the dominant SC topic areas in the last three decades.

According to the Association for Supply Chain Management (APICS), the MPS is a line on the master schedule grid that reflects the anticipated build schedule of those items assigned to it, and it represents the items that a company plans to produce that are expressed as specific configurations, quantities, and dates. The MPS is determined by the SC planning environment according to: (i) its strategies (make to stock, make to order, engineer to order, configure to order, assemble to order, among others.); (ii) the number and type of involved stakeholders (suppliers, warehousers, manufacturers, distributors or retailers); (iii) structure (hierarchy with its tiers and relationships); and (iv) the nature of activities (production, distribution and/or procurement).

In the specific segment of the SC literature that focuses on the MPS, proposing new resolution and optimisation models has been a recurrent approach. Chern et al. [13] put forward a multi-objective MPS resolution model with a heuristic method based on a genetic algorithm. Grillo et al. [14] use the fuzzy set theory to model uncertainty and propose a metaheuristic particle swarm optimisation (PSO) technique as a solution method. A method to achieve an optimal MPS in an uncertain environment is proposed by Sutthibutr and Chiadamrong [15], based on a multi-objective linear fuzzy model with an α-cut analysis. Arani and Torabi [16] integrate physical/material tactical plans with financial ones to account for their reciprocal effects. Ghasemy et al. [17] propose a mixed integer nonlinear programming model with probabilistic constraints to determine centralised planning, viewed from the social sustainability perspective under uncertainty. Martin et al. [18] address the uncertain MPS with two robust optimisation approaches. The MPS problem for a centralised SC of replenishment, production and distribution is tackled by Peidro et al. [19] by presenting a fuzzy multi-objective linear programming approach.

According to Orozco-Romero et al. [20], the DT approach is a solution that enables both real-time digital monitoring and control and automatic decision making. Marmolejo-Saucedo et al. [4] review the scientific literature on DTs in SC management. The association of DTs with disruptive risk management and resilience in the SC is noteworthy. In this line, Barykin et al. [21] attribute the need to build DTs to the poor reliability and stability of SCs due to errors in their operation, and assert that DT can generate information on the impact of such errors, and can influence SC performance by observing different scenarios that simulate the location of errors and their duration, and to analyse recovery policies. Ivanov et al. [22] explain the SC DT concept and propose a framework for risk management. Ivanov and Das [23] identify the need to implement such a partnership to map supply networks and to ensure their visibility as a tool to recover from disruption by taking the disruptive effect of the COVID-19 pandemic as an example. Dolgui et al. [24] propose reconfigurability as a SC parameter that characterises the SC in an uncertain and changing environment by addressing the notion of a reconfigurable SC, or a X-network, with DT as a basis for its design. SCs' resilience to fluctuations of make-to-order environments in customised production cases is addressed by Park et al. [25], who propose a logistics CPS based on DT technology. More closely in line with the objectives of the present paper, Wang et al. [26] address the SC planning problem from a DT perspective by, detailing its benefits and potential compared to traditional approaches.

Regarding the use of AAI as a support for production planning in the SC domain, it is worth noting that most contributions focus on the operational decision level. Of those dealing with planning at the tactical decision level, most either focus on inventory replenishment and dynamic supplier selection problems, or pose planning problems, but by means of approaches prior to using deep reinforced learning (DRL) mechanisms with which to tackle large sets of states and actions by completing training in reasonable time lapses with, for example, artificial neural networks (ANN) or proximal policy optimisation (PPO). More in line with our research, Alves and Mateus [27] consider a DRL approach based on a second version of proximal policy optimisation (PPO2) to solve the problem of a four-step SC with two nodes per step and stochastic demands. For Peng et al. [28], the optimisation approach is similar, but the considered SC structure is simpler, based on a single factory and warehouse that does not contemplate supply steps. In a study restricted to the semiconductor sector SC, Lauer and Legner [29] describe a framework for measuring instability in the MPS based on machine learning.

Finally, the application of the ZDM philosophy in the SC domain has been, albeit sparsely, also addressed by researchers. Most have focused more on the quality management discipline than on OPC, and the zero-defect outcome comes indirectly from applying other strategies or philosophies. For Siddh et al. [30], the zero-defect outcome is the effect of integrating lean six sigma into the SC as their central idea states that if you can know how many defects the process has, you can also systematically figure out how to eliminate them. Pardamean and Wibisono [31] propose a framework to explain the impact of six sigma on SC performance based on increasing process capability in the value stream by seeking zero defects and reducing process variation. Poornachandrika and Venkatasudhakar [32] present a behavioural process and a system model for achieving zero defects with a case study conducted in an automotive company. Unlike the above authors, Thakur and Mangla [33] use the zero-defects concept in the SC as the effect of sustainable practices.

It can be concluded that the literature on the MPS problem in the SC is numerous, varied and adds value to this research in terms of: (i) the use of AAI systems to support production planning in the SC domain is limited and mostly focused on DRL-based methods; (ii) conceptual framework proposals based on RL-driven DT are limited; (iii) the zero-defects concept in the SC domain is not approached as a *per se* strategy, but appears as the effect of applying other strategies.

4 Proposal

The MPS plays a crucial role in SC4.0 and has been a sustained driver of research into new planning technologies, which has provided continuous scientific development, and generated new models with a wide range of approaches. However, the growing scale and complexity of the MPS has influenced the persistence of knowledge gaps, especially in today's dynamic environment where new technological developments occur at an ever-increasing speed.

The proposed conceptual framework (Fig. 1) is characterised by virtually replicating the MPS by merging physical and virtual processes and resources in a DT. Infrastructure, data and information are elements that belong to the manufacturer's sphere. The scope of this replication extends from the manufacturer sphere (the centre of the SC) to the other actors involved in it by means of cloud-computing tools.

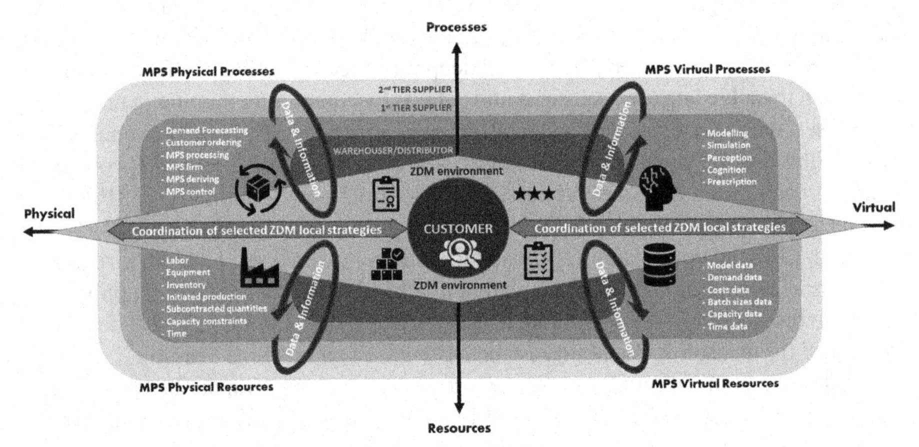

Fig. 1. Conceptual framework of DT-based and ZDM-oriented manufacturer's MPS

Within this framework, the SC is understood as a single domain for all the intervening actors, in which they use personalised blocks of data and information about MPS, but from a single common origin: the DT. This scheme not only facilitates the flow of data and information about production planning between actors, but also creates a coordination channel for individual zero-defect strategies in the SC that makes it possible to: (i) enable collaborative manufacturing with the DT as a means of sharing data and information about processes and resources; (ii) allow, for each involved stakeholder, the monitoring of those MPS process parameters that need to be shared in this collaborative manufacturing context, to improve early defect detection, or even prediction, as a way to empower prevention policies; (iii) enhance data storage, analysis and visualisation by unifying these performances through the DT; (iv) collaboratively launch rescheduling production across the entire SC in only one action that is generated and spread by the DT. In a nutshell; 1) collaborative manufacturing; 2) process monitoring; 3) data management enhancement; and 4) rescheduling ability. Four of the seven ZDM system [34] areas would be gathered and considered in this model to, therefore, favour a zero-defect goal within the SC.

The implementation of the DT for SC master planning according to the described framework requires several stages. The first is to develop the manufacturer's specific domain before extending it to other actors. The virtual process in this restricted DT space is described below as kernel of the model.

The process is based on the DRL method and is developed by two elements: the training environment and the DRL agent (Fig. 2).

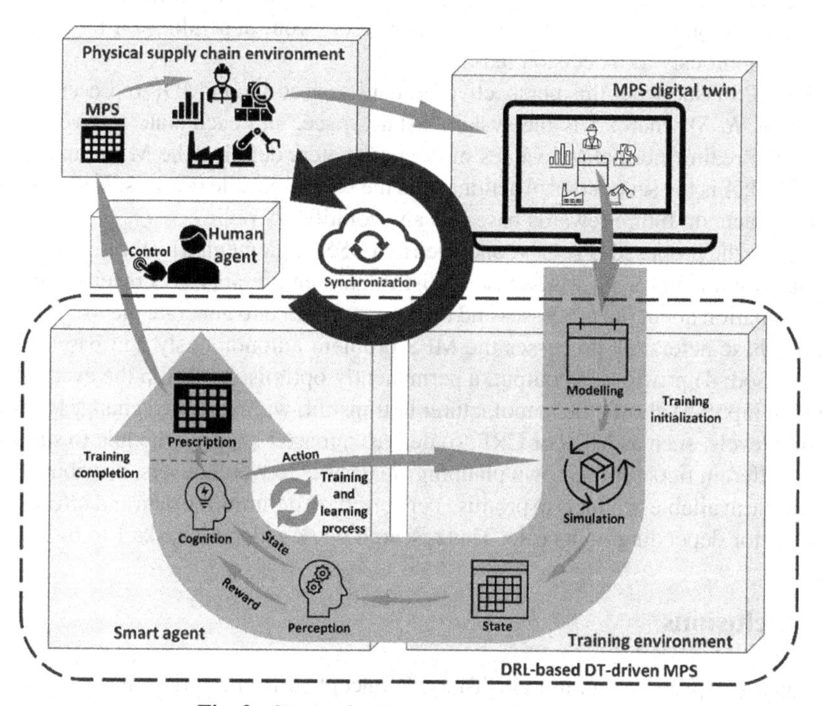

Fig. 2. Setup of DRL-based DT-driven MPS

Basically, the training environment is the MPS modelled in such a way that it is made up of: 1) an observation space; 2) an action space; 3) an initial state; and 4) the action function. The observation space specifies the variables of the MPS issue and delimits the boundaries between which they may vary. The action space determines what actions on the MPS issue can be decided, and to what extent. The initial state represents the state of the MPS in the first time period considered in the master planning, before the application of any action, and is defined by the value adopted by the MPS variables within the observation space in that period. Finally, the action function defines what varies from a state to the next, after applying an action belonging to the valid action space. The DRL agent must play its role in the arena shaped by the above-described environment. In essence, this is a DRL algorithm that collects information about the current MPS state in the training environment and acts on it by triggering an advance to a new state. For this step, the environment grants the agent a reward, whose value depends on a specific policy that assesses how much the new state improves the MPS. With this reward, and by observing the new MPS state, the agent is prepared to perform a new action, which will lead to a new state and a new reward, and so on cycle after cycle.

States and its rewards are stored so that, after enough cycles, the agent covers one part of the observation space that is large enough to start triggering the appropriate action for each MPS state which, from this one, more quickly leads towards either the optimal solution to the issue or a suboptimal one that is accepted as being valid. With it, the training phase finishes, and the agent is trained to continue taking actions in the MPS either semi-autonomously with a prescriber role or even, depending on its reliability level, autonomously as a decision maker.

The MPS issue from this perspective is characterised by an MDP represented by a tuple (S, A, R, δ) where: S is the system's state space, and each state is a vector that collects the real or normalised values of the parameters defining the MPS during each time period; A is the set of control actions; R is the set of possible rewards; δ is a discount factor that acts on future rewards based on an evolutionary policy.

In short, the proposed DT: 1) is conceived as a DSS implemented by the manufacturer, and shared with suppliers, warehousers, distributors and retailers; 2) receives the data and information about the processes and resources required to generate the MPS as input from all these actors; 3) processes the MPS problem autonomously and based on the DRL method; 4) provides, as output, a permanently optimised MPS in the event of any change in input; 5) allows the manufacturer to transmit, without delay, changes to lower planning levels, such as MRP or CRP; 6) derives a master supply schedule to suppliers at their different tiers for their own planning; 7) derives to warehousers, distributors and retailers the available products to promise per period; 8) delimits the data and information of each actor depending on its role. This research work addresses tasks 1 to 6.

5 Conclusions

This paper has proposed an initial DT-based conceptual framework to model, optimise and prescribe the MPS in an SC with SC4.0 attributes and a ZDM context. This framework has focused on optimisation algorithms to solve the MPS problem in the specific described environment, based on applying DT and DRL techniques.

The proposed DT-based model, designed to accommodate the set of actors in the SC, along with their physical and virtual processes and resources, has been described. The DRL-based DT-driven MPS setup has also been presented.

Both the described framework and its configuration are considered to be a first contribution of this research. Its design aims to improve SC performance by reinforcing its digitisation, intelligence, visibility, interconnectedness, organisation and sustainability attributes, which is the goal for any traditional supply chain that to transform into SC4.0 is pretended. DT technology is distinguished by the potential to simultaneously and positively influence all these aspects because: (i) digitisation is an intrinsic property of a DT; (ii) while the commonest purpose of a DT is to simulate, analyse, predict or optimise, the paradigm admits moving one step further towards the action of autonomously prescribing, an ability that lies in the intelligence attribute; (iii) a model in which the DT replicates a specific planning subject (e.g. the MPS) for its shared use across the entire SC has the capacity to take visibility, interconnectedness and organisation qualities to a higher level; (iv) a more effective ZDM strategy facilitated by the model design contributes to SC sustainability.

DRL-based modelling can help to solve the problem of correlating immediate planning actions with their long-term consequences, and to allow big data problems to be tackled. Unlike analytical or heuristic approaches, the DRL-based modelling approach provides an acceptable solution to that problem in a real environment, such as manufacturing, where feedback usually befalls delays in time. It has also been shown that DRL systems are effective tools for dealing with problems for which a numerical resolution is harder because of the large number of possible states.

This proposal has some limitations. The model does not foresee the inclusion of financial considerations. Moreover, the value of the resources involved in the MPS by the actors intervening in the SC means that it is advisable to restrict the DT's prescriptive action in a first stage, so that the final confirmation depends on the human operator. This recommendation would continue to be advisable until the system's reliability has been properly verified.

Regarding the research perspectives, this conceptual framework has to be considered an initial starting point and roadmap for modelling, applications and empirical validations in a real-world SC MPS case study. Additionally, studying if the modelling approach can be extended to other planning levels like MRP, CRP or scheduling is necessary, along with which assumptions and restrictions. This will require further research.

While the proposed conceptual framework accommodates all the actors in the SC, developing the model beyond the manufacturer and its suppliers at the two closest tiers is challenging, and opens up a supplementary research line. The same conclusion is reached for the task of incorporating additional supplier tiers into the previous two, plus logistics warehousers, wholesale distributors, retailers and, finally, customers.

Finally, the described conceptual framework, and the technical background behind the proposed DT, can be adapted to other novel alternative tactical planning frameworks, such as the adaptive sales and operations planning (AS&OP), which derive from the demand-driven adaptive enterprise (DDAE) model, by substituting the MPS subject for other different ones; e.g., replenishment of items in the buffers identified at the tactical level. It also would allow it being modelling as a non-linear and stochastic and/or fuzzy problem, and even being formulated as an MDP, to face uncertainty. This would be a promising future research line to open.

Acknowledgments. The research leading to these results received funding from the European Union H2020 Program with grant agreement No. 825631 "Zero Defect Manufacturing Platform (ZDMP)" and with grant agreement No. 958205 "Industrial Data Services for Quality Control in Smart Manufacturing (i4Q)" and from the Spanish Ministry of Science, Innovation and Universities under grant agreement RTI2018-101344-B-I00 "Optimisation of zero-defects production technologies enabling supply chains 4.0 (CADS4.0)".

References

1. Marmolejo-Saucedo, J.A., Hartmann, S.: Trends in digitization of the supply chain: a brief literature review. EAI End. Trans. Energy Web **7**(29), e8 (2020)

2. Büyüközkan, G., Göçer, F.: Digital supply chain: literature review and a proposed framework for future research. Comput. Ind. **97**, 157–177 (2018)
3. Feldt, J., Kourouklis, T., Kontny, H., Wagenitz, A., Teti, R., D'Addona, D.M.: Digital twin: revealing potentials of real-time autonomous decisions at a manufacturing company. Procedia CIRP **88**, 185–190 (2020)
4. Marmolejo-Saucedo, J.A., Hurtado-Hernandez, M., Suarez-Valdes, R.: Digital twins in supply chain management: a brief literature review. In: Vasant, P., Zelinka, I., Weber, G.-W. (eds.) ICO. AISC, vol. 1072, pp. 653–661. Springer, Cham (2020). https://doi.org/10.1007/978-3-030-33585-4_63
5. Angione, G., Cristalli, C., Barbosa, J., Leitão, P.: Integration challenges for the deployment of a multi-stage zero-defect manufacturing architecture. In: International Conference on Industrial Informatics (INDIN), Institute Electrical and Electronics Engineers Inc., pp. 1615–1620 (2019)
6. Usuga, J.P., Lamouri, S., Grabot, B., Pellerin, R., Fortin, A.: Machine learning applied in production planning and control: a state-of-the-art in the era of industry 4.0. J. Intell. Manuf **31**(6), 1531–1558 (2020)
7. Abu-Bakar, M., Abbas, I., Kalal, M., Alsattar, H., Bakhayt, A.G., Kalaf, B.: Solution for multi-objective optimisation master production scheduling problems based on swarm intelligence algorithms. J. Comput. Theoret. Nanosci. **14**, 5184–5194 (2017)
8. Ould-Louly, M.A., Dolgui, A.: The MPS planning under lead time uncertainty. In: Proceeding of the Workshop on Production Planning and Control, pp. 148–155 (2020)
9. Stich, V., Adema, J., Blum, M., Reschke, J.: Supply chain 4.0: Logistikdienstleister im Kontext der vierten industriellen Revolution. In: Voß, P.H. (ed.) Logistik – eine Industrie, die (sich) bewegt, pp. 63–76. Springer, Wiesbaden (2015). https://doi.org/10.1007/978-3-658-10609-6_6
10. Frederico, G.F., Garza-Reyes, J.A., Anosike, A., Kumar, V.: Supply chain 4.0: concepts, maturity and research agenda. Supply Chain Manage. **25**, 262–282 (2019)
11. Zekhnini, K., Cherrafi, A., Bouhaddou, I., Benghabrit, Y., Garza-Reyes, J.A.: Supply chain management 4.0: a literature review and research framework. Benchmarking **28**, 465–501 (2020)
12. Maryniak, A., Bulhakova, Y., Lewoniewski, W., Bal, M.: Diffusion of knowledge in the supply chain over thirty years - thematic areas and sources of publications. In: Lopata, A., Butkienė, R., Gudonienė, D., Sukackė, V. (eds.) ICIST. CCIS, vol. 1283, pp. 113–126. Springer, Cham (2020). https://doi.org/10.1007/978-3-030-59506-7_10
13. Chern, C.-C., Lei, S.-T., Huang, K.-L.: Solving a multi-objective master planning problem with substitution and a recycling process for a capacitated multi-commodity supply chain network. J. Intell. Manuf. **25**, 1–25 (2014)
14. Grillo, H., Peidro, D., Alemany, M.M.E., Mula, J.: Application of particle swarm optimisation with backward calculation to solve a fuzzy multi-objective supply chain master planning model. Int. J. Bio-Inspired Comput. **7**, 157–169 (2015)
15. Sutthibutr, N., Chiadamrong, N.: Applied fuzzy multi-objective with α-cut analysis for optimizing supply chain master planning problem. In: ACM International Conference Proceeding Series, Association for Computing Machinery, pp. 84–91 (2019)
16. Arani, H.V., Torabi, S.A.: Integrated material-financial supply chain master planning under mixed uncertainty. Inf. Sci. **423**, 96–114 (2018)
17. Ghasemy-Yaghin, R., Sarlak, P., Ghareaghaji, A.A.: Robust master planning of a socially responsible supply chain under fuzzy-stochastic uncertainty (a case study of clothing industry). Eng. Appl. Artif. Intell. **94**, 103715 (2020)
18. Martín, A.G., Díaz-Madroñero, M., Mula, J.: Master production schedule using robust optimization approaches in an automobile second-tier supplier. CEJOR **28**(1), 143–166 (2020)

19. Peidro, D., Mula, J., Alemany, M.M.E., Lario, F.-C.: Fuzzy multi-objective optimisation for master planning in a ceramic supply chain. Int. J. Prod. Res. **50**, 3011–3020 (2012)
20. Orozco-Romero, A., Arias-Portela, C.Y., Saucedo, J.: The use of agent-based models boosted by digital twins in the supply chain: a literature review. In: Vasant, P., Zelinka, I., Weber, G.-W. (eds.) ICO. AISC, vol. 1072, pp. 642–652. Springer, Cham (2020). https://doi.org/10.1007/978-3-030-33585-4_62
21. Barykin, S.Y., Bochkarev, A.A., Kalinina, O.V., Yadykin, V.K.: Concept for a supply chain digital twin. Int. J. Math. Eng. Manage. Sci. **5**, 1498–1515 (2020)
22. Ivanov, D., Dolgui, A., Das, A., Sokolov, B.: Digital supply chain twins: managing the ripple effect, resilience, and disruption risks by data-driven optimization, simulation, and visibility. In: Ivanov, D., Dolgui, A., Sokolov, B. (eds.) Handbook of Ripple Effects in the Supply Chain. ISORMS, vol. 276, pp. 309–332. Springer, Cham (2019). https://doi.org/10.1007/978-3-030-14302-2_15
23. Ivanov, D., Das, A.: Coronavirus (COVID-19/SARS-CoV-2) and supply chain resilience: a research note. Int. J. Integr. Supply Manage. **13**, 90–102 (2020)
24. Dolgui, A., Ivanov, D., Sokolov, B.: Reconfigurable supply chain: the X-network. Int. J. Prod. Res. **58**, 4138–4163 (2020)
25. Park, K.T., Son, Y.H., Noh, S.D.: The architectural framework of a cyber physical logistics system for digital-twin-based supply chain control. Int. J. Prod. Res., 1–22 (2020)
26. Wang, Y., Wang, X., Liu, A., Gao, R.X., Ehmann, K.: Digital twin-driven supply chain planning. Procedia CIRP **93**, 198–203 (2020)
27. Alves, J.C., Mateus, G.R.: Deep reinforcement learning and optimization approach for multi-echelon supply chain with uncertain demands. In: Lalla-Ruiz, E., Mes, M., Voß, S. (eds.) ICCL. LNCS, vol. 12433, pp. 584–599. Springer, Cham (2020). https://doi.org/10.1007/978-3-030-59747-4_38
28. Peng, Z., Zhang, Y., Feng, Y., Zhang, T., Wu, Z., Su, H.: Deep reinforcement learning approach for capacitated supply chain optimization under demand uncertainty. In: Proceedings Chinese Automation Congress, CAC, Institute of Electrical and Electronics Engineers Inc., pp. 3512–3517 (2019)
29. Lauer, T., Legner, S.: Plan instability prediction by machine learning in master production planning. In: International Conference on Automation Science and Engineering (CASE), Institute of Electrical and Electronics Engineers Inc., pp. 703–708 (2019)
30. Siddh, M.M., Soni, G., Gadekar, G., Jain, R.: Integrating lean six sigma and supply chain approach for quality and business performance. In: International Conference on Business and Information Management, ICBIM, Institute of Electrical and Electronics Engineers Inc., pp. 53–57 (2014)
31. Pardamean, G.D., Wibisono, E.: A framework for the impact of lean six sigma on supply chain performance in manufacturing companies. In: IOP Conference Series: Materials Science and Engineering, Institute of Physics Publishing Ltd., vol. 528 (2019)
32. Poornachandrika, V., Venkatasudhakar, M.: Quality transformation to improve customer satisfaction: using product, process, system and behaviour model. In: IOP Conference Series: Materials Science and Engineering, Institute of Physics Publishing Ltd., vol. 923 (2020)
33. Thakur, V., Mangla, S.K.: Change management for sustainability: evaluating the role of human, operational and technological factors in leading Indian firms in home appliances sector. J. Clean. Prod. **213**, 847–862 (2019)
34. Lindström, J., Kyösti, P., Birk, W., Lejon, E.: An initial model for zero defect manufacturing. Appl. Sci. **10**, 4570 (2020)

Intelligent Decision Making

Matheuristic Algorithms for Production Planning in Manufacturing Enterprises

Eduardo Guzman(✉), Beatriz Andres, and Raul Poler

Research Centre on Production Management and Engineering (CIGIP), Universitat Politècnica de València (UPV), Calle Alarcón, 03801 Alcoy, Alicante, Spain
eguzman@cigip.upv.es

Abstract. Production systems are moving towards new levels of smart manufacturing, which means that production processes become more autonomous, sustainable, and agile. Additionally, the increasing complexity and variety of individualized products makes manufacturing a challenge, since it must be produced by consuming the least number of resources, generating profitability. In mathematical perspective, most production planning problems, such as real-world scheduling and sequencing problems, are classified as NP-Hard problems, and there is most likely no polynomial-time algorithm for these kinds of problems. In addition, advances in information and communication technologies (ICT) are increasing, leading to an already existing trend towards real-time scheduling. In this context, the aim of this research is to develop matheuristic algorithms for the optimization of production planning in the supply chain. The development of matheuristic algorithms allows finding efficient solutions, achieving shorter computational times, providing companies with smart manufacturing skills to quickly respond to the market needs.

Keywords: Scheduling · Matheuristics · Supply chain · Production planning

1 Introduction

Nowadays, the rapid economic growth of markets, the competitive pressure and the increasingly turbulent business environments are increasingly forcing companies, particularly small and medium-sized enterprises (SMEs), to innovate in their industrial manufacturing systems. SMEs currently represent 99.8% of companies in the non-financial business sector of the European Union (EU-28) [1]. The market in which these companies operate today is intensely dynamic, which makes effective supply chain (SC) management central to improving organizational performance.

Today, there is great an interest from researchers to improve the performance of companies and SCs in general. An example of the improvement in performance and innovation is what is present in the automotive industry. However, this and other industries have had to respond and adapt to the continuous changes of the organizational environment, with the aim of providing high quality and personalized products and services. Consequently, SCs are not static since they must respond to continuous changes,

© IFIP International Federation for Information Processing 2021
Published by Springer Nature Switzerland AG 2021
L. M. Camarinha-Matos et al. (Eds.): DoCEIS 2021, IFIP AICT 626, pp. 115–122, 2021.
https://doi.org/10.1007/978-3-030-78288-7_11

adapting their techniques of control, and coordinating and managing the change in the way operation and configuration of companies. Moreover, enterprises have to manage their evolution towards participating in collaborative networks [2].

In order to deal with these dynamic environments, advanced tools and techniques have to be designed to provide SMEs affordable tools, in terms of cost, usability, and computationally efficiency, enhancing enterprises' competitiveness in current global changing markets. The techniques to be provided can be based on different approaches, for example, mathematical programming and analytical techniques. However, most real-world planning problems are too complex to be mathematically modelled. At the same time, its resolution, with commercial solvers, is not computationally efficient when the planning problems to be solved consider many variables and a large amount of data.

Combinatorial optimization problems are present in a large number of services related to life improvement, such as public transport, delivery services, shift scheduling in hospital centers [3], etc. and in manufacturing, such as production scheduling, operations sequencing [4], etc. These problems are usually presented as NP-Hard, which means that exact techniques and some algorithms cannot solve them in an effective calculation time, when the problem has become too large.

Therefore, it is necessary to focus research efforts on the study and generation of techniques and tools that improve the way in which available resources are used, both in the SC and in the services used in the society, in general. In accordance with this reality, the search for solutions to this type of planning problems continues to be a relevant research topic. Finding better solutions in quality and time has a significant value since intractable production planning problems with a large amount of data and variables would have a solution in an effective computational time. Therefore, the following research question is addressed, in this paper, are:

RQ1. In which kind of scenarios are matheuristic algorithms faster or more efficient than linear programming models or metaheuristic algorithms?
RQ2. How matheuristic algorithms contribute to applied artificial intelligence systems?
RQ3. How matheuristic algorithms solve complex production scheduling problems?

To provide a response to the research questions posed, the original contribution proposed in this research focuses on the development of matheuristic algorithms to solve manufacturing planning problems both individually (enterprise level) and globally (SC level). Accordingly, the document is structured as follows. Section 2 examines the utility of matheuristic in applied artificial intelligence systems. Section 3 proposes brief state of the art of the matheuristic algorithms. Section 4 describes the contribution and innovation of this research. Finally, Sect. 5 covers the conclusions of the developed work and future lines of research.

2 Matheuristics for Applied Artificial Intelligence Systems

Manufacturing systems are becoming increasingly dynamic [5], due to the new requirements demanded by the industry. Over time, classical approaches of decision-making assistance, such as Enterprise Resource Planning (ERP) and Decision Support System

(DSS), have been changing or adapting to new technologies, such as machine learning, data mining and big data [6]. Currently, manufacturing processes seek to adapt to novel approaches, such as industry 4.0 or the internet of things.

Regarding classic production scheduling approaches that analyze the operation time of the production sequences, the configuration times and even the maintenance activities [7], evolve towards intelligent scheduling approaches that seek to respond dynamically to the environment. In this regard, smart scheduling uses intelligent algorithms to process and analyze information from sensors and wireless communication devices of the machines. The collection of real-time information, not only allows to compute scheduling plans using optimization techniques but also to recompute the production scheduling, attending to the changes that could occur in the production environment [8]. This means that the initial production schedule configuration is modified due to events that may unexpectedly appear in the production process, such as machine malfunctions, the reception of new orders or modifications in the execution priorities of the work to be carried out [9]. Production scheduling problems are characterized by the large amount of data associated with the problem and in a collaborative context, the problem becomes even more difficult when a production plan has to be rescheduled since in collaborative planning, both customers and suppliers must continuously share information to plan their activities and this data exchange must be relevant and timely for all members of the supply chain involved [10]. Currently, Artificial Intelligence (AI) systems support companies in performing efficient data analysis through predictive analytics which is becoming an important part of companies as they seek to predict future events that may affect the production process.

In this context, the effectiveness of the different types of metaheuristic algorithms to solve these types of problems is determined by the ability to adapt them to the problem and its unique characteristics while avoiding falling into the local optimum. Currently, the approaches to artificial intelligence and machine learning, which is a subfield of AI, have gained popularity in recent years, and techniques such as Learnheuristics [11] (combination of metaheuristics and machine learning) are showing their efficiency in this field [12]. In order to reschedule a plan and find optimal or near-optimal solutions, the processing time required by mathematical models or some metaheuristics to solve this type of problems may be inefficient and require many hours or possibly days. In this sense, combining machine learning with matheuristic algorithms can be helpful since mathematical algorithms present better performance and computationally more efficient solutions by taking advantage of the experience of commercial or free solvers and the advantages of heuristic or metaheuristic algorithms [13, 14].

3 Literature Review

There is a wide variety of papers describing different models and algorithms to solve procurement, production, distribution problems. Nevertheless, many of these techniques correspond to mathematical models, heuristic and metaheuristic algorithms [15]. The application of these techniques depends on the application area, i.e. SC planning under uncertainty [16], closed loop SC [17], SC sustainable management [18], or green SC management [19]. These studies reviewed the models and algorithms employed to solve optimization problems in their specific field.

In these reviews, very few mention the use of combined or hybrid algorithms, such as matheuristic algorithms. These algorithms are performed by *"the interoperation of metaheuristics and mathematical programming techniques"* [20]. According to Ball [21] and Talbi [22], combinations or hybridizations of matheuristics can be classified into three approaches 1) decomposition approaches, the problem is decomposed into subproblems to be solved optimally; 2) improvement heuristics or metaheuristics, the mathematical programming model will be used to enhance an initial solution obtained by some heuristic or metaheuristic method; and 3) approaches employing the mathematical programming model to provide approximate solutions, in that a relaxation of the problem towards optimality is solved. The method presented in our study, consists of a combination of a genetic algorithm and linear programming models, fall into categories 2) and 3) of this classification.

Cabrera-Guerrero et al. [23] demonstrate that the combination of techniques, or hybridization, can be advantageous to solve complex problems. Verbiest et al. [24] uses a combination of an iterated local search algorithm (metaheuristic) with a Mixed Integer Linear Programming (MILP) model, to optimize production lines, design of installed line and allocation of products. This study compares the matheuristic approach with an exact method (MILP), verifying that the matheuristic offers efficient solutions, in a shorter calculation time. Worth to highlight is the work of Ta et al. [25], in which the solution given by a genetic algorithm is compared with the solution obtained through the implementation of a matheuristic algorithm, in the context of scheduling problem, concluding that the matheuristic algorithm behaves more efficiently than the genetic algorithm. According to the results of the works analyzed, it can be concluded that matheuristic techniques are suitable for solving problems in realistic instances and allow obtaining good results in acceptable computing times.

4 Research Contribution and Innovation

In general, both in the literature and in industry, mathematical programming models are generally one of the standard approaches to solve scheduling problems. In this study, we present the resolution of the job shop scheduling problem (JSP) with a matheuristic algorithm that hybridizes a Mixed Integer Linear Programming (MILP) model and a Genetic Algorithm (GA). MILP formulations for JSP exist since the 1960s, since the significant improvement of MILP solvers in the last years, it is relevant to perform a comparison of standard JSP models using modern optimization software such as GUROBI and a matheuristic algorithm, with this comparison we will answer the research questions RQ1 and RQ3.

The selected MILP is a disjunctive model based on Ku and Beck [26]. The job shop scheduling problem is given by a J finite set of n jobs or parts and a finite set M of m machines. For each job $j \in J$, the list $\left(\sigma_1^j, \ldots \sigma_h^j, \ldots \sigma_m^j\right)$ of machines with the processing order of job j is provided. σ_h^j is the h-th operation of job j. p_{ij} represents the processing time of job j on machine i. Only one job at a time can be processed by each machine, and a job, once it starts on a given machine, must finish processing on such machine without interruption.

$$\min \text{Cmax} \tag{1}$$

$$\text{s.t.} \quad x_{ij} \geq 0, \quad \forall j \in J, i \in M \tag{2}$$

$$x_{\sigma_h^j, j} \geq x_{\sigma_{h-1}^j, j} + p_{\sigma_{h-1}^j, j}, \quad \forall j \in J, h = 2, \ldots m \tag{3}$$

$$x_{ij} \geq x_{ik} + p_{ik} - V \cdot z_{ijk}, \quad \forall j, k \in J, j < k, i \in M \tag{4}$$

$$x_{ik} \geq x_{ij} + p_{ij} - V \cdot (1 - z_{ijk}), \quad \forall j, k \in J, j < k, i \in M \tag{5}$$

$$Cmax \geq x_{\sigma_m^j, j} + p_{\sigma_m^j, j}, \quad \forall j \in J \tag{6}$$

$$z_{ijk} \in \{0, 1\} \quad \forall j, k \in J, i \in M \tag{7}$$

$$z_{ij} \in \mathbb{Z} \quad \forall j, k \in J \tag{8}$$

The aim to find a schedule of jobs on machines that minimizes the makespan [26]. Constraint (2) guarantees that each job's start time is equal to or greater than 0. Constraint (3) assures that each operation of a job is carried out in the required order. Disjunctive constraints (4) and (5) establish there cannot be two jobs scheduled on one machine at the same time. It is necessary to assign V a value large enough to guarantee the correctness of (4) and (5), $V = \sum_{j \in J} \sum_{j \in M} p_{ij}$ considering that the completion time of any operation must not be greater than the sum of the processing times of all operations. Constraint (6) guarantees that the makespan is the longest completion time of the last operation of all jobs as a minimum [26].

The aim of this section is to provide a matheuristic approach to solve the job shop scheduling problem quickly and efficiently, in particular for large-size problems. To this extent, we design a matheuristic approach applying a linear programming model within the metaheuristic procedure (Genetic algorithm). The quality of the solutions is improved by integrating dispatch rules with the GA to generate an efficient initial population, including: First In First Out- FIFO; Last In First Out - LIFO; Shortest Remaining Operation Time – SROT; Longest Remaining Operation Time – LRPT; Shortest Operation Time - SOT; Less Remaining Operations – LRO; Most Remaining Operations – MRO; Least Set-Up – LSU; Longest Operation Time – LOT; Work In Next Queue – WINQ; Due Date – DD; Static Slack - SS; Dynamic Slack - DS; Relative Dynamic Slack - RDS; SS/Remaining Operation Time – SS/TPR; DS/Remaining Operation Time – DS/TPR; SS/Remaining Operations – SS/RO; DS/Remaining Operations – DS/RO.

GA generates an initial population (set of chromosomes) at 50% randomly and the rest of the population is generated through dispatching rules, due to the randomness of chromosomes it is difficult to obtain an appropriate fitness value, so dispatching rules are used to improve GA speed.

All chromosomes in the population are evaluated in each generation (fitness) using the relaxed disjunctive mathematical model. A repair strategy is used to avoid infeasible chromosomes. This strategy corrects the sequence of an individual in the population if it is non-viable (non-viability arises from non-compliance with precedence constraints, that is, when a job's predecessor is processed after its successor job) then calculates a new sequence [27]. Fitness values are considered in mating to form new offspring. Therefore, selecting chromosomes according to the most suitable fitness values allows the matheuristic to obtain better solutions. The roulette wheel method is used as a selection operator to select an individual from the population. The mating is produced by two parent chromosomes to obtain a child chromosome using the Partially Mapped Crossover Operator, then mutating the daughter chromosome using Swap Mutation Operator. The flow chart of matheuristic algorithm is illustrated in Fig. 1.

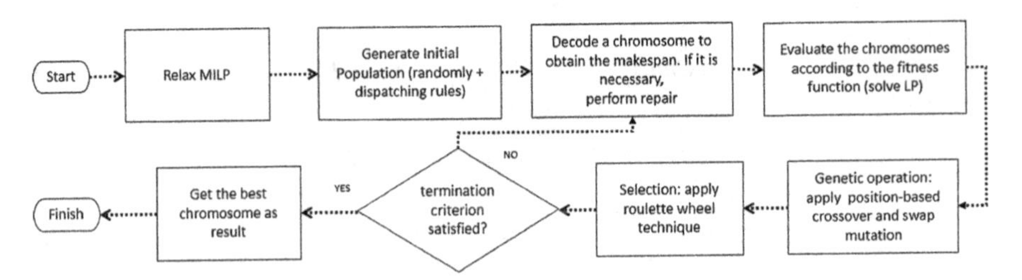

Fig. 1. Flow chart of matheuristic algorithm.

For the assessment of the performance of the proposed matheuristic, we first evaluate the behavior of the MILP for job shop scheduling problem, for this, we use a Taillard instance (ta02) [28] consisting of 15 jobs and 15 machines, the JSP is NP-hard for $n \geq 3$ and $m \geq 2$ [26]. To solve this instance, we use the GUROBI solver, the MILP obtains an optimal solution at 7057.71 s and a makespan of 1244. Computational tests performed were run on an Intel (R) Core (TM) I5-8500 CPU with 3.00 GHz and 8 GB RAM.

To compare matheuristic efficiency to the MILP, we establish a stopping parameter in the matheuristic of 60 s. The proposed matheuristic obtains a makespan of 1399.0, this means that the matheuristic obtains a GAP of 12.45%, for this reason we can conclude that the matheuristic is efficient, for this type of problems obtaining good solutions in relatively shorter calculation time. Therefore, the future lines of research are to improve the genetic algorithm since the genetic operators used are the standard ones and operators designed for the concrete problem would obtain better performance, as well as to try other metaheuristics and new instances with different characteristics of processing times.

5 Conclusions and Further Work

This study analyzes the evolution suffered in the manufacturing research area, due to the new requirements associated to the changing and global markets. New production paradigms offer great opportunities and challenges, as they support the transformation of technology and market conditions. The optimization of manufacturing processes of a company will be determined by the appropriateness of tools and the size of the data needed to model and solve a planning problem. This research focuses on the development of tools to generate matheuristic algorithms applicable to solve manufacturing planning problems, both at the enterprise and SC levels, achieving the integral optimization of manufacturing assets.

The proposed tools will be based on a methodology that describes the best combination of metaheuristic algorithms and exact methods, depending on (i) the type of optimization problem; (ii) the type of input and output data; and (iii) the amount of data that the company or the supply chain handles.

Future lines of research include the design of efficient matheuristics, to reduce the calculation time when solving real-sized enterprise and SC problems, generating near-optimal or good solutions. The matheuristics should be as general as possible to be applied in different industries and sectors, without losing the accurateness of the planning problem modelled and the efficiency on the computation time.

Acknowledgments. Funding for this work has been provided by the Conselleria de Educación, Investigación, Cultura y Deporte - Generalitat Valenciana for hiring predoctoral research staff with Grant (ACIF/2018/170) and European Social Fund with Grant Operational Program of FSE 2014–2020, the Valencian Community.

References

1. European Commission. Annual Report on European SMEs 2016/2017: focus on self employment (2017). https://doi.org/10.2873/742338
2. MacCarthy, B.L., Blome, C., Olhager, J., Srai, J.S., Zhao, X.: Supply chain evolution – theory, concepts and science. Int. J. Oper. Prod. Manag. **36**(12), 1696–1718 (2016). https://doi.org/10.1108/IJOPM-02-2016-0080
3. Guzmán Ortiz, E., Andres, B., Fraile, F., Poler, R., Ortiz Bas, Á.: Fleet management system for mobile robots in healthcare environments. J. Ind. Eng. Manage. **14**(1), 55 (2021). https://doi.org/10.3926/jiem.3284
4. Andres, B., Guzman, E., Poler, R.: A novel MILP model for the production, lot sizing, and scheduling of automotive plastic components on parallel flexible injection machines with setup common operators. Complexity **2021**, 16 (2021). https://doi.org/10.1155/2021/6667516
5. Dolgui, A., Ivanov, D., Sethi, S.P., Sokolov, B.: Scheduling in production, supply chain and Industry 4.0 systems by optimal control: fundamentals, state-of-the-art and applications. Int. J. Prod. Res. **57**(2), 411–432 (2019). https://doi.org/10.1080/00207543.2018.1442948
6. Koźlak, J., Sniezynski, B., Wilk-Kołodziejczyk, D., Leśniak, A., Jaśkowiec, K.: Multi-agent environment for decision-support in production systems using machine learning methods. In: Rodrigues, J.M.F., et al. (eds.) ICCS 2019. LNCS, vol. 11537, pp. 517–529. Springer, Cham (2019). https://doi.org/10.1007/978-3-030-22741-8_37
7. Alemão, D., Rocha, A.D., Barata, J.: Production scheduling requirements to smart manufacturing. In: Camarinha-Matos, L.M., Almeida, R., Oliveira, J. (eds.) DoCEIS 2019. IAICT, vol. 553, pp. 227–237. Springer, Cham (2019). https://doi.org/10.1007/978-3-030-17771-3_19
8. Rossit, D.A., Tohmé, F., Frutos, M.: Industry 4.0: smart scheduling. Int. J. Prod. Res. **57**(12), 3802–3813 (2019). https://doi.org/10.1080/00207543.2018.1504248
9. Rossit, D., Tohmé, F.: Scheduling research contributions to smart manufacturing. Manuf. Lett. **15**, 111–114 (2018). https://doi.org/10.1016/j.mfglet.2017.12.005
10. Andres, B., Poler, R.: Models, guidelines and tools for the integration of collaborative processes in non-hierarchical manufacturing networks: a review. Int. J. Comput. Integr. Manuf. **2**(29), 166–201 (2016). https://doi.org/10.1080/0951192X.2014.1003148
11. Calvet, L., De Armas, J., Masip, D., Juan, A.A.: Learnheuristics: hybridizing metaheuristics with machine learning for optimization with dynamic inputs. Open Math. **15**(1), 261–280 (2017). https://doi.org/10.1515/math-2017-0029

12. de Sousa Jr., W.T., Montevechi, J.A.B., de Carvalho Miranda, R., de Oliveira, M.L.M., Campos, A.T.: Shop floor simulation optimization using machine learning to improve parallel metaheuristics. Expert Syst. Appl. **150** (2020). https://doi.org/10.1016/j.eswa.2020.113272
13. Motta Toledo, C.F., De Oliveira, L., De Freitas Pereira, R., França, P.M., Morabito, R.: A genetic algorithm/mathematical programming approach to solve a two-level soft drink production problem. Comput. Oper. Res. **48**, 40–52 (2014). https://doi.org/10.1016/j.cor.2014.02.012
14. Bin Woo, Y., Kim, B.S.: Matheuristic approaches for parallel machine scheduling problem with time-dependent deterioration and multiple rate-modifying activities. Comput. Oper. Res. **95**, 97–112 (2018). https://doi.org/10.1016/j.cor.2018.02.017
15. Mula, J., Peidro, D., Díaz-Madroñero, M., Vicens, E.: Mathematical programming models for supply chain production and transport planning. Eur. J. Oper. Res. **204**(3), 377–390 (2010). https://doi.org/10.1016/j.ejor.2009.09.008
16. Peidro, D., Mula, J., Poler, R., Lario, F.C.: Quantitative models for supply chain planning under uncertainty. Int. J. Adv. Manuf. Technol. **43**(3–4), 400–420 (2009). https://doi.org/10.1007/s00170-008-1715-y
17. Stindt, D., Sahamie, R.: Review of research on closed loop supply chain management in the process industry. Flex. Serv. Manuf. J. **26**(1–2), 268–293 (2012). https://doi.org/10.1007/s10696-012-9137-4
18. Brandenburg, M., Govindan, K., Sarkis, J., Seuring, S.: Quantitative models for sustainable supply chain management: developments and directions. Eur. J. Oper. Res. **233**(2), 299–312 (2014). https://doi.org/10.1016/j.ejor.2013.09.032
19. Malviya, R.K., Kant, R.: Green supply chain management (GSCM): a structured literature review and research implications. Benchmarking Int. J. **22**(7), 1360–1394 (2015). https://doi.org/10.1108/BIJ-01-2014-0001
20. Boschetti, M.A., Maniezzo, V., Roffilli, M., Bolufé Röhler, A.: Matheuristics: optimization, simulation and control. In: Blesa, M.J., Blum, C., Di Gaspero, L., Roli, A., Sampels, M., Schaerf, A. (eds.) HM 2009. LNCS, vol. 5818, pp. 171–177. Springer, Heidelberg (2009). https://doi.org/10.1007/978-3-642-04918-7_13
21. Ball, M.O.: Heuristics based on mathematical programming. Surv. Oper. Res. Manag. Sci. **16**(1), 21–38 (2011). https://doi.org/10.1016/j.sorms.2010.07.001
22. Talbi, E.G.: A unified taxonomy of hybrid metaheuristics with mathematical programming, constraint programming and machine learning. In: Talbi, E.G. (ed.) Hybrid Metaheuristics. SCI, vol. 434, pp. 7–36. Springer, Heidelberg (2013) https://doi.org/10.1007/978-3-642-30671-6_1
23. Cabrera-Guerrero, G., Lagos, C., Castañeda, C., Johnson, F., Paredes, F., Cabrera, E.: Parameter tuning for local-search-based matheuristic methods. Complexity**2017** (2017). https://doi.org/10.1155/2017/1702506
24. Verbiest, F., Cornelissens, T., Springael, J.: A matheuristic approach for the design of multiproduct batch plants with parallel production lines. Eur. J. Oper. Res. **273**, 933–947 (2018). https://doi.org/10.1016/j.ejor.2018.09.012
25. Ta, Q.C., Billaut, J.-C., Bouquard, J.-L.: Matheuristic algorithms for minimizing total tardiness in the m-machine flow-shop scheduling problem. J. Intell. Manuf. **29**(3), 617–628 (2015). https://doi.org/10.1007/s10845-015-1046-4
26. Ku, W.Y., Beck, J.C.: Mixed Integer Programming models for job shop scheduling: a computational analysis. Comput. Oper. Res. **73**, 165–173 (2016). https://doi.org/10.1016/j.cor.2016.04.006
27. Kundakci, N., Kulak, O.: Hybrid genetic algorithms for minimizing makespan in dynamic job shop scheduling problem. Comput. Ind. Eng. **96**, 31–51 (2016). https://doi.org/10.1016/j.cie.2016.03.011
28. Taillard, E.: Benchmarks for basic scheduling problems. Eur. J. Oper. Res. **64**(2), 278–285 (1993). https://doi.org/10.1016/0377-2217(93)90182-M

Assessment of Sentinel-2 Spectral Features to Estimate Forest Height with the New GEDI Data

João E. Pereira-Pires[1](✉), André Mora[1], Valentine Aubard[2], João M. N. Silva[2], and José M. Fonseca[1]

[1] Centre of Technology and Systems/UNINOVA, School of Science and Techonology, NOVA University of Lisbon, 2829-516 Caparica, Portugal
je.pires@campus.fct.unl.pt, {atm,jmf}@uninova.pt
[2] Forest Research Centre, School of Agriculture, University of Lisbon, 1349-017 Lisboa, Portugal
{vaubard,joaosilva}@isa.ulisboa.pt

Abstract. The unprecedent availability of vertical structure forest data provided by NASA Global Ecosystem Dynamics Investigation (GEDI), allows the validation of new methodologies based on other Remote Sensing (RS) sensors for monitoring forest parameters, such as Forest Height (FH). Previously, studies on FH estimation implied in-situ measurements or acquiring LiDAR data, which was limited and expensive. Opposing to the sampling nature of GEDI mission, Sentinel-2 optical products has a high revisiting frequency and a high spatial resolution favoring the implementation of forest monitoring methodologies. This work presents a study on the correlation and usability of linear and exponential regressions for estimating FH through Sentinel-2 imagery. It was also exploited the advantages of making estimations by study area, or by specific land cover types. Overall, a R^2 of 0.66 and a RMSE of 2.91 m were achieved, and in case of specifying the vegetation type were 0.83 and 2.40 m, respectively.

Keywords: GEDI · Sentinel-2 · Remote sensing · Forest height · Parametric regressions · LiDAR

1 Introduction

Forests ecosystems are the biggest carbon storages of the planet, playing an important role in its sustainability, preserving Earth climate [1, 2]. Forest management and monitoring are essential activities to assure the conservation of this ecosystems. Among the vertical structure parameters, Forest Height (FH) is a fundamental variable for describing forest areas. Furthermore, FH is commonly used for Aboveground Biomass (AGB) estimation [2, 3], which is an indicator of the forest fuel load. The information relatively to the fuel load is important for preparing wildfire management planning, by enabling an efficient scheduling of fuel treatments with the goal of reducing fire hazard. Besides

© IFIP International Federation for Information Processing 2021
Published by Springer Nature Switzerland AG 2021
L. M. Camarinha-Matos et al. (Eds.): DoCEIS 2021, IFIP AICT 626, pp. 123–131, 2021.
https://doi.org/10.1007/978-3-030-78288-7_12

controlling the forest fuel load, other proactive strategies, such as the implementation of fire and fuel breaks (FB) [4], rely on periodic treatments and monitoring their fuel load [5–7].

Some regions of the globe are strongly affected by wildfires, in particular the Mediterranean Europe (Portugal, Spain, France, Italy, and Greece) [8]. In Portugal, the Portuguese Institute for Nature Conservation and Forests (ICNF) implemented a Fuel Break Network (FBN), preventing wildfires and creating new opportunities for firefighting. FBs efficiency depends on the control of their fuel load [5–7].

The in-situ measurement of FH is not a suitable strategy for acquiring the periodic data needed for forest monitoring. The growing number of available Remote Sensing (RS) sensors lead to the development of new methodologies for estimating the FH. Although airborne platforms usually provide higher quality data, they do not have the time coverage to ensure the periodic availability of FH estimations, opposing to spaceborne platforms. Within the RS sensor types, Light Detection and Ranging (LiDAR) is the most suitable for estimating the FH [1, 3, 9]. However, LiDAR technologies are usually carried by aircrafts, having limited coverage and providing sparse measurements in time and space [1, 3, 9]. Adding to this, LiDAR data can be very expensive.

Spaceborne LiDAR was not optimized for vegetation analysis, until the recent NASA Global Ecosystem Dynamics Investigation (GEDI) dedicated to measuring the vertical structure of vegetation [1, 9]. Nevertheless, GEDI is just a sampling mission, not being suitable for regular monitoring. Other RS sensors, such as Optical and Synthetic Aperture Radar (SAR), have dedicated spaceborne platforms (Landsat, Sentinel-1, Sentinel-2), acquiring data with high revisiting frequency, being suitable for vegetation monitoring.

This article presents a study on how FH can be estimated, in a regular basis, from Remote Sensing Optical spectral features (SF, i.e., reflectance bands and spectral indices) for monitoring the FBs. A comparison between Sentinel-2 Level 2A products, SF and the height above the ground (here used as FH) measurements from GEDI Level 2B products will be made, assessing which are the best SF to estimate the FH. As suggested in previous studies [9], ecological features influence the measured reflectance values, so beyond the overall analysis, local analysis will be performed. The study will also assess the proposed technique sensitivity to different forest types. The results will be assessed by the Root Mean Square Error (RMSE) and Coefficient of Determination (R^2) relatively to parametric regressions, and the Pearson's Correlation.

The article was written through five sections, with Sect. 1 concerning Introduction and Sect. 2 the relationship with Applied Artificial Intelligence (AI) Systems. In Sect. 3 materials are presented (regions of interest, Remote Sensing data, and the used Spectral Indices); Sect. 4 presents results, including which are the best achieved regressions overall, locally, and by land cover type; finally, in Sect. 5 results are compared with previous studies, and conclusions are drawn.

2 Relationship with Applied Artificial Intelligence Systems

DoCEIS 2021 is dedicated to Technological Innovation for Applied AI Systems. This article proposes a feature selection pre-processing stage for FH estimation framework based on Artificial Intelligence methods (which will be a product of the PhD work where this article is framed). In this study, the best Remote Sensing SF for the estimation of FH in several Portuguese regions (within the FBN) with heterogenous ecological features were selected. It was also studied the impact of estimating the FH locally and/or by land cover type. Summing up the question this manuscript proposes to answer which are the best SF to estimate the FH.

3 Materials and Methods

3.1 Study Areas

Four regions where fuel load treatments occurred during 2019 were selected within the Portuguese FBN. These treatments were detected using the methodologies presented in [5–7] and confirmed by ICNF. For each region, and to generate a more complete dataset, several samples from the treated areas and surrounding non-treated areas were select, providing low and high FH measurements. These regions are in different parts of the country, being subjected to different ecological conditions and land cover types (see Table 1, [10]).

3.2 Remote Sensing Data

For this study, data from GEDI and Sentinel-2 were used. GEDI is a LiDAR sensor onboard of the International Space Station, operating since April 2019 and optimized for forest monitoring. This mission has a global coverage between ~51.6°N and ~51.6°S latitudes and, according to [1, 9], it is expected to sample 4% of Earth's land surface. The GEDI Level-2B products provide Canopy Cover and Vertical Profile metrics (with a 25 m spatial resolution), being the height above the ground, the metric used in this study as the FH (available in layer rh 100). To guarantee the quality of data, only samples with the quality flags set (layers l2a_quality_flag and l2b_quality_flag) were used.

Sentinel-2 is the platform carrying the Multi-Spectral Instrument (MSI), an optical sensor from the Copernicus mission. The spatial resolution for the spectral bands is 10 m for visible and Near Infrared (NIR) bands, 20 m for red edge, Narrow NIR, and Short Wave Infrared (SWIR) bands, and 60 m for coastal aerosol, cirrus, and water vapor bands [5]. This mission is composed by two satellites allowing this constellation to achieve a 5-days revisiting period. Sentinel-2 Level-2A products available in Copernicus Open Access Hub were used. Level-2A category corresponds to Bottom-of-Atmosphere products, being the atmospheric corrections performed by Sen2Cor algorithm [11]. Although several reflectance bands have the spatial resolution of 10 m, due to the spatial resolution of 25 m from GEDI, the Sentinel-2 20 m resolution bands and the visible spectrum bands resampled to 20 m were used. For the NIR band, instead of using B08 (NIR) resampled to 20 m, B8A (NIR – narrow band) was used.

The study period was March 2020 to September 2020, having been selected 100 samples (25 per region) from GEDI. For each sample date, the closest corresponding Sentinel-2 observation, was used. From this dataset, 50 samples were from Eucalyptus Forests, 33 from Pine Forests, and 17 from Cork Tree Forests (Table 2).

Table 1. Description of the regions of interest.

Region of interest – County	Relative location in Country	Land cover type
Amieira – Gavião	Inland South Center	Eucalyptus and Cork tree forests
Besteiros – Portalegre	Inland South Center	Eucalyptus, Pine, and Cork tree forests
Capinha – Fundão	Inland North Center	Eucalyptus forests
Famalicão – Guarda	Inland North Center	Pine forests

3.3 Methods

In Remote Sensing is common to use derivatives from reflectance measurements, such as spectral indices. The selected indices for the analyses are presented in Table 2. Equations (1), (2), (3), (4), (5) correspond to normalized spectral differences [1, 6, 7]. Equations (1) and (2) are the Normalized Difference Vegetation Index (NDVI), using the Red an NIR band, respectively; (3) and (4) are the Normalized Difference Moisture Index (NDMI), using the respective SWIR bands; and NDSWIR, which is the Normalized Difference between SWIR bands. The other indices are optimized for the vegetation: Enhanced Vegetation Index (EVI) and Modified Soil-Adjusted Vegetation Index 2 (comparing this with MSAVI1, it has the advantage of not using the L parameter).

The goal for this study is to define which are the best Remote Sensing SF for FH estimation by comparison with GEDI data. The full dataset is used for the analysis, being grouped by land cover, region of interest, and by both criteria. Firstly, the Pearson's correlation with the FH is computed for all selected features. The features more correlated with the FH were selected for further analysis. Next, two parametric regressions (Linear – $a * x + b$; Exponential – $a * \exp(b * x)$) were tested, being evaluated by the R^2, indicating which is the best regression. Finally, the RMSE is computed being assessed the uncertainty of the estimation.

Table 2. Spectral indices used in this study.

Spectral index	Equation
$NDVI_{664nm} = (B8A - B04)/(B8A + B04)$	(1)
$NDVI_{559nm} = (B8A - B03)/(B8A + B03)$	(2)
$NDMI_{1610nm} = (B8A - B11)/(B8A + B11)$	(3)
$NDMI_{2200nm} = (B8A - B12)/(B8A + B12)$	(4)
$NDSWIR = (B11 - B12)/(B11 + B12)$	(5)
$EVI = 2.5 * (B8A - B04)/(B8A + 6 * B04 - 7.5 * B02 + 1)$	(6)
$MSAVI2 = \left(2 * B8A + 1 - \mathrm{sqrt}\left((2 * B8A + 1)^2 - 8 * (B8A - B04)\right)\right)/2$	(7)

The results will be obtained by group (land cover and region of interest) and overall considering all cases. This strategy will show the advantages of grouping the data.

4 Discussion and Results

The detailed results are presented in Fig. 1, Fig. 2, and Fig. 3. It is shown the Pearson's Correlation between the SF and FH and the other figures show the R^2 for linear and exponential regressions using those variables. It is used a color scale, Green to Red, being the greener values the best results.

Region of Interest	Land Cover	Spectral Features														
		B02	B03	B04	B05	B06	B8A	B11	B12	NDVI 664	NDVI 559	NDMI 1610	NDMI 2200	NDSWIR	EVI	MSAVI2
-	Eucalyptus	0.85	0.87	0.87	0.85	0.66	0.48	0.85	**0.89**	0.87	0.84	**0.89**	**0.91**	0.83	0.79	0.86
	Pine	0.53	**0.67**	**0.66**	**0.66**	0.39	0.37	0.51	0.50	0.58	0.53	0.32	0.35	0.39	0.34	0.57
	Corktree	0.52	0.61	0.61	**0.70**	0.58	0.57	**0.81**	**0.72**	0.48	0.41	0.61	0.57	0.39	0.16	0.46
Amieira	-	0.80	0.82	**0.83**	**0.83**	0.74	0.73	**0.88**	**0.86**	0.80	0.76	0.81	0.78	0.56	0.74	0.80
Besteiros		0.77	**0.81**	0.76	0.77	0.52	0.47	**0.81**	**0.81**	0.70	0.77	0.70	0.71	0.54	0.45	0.71
Capinha		0.93	0.92	0.92	0.89	0.68	0.26	0.88	0.92	**0.96**	**0.96**	0.90	**0.94**	0.88	0.92	**0.94**
Famalicão		0.52	**0.69**	**0.65**	**0.65**	0.43	0.40	0.53	0.49	0.58	0.55	0.31	0.34	0.37	0.33	0.57
Amieira	Eucalyptus	0.92	0.92	0.92	0.91	0.77	0.73	0.94	0.94	**0.95**	0.94	**0.96**	**0.95**	0.93	0.94	0.94
	Corktree	0.10	0.28	0.21	0.38	**0.57**	**0.69**	**0.70**	0.44	0.09	0.02	0.36	0.06	0.28	0.46	0.10
Besteiros	Eucalyptus	0.91	**0.93**	0.86	0.90	0.69	0.57	**0.93**	**0.92**	0.82	0.89	**0.92**	0.90	0.61	0.54	0.81
	Pine	**0.82**	0.80	0.77	0.68	0.16	0.01	**0.82**	**0.84**	0.67	0.67	0.72	0.74	0.69	0.51	0.69
	Corktree	0.89	**0.94**	0.89	**0.97**	0.74	0.65	**0.94**	0.92	0.78	0.70	0.78	0.80	0.84	0.39	0.78
Capinha	Eucalyptus	0.93	0.92	0.92	0.89	0.68	0.26	0.88	0.92	**0.96**	**0.96**	0.90	**0.94**	0.88	0.92	**0.94**
Famalicão	Pine	0.52	**0.69**	**0.65**	**0.65**	0.43	0.40	0.53	0.49	0.58	0.55	0.31	0.34	0.37	0.33	0.57
Overall		0.72	**0.79**	**0.78**	**0.78**	0.56	0.46	0.75	0.76	0.76	0.73	0.69	0.71	0.66	0.60	0.75

Fig. 1. Absolute values of pearson's correlation, in bold the best values by group. Scale Green-white-red for best values by group. (Color figure online)

The results from the Pearson's correlation are presented Fig. 1. From the overall results correlations above the 0.75 were achieved, which shows that there is in fact a relation between the SF and GEDI's FH. The bands exhibit a better correlation than the indices, being bands 3, 4 and 5 the ones with higher correlation. Within the indices, $NDVI_{664nm}$ and MSAVI2 are the most suitable.

Grouping data by region of interest led to better results than grouping by land cover type (Fig. 1). Relatively to land cover type the best class was the Eucalyptus Forest (0.91 for $NDMI_{2200nm}$) and the worst was Pine Forest class (0.67 for B03). When grouping by region of interest, Capinha was the best region achieving 0.96 (note that in this region there were only Eucalyptus Forest) for both NDVIs, and the worst region was Famalicão with correlation of 0.69 for B03. With this criterion, with exception of Capinha, spectral bands exhibit again a better correlation with FH.

The highest correlations were achieved for data grouped by region of interest and land cover type, being Besteiros the best example (that has the three land cover types dealt in this study) achieving an overall correlation of 0.81 for B12, and when divided by forest type it has achieved 0.93 for B11 in Eucalyptus; 0.84 for B12 in Pine; and 0.97 for B05 in Cork trees.

The R^2 values for each regression and all defined groups are presented in Fig. 2 and Fig. 3. The comparison of the overall values shows that the exponential regression

Region of Interest	Land Cover	Spectral Features														
		B02	B03	B04	B05	B06	B8A	B11	B12	NDVI 664	NDVI 559	NDMI 1610	NDMI 2200	NDSWIR	EVI	MSAVI2
-	Eucalyptus	0.72	0.75	0.76	0.72	0.44	0.23	0.73	**0.79**	0.76	0.70	**0.79**	**0.83**	0.68	0.63	0.74
	Pine	0.28	**0.44**	**0.43**	**0.43**	0.15	0.14	0.26	0.25	0.33	0.28	0.10	0.12	0.15	0.11	0.33
	Corktree	0.27	0.38	0.37	**0.49**	0.34	0.33	**0.65**	**0.51**	0.23	0.17	0.38	0.33	0.16	0.03	0.21
Amieira	-	0.64	0.67	0.68	**0.69**	0.54	0.53	**0.78**	**0.74**	0.64	0.58	0.65	0.60	0.31	0.55	0.64
Besteiros		0.59	**0.65**	0.58	0.59	0.27	0.22	**0.65**	**0.66**	0.49	0.59	0.50	0.50	0.29	0.21	0.51
Capinha		0.86	0.85	0.84	0.79	0.46	0.07	0.77	0.85	**0.92**	**0.92**	0.82	0.88	0.77	0.85	**0.89**
Famalicão		0.27	**0.48**	**0.42**	**0.42**	0.19	0.16	0.28	0.24	0.34	0.30	0.10	0.12	0.14	0.11	0.32
Amieira	Eucalyptus	0.85	0.84	0.85	0.82	0.59	0.53	0.89	0.89	**0.90**	0.89	**0.92**	**0.91**	0.87	0.89	0.89
	Corktree	0.01	0.08	0.04	0.14	**0.33**	**0.47**	**0.49**	0.19	0.01	0.00	0.13	0.00	0.08	0.21	0.01
Besteiros	Eucalyptus	0.83	**0.86**	0.74	0.80	0.48	0.33	**0.87**	**0.85**	0.68	0.80	**0.85**	0.81	0.37	0.30	0.65
	Pine	**0.67**	0.64	0.59	0.46	0.03	0.00	**0.68**	**0.70**	0.45	0.45	0.52	0.55	0.47	0.26	0.47
	Corktree	0.79	**0.89**	0.79	**0.95**	0.55	0.43	**0.89**	0.84	0.60	0.49	0.61	0.64	0.70	0.15	0.60
Capinha	Eucalyptus	0.86	0.85	0.84	0.79	0.46	0.07	0.77	0.85	**0.92**	**0.92**	0.82	0.88	0.77	0.85	**0.89**
Famalicão	Pine	0.27	**0.48**	**0.42**	**0.42**	0.19	0.16	0.28	0.24	0.34	0.30	0.10	0.12	0.14	0.11	0.32
Overall		0.52	**0.63**	**0.61**	**0.61**	0.32	0.21	0.56	0.58	0.58	0.54	0.48	0.51	0.44	0.37	0.56

Fig. 2. R^2 values for linear regression.

has the best estimation. It achieves a R^2 of 0.67 for B05, opposing to 0.63 for B03 in the linear regression. Again, the best spectral features when analyzing the overall data are spectral bands. Inspecting all the proposed approaches, most estimations were better when using the exponential regression. As expected, relatively to the grouping criterion, the same conclusions are reached, being the highest R^2 obtained, 0.96, for the exponential regression for Besteiros Cork tree with the B05. The best SF and regression for each group is presented in Table 3. The uncertainty of FH estimations was assessed by the RMSE, being presented in Table 3 the results for the best regressions defined before. To understand the impact of the RMSE value, it is also presented the range of FH measurements and FH mean for each regression. The average RMSE of all regressions is 2.33 m and there are not values greater than 4.00 m. Since FH values range between 3 m and 22 m, it shows that spectral features are suitable for measuring FH according to GEDI data.

Region of Interest	Land Cover	Spectral Features														
		B02	B03	B04	B05	B06	B8A	B11	B12	NDVI 664	NDVI 559	NDMI 1610	NDMI 2200	NDSWIR	EVI	MSAVI2
-	Eucalyptus	0.72	0.77	**0.79**	0.76	0.49	0.24	0.78	**0.83**	0.77	0.72	0.76	**0.81**	0.69	0.66	0.78
	Pine	0.28	**0.48**	**0.50**	**0.50**	0.16	0.15	0.29	0.27	0.34	0.26	0.09	0.11	0.14	0.10	0.34
	Corktree	0.30	0.40	0.40	**0.50**	0.37	0.38	**0.63**	**0.52**	0.25	0.18	0.38	0.34	0.19	0.03	0.23
Amieira	-	0.63	0.66	0.69	**0.70**	0.55	0.58	**0.76**	**0.72**	0.62	0.56	0.62	0.59	0.40	0.56	0.64
Besteiros		0.60	**0.67**	0.57	0.59	0.27	0.23	**0.63**	**0.65**	0.46	0.58	0.45	0.47	0.28	0.18	0.49
Capinha		**0.92**	0.91	0.90	0.86	0.52	0.08	0.82	0.87	0.91	**0.93**	0.79	0.85	0.77	0.86	**0.92**
Famalicão		0.28	**0.55**	**0.53**	**0.52**	0.21	0.18	0.35	0.29	0.36	0.29	0.09	0.11	0.13	0.09	0.35
Amieira	Eucalyptus	0.88	0.87	0.88	0.87	0.65	0.60	0.91	0.92	0.92	0.90	**0.94**	**0.95**	0.91	**0.95**	0.91
	Corktree	0.01	0.07	0.04	0.13	**0.31**	**0.45**	**0.44**	0.19	0.01	0.00	0.15	0.01	0.09	0.18	0.01
Besteiros	Eucalyptus	0.85	0.87	0.76	0.74	0.48	0.34	0.85	**0.89**	0.72	0.88	**0.94**	**0.92**	0.45	0.27	0.71
	Pine	**0.67**	0.61	0.56	0.42	0.02	0.00	**0.65**	**0.68**	0.43	0.44	0.48	0.52	0.44	0.25	0.46
	Corktree	0.81	**0.93**	0.83	**0.96**	0.59	0.48	**0.91**	0.89	0.60	0.47	0.61	0.66	0.72	0.14	0.60
Capinha	Eucalyptus	**0.92**	0.91	0.90	0.86	0.52	0.08	0.82	0.87	0.91	**0.93**	0.79	0.85	0.77	0.86	**0.92**
Famalicão	Pine	0.28	**0.55**	**0.53**	**0.52**	0.21	0.18	0.35	0.29	0.36	0.29	0.09	0.11	0.13	0.09	0.35
Overall		0.54	**0.66**	**0.66**	**0.67**	0.35	0.22	0.60	0.61	0.59	0.54	0.46	0.49	0.44	0.33	0.59

Fig. 3. R^2 values for exponential regression.

Table 3. Regression (R) method (E- Exponential; L – Linear) by group and respective uncertainty.

Group	R	SF	RMSE (m)	FH range (m)	FH mean	No of samples
Eucalyptus	E	B12	2.40	[3.28; 21.14]	9.22	50
Pine	L	B05	3.68	[4.65; 21.86]	10.32	33
Cork tree	L	B11	1.71	[4.26; 16.47]	8.91	17
Amieira	L	B11	1.76	[3.28; 15.38]	7.26	25
Besteiros	L	B12	2.40	[5.07; 20.40]	9.96	25
Capinha	E	$NDVI_{559nm}$	2.44	[3.66; 21.14]	10.77	25
Famalicão	E	B03	3.97	[4.65; 21.86]	10.13	25
Amieira – Eucalyptus	E	$NDMI_{2200nm}$	1.33	[3.28; 15.38]	6.64	15
Amieira – Cork Tree	L	B11	2.07	[4.26; 13.14]	8.18	10
Besteiros – Eucalyptus	E	$NDMI_{1610nm}$	2.33	[5.07; 20.40]	9.20	10
Besteiros – Pine	L	B12	1.45	[7.51; 13.89]	10.77	8
Besteiros – Cork Tree	E	B05	0.71	[7.17; 13.81]	9.95	7
Capinha – Eucalyptus	E	$NDVI_{559nm}$	2.44	[3.66; 21.14]	10.77	25
Famalicão – Pines	E	B03	3.97	[4.65; 21.86]	10.12	25
Overall	E	B05	2.91	[3.28; 21.86]	9.53	100

5 Conclusions and Future Work

GEDI measurements offer a new opportunity to define new methodologies for forest monitoring. This article presented an exploratory study about the relation between SF and the FH measurements from GEDI. It was verified that a relation exists and may be used for predicting this parameter. A comparison between the RMSE achieved by this study and [3], shown that the values were similar, although here they were applied for smaller areas, and there were used less samples. As in [9], where the local calibration was exploited with good results, this work verified the same. Beyond that, this study shown that joining the local information to the land cover will further improve results. Although increasing the information about the region, where the estimation is being applied, leads to less generic methods, being applicable to smaller areas. The best approach may be to use the regression considering only the land cover, which already improves the estimation, and it still is a generic approach to the problem. It was also shown that different land covers have different results. Eucalyptus forest achieved the best results, probably due its dense occupation of the soil, being more robust to the impact of other terrain characteristics in the reflectance measurements, opposing to Pine forest that usually are not as well behaved as the previous. Finally, the fact that the relation is not strictly linear was expected because the spectral features are not sensible only to FH, but also to the AGB, and other forest parameters.

In continuation of this work, non-parametric regressions will be applied to understand if there is an improvement on the estimation. The generation of larger datasets and considering new land covers. Also, the definition of a FH estimation methodology with resource to optical Remote Sensing data.

Acknowledgments. The authors would like to acknowledge Fundação de Ciências e Tecnologia (FCT) for funding the projects FUELMON (PTDC/CCI-COM/30344/2017) and foRESTER (PCIF/SSI/0102/2017), and the Research Units, Centre of Technology and Systems (UIDB/00066/2020) and Forest Research Centre (UIDB/00239/2020). João Eduardo Pereira-Pires thanks the Fundação para a Ciência e Tecnologia (FCT), Portugal for the Ph.D. Grant 2020.05015.BD.

References

1. Potapov, P., et al.: Mapping global forest canopy height through integration of GEDI and landsat data. Remote Sens. Environ. **253**(October 2020), 112165 (2021). https://doi.org/10.1016/j.rse.2020.112165
2. Ku, N.W., Popescu, S.C.: A comparison of multiple methods for mapping local-scale mesquite tree aboveground biomass with remotely sensed data. Biomass Bioenerg. **122**(January), 270–279 (2019). https://doi.org/10.1016/j.biombioe.2019.01.045
3. Lang, N., Schindler, K., Wegner, J.D.: Country-wide high-resolution vegetation height mapping with Sentinel-2. Remote Sens. Environ. **233**(April), 111347 (2019). https://doi.org/10.1016/j.rse.2019.111347
4. Ascoli, D., Russo, L., Giannino, F., Siettos, C., Moreira, F.: Firebreak and fuelbreak. In: Manzello, S.L.: Encyclopedia of Wildfires and Wildland-Urban Interface (WUI) Fires. Springer, Cham, pp. 1–9 (2018). https://doi.org/10.1007/978-3-319-51727-8
5. Aubard, V., Pereira-Pires, J.E., Campagnolo, M.L., Pereira, J.M.C., Mora, A., Silva, J.M.N.: Fully automated countrywide monitoring of fuel break maintenance operations. Remote Sens. **12**(18), 2879 (2020). https://doi.org/10.3390/rs12182879
6. Pereira-Pires, J.E., Aubard, V., Ribeiro, R.A., Fonseca, J.M., Silva, M.N., Mora, A.: Semi-automatic methodology for fire break maintenance operations detection with Sentinel-2 imagery and artificial neural network (2020). https://doi.org/10.3390/rs12060909
7. Pereira-Pires, J.E., et al.: Pixel-based and object-based change detection methods for assessing fuel break maintenance. In: 2020 International Young Engineers Forum (YEF-ECE), pp. 49–54, July 2020. https://doi.org/10.1109/YEF-ECE49388.2020.9171818
8. San-Miguel-Ayanz, J., et al.: Forest Fires in Europe, Middle East and North Africa 2017 (2018)
9. Healey, S.P., Yang, Z., Gorelick, N., Ilyushchenko, S.: Highly local model calibration with a new GEDI LiDAR asset on Google Earth engine reduces landsat forest height signal saturation. Remote Sens. **12**(17), 2840 (2020). https://doi.org/10.3390/rs12172840

10. Direção-Geral do Território. Especificações técnicas da Carta de Uso e Ocupação do Solo (COS) de Portugal Continental para 2018. Relatório Técnico. Direção-Geral do Território (2019)
11. Main-Knorn, M., Pflug, B., Louis, J., Debaecker, V., Müller-Wilm, U., Gascon, F.: Sen2Cor for Sentinel-2. In: Image and Signal Processing for Remote Sensing XXIII, p. 3, October 2017. https://doi.org/10.1117/12.2278218

Assessing Normalization Techniques for TOPSIS Method

Nazanin Vafaei(✉), Rita A. Ribeiro, and Luis M. Camarinha-Matos

CTS-UNINOVA and School of Science and Technology, NOVA University of Lisbon, 2829-516 Caparica, Portugal
{Nazanin.vafaei,rar,cam}@uninova.pt

Abstract. In recent years, data normalization is receiving considerable attention due to its essential role in decision problems. Especially, considering the new developments in Big data and Artificial Intelligent to handle heterogeneous data from sensors, normalization's role as a preprocessing step for complex decision problems is more distinguished. However, selecting the best normalization technique among several introduced techniques in the literature is still an open issue. In this study we focus on evaluating normalization techniques in Multi-Criteria Decision Making (MCDM) methods namely for Technique for Order of Preference by Similarity to Ideal Solution (TOPSIS) to recommend the most proper technique. A small numerical example, borrowed from literature, is used to show the applicability of the proposed assessment framework using several metrics for recommending the most suitable technique. This study helps decision makers to improve the accuracy of the final ranking of results in decision problems by selecting the best normalization technique for the related case study.

Keywords: Normalization · MCDM · TOPSIS · Decision making · Data fusion · Aggregation · Big data · Artificial Intelligence

1 Introduction

Nowadays, selecting the optimal solution/alternative based on multiple criteria for a given decision problem is a major task for decision makers due to the availability of criteria with different scales/ranges. Multi-Criteria Decision Making (MCDM) is used by most decision makers to deal with the decision problems. They carry out each MCDM method by defining a decision matrix that consists of a set of alternatives Ai (i = 1, …, m), criteria Cj (j = 1,…, n), the relative importance of the criteria (or weights) Wj, and rij, corresponding the rating of alternative i with respect to criteria j [1]. Most of the criteria are measured on different scales (e.g., weight, height, temperature, etc.) while they need to be defined in the same scale/range to enable decision makers to make a valid comparison and selection of the best solution. In other words, decision makers need some preprocessing to produce comparable and dimensionless data from heterogeneous input data sets that is called normalization process. Generally, MCDM methods have four main steps as [2]:

© IFIP International Federation for Information Processing 2021
Published by Springer Nature Switzerland AG 2021
L. M. Camarinha-Matos et al. (Eds.): DoCEIS 2021, IFIP AICT 626, pp. 132–141, 2021.
https://doi.org/10.1007/978-3-030-78288-7_13

1) Determine the decision matrix
2) Normalize the criteria values in the decision matrix
3) Calculate weighted normalized values
4) Aggregation process (which differs for each MCDM method)
5) Sort alternatives in a decreasing ordering.

There are some research papers about the importance of normalization techniques in MCDM methods [3–9]. They discuss the fact that different normalization techniques may address different ranking of alternatives. So, selecting an improper normalization technique may cause deviation from the original solution. Therefore, normalization has an essential role in most MCDM methods and using the most proper technique will help decision makers to improve the accuracy of the final solution.

Furthermore, new developments in big data and Artificial Intelligence (AI) and the integration with MCDM methods provide novel aspects for handling collected data from heterogeneous sensors. These big data from sensors need a normalization process to produce dimensionless input data sets to be used in decision problems. So, normalization techniques have important role in these new points of view of science.

Several normalization techniques are introduced in the literature along with different MCDM methods [1]. In this study, we analyze the effects of different normalization techniques on the Technique for Order of Preference by Similarity to Ideal Solution (TOPSIS) method (to get more details about TOPSIS please see [7]). Thus, the main research question related to this study is: *Which normalization technique is the most appropriate for usage with the TOPSIS method?*

This paper shows the applicability of the assessment framework proposed by [8] and compares the suitability of different normalization techniques using the TOPSIS method. In order to test the mentioned framework, a case study was borrowed from [10], which analyzed the effects of five normalization techniques as Max, Max-Min, Sum, Vector, and Fuzzification (Gaussian) with the TOPSIS method. The obtained results are compared with the results of initial work from [10].

2 Contribution to Applied Artificial Intelligence Systems

In recent years, with the advent of big data, organizations deal with complex decision problems consisting of large amounts of data. So, the integration of MCDM and Artificial Intelligence (AI) techniques is considered and reached success in handling real-world problems [11]. This integration enables decision makers to better structure complex decision problems in static and distributed environments. Doumpos and Grigoroudisby [11] mention that these help as "*handling of massive data sets, the modelling of ill-structured information, the construction of advanced decision models, and the development of efficient computational optimization algorithms for problem solving*".

Several AI techniques are introduced in the literature which are used with integration MCDM, such as Fuzzy Logic (FL), Genetic Algorithm (GA), Neural Network (NN), Heuristic or meta-heuristics, Knowledge-Based (KB), Expert Systems (ES), Tabu-Search (TS), Simulated-annealing (SA), Dampster Shafer (DS), and Self-Organizing-Map (SOM). However, FL is the most popular technique to be used with MCDM methods (e.g., Fuzzy-AHP, Fuzzy-ANP, and Fuzzy-TOPSIS, etc.) [12].

There are some researches on implementing AI techniques with MCDM methods such as Ho [13] that uses 8 meta-heuristics along with AHP, Pan [14] applies Fuzzy-AHP for bridge construction methods selection, Sheu [15] uses Fuzzy-AHP, Fuzzy-TOPSIS, and Fuzzy-MCDM for global logistic operational model, Kulturel-Konak et al. [16] apply TS for system redundancy allocation problem, Efendigil et al. [17] implement ANN and Fuzzy-AHP for third-party logistics providers selection, and Wu et al. [18] use Fuzzy-ANP for site selection problem.

3 Assessment Framework for Evaluation of Normalization Techniques

As mentioned above, normalization is a vital step of most MCDM decision problems that "transfers" all criteria to the same scale and provides an effective comparison between alternatives to select the optimal solution. Numerous normalization techniques have been introduced in the literature. For instance, Jahan and Edwards [1] listed 31 techniques and addressed the pros and cons of them and pointed the influence effects of normalization on the results of MCDM methods in material selection decision problems. The authors of [1] also discuss the different features that should be considered to evaluate a normalization technique namely ranking reversal, symmetry, handling negative values, and capability in removing scales. Furthermore, Vafaei et al. [8] added data type and topology to the initial features from [1] as an important aspect for considering in the evaluation process.

Among several introduced normalization techniques in the literature [1], some of them are more well-known and implemented for the specific mission or MCDM methods. For example, Vector normalization is often applied with TOPSIS method, Target base normalization technique is utilized for material selection decision problems, and Sum is used with AHP (Analytical Hierarchy Process) method [1]. However, there are no clear reasons in the literature for these specific usages, which motivated us to evaluate different normalization techniques in MCDM decision problems.

Some research papers investigated the evaluation of the effects of normalization techniques in MCDM decision problems using various metrics. For instance, Celen [3] analyzed the effect of four normalization techniques (Max, Max-Min, Sum, and Vector) in TOPSIS method using consistency conditions metrics and showed that Vector is the most appropriate normalization technique for the used case study [3]. Also, Charaborty and Yeh [4, 5] used Ranking Consistency Index (RCI) for evaluating the same normalization techniques (Max, Max-Min, Sum, and Vector) for TOPSIS [4] and SAW [5] methods. In another study, Lakshmi and Venkatesan [5] assessed five normalization techniques namely Max, Max-Min, Sum, Vector, Fuzzification (Gaussian membership function) with TOPSIS method using time and space complexity in MATLAB software and selected Sum normalization technique as the best for the case study. In addition, Mathew et al. [6] implemented Spearman correlation to evaluate 6 normalization techniques for the weighted aggregated sum product assessment (WASPAS) method and suggested Max-Min technique as the most suitable normalization for the case study. Recently, Vafaei et al. [7–9, 19, 20] developed an assessment framework to evaluate different normalization techniques for MCDM methods. The proposed assessment framework is consisted of several metrics that are presented in Fig. 1.

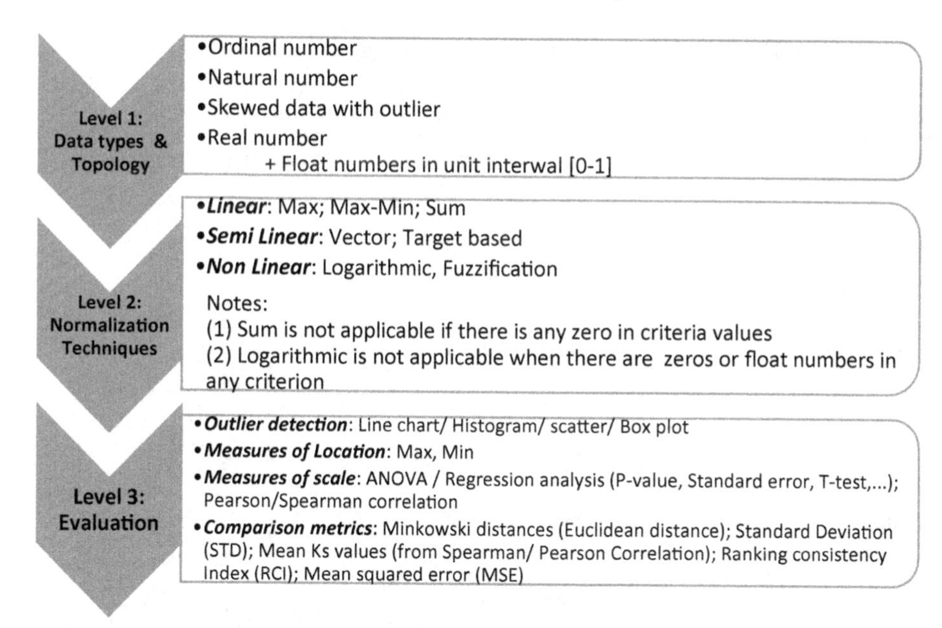

Fig. 1. Three level of the evaluation framework (adopted from [8]).

In this study, we show the applicability of the evolved framework that is proposed by [8]. Figure 1 shows that the first level of this framework is related to distinguishing the data type and topology of the input data sets. Proceeding to the second level enables decision makers to select the normalization techniques. Following, the third level that is the main part of the framework, includes several metrics to assess the used normalization techniques in the decision problems and recommend the most proper normalization techniques for the related case study (for more detail about the assessment framework please see [8]).

In the next section, we show the usage of this assessment framework using a case study that is borrowed from [10]. The related case study from [10] assessed five normalization techniques i.e. Max, Max-Min, Sum, Vector, Fuzzification (Gaussian membership function). So, in order to provide the possibility of benchmarking between our results and the initial results from the author we use the same normalization techniques. The formulas of the mentioned normalization techniques are presented in Table 1. It is noticeable that benefit formulas refer to the higher values the better and cost formulas represent the lower value is desirable.

Table 1. Well-known normalization techniques (adapted from [10]).

Normalization technique	Condition of use	Formula
Linear: Max	Benefit criteria	$n_{ij} = \frac{r_{ij}}{r_{max}}$
	Cost criteria	$n_{ij} = 1 - \frac{r_{ij}}{r_{max}}$
Linear: Max-Min	Benefit criteria	$n_{ij} = \frac{r_{ij} - r_{min}}{r_{max} - r_{min}}$
	Cost criteria	$n_{ij} = \frac{r_{max} - r_{ij}}{r_{max} - r_{min}}$
Linear: Sum	Benefit criteria	$n_{ij} = \frac{r_{ij}}{\sum_{i=1}^{m} r_{ij}}$
	Cost criteria	$n_{ij} = \frac{1/r_{ij}}{\sum_{i=1}^{m} 1/r_{ij}}$
Semi-Linear: Vector	Benefit criteria	$n_{ij} = \frac{r_{ij}}{\sqrt{\sum_{i=1}^{m} r_{ij}^2}}$
	Cost criteria	$n_{ij} = 1 - \frac{r_{ij}}{\sqrt{\sum_{i=1}^{m} r_{ij}^2}}$
Non- Linear: Fuzzification (membership function)	Benefit & cost criteria	E.g. trapezoidal: $f(x, a, b, c, d) = \begin{cases} 0 & x \le a \\ \frac{x-a}{b-a} & a \le x \le b \\ \frac{d-x}{d-c} & c \le x \le d \\ 0 & d \le x \end{cases}$

4 Comparison of Normalization Techniques with an Illustrative Example for TOPSIS Method

To test the applicability of the proposed assessment framework, we applied metrics from the framework to the small illustrative example borrowed from [10]. This case study analyzed and recommended normalization techniques for TOPSIS method in a car selection problem. It consists of 4 alternatives (A1, …, A4) regarding different car brands (Civic Coupe, Saturn Coupe, Ford Escort, and Mazda Miata) and 4 criteria (C1, …, C4) related to the car characteristics (style, reliability, fuel-eco, and cost). The decision matrix with the input data is depicted in Table 2.

Table 2. Decision matrix input data (borrowed from [10])

	C1	C2	C3	C4
A1	7	9	9	8
A2	8	7	8	7
A3	9	6	8	9
A4	6	7	8	6

The authors of [10] used five normalization techniques (Max, Max-Min, Sum, Vector, and Fuzzification (using Gaussian membership function)) to analyze the effects of using different normalization techniques on the TOPSIS method. They calculated the relative closeness and ranking of alternatives, with TOPSIS, using the selected normalization techniques for this case study (Table 3). For more details about the TOPSIS method please see [7].

Table 3. Relative closeness (RC) and Ranking of alternatives (R) the case study from [10]

	Vector		Max-Min		Sum		Max		Fuzzification (Gaussian)	
	RC	R	RC	R	RC	R	RC	R	RC	R
A1	0.74	1	0.88	1	0.38	1	0.26	4	0.75	1
A2	0.41	3	0.28	4	0.26	3	0.31	1	0.45	3
A3	0.17	4	0.31	3	0.009	4	0.29	3	0.02	4
A4	0.44	2	0.45	2	0.32	2	0.30	2	0.62	2

As Table 3 depicts, there is no consensus between the five selected normalization techniques for ranking alternatives. The work described in [10] calculated time complexity and space complexity for each normalization technique with the help of MATLAB and recommended the Sum normalization technique as the best one for the case study, using the TOPSIS method.

Now, we apply the proposed assessment framework and recommend the most appropriate normalization technique for the related case study and compare our results with the obtained results by the authors of [10].

In the first level of the assessment framework the topology of input data is considered. However, in this case study the decision matrix contains integer numbers between [6–9] without any outliers or decimal numbers, and zero. So, we skip the first level and proceed to the second level for selecting the normalization techniques to be assessed.

As mentioned before, the authors of [10] analyzed the effect of five normalization techniques (Max, Max-Min, Sum, Vector, and Fuzzification (using Gaussian membership function)) i.e. at least one normalization technique from three categories (Linear, Semi-linear, and Non-linear) that are mentioned in the second level of the assessment framework (Fig. 1) are selected.

The third level of the proposed assessment framework consists of several metrics from four classes (outlier detection; measures of location; measures of scale; and comparison methods). As mentioned above, the decision matrix includes integer numbers in the interval [6–9] without any outliers, decimal numbers and zero. Therefore, metrics for determining outliers are useless and we omitted these class of metrics for this case study. For the rest of the metrics, we focused on the comparison metrics namely Minkowski distances (Euclidean distance), Standard Deviation (STD), Mean Ks values (from Spearman/Pearson Correlation), Ranking consistency Index (RCI), and Mean squared error (MSE). For details about calculating Euclidean distance and STD please see [19] and for calculation of Mean Ks value and RCI please see [7].

For calculating MSE for aggregated data sets, it is obtained from the average of mean squared error for each normalization technique with other normalization techniques using the ranking of alternatives [21, 22]. It should be noticed that the favorable result for MSE is the lower value the better because it is desirable to have less error when comparing different normalization techniques [8]. For the rest of the metrics (Euclidean distance, STD, RCI, and Mean Ks) the higher values are better and more desirable [8]. The results of MSE are depicted in Table 4.

Table 4. MSE for the borrowed case study from [10] for TOPSIS method

	Vector	Max-Min	Sum	Max	Fuzzification (Gaussian)	MSE	Rank
Vector	–	0.5	0	3.5	0	1	2
Max-Min	0.5	–	0.5	0.5	0.5	0.5	1
Sum	0	0.5	–	3.5	0	1	2
Max	3.5	0.5	3.5	–	3.5	2.75	5
Fuzzification (Gaussian)	0	0.5	0	3.5	–	1	2

Implementing different metrics from the third level of the proposed assessment framework as Euclidean distance, STD, RCI, and Mean Ks plus the results of MSE are provided comparable results (Table 5).

Table 5. Results of different metrics of assessment framework using TOPSIS method for the borrowed case study from [10].

	Euclidean	STD	RCI	MSE	Mean Ks
Max	0.8094	0.2337	10.75	1	0.5211
Max-Min	0.9587	0.2768	9	0.5	0.3364
Sum	0.5648	0.1630	10.75	1	0.5690
Vector	0.0748	0.0216	6.25	2.75	−0.5452
Fuzzification (Gaussian)	1.1016	0.3180	10.75	1	0.5694

Table 6 shows the ordering of normalization techniques with respect to each used metrics. The different metrics produced different ranks for the chosen techniques and still recommending the most appropriate normalization technique is impossible just by looking at the results. Thus, plurality voting (PV) is used to sum up the obtained results of metrics [8]. PV counts the number of times that a normalization technique being the first ranking/ordering with respect to the applied metrics. So, the normalization technique that has the large number of times being the first ranked would be recommended as a more appropriate technique [8].

Table 6. Ordering of normalization techniques with respect to the metrics and using plurality voting

	Euclidean↑	STD↑	RCI↑	MSE↓	Mean Ks↑	PV
Max	3	3	1	2	3	1
Max-Min	2	2	4	1	4	1
Sum	4	4	1	2	2	1
Vector	5	5	5	5	5	0
Fuzzification (Gaussian)	1	1	1	2	1	4

From the obtained results (Table 6) using the proposed assessment framework and plurality voting, the Fuzzification (Gaussian) normalization technique is the best one due to having the large number of times being the first order considering the implemented metrics, while the approach by [10], recommended the Sum normalization technique.

Comparing the results of both approaches, we believe our framework provides more robust and reliable results than the ones obtained by [10], because we cover a wide range of metrics (STD, Euclidean distance, Mean Ks, RCI, and MSE). On the other hand, implementing PV enabled us to aggregate the obtained results from different used metrics. In this case study, the authors of [10] just calculated time and space complexity with MATLAB, and these results are highly dependent on the style of MATLAB users/programmers. For instance, someone can code Sum normalization technique in a manner that obtains time and space complexity twice higher than someone else. Therefore, our proposed framework ensures more accurate and reliable results to support decision makers.

5 Conclusions

This paper addressed the applicability and robustness of the assessment framework to evaluate different normalization techniques and recommend the most appropriate technique for the TOPSIS method. A case study borrowed from [10] was used to analyze the effects of five chosen normalization techniques namely Max, Max-Min, Sum, Vector, and Fuzzification (Gaussian) and recommended the Fuzzification (Gaussian) as the best technique to be used in the related case study. Moreover, the obtained results were compared with the initial results by the authors of [10] and showed that our results are more accurate and robust than the initial results due to the implementation of several metrics from the assessment framework.

There are several normalization techniques introduced in the literature [1] which are not evaluated yet. In future we plan to evaluate further normalization techniques for different MCDM methods (e.g. PROMETHEE, MOORA, COPRAS, and etc.) using the proposed framework. Also, the validation of the assessment framework has not been done with real-world case studies, which is planned as future work.

Acknowledgements. This work was funded in part by the Center of Technology and Systems (CTS) and the Portuguese Foundation for Science and Technology (FCT) through the Strategic Program UIDB/00066/2020.

References

1. Jahan, A., Edwards, K.L.: A state-of-the-art survey on the influence of normalization techniques in ranking: Improving the materials selection process in engineering design. Mater. Des. **65**(2015), 335–342 (2015). https://doi.org/10.1016/j.matdes.2014.09.022
2. Tzeng, G.-H., Huang, J.-J.: Multiple Attribute Desicion Making: Methods and Applications. Taylor & Francis Group, Boca Raton, FL. 33487–2742 (2011)
3. Celen, A.: comparative analysis of normalization procedures in topsis method: with an application to Turkish deposit banking market. Informatica **25**(2), 185–208 (2014)
4. Chakraborty, S., Yeh, C.-H.: A simulation comparison of normalization procedures for TOPSIS. In: 2009 International Conference on Computers and Industrial Engineering, pp. 1815–1820. IEEE, Troyes (2009). https://doi.org/10.1109/iccie.2009.5223811
5. Chakraborty, S., Yeh, C.-H.: A simulation based comparative study of normalization procedures in multiattribute decision making. In: AIKED'07 Proceedings of the 6th Conference on 6th WSEAS International Conference on Artificial Intelligence, Knowledge Engineering and Data Bases, vol. 6, pp. 102–109, World Scientific and Engineering Academy and Society (WSEAS) Stevens Point, Wisconsin, USA (2007)
6. Mathew, M., Sahu, S., Upadhyay, A.K.: Effect Of Normalization Techniques In Robot Selection Using Weighted Aggregated Sum Product Assessment (2017)
7. Vafaei, N., Ribeiro, R.A., Camarinha-Matos, L.M.: Data normalisation techniques in decision making: case study with TOPSIS method. Int. J. Inf. Decis. Sci. **10**(1), 19 (2018). https://doi.org/10.1504/IJIDS.2018.090667
8. Vafaei, N., Ribeiro, R.A., Camarinha-Matos, L.M.: Selecting normalization techniques for the analytical hierarchy process. In: Technological Innovation for Life Improvement. DoCEIS 2020. IFIP Advances in Information and Communication Technology, pp. 43–52. Springer, Cham (2020). https://doi.org/10.1007/978-3-030-45124-0_4
9. Vafaei, N., Ribeiro, R.A., Camarinha-Matos, L.M.: Selection of normalization technique for weighted average multi-criteria decision making. In: Camarinha-Matos, L.M., Adu-Kankam, K., Julashokri, M. (eds.) Technological Innovation for Resilient Systems. DoCEIS 2018. IFIP Advances in Information and Communication Technology, vol 521, pp. 43–52. Springer, Cham, (2018). https://doi.org/10.1007/978-3-319-78574-5_4
10. Lakshmi, T.M., Venkatesan, V.P.: A comparison of various normalization in techniques for order performance by similarity to ideal solution (TOPSIS). Int. J. Comput. Algorithm **3**(3) (2014)

11. Doumpos, M., Grigoroudis, E.: Multicriteria Decision Aid and Artificial Intelligence. John Wiley & Sons, Ltd, Chichester, UK (2013). https://doi.org/10.1002/9781118522516
12. Aliasi, M.A., Zaiton, S., Hashimi, M., Samsudin, S.: Multi crteria decision making and its applications: a literature review. J. Teknol. Mklm. **20**(2), 129–152 (2008)
13. Ho, W.: Integrated analytic hierarchy process and its applications – a literature review. Eur. J. Oper. Res. **186**(1), 211–228 (2008). https://doi.org/10.1016/j.ejor.2007.01.004
14. Pan, N.-F.: Fuzzy AHP approach for selecting the suitable bridge construction method. Autom. Constr. **17**(8), 958–965 (2008). https://doi.org/10.1016/j.autcon.2008.03.005
15. Sheu, J.-B.: A hybrid neuro-fuzzy analytical approach to mode choice of global logistics management. Eur. J. Oper. Res. **189**(3), 971–986 (2008). https://doi.org/10.1016/j.ejor.2006.06.082
16. Kulturel-Konak, S., Coit, D.W., Baheranwala, F.: Pruned Pareto-optimal sets for the system redundancy allocation problem based on multiple prioritized objectives. J. Heuristics **14**(4), 335–357 (2007). https://doi.org/10.1007/s10732-007-9041-3
17. Efendigil, T., Önüt, S., Kongar, E.: A holistic approach for selecting a third-party reverse logistics provider in the presence of vagueness. Comput. Ind. Eng. **54**(2), 269–287 (2008). https://doi.org/10.1016/j.cie.2007.07.009
18. Wu, C.-R., Lin, C.-T., Chen, H.-C.: Integrated environmental assessment of the location selection with fuzzy analytical network process. Qual. Quant. **43**(3), 351–380 (2009). https://doi.org/10.1007/s11135-007-9125-z
19. Vafaei, N., Ribeiro, R.A., Camarinha-Matos, L.M., Valera, L.R.: Normalization techniques for collaborative networks. Kybernetes **49**(4) (2019). https://doi.org/10.1108/k-09-2018-0476
20. Vafaei, N., Ribeiro, R.A., Camarinha-Matos, L.M.: Normalization techniques for multi-criteria decision making: analytical hierarchy process case study. In: Camarinha-Matos, L.M., Falcao, A., Vafaei, N., Najdi, S (eds.) DoCEIS 2016. IFIP Advances in Information and Communication Technology Technological Innovation for Cyber-Physical Systems, pp. 261–269. Springer, Cham, Lisbon, Portugal (2016). https://doi.org/10.1007/978-3-319-31165-4_26
21. Felinto de Farias Aires, R., Ferreira, L., Galdino de Araujo, A., Borenstein, D.: Student selection in a Brazilian university: using a multi-criteria method. J. Oper. Res. Soc. **69**(4), 528–540 (2018). https://doi.org/10.1057/s41274-017-0242-3
22. de F. Aires, R.F., Ferreira, L.: A new approach to avoid rank reversal cases in the TOPSIS method. Comput. Ind. Eng. **132**, 84–97 (2019). https://doi.org/10.1016/j.cie.2019.04.023

How Can e-Grocers Use Artificial Intelligence Based on Technology Innovation to Improve Supply Chain Management?

Mar Vazquez-Noguerol[1](✉), Carlos Prado-Prado[1], Shaofeng Liu[2], and Raul Poler[3]

[1] Grupo de Ingeniería de Organización (GIO), Business Organization and Marketing Department, School of Industrial Engineering, University of Vigo, Galicia, Spain
marfernandezvazquez@uvigo.es

[2] Plymouth Business School, University of Plymouth, Plymouth, UK

[3] Research Centre on Production Management and Engineering (CIGIP), Universitat Politècnica de València, Alicante, Spain

Abstract. The digital transformation among grocery sales is in full swing. However, some retailers are struggling to adapt to technological innovation in the grocery industry to achieve digital excellence. The purpose of this article is to analyse artificial intelligence systems applied in e-commerce that could be implemented in online grocery sales. Unlike other online businesses, grocery sales face logistical challenges that differentiate them, such as fresh product conservation and tight delivery times. Through a literature review, this study aims to provide researchers and practitioners with a starting point for the selection of technological innovation to solve e-grocery problems.

Keywords: Artificial intelligence · Digital transformation · E-commerce · Grocery sales · Applied systems

1 Introduction

The online sale of food products is gaining considerable commercial interest and generating numerous business opportunities. Traditional grocery sales must adapt to the digital transformation where online sales present great difficulties not identified in other sectors [1, 2]. In addition to the logistical efforts required to preserve the quality of perishable products [3], complications are exacerbated by tight delivery times [4]. All these difficulties give rise to the need for artificial intelligence (AI) systems to tackle the digital transition existing in the online grocery retail trade [5].

AI systems deal with computer programs that possess own decision-making capability to solve problems in the areas of representation of knowledge, learning, prediction, reasoning and perception [6]. The first AI system applied to the online channel of grocery sales was developed as a support for decision-making [7]. Grocery sellers can select the most suitable transport operating system in terms of cost, distance and time through this tool. That research line was followed by another author who combined an agent-based

© IFIP International Federation for Information Processing 2021
Published by Springer Nature Switzerland AG 2021
L. M. Camarinha-Matos et al. (Eds.): DoCEIS 2021, IFIP AICT 626, pp. 142–150, 2021.
https://doi.org/10.1007/978-3-030-78288-7_14

simulation with inventory optimization [8], in which the use of geographic network data reduces transport distances. One year later, the same author completed the previously developed system by presenting a simulation and optimization-based decision support system [9]. The computational experiments are able to model demand patterns and logistics processes by integrating data on the shelf life and preferences for items.

Moreover, some studies look at how technological innovation can be used to forecast demand. On the one hand, a regression and machine learning model was created to offer personalization to shoppers [10]. The designed AI systems use a mixture of discourse exploration and code-based reconstruction of key features from shopping lists. On the other hand, a model for accurately predicting the demand distribution was proposed with linear regression methods [11]. These researchers achieve cost minimization by attending to the behaviour of the digital consumers.

The development of AI systems to solve the challenges in e-grocery has been particularly oriented to manage customer demand and online order delivery. However, the number of publications looking at technological innovation is limited. Therefore, this study has a twofold motivation: (i) identify the most prevalent techniques of AI that are applied in e-commerce and (ii) introduce the potential AI techniques that can be employed in the digital transformation of grocery sales. To carry out this study, the following research question was defined:

RQ: What is the current state of research on the development of AI techniques in e-commerce and which of those techniques can be adapted to e-grocery?

2 Contribution to Applied Artificial Intelligence Systems

The term e-grocery refers to the online sale of food products. Paying special attention to the online channel, this study has focused on discovering techniques to improve the digital transformation. In this context, digital transformation is the integration of technology into business, fundamentally improving how to offer value to customers. This value is of great importance as the boundaries between traditional and electronic commerce disappear [12].

Grocery retailers must allocate a significant portion of revenue to investing in digital transformation. Until now, technological innovation in this sector has only been carried out with simple algorithms [7–11]. Mathematical models have also been understood as AI techniques that allow automated planning [13].

Implementation could increase if AI techniques employed in other sectors were analysed. Therefore, the main objective of this research is to discover AI applications in e-commerce for promoting technological advancements, which will allow grocery sellers to achieve greater flexibility to adapt to the online channel.

The systematic literature review carried out in this article presents AI tools such as machine learning, neural networks and recommendation systems. These publications offer general frameworks, systems, algorithms and methods that are easily applicable to other sectors. If these e-commerce tools were applied in e-grocery, AI techniques would help grocery sellers to improve forecasting and decision-making, customer acquisition and organizational productivity.

In this way, the proposed study is a major contribution as it shows that there are few developed techniques for innovation in the supply chain of e-grocers, which makes this line of research of great future interest for researchers and companies. From this analysis, we identify potential gaps and opportunities for research and practical improvement and devise guidelines for futures studies.

3 A Systematic Literature Review

The literature review constitutes the main part of the research process [14] because the purpose of this study is to analyse the research carried out on e-commerce taking into account the relationship between technological innovation and applied AI systems. It seems that there are several tools used to manage the supply chain, but none from the point of view of e-commerce [15]. In order to fulfil the proposed objective of this study, the content must follow a clear and decided process structure [16], for which a four-step review methodology is developed [17]. The following four subsections provide the details of each of the four steps.

3.1 Material Collection

The scope of the study begins with selection of the SCOPUS and Web of Science databases. The main search criteria were narrowed according to the keywords of the research question 'artificial intelligence' and 'e-commerce' in the search fields: article title, abstract and keywords. Additional sets of selection criteria stipulate the following: the article is written in English and the document type is an article. The search period is adjusted to the last ten years, ranging from 2011 to 2020. Finally, the search was adapted to the subject areas such as computer science, engineering, decision sciences and mathematics. The search criteria used were adapted to each specific database to guarantee the robustness of the search. The search was carried out in January 2021. The selection process of the publications considered in this study can be summarised as follows. From the first search in the both selected databases, a total of 137 references were identified. After eliminating duplicates, 126 articles remained. Once the set of articles has been selected, we applied a second set of criteria to exclude irrelevant articles. Each author of this paper read every article to ensure that it had the required quality. We defined a customized article inclusion protocol to review titles, keywords and abstracts [18]. The analysis of articles was compared by the authors, discussing criteria and results [19]. Application of these criteria reduced the number of selected publications for analysis and synthesis to 42.

3.2 Descriptive Analysis

In this phase, the 42 selected articles were analysed. The characteristics evaluated were: journal and year of publication. The journal 'Sustainability' stands out from the other publications as it appears 5 times. It is followed by the sources: 'Electronic Markets' and 'International Journal of Innovative Technology and Exploring Engineering'. By analysing the publication years, information is obtained on the evolution of research works carried out during the last 10 years. It is noteworthy that over 76% of the papers were published between 2019 and 2020. None of the other years represents more than

8% on its own, as shown in Fig. 1. The consequence of the distribution in time may be the result of a lack of practical application of the value contributed by these AI tools until 2019.

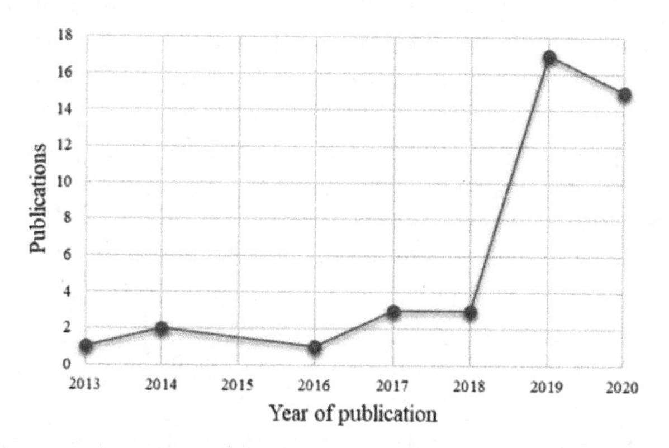

Fig. 1. Classification of articles according to the time distribution

3.3 Category Selection

In order to examine the 42 publications, we broke them down into fundamental parts on the basis of a specific set of characteristics feeding back to our research question. These features were: 'AI techniques' and 'Outcome'. To develop the analysis, we first determined the scientific sources that report a comprehensive list of AI techniques in practice and scientific literature [20, 21]. We analyse the AI techniques that the publications focused on according to: AI neural networks, Fuzzy logic, Agent-based systems, Genetic algorithm, Data mining, Support vector machines, Decision support systems, Machine Learning, Expert systems, Bayesian networks, Recommendation system, DVA and Chatbot, AI algorithms or General forms of AI. This last group includes those publications where more than three techniques are discussed. They are usually conceptual publications where the most applied AI tools are determined and where comparisons are made between them. Regarding the outcome, the publications have been classified according to how they develop the topic: approach, system, framework, method, literature review, application or algorithm.

3.4 Material Evaluation

In this stage, the analysed articles were validated according to the approaches selected through a deductive and inductive process. The evaluation ensured that the studies were appropriate and that they had sufficient information to be able to apply the parameters considered for the classification. The analysis helped the organization, categorization, structure, and the main findings of the review to be examined.

4 Research Contribution and Innovation

This section shows the results of the review carried out. Moreover, the studies were analysed in relation to the technique or outcome they were aimed at. Table 1 details the results obtained from the categorization of the reviewed articles.

Table 1. Summary of the categorization of the literature

AI Technique	Amount	Studies
Machine learning	10	[22, 31, 32, 35, 40, 45, 48, 52, 54, 62]
Recommendation system	7	[23, 30, 31, 40, 44, 47, 63]
AI neural networks	6	[32, 38, 44, 53, 54, 61]
General forms of AI	6	[24, 27, 34, 39, 41, 42]
Support vector machines	6	[44, 45, 48, 53, 54, 62]
DVA and Chatbot	6	[30, 33, 49, 53, 57, 60]
AI algorithms	6	[26, 28, 29, 48, 56, 58]
Data mining	5	[37, 52, 61–63]
Genetic algorithm	4	[25, 45, 59, 61]
Decision support systems	4	[37, 38, 46, 55]
Fuzzy logic	3	[25, 37, 61]
Agent-based/multi-agent systems	3	[36, 43, 51]
Expert systems	1	[50]
Bayesian networks	1	[38]

As outlined above, this summary shows the frequency of AI techniques. Since some research employs more than one technique, the total frequency of some methods is greater than the number of publications. To be precise, 19 publications (45%) use a single-technique approach, 9 articles (21%) develop a double-technique, 8 (19%) have a multi-technique, and 6 (only 14%) present a more global view on AI systems. The most used technique is machine learning (over 15%). The second-most-frequent technique was recommendation system (10% times).

Another aspect on which the literature in this review is based is the outcome of the study. In this categorization, for each publication we define a unique outcome (an algorithm, a system, a framework, a method, a model, a literature review, an application or an approach). Figure 2 presents the outcomes with an experimental/practical orientation.

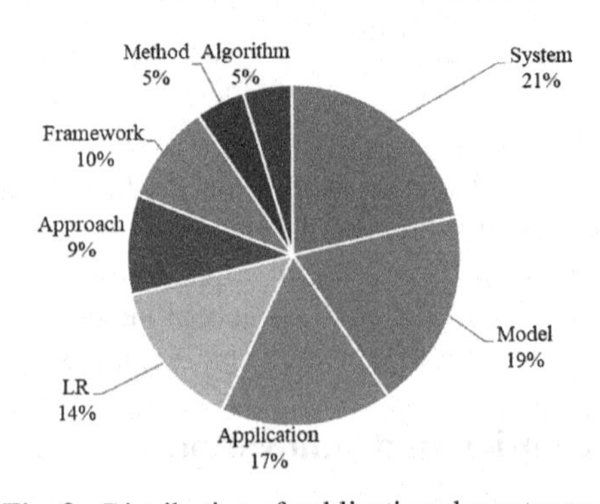

Fig. 2. Distribution of publications by outcomes

5 Conclusions and Future Work

E-commerce increasingly fosters competitiveness and there is a constant need for the application of new methods and technologies [36]. AI techniques are presented as a great opportunity, but they should be approached in the right way since only a third of the projects are successful [35]. Although some research provided insights into the application of AI techniques in e-grocery, there are still many scientific gaps.

The main opportunity for research identified in this study is the need to conduct studies on the implementation of AI techniques in real-world practice. The state of the art could be characterized by lot of theoretical and not so much applied research. Future investigations should include such practical application in companies and with real data, showing quantitative results.

Our research highlights that the most employed AI techniques in e-commerce are e-learning, neural networks and recommendation systems. These publications present systems and algorithms, but there is a lack of methods and approaches for AI systems. In this sense, an interesting future line of research is presented: researchers should focus on developing AI applied systems to find out how technological innovation improves the supply chain management.

Moreover, this literature review highlights many studies focused on consumer behaviour, on how to improve the level of service through either chatbots, algorithms or data mining [33, 39, 52, 62]. Systems of this type allow a relationship to be built between the elements and for each user to make the most appropriate decision. The value contributed in these investigations is very broad, but they do not analyse how these tools facilitate supply chain management. This approach is presented as an interesting line of research to develop in future studies.

Finally, a research gap has been identified in the application of AI techniques in e-grocery. Some tools analysed in this study developed for e-commerce are not so easily adaptable to e-grocers. This case is applicable to algorithms, frameworks and applications focused on logistics, which must be adapted to solve the logistical complications of grocery sellers such as fresh product conservation and tight order delivery times. Publications could focus on implementing ant colony algorithms to improve the distribution of fresh products. This aspect was not taken into account in the publication dealing with colony algorithms in e-commerce [26] and with digital voice assistants [57, 60]. Those authors have not taken into account the implications of using this technique in the management of foodstuff supply chains. This offers a guideline for future studies where the technological innovation will lead to more accurate forecasting and decision-making. As a result, it will be possible to improve customer acquisition and the organizational productivity of e-grocers.

References

1. Seidel, S., Mareï, N., Blanquart, C.: Innovations in e-grocery and logistics solutions for cities. Transp. Res. Proced. **12**, 825–835 (2016)
2. Wollenburg, J., Holzapfel, A., Hübner, A., Kuhn, H.: Configuring retail fulfillment processes for omni-channel customer steering. Int. J. Electron. Commer. **22**(4), 540–575 (2018)

3. Fredriksson, A., Liljestrand, K.: Capturing food logistics: a literature review and research agenda. Int. J. Logist. Res. Appl. **18**(1), 16–34 (2015)
4. Lau, H., Nakandala, D., Shum, P.K.: A business process decision model for fresh-food supplier evaluation. Bus. Process Manag. J. **24**(3), 716–744 (2018)
5. Dannenberg, P., Fuchs, M., Riedler, T., Wiedemann, C.: Digital transition by COVID-19 pandemic? The German food online retail. Tijdschrift voor economische. **111**(3), 543–560 (2020)
6. Leo Kumar, S.P.: State of the art-intense review on artificial intelligence systems application in process planning and manufacturing. Eng. Appl. Artif. Intell. **65**, 294–329 (2017)
7. Al-nawayseh, M.K., Alnabhan, M.M., Al-Debei, M.M., Balachandran, W.: An adaptive decision support system for last mile logistics in E-commerce: a study on online grocery shopping. Int. J. Decis. Support Syst. Technol. **5**(1), 40–65 (2013)
8. Fikar, C., Mild, A., Waitz, M.: Facilitating consumer preferences and product shelf life data in the design of e-grocery deliveries. Eur. J. Oper. Res. 1–47 (2019)
9. Fikar, C.: A decision support system to investigate food losses in e-grocery deliveries. Comput. Ind. Eng. **117**, 282–290 (2018)
10. Mackenzie, A.: Personalization and probabilities: impersonal propensities in online grocery shopping. Big Data Soc. **5**(1) (2018)
11. Ulrich, M., Jahnke, H., Langrock, R., Pesch, R., Senge, R.: Distributional regression for demand forecasting in e-grocery. Eur. J. Oper. Res. 9–58 (2019)
12. Mishra, N., Mukherjee, S.: Effect of artificial intelligence on customer relationship management of amazon in Bangalore. Int. J. Manag. **10**(4) (2019)
13. Vazquez-Noguerol, M., Comesaña-Benavides, J., Poler, R., Prado-Prado, J.C.: An optimisation approach for the e-grocery order picking and delivery problem. Cent. Eur. J. Oper. Res. 1–30 (2020)
14. Wee, B.V., Banister, D.: How to write a literature review paper? Transp. Rev. **36**(2), 278–288 (2016)
15. Toorajipour, R., Sohrabpour, V., Nazarpour, A., Oghazi, P., Fischl, M.: Aetificial intelligence in supply chain management: a systematic literature review. J. Bus. Res. **122**, 502–517 (2021)
16. Seuring, S., Stefan, G.: Conducting content-analysis based literature reviews in supply chain management. Supply Chain Manag.: Int. J. **17**(5), 544–55 (2012)
17. Mayring, P.: Qualitative Inhaltanalyse – Grundlagen und Techniken, vol. 3, pp. 58. Beltz Verlag, Weinheim (2010)
18. Orwin, R.G., Cooper, H., Hedges, L.V.: The Handbook of Research Synthesis, pp. 139–162. Russell Sage Found, New York (1994)
19. Miles, M.B., Huberman, A.M.: Qualitative Data Analysis: An Expanded Sourcebook (1994)
20. Chen, S.H., Jakeman, A.J., Norton, J.P.: Artificial Intelligence techniques: an introduction to their use for modelling environmental systems. Math. Comput. Simul. **78**, 379–400 (2008)
21. Min, H.: Artificial intelligence in supply chain management: theory and applications. Int. J. Logist. Res. Appl. **13**, 13–39 (2010)
22. Khrais, L.T.: Role of artificial intelligence in shaping consumer demand in e-commerce. Fut. Int. **12**(12), 226 (2020)
23. Cabrera-Sánchez, J.P., Ramos-de-Luna, I., Carvajal-Trujillo, E., Villarejo-Ramos, Á.F.: Online recommendation systems: factors influencing use in e-commerce. Sustain. **12**(21), 8888 (2020)
24. Bandara, R., Fernando, M., Akter, S.: Privacy concerns in e-commerce: a taxonomy and a future research agenda. Electr. Mark. 1–19 (2019)
25. Leung, K.H., Lee, C.K., Choy, K.L.: An integrated online pick-to-sort order batching approach for managing frequent arrivals of B2B e-commerce orders under both fixed and variable time-window batching. Adv. Eng. Inform. **45**, (2020)

26. Feng, Z.: Constructing rural e-commerce logistics model based on ant colony algorithm and artificial intelligence method. Softw. Comput. 1–10 (2019)
27. Sima, V., Gheorghe, I.G., Subić, J., Nancu, D.: Influences of the industry 4.0 revolution on the human capital development and consumer behavior: a systematic review. Sustain. **12**(10), 4035 (2020)
28. Miikulainen, R., et al.: Ascend by evolve: AI-based massively multivariate conversion rate optimization. AI Mag. **41**(1), 44–60 (2020)
29. Li, S.: Structure optimization of e-commerce platform based on artificial intelligence and blockchain technology. Wirel. Commun. Mob. Comput. **2020** (2020)
30. Yang, G., Ji, G., Tan, K.H.: Impact of artificial intelligence adoption on online returns policies. Ann. Oper. Res. 1–24 (2020)
31. Suresh, A., Carmel Mary Belinda M.J.: A comprehensive study of hybrid recommendation systems for e-commerce applications. Int. J. Adv. Sci. and Technol. **29**(3), 4089–4101 (2020)
32. Manikandan, S., Chinnadurai, M.: Evaluation of students' performance in educational sciences and prediction of future development using tensorflow. Int. J. Eng. Educ. **36**(6), 1783–1790 (2020)
33. Adam, M., Wessel, M., Benlian, A.: AI-based chatbots in customer service and their effects on user compliance. Electron. Mark. 1–19 (2020)
34. Glinkina, O.V., Ganina, S.A., Maslennikova, A.V., Solostina, T.A., ViktorovnaSoloveva, M.: Digital changes in the economy: advanced opportunities for digital innovation. Int. J. Manag. **11**(3) (2020)
35. Pearson, A.: Personalisation the artificial intelligence way. J. Digit. Soc. Med. Mark. **7**(3), 245–269 (2019)
36. Park, J., Rahman, H.A., Suh, J., Hussin, H.: A study of integrative bargaining model with argumentation-based negotiation. Sustain. **11**(23), 6832 (2019)
37. Leung, K.H., Luk, C.C., Choy, K.L., Lam, H.Y., Lee, C.K.: A B2B flexible pricing decision support system for managing the request for quotation process under e-commerce business environment. Int. J. Prod. Res. **57**(20), 6528–6551 (2019)
38. Xu, Y.Z., Zhang, J.L., Hua, Y., Wang, L.Y.: Dynamic credit risk evaluation method for e-commerce sellers based on a hybrid artificial intelligence model. Sustain. **11**(19), 5521 (2019)
39. Ingaldi, M., Ulewicz, R.: How to make e-commerce more successful by use of Kano's model to assess customer satisfaction in terms of sustainable development. Sustain. **11**(18), 4830 (2019)
40. Su, X., Sperlì, G., Moscato, V., Picariello, A., Esposito, C., Choi, C.: An edge intelligence empowered recommender system enabling cultural heritage applications. IEEE Trans. **15**(7), 4266–4275 (2019)
41. Nazim Sha, S., Rajeswari, M.: Creating a Brand Value and Consumer Satisfaction in E-Commerce Business Using Artificial Intelligence with the Help of Vosag Technology (2019)
42. Rao, N.T., Bhattacharyya, D.: Applications of Artificial Intelligence and ML in Business (2019)
43. Lee, Y.S., Sikora, R.: Application of adaptive strategy for supply chain agent. Inform. Syst. e-Bus. Manag. **17**(1), 117–157 (2019)
44. Suryana, N., Basari, A.S.H.: Involve convolutional-NN to generate item latent factor consider product genre to increase robustness in product sparse data for e-commerce. J. Phys. **1201**(1) (2019)
45. Vanneschi, L., Horn, D.M., Castelli, M., Popovič, A.: An artificial intelligence system for predicting customer default in e-commerce. Expert Syst. Appl. **104**, 1–21 (2018)
46. Salem, A.B.M., Parusheva, S.: Developing a web-based ontology for e-business. Int. J. Electron. Commer. Stud. **9**(2), 119–132 (2018)
47. Zhao, L., Pan, S.J., Yang, Q.: A unified framework of active transfer learning for cross-system recommendation. Artif. Intell. **245**, 38–55 (2017)

48. Tang, L., Wang, A., Xu, Z., Li, J.: Online-purchasing behavior forecasting with a firefly algorithm-based SVM model considering shopping cart use. Eurasia J. Math. Sci. Technol. Educ. **13**(12), 7967–7983 (2017)
49. Peng, M., Qin, Y., Tang, C., Deng, X.: An e-commerce customer service robot based on intention recognition model. J. Electron. Commer. Organ. **14**(1), 34–44 (2016)
50. Chhabra, M., Das, S., Sarne, D.: Expert-mediated sequential search. Eur. J. Oper. Res. **234**(3), 861–873 (2014)
51. Chen, S., Hao, J., Weiss, G., Tuyls, K., Leung, H.F.: Evaluating Practical Automated Negotiation Based on Spatial Evolutionary Game Theory, pp 147–158. Springer, Cham. (2014)
52. Tran, P.Q., Thanh, N., Vu, N., Thanh, H., Xuan, H.: Effective opinion words extraction for food reviews classification. Int. J. Adv. Comput. Sci. Appl. **11**(7) (2020)
53. Xu, Y., et al.: A healthcare-oriented mobile question-and-answering system for smart cities. Trans. Emerg. Telecommun. Technol. **9**(3), 2977 (2020)
54. Kumar, S., Gahalawat, M., Roy, P.P., Dogra, D.P., Kim, B.G.: Exploring impact of age and gender on sentiment analysis using machine learning. Electron. **9**(2), 374 (2020)
55. Methenitis, G., Kaisers, M., La Poutré, H.: Degrees of rationality in agent-based retail markets. Comput. Econ. 1–21 (2019)
56. Sun, L., Chen, P., Xiang, W., Chen, P., Gao, W.Y., Zhang, K.J.: SmartPaint: a co-creative drawing system based on generative adversarial networks. Front. Infor. Technol. Electron. Eng. **20**(12), 1644–1656 (2019)
57. Hsiao, W.H., Chang, T.S.: Exploring the opportunity of digital voice assistants in the logistics and transportation industry. J. Enterp. Inf. Manag. (2019)
58. Ribeiro, M.R., Barioni, M.C.N., de Amo, S., Roncancio, C., Labbé, C.: StreamPref: a query language for temporal conditional preferences on data streams. J. Intell. Inf. Syst. **53**(2), 329–360 (2019)
59. Manahov, V., Zhang, H.: Forecasting financial markets using high-frequency trading data: examination with strongly typed genetic programming. Int. J. Electron. Commer. **23**(1), 12–32 (2019)
60. West, E.: Amazon: Surveillance as a service. Surveill. Soc. **17**(1/2), 27–33 (2019)
61. Zhang, J., Williams, S.O., Wang, H.: Intelligent computing system based on pattern recognition and data mining algorithms. Sustain. Comput. Inform. Syst. **20**, 192–202 (2018)
62. Catal, C., Guldan, S.: Product review management software based on multiple classifiers. Iet Softw. **11**(3), 89–92 (2017)
63. Inbarani, H., Thangavel, K.: Rough Web Intelligent Techniques for Page Recommendation. Intelligent Techniques in Recommendation Systems. pp. 170–191. IGI Global (2013)

A Conceptual Framework of Human-System Interaction Under Uncertainty-Based on Shadow System Perspective

Qingyu Liang(✉) and Juanqiong Gou

School of Economic and Management, Beijing Jiaotong University, Beijing, China
{qingyu.liang,jqgou}@bjtu.edu.cn

Abstract. Instability is the norm, and emergency management has gradually become the general situation of organizations. Due to the enterprise business systems are developed to handle certain business under a planned and controlled assumption, cannot solve the uncertain business. Instead, a large number of uncertain business mainly rely on people's interactives which bring diverse perspectives and sharing knowledge to solve. This paper interprets the representation of shadow system under uncertainty and further analyzes one type of obstacle of human-system interaction based on empirical analysis. Finally, this paper designs a conceptual framework about the feedback and enabling between shadow system and legitimate system to solve this obstacle.

Keywords: Uncertainty · Business system · Shadow system · Human-system interaction · Conceptual framework

1 Introduction

Instability is the norm, and VUCA (volatility, Uncertainty, Complexity, Ambiguity) has gradually become synonymous with today's world. VUCA has been variously used to describe an environment that defies confident diagnosis and befuddles executives [1]. VUCA brings challenges to many areas of management, including design innovation, organizational structure, strategic planning, ecosystem, talent management, partnership, and so on [2]. Though the words of VUCA do have related meanings, it's the differences among them that are most valuable for researchers [1]. This paper just focuses on uncertainty which is the research background and basic assumption of our research.

Taylor's scientific management theory emphasizes that the best scientific management should be based on clearly defined laws, regulations, and principles [3]. Many theories and solutions are proposed under a certain environment which means that the organization's management and business under a planned and controlled situation. Similarly, the process of IS development (ISD) is also needed to be rationally planned and controlled which is the most basic assumption [4]. The information systems are developed to improve the operational performance of organizations but also used to

© IFIP International Federation for Information Processing 2021
Published by Springer Nature Switzerland AG 2021
L. M. Camarinha-Matos et al. (Eds.): DoCEIS 2021, IFIP AICT 626, pp. 151–160, 2021.
https://doi.org/10.1007/978-3-030-78288-7_15

fix employees' operation processes, to ensure that the business can be controllable, predictable, and planned. So, the traditional organization and business management, as well as the ISD, are all based on a certain and controllable situation.

The operation of the largest and most successful business organizations in the world is supported by ERP (Enterprise resource planning) systems [5, 6]. ERP systems are the main information system in organizations. As the name of ERP contains the word planning, it's been developed under a planned and controlled situation leading to its hard to solve the uncertainty. However, when uncertainty occurs, it mainly needs robust communication and teamwork of people that bring together diverse perspectives, teams and organizations can respond adequately to uncertainty [7]. So, the information system is useless when facing uncertainty, instead, a large amount of uncertainty mainly depends on interaction and collaboration between people to handle.

This phenomenon that the people don't use the formal modes of the organization which called legitimate system (i.e., a pattern of common recognition among members of an organization) to handle the business of the organization, but use other informed ways which organization did not make any provision and acknowledge to handle business, is called Shadow systems [8]. In today's digital age, legitimate systems are mainly reflected in various business systems in enterprises, carried the fixed business process and organization's policies. But the form of the shadow system has not yet been recognized by everyone. Some scholars use the new term "*shadow IT*" [9] to explain this phenomenon that the business departments and users independently implement their solutions outside of the organization's IT service [9] (e.g., Excel, database, cloud services, mobile devices, and so on).

However, the authors think that Shadow IT is just one type of representation from the perspective of IT governance. The social activities like robust communication and teamwork of people to solve the uncertainty business which enterprise's business system cannot are another representation of shadow system under uncertainty assumption. So, this paper wants to explain under the uncertainty assumption, what are the obstacles of human-system interaction? what is the appearance of the shadow system brought by these obstacles? And how do we analyze and use this type of shadow system? Specifically, we seek to address the following research questions:

(a) ***What representation of the shadow system brought by human-system interaction's obstacles under uncertainty?***
(b) ***How to design the ideal framework of the human-system interaction under uncertainty to solve the obstacles?***

In addressing these research questions, the aim of our study is twofold. First, we interpret the representation of the shadow system under uncertainty, enrich the connotation of the shadow system. Secondly, in addition to academic significance, our research also aims to provide a way to solve the obstacles of human-system interaction under uncertainty.

The paper is organized as follows. The first section has established our motivation and the research questions. In the second section, we introduce the relationship between our research and this conference's theme "A*rtificial Intelligence Application*". In the third section, we review the relevant literature about our research perspective about shadow system, and emphasis the research significance. The fourth section analyzes the shadow system under uncertainty. The fifth section of this paper presents the obstacles of human-system interaction. In the sixth section, the authors design the feedback and enabling cycle between the shadow system and the legitimate system under an idealized state. The seventh section is the conclusion and research challenge. And the last section is the future work.

2 Relation to Applying AI

AI refers to a machine that imitates human intelligence, including perception, reasoning, learning, interaction, etc. [10], which can be broadly defined as an intelligent system with the ability to think and learn [11]. The development of AI technology has brought opportunities for enterprises to handle VUCA. For example, the decision-making process is characterized by uncertainty, complexity, and ambiguity [12]. The big data processing and analysis capabilities of AI can expand human cognition when dealing with complexity, and AI's anomaly detection and sentiment analysis capabilities can help humans deal with uncertainties and ambiguities. [13].

Meanwhile, the growing consensus that human intelligence and artificial intelligence are complementary has led to Human-AI hybrid systems, which emphasizes that when we focus on the ability of AI, we cannot ignore the importance of human wisdom. This paper regards the social discussion of employees when facing uncertainty as one type of shadow system. So, the social data is also one representation of the shadow system, to which we need to pay attention. However, these social data contain a lot of human wisdom, experience, or others, needing us to mine them by AI technology.

The authors think that when we discuss the application of AI, we need to first determine an application scenario and a specific problem in this scenario. Secondly, we must not ignore human beings, because the current application of AI must be based on Human-AI hybrid systems [14]. Third, we need to conduct an "idealized design" [15], meaning not to focus on near-term obstacles but to think big without feeling constrained by the status quo [16].

Following these three steps mentioned above, firstly this paper focuses on the shadow system problem generated by human-system interaction under uncertainty. Secondly, social data as one type of representation of the shadow system under uncertainty, which contains human's wisdom needs to be mined by AI. Finally, we design the feedback and enabling cycle between the shadow system and the legitimate system under the ideal state.

3 Literature Review

Shadow system is a phenomenon, which means that the people don't use the formal modes to handle the business, but use other informed ways which organization did not make any provision and acknowledge to handle business [8]. The formal model called legitimate system means it gets common recognition among members of an organization [8]. The shadow system is generated automatically after the legitimate system is set up. Because legitimate systems are not 100% perfect, the organization needs to fill gaps in formal structures to cope with tasks or to substitute neglected formal structures [17]. Therefore, when discussing shadow systems, legitimate systems must be considered.

In the current published literature, the current definition of the shadow system has not yet been unified by scholars. Some scholars think many terms that have similar meanings to the shadow system, like shadow IT, feral systems, workarounds system, etc. Among them, the most popular term is "shadow IT", which refers to the "information technology (IT) for business processes is not only provided by the IT department of the organization. Business departments and users independently implement their solutions outside of the organization's IT service management." [9].

The phenomenon of the shadow system needs to be paid attention to by scholars and business managers. Because the shadow system has many benefits and many threats. The benefits of the shadow system to the organization mainly around the creativity, innovation, and stability and order brought by the shadow system [18]. Because the shadow system can help to overcome the shortcomings of the legitimate system [18] and improve the organization's innovation ability and the speed of change. [17] At the same time, the shadow system can help practitioners and researchers improve enterprise systems [19]. However, the shadow system also has a lot of threats. For example, the existence of the shadow system weakens the enterprise's IT governance [20], maybe even overthrew the legitimate system [19]. The shadow system is also thought to violate the compliance rules [21], increasing security risks [22], and so on.

The concept of the shadow system was first proposed in the field of organization management [8]. Due to its covert characteristics, it is not easy to be discovered and managed by managers. So, with the development of information technology, all sorts of IT products used by people let shadow system can be seen digitally. So, the authors think shadow IT is just a digital representation of the shadow system.

As we can see, the existing literature mainly focuses on the shadow system from the perspective of IT, which regards shadow system as an information system [17] or others. However, the authors think the shadow system represents one organization's phenomenon, which has many interpretations. The authors think that under the current uncertainty assumption, the phenomenon of the shadow system will become more and more prominent, and we need more interpretation.

4 Shadow System Under Uncertainty

Under the current uncertain environment, represented by uncertain business, cross-boundary business, innovation business, and emergent businesses, and so on becoming the main part of the organization's daily business. Due to the enterprise's business systems are developed to handle certain business under a planned and controlled situation, leading to its hard to solve the uncertainty business. So, a large number of uncertain businesses mainly rely on people to solve.

About causes of uncertainty, there are two reasons. One is due to lacking knowledge [23], the other is due to the complexity of the system [4, 23]. So, when facing uncertainty, people need to collaborate, with robust communication and teamwork that bring together diverse perspectives [7] and sharing knowledge to identify and handle uncertainty [2]. Therefore, the author thinks that the cause of the shadow system generation is the flexibility of the business system not well when facing the uncertain business. And the main way for people to handle business is interaction and discussion, with forms about offline face-to-face discussion, online social software discussion, etc. Hence, social interaction is one obvious representation of the shadow system under uncertainty.

As shown in Fig. 1 below, facing uncertainty, business systems are becoming less and less valuable, and people are getting busier and busier. The shadow system, which stands by social interaction becomes the main way for employees to quickly develop solutions to meet emergency needs.

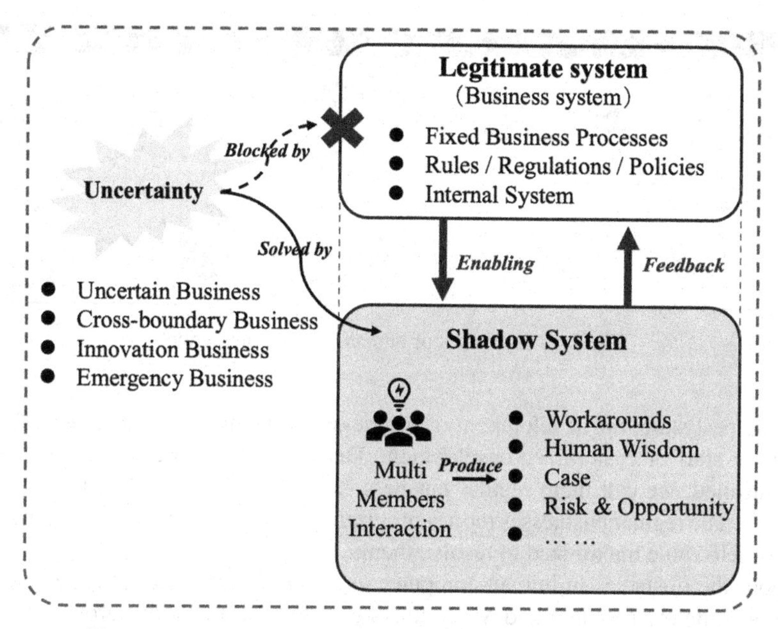

Fig. 1. The relationship between uncertainty and shadow system

According to Clark [24], "much of what matters about human intelligence is hidden not in the brain, nor the technology, but in the complex and iterated interactions and collaborations between the two". So, the shadow system is a treasure for the organization. As shown in Fig. 1 above, a large number of workarounds, human wisdom, human experience, case, risk, and opportunity will be retained in the shadow system after the uncertain events are solved by people. Consequently, the authors think the enterprise needs to utilize the treasure come from the shadow system to improve the flexibility of the business system under uncertainty. As shown in Fig. 1 above, this paper mainly focuses on the enabling and feedback between the shadow system and the legitimate system.

Through the above description, the authors propose the representation of the shadow system under uncertainty is social interaction. And the reason is that the business system is useless when facing uncertain business. To explore the reality in the enterprise, we have conducted several interviews, which we will discuss in the next section.

5 Human-System Interaction Obstacle

This section mainly analyzes the obstacles between the employees and the business systems. Employees represent the shadow system, and the business system represents the legitimate system. We have conducted several interviews with one company's employees and Beijing Jiaotong University's MBA students. And the authors divide three states of human-system interaction, as shown in Fig. 2 below.

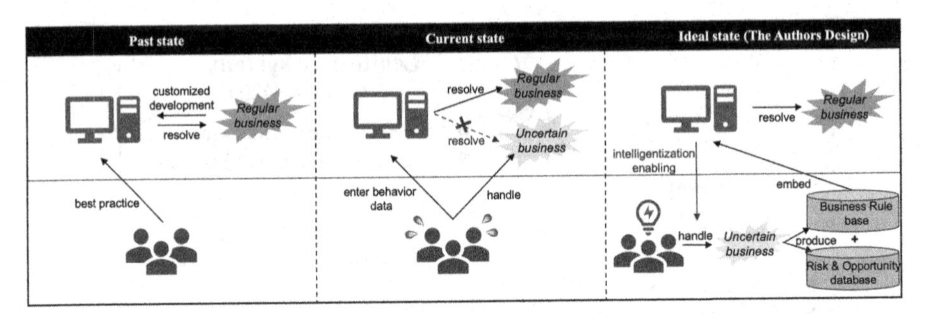

Fig. 2. Three states of human-system interaction

In the past state, the development of business systems mainly comes from the best practice of staff or customized development. Due to these businesses can be planned and controlled, we call them regular business, which the business system can handle efficiently. The regular businesses represent certainty which business information system can play self-value maximized to resolve them.

About the obstacles in human-computer interaction in the current state, we interviewed a company manager and MBA students in the form of focus groups. We have compiled the following two representative interview data from numerous interview data. The manager of the enterprise we interviewed said:

"Our company has 12 people in total, but we have specially arranged a colleague to enter data into our BCP system (The business system) regularly because the headquarters will review our work through this system. This system has become a burden on our work, rather than helping us."

Similarly, an MBA student said:

"WeChat and QQ (Both Chinese social APP) have become my main way to handle my daily work in my company. Many uncertain events require me to discuss with different apartment colleagues or call other company employees by different social apps."

Under uncertainty, the uncertain businesses are mainly solved by employees, while business systems are becoming more and more useless. Moreover, to manage and control businesses, it needs employees to input data in the information system which they handle offline, to guarantee the data recorded by the information system can truly reflect the real business situation. Hence, employees do not only deal with business, they need to take extra time to enter data, which increases the huge workload. According to our data analysis of interviews, we find a large number of Chinese enterprises are in this stage now.

To solve this obstacle, our "idealized design" aims to extract the knowledge, which contains workarounds, human wisdom, employees' experience, and so on in the shadow system as mentioned in Fig. 1. And then, designing this knowledge as some databases or microservices embedding into the business system, to improve the flexibility and intelligence of the business system, to better-enabling frontline employees. The details we will introduce in the next section.

6 Human-System Interaction Obstacle

Based on the analysis of obstacles in the human-system interaction in Sect. 5, this part aims to propose a conceptual framework of feedback and empowerment between shadow system and legitimate system, As shown in Fig. 3 below.

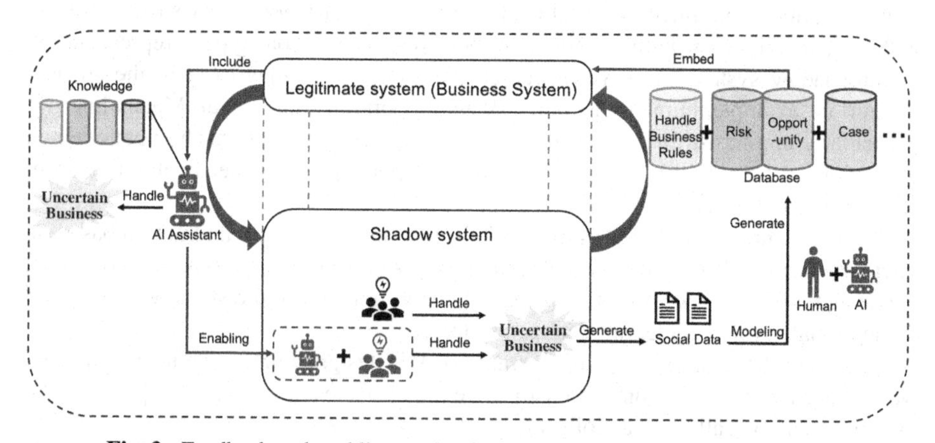

Fig. 3. Feedback and enabling cycle of shadow system and legitimate system

According to the introduction of shadow system under uncertainty in part 4 above, and empirical analysis in part 5, we can see that human's social data among people can be regarded as one representation of shadow system. However, the authors emphasize again that social data refers to the interactive data that employees aim to handle uncertain businesses that an enterprise's business system (legitimate system) cannot handle.

The authors think that social interaction data contains human wisdom, human experience, risk, opportunity. Because people's discussion and communication are the processes of transforming uncertainty into definite risks or opportunities, and at the same time, they will discuss some solutions to resolve uncertain events. Therefore, through the analysis and modeling of social interaction data, we can transfer the neglected social data into all kinds of databases and microservices, as shown in Fig. 3.

And we can embed these databases and microservices into the business system to improve the flexibility and intelligence of the business system. The reason we design databases and microservices is organizations are looking to expand the capabilities of their systems by integrating new modules, or addons, but not spend a lot of manpower and money to develop new information systems [25]. So, our design is suited for the current information system development line.

After completing the feedback from the shadow system to the legitimate system, we also need to pay attention to the enabling of the business system to frontline employees. In the process of enabling frontline employees, we are based on the perspective of human-AI collaboration. We must admit that when an enterprise encounters uncertain events in the future, it still needs employees to solve the problem. But through our design, the role of the information system is displayed when the same uncertainty event occurs. For example, the rules database is designed to record the handle ways from employees, when the same event occurs, AI assistant can replace people to resolve. However, it can also provide reference to the processing of similar events.

7 Conclusion and Research Challenge

This paper firstly introduces the relationship between uncertainty and the shadow system in the organization. The authors think that social interaction is one type of representation of the shadow system. And we discussed the content that may exist in the shadow system, for example, human wisdom, risk and opportunity, and so on. Meanwhile, we particularly emphasize that under the current uncertain assumption, the phenomenon of shadow systems will become more and more popular, and it needs attention from scholars and enterprise managers.

Then the authors analyzed a type of obstacle in human-system interaction based on interviews with MBA students and one company's manager. For solving this obstacle, we design a framework about feedback and enabling between the shadow system and the legitimate system under an idealized state.

Although the authors' conceptual framework is designed under the idealized state, we still need to pay attention and try to solve the obstacles in our research process. We mainly face two challenges as follows:

- The degree of CEO attention. When the authors serve as consultants for several cooperative enterprises, we emphasize that CEOs should pay attention to the social data of employees. We found that one enterprise CEO attaches great importance to social data and has developed timely social functions in their business system. However, he does not know how to use the data, and the employees are not required to use it compulsorily, resulting in timely social functions that not be used persistently. And some CEOs believe that social data is not very useful, and believe that employees only need to follow business rules and complete business through legitimate systems to achieve their goals. However, the CEO should play the main role and lead the enterprise to control VUCA [2, 16]. Hence, the obstacles of the CEO's understanding and acceptance of the shadow system need to be further research.
- Social data privacy issues. Currently, many social apps as one public social software have unclear boundaries between public and private data. At the same time, many people believe that social data is their privacy and are unwilling to share it. In the

focus group interview process, we asked MBA students to review their social data about handling business and let them voluntarily share it in class. MBA students excited found their social data contain many solutions they used to solve uncertain events, and they all began to imagine how to use them in the future.

8 Future Work

In the current research, the data we mainly analyze comes from WeChat APP. We let MBA students voluntarily contribute social data which comes from the discussion in their daily work. To handle the obstacles mentioned above in future challenges, the next phase work of our research is to develop a simulation platform for a case enterprise. With the help of a simulation platform to implement our ideal design framework of feedback and empowerment between shadow system and legitimate system. There are two main reasons:

- The real information systems and business of the enterprise are complex, cannot be easily tested, and implement our ideal design framework. And it is hard for CEO to recognize our ideal design and implement it when they do not see actual results. So, through the development of a simulation platform, which is convenient for us to experiment. Meanwhile, allows the CEO to visually see our experiment results.
- Due to the privacy of social data and the inseparability of data related to private life and business discussions, it is difficult to collect useful data. By designing communication function in the virtual simulation platform, when multiple people are playing games together, facing the uncertain events needs to make decisions, players from different departments can set up discussion groups, and social data will be collected by the platform automatically.

Acknowledgments. Funding for this research was provided by the Fundamental Research Funds for the Central Universities (2021YJS050)

References

1. Bennett, N., Lemoine, G.J.: What a difference a word makes: understanding threats to performance in a VUCA world. Bus. Horiz. **57**, 311–317 (2014)
2. Millar, C.C.J.M., Groth, O., Mahon, J.F.: Management innovation in a VUCA world: challenges and recommendations. Calif. Manage Rev. **61**(1), 5–14 (2018)
3. Taylor, F.W.: The Principle of Scientific Management. Harper Brothers, New York (1911)
4. Benbya, H., Nan, N., Tanriverdi, H., Yoo, Y.: Complexity and information systems research in the emerging digital world. MIS Q. **44**(1), 1–17 (2020)
5. Liang, H., Saraf, N., Hu, Q., Xue, Y.: Assimilation of enterprise systems: the effect of institutional pressures and the mediating role of top management. MIS Q. **31**(1), 59–87 (2007)
6. Morris, M.G., Venkatesh, V.: Job characteristics and job satisfaction: understanding the role of enterprise resource planning system implementation. MIS Q. **34**(1), 143–161 (2010)

7. Baran, B.E., Woznyj, H.M.: Managing VUCA: the human dynamics of agility. Organ. Dyn. (2020). https://doi.org/10.1016/j.orgdyn.2020.100787
8. Stacey, R.: Complexity and Creativity in organizations. Berrettkoehler, SanFrancisco, CA (1996)
9. Zimmermann, S., Rentrop, C., Felden, C.: Managing shadow IT instances–a method to control autonomous IT solutions in the business departments. In: Twentieth Americas Conference on Information Systems. Savannah (2014)
10. Rai, A., Constantinides, P., Sarker, S.: Editor's comments: next-generation digital platforms: toward human–AI hybrids. MIS Q. **43**(1), iii–ix (2019)
11. Russell, S., Norvig, P.: Artificial Intelligence: A Modern Approach, 3rd edn. Pearson (2015)
12. Choo, C.W.: Towards an information model of organizations. Cana. J. Inform. Sci. **16**(3), 32–62 (1991)
13. Jarrahi, M.H.: Artificial intelligence and the future of work: human-AI symbiosis in organizational decision making. Bus. Horiz. **61**(4), 577–586 (2018)
14. Aleksander, I.: Partners of humans: a realistic assessment of the role of robots in the foreseeable future. J. Inf. Technol. **32**(1), 1–9 (2017)
15. Ackoff, R.L., Magidson, J., Addison, H.: Idealized Design. FT Press (2006)
16. Schoemaker, P.J.H., Sohvi, H., David, T.: Innovation, dynamic capabilities, and leadership. Calif. Manage. Rev. **61**(1), 15–42 (2018)
17. Behrens, S., Sedera, W.: Why do shadow systems exist after an ERP implementation? lessons from a case study. In: The 8th Pacific Asia Conference on Information Systems, pp. 1712–1726. Shanghai, China (2004)
18. Behrens, S.: Shadow systems: the good, the bad and the ugly. Commun. ACM **52**(2), 124–129 (2009)
19. Jones, D., Behrens, S., Jamieson, K., Tansley, E.: The rise and fall of a shadow system: lessons for enterprise system implementation. ACIS (2004)
20. Huber, M., Zimmermann, S., Rentrop, C., Felden, C.: The influence of shadow IT systems on enterprise architecture management concerns. In: Themistocleous, M., Morabito, V. (eds.) EMCIS 2017. LNBIP, vol. 299, pp. 461–477. Springer, Cham (2017). https://doi.org/10.1007/978-3-319-65930-5_37
21. Panko, R.R.: Spreadsheets and Sarbanes-Oxley: regulations, risks, and control frameworks. Commun. Assoc. Inf. Syst. **17**, 647–676 (2006)
22. Silic M, Back.: A shadow IT – a view from behind the curtain. Comput. Secur. **45**, 274–283 (2014)
23. Brugnach, M., Pahl-Wostl, C., Lindenschmidt, K.E., Janssen, J., Gaber, N.N.: Complexity and uncertainty: rethinking the modelling activity. Dev. Integr. Environ. Asses. **3**(08), 49–68 (2008)
24. Clark, A.: Mindware: An Introduction to the Philosophy of Cognitive Science. Oxford University Press, New York (2001)
25. Beatty, R.C., Williams, C.D.: ERP ii: best practices for successfully implementing an ERP upgrade. Commun. ACM **49**(3), 105–109 (2006)

A New Challenge for Machine Ethics Regarding Decision-Making in Manufacturing Systems

Esmaeil Kondori(✉) and Rui Neves-Silva

School of Science and Technology, NOVA University of Lisbon, 2829-516 Caparica, Portugal
kondori@campus.fct.unl.pt, rns@fct.unl.pt

Abstract. In order to deal with increasingly complex manufacturing systems, we need to make sophisticated decisions. A new challenge emerges when dealing with presenting a new decision – making model merged by an off-line (production data including; staffs, machinery, materials) and on-line (sensors, actuators) data to render a shared responsibility of decision´s consequences between machine and human through giving weight to the taken decisions. Undoubtedly, to make an accurate fair prediction, this presented model should follow the ethical rules. However, the mostly past research works about relationship between machine and ethics mainly have focused on human and his responsibility in applying of technology and only humans have engaged in ethical issues. In light of the digital era especially applying AI and Machine learning, necessarily a new approach should be applied to the interplay between the machine, ethics, and human by adding an ethical dimension to those machines which involve with decision making.

Keywords: Sliding decision - making · Machine ethics · Smart manufacturing systems · Artificial intelligence

1 Introduction

At the early stage of the fourth industrial revolution, 'Industrie 4.0', machines (through current paper machine means ordinary physical machines, autonomous robots, as well as purely algorithmic systems) increasingly penetrate many aspects of our routine life, and gradually are finding their key positions especially in manufacturing systems by making intelligent interactions between physical and autonomous components and expected to be a growing factor in the future superiorities [1]. This means in the age of machines [2], despite all warnings, the interaction between human and machine is entering in the new environment, and systems, with the focus on manufacturing systems, will experience a new integration of humans - automation model via diverse elements such as informatics, robotics, mobile devices and sensors [3]. Simultaneously, the concerns connected to ethical decision-making, which has been challenging issues, significantly has drawn both public and experts' attention [4, 5]. Since many aspects of machines´ behavior are ethically relevant [6], so in this field, most of attempts have focused, how to design, employ, and then to evaluate a machine which could act ethically in its performances and also in relation with other agents and humans with minimum cause harm [7].

© IFIP International Federation for Information Processing 2021
Published by Springer Nature Switzerland AG 2021
L. M. Camarinha-Matos et al. (Eds.): DoCEIS 2021, IFIP AICT 626, pp. 161–172, 2021.
https://doi.org/10.1007/978-3-030-78288-7_16

Despite serious warnings from eminent thinkers about the risk of applying these technologies (because applying automating ethical decision-making operates the risk of taking humans entirely out of the ethical decision-making process), seemingly humans inevitably have been convicted to employ these complex technologies, however, these warnings stand in contrast to the current innovation of technologies [8]. Till now, several works have been executed on machines through complex manufacturing systems [9] and exploring the notions of the use of them, but ethic of machine is still under study. As a pioneer, Kantian [10] proposed his ethical theory by putting the "ethic" into ethical machines.

Dealing with this issue is so crucial, because by clarifying the aspects of machine ethics and then ethical decision making, in a calculated fair approach, we can share the responsibility between human and machine during decision process.

The rest of this paper is structured as follows. Section 2 renders the relationship between our work and the scope of the conference. Section 3 discusses about autonomy and its role in ethical decision making, its importance, and justification of used terminology throughout the paper. Section 3 presents a framework regarding machine ethics, its important, and main challenges in front of it. Section 4 talks about machine responsibility and type of responsibilities. Section 5 present the research approach to this work and Sect. 6 presents conclusion.

2 Relationship to Technological Innovation for Applied AI Systems

Human´s decision situations have been studied by several research communities such as artificial intelligence, psychology, cognitive science, and decision science [11]. As a pioneer of the field of decision support systems, Herbert Simon made key contributions to enhance our understanding of the decision-making process. He suggested for the first time that the decision-making model of human beings be based on three phases: (1) Intelligence phase, (2) Design phase, and (3) Choice phase [12]. On the other hand, some efforts from other authors led to various models which have been developed to simulate decision behaviors, where [13] classified them into three major categories including: (1) economical approach, (2) psychological approach, and (3) synthetic engineering-based approach.

Among them, some research concentrated simulation-supported planning of manufacturing systems. But this sort of simulation (manufacturing processes) is mainly focused on machinery, facilities and the material which flow into production line [13, 14]. The main weak point of these efforts is that they only consider an operation-based approach [11]. In other words, solely the operative functions are modelled with no attention (or minimum attention) to the role of the staffs´ decisions. In fact, by neglecting the influence of human decision making in manufacturing operations, it changes its role to a passive one [14, 15].

Nowadays, in accordance with emerging new manufacturing paradigm, staffs' decisions at shop floor level are gradually finding its actual position and considered as an active component during decision situations. Considering the human in an active role [16], there is a huge insight gain about decisions and leads the process towards a measured action as a final target. To satisfy this, we must support the decision situations by calculated prediction, extracted knowledge, and different scenarios about handling the manufacturing systems.

In this way, by merging both past (off-line) and real-time (on-line) data collected by embedded sensors from manufacturing systems [17, 18]. Getting support from digital twins as a powerful solution which paves the way into a high-level prediction of future events, as a testbed of adopting decision, our machine (AI core) will be fed by collected data then can be trained.

Aligning with the scope of the conference, in this work we are going to propose a decision-making model with the capability of sharing the responsibility of taken decisions ethically. This model will benefit digital twins in order to provide real – time (on-line) data through the installed sensors and at the same time will be supported by past (off-line) data collected from manufacturing system, e.g., production data including staffs, machinery, materials ... to balance the responsibility of decision´s consequences between machine and human. In fact, the proposed model through this work is an AI-based decision model as it benefits merged collected data in order to make prediction.

Developing this notion, allows us to do virtual what-if experiments before we try things out for real [14].

3 Autonomy Role in Ethical Decision Making

Autonomy is a vital structure in defining human-machine interaction and broadly changes through machine platforms. Levels of machine autonomy, ranging from teleoperation to fully autonomous systems (e.g. in a fully advanced manufacturing system), have affect the way in which humans and machine interact with each another [19].

According to one of the most famous definition, a machine is a task-oriented device which uses sensors and other information, to be able to physically change its environment, move, and have both the energy and capability to autonomously take decision regarding how to carry out its tasks. In fact, one pivotal characteristic of an autonomous machine is the ability to reply properly to a wide range of situations but based on some defined ethical principles. The main sign of such an ethical agent is demonstrating the autonomy (in different levels as mentioned) in decision making process. Regarding industrial systems, it is expected that future manufacturing systems will still count on collaborations between humans and machine albeit in totally renewed arrangements and in higher levels of autonomy to improve their competitive advantage in order to operate without external interventions [3, 6].

A key component in this new paradigm will be intelligent autonomy and fortified human-machine collaboration.

Entering digital era, and applying new independent advanced machines, many ethical issues are raised because of capability of these machines, in taking independent decision and acting.

However, the most important bottleneck we usually encounter is ethical issues related to design as well as to run of such systems. Whether in practice or in theory, there are many difficulties in front of attributing ethical decision making to machines independently of human intention or will. However, significant improvement in the intelligent automation is promising that in the near future autonomous small-scale machines and safe large-scale machines will be applied in a structured collaboration framework with humans as part of advanced manufacturing systems [6, 20].

4 What is Machine Ethics?

Nowadays, emerging field of machine ethics has attracted a lot of attentions [10] and many believe, assigning control over vital decisions to machines requires machines do actions in an appropriate ethical way [21].

The destination of machine ethics might be one of the following argued expressions including capability to design machines which are eligible as "artificial moral agents" [22]; which can follow ethical rules; which can make ethical decision; and which have "an ethical aspect [23]. On top of this issue, a fundamental question that must be answered is how a machine achieves at its ethical conclusions during ethical decision-making process [6]. Regarding this and during decision process, two distinctive approaches have been considered: 'top-down' and 'bottom-up' methods [24]. Top-down approach assumes humans have collected adequate insight on a specific subject so decision making algorithms will be codified by the machine programmer to generate the predictable results: in fact, through this approach, the machine is trained with accordance what a human perceives as an ethical behaviour, which one needs to be determined and the appropriate time to be applied. According to bottom-up approach, the machine designer builds an open-ended system that is capable to gather needed data from its surroundings, to be able to anticipate the outputs of its measures, to opt from among existing alternatives and, more crucially, has the ability to learn from its prior experiences [24].

The final goal of machine ethics, (we believe and, in the following), is that a machine can apply an ideal ethical principle or set of principles [25] to be able to create a shared responsibility of decision´s consequences with human.

4.1 Why Machine Ethic is Important?

Designing then building ethical machines is a practicable, not a theoretical attempt. Acting to design, will ensure that growingly autonomous machines will not a reason of harm to humans and other entities qualified of ethical consideration [26]. Autonomous machines are increasingly taking over human tasks in any levels of decision process in manufacturing systems, while in the beginning, machines were replaced with workers only in assembly lines and workshop floors to carry out uncomplicated and restricted assignments.

With the advent of new technologies especially those which were employed in manufacturing systems, not only simple jobs that were previously carried out purely by human, but complicated ones gradually are being transferred to machines and robots. Due to this notion, Picard [27] says, "the greater the freedom of a machine, the more it will need moral standards".

For this reason, recently *Machine Ethics* have drawn much attentions and many researchers have been showing a great interest to this issue.

As discussed, in light of digital era, machines in a serious way and increasingly have imposed themselves to human in various domains, from agriculture to industry. Through the interactions, machines take over many types of decisions and activities which before performed by humans. Therefore, by replacing humans with machines, performing more interactions between this combination, meaningfully will decrease human control over decisions and from another side will lead to an increased number of decisions which are made by machines.

In this sense, the essence of ethics plays a crucial role in decision making to consider substantial problems in sharing of responsibility [28] between machine and human. Clearly, the consequences of taken decisions should reduce the possibility of negative results for humans and/or to mitigate the negative effects machines can cause [21].

Coming back to the topic, why the field of machine ethics important? The following reasons can be brought to answer this question.

First, to abandon this aspect of machine could have serious negative consequences through the decision process especially in manufacturing systems during human – machine interactions. Second, as previously discussed, the main concern is whether these machines will demonstrate ethical behaviour or not. So, the future of machine ethics, especially AI may be at risk [25]. An integral concern connected to AI is different as the huge amount of data must be applied to train AI algorithms. In fact, "AI is fueled by data;" hence, it encounters ethical challenges related to data collection, including consent, IP, and privacy [29], and especially GDPR (General Data Protection Regulation).

4.2 Challenges in Front of Machine Ethics

As prior argued, with the advent of new field of machine ethics, the fundamental concern is how to be added an ethical aspect to the machines [25].

By entering to the era of the fourth industrial revolution 'Industry 4.0', this concern accelerated as companies try to digitalize the industrial processes, especially those that are driven by AI and intelligent machine learning to make efficient the manufacturing systems, because according to [30], automating ethical decision-making can situate a direct risk to a user's ethical autonomy.

Due to the traditional mindset in manufacturing systems, there is a historic mistrust proximity to machine on the shop floor among industrial staffs and they psychologically feel a strong segregation in this relation. This segregation has made a big problem in human – machine collaborations and caused to reduce workflow efficiency [31].

In short, as [32] says, the potential downsides to machine ethics include technical safety, transparency and privacy, fundamental values, bias in data, training sets, unemployment / lack of purpose & meaning, growing social unfairness, environmental effects, automating ethics, human rights, effects on the human spirit and etc. As discussed in *Introduction* sector, ethic of machine is still under study. But as an initial definition, the concept of ethics is to bear the consequences of taken decisions in order to maximize the benefits and minimize the risks to a society (manufacturing system) uses the machine. However, it is still a challenging issue to ethical theory to be applied in the mentioned field.

5 Can Machines Be Responsible?

One of the fundamental subjects that must be considered and find a transparent answer for is human-machine interactions in manufacturing systems, in which concerns are growing; "When a machine makes mistakes, who is responsible?' How can we share the responsibility in human-machine model?

Since in near future machines, according to their capacity, they will be assigned to undertake more tasks especially those are related to human's safety, health, and his live, therefore human will have to make confidence whether those are appropriately following ethical principles and also consider if there is a risk that could cause harm.

In this regard, namely, to be able to propose a reliable model that can bring us a solution which can solve aforementioned problem, we need to develop new concept based on dynamic models that sensitively reacts to any changes, even a minor, just like the real thing is something new, a digital twin can take this responsibility.

To have accurate predictions or to make an accurate estimation as the basis of robust decision-making process during a manufacturing system, accessibility to a timely real data from real system is crucial. In fact, the models need to be fed by real – time data to be able to help us in making accurate predictions. Since all discussed decision-making models benefiting from static models, consequently it is not expected to access to exact predictions. In this regard, we need to detect the fundamental KPIs, those deeply effect on our proposed decision model (sliding decision making model) through a manufacturing system.

Clearly, by employing digital twins, as a fashion method, this work tries to overcome this pitfall.

In the meantime, a few researchers [33] claim that, in the predictable future of technology, "machines will take zero responsibility" for their actions, and humans will be the ultimate responsible for any outcome.

As earlier discussed, some academic reports, for instance [34] believe that it would be threatening if be given a full responsibility to machines for their actions, as they might go out of control even from the programmers [6].

To answer this issue, two prevalent approaches about a machine's ethics responsibility should be addressed: classical approach and pragmatic approach.

Based on classical approach there is no responsibility to machines for the actions under any situation. This approach views them as mechanical facilities or servants. But in contrast, pragmatic approach assumes 'artificial ethics' can be attributed to machines and then machines can be viewed as responsible for their decisions and actions [35].

5.1 Types of Human Ethical Responsibility, Can be Extended to Machines?

To be able to share ethical responsibility through decision making process in any situation including manufacturing systems between human and machine, firstly we need to know types of responsibilities which are toward human and secondly, whether such types of responsibilities can be extended to machines. Therefore, according to [36], human ethical responsibility can be split into three types: causal responsibility, role responsibility, and liability responsibility.

In causal responsibility, an individual will be responsible for everything caused by him/her, namely his/her actions. In role responsibility, based on a person's role in a certain area, in short, the task is the responsibility. But liability responsibility identifies who is eligible to be "admired or blamed" for especial measures or conclusions. According to [35], causal responsibility can be dedicated to non-humans e.g., machines.

Since machines come in different varieties then not all types have the ability to bear responsibilities, in fact taking responsibility among them directly depends on how autonomous they are. For example, a thoroughly advanced autonomous machine in a production line can be considered to bear some causal responsibility as it has ability to make decision that leads to outputs in an extensive range of environments while the responsibility of a machine with low autonomy, typically is on the human that controls it [6]. In the meantime, the autonomy level of machine that comes from its training rate, and already defined related manufacturing systems' KPIs, then machine´s responsibility during decision process can be determined. In other word, when actions are carried out autonomously by a machine, the consequences of the actions are assessed by the AI-based system. In this regard, through a human - machine interaction, to be able to share the accurate responsibility, first the limitations of a human and the machine should be understood.

Usually under certain conditions, human makes poor predictions. Humans often overweight crucial information and are careless for statistical properties. Machines often show better outcomes than humans in complex interactions where there are different indicators, especially dealing with big data. Hence, based on our proposed decision-making model, obviously it is expected to have a more responsive machine in the aforementioned situations. Using big data, the machine training rate will increase, and it means we will have a machine with a high-level autonomy. As we face more growing dimensions of interaction, the capability of a human to make an accurate prediction will diminish, especially comparison to machines, and it means machine should bear more responsibility than before.

6 Research Approach

Since this paper is a part of a PhD thesis, we expect at the end of this work, combining off-line and on-line data collected during our research, then training the machine (AI core), and applying the collected data in a real case study in a manufacturing system, we can develop our model and propose a decision-making model that ethically balance the responsibility through human – machine interaction.

Regarding to the thesis topic, we are going to answer to a part of thesis main research question in this work.

How to model a decision-making process within a manufacturing system that capable to balance then share a reasoned ethical responsibility between human and machine?

It was expected to be discussed the results of case study, but as this model is in its early development stage, naturally it is being discussed theoretically, however, as one our main target, we are going to apply this model in the next phase of its development on a real case study in a manufacturing system. Thus, we already have put this part as the pillar of our PhD work that will be considered.

6.1 Sliding Decision Making Model

In this section, we would like to propose sliding decision making as a possible solution. As said, solely having the capacity for ethical performing never guarantee ethically aligned decision making. In this regard, a machine which is trained by both off-line (production data including staffs, machinery, materials) and on-line (installed sensors and actuators) accurate data within a manufacturing system can bring us a strong insight in the modeling of ethical-based decision making.

Dealing with the suggested ethical decision-making model, some steps and features need to be considered. We also will debate how these features of autonomy and choice could have consequences for attributing ethical responsibility to machines.

To be able to enrich our database (by collecting data from the mentioned sources) and in order to train our machine, a 6-stage process is suggested as following:

1 Collecting data from installed sensors to provide real-time data.
2 Collecting data from multi off-line sources, e.g. production line, staffs, equipment, materials, … to provide past data.
3 Analyzing the collected data by categorizing and integrating.
4 Extracting the patterns according to the collected data from its experience.
5 Enriching the database by gathering huge (big) data and training our machine (AI core) via collected data.
6 Making decision aligned with ethical principles for doing appropriate prediction.

Completing aforementioned steps, by applying the past data from off-line sources, and also receiving real-time data from embedded sensors (applying digital twins), now the collected data can be analyzed, and machine is capable to detect and extract the repeated behaviors as the structured patterns based on its experiences to take high-quality decisions that are compatible with ethical principles. Through a manufacturing system, these machines will make gradually complicated and take vital decisions related to humans and other agents, so we need to know whether their decisions are reliable and ethically defensible or not. According to its autonomy level, sliding decision making model must assess the ethical implications of their probable proceedings in order to fair sharing the responsibility within human-machine interplay.

To reach this goal in our sliding decision-making model, quantifying the uncertainty and the risk connected to the decision process is vital in determining the amount of responsibility to be transferred to the machine. Applying already detected manufacturing system´s KPIs and at the same time by merging them with collected data, now the proposed model has this chance to be trained by appropriate data.

However, designing such machines is not so easy. Hence, we will need to keep the machines responsive about the taken measures and decisions, because the proposed decision-making model needs that the taken decisions be transparent and logically be strong.

To reach to what argued above, generally we should perform two actions:

Firstly, enhance machine ethics in a decision process by taking the two following ways to be able to add an ethical aspect of a machine:

a. Enhancing the core behavior of the machine by training and in result, increasing its autonomy level, to follow ethical performances.
b. Enhancing the behavior of decision-makers, who uses the machine.

And in the second measure, we should enhance the behavior of machine or human (decision makers) by taking the following measures:

i) By improving the decisions even at individual level,
ii) By improving how decision-makers fit within ethical decisions, as a broader social system [36].

6.2 Methodology

In terms of making ethical decisions, sliding decision making model will act based on the autonomy level that the machine is codified. In fact, in its specific autonomy level, the trained machine will benefit from freedom degree assigned to that level to make decision. Therefore, the proposed model will evaluate the implications of taken decisions with accordance to the characteristics of that level, its limitations, and its degree of freedom. So, in our discussion about ethically sharing responsibility between human and machine in a manufacturing system, sliding decision model will act to share the responsibility according to the degree of machine autonomy. More transparent, the more formulated and codified by human and his trace is more visible, the lower autonomy level then the weight of responsibility for those probable mistakes lies squarely with the machines' designer or owner. In contrast, if the measures that are conducted by machine have arrived from its experiences during its training by collected data with minimum human interferences ('bottom-up' approach), means higher autonomy level and clearly the burden of responsibility for the probable mistakes and ethical consequences is more obviously on the machine's shoulders.

Training machines and make them more intelligent means, augmentation in their level of autonomy and independencies. With this, practically we increase their capability in decision making and by advances in their autonomy level, machines will follow ethical principles in sharing and balancing the responsibility with human, as they aware of the consequences of their actions, therefore will take responsibility about already taken decisions without human presence. In fact, as humans does not play a significant role in their decision-making consequences, hence in this situation, based on the proposed decision model, machines have to bear more responsibilities during humans-machine interactions.

7 Conclusion

The future of machine ethics debate has a strong dependency on improvements in both technology and ethical theory from human-machine collaboration point of view.

Once autonomous machines can and will be ethical agents that have capability to make ethical decisions by accepting their responsibility in a balanced human-machine interaction. Here, the fundamental question would be: who will be responsible for the actions performed by autonomous ethical machines? In our proposed decision-making model, i.e. sliding decision making model, the responsibility in decision making has a direct correlation with machine autonomy level. According to this model, three scenarios will be raised:

Low-autonomous machines, Semi-autonomous machines, and High-autonomous machines.

In first scenario, as long as machines perform based on designs and programs invented by humans, the designer is responsible for any consequences. In second scenario, things will undoubtedly get complicated. What can be said here is to get rid of this risky situation, strongly recommended to be increased the autonomy level of machine to be changed to high-autonomous machine.

In third and last scenario, a trained machine which learns from its experiences while is capable to boost its own decision making, can bring us a higher autonomy level that with this specification, responsibility may shift entirely from human to the machine while is needless of the direct effect of programs, designer, or humans.

All already discussed aforementioned scenarios come back to the machine autonomy levels and its degree of freedom (by quantifying the uncertainty and the risk involved in the decision-making process) the risk in making decisions by sharing responsibility within human-machine interactions.

At the end as previously argued, since the ethics in this work mean taking responsibility regarding made decisions using obtained autonomy, the proposed decision-making model will deal with already collected merged data in our case study in a manufacturing system, and in correspondence with training rate, the proposed model most likely will act aligned with ethical performances, however this phase is still under study and reaching to this, is one of the main goal in our PhD work.

Acknowledgements. This work benefited from partial support from Fundação para a Ciência e Tecnologia through the program UIDB/00066/2020 (CTS – Center of Technology and Systems).

References

1. Lumbreras, S.: The Limits of Machine Ethics, Institute for Research in Technology, Universidad Pontificia Comillas, Madrid 28001, Spain
2. Veruggio, G., Operto, F., Bekey, G.: Roboethics: social and ethical implications. In: Siciliano, B., Khatib, O. (eds.) Springer Handbook of Robotics, pp. 2135–2160. Springer, Cham (2016). https://doi.org/10.1007/978-3-319-32552-1_80
3. Fletcher, S.R., Webb, P.: Industrial robot ethics: the challenges of closer human collaboration in future manufacturing systems. In: Ferreira, M.I.A., J., Silva Sequeira, Tokhi, M.O., Kadar, E.E., Virk, G.S. (eds.) A World with Robots. ISCASE, vol. 84, pp. 159–169. Springer, Cham (2017). https://doi.org/10.1007/978-3-319-46667-5_12
4. Shi, Y., Sun, C., Li, Q., Cui, L., Yu, H., Miao, C.: A fraud resilient medical insurance claim system. In: AAAI, pp. 4393–4394 (2016)
5. Zheng, Y., Yu, H., Cui, L., Miao, C., Leung, C., Yang, Q.: Smarths: An ai platform

6. Alaieri, F., Vellino, A.: Ethical decision making in robots: autonomy, trust and responsibility. In: Agah, A ., Cabibihan, J.J., Howard A.M., Salichs, M.A., He, H., (eds.) Social Robotics: 8th International Conference, ICSR 2016, Kansas City, MO, USA, November 1-3, 2016 Proceedings Lecture Notes in Computer Science LNCS 9979 Springer International Publishing Cham 159 168 (2016) https://doi.org/10.1007/978-3-319-47437-3
7. Millar, J.: An ethics evaluation tool for automating ethical decision-making in robots and self-driving cars, Carleton University, Ottawa, Canada. Appl. Artif. Intell. **30**(8), 787–809 (2016)
8. J., Torresen: A review of future and ethical perspectives of robotics and AI. Front. Robot. AI **4**, 75 (2018). https://doi.org/10.3389/frobt.2017.00075
9. Luxton, D.D.: Recommendations for the ethical use and design of artificial intelligent care providers. Artif. Intell. Med. **62**(1), 1–10 (2014). https://doi.org/10.1016/j.artmed.2014.06.004
10. Tonkens, R.: A challenge for machine ethics. Minds Mach. **19**(3), 421–438 (2009). https://doi.org/10.1007/s11023-009-9159-1
11. Robinson, S., et al.: Modelling and improving human decision making with simulation. In: Peters, B.A., Smith, J.S., Medeiros, D.J., Rohrer, M.W., (eds.) Winter Simulation Conference (2001)
12. Rizun, N., Taranenko, Y.: Simulation models of human decision-making processes. Manage. Dyn. Knowl. Econ. **2**(2), 241–264 (2014)
13. Kim, N., Joo, J., Rothrock, L., Wysk, R., Son, Young-Jun.: Human behavioral simulation using affordance-based agent model. In: Jacko, J.A. (ed.) HCI 2011. LNCS, vol. 6761, pp. 368–377. Springer, Heidelberg (2011). https://doi.org/10.1007/978-3-642-21602-2_40
14. Zülch, G., Modelling and Simulation of Human Decision-Making in Manufacturing Systems. 1-4244-0501-7/06/. IEEE (2006)
15. Lin, T.: Modelling of Human Decision Making via Direct and Optimization-based Methods for Semi-Autonomous Systems. University of California, Berkeley (2015)
16. Aerts, D., Sassoli de Bianchi, M., Sozzo, S., Veloz, T.: Modeling Human Decision-making: An Overview of the Brussels Quantum Approach (2018). arXiv:1807.11036v1 [q-bio.NC]
17. Szipka, K.: Modelling and Management of Uncertainty in Production Systems - from Measurement to Decision. KTH Royal Institute of Technology Department of Production Engineering Manufacturing and Metrology Systems (2018)
18. Hoc, J.M.: From human – machine interaction to human – machine cooperation. Ergonomics **43**(7), 833–843 (2010). https://doi.org/10.1080/001401300409044
19. Beer, J.M., Fisk, A.D., Rogers, W.A.: Toward a framework for levels of robot autonomy in human-robot interaction. J. Hum. Robot. Interact. **3**(2), 74 (2014). https://doi.org/10.5898/JHRI.3.2.Beer
20. Kavathatzopoulos, I., Asai, R.: Can machines make ethical decisions? In: Papadopoulos, H., Andreou, A.S., Iliadis, L., Maglogiannis, I. (eds.) AIAI 2013. IAICT, vol. 412, pp. 693–699. Springer, Heidelberg (2013). https://doi.org/10.1007/978-3-642-41142-7_70
21. Tolmeijer, S., Kneer, M., Sarasua, C., Christen, M., Bernstein, A.: Implementations in machine ethics: a survey. ACM Comput. Surv. **53**(6), 1–38 (2021). https://doi.org/10.1145/3419633
22. Anderson, S.L., Anderson, M., Anderson, S.L.: Machine metaethics. In: Anderson, M., Anderson, S.L. (eds.) Machine Ethics, pp. 21–27. Cambridge University Press, Cambridge (2011). https://doi.org/10.1017/CBO9780511978036.004
23. Anderson, M., Anderson, S.L.: Guest editors' introduction: machine ethics. IEEE Intell. Syst. **21**(4), 10–11 (2006)
24. Allen, C., Smit, I., Wallach, W.: Artificial morality: top-down, bottom-up, and hybrid approaches. Ethics Inf. Technol. **7**(3), 149–155 (2005)
25. Anderson, M., Anderson, S.L.: Machine ethics: creating an ethical intelligent agent. AI Mag. **28**(4), 15–26 (2007)

26. Mittelstadti, B.: AI ethics – too principled to fail?
27. Picard, R.W., et al.: Affective Computing. MIT Press, Cambridge (1995)
28. Sparrow, R.: Killer robots. J. Appl. Philos. **24**(1), 62–77 (2007)
29. Taddeo, M., Floridi, L.: How AI can be a force for good. Science **361**(6404), 751–752 (2018)
30. Millar, J.: Technology as moral proxy: autonomy and paternalism by design. IEEE Technol. Soc. Mag. **34**(2), 47–55 (2015). https://doi.org/10.1109/MTS.2015.2425612
31. Santis, A., Siciliano, B.: Safety issues for human–robot cooperation in manufacturing systems. Tools and Perspectives in Virtual Manufacturing (2008)
32. Artificial Intelligence and Ethics: Sixteen Challenges and Opportunities, Brian Patrick Green, director of Technology Ethics at the Markkula Center for Applied Ethics
33. Asaro, P.: Robots and responsibility from a legal perspective. In: IEEE International Conference on Robotics and Automation, Rome, Italy (2007)
34. Johnson, D.G.: Computer systems: moral entities but not moral agents. Ethics Inf. Technol. **8**(4), 195–204 (2006)
35. Dodig-Crnkovic, G., Persson, D.: Sharing moral responsibility with robots: a pragmatic approach. In: Tenth Scandinavian Conference on Artificial Intelligence, SCAI 2008, pp. 165–168 (2008)
36. Jarvik, M.: How to understand moral responsibility? TRAMES. J. Humanit. Soc. Sci. **7**(3), 147–163 (2003)

Smart Energy Management

Towards a Hybrid Model for the Diffusion of Innovation in Energy Communities

Kankam O. Adu-Kankam[1,2(✉)] and Luis M. Camarinha-Matos[1(✉)]

[1] Nova University of Lisbon, School of Science and Technology, UNINOVA - CTS, Campus de Caparica, 2829-516 Monte Caparica, Portugal
cam@uninova.pt

[2] School of Engineering, University of Energy and Natural Resources (UENR), P. O. Box 214, Sunyani, Ghana

Abstract. The need for comprehensive models to simulate the diffusion of innovations in communities or social systems has become eminent. Existing models such as the Diffusion of Innovation expound how ideas, products, or innovations gain acceptance and spread over time. Other analogous models, such as the Transtheoretical Model also claim that people do not change behaviours quickly and decisively. Instead, they change in a continuous and cyclical process of internal decision-making. Although these two models are used to address adoption, it may be observed that one addresses it from a behavioural point of view while the other from the characteristics of the innovation perspective. In this study, we propose and develop a hybrid model based on these two. We expect that a composite model with enhanced attributes can be deployed as a decision support tool to enhance the diffusion of innovations particularly within energy communities. The study sought to conduct a structural and contextual analysis of these models hoping to find reasonable grounds for merging them.

Keywords: Transtheoretical model · Diffusion of innovation model · Behaviour change · Hybridization · Energy communities

1 Introduction

It is generally acknowledged that the Earth's resources are depleting rapidly. The demand for these resources surpasses the planet's capability to supply, which has adverse effects on the environment, resulting in climate change. This phenomenon poses severe threats to societies due to overutilization of its natural resources. Social Innovations in the Energy Transition (SIET) is a novel and rapidly evolving concept that has been proposed to significantly contribute to the reduction in overexploitation, particularly, in energy related resources. It has been proposed in several studies including [1] to offer tools to support existing social structures at transforming their energy needs towards a sustainable one. Its impacts are expected to occur at the level of individual behaviour change and collective lifestyles in communities [1].

© IFIP International Federation for Information Processing 2021
Published by Springer Nature Switzerland AG 2021
L. M. Camarinha-Matos et al. (Eds.): DoCEIS 2021, IFIP AICT 626, pp. 175–188, 2021.
https://doi.org/10.1007/978-3-030-78288-7_17

SIET, like many other emerging concepts, lacks a unified definition, however, from the perspectives of [1], "it represents social innovations that can contribute to the energy transition." The mentioned authors argued that such innovations may also entail the introduction of new energy related activities such as energy production, storage, distribution, consumption, as well as new energy-related behaviours.

Like many new innovations, SIET is likely to face some barriers towards its general acceptance and diffusion. Rogers in [2], maintained that behavioural barriers significantly affect the rate of adoption of many innovations. For instance, the rate of adoption for technologies such as the internet, per households, in the United States increased from 10% to 88.3% between 1993 and 2016, and for personal computers from 20.7% to 89.30% between 1992 and 2016 [3], a period spanning more than two decades for each technology. Other studies like [4] have also claimed that resistance to adoption is usually rooted in social and behavioural concepts like attitudes and value systems, therefore, solutions to diffusion could not only be technological, but also may include new ways of collaboration, decision-making, and mobilizing society [1]. Some studies that have also suggested and adopted the idea of collaboration to solve similar problems in energy communities are found in [5–8].

The objective of this study is to propose and develop a hybrid and multi-dimensional model that can be used as a decision support tool to equip community managers or innovators in managing or facilitating the general diffusion of innovations in communities. Although the proposed model could have a generic use, we expect to test it in subsequent studies using the diffusion of SIET as a case study. We consider a software simulation environment using Agent-based simulation techniques. This technique can help to represent the community, its members and the interaction between them using software agents in an agent-based model (ABM). An advantage of ABMs includes the facts that agents can be modelled to exhibit autonomous behaviours which may include autonomous decision making. They can be modelled to be proactive or goal-oriented, thus, having goals to achieve. Furthermore, these agents can be modelled to be cognitive/perceptive thus having a sense of awareness and finally, being adaptive to their environments.

The approach to the development of the hybrid model involves a structural and contextual analysis of two key models. These are: (a) the Diffusion of Innovation Model (DIM) and (b) the Transtheoretical Model (TTM). These models are selected because available literature reveals that (a) the TTM is one of the most widely applied models for behavioural studies, and (b) the DIM is also considered in literature as the leading model in the studies of diffusion. The hybrid model is expected to be novel in nature and characteristics. It is also expected to be multi-dimensional having a behavioural dimension and an innovation dimension simultaneously. We anticipate that the model can be useful for studying several cases of diffusion, particularly in cases that are similar to SIET, which is claimed in [1] as a multifaceted problem having dimensions that are technological, social, and behavioural. We call the hybrid model the "**Hy**brid **Tra**nstheoretical and Diffusion of **In**novation Model" (HyTraIn model). The following research questions (RQs) are therefore used to guide the present study.

RQ-1. How do DIT and TTM models compare from both the contextual and structural perspectives?

RQ-3. Based on the observed contextual and structural similarities or differences, how can these models be hybridized into a single model?

2 Relationship with Applied Artificial Intelligence

Digital Twins (DT) are emerging to play essential roles in bridging the divide between physical and virtual spaces and helping to provide efficient, and intelligent services [9]. Its incorporation into the power grid could enable the integration of intelligence in the form of smart software agents which can provide optimum grid management in aspects such as autonomous control and decision-making [10]. By coupling these two spaces, preferences of physical entities such as households could be delegated to DTs [11] such that DT could make some decisions on behalf of the physical twin.

This current study is a partial aspect of an ongoing Ph.D. research. In the study, we propose the idea of "Collaborative Networks of Influencers." The study attempts to harness the influential roles played by community role-models or opinion leaders to facilitating the diffusion of SIET. Physical entities within the community could have a digital replica of themselves in the form of Cognitive Household Digital Twins (C-HDT). In [12], a Cognitive Digital Twins is described as a "digital reflection of the user, intended to make decisions and carry out tasks on the user's behalf." In this case, a C-HDT could be automated with a digital profile that reflects a set of attributes such as the physical twin's value system, consumption preferences, sustainability choices, etc. These C-HDTs could be delegated to make decisions on behalf of their physical twin based on their digital profile. Such decision may include adoption of innovation and other behavioural issues that conforms to their predefined digital profiles. The idea of C-HDTs can help increase the level intelligence and smartness of households.

3 Related Literature

A comprehensive study in [1] provides an overview of SIET. It discusses its potential contribution to the energy transition and identifies its potential effects. Other studies, like [13], have argued that it is difficult to have a comprehensive definition for SIET due to the complexity and multidisciplinary nature of the concept. An European Commission (EC) funded project named SONNET, attempts to understand ways and conditions under which SIET can contribute to the commission's strategy for clean the energy transition [14]. Another EC sponsored project called Social Innovation Modelling Approaches to Realizing Transition to Energy Efficiency and Sustainability (SMARTEES), is described in [15]. It aims at supporting the energy transition to improve policy design by developing alternative and robust policy pathways that foster citizen inclusion. COMETS (Collective Action Models for the Energy Transition and Social Innovation) [16], is also another EC projects intended to fill the knowledge gaps around citizen engagement in the energy transition.

Although several ideas and projects including the ones discussed above seek to address SIET, available literature reveals a gap in the availability and diversity of models to study diffusion of these concepts. In studies relating to diffusion, the DIM model in its unmodified form is often utilized. However, in its unmodified form, the DIM has limited capabilities to address diffusion from a multidimensional perspective. Therefore, this proposed model could be useful in complimenting existing ones and could help to advance knowledge in this area.

4 Analysis of Base Models

We hereby introduce some key terms that are used in the analysis. These are: (a) Decision Making Entity (DME) - the entity that is being influenced to either change behaviour or adopt an innovation, (b) Elements of Influence (EI) - the forces that drive change. These are pieces of information that are tailored strategically to suit the demands of a DME, and to induce in a change.

4.1 Diffusion of Innovation Model (DIM)

Figure 1 provides a structural representation of the DIM model [2]. This model expounds on how ideas, products, or innovations gain acceptance and spread through a social system. The model focuses on the innovation´s characteristics such as its relative advantage, compatibility, complexity, trialability, and observability [2]. Some application of this model in the energy sector include studies such as [17]. The diagram shows the five distinct stages of the involved process and their sequence of progression. It also shows the transitions that connect the various stages. The communication channels represent the medium through which information is disseminated. Furthermore, the figure reveals two categories of stages. These are (a) covert actions stages and (b) overt actions stages. A covert action occurs internally within a DME, such as mental activities, which are often not physically visible to an observer. Overt actions, on the other hand, are actions that are physical and can be seen by an observer.

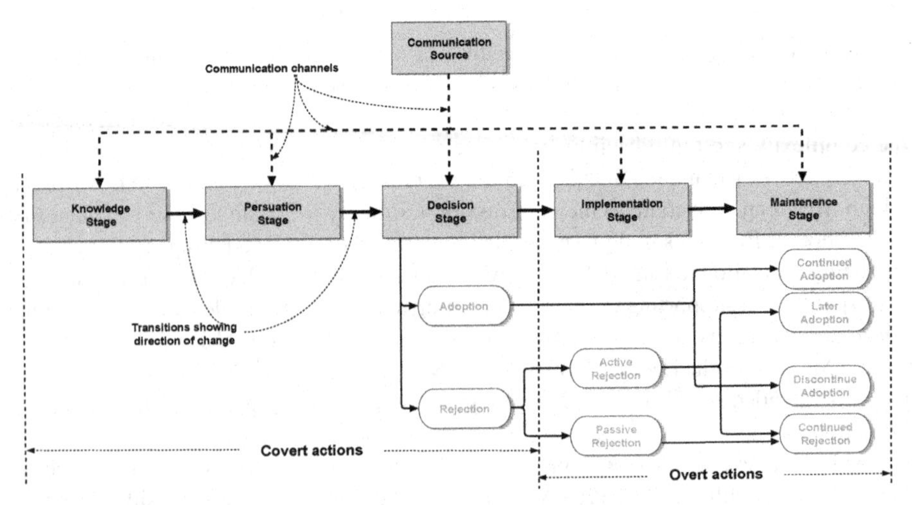

Fig. 1. A model of the diffusion of innovation before hybridization

Table 1 provides further details about the key attributes that characterize each stage in Fig. 1. It also provides information about how different elements of influence are tailored to influence the DME at any stage of the mode.

Table 1. The various stages of the DIT, corresponding attributes and elements of influence [2]

Stages	Key attributes	Elements of influence
1 Knowledge	1. DME is aware of the existence of the innovation [2] *Contextually, "awareness" is the central attribute of this stage*	*Tailored to increase awareness and knowledge about the innovation*
2 Persuasion	1. DME seeks more information to evaluate the pros and cons of the innovation [2] 2. DME seeks social reinforcement from near peers in making a final decision [2] 3. DME forms either a favourable or unfavourable impression about the innovation [2] *Contextually, "deliberations and social reinforcement" are central attributes of this stage. The DMEs deliberate whether to adopt or reject the innovation while seeking social reinforcement for their decision*	*Usually tailored to increase knowledge about the innovation and also facilitate persuasion through social bonding, based on common values*
3 Decision	1. DMEs may try the innovation on a probationary basis to determine its usefulness in their situation [2 2. Trying the innovation reduces inherent uncertainty about its consequences [2] 3. The outcome of this process is either a rejection or acceptance of the innovation [2] *Contextually, "incipience" is the central attribute of this stage. gradual incipience of the desire either to adopt or reject the innovation is observed*	*Usually tailored to facilitate the decision of the DME through easy access and engagement with the innovation. Technical information is also provided at this stage*
4 Implementation	1. DMEs actively participate in the innovation and seek more information such as: · How to use the innovation effectively? · What operational problems are likely to be encountered? · Where to obtain the innovation? · How to solve problems concerned with the innovation? [2] *Contextually, "commitment" is the central attribute of this stage. The DMEs actively commit themselves to innovation*	*Usually tailored to aid in the form of "supportive messages" to the DME to strengthen decision and prevent "cognitive dissonance" from occurring*
5 Confirmation	1. DME seeks reinforcement of an innovation-decision 2. DME may reverse the decision if exposed to conflicting messages about the innovation *Contextually, "sustenance" is the central attribute of this stage. DMEs actively engage the behaviour and tries to avoid relapse*	*Designed to provide supportive messages to the DME to strengthen decision and prevent "cognitive dissonance" from occurring*

4.2 The Transtheoretical Model (TTM)

Figure 2 is a structural representation of the TTM model. This model assumes that people do not change behaviours quickly and decisively, but rather, in a continuous and cyclical process of internal decision-making [18]. Some application of this model in the energy domain include [19]. The figure also shows the five distinct stages of the change process and their progression sequence from one stage to the other. It also shows the transitions that connect the various stages as well as the communication channels, covert actions stages and overt actions stages.

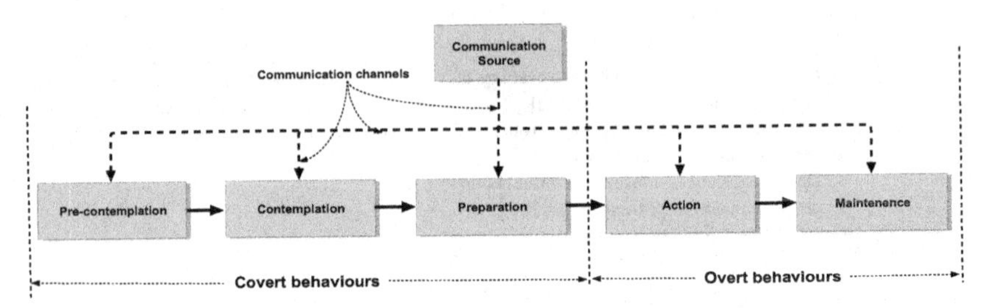

Fig. 2. A representation of the transtheoretical model before hybridization

Table 2 also provides further details about the key attributes that characterize each stage of the TTM. It also provides information about the various elements of influence.

Table 2. The various stages of the TTM, corresponding attributes and elements if influence [18]

Decision process	Key characteristics	Elements of influence
1 Pre-contemplation	DME has no intention to change behaviour in the foreseeable future. DME may lack knowledge of the effect of the problematic behaviour [18]. *Contextually, "ignorance" is the central attribute of this stage. The DME is ignorant about their problematic state*	*Usually tailored to provide information that could increase* awareness and *knowledge about the problem*
2 Contemplation	DME is aware of the problem and is seriously thinking about overcoming it but has not yet committed to acting [18]. DME seeks social reinforcement from peers in making final decisions. *Contextually, "deliberations and social reinforcement" are central attributes of this stage. DME deliberates about the behaviour change whilst seeking social reinforcement for their decision*	*Usually tailored to increase knowledge about the behaviour and also facilitate persuasion through social bonding and also based on common values*
3 Preparation	DME is intending to take action immediately and report on small behavioural changes achieved [18] *Contextually, "incipience" is the central attribute of this stage. Incipience of the desired change is observed*	*Tailored to aid decision of the DME and encourage small changes at a time*

(continued)

Table 2. *(continued)*

Decision process	Key characteristics	Elements of influence
4 Action	DMEs modifies their behaviour, experiences, and/or environment to overcome the problematic behaviours [18] *Contextually, "commitment" is the central attribute of this stage. DMEs actively engage in the behaviour change and commits to sustaining it*	*"supportive messages" to the DMEs to strengthen their decision and prevent "cognitive dissonance" from occurring*
5 Maintenance	In this stage, the DME works hard to maintain the choice of behaviour, hoping to prevent relapse and consolidate the gains attained. [18]. *Contextually, "sustenance" is the central attribute of this stage. DMEs actively engage the behaviour and tries to avoid relapse*	*"supportive messages" to the DMEs to strengthen decision and prevent "cognitive dissonance" from occurring*

4.3 Structural Comparison Between DIT and TTM

Considering Figs. 1 and 2, the following structural similarities are observed:

a. **The number of stages and transitions**: Each of the two models is comprised of five key stages connected by four transitions.
b. **Covert Stages:** The first three stages for both models are covert action stages.
c. **Overt Stages:** The last two stages for both models are overt action stages.
d. **Communication channels:** The communication channels for both models are similar. They both support centralized or decentralized sources of information. The observed structural similarities between the models form good grounds to propose a merger without compromising the structural integrity of both models.

4.4 Contextual Comparison, Hybridization, and Redefinition

From Tables 1 and 2, the following contextual similarities differences are observed:

1. **Pre-contemplation (TTM) and knowledge (DIT) stages.** These first two stages have opposing attributes. DMEs in the pre-contemplation stage are described as being ignorant of the existence of a problem. On the contrary, DMEs in the knowledge stage possess knowledge of the innovation. This, therefore, forms two opposing attributes. However, their respective elements of influence are contextually similar. They are both tailored to provide information that is aimed at increasing awareness and knowledge in the DMEs. Based on this contextual similarity, we propose the hybridization of these two stages into one (Fig. 3). We call the hybrid stage the ***"awareness stage"****and define it as the stage where a DME is provided with information about the "phenomenon" to increase knowledge and awareness about it.* The phenomenon here could represent innovation or behaviour.
2. **Contemplation (TTM) and Persuasion (DIT) stages**
   There is a common central attribute for these two stages. This can be described as "deliberations and social reinforcement." It can further be observed that the elements of influence for both stages are usually tailored to increase knowledge and

also facilitate social reinforcements. Social bonds, such as shared values are also vital here. This therefore suggests that by hybridizing these two stages, we could tailor a common set of elements of influences that will focused on enhancing the deliberation process of the DME and also facilitate social reinforcement. We propose the hybridization of these two stages into one (Fig. 3) and rename it as "***deliberation stage***". *It can be defined as the stage where the DME has knowledge of the existence of the "phenomenon" and is contemplating adjustments towards probable engagement or disengagement with the phenomenon.* The adjustment may represent adoption or a change.

3. **Preparation (TTM) and decision (DIT) stages**
   These two stages also have a common and central attribute. This is described as "incipience." The elements of influences are tailored to aid the DME´s decision-making process. The elements of influence could also be focused on the encouragement of small changes at a time. This means that by hybridizing these two stages into one, the actions/activities that occur in this composite could be influenced by elements of influences that are tailored to enable decision making and encourage small changes. We thus propose the hybridization of these two stages into one (Fig. 3) and rename it as "***incipient stage,***" *which can be defined as the stage where the DME begins to show interest in the "phenomenon" and initiates actions to experience the phenomenon. The DME will form an opinion that could be favourable or unfavourable towards it.*
4. **Action (TTM) and implementation (DIT) stages**
   The central attributes in these two stages can be described as commitment. The elements of influence from these stages are tailored to reinforce or strengthen the commitment and decision of the DME and to prevent relapse. Again, we propose the hybridization of these two stages into one (Fig. 3) and rename it as "***commitment stage***". *It is defined as the stage where the DMEs actively engage themselves with the phenomenon and make environmental or personal modifications to sustain the phenomenon and prevent relapse.*
5. **Maintenance (TTM) and Confirmation (DIT) stages.**
   Finally, the central attributes in these last two stages can be described as sustenance. The elements of influence are tailored to strengthen the DME´s decision and to prevent relapse or cognitive dissonance. We also propose the hybridization of these two stages into one (Fig. 3) and rename it as "***sustenance stage.***"*This hybrid stage is defined as the stage where the DME actively works to sustain the phenomenon and tries to avoid/prevent relapse/cognitive dissonance from occurring.* Cognitive dissonance describes the mental state of discomfort that results from holding two conflicting beliefs, values, or attitudes. People tend to seek consistency in their attitudes and perceptions, so this conflict causes feelings of unease or discomfort and could affect the decision of the DME [20].

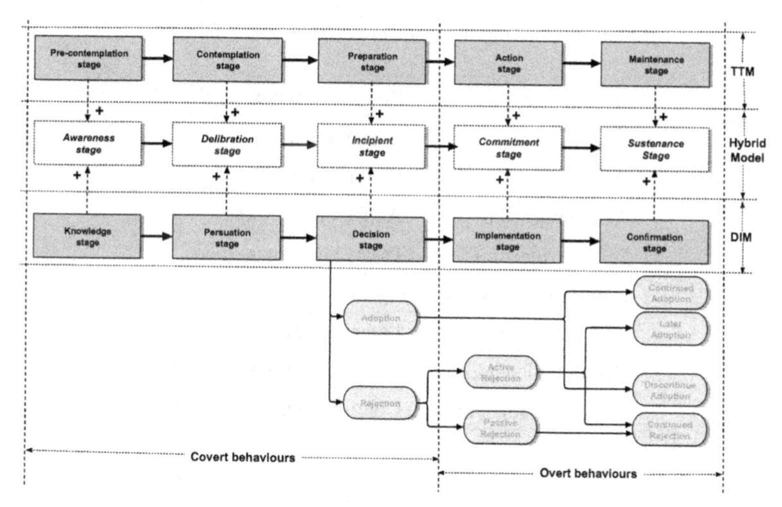

Fig. 3. The hybridization process of DIT and TTM models.

4.5 The Hybrid Transtheoretical and Diffusion of Innovation Model (HyTraIn)

Figure 4 shows the outcome of the hybridization process. It represents the final version of HyTrain model. It is essential to indicate here that the hybridization only occurred at the primary section of the HyTrin model. The stages indicated as the secondary section was not hybridized. Therefore, their functions remained the same as the original DIT model. However, these stages need to be redefined so as to conform with the intent and purposes of the HyTraIn model. The redefinition is shown in Table 3. Engagement here means that the DME gets involved with the phenomenon. Disengagement means the DME does not get involved with the phenomenon. In future implantation using the Anylogic simulation platforms, DMEs will be modelled as software agents and the various stage of the HyTraIn model shall be simulated as internal states of the DME. These internal states shall be modelled using charts. The transition between states will also be controlled using inbuilt transition triggers that are activated based on several signals such as condition, messages, timeout rates etc. The elements of influence will be modelled using system dynamics stock and flow blocks and the communication between DMEs will be achieved through inbuilt communication networks in Anylogic.

Table 3. Redefining the primary sections of the DIT model

Original stages	Redefined stages
Adoption	Engagement
Rejection	Disengagement
Active rejection	Active engagement
Passive rejection	Passive disengagement
Continued adoption	Continued engagement
Later adoption	Later engagement
Discontinued adoption	Discontinued engagement
Continued rejection	Continued disengagement

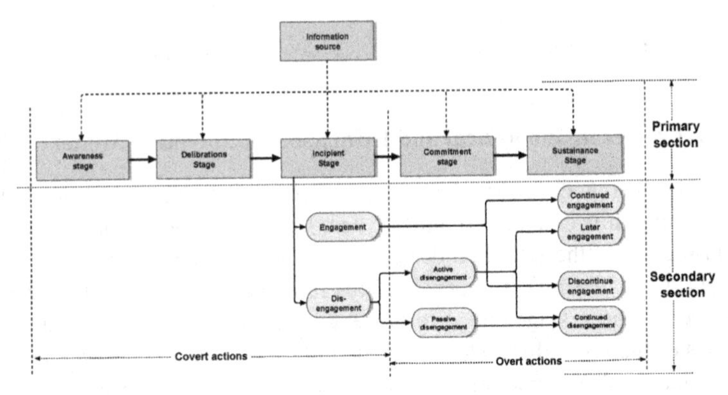

Fig. 4. The final HyTraIn model.

5 Demonstration of the Modelling Technique

Full implementation of this model shall be advanced in subsequent studies using a multi-method simulation approach. The method shall integrates system dynamics, agent-based, and discrete event simulation techniques in a single simulation platform called the Anylogic [21]. By adopting this approach, CHDTs shall be modelled as DMEs using software agents to represent them. The community shall also be modelled as constituting of several interconnected software agents using diverse network topologies to represent the communication channels for message passing. As a brief introduction to the modelling technique, we use Fig. 5, DME-1 to represent a C-HDT. This CHDT as an example has a digital profile shown as comprising of 3 values and 3 attributes. The C-HDT also possess an input, a decision block and an output.

The impact of these messages on the C-HDT is modelled using a probability distribution function modelled as a *uniform distribution (x, y)*, where *x* is the minimum impact induced by the message and y the maximum. Since the distribution is a continuum and oscillates between these boundaries it could be used to simulate some dynamics in the degree of impact caused by these messages. The impact of these messages will trigger

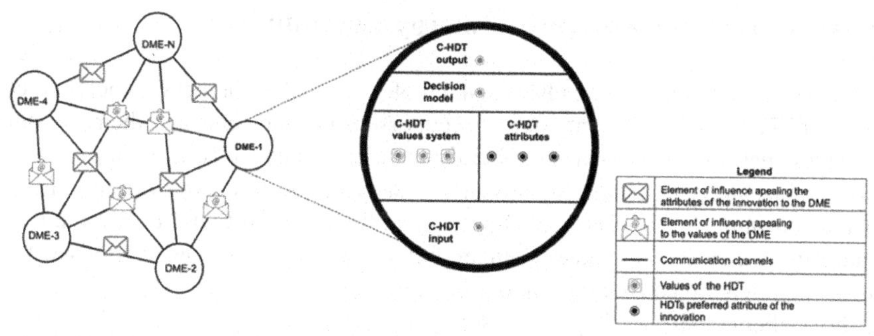

Fig. 5. A mesh network of interconnected software agents showing the exchange of elements of influences and digital profile of a C-HDT.

an internal behaviour in the c-HDT which can be visualized at the output as Shown in Fig. 6. These internal behaviours are used to make decision within the decision block of the C-HDT. C-HDTs will only accept and consume compatible messages. Non compatible messages are rejected and cannot trigger any behaviour. A message is considered compatible if its content matches with any one of the predefined set of attributes for the recipient C-HDT. The cognitive capability of these C-HDTs is derived from their ability to recognize compatible messages from non-compatible ones. as the number of compatible messages increases, the magnitude of its oscillations also increases until the decision threshold is reached or exceeded. at this point the CHDT makes a decision. The types of messages to disseminate, time and frequency of dissemination shall be decided by a community manager in collaboration with the influencers. The community manager and the network of collaborators will adopt the hyTraIN model as the main decision support tool.

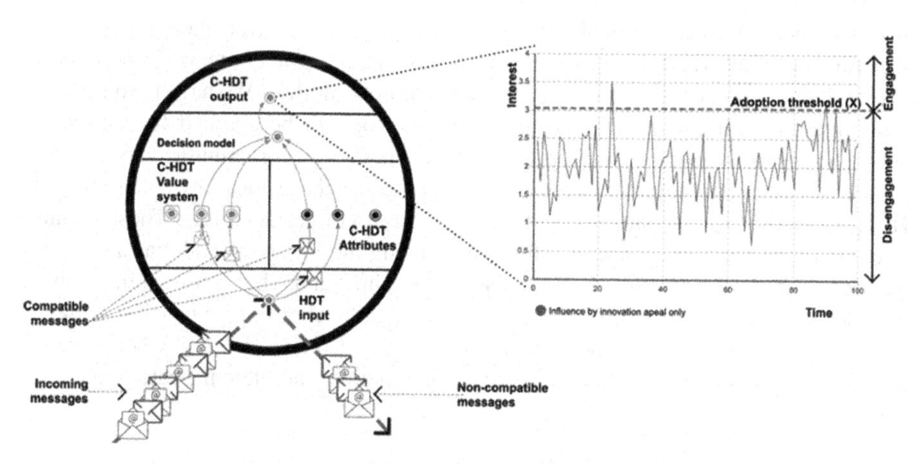

Fig. 6. A C-HDT showing incoming, compatible, and non-compatible messages.

6 Application of Concepts to Energy Communities

Delegation of deferrable loads (DDL) refers to the process whereby consumers/prosumers within a community accept to delegate the control of their household appliances such as dishwashers, tumble dryers and washing machines to an external entity such as an aggregator or a community manager for purposes of promoting sustainable consumption [5]. These appliances are often referred to as "deferrable loads" because users can defer or delay their preferred time of use to later periods without causing significant inconvenience to them.

The challenge with DDL is that it solely depends on the willingness of the user to participate. potential adopters are often faced with barriers such as perceived inconvenience, fear of losing comfort, or the fear of not being in control. ddl could therefore be considered a good example of siet whose acceptance and diffusion can severely be hampered by these barriers which can be considered as a mix of social and behavioural concerns. by adopting the concepts discussed in this study, users could define their preferences relating to the DDL and Delegate them to their C-HDTs. For example, a CHDT could accept a DDL proposal based on the level of flexibility offers. other attributes about DDL that could appeal to the value system of the C-HDT may include benefits to the user, benefits to the community, immediate impact on the environment, level of social inclusion and cohesion, etc. These DDL attributes could carefully be crafted into pieces of elements of influence and disseminated through existing communication channels in the form of messages. our proposed C-HDTS, through their cognitive abilities, can identify attributes of DDL that suit their digital profiles and can decide to whether to engage or disengage.

7 Conclusion and Future Work

In this study, we have analysed the Diffusion of Innovation and Transtheoretical models' structural and contextual properties. Based on this analysis's outcome, we have proposed a hybrid model that encompasses the attributes of both models. We have partially illustrated the modelling approach and the modelling tools to be adopted for subsequent studies. The application of the proposed concepts in energy communities has also been discussed briefly. In future studies, we shall advance these ideas by integrating the HyTraIn model as a decision support tool for a group of collaborators. These collaborators (Collaborative Network of Influencers), using the HyTraIn model as a tool, will decide which elements of influence to disseminate, how and when to disseminate them, what level of impact is expected to be achieved, what level of impact is being achieved, when to transition and implement subsequent stages of the model, and when to repeat the cycle etc. It is expected that these ideas could help to facilitate the rate of adoption SIETs in communities.

Acknowledgment. Project CESME (Collaborative & Evolvable Smart Manufacturing Ecosystem and the Portuguese FCT program UIDB/00066/2020 (CTS – Center of Technology and Systems) for providing financial support for this work.

References

1. Hoppe, T., de Vries, G.: Social innovation and the energy transition. Sustainability **11**(1), 141 (2018). https://doi.org/10.3390/su11010141
2. Rogers, E.M.: Diffusion of Innovation, 3rd edn. The Free Press, New York (1983)
3. Ritchie, H., Roser, M.: Technology Adoption. Our World in Data, 02 October 2017. https://ourworldindata.org/technology-adoption. Accessed 12 Feb 2021
4. Wolsink, M.: The research agenda on social acceptance of distributed generation in smart grids: Renewable as common pool resources. Renew. Sustain. Energy Rev. **16**(1), 822–835 (Jan. 2012). https://doi.org/10.1016/j.rser.2011.09.006
5. Adu-Kankam, K.O., Camarinha-Matos, L.M.: A collaborative approach to demand side energy management. In: Camarinha-Matos, L.M., Afsarmanesh, H., Ortiz, A. (eds.) PRO-VE 2020. IAICT, vol. 598, pp. 393–405. Springer, Cham (2020). https://doi.org/10.1007/978-3-030-62412-5_32
6. Adu-Kankam, K.O., Camarinha-Matos, L.M.: Towards collaborative virtual power plants: trends and convergence. Sustain. Energy Grids Netw. **16**, 217–230 (2018). https://doi.org/10.1016/j.segan.2018.08.003
7. Adu-Kankam, K.O., Camarinha-Matos, L.M.: A Framework for behavioural change through incentivization in a collaborative virtual power plant ecosystem. In: Camarinha-Matos, L.M., Farhadi, N., Lopes, F., Pereira, H. (eds.) DoCEIS 2020. IAICT, vol. 577, pp. 31–40. Springer, Cham (2020). https://doi.org/10.1007/978-3-030-45124-0_3
8. Adu-Kankam, K.O., Camarinha-Matos, L.M.: Towards collaborative virtual power plants. In: Camarinha-Matos, L.M., Adu-Kankam, K.O., Julashokri, M. (eds.) DoCEIS 2018. IAICT, vol. 521, pp. 28–39. Springer, Cham (2018). https://doi.org/10.1007/978-3-319-78574-5_3
9. Nazarenko, A.A., Camarinha-Matos, L.M.: The role of digital twins in collaborative cyber-physical systems. In: Camarinha-Matos, L.M., Farhadi, N., Lopes, F., Pereira, H. (eds.) Technological Innovation for Life Improvement: 11th IFIP WG 5.5/SOCOLNET Advanced Doctoral Conference on Computing, Electrical and Industrial Systems, DoCEIS 2020, Costa de Caparica, Portugal, July 1–3, 2020, Proceedings, pp. 191–205. Springer International Publishing, Cham (2020). https://doi.org/10.1007/978-3-030-45124-0_18
10. Ahmad, T., et al.: Artificial intelligence in sustainable energy industry: Status Quo, challenges and opportunities. J. Clean. Prod. **289**, 125834 (2021). https://doi.org/10.1016/j.jclepro.2021.125834
11. Xiang, F., Huang, Y., Zhang, Z., Zuo, Y.: Digital twin driven energy-aware green design. In: Digital Twin Driven Smart Design, pp. 165–184. Elsevier (2020). https://doi.org/10.1016/B978-0-12-818918-4.00006-3
12. Somers, S., Oltramari, A., Lebiere, C.: Cognitive twin: a cognitive approach to personalized assistants. In: Spring Symposium on Combining Machine Learning and Knowledge Engineering in Practice, vol. 2600 (2020)
13. Koukoufikis, G.: Social innovation and the energy transition - towards a working definition. Eur. Com. Jt. Res. Cent. (2021). doi: https://doi.org/10.13140/RG.2.2.19905.58720.
14. Center for Energy and the Environment: H2020- SONNET Social Innovation for the Energy Transition. https://www.zhaw.ch/en/sml/institutes-centres/cee/research-consulting/h2020-sonnet-social-innovation-for-the-energy-transition/. Accessed 08 Feb 2021
15. "SMARTEES-LOCAL SOCIAL INNOVATION". https://local-social-innovation.eu/. Accessed: 08 Feb 2021
16. "The COMET Project". http://www.comets-project.eu/index.php?option=com_sppagebuilder&view=page&id=62. Accessed 08 Feb 2021

17. Boumaiza, A., Abbar, S., Mohandes, N., Sanfilippo, A.: Innovation diffusion for renewable energy technologies. In: 2018 IEEE 12th International Conference on Compatibility, Power Electronics and Power Engineering (CPE-POWERENG 2018), vol. 8, pp. 1–6 (2018) doi: https://doi.org/10.1109/CPE.2018.8372592
18. Prochaska, J., Norcross, J.: Systems of Psychotherapy A Transtheoretical Analysis, 8th edn., pp. 489–496. Cengage Learning, Stamford, USA (2013)
19. He, H.A., Greenberg, S., Huang, E.M.: One size does not fit all: applying the transtheoretical model to energy feedback technology design. In: CHI 2010: Sense and Sustainability, pp. 927–936 (2010)
20. Cherry, K.: What is Cognitive Dissonance? (2020). https://www.verywellmind.com/what-is-cognitive-dissonance-2795012. Accessed 04 Feb 2021
21. AnyLogic. AnyLogic: Simulation Modeling Software (2018). https://www.anylogic.com/. Accessed 13 Feb 2020

Towards Extension of Data Centre Modelling Toolbox with Parameters Estimation

Yulia Berezovskaya[1(✉)], Chen-Wei Yang[1], and Valeriy Vyatkin[1,2]

[1] Department of Computer Science, Electrical and Space Engineering, Luleå University of Technology, Luleå, Sweden
{yulia.berezovskaya,chen-wei.yang}@ltu.se

[2] Department of Electrical Engineering and Automation, Aalto University, Espoo, Finland

Abstract. Modern data centres consume a significant amount of electricity. Therefore, they require techniques for improving energy efficiency and reducing energy waste. The promising energy-saving methods are those, which adapt the system energy use based on resource requirements at run-time. These techniques require testing their performance, reliability and effect on power consumption in data centres. Generally, real data centres cannot be used as a test site because of such experiments may violate safety and security protocols. Therefore, examining the performance of different energy-saving strategies requires a model, which can replace the real data centre. The model is expected to accurately estimate the energy consumption of data centre components depending on their utilisation. This work presents a toolbox for data centre modelling. The toolbox is a set of building blocks representing individual components of a typical data centre. The paper concentrates on parameter estimation methods, which use data, collected from a real data centre and adjust parameters of building blocks so that the model represents the data centre most accurately. The paper also demonstrates the results of parameters estimation on an example of EDGE module of SICS ICE data centre located in Luleå, Sweden.

Keywords: Data centre · Modelling · Power consumption · Parameter estimation · Matlab/Simulink

1 Introduction

Data centres are sizable consumers in the energy grid and comparable to industrial plants in terms of energy consumption [1]. Modern data centres use more and more renewable energy sources, which tend to intermittent energy production [2]. Data centres are expected to flexibly respond to changes in energy supply and possible restrictions from the energy grid and remain highly available and reliable. To meet these expectations, the promising approach is flexible control methods, which adapt the data centre energy use based on resource requirements during the data centre operation.

The subject of my PhD study is the development of energy-efficient control in data centres. Any data centre can be thought of as a distributed system of interdependent

© IFIP International Federation for Information Processing 2021
Published by Springer Nature Switzerland AG 2021
L. M. Camarinha-Matos et al. (Eds.): DoCEIS 2021, IFIP AICT 626, pp. 189–196, 2021.
https://doi.org/10.1007/978-3-030-78288-7_18

components, which are too complex for centralised management. As a part of my PhD research, a design of multi-agent control to reach energy efficiency in data centres was presented in [3]. Further elaborating the multi-agent control requires the data centre model, which is expected to substitute a real data centre as a system under control. In our previous work [4], we developed a modular Simulink toolbox, which is formed as a set of blocks for modelling individual data centre components such as servers, and components of a cooling system. The toolbox allows constructing the models of data centres of arbitrary configurations. The models are capable of estimating the energy consumption and predicting the thermal evolution inside the data centre.

Most of the blocks in the toolbox have their internal parameters, which depend on the type of modelled component. The accuracy of modelling results is mainly determined by the selection of those parameters. The current edition of the toolbox uses rough estimates of the parameters. The parameters estimation for the toolbox is not scalable as the parameters are only accurate for a specific datacenter configuration. Any other configuration requires a redefinition of model parameters, which can be achieved by either a) using datasheets of data centre components, or b) extracting the parameter values from the real data. This research work aims to introduce data-driven methods to estimate the modelling parameters for any given datacentre configuration. The work also considers an extension of the toolbox with the proposed methods.

This work deals with parameters of the toolbox block called the Server block. That block is responsible for the modelling of the main IT component. The main contributions of the work:

- presenting two data-driven procedures for parameters estimation: the regression-based estimation and the simulation-based optimisation;
- extension the toolbox with both procedures implemented as Matlab scripts;
- employment of both procedures to real data from the EDGE module of SICS ICE data centre located in Luleå, Sweden [5];
- demonstrating the pros and cons of both procedures.

The rest of the paper is organised as follows. Section 2 provides an overview of related works in the area of parameter estimation for data centre models as well as the relationship of the work to applied artificial intelligence. Section 3 describes the parameters, which require the estimation. Section 4 describes the general procedures for parameters estimation. Section 5 considers the results of parameters estimation and compares two proposed procedures and the conclusion.

2 Related Works

This section considers works, which concentrate on approaches to modelling and models parameters estimation. The main approaches are white-box modelling and black-box identification [6]. The white-box models use scientific relations for describing the process. Parameters of the processes are known constants or they come from specifications of the modelled components. For example, server power consumption modelling requires power parameters of the corresponding CPU and server fan. From the authors' experience, it is not so easy to get the required parameters for the CPU and the server fan. As an idea of the toolbox is in modelling data centres of any configuration, the modelling approach used in it is a so-called grey-box, which utilises scientific relations and requires additional techniques for parameter estimation.

As this work deals with the server power modelling, we are interested in modelling approach and parameters estimation for such components as CPUs and server fans. In [7], authors provide a detailed survey of works, which concentrate on modelling the energy consumption of all components of data centres including servers and their components.

The work [8] demonstrates that the CPU power consumption depends linearly on its utilisation. This work describes the experiments on specific CPUs to get their power parameters. However, it is not always possible to conduct experiments with each type of CPU presented in the modelled data centre. In [9], the authors also deal with the linear relationship between the CPUs power consumption and its utilisation, but there are no clear recommendations on parameters selection.

For the server fans, there also exists works, which consider modelling their power consumption. In [9], the authors present the cubic polynomial model of fan power consumption, but there is no explanation on how its parameters were obtained. The work [10] describes the experiment on a specific server fan to get parameters for its power model, which is a cubic polynomial. However, it is not always possible to conduct experiments with each type of server fan utilised in the modelled data centre.

Thus, this work is inspired by the necessity to have reliable procedures for parameters estimation in the server power model. The work presents estimation procedures based on data about CPUs utilisation, server fans speed and power consumption of servers. Those data are collected from the real data centre. One of the suggested procedures is based on a regression model, which is a common machine learning algorithm. So the paper relates to artificial intelligence systems in way of using machine learning algorithms.

3 Parameters Estimation

This work deals with parameters of the Server block, which estimates the power consumption of the server as a sum of the power of its main components: CPUs and server fans. The total power consumption of the server can be calculated by (1), which is combination of equations for CPU and server fan power consumption used in the toolbox [4].

$$P_{SRV} = \sum_{i=1}^{n} \left(P_{CPU,idle} + \left(P_{CPU,max} - P_{CPU,idle}\right) Util_i\right) + \sum_{i=1}^{m} \frac{P_{SF,max}}{RPM_{max}^3} RPM_i^3. \quad (1)$$

Here, n is number of CPUs on the server; $Util_i$ is utilisation of ith CPU; m is number of server fans on the server; RPM_i is rotation speed of ith server fan.

From Eq. (1) inner parameters of the server block: the CPU power consumption in idle mode ($P_{CPU,idle}$); the CPU peak power consumption ($P_{CPU,max}$); the server fan peak power consumption ($P_{SF,max}$); the server fan maximum rotation speed (RPM_{max}).

This work suggests two ways for parameter estimation: regression-based estimation and simulation-based optimisation.

The *regression-based estimation* performs the following steps:

1. Constructing the regression model which reflects the relationship between the values of the independent variables (predictors) and the explanatory variable (responses);
2. Planning the experiments on the real facility to measure values of the predictors and responses;
3. Pre-processing measured data;
4. Determining the coefficients of the regression model;
5. Statistical analysis of the results.

The *simulation-based optimisation* performs the following steps:

1. Collecting data from the real facility;
2. Constructing a model of a component whose parameters require estimation;
3. Setting inputs of the model to the data from the real facility;
4. Running the optimisation method, which minimises the mean deviation among modelling results and real values (cost function) and takes parameter values corresponding to the minimum as required ones.

The following subsections discuss the implementation of both ways for estimation parameters of building blocks in the data centre modelling toolbox. This section deals with estimating the parameters from the Eq. (1). The model takes the assumption that all CPUs on the server are identical to each other, the same works for all the server fans. It means that all the CPUs and all the server fans have the same parameter values.

3.1 Regression-Based Estimation

Based on (1) the server power can be presented as linear regression model:

$$P_{SRV} = a_0 + a_1 \cdot X_1 + a_2 \cdot X_2. \tag{2}$$

In (2) regression coefficients represent the server block parameters:

$$a_0 = n \cdot P_{CPU,idle};\;\; a_1 = P_{CPU,max} - P_{CPU.idle};\;\; a_2 = \frac{P_{SF,max}}{RPM_{max}^3}. \tag{3}$$

In (2) predictors represent the server block inputs:

$$X_1 = \sum\nolimits_{i=1}^{n} Util_i;\;\; X_2 = \sum\nolimits_{i=1}^{m} RPM_i^3. \tag{4}$$

To find regression coefficients, the measured values of predictors (X_1 and X_2) and response (P_{SRV}) are required. For that aim, the experiment in the real data centre is conducted. An experimenter can control the CPUs utilisation directly. Whereas server fans speeds depend on the corresponding CPUs temperature, thus they are uncontrollable by the experimenter.

The experiment plan:

1. Set the experiment duration (T);
2. Split the experiment time into two or more periods;
3. Set the utilisation of all CPUs so that it is 100% and 0% during the first and second periods (if there are other periods the utilisation can have arbitrary value but it should be constant during the period);
4. Measure the rotation speed of all server fans and power consumption of all servers during the periods;
5. Save measurements as time-series.

The result of the experiment is measured data, such as the servers power consumption and the rotation speed of server fans saved as separate time-series for each server and server fan.

Before starting the calculation of parameters, the measured data requires pre-processing.

Measurements pre-processing:

1. Remove explicit outliers from the data set;
2. Smooth out the data in the data set by filtering;
3. Carry out centring the predictors and the response to get rid of intercept in the regression model;
4. Perform standardisation of the predictors and the response in the regression model.

At last, when all data are prepared, it is possible to calculate the parameters. For each server, parameters are found using matrix form of linear regression model (5).

$$P_N = X_N \cdot \alpha. \tag{5}$$

In (5) P_N is a centred and standardised vector of measured values of server power consumption; X_N is a centred and standardised matrix of measured values of CPU utilisation (the first column), and cube rotation speed of the server fans (the second column); α is a vector of parameters. Traditionally, the method of least squares is used to obtain the values of α, which is reduced to solving a system called normal Eqs. (6) with a positive definite symmetric matrix.

$$X_N' \cdot P_N = \left(X_N' \cdot X_N\right) \cdot \alpha. \tag{6}$$

The vector α can be determined as in (7), as the system matrix is small, it is only 2×2.

$$\alpha = \left(X_N' \cdot X_N\right)^{-1} \cdot X_N' \cdot P_N. \tag{7}$$

Use the vector α to calculate coefficients represented by (3).

Statistical analysis of the results is in testing the hypothesis that coefficients calculated for different servers are from the same distribution with the same mean value.

Section 5 demonstrates the implementation and results of the equation-based estimation procedure for data measured in the real data centre.

3.2 Simulation-Based Optimisation

The simulation-based optimisation is another procedure to estimate server parameters. This procedure minimises the cost function (8), which estimates the mean deviation among modelling results and real values [11, 12].

$$J\left(P_{CPU,idle}, P_{CPU,max}, P_{SF,max}, RPM_{max}\right) = \frac{1}{2m}\sum_{t=1}^{m}\left(P_{SRV,real}(t) - P_{SRV,model}(t)\right)^2 \quad (8)$$

In (8), $P_{SRV,real}(t)$ is the real server power at time t; $P_{SRV,model}(t)$ is the server power calculated by the model at the same time t; and m is the number of timestamps.

The parameters estimation process goes through the following steps. The first step is in the server model preparation:

(1) the initial value, lower and upper bounds of all parameters are determined;
(2) the time-series with data about the CPU usage, the rotational speed of corresponding local fans, are set as input values of the auxiliary model;
(3) the server model provides modelled values of the server power consumption, which is used for calculation the cost function (8).

The second step consists in running the optimisation process (Matlab function: fmincon) which runs the server model with the current parameters to calculate the cost function value, then generate new parameter values and reruns the server model until the global minimum for cost function is found. The parameter values corresponding to the found minimum is considered as the desired parameter values.

The next section demonstrates the implementation and results of the simulation-based optimisation procedure for data measured in the real data centre.

4 Results and Discussion

To evaluate the proposed earlier procedures for the server parameters estimation, the data were collected in the Edge module of the SICS ICE facility located in Luleå, Sweden [5]. Table 1 demonstrates the profile of the CPUs utilisation during the data collection experiment.

Table 1. The CPUs utilisation profile during the data collection experiment.

Time:	0–3 h	3–6 h	6–9 h	9–10 h	10–11 h	11–12 h
Utilisation:	100%	50%	75%	100%	0%	80%

Figure 1 demonstrates the results of the server parameters estimation with the equation-based and the simulation-based procedures. Both procedures shows the similar results. The mean absolute error (MAE): for the equation-based procedure is 5.5 W; for

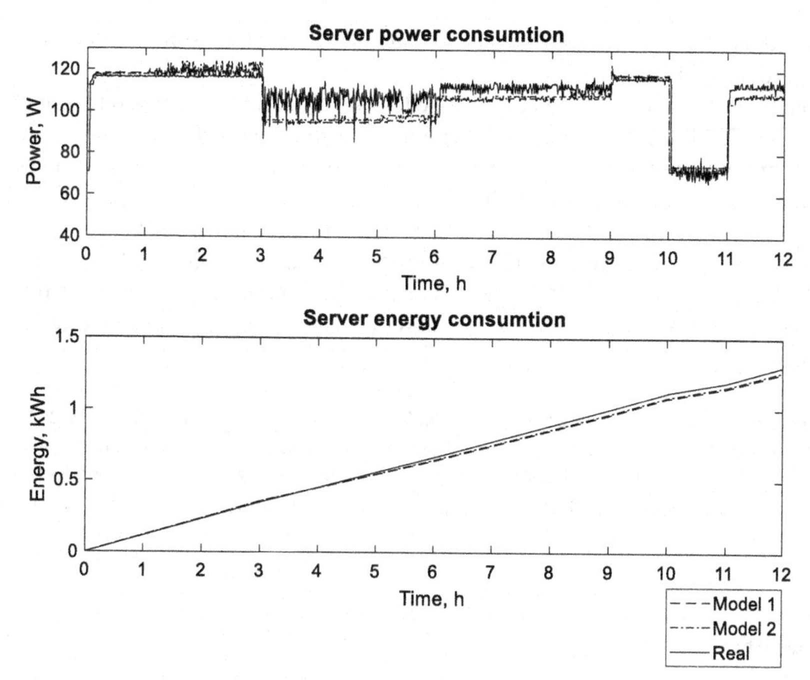

Fig. 1. Comparing the modelling results and real data: server power consumption and server energy consumption.

the simulation-based optimisation is 5.1 W. The mean absolute percent error (MAPE): for the equation-based procedure is 5.1%; for the simulation-based optimisation is 4.8%.

Both procedures demonstrate quite realistic results, and they are added as scripts to the toolbox so that they can be used for parameters estimation. Comparing the MAE and MAPE for both procedures the best one can be selected, and parameters obtained with it can be applied as the server model parameters.

It is worth mentioning, that the equation-based estimation procedure takes much less time than the simulation-based optimisation. However, for the server fan, it can estimate only the composite parameter $\left(\frac{P_{SF,max}}{RPM_{max}^3}\right)$, when the simulation-based optimisation is able to estimate all parameters separately. In addition, the equation-based estimation can be used only if corresponding equation is quite easy such as linear equation. Thus, the toolbox provides with both procedures, so the decision, which one should be used, is made in each individual case relying on timing and accuracy requirements.

5 Conclusion

In this paper, we proposed and implemented two procedures for parameters estimation at server power modelling. The toolbox [4] has been extended with two scripts implementing the estimation of the parameters. The procedures have been employed to the estimation of parameters of server power model. Section 5 demonstrates the results of parameters estimation using the proposed procedures. The models constructed with the estimated parameters demonstrate that the calculated power consumption of the server is close to the real data.

The future work is going to be developed in two directions. The first one is in implementation of additional techniques for parameters estimation such as on-line parameters estimation, and utilising neural networks for estimation parameters. The second one is in the estimation of parameters for all building blocks in the data centre modelling toolbox [Ber]. The special interest here is parameters determining the thermal behaviour of data centres, namely temperature evolution of all CPUs and air inside the data centre. The idea here is to extend the toolbox with all possible techniques of parameters estimation and each time at model constructing use those, which demonstrate most accurate results at modelling.

Acknowledgments. This project has been funded by partners of the ERA-Net SES 2018 joint call RegSys (www.eranet-smartenergysystems.eu) – a network of 30 national and regional RTD funding agencies of 23 European countries. As such, this project has received funding from the European Union's Horizon 2020 research and innovation programme under grant agreement no. 775970.

References

1. Bertoldi, P.: A market transformation programme for improving energy efficiency in data centres. In: Proceedings of the MELS: Taming the Beast, ACEEE Summer Study on Energy Efficiency in Buildings, Pacific Grove, CA, USA (2014)
2. Koronen, C., Åhman, M., Nilsson, L.J.: Data centres in future European energy systems—energy efficiency, integration and policy. Energy Effi. **13**, 129–144 (2020)
3. Berezovskaya, Y., Yang, C.-W., Vyatkin, V.: Towards multi-agent control in energy-efficient data centres. In: IECON 2020 the 46th Annual Conference of the IEEE Industrial Electronics Society (2020)
4. Berezovskaya, Y., Yang, C.-W., Mousavi, A., Vyatkin, V., Minde, T.B.: Modular model of a data centre as a tool for improving its energy efficiency. IEEE Access **8**, 46559–46573 (2020)
5. Boyd, S., Vandenberghe, L.: Convex Optimization, Cambridge. Cambridge University Press, New York (2004)
6. Schneider, J.J., Kirpatrick, S.: Stochastic Optimisation. Springer-Verlag, Heidelberg, Berlin (2006)
7. Montgomery, D.C.: Design and Analysis of Experiments. Wiley, New York (2013)
8. URL of SICS ICE Data Centre located in Luleå, Sweden. https://www.ri.se/en/ice-datacenter/about-ice-datacenter. Accessed 11 Feb 2021
9. Sohlberg, B., Jacobsen, E.W.: Crey box modelling - branches and experiences. IFAC Proc. Vol. **41**(2), 11415–11420 (2008)
10. Dayarathna, M., Wen, Y., Fan, R.: Data center energy consumption modeling: a survey. IEEE Comun. Surv. Tutor. **18**(1), 732–794 (2016)
11. Basmadjian, R., Ali, N., Niedermeier, F., de Meer, H., Giuliani, G.: A methodology to predict the power consumption of servers in data centres (2011)
12. Wang, Z., Bash, C., Tolia, N., Marvah, M., Zhu, X., Ranganathan, P.: Optimal fan speed control for thermal management of servers. In: Proceedings of the ASME/Pacific Rim Technical Conference and Exhibition on Packaging and Integration of Electronic and Photonic Systems, MEMS, and NEMS (InterPACK) (2009)

Power Transformer Design Resorting to Metaheuristics Techniques

Pedro Alves[1], P. M. Fonte[1,2,3], and R. Pereira[1,2,3](✉)

[1] Instituto Superior de Engenharia de Lisboa, Instituto Politécnico de Lisboa, Lisboa, Portugal
{pedro.fonte,rita.pereira}@isel.pt
[2] LCEC/ISEL- Low Carbon Energy Conversion Research Group, R. Conselheiro Emídio Navarro 1,
1959-007 Lisbon, Portugal
[3] ISRC, Interdisciplinary Studies Research Center, Rua Dr. António Bernardino de Almeida, 431, 4200-072 Porto, Portugal

Abstract. Power transformers have a key role in the power system grids. Their manufacturing and design must consider several aspects, such as technical limits, legal constrains, security constrains and manufacturing price. Considering only power transformers' active parts, it is possible to identify 20 manufacturing specific parameters, and in economic point of view, 13 variables are also considered. Using a classic approach, variables are chosen accordingly with the defined constraints, followed by a sensitivity analysis preformed to each variable, to optimize the manufacturing cost. This procedure can be time consuming and the optimum may not be reached. In this paper, genetic algorithms are used. An innovative approach through the introduction of genetic compensation concept in mutation operator is detailed. Results pointed out an increased performance and consistency when compared with the classical approach.

Keywords: Power transformer · Genetic algorithms · Genetic compensation

1 Introduction

Power transformers design is a challenging task requiring simultaneously an agreement between imposed constraints, such as standards and specifications, and keeping manufacturing cost as low as possible. Several design improvements were made to increase power transformer efficiency and decrease manufacturing cost. One example was replacing conventional steel by amorphous laminated steel, resulting in no load losses reduction, about 70% [1]. According to [2], four power transformer designing methodologies can be considered: i) Experimental methods – where binding analytical methods with experimental measurements, results in a precise mathematical model; ii) Equivalent electric circuit – this modeling technique results into a semi-empirical model, but outcomes are satisfactory and this method still be used in industry; iii) Numerical methods – a common tool used to study and model power transformers, being finite elements

© IFIP International Federation for Information Processing 2021
Published by Springer Nature Switzerland AG 2021
L. M. Camarinha-Matos et al. (Eds.): DoCEIS 2021, IFIP AICT 626, pp. 197–205, 2021.
https://doi.org/10.1007/978-3-030-78288-7_19

methods usually applied; iv) Stochastic methods - including artificial intelligence (AI) methods, such as particle swarm optimization (PSO), artificial neural networks (ANN), ant colony optimization (ACO) or genetic algorithms (GA), are rising up.

In literature and among other AI methods, PSO is used for power transformers winding modelling in [3]. ACO technique in used in [4] for power transformer nominal power design and for total cost minimization in [5]. NN are used in [6] for no load losses reduction, for magnetization current minimization in [7], to support winding material selection in [8] or to minimize manufacturing cost in [9]. GA, on their turn are used in [10] to minimize leakage magnetic field, in [11], to minimize both losses and manufacturing costs, in [12] for total cost minimization, or in [13] to minimize only the manufacturing cost.

In this paper, GA is used to minimize power transformer manufacturing cost and an innovative parameter, named as genetic compensation (GC) is included into mutation operator. This paper is organized as follows: in Sect. 2 a relationship to applied AI systems is addressed. In Sect. 3, the GA used is described and the GC parameter developed is detailed. In Sect. 4, the developed methodology is analyzed and in Sect. 5 conclusions are pointed out.

2 Relationship to Applied Artificial Intelligence Systems

In power transformer design is possible to apply traditional methods as the ones described in i–iii (Sect. 1). However, state-of-the art tools based on AI techniques are being used and are reveling new approaches which are less time consuming and allowing available resources optimization. For power transformer design, and if only transformer' active parts are considered, 20 construction parameters must be taken into account. Some of them are detailed in Table 1.

Table 1. Intrinsic power transformer parameters examples for 630 kVA, 20/0.4 kV.

Variable	Value	Description
BIL_{HV-LV}	$150e^{-3}$; $10e^{3}$[V]	Basis insulation for high voltage and low voltage
g_{HV-LV}	8856 [kgm^{-3}]	High voltage (HV), low voltage (LV) specific mass
$LDSP_{HV-LV}$	1; 0.909	HV and LV winding spatial direction factor
$T_{o,max}$	100 [°C]	Oil maximum temperature
$T_{w,max}$	100 [°C]	Winding maximum temperature
$Induced_{max}$	$6e^{3}$ [V]	Maximum induced voltage for 0.28 mm insulation
P_{HV-LV}	$2.0968e^{-8}$ [Ωm]	LV and LV winding resistivity

In addition, and considering the economic point of view, 13 parameters must be considered, where some of them are shown in Table 2. So, this is a complex multidimensional problem that is subjected to a large amount of constraints. The traditional approach described in [14] was implemented and used as comparison basis with the

GA developed method. This traditional and semi empirical method implementation was useful, not only to contextualize the design approach using AI, but also to understand the system variables and their corresponding outcomes.

There are several AI techniques used in power transformer design, as the ones [1–13] mentioned in Sect. 1. All of them have a couple of important features in common, which are the improvement of methods efficiency and optimization. Here, the optimization can be economic, by means of cost reduction resulting in manufacturing energy savings or by using more suitable materials avoiding unnecessary losses (economic or even electrical losses). This paper contribution to applied intelligence systems field, is in line with the previously referred literature, however, an additional and important contribution is given in what concerns to the GA performance, as detailed in Sect. 3.

Table 2. Economic power transformer parameters examples.

Variable	Units	Description
A	[$\$W^{-1}$]	No load losses cost
B	[$\$W^{-1}$]	Load losses cost
$uc_{1,2}$	[$\$kg^{-1}$]	High voltage and low voltage winding costs
uc_6	[$\$kg^{-1}$]	Mineral oil cost
C_{lab}	[$]	Labor cost

3 Power Transformer Design Model

To apply the GA on the power transformer design is mandatory to define the model parameters. Those parameters are given by the chromosomes alleles as described in Table 3.

Table 3. Chromosome alleles considered in GA definition.

Allele	Variable (x_i)	Description
1	Turns_LV	Low voltage winding turns
2	D	Core width
3	FD	Magnetic induction
4	G	Core window' height
5	t_LV	Low voltage conductive tape thickness
6	d_HV	High voltage conducting wire diameter

The fitness function shown in Eq. (1) aggregates all the calculus defined in [14] and receive as inputs the parameters shown in Table 3.

$$[CTM,\ TOC,\ dvar] = f(x_i) \tag{1}$$

In (1) the fitness function depends on CTM parameter, which is the power transformer manufacturing cost; Also, it's possible to consider other parameter, defined as TOC, which is the power transformer total ownership cost. The output parameter, defined as *dvar* is the variables set which are subjected to the constraints shown in Table 4. Costs are obtained by following the dimensioning equations presented in [14] and are subdivided in materials (LV/HV winding, magnetic material, insulation, duct strips, etc.), manufacturing and sales margin.

Table 4. Constrained variables.

Constraint	Variable (x_i)	Description
1	$dvar_1$	Induced voltage (equal constraint)
2	$dvar_2$	Turns ratio (equal constraint)
3	NLL	No load losses
4& 5	LL_LV; LL_HV	Load losses for low and high voltage
6 & 7	TL_LV; TL_HV	Total losses for low and high voltage
8	TLRTT	Heat transfer
9	U_k	Short-circuit impedance
10	AOR	Heat increasing
11 & 12	Induced_LV, HV	Induced voltage on low and high voltage windings
13 &14	Impulse_LV, HV	Voltage impulse on low and high voltage windings
15	TH_min	Tank height

3.1 GA Operator's Characterization

In this section the GA operators, namely selection, crossover, mutation, elitism and stopping criteria are characterized. Selection can be made using: i) proportional method; ii) ranking selection; iii) tournament selection and iv) stationary selection [15]. Considering the power transformer design case study, it is important to guarantee that selection method can include constraints. Despite being possible to use penalties in the decision variable in both, ranking selection and proportional method, this is a complex implementation process because it implies an exhaustive analysis of all decision variables. To obliviate this difficulty, the tournament selection is pointed out by [16] as a solution that enables comparing individuals, relating them with the decision variable and also allowing to make this comparison taking into account the accomplishment of the defined constraints. So, in this case study, a binary tournament selection with constraints, based on [16] is performed.

Crossover operator allows to produce offspring, i.e., allows to produce a set of new possible solutions for the problem. The common crossover types are single point, multipoint and uniform. Because no major differences were noticed by using different crossover types, in this case study single point crossover is performed.

Mutation operator allows to change randomly an allele position, changing the chromosome genetics and is used to ensure the searching for a solution in the overall variables' domain. In [17] is demonstrated that a mutation coefficient higher value can be need for complex problems, as the one considered in this case study. However, the mutation effect can result in new individuals less fit, being this setback solved by natural selection that will eliminate these individuals in future generations. Last studies, showed that in nature, has been observed that mutation tends to be softened, decreasing the pure random mutation characteristic. This phenomenon is defined as GC [18] and will be modeled and implemented as detailed in Sect. 3.2.

Elitism guarantees that the most fit individuals of a previous generation are copied and inserted in the next generation, resulting in a better and quicker algorithm convergence [19]. When a problem with constraints is considered, the elitism operator needs to be adapted, assuring that only parents that satisfy the constraints are chosen and only replace the offspring that don't satisfy the constraints or have worst fitness value than the parents. In this case study 2 stopping criteria were used. The generation limit empirically defined as one hundred times bigger than variables number, and stall. If the GA is still running without an improvement of the fitted individual, then the stall stopping criteria acts.

3.2 Mutation with Genetic Compensation Effect

For a more effective mutation based on nature genetic compensation, the following procedure is applied: when a viable solution occurs, the mutation domain is limited by a range defined around the fitness value of the better fitted individual. For example, assuming a variable domain between 0 and 100 that accomplish the imposed constraints and that for a time instant the most fitted individual for that variable is 15, for that time ahead the mutation will be only possible for a range around 15. If a compensation rate of 10% is chosen, then mutation occurs between 13 and 17 instead between 0 and 100. The proposed approach may slightly increase the risk of falling into a local minimum. The mathematical formulation of this mutation with GC effect is given by (2).

$$x_i^{mutant} = x_i^{best} \times [1 + C_{gencomp} \times (2RAND - 1)] \quad (2)$$

Where x_i^{mutant} is the new i allele value, x_i^{best} is the best i allele value, $C_{gencomp}$ is the GC effect rate and *RAND* is a random value between 0 and 1.

3.3 GA Parameters Definition

In this case study a 200 population size is considered and was defined by GA performance analysis, through tests with 10, 20, 50, 100, 200, 500 and 1000 individuals, which results are shown in Fig. 1.

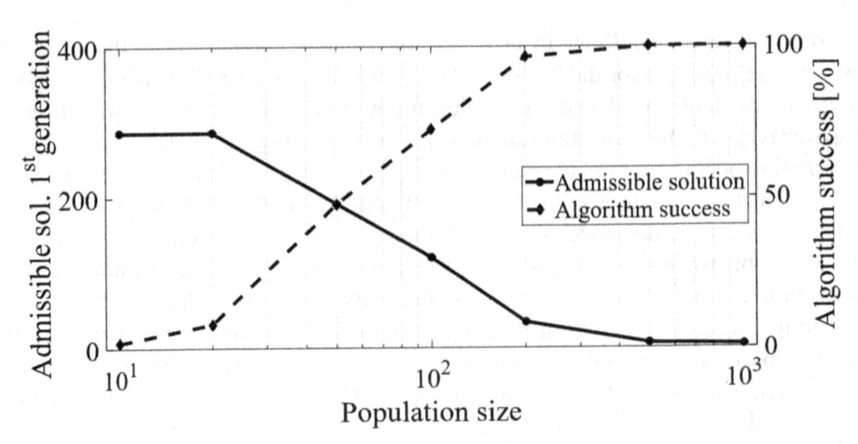

Fig. 1. Population size definition based on admissible solution and algorithm success.

The considered crossover coefficient is 1 (100%) and was also defined by GA performance analysis, through tests shown in Fig. 2, considering 0.01, 0.08, 0.4, 0.8 and 1 crossover coefficient values. Elitism coefficient was considered 5%, the stall stopping criteria was defined at 50 generations and every set of parameters was tested 43 times. The best combination of mutation and GC was found to be 50% and 5%, respectively, as shown in Fig. 3. The corresponding processing time is shown in Fig. 4.

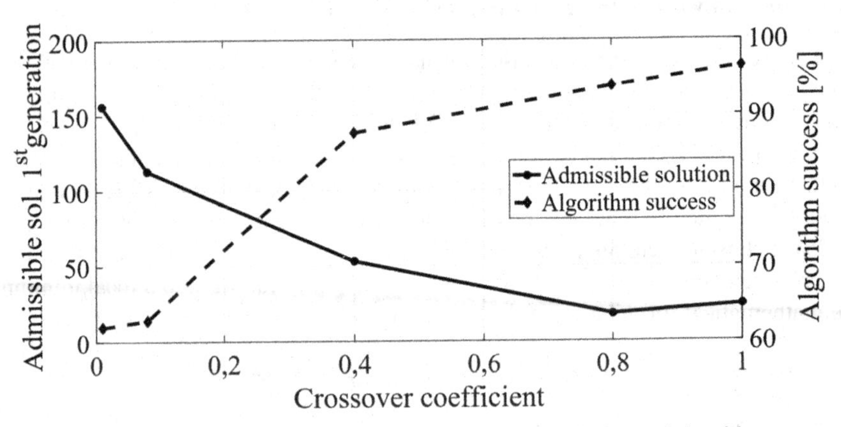

Fig. 2. Crossover coefficient definition based on admissible solution and algorithm success.

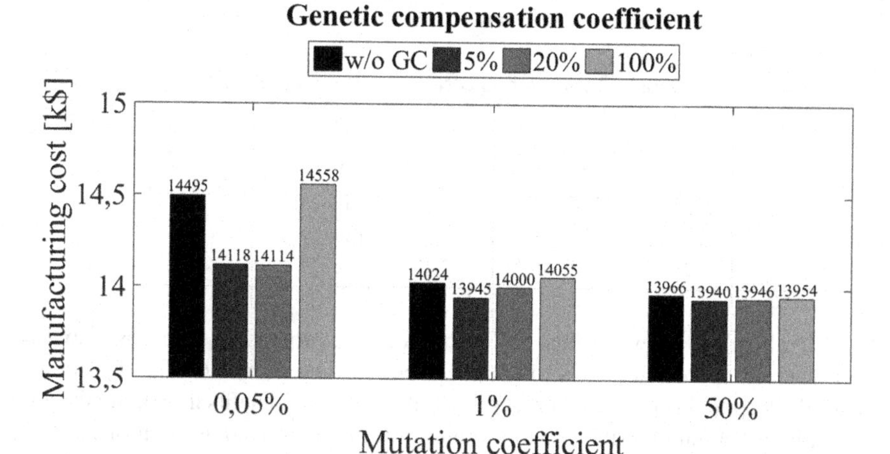

Fig. 3. Mutation coefficient with genetic compensation effect on manufacturing cost.

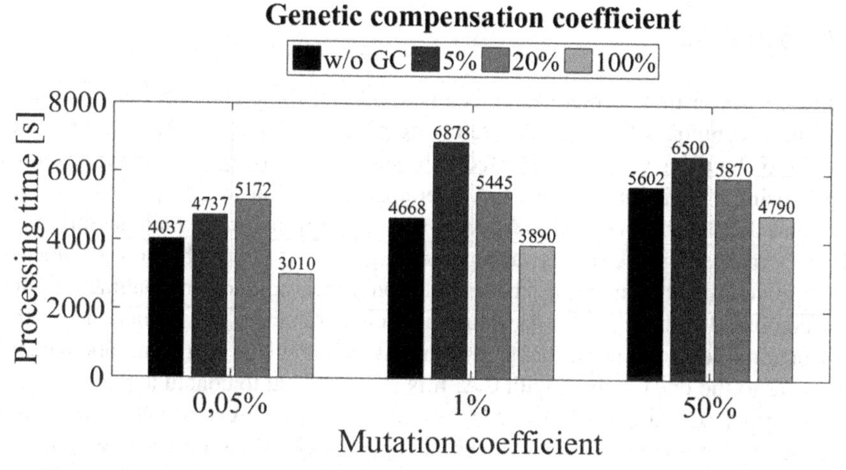

Fig. 4. Mutation coefficient with genetic compensation effect on processing time.

4 Case Study Analysis

Using the traditional power transformer design described in [14] the manufacturing cost is optimized through a sensibility analysis performed by brute-force (BF), consisting in thorough search of the best solution among all admissible solutions, that satisfy the manufacturing requirements and resulting in a benchmark definition. The obtained results are shown in Table 5.

As observed in both Fig. 3 and Fig. 4, GA with GC effect contributes for a manufacturing cost decreasing but the processing time is always superior than the values observed in Table 5. Using the GA with GC effect it is possible to obtain a manufacturing cost of $13 940, inferior to the manufacturing costs registered in Table 5 and

Table 5. Best results obtained with brute-force.

Iteration	Manufacturing cost [$]	Processing time [s]
1	14 672	114
2	14 275	236
3	14 026	47
4	13 945	149

inferior to all values shown in Fig. 3. Nevertheless, the processing time was 43.6 times bigger when compared with the 4th iteration shown in Table 5, with 6500 s of processing time used. Despite this increased processing time, there are benefits in running the algorithm without defining feasible starting values. Starting with random solutions, GA can achieve optimal or quasi-optimal solutions. These tools can show good performances in problems without obvious first feasible solutions.

5 Conclusions

Traditional power transformer design is a method that show good results, however the use of new techniques based on AI are taking place and evolving. This paper shows a contribution by using GA with GC effect. The study was performed by comparison with the BF, using 4 iterations. For the GA operator's definition several performance tests were made, regarding the minimization of the power transformer manufacturing cost, but also considering GA success and processing time. It is possible to conclude, that GA improved the attainment of a better solution, reaching a lower manufacturing cost when compared with BF result. As values of some parameters got smaller and reaching construction tolerances, no further steps were taken in BF. The best result obtained with BF is near to the one obtained with GA. It is also possible to conclude that processing time using GA exceeds the one needed by the BF. However, GA starts performing a blind search without predefined known values as happens with the semi empirical methods, being an adequate exploratory tool to study new transformers models. When traditional methods are used, several iterations must be performed to obtain improved results, so the overall time process should be also considered. The introduction of the GC showed promising results increasing the search capacity. These values can be improved with future research regarding GC coefficient. For future developments, results comparison with other AI techniques, such as PSO or ACO will be addressed.

References

1. Mehta, R.M.P.H.D.: A review on transformer design optimization and performance analysis using artificial intelligence techniques. Int. J. Sci. Res. **3**(9), 726–733 (2014)
2. Amoiralis, E.I., Tsili, M.A., Georgilakis, P.S.: The state of the art in engineering methods for transformer design and optimization: a survey. J. Optoelectron. Adv. Mater. **10**(5), 1149–1158 (2008)

3. Aghmasheh, R., Rashtchi, V., Rahimpour, E.: Gray box modeling of power transformer windings based on design geometry and particle swarm optimization algorithm. IEEE Trans. Power Deliv. **33**(5), 3284–3293 (2018)
4. Folorunso, O., Oriaifo, P.A., Idiagi, N.S., Ogujor, E.A.: Application of anto colony ptimization in distribution transformer sizing. Niger. J. Technol. (NIJOTECH) **36**(4), 1233–1238 (2017)
5. Fouzai, M., Zouaghi, T.: Ant colony algorithm applied to power transformer optimization. In: International Conference on Electrical Engineering and Software Applications, pp. 1–5 (2013)
6. Finocchio, M.A.F., Lopes, J.J., de França, J.A., Piai, J.C., Mangili, Jr. J.F.: Neural networks applied to the design of dry type transformers: an example to analyze the winding temperature and elevate the thermal quality. Int. Trans. Electr. Energ. Syst. **27**(e2257), 1–10 (2017)
7. Adly, A.A.: Computation of inrush current forces on transformer windings. IEEE Trans. Magnet. **37**(4), 2855–2857 (2001)
8. Amoiralis, E.I., Georgilakis, P.S., Tsili, M.A., Kladas, A.G.: Artificial intelligence combined with hybrid FEM-BE techniques for global transformer optimization. IEEE Trans. Magnet. **43**(4), 1633–1636 (2007)
9. Geromel, L.H., Souza, C.R.: The application on intelligent systems in power transformer design. In: IEEE Canadian Conference on Electric & Computer Engineering, pp. 285–290 (2002)
10. Mohammed, S.M., Vural, R.A.: NSGA-II + FEM based loss optimization of three-phase transformer. IEEE Trans. Indus. Electron. **66**(9), 7417–7425 (2019)
11. Elia, S., Fabbri, G., Nisticò, E., Santini, E.: Design of cast-resin distribution transformers by means of genetic algorithms. In: International Symposium on Power Electronics, Electrical Drives, Automation and Motion, pp. 1473–1477 (2006)
12. Zhang, S., Hu, Q., Wang, X., Wang, D.: Research of transformer optimal design modeling and intelligent algorithm. Chin. Control Decis. Conf. **3**, 213–218 (2011)
13. Yang, S., Jianrong, L., Xueliang, F., Haifang, W., Honghui, L.: Application research based on improved genetic algorithm in cloud task scheduling. J. Intell. Fuzzy Syst. **38**(1), 239–246 (2020)
14. Georgilaki, P.S.: Spotlight on Modern Transformer Design. Springer, vol. 53, no. 9 (2009)
15. Goldberg, D.E., Deb, K.: A comparative analysis of selection schemes used in genetic algorithms. In: Foundations of Genetic Algorithms, vol. 1, pp. 69–93 (1991)
16. Coello, C.A.C., Montes, E.M.: Constraint-handling in genetic algorithms through the use of dominance-based tournament selection. Adv. Eng. Inf. **16**(3), 193–203 (2002)
17. Tate, D.M., Smith, A.E.: Expected allele coverage and the role of mutation. In: 5th International Conference on Genetic Algorithms, pp. 31–37, USA (1993)
18. Grether, G.F.: Environmental change, phenotypic plasticity, and genetic compensation. In: The American Naturalist, vol. 166, no. 4 (2005)
19. Deb, K., Pratap, A., Agarwal, S., Meyarivan, T.: A fast and elitist multiobjective genetic algorithm: NSGA-II. IEEE Trans. Evol. Comput. **6**(2), 182–197 (2002)

Communications and Electronics

Detection of Signaling Vulnerabilities in Session Initiation Protocol

Diogo Pereira[1](✉) and Rodolfo Oliveira[1,2](✉)

[1] Departamento de Engenharia Electrotécnica e de Computadores, Faculdade de Ciências e Tecnologia, FCT, Universidade Nova de Lisboa, 2829-516 Caparica, Portugal
dfca.pereira@campus.fct.unl.pt, rado@fct.unl.pt
[2] Instituto de Telecomunicações, 1049-001 Lisbon, Portugal

Abstract. This paper investigates the detection of abnormal sequences of signaling packets purposely generated to perpetuate signaling-based attacks in computer networks. The problem is studied for the Session Initiation Protocol (SIP) using a dataset of signaling packets exchanged by multiple end-users. The paper starts to briefly characterize the adopted dataset and introduces a few definitions to propose a deep learning-based approach to detect possible attacks. The solution is based on the definition of an orthogonal space capable of representing the sampling space for each time step, which is then used to train a recurrent neural network to classify the type of SIP dialog for the sequence of packets observed so far. When a sequence of observed SIP messages is unknown, this represents possible exploitation of a vulnerability and in that case, it should be classified accordingly. The proposed classifier is based on supervised learning of two different sets of anomalous and non-anomalous sequences, which is then tested to identify the detection performance of unknown SIP sequences. Experimental results are presented to assess the proposed solution, which validates the proposed approach to rapidly detect signaling-based attacks.

Keywords: Deep learning · Multimedia networks · SIP protocol

1 Introduction

Nowadays, the Session Initiation Protocol (SIP) [1] plays an important role in the telecommunications arena. SIP supports a plethora of communication services, including voice calls and legacy Public Switched Telephone Network systems through Voice over Internet Protocol (VoIP) [2]. Not less important is the SIP role on cellular networks, where it is used to support all IP Multimedia Subsystem (IMS) services' signaling [3, 4], including multimedia and non-multimedia services. The SIP protocol allows the establishment of sessions through adequate authentication mechanisms and signaling control flows that are dynamic enough to accommodate several purposes, e.g., session initiating, maintaining, and terminating between two peers.

© IFIP International Federation for Information Processing 2021
Published by Springer Nature Switzerland AG 2021
L. M. Camarinha-Matos et al. (Eds.): DoCEIS 2021, IFIP AICT 626, pp. 209–217, 2021.
https://doi.org/10.1007/978-3-030-78288-7_20

The security of the SIP protocol is an important aspect given its importance in the telecommunication operators and in supporting non-commercial VoIP services. It is well-known that SIP is exposed to a significant number of vulnerabilities [5, 6]. In this paper, we are interested in exploring the vulnerabilities caused by the combination of different signaling patterns, which can cause denial-of-service, unauthorized access to a call, billing errors, and other types of attacks [5]. Consequently, it is important to identify potential malicious SIP signaling sequences received by the SIP servers, including new signaling sequences never observed before. While the already known potential malicious sequences can be detected in an automated way, the SIP sequences never observed before need to be analyzed by domain experts who can then assess their level of vulnerability. However, the detection of anomalous SIP signaling sequences is challenging due to the high number of different signaling sequences, the order of the messages in the dialog, and the dialogs' variable length.

Motivated by the advantages of adopting deep learning techniques and admitting that a SIP server can access all SIP messages as they occur over time, in this paper we propose a deep learning scheme to detect anomalous and/or unknown SIP signaling sequences as they transverse the SIP servers. Apart from describing the proposed solution, this paper also reports its performance evaluation tested with practical data.

1.1 Research Question and Contribution

The research question tackled in this paper has to do with the design of innovative learning and classification methodologies capable of identifying unknown or abnormal SIP sequences in the shortest amount of time. The research question is stated as follows:

Considering that a SIP server, or a SIP agent, has access to all SIP messages as they occur over time, is it possible to classify SIP signaling patterns, so that the detection of abnormal or unknown SIP dialogs can be quickly done in an efficient manner? Additionally, is it possible to predict abnormal or unknown SIP dialogs when only a few elements of the SIP signaling sequence are known?

The main contributions of this work are: (1) an innovating modeling approach, capable of representing the knowledge related with the SIP sequences; (2) the knowledge model is then explored in a deep learning scheme, based on Long Short-term Memory (LSTM) Recurrent Neural Networks (RNN); (3) a statistical analysis is proposed to automatically detect unknown SIP sequences; (4) the proposed methodology is evaluated using practical data, showing that the detection of unknown SIP dialogs can reach 99.84%, which demonstrates the practical advantage of the proposed scheme.

1.2 Related Work

The SIP [1] is an application-layer protocol designed to initiate, maintain, and terminate multimedia sessions through the exchange of SIP messages between each user agent. Each SIP message can be either a request or a response. Initially, a SIP message must be sent with a request that can be identified by a specific method. In response to one of those methods, a response SIP message is sent with a specific code. Every SIP request exchanged between agents initiate a SIP transaction, and multiple SIP transactions exchanged between two peers form a SIP dialog, which represents the peer-to-peer relationship over time. A user agent can identify the different dialogs through the SIP Call-ID, i.e., a unique identifier for every dialog's message.

The vulnerabilities of the SIP protocol have been identified in several works such as [5, 6]. These include service interruption, service destruction, or unauthorized access to previously reserved computing resources. SIP service interruption can be caused by flooding attacks, and different solutions include threshold-based classifiers that compare the traffic patterns with the prior statistics [7]. Malformed SIP messages are another way of compromising SIP. Malicious SIP messages are usually detected through intrusion detection systems or identification of deviations from a priori statistics [8]. Another class of SIP vulnerability, aka SIP signaling vulnerability, take advantage of defective implementations of the protocol, where protocol implementation issues can be explored by sending SIP messages to allow improper authentication mechanisms [5]. A mitigation approach for this type of vulnerability was proposed in [9], where a rule-based methodology is used according to the contextual information of the SIP traffic. More recently, the work in [10] has proposed a methodology based on the SIP sequences and their timings that are then used to detect deviations that may represent vulnerabilities. Although different SIP signaling vulnerabilities have already been proposed in [9, 10], this work is not assuming a fixed probabilistic model of the SIP operation. Contrarily, we propose a methodology capable of learning from past SIP sequences, which is used to detect unknown SIP dialogs that can be further categorized by domain experts. Moreover, the vulnerability of the abnormal dialogs can also be evaluated based on prior trustworthy SIP data.

2 Applied Artificial Intelligence Systems

A wide range of services has been supported by innovative applied Artificial Intelligence (AI) systems that have been applied in several areas, such as e-commerce, banking, and social media, just to mention a few. While in several application scenarios the amount of data and time constraints are not a big concern, in other applications the AI systems need to cope with very large amounts of data and a quick response might be required. Traditionally, the security of individuals and computational systems has been an area of massive adoption of AI systems. In this work, we address the security of the SIP protocol, an important tool for network operators and society in general. This work is mainly centered on the adoption of AI tools to learn from prior SIP data and to classify SIP dialogs in the shortest amount of time. Recent advances in AI, particularly on deep learning techniques that deal with sequential data are natural candidates to be used in the classification of SIP dialogs. However, the high volume of signaling traffic on the network operator servers needs well-tailored solutions capable of making an accurate decision using the minimum amount of data so that they achieve a quick response. Our work aims at fulfilling this challenge, by adopting state-of-art deep learning techniques based on RNNs that are feed with real-time SIP packets traversing the SIP servers. The focus is on the efficient classification of SIP dialogs observed so far, as well as on the detection of unknown SIP dialogs never observed before.

3 Modeling, Learning, and Classification

3.1 System Model

A **SIP message** $m_k, k \in \mathcal{M} = \{1, 2, \ldots, M\}$, represents a specific type of SIP request or SIP response. The total number of types of SIP requests plus responses is denoted by M, and $\mathcal{M}$ represents the set of all types of SIP messages. A SIP dialog is composed of SIP messages. More specifically, a **SIP dialog** is a sequence of consecutive SIP messages represented by $\boldsymbol{d}_k =< m^{(1)}, m^{(2)}, \ldots, m^{(L_d)} >$, where $m^{(j)}$ represents the $j-th$ message of the SIP dialog. L_d represents the SIP dialog length. All SIP messages contained in a SIP dialog share the same SIP Call-ID, and sender and receiver URIs. Given the number of possible SIP methods in a request and possible reply codes in a response, the number of different dialogs that can be created between the user agents is high. Besides that, the dialogs can be legitimate or anomalous.

An **observation** k taken by a user agent or a SIP server is a sequence of consecutive SIP messages represented by $\boldsymbol{o}_k = \langle m^{(1)}, m^{(2)}, \ldots, m^{(L_o)} \rangle$. Each SIP message is represented by $m^{(h)} = m_i, i \in \mathcal{M}, h \in \{1, 2, \ldots, L_o\}$. The symbol L_o represents the length of the observation.

A requirement to meet when working with sequential neural networks is that the length of the input data must be described over consecutive discrete-time events. The set of events is represented by the observation. However, because the length of the observations can be variable, we transform each observation into a fixed-length stuffed sequence, denoted as a pad sequence. A **pad sequence** $\boldsymbol{s}_k$ associated to the observation $\boldsymbol{o}_k$, is a sequence of length $L_N = L_o + n$, where n represents the number of zeros added to the observation as follows, $\boldsymbol{s}_k = < \underbrace{\boldsymbol{o}_k, 0, 0, \ldots, 0}_{(n)} >$. L_N represents a fixed length in all pad sequences. Another aspect that must be evaluated is the type of data handled by the neural network, i.e., numerical, or categorical data, since it influences how the input data is normalized. The SIP methods and responses are categorical data, and its encoding is done through an **encoded SIP message** $\boldsymbol{m}_i^{'}$, which represents a Boolean vector describing the SIP message m_i. This vector has a length of $L_M = M + 1$, where 1 represents the zero-pad symbol and is obtained using a One Hot Encoder [12].

3.2 Deep Learning and Classification

The learning of the SIP dialogs observed in a server is tackled in this subsection through the adoption of a recurrent neural network, more specifically a LSTM.

Since the goal of this work is to classify the input data in multiple SIP dialogs contained in trustworthy or non-trustworthy datasets, it was designed the LSTM architecture to detect an observed input sequence of L_o SIP messages. This architecture is presented in Fig. 1, consisting of one LSTM RNN model and an Unknown SIP Dialogs' Classifier. The LSTM RNN model receives a $1 \times L_N \times M$ input sequence $\boldsymbol{s}_k$, produced by the Pad Sequence and the One Hot Encoder. Then the LSTM layer processes one step at each L_N discrete time units of $\boldsymbol{s}_k$ and returns a $1 \times N$ sequence, $\boldsymbol{h}_0$, with real values in the interval $[-1, 1]$. The Dense layer receives the LSTM output and generates the output vector, $\boldsymbol{y}_k$, a $1 \times N$ sequence with real values in $[0, 1]$. The variable N stands for the total number of unique SIP dialogs contained in the trustworthy dataset. Through this output vector, it is possible to identify the most probable dialog by finding the position with maximum value.

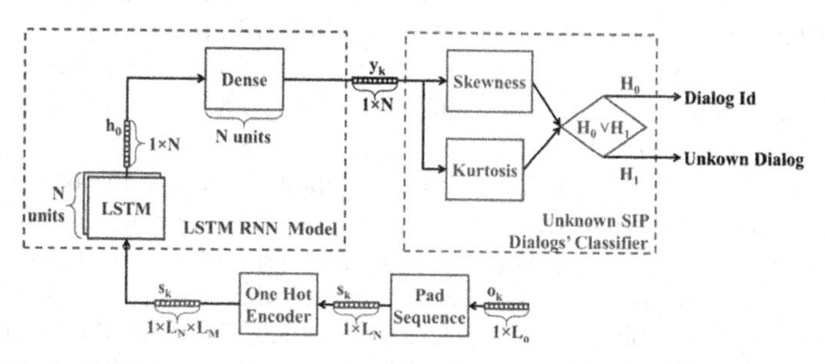

Fig. 1. LSTM architecture, including the unknown SIP dialog's classifier.

3.3 Unknown SIP Dialogs' Detection

The unknown SIP dialogs are the ones not included in the training datasets of trustworthy and non-trustworthy dialogs. The goal behind the detection of unknown SIP dialogs is to identify SIP dialogs not included in the training datasets and thus detect SIP dialogs never observed before. The output of the LSTM RNN model is used as input of the unknown SIP dialogs' classifier. From this input, it is computed the central moments to evaluate if they can be used to distinguish unknown SIP dialogs. Next, we describe a semi-supervised threshold-based classifier used to distinguish known and unknown SIP dialogs.

The classifier starts to compute the normalized kurtosis and skewness of each observed SIP dialog. The kurtosis and skewness thresholds are given by $\lambda_k = \mu_k - \sigma_k^2$ and $\lambda_s = \mu_s - \sigma_s^2$, respectively, where μ_k and μ_s represent the mean of the kurtosis and skewness values computed from the LSTM RNN model outputs for all SIP dialogs in the training set, and σ_k^2 and σ_s^2 represent the variance of the kurtosis and skewness values, respectively.

A SIP dialog is classified as a known dialog, hypothesis H_0, or unknown dialog, hypothesis H_1, according to the following conditions:

$$H_0 : \mu^3 \geq \lambda_s, \mu^4 \geq \lambda_k,$$

$$H_1 : \mu^3 < \lambda_s, \mu^4 < \lambda_k,$$

where μ^3 and μ^4 represent the skewness and kurtosis of the LSTM output obtained with the SIP dialog to classify.

4 Performance Evaluation

To validate the performance of the architecture proposed in Sect. 3, it was adopted the SIP dataset created in [11]. Regarding the characteristics of this dataset, it contains 1492 types of SIP dialogs, which correspond to a total of 18782 SIP dialogs. The length of these SIP dialogs is between 2 and 56, and the number of unique SIP messages (M) is 17. Through this information, we can identify some of the variables previously defined in Subsects. 3.1 and 3.2, particularly, $L_N = 56$, $L_M = 18$, and $N = 1492$.

Three different datasets were used to train, validate, and test the proposed neural network architecture. The datasets were randomly divided containing 50%, 20%, and 30% of the transactions exchanged on the SIP dataset, representing the training, validating, and testing datasets, respectively. Finally, the results here reported were computed in Python running over a 64bit Ubuntu 18.04.5 LTS with 128 GB of RAM and running over an Intel(R) Core(TM) i7-9800X CPU @ 3.80 GHz and GeForce RTX 2080 Ti 11 GB. Regarding the execution in a RTX 2080 Ti, its advantage is mainly observed for training the neural network. Equivalent or even lower computational times can be achieved by implementing the neural network in dedicated hardware (e.g. adopting FPGAs).

To perform the detection of the most likely SIP dialog for each given sequence of SIP dialogs the LSTM RNN model was trained for 500 epochs and the detection probability is reported in Table 1. The detection probability shows that the LSTM RNN model can classify all the dialogs it learned, since it detects all the SIP dialogs belonging to the training set. However, the same cannot be stated for the validation and test datasets, because the detection probability is lower than 100%. The lower performance is due to the existence of SIP dialogs that were never learned before. This is a consequence of their lower occurrence in the SIP dataset meaning that when they were distributed over each dataset they were placed in the test and validation datasets.

Table 1. Detection probability of the LSTM RNN model in each dataset.

Dataset	Train	Validation	Test	Joint datasets
Detection probability	100.00%	93.54%	92.80%	96.60%

The detection performance of the proposed model is also depicted in Fig. 2, where the prediction performance is studied as a function of the relative amount of information that constitutes the SIP dialog, i.e., L_o/L_d. In this test, the model uses as inputs an increasing sequence of SIP messages until reaching the complete SIP dialog. For each added new message it is checked if the model is capable of successfully classifying that specific dialog. The results show that the proposed model correctly predicts some dialogs with the minimum amount of information available, close to 1.79%. However, to correctly identify 50% of the dialogs it is required to know approximately 85.71% of the information of the SIP dialog. Finally, when the complete SIP dialog is known ($L_o/L_d = 100\%$) we enter the detection stage where its probability is close to 0.9660. Additionally, the average detection computing time is 1.969 ms.

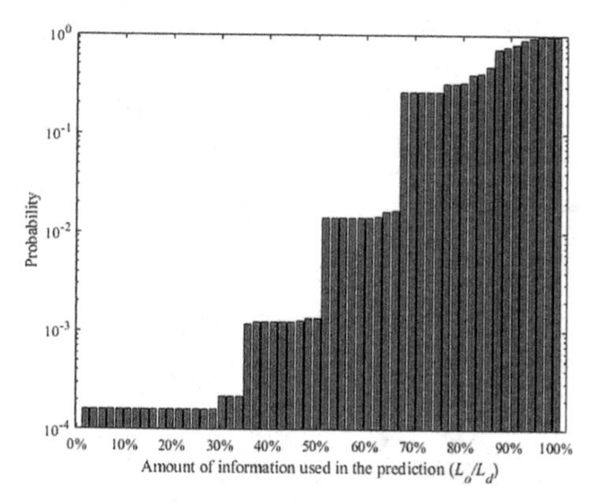

Fig. 2. SIP dialogs prediction probability over the amount of available information.

Table 2. Unknown SIP dialogs classifier metrics.

$P_D = \frac{TP}{TP+FN}$	$P_{FA} = \frac{FP}{TN+FP}$
99.84%	7.24%

As referred above, there are SIP dialogs that are mis-detected by the proposed LSTM RNN model. Thus, it is important that these dialogs are classified as unknown, to prevent the occurrence of attacks. The classification of unknown SIP dialogs was achieved through the addition of a classifier that was parametrized to distinguish between the dialogs that were already trained and the unknown ones. The classifier is based on the skewness and kurtosis of the LSTM RNN model's output, as explained in Subsect. 3.3, and the decision is based on two thresholds, $\lambda_k = 0.9816$, and $\lambda_k = 0.96826$ that were computed using the training dataset. Concerning the performance of the classifier, Fig. 3 illustrates the distribution of the dialogs classified into four different labels. These labels present the dialogs that were correctly classified as unknown and already trained, respectively, true positive and true negative, but also the dialogs that were misclassified (false negative and false positive). Through the labels, we have computed the probability of correctly classifying the dialogs as unknown (P_D) and the probability of misclassifying a trustworthy dialog (P_{FA}). The results are presented in Table 2, showing that the proposed classifier can detect 99.84% of the unknown SIP dialogs. This is an important result since it can be used to detect possible vulnerabilities through the appropriate evaluation of the SIP dialogs by domain experts capable of assessing its vulnerability level.

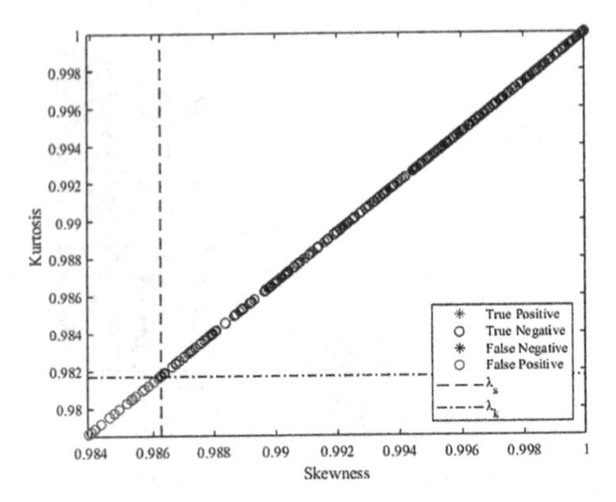

Fig. 3. Performance of the unknown SIP dialog's classifier.

5 Conclusions

Giving the high importance of SIP security for telecommunication companies and non-commercial VoIP services, this paper proposed a dynamic methodology capable of identifying important protocol vulnerabilities related to SIP signaling. More concretely, we have proposed an innovative methodology to detect SIP sequences according to prior data, which can be labeled as trustworthy or non-trustworthy data. Additionally, a statistical methodology is also described to detect unknown SIP dialogs that can constitute an important source of attacks. The experimental assessment described in the paper and its results show the effectiveness of the proposed methodology to improve the security of SIP-based services.

References

1. Rosenberg, J., et al.: Sip: session initiation protocol. RFC 3261, RFC Editor, June 2002
2. Uzelac, A., Lee, Y.: Voice over ip (voip) sip peering use cases. RFC 6405, RFC Editor, November 2011
3. Khlifi, H., Grégoire, J.: IMS application servers: roles, requirements, and implementation technologies. IEEE Internet Comput. **12**(3), 40–51 (2008)
4. Achour, A., Haddadou, K., Kervella, B., Pujolle, G.: A SIP-SHIM6-based solution providing interdomain service continuity in IMS-based networks. IEEE Commun. Mag. **50**(7), 109–119 (2012)
5. Sisalem, D., Kuthan, J., Ehlert, S.: Denial of service attacks targeting a sip voip infrastructure: attack scenarios and prevention mechanisms. IEEE Netw. **20**(5), 26–31 (2006)
6. Geneiatakis, D., et al.: Survey of security vulnerabilities in session initiation protocol. IEEE Commun. Surv. Tuts. **8**(3), 68–81 (2006)
7. Tas, I.M., Unsalver, B.G., Baktir, S.: A Novel SIP based distributed reflection denial-of-service attack and an effective defense mechanism. IEEE Access **8**, 112574–112584 (2020)
8. Hentehzadeh, N., Mehta, A., Gurbani, V.K., Gupta, L., Ho, T.K., Wilathgamuwa, G.: Statistical analysis of self-similar session initiation protocol (sip) messages for anomaly detection. In: 2011 4th IFIP International Conference on New Technologies, Mobility and Security, pp. 1–5 (2011)

9. Lahmadi, A., Festor, O.: A framework for automated exploit prevention from known vulnerabilities in voice over ip services. IEEE Trans. Netw. Serv. Manag. **9**(2), 114–127 (2012)
10. Golait, D., Hubballi, N.: Detecting anomalous behavior in voip systems: a discrete event system modeling. IEEE Trans. Inf. Forens. Secur. **12**(3), 730–745 (2017)
11. Nassar, M., State, R., Festor, O.: Labeled VoIP data-set for intrusion detection evaluation. In: Aagesen, F.A., Knapskog, S.J. (eds.) EUNICE 2010. LNCS, vol. 6164, pp. 97–106. Springer, Heidelberg (2010). https://doi.org/10.1007/978-3-642-13971-0_10
12. Harris, D., Harris, S.: Digital Design and Computer Architecture, 2nd edn. Morgan Kaufmann Publishers Inc., San Francisco (2012)

Interference Power Characterization in Directional Networks and Full-Duplex Systems

Ayman T. Abusabah[1,2(✉)], Rodolfo Oliveira[1,2], and Luis Irio[1,2]

[1] Departamento de Engenharia Electrótecnica e de Computadores, Faculdade de Ciências e Tecnologia, Universidade Nova de Lisboa, 2825-149 Caparica, Portugal
[2] Instituto de Telecomunicações, Aveiro, Portugal

Abstract. This paper characterizes the aggregate interference power considering both directional millimeter-wave (mmWave) and In-Band Full-Duplex (IBFDX) communications. The considered scenario admits random locations of the interferers. The analysis considers a general distance-based path loss with a sectored antenna model. The interference caused to a single node also takes into account the residual self-interference due to IBFDX operation. The main contribution of the paper is the characterization of the interference caused by both transmitting nodes and full-duplex operation for different parameters and scenarios.

Keywords: In-Band Full-Duplex wireless communications · Directional beamforming · Millimeter-Wave · Interference characterization · Performance analysis

1 Introduction

In In-Band Full-Duplex (IBFDX) wireless communications, the a transceiver can simultaneously transmit and receive over the same frequency band. Compared with half-duplex communication systems, e.g., time division duplexing (TTD) and frequency division duplexing (FDD), the full-duplex systems can potentially double the capacity of the communication link, by reducing the residual self-interference (SI) through passive and active methods [1, 2]. On the other hand, directional communication is a promising technology that has an advantage in overcoming the high isotropic path loss at millimeter-wave (mmWave) bands, [3]. Rigorously speaking, directional communication networks will change the conventional concepts about the interference, because the nodes align their beams according to specific directions.

The characterization of interference in wireless networks has been a topic of extensive research in the last years [4]. The aggregate interference is usually modeled through advanced stochastic geometry techniques [5] that have into account the spatial position of each interferer and its radio channel to determine the amount of interference caused to a specific node [4]. In [6], the authors have adopted the concepts of aligned

© IFIP International Federation for Information Processing 2021
Published by Springer Nature Switzerland AG 2021
L. M. Camarinha-Matos et al. (Eds.): DoCEIS 2021, IFIP AICT 626, pp. 218–225, 2021.
https://doi.org/10.1007/978-3-030-78288-7_21

gain and misaligned gain to derive a coverage model for the signal-to-interference-plus-noise ratio (SINR). The spatial interference caused by multiple simultaneous and uncoordinated transmissions occurring in the mmWave band was studied in [7] to characterize the collision probability as a function of the density of the transmitting nodes and antenna patterns. The authors in [8] have also considered the effect of non-binary object blockage in the aggregate interference, by assuming that a single obstacle can cause a partial blockage. The modeling of interference in cellular MIMO beamforming mmWave communications was also tackled in [9], by considering two models (inverse Weibull and inverse Gaussian) and a mixture of them. On the other hand, the difficulty in the mathematical modeling process has limited the amount of the study for the statistical characterization of residual SI. The authors in [10] have computed the strength of the residual SI and the amount of cancellation. In particular, the authors assumed a narrow-band model for the characterization of the residual SI power, i.e., it is assumed that the coherence time of the channel is more than the time of the signal. The distribution of the residual SI power was compared with other known distributions in [11]. Closed-form approximations were presented in [12] and [13]. The work in [14] estimates the channel with a single tap delay. While the aforementioned works deal with each type of interference individually, this work considers the characterization of the interference in directional networks jointly with the residual SI from IBFDX systems.

1.1 Motivation and Research Question

The key to success when designing the IBFDX system is to minimize the residual SI. Mainly, the cancelation of the SI is proportional to the accuracy of the estimated channels. Moreover, directional beamforming plays a major role in boosting the communication quality. In such systems, multiple nodes may act as interference sources toward a specific node. Therefore, it is crucial to study the joint interference caused by not only IBFDX systems, but also by directional beamforming. The study aims to answer the following research questions:

- Question 1: What is the best distribution to model the interference power when jointly considering IBFDX and directional communication?
- Question 2: How can the estimation errors effect on the interference power?
- Question 3: What is the influence of gain pattern parameters (main lobe, sidelobes, and beamwidth) on the interference power?

2 Relationship to Applied Artificial Intelligence Systems

Nowadays artificial intelligence (AI) systems play an important role in several sectors, leveraging the added value of a multitude of services through more customized practices that allow a better fit between the service demand and its operational features. Big efforts are usually required to process a large amount of offline data in AI systems, while online applications supported by AI, such as autonomous driving, require very low latency. The low latency requirement includes not only efficient AI algorithms, but also low latency and high throughput communication links. This work is mainly centered on improving the throughput of existing wireless communication systems, which are and will be even more important to deploy a plethora of AI systems capable of addressing mobile and low latency services.

3 System Model

In the system model we consider that the transimmters (aka nodes) are located in the spatial region of interest according to a Poisson Point Process (PPP) Π with density λ over a ring with an inner radius, R_{I}, and an outer radius, $R_{\mathcal{O}}$, i.e., $R_{\mathrm{I}} \leq r \leq R_{\mathcal{O}}$. For the particular case of $R_{\mathrm{I}} = 0$ a circular region is considered. Without loss of generality, we condition on a node at the origin, which according to Slivnyak's theory in stochastic geometry [15], yields to a homogeneous PPP with the corresponding density λ. The reference node is supposed to perform IBFDX to communicate with a corresponding node. At a given time slot, we assume that one or more nodes, except the one connected with the reference node, cause interference. The goal is mainly to characterize the power of the interference caused by multiple transmitting nodes and the the residual SI power caused by IBFDX operation.

We adopt an active analog canceler full-duplex model [13] that cancels the SI at the angular carrier frequency $\omega_c = 2\pi f_c$. The model considers the residual interference after the SI signal has been canceled by a generic post-mixer active analog canceller. Analogue cancellation schemes can achieve a substantial amount of cancellation [10] (up to 40–50 dB), achieving higher cancellation than the digital one. This can be due to the cancellation of the transmitter impairments. Moreover, if analog cancellation and digital cancellation are sequentially combined, the performance of the digital cancellation depends on the analog cancellation performance, as reported in [16]. Consequently, it is recommended to use analog cancellation techniques before the digital cancellation. The proposed model considers the residual SI signal in an analog post-mixer canceler after the SI signal is upconverted.

The up-converted SI signal, $x(t)$, is transmitted over the full-duplex channel with gain and delay denoted by h and τ, respectively. The estimated channel parameters, delay and gain, $\hat{\tau}$ and $\hat{h}$, respectively, are injected in the cancelation loop to obtain the residual SI signal, $y_{res}(t)$, as depicted in Fig. 1.

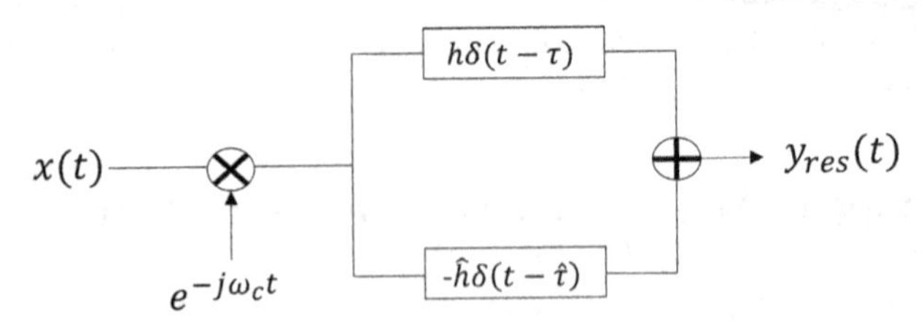

Fig. 1. Block diagram of IBFDX system.

Based on Fig. 1, $y_{res}(t)$ represents the residual SI signal which can be expressed as follows

$$y_{res}(t) = hx(t-\tau)e^{j\omega_c(t-\tau)} - \hat{h}x\big(t-\hat{\tau}\big)e^{j\omega_c(t-\hat{\tau})}, \tag{1}$$

where h is the channel gain and $\hat{h}$ is the estimated gain given by $\hat{h} = \epsilon h$, where $(1 - \epsilon)$ is the estimation error of the gain, $\epsilon \geq 0$. The estimation error of the phase is given by $\phi = \omega_c\big(\tau - \hat{\tau}\big)$. We highlight that The estimated channel parameters $\hat{h}$ and $\hat{\tau}$ can be done using different approaches that are already available in the literature [17].

Considering that $x(t - \tau) = x\big(t - \hat{\tau}\big)$, then (1) can be written as follows

$$y_{res}(t) = x(t)hc, \tag{2}$$

where $c = \Big(e^{j\omega_c(t-\tau)} - \epsilon e^{j\omega_c(t-\hat{\tau})}\Big)$ is a constant. Assuming that $x(t)$ and h are independent random variables (RVs), then, the residual SI power can be represented as

$$P_{y_{res}} = \big(X^2\big)\big(H^2\big)C, \tag{3}$$

where $C = \big(1 + \epsilon^2 - 2\epsilon\cos(\phi)\big)$ is again a constant. Based on (3), the residual SI power is proportional to the power of the transmitted signal, the power of the SI channel, and estimation errors.

Considering a large-scale, distance-based path loss and small-scale fading for modeling the wireless channel between any communicating pairs. Therefore, the received power caused by an i-th node and seen at the reference node is given by

$$P_i = P_t\Psi_i G_{i,\mathcal{J}} G_{\mathcal{J},i}(r_i)^{-\alpha}, \tag{4}$$

where P_t is the same transmitted power across all nodes. We also consider both Rayleigh and Rician small-scale fading channels in which Ψ_i is drawn from a Gamma distribution as shown later. $G_{i,\mathrm{I}}$ and $G_{\mathrm{I},i}$ represent the gain of an i-th transmitting node and the gain of the reference node, respectively. $\alpha > 2$ is the large-scale path loss coefficient, and r_i is the distance between an i-th node and the reference node.

The Rayleigh channel can describe the stochastic fading when there is no line-of-sight (LoS) signal. When the channel is a Rayleigh distributed, $\boldsymbol{\Psi_i}$ can be drawn from an exponential distribution with mean $1/\boldsymbol{\mu}$, therefore, it can be expressed by a Gamma distribution with the shape parameter, $\boldsymbol{k} = 1$, and the scale parameter, $\boldsymbol{\theta} = \frac{1}{\mu}$, as follows

$$\Psi_i \sim \mathrm{Exp}(\mu) \sim \mathrm{Gamma}(k, \theta). \tag{5}$$

On the other hand, the Rician fading channel can be characterized through K and Ω where K is the ratio between the LoS power and the non-LoS power, and Ω represents the total power from LoS and non-LoS. Then, the received signal amplitude is Rician distributed with parameters $\nu^2 = \frac{K\Omega}{1+K}$ and $\sigma^2 = \frac{\Omega}{2(1+K)}$. $K_{dB} = 10\log_{10}(K)$ is the decibels representation of K. By definition, if $X \sim Rice(\nu, \sigma)$, then $(\frac{X}{\sigma})^2$ follows a non-central Chi-squared distribution with non-centrality parameter $(\frac{\nu}{\sigma})^2$. Consequently, moment matching can then be used to obtain a simplified Gamma approximation for Ψ_i as $\Psi_i \sim \mathrm{Exp}(\mu) \sim \mathrm{Gamma}(k, \theta)$, where the shape parameter, k, and scale parameter, θ, are given by

$$k = \frac{(\nu^2 + 2\sigma^2)^2}{4\sigma^2\big(\nu^2 + \sigma^2\big)}, \theta = \frac{4\sigma^2\big(\nu^2 + \sigma^2\big)}{(\nu^2 + 2\sigma^2)^2}. \tag{6}$$

Regarding the beamforming model, we asume that all nodes are capable of performing directional beamforming. We adopt an antenna model to represent the gain patterns G_T and G_R at the transmitting and receiving node, respectively, as follows

$$G_{T,R}(\theta) = \begin{cases} G_{T,R}^{max}, & |\theta| \leq \omega/2 \\ G_{T,R}^{min}, & |\theta| \geq \omega/2 \end{cases} \tag{7}$$

where G^{max} and G^{min} are the gains of main and sidelobes, respectively, defined by beamwidth $\omega \in (0, 2\pi)$ and the bore-sight angle direction $\theta \in (-\pi, \pi)$. We assume that all nodes are located on the same plane, i.e., no variation in beam pattern over the elevation angle. While the sectorized antenna modeling is quite simple, some useful applications with some simplifying assumptions can be obtained and utilized as claimed in [5] and adopted in [13] for establishing innovative MAC policies.

Based on (4), the aggregate interference power caused to the reference node is formulated as

$$I_o = \sum_{i=1}^{N} P_i, i \in \Pi, \tag{8}$$

where N is a RV characterized by a homogeneous PPP that represents the number of active transmitters over the region represented by the area $A = \pi\left(R_{\mathcal{O}}^2 - R_{\mathrm{I}}^2\right)$. Therefore, the probability of n nodes being inside a region A is given by

$$P[N = n] = \frac{(\lambda|A|)^n}{n!} e^{-\lambda|A|}. \tag{9}$$

Finally, the aggregate interference power at the reference node is the residual SI power given by (3) and the interference power given by (9), which can be written as

$$P_{tot} = P_{y_{res}} + I_o. \tag{10}$$

4 Performance Analysis

The validation has been performed using the Monte Carlo simulation results where 10^6 iterations were run. The carrier frequency is set to 60 GHz. The power of the residual SI in (3) and the aggregate interference power in (8) are generated from empirical data. The samples of the SI signal are generated from Normal distribution, i.e., $X \sim \mathcal{N}(0, \sigma_x^2)$ with $\sigma_x^2 = \frac{1}{2}$. The SI channel is assumed to be Rician distributed, i.e., $H \sim Rice(\nu, \sigma)$. Ψ_i are generated from a Gamma distribution, where k and θ are identified for a Rayleigh channel and for a Rician channel. The network and channel parameters are listed in Table 1, unless otherwise specified.

Table 1. Network and channel parameters

f_c	60 GHz	P_t	1 mW	σ_x^2	0.5	Ω	1 mW
ϵ	0.9	K_{dB} for SI channel	10	σ_h^2	0.5	α	4
ϕ	10°	K_{dB} for directional channel	0	R_I, R_O	1 m, 5 m	G^{max}	1
μ	2	ω	{45°, 60°}	λ	50 node/m^2	G^{min}	{0.05, 0.1}

For sake of defining the best distribution in representing the aggregate interference power, different known distributions were generated using empirical data. Figure 2 plots the PDF of the distributions exhibiting the best accuracy (Exponential, Weibull, Nakagami, Gamma, Rayleigh, Generalized Extreme Value (GEV), and Lognormal) against the PDF of the empirical data considering a Rician Fading channel for directional communication. As can be seen, GEV distribution exhibits the best accuracy in representing the aggregate interference power. The CDFs of the aggregate interference power are depicted in Fig. 3 for fast fading (Rician and Rayleigh) channels. Different gain levels of the beam sidelobes and different beamwidths are considered. The results reflect the incremental effect on the interference power due to the increase in the sidelobes gain ($G^{min} = 0.05, 0.1$ were adopted in the comparison). On the other hand, the results show that the interference power decreases when adopting small ω values (narrower beams), due to the concentration of higher power in specific and smaller spatial regions ($\omega = 45°, 60°$ were adopted in the comparison). We conclude that although the proposed modeling methodology is quite simple, the simulated CDFs comply with different network and channel parameters.

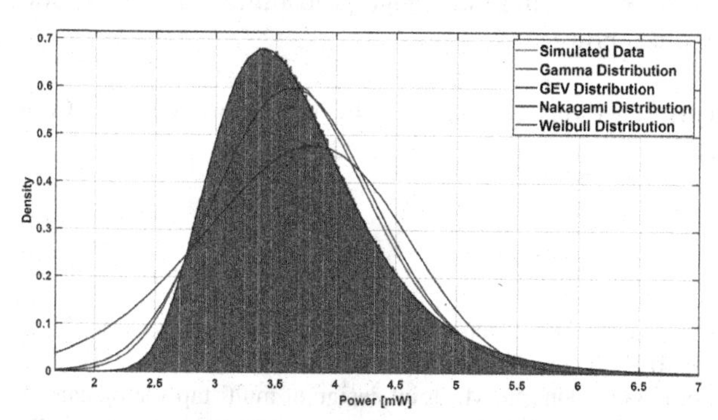

Fig. 2. The PDF of the aggregate interference power with PDFs of other known distributions considering a Rician channel for directional communication: $K_{dB} = 0$, $\omega = 45°$, and $G^{min} = 0.1$.

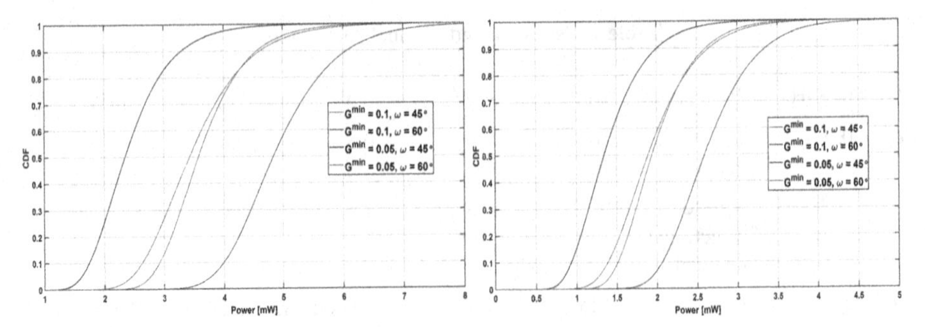

Fig. 3. CDFs of the aggregate interference power P_{tot} considering 1) a Rician fading channel for directional communication with $K_{dB} = 0$ at the left side 2) a Rayleigh fading channel for directional communication: $\mu = 2$ at the right side.

5 Conclusions

In this paper, we have studied the distribution of the aggregate interference power due to: 1) the residual SI power in IBFDX, 2) the interference caused to a single node in directional beamforming networks. The work takes the initial step for investigating theoretical approximations of the aggregate interference power. Based on an extensive comparison with known distributions, it is shown that the GEV distribution exhibits the best accuracy in representing the aggregate interference power. The aggregate interference power distribution shown in this work can be adopted in providing technical criteria for mitigating the level of the interference in practical directional communication when considering IBFDX systems. For example, the optimal antenna parameters can be computed according to a given interference level. In general, the interference characterization can be utilized to define several points related to the performance analysis of both directional communication and IBFDX systems. For instance, the communication systems capacity can be enhanced by deriving the outage probability using the characteristics of the aggregate interference power.

Acknowledgements. This work was supported by the Marie Skłodowska-Curie project number 813391, TeamUp5G.

References

1. Kolodziej, K.E., Perry, B.T., Herd, J.S.: In-band full-duplex technology: techniques and systems survey. IEEE Trans. Microw. Theory Tech. **67**(7), 3025–3041 (2019)
2. Alexandropoulos, G.C., Duarte, M.: Joint design of multi-tap analog cancellation and digital beamforming for reduced complexity full duplex MIMO systems. In: IEEE International Conference on Communications (ICC), Paris, pp. 1–7 (2017)
3. Yang, H., Herben, M.H.A.J., Akkermans, I.J.A.G., Smulders, P.F.M.: Impact analysis of directional antennas and multiantenna beamformers on radio transmission. IEEE Trans. on Veh. Technol. **57**(3), 1695–1707 (2008)
4. Haenggi, M., Ganti, R.: Interference in large wireless networks. Found. Trends Netw. **3**, 127–248 (2009)

5. Di Renzo, M.: Stochastic geometry modeling and analysis of multi-tier millimeter wave cellular networks. IEEE Trans. Wirel. Commun. **14**(9), 5038–5057 (2015)
6. Rebato, M., Park, J., Popovski, P., De Carvalho, E., Zorzi, M.: Stochastic geometric coverage analysis in mmWave cellular networks with realistic channel and antenna radiation models. IEEE Trans. Commun. **67**(5), 3736–3752 (2019)
7. Singh, S., Mudumbai, R., Madhow, U.: Interference analysis for highly directional 60-GHz mesh networks: the case for rethinking medium access control. IEEE/ACM Trans. Netw. **19**(5), 1513–1527 (2011)
8. Niknam, S., Natarajan, B., Barazideh, R.: Interference analysis for finite-Area 5G mmWave networks considering blockage effect. IEEE Access **6**, 23470–23479 (2018)
9. Elkotby, H., Vu, M.: Interference modeling for cellular networks under beamforming transmission. IEEE Trans. Wireless Commun. **16**(8), 5201–5217 (2017)
10. Sahai, G.P., Dick, C., Sabharwal, A.: On the impact of phase noise on active cancelation in wireless full-duplex. IEEE Trans. Veh. Technol. **62**(9), 4494–4510 (2013)
11. Abusabah, A.T., Irio, L., Oliveira, R.: In-band full-duplex residual self-interference approximation in multi-tap delay fading channels. In: 2020 International Wireless Communications and Mobile Computing (IWCMC), Limassol, Cyprus, pp. 635–640 (2020)
12. Abusabah, A.T., Irio, L., Oliveira, R., da Costa, D.B.: Approximate distributions of the residual self-interference power in multi-tap full-duplex systems. IEEE Wireless Commun. Lett. https://doi.org/10.1109/lwc.2020.3042754
13. Irio, L., Oliveira, R.: Distribution of the residual self-interference power in in-band full-duplex wireless systems. IEEE Access **7**, 57516–57526 (2019)
14. Quazi, A.: An overview on the time delay estimate in active and passive systems for target localization. IEEE Trans. Acoust. Speech Signal Process. **29**(3), 527–533 (1981)
15. Baccelli and B. Blaszczyszyn. Stochastic Geometry and Wireless Networks. Now Publishers, Delft, The Netherlands (2009)
16. Duarte, M.: Full-duplex wireless: Design, implementation and characterization" Ph.D. dissertation, Rice Univ., Houston, TX, USA, April 2012
17. Choi, Y., Shirani-Mehr, H.: Simultaneous transmission and reception: algorithm, design and system level performance. IEEE Trans. Wireless Commun. **12**(12), 5992–6010 (2013)

FEM-Parameterized Sensorless Vector Control of PMSM Using High-Frequency Voltage Injection

Gergely Szabó(✉) and Károly Veszprémi

Department of Electric Power Engineering, Budapest University of Technology and Economics
Budapest, Budapest 1111, Hungary
{szabo.gergely,veszpremi.karoly}@vet.bme.hu

Abstract. The authors of the paper present the high-frequency voltage injection-based sensorless vector control method, where the test signals are injected in the estimated common coordinate system. During the modeling process a custom designed permanent magnet synchronous machine is used and its parameters are calculated using measurements combined with finite element method (FEM). The authors present an enhanced PLL-based estimator, and detail the limitations of the sensorless algorithm using the FEM results. Simulation results will be presented, where the sensorless method is combined with an incremental encoder, demonstrating the low-frequency region performance of the proposed algorithm.

Keywords: High-frequency voltage injection · FEM · Sensorless vector control · Low-frequency performance · Incremental encoder

1 Introduction

The injection-based vector control techniques can provide good performance in low-frequency regions, where many of the sensorless methods fail [1, 2]. Since most of the controlled electric drives involve a voltage source inverter, therefore voltage injection is an obvious choice. Based on the place of injection rotating and synchronous methods can be distinguished. The first solution adds test signals to the terminal voltages in the stationary reference frame [3, 4], while the latter one adds test signals in the estimated common coordinate system [5, 6].

In case of an actuator a usual speed-torque profile starts from standstill no-load condition, followed by a light-load speed up region and the cycle ends with a low-speed or standstill operation with high load. This common cycle covers wide range of rotational speed with various load condition. Assuming a permanent magnet synchronous machine as the rotating machine of the actuator, the implementation of a vector control algorithm requires good dynamic and precise tracking of the rotor position.

This can be achieved with a high-bandwidth and high-resolution encoder, but this could increase the system's cost. Another solution can be a cheaper encoder with additional algorithms to fulfill the requirements. The combination of high-frequency injection

© IFIP International Federation for Information Processing 2021
Published by Springer Nature Switzerland AG 2021
L. M. Camarinha-Matos et al. (Eds.): DoCEIS 2021, IFIP AICT 626, pp. 226–239, 2021.
https://doi.org/10.1007/978-3-030-78288-7_22

methods with lower cost encoders could be a reasonable alternative. In such systems in the low-frequency region the common coordinate system's angle is estimated based on the injection method, but in higher frequencies the estimation is overtaken by the physical encoder's processed signal. The design of the injection method and also the vector control algorithms require the machine parameters, which can be obtained through the combination of measurement evaluation and finite element analysis. Nevertheless, the system performance can be improved, if these methods involve the saturation characteristics of the machine, but not the static parameters.

The authors present the finite element method analysis of the used permanent synchronous motor, combined with measurement result evaluations in Sect. 2. This investigation's target is to obtain the machine parameters that are required for the high-frequency voltage injection method and the conventional vector control algorithm. Section 3 details the high-frequency voltage injection method including a dynamic model, used in the angle estimation. Section 4 gives an overview of the vector-controlled system with the combination of high-frequency injection and incremental encoder, including simulation results.

2 Analysis of PMSM

2.1 Finite Element Method Analysis

The presented rotating machine analysis is the combination of measurement data evaluation and finite element method (FEM). The measurements were the standard no-load and short circuit measurements at different mechanical speeds. The first one is used to calculate the pole flux Ψ_p, while the second one is used to validate the torque profile with the FEM results. Table 1 summarizes the motor parameters priory to the FEM.

Table 1. Permanent magnet synchronous machine parameters

Parameter	Value	Source
P_n	2 kW	Design parameter
U_n	330 V	Design parameter
I_n	3.5 A_{RMS}	Nominal load measurement
n_n	3000 RPM	Design parameter
R	2.71 Ω	RLC measurement
Ψ_p	0.335 Vs	No-load measurement
p	2	Design parameter
J	0.0036 kgm^2	Design parameter
F	0.0011 Nms	Design parameter

2.2 Finite Element Method Analysis

The inputs of this analysis are the known motor topology including the applied materials. In the first step they used to calculate $\boldsymbol{d}-\boldsymbol{q}$ axes fluxes, which are the functions of direct-axis $\boldsymbol{i_d}$ and quadrature-axis $\boldsymbol{i_q}$ currents [7]. During the analysis the $\boldsymbol{d}$ axis was bound to the rotor's circumferential flux density distribution's positive peak.

In the first setup, the rotor is set into $\boldsymbol{\alpha_{elec}} = \mathbf{0}°$ position, as shown in Fig. 1(a), to calculate the $\boldsymbol{d}$ axis flux $\boldsymbol{\Psi_d}(\boldsymbol{i_d}, \boldsymbol{i_q})$. In the second setup the rotor is positioned in $\boldsymbol{\alpha_{elec}} = 90°$ direction, as shown in Fig. 1(b), in order to calculate progression of $\boldsymbol{q}$ axis flux $\boldsymbol{\Psi_q}(\boldsymbol{i_d}, \boldsymbol{i_q})$. For both cases all the possible $\bar{\boldsymbol{i}} = \boldsymbol{i_d} + \boldsymbol{j i_q}$. combinations were examined on the $[-2\hat{\boldsymbol{I}}_{\boldsymbol{n}}\ \ 2\hat{\boldsymbol{I}}_{\boldsymbol{n}}]$ current interval with $\boldsymbol{\Delta i} = 0.4\boldsymbol{A}$ resolution, and the result are shown in Fig. 2(a) and (b) for the selected machine.

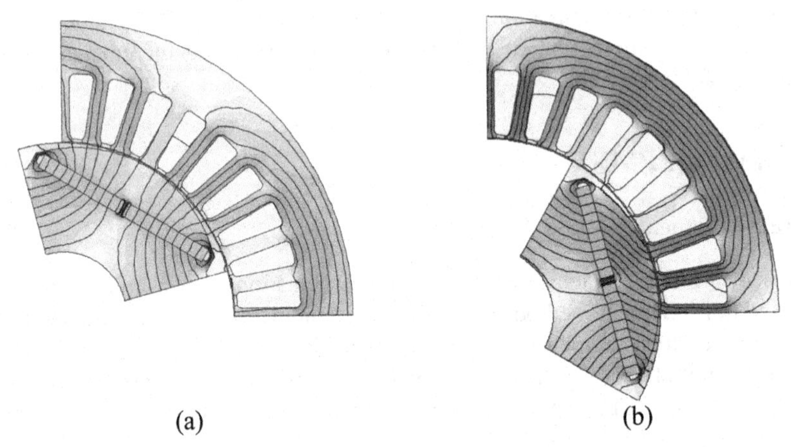

Fig. 1. Flux and inductance calculation in (a) $\boldsymbol{\alpha_{elec}} = \mathbf{0}°$ direction alignment, (b) $\boldsymbol{\alpha_{elec}} = \mathbf{90}°$ direction alignment

With the known progression of $\Psi_d(i_d, i_q)$ and $\Psi_q(i_d, i_q)$ fluxes the self- and cross-coupling inductances can be calculated with partial derivative or their approximation for numerical approaches as follows,

$$L_d(i_d, i_q) = \frac{\partial \Psi_d(i_d, i_q)}{\partial i_d} \approx \left. \frac{\Delta \Psi_d(i_d, i_q)}{\Delta i_d} \right|_{i_q=\text{const.}}, \tag{1}$$

$$L_{dq}(i_d, i_q) = \frac{\partial \Psi_d(i_d, i_q)}{\partial i_q} \approx \left. \frac{\Delta \Psi_d(i_d, i_q)}{\Delta i_q} \right|_{i_d=\text{const.}}, \tag{2}$$

$$L_q(i_d, i_q) = \frac{\partial \Psi_q(i_d, i_q)}{\partial i_q} \approx \left. \frac{\Delta \Psi_q(i_d, i_q)}{\Delta i_q} \right|_{i_d=\text{const.}}, \tag{3}$$

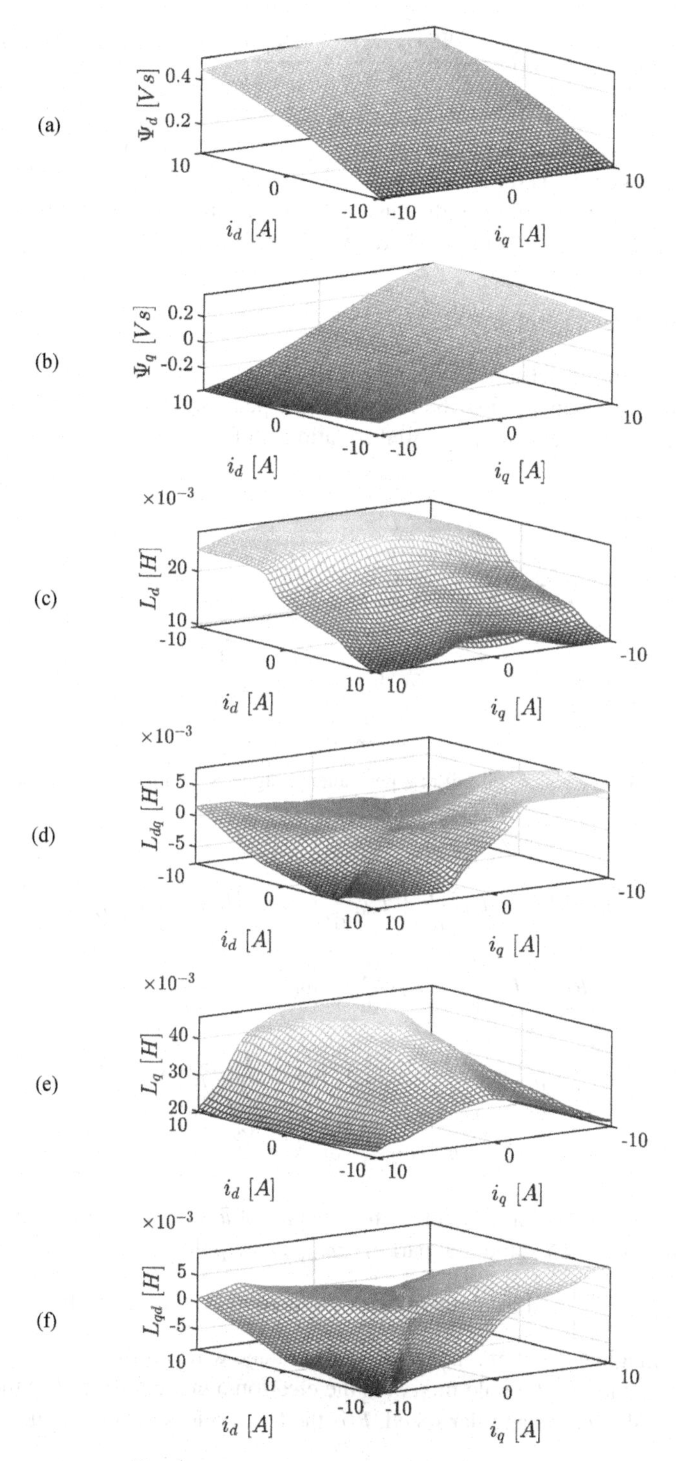

Fig. 2. Progression of fluxes and inductances

$$L_{qd}(i_d, i_q) = \frac{\partial \Psi_q(i_d, i_q)}{\partial i_d} \approx \left.\frac{\Delta \Psi_q(i_d, i_q)}{\Delta i_d}\right|_{i_q=\text{const.}} \tag{4}$$

where L_d is the direct axis self-inductance, L_{dq} is the quadrature-to-direct axis cross-coupling inductance, L_q is the quadrature axis self-inductance and L_{qd} is the direct-to-quadrature axis cross-coupling inductance. Based on these calculations the nominal values of L_d and L_q are 15.06 mH and 36.23 mH respectively.

2.3 Mathematical Model of PMSM

A permanent magnet synchronous machine in $d-q$ reference frame, bound to the rotor's circumferential flux density distribution's positive peak, can be modeled as shown in Fig. 3 and with the system of differential equations in Eqs. 5–8.

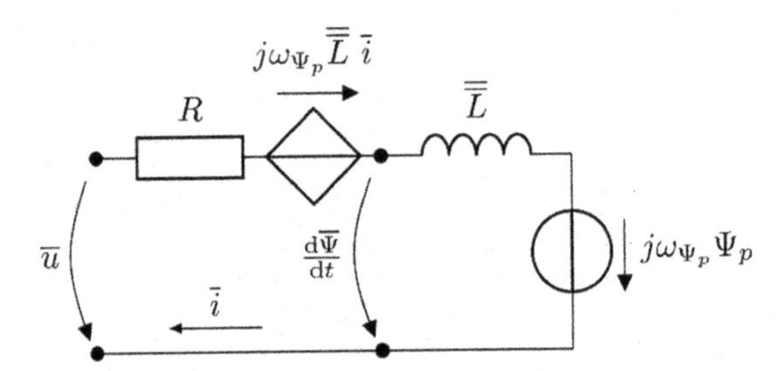

Fig. 3. Equivalent circuit of a permanent magnet synchronous machine

$$u_d = Ri_d + L_d\frac{di_d}{dt} + L_{dq}\frac{di_q}{dt} - \omega_{\psi_p}(L_{qd}i_d + L_q i_q), \tag{5}$$

$$u_q = Ri_q + L_q\frac{di_q}{dt} + L_{qd}\frac{di_d}{dt} + \omega_{\psi_p}(L_d i_d + L_{dq}i_q + \Psi_p), \tag{6}$$

$$m = \frac{3}{2}p\left((L_d - L_q)i_d i_q + \Psi_p i_q + L_{dq}i_q^2 - L_{qd}i_d^2\right), \tag{7}$$

$$(m - m_l - F\omega) = J\frac{d\omega}{dt}, \tag{8}$$

where u_d is the $\boldsymbol{d}$ axis voltage which is the real part of $\bar{u}$, R is the stator resistance, i_d is the $\boldsymbol{d}$ axis current which is the real part of $\bar{i}$, ω_{ψ_p} is the pole flux's angular speed and in Fig. 3 $\overline{\overline{L}} = \begin{bmatrix} L_d & L_{dq} \\ L_{qd} & L_q \end{bmatrix}$ and its elements are described in Eqs. 1–4, i_q is the q axis current which is the imaginary part of $\bar{i}$, u_q is the q axis voltage which is the imaginary part of $\bar{u}$, Ψ_p is the magnitude of the pole flux, m is the electromagnetic torque, J is the moment of inertia, ω is the rotor's angular speed, F is the friction loss factor, p is the number of pole pairs.

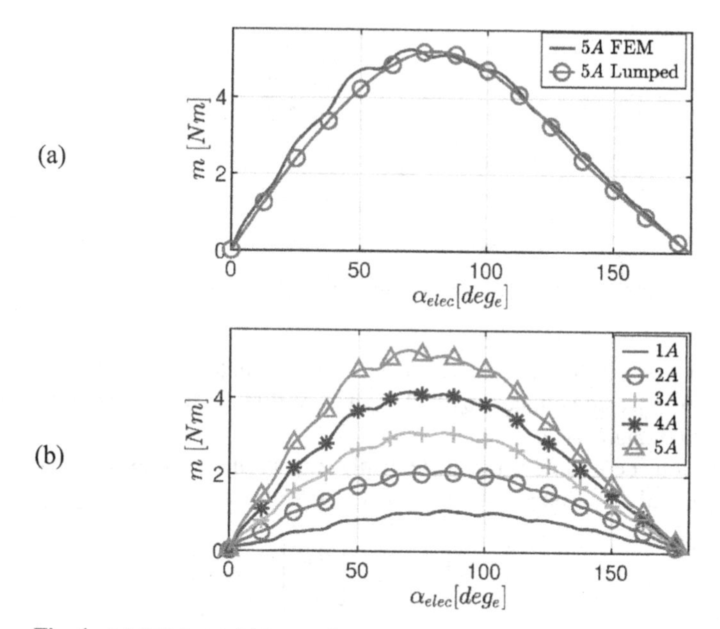

Fig. 4. (a) FEM and (b) lumped-parameter model calculated torque profiles

The machine's torque profile was calculated over one pole pitch on the $[0\ \hat{I}_n]$ interval with $\Delta i = 1A$ and $\Delta\,\alpha_{elec} = 1°$ resolutions and its results are shown in Fig. 4(a). These curves were used to validate the saturating lumped-element model, by comparing the torques of each calculation methods. For $\hat{I} = 5$ A stator current vector Fig. 4(b) shows the differences between the FEM and lumped-element model's torque. The main differences between the two calculation methods, that the latter one does not include the cogging torque, but it provides reasonable accuracy and fast results.

3 High-Frequency Synchronous Injection

3.1 Mathematical Model

In case of synchronous injection, high-frequency voltage signals are injected in the estimated $\hat{d} - \hat{q}$ frame, which is illustrated in Fig. 5.

Figure 5 also gives the angle error's definition used during the modeling process as follows,

$$\alpha_e = \alpha_{\Psi_p} - \hat{\alpha}_{\Psi_p}. \tag{9}$$

The mathematical modeling of the method was carried out using complex phasors, where complex rotating vector is bound to the sine wave. Equation 10 shows the time signals and also the corresponding complex components.

$$\begin{bmatrix} \hat{u}_{dh} \\ \hat{u}_{qh} \end{bmatrix} = \begin{bmatrix} u_h sin(\omega_h t) \\ -u_h cos(\omega_h t) \end{bmatrix} \Longleftrightarrow \begin{bmatrix} \hat{u}_{dh} \\ \hat{u}_{qh} \end{bmatrix} = \begin{bmatrix} u_h \\ -ju_h \end{bmatrix}, \tag{10}$$

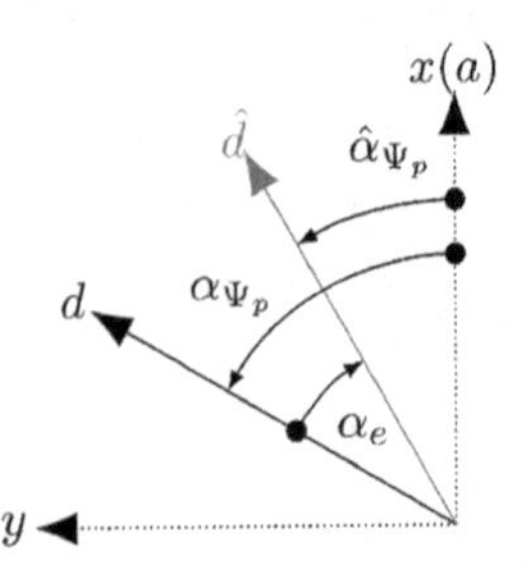

Fig. 5. Angle relations of the real d and estimated ($\hat{d}$) coordinate systems

where $\hat{u}_{dh}$ and $\hat{u}_{qh}$ are the injected voltages in the estimated $\hat{d} - \hat{q}$ frame, u_h is the amplitude of the injected voltages, $\omega_h = 2\pi f_h$, where f_h is the frequency of the injected voltages, j is the imaginary unit.

Using previous definition of the angle displacement, the projections of the injected voltages on the real $d - q$ axes can be calculated as follows,

$$\begin{bmatrix} u_{dh} \\ u_{qh} \end{bmatrix} = \overline{\overline{R}}(\alpha_e) \begin{bmatrix} \hat{u}_{dh} \\ \hat{u}_{qh} \end{bmatrix}, \tag{11}$$

where $\overline{\overline{R}}$ is the rotation operator, and it can be expressed as

$$\overline{\overline{R}}(\alpha) = \begin{bmatrix} \cos(\alpha) & \sin(\alpha) \\ -\sin(\alpha) & \cos(\alpha) \end{bmatrix}. \tag{12}$$

This method requires the high-frequency current components in the stationary $x - y$ reference frame, since in a real system this is the only point where measurements can be performed. Thus, using applied voltage components, Ohm's law can be used in the form as shown in Eq. 13.

$$\begin{bmatrix} u_{dh} \\ u_{qh} \end{bmatrix} = \overline{\overline{Z}}_h \begin{bmatrix} i_{dh} \\ i_{qh} \end{bmatrix} = \overline{\overline{Z}}_h \, \overline{\overline{R}}\left(\alpha_{\Psi_p}\right) \begin{bmatrix} i_{xh} \\ i_{yh} \end{bmatrix}, \tag{13}$$

where i_{dh} and i_{qh} are the high-frequency current components in the $d - q$ reference frame, $\overline{\overline{Z}}_h$ is the high-frequency impedance matrix that can be derived from Eqs. 5–8 at the injection frequency as

$$\overline{\overline{Z}}_h = \begin{bmatrix} R + j\omega_h L_d - \omega_{\Psi_p} L_{qd} & j\omega_h L_{dq} - \omega_{\Psi_p} L_q \\ j\omega_h L_{qd} + \omega_{\Psi_p}\left(L_d + \frac{\Psi_p}{i_d}\right) & R + j\omega_h L_q + \omega_{\Psi_p} L_{dq} \end{bmatrix} \approx$$

$$\begin{bmatrix} R + j\omega_h L_d & 0 \\ 0 & R + j\omega_h L_q \end{bmatrix} = \begin{bmatrix} Z_{h11} & 0 \\ 0 & \bar{Z}_{h22} \end{bmatrix}. \tag{14}$$

Equation 14 shows that some simplifications can be performed, because the anti-diagonal elements and also the $\omega_{\Psi_p} L_{qd}$ and $\omega_{\Psi_p} L_{dq}$ terms in the main-diagonal can be neglected, since their contribution to the output is much smaller than the other elements'.

Reorganizing Eq. 13, the high-frequency current components in the $x-y$ frame can be expressed as follows,

$$\begin{bmatrix} i_{xh} \\ i_{yh} \end{bmatrix} = \bar{\bar{R}}^{-1}(\alpha_{\Psi_p})\bar{\bar{Z}}_h^{-1}\bar{\bar{R}}(\alpha_e)\begin{bmatrix} \hat{u}_{dh} \\ \hat{u}_{qh} \end{bmatrix}. \tag{15}$$

3.2 Mathematical Model

The common coordinate system's angle can be estimated with a phase-locked loop (PLL) structure, as shown in Fig. 6.

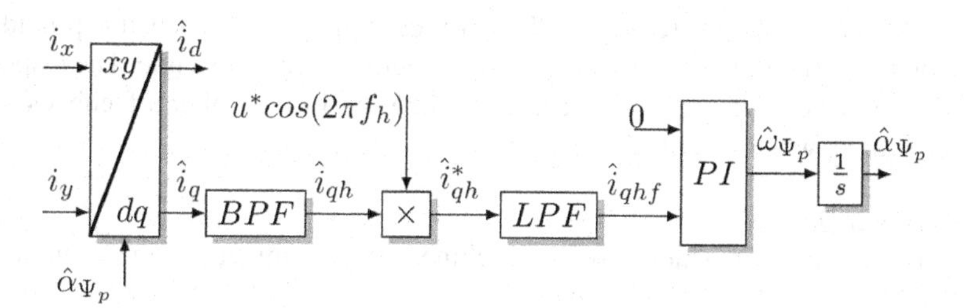

Fig. 6. Phase-locked loop

The stationary reference frame currents are transformed into the estimated common coordinate system, resulting $\hat{i}_d$ and $\hat{i}_q$ components. Thereafter, they are filtered using a band-pass filter *BPF* to obtain the high-frequency components $\hat{i}_{dh}$, $\hat{i}_{qh}$ and they can be modeled as

$$\begin{aligned} \hat{i}_{dh} =& \left(\cos^2(\alpha_e)\frac{1}{\bar{Z}_{h11}} + \sin^2(\alpha_e)\frac{1}{\bar{Z}_{h22}}\right)\hat{u}_{dh} \\ &+ \sin(\alpha_e)\cos(\alpha_e)\left(\frac{1}{\bar{Z}_{h11}} - \frac{1}{\bar{Z}_{h22}}\right)\hat{u}_{qh}, \end{aligned} \tag{16}$$

$$\begin{aligned} \hat{i}_{qh} =& \sin(\alpha_e)\cos(\alpha_e)\left(\frac{1}{\bar{Z}_{h11}} - \frac{1}{\bar{Z}_{h22}}\right)\hat{u}_{dh} \\ &+ \left(\sin^2(\alpha_e)\frac{1}{\bar{Z}_{h11}} + \cos^2(\alpha_e)\frac{1}{\bar{Z}_{h22}}\right)\hat{u}_{qh}. \end{aligned} \tag{17}$$

Equations 16–17 offer three solutions for the synchronous injection. In the first one both $\hat{u}_{dh}$ and $\hat{u}_{qh}$ voltages are used, often called as synchronous rotating injection. The other two solutions use only one of the available voltages, but in most of the cases $\hat{u}_{dh}$ voltage is used. In this case, which method is used in the further modeling, we are interested only in $\hat{i}_{qh}$, which can be reduced to the following expression,

$$\hat{i}_{qh} = \sin(\alpha_e)\cos(\alpha_e)\left(\frac{1}{\bar{Z}_{h11}} - \frac{1}{\bar{Z}_{h22}}\right)\hat{u}_{dh} \tag{18}$$

and its time domain equivalent is

$$\hat{i}_{qh}(t) = u_h \sin(\alpha_e)\cos(\alpha_e)\left|\bar{Y}^*\right|\sin\left(\omega_h t + \mathrm{arc}\left(\bar{Y}^*\right)\right), \tag{19}$$

where $\bar{Y}^* = \frac{1}{\bar{Z}_{h11}} - \frac{1}{\bar{Z}_{h22}}$.

In the next step $\hat{i}_{qh}(t)$ is fed into the phase detector part of the PLL and it is multiplied with a cosine function having the same frequency as the injected voltages and amplitude u^*, resulting $\hat{i}_{qh}^{\ *}$. Thereafter a low-pass filer LPF is applied on $\hat{i}_{qh}^{\ *}$ and its output is $\hat{i}_{qhf}^{\ *}$ which is shown in Eq. 20.

$$\hat{i}_{qhf}(t) = \frac{1}{2} u^* u_h \sin(\alpha_e)\cos(\alpha_e)\left|\bar{Y}^*\right|\sin\left(\mathrm{arc}\left(\bar{Y}^*\right)\right). \tag{20}$$

In the last step, $\hat{i}_{qhf}(t)$ is fed into a PI controller with zero reference, that provides an estimation for the common coordinate system's angular speed and angle. The inspection of Eq. 20 describes four possible scenarios, when the PI controller's feedback signal takes zero value, which are the following:

- u_h or u^* equals zero,
- $\left|\bar{Y}^*\right|$ becomes zero, in which case the machine is fully symmetrical in magnetic point of view,
- $\mathrm{arc}\left(\bar{Y}^*\right)$ becomes zero, which is analogue to the case before,
- $\sin(\alpha_e)\cos(\alpha_e)$ becomes zero, because the angular displacement between the real and estimated coordinate systems disappears.

The second and third cases point out the limitations of the injection method, which is magnetic symmetry, when the $\boldsymbol{d}$ and q axes impedances are equal. This symmetry can be the result of the machine's topology, for which a good example is a surface mounted permanent magnet synchronous machine, where these impedances are equal or very close to each other even in saturated cases. On the other hand, $\left|\bar{Y}^*\right|$ and $\mathrm{arc}\left(\bar{Y}^*\right)$ could become zero due to saturation effects at some combination of i_d, i_q currents.

Taking into account sensing and signal-to-noise considerations, in case of the machine-under-test the i_d, i_q combinations where the L_d/L_q ratio falls below 1.5 are considered as prohibited current pairs, where high-frequency injection cannot be applied. This region is illustrated in Fig. 7 which should be taken into account in current reference calculation. One affected algorithm is the field weakening current reference calculation, but the injection-based sensorless method is meant to operate in low-frequency regions, not in the working points above the nominal speed. Another affected algorithm is the maximum torque-per-ampere (MTPA), which is worth to implement to utilize the machine's saliency [8].

The tuning of the PLL's PI controller can be performed using the proposed dynamic model by authors in [9] and its reduced form is shown in Fig. 8.

The components of this block diagram are the following:

- $G_{PI}(s)$ is the PI controller and its transfer function is

$$G_{PI}(s) = A_p\left(1 + \frac{1}{sT_i}\right), \tag{21}$$

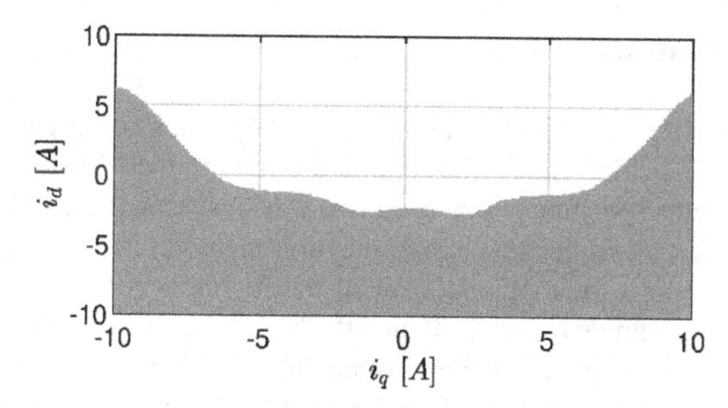

Fig. 7. Prohibited current combinations, where $L_d/L_q < 1.5$

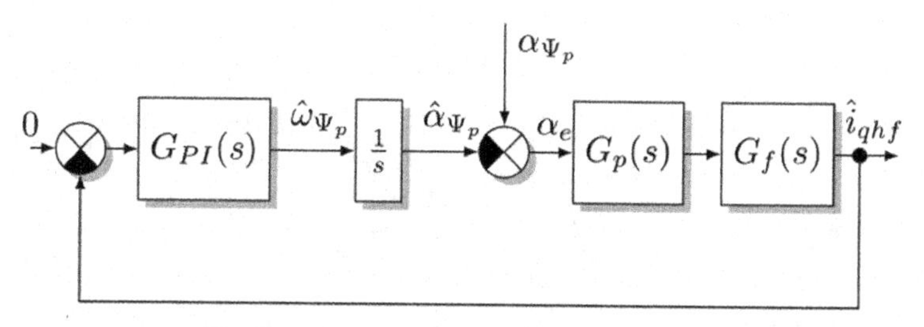

Fig. 8. Dynamic model of the PLL structure

where A_p is the proportional gain, T_i is the integral time,

- $G_p(s)$ is process' block and its transfer function can be modeled as

$$G_p(s) = \frac{p_1 s^2 + p_2 s + p_3}{(s - \lambda_d)(s - \lambda_q)}, \tag{22}$$

where p_1, p_2, p_3 parameters are the function of the machine parameters, λ_d, λ_q are the eigenvalues of the $d-$ and $q-$ axes impedances,

- $G_f(s)$ is a low-pass filter and its transfer function is

$$G_f(s) = \frac{1}{sT_f + 1}, \tag{23}$$

where T_f is the filter's time constant.

This dynamic model offers two solutions for the PI controller's tuning. In the first approach the nominal L_d, L_q values are used and the controller is tuned to have high phase margin considering the prohibited current regions. This results a stable control in the low-frequency region, but its performance will be limited, so high dynamic changes in the common coordinate system's angle cannot be tracked. The other approach takes into account the saturation effects in the direct and quadrature axes, and constantly updates the proposed $G_p(s)$ process model. This is more complex algorithm, but it could provide better dynamics in the target application.

4 Drive Simulation

Figure 9 illustrates the simulated system. The PMSM block represents the saturating, lumped-parameter machine and it was parameterized with the FEM results.

The rotor's angular position is sensed in two ways, with an incremental encoder and with the presented high-frequency signal injection method. The final angle, $\hat{\alpha}_{\Psi_p}$ used for the coordinate transformations is obtained by the linear combination of processed incremental encoder's angle $\hat{\alpha}_{\Psi_p,\mathrm{inc}}$[10], and the high-frequency injection's $\hat{\alpha}_{\Psi,HF}$ estimation. The latter one dominates the low-frequency region, which is below 15 Hz electrical frequency in the simulations, while the encoder's signal overtakes the estimation in high-frequency region.

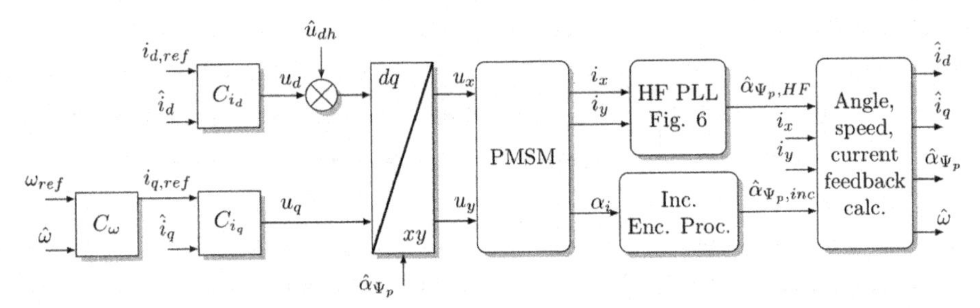

Fig. 9. Cascade control loop with the estimator

This combination of angle estimations combines both solution's advantages. In the low-frequency region with the voltage injection method rotor initial electrical position tracking and good resolution angle estimation can be achieved. On the other hand, at higher frequencies the encoder's angle provides good dynamic and precise estimation, when the high-frequency injection fails due to bad signal-to-noise ratio.

In the presented control loop all of the controllers, C_{i_d}, C_{i_q} and C_ω are PI type controllers as shown in Eq. 8. Table 2 summarizes the controller parameters [11].

Table 2. Controller parameters.

Controller	Ap	Ti
d-axis current	7.89	2.13 ms
q-axis current	24.39	4.83 ms
Angular speed	0.17	79.51 ms
HF PLL	9375	28.4 ms

These parameters were obtained assuming the nominal motor parameters, and they were modified online based on the estimated saturation of the machine.

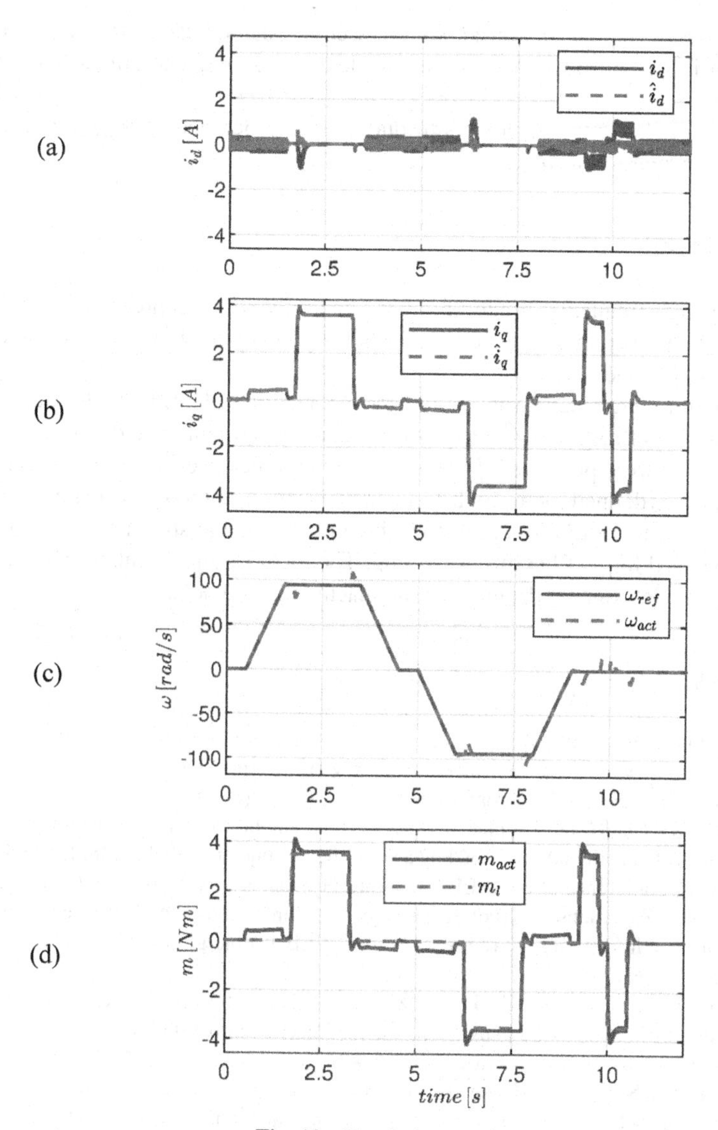

Fig. 10. Simulation results

The test cycle includes all the four quadrants with applied load torque during the motoring states as shown in Fig. 10. At the end of the cycle, zero frequency performance is examined with active load torque in both directions. Figures 10(a)–(b) show the actual i_d, i_q currents and their estimations $\hat{i}_d$ and $\hat{i}_q$. Figure 10(c) shows the mechanical speed reference ω_{ref} and the actual ω_{act} shaft angular speed.

These first three figures clearly show, that this angle estimation method can be used for vector control, and stable speed-current cascade control can be achieved. At low-speed region the estimation depends on the injection method, therefore in that frequency range current ripples can be observed. As the electric speed increases, the vector control is executed using the encoder's angle, meanwhile the high-frequency signal's amplitude reaches zero.

Figure 10(d) shows the machine's torque, which is denoted as m_{act}, and the load torque, which is denoted as m_l.

5 Conclusion

In this paper high-frequency synchronous voltage injection was presented, and it was combined with an incremental encoder to achieve good dynamic vector control on the whole frequency range.

The machine parameters were calculated using finite element method and measurement results evaluation. The analytical results and mathematical description of the injection method were presented, based on the comprehensive FEM analysis, a novel prohibited range is defined for the high-frequency injection method. The angle estimation was performed with a PLL structure, for which new dynamic structure was proposed, which can be used for its PI controller tuning. The FEM results can also be involved in this dynamic model, since it depends on the machine parameters.

References

1. Lin, X., Huang, W., Jiang, W.: Position sensorless direct torque control for pmsm based on pulse high frequency stator flux injection at low speed. In: 2019 IEEE 28th International Symposium on Industrial Electronics (ISIE), pp. 366–371 (2019)
2. Medjmadj, S., Diallo, D., Delpha, C., Yao, G.: A salient-pole pmsm position and speed estimation at standstill and low speed by a simplified hf injection method. In: IECON 2017 - 43rd Annual Conference of the IEEE Industrial Electronics Society, pp. 8317–8322 (2017)
3. Liu, J.M., Zhu, Z.Q.: Sensorless control strategy by squarewaveform high-frequency pulsating signal injection into stationary reference frame. IEEE J. Emerg. Sel. Top. Power Electron. **2**(2), 171–180 (2014)
4. Wang, G., Xiao, D., Zhang, G., Li, C., Zhang, X., Xu, D.: Sensorless control scheme of ipmsms using hf orthogonal square-wave voltage injection into a stationary reference frame. IEEE Trans. Power Electron. **34**(3), 2573–2584 (2019)
5. Jang, J.-H., Sul, S.-K., Ha, J.-I., Ide, K., Sawamura, M.: Sensorless drive of surface-mounted permanent-magnet motor by high frequency signal injection based on magnetic saliency. IEEE Trans. Ind. Appl. **39**(4), 1031–1039 (2003)
6. Kim, S., Ha, J., Sul, S.: Pwm switching frequency signal injection sensorless method in ipmsm. IEEE Trans. Ind. Appl. **48**(5), 1576–1587 (2012)
7. Stumberger, B., Stumberger, G., Dolinar, D., Hamler, A., Trlep, M.: Evaluation of saturation and cross-magnetization effects in interior permanent-magnet synchronous motor. IEEE Trans. Ind. Appl. **39**(5), 1264–1271 (2003)
8. Kim, H., Lee, Y., Sul, S., Yu, J., Oh, J.: Online mtpa control of ipmsm based on robust numerical optimization technique. IEEE Trans. Ind. Appl. **55**(4), 3736–3746 (2019)
9. Szabó, G., Veszprémi, K.: Sensorless vector control of permanent magnet synchronous machine using high-frequency signal injection. Acta Polytechnica Hungarica **17**(4), 145–163 (2020)

10. Ilmiawan, A.F., Wijanarko, D., Arofat, A.H., Hindersyah, H., Purwadi, A.: An easy speed measurement for incremental rotary encoder using multi stage moving average method. In: International Conference on Electrical Engineering and Computer Science (ICEECS) 2014, pp. 363–368 (2014)
11. Wang, L., Chai, S., Yoo, D., Gan, L., Ng, K.: PID and predictive control of electrical drives and power converters using MATLAB/Simulink. Wiley, New York (2015)

Classification Systems

Deep Learning-Based Automated Detection of Inappropriate Face Image Attributes for ID Documents

Amineh Mazandarani[1](✉), Pedro Miguel Figueiredo Amaral[1](✉), Paulo da Fonseca Pinto[1](✉), and Seyed Jafar Hosseini Shamoushaki[2](✉)

[1] Faculdade de Ciências e Tecnologia, Universidade Nova de Lisboa, Lisbon, Portugal
a.mazandarani@campus.fct.unl.pt, {pfa,pfp}@fct.unl.pt
[2] University of Coimbra, Lisbon, Portugal
jafar@isr.uc.pt

Abstract. A face photo forms a fundamental element of almost every identity document such as national ID cards, passports, etc. The governmental agencies issuing such documents may set slightly different requirements for a face image to be acceptable. Nevertheless, some are too critical to avoid, such as mouth closedness, eyes openness and no veil-over-face. In this paper, we aim to address the problem of fully automating the inspection of these 3 characteristics, thereby enabling the face capturing devices to determine, as soon as a face image is taken, if any of them is invalid or not. To accomplish this, we propose a deep learning-based approach by defining model architectures that are lightweight enough to enable real-time inference on resource-constrained devices with a particular focus on prediction accuracy. Lastly, we showcase the performance and efficiency of our approach, which is found to surpass two well-known off-the-shelf solutions in terms of overall precision.

Keywords: Image quality verification · Deep learning · Face detection · Binary classification

1 Introduction

It has always been quite common for an identity document to contain a face image of its holder to facilitate the recognition of his/her identity. Consequently, the face is known to be the most important biometric trait and, in respect to other traits, offers several advantages such as: non-intrusive acquisition; minimal hardware requirements thanks to camera technology advances; and easy capture process without any intervention of the individual. Over the past decade, electronic ID documents started to replace their traditional equivalents and thus information comes embedded into an internal chip, whether it is demographic details or biometric features like the face image. As a result, AI-powered biometrics inspection has been enabled for automated real-time identity verification [1, 2].

© IFIP International Federation for Information Processing 2021
Published by Springer Nature Switzerland AG 2021
L. M. Camarinha-Matos et al. (Eds.): DoCEIS 2021, IFIP AICT 626, pp. 243–253, 2021.
https://doi.org/10.1007/978-3-030-78288-7_23

In 2002, the International Civil Aviation Organization (ICAO) asked a group of experts to establish a specific physical feature of an individual as a biometric identifier that can be read by a machine to confirm his/her identity [3]. The group made the decision and selected the face as the primary globally interoperable biometric feature for machine-assisted identity verification (MAIV) in machine readable travel documents. The face typically poses some limitations in comparison with other features (fingerprint, for example) if face images do not fulfill minimum quality requirements, suggesting that for highly successful MAIV the images are required to meet certain strict quality standards. Therefore, following on from that decision, the ISO/IEC 19794–5 standard [4] defines a set of rules for a proper face image acquisition procedure along with scene conditions and proposes some guidelines and plenty of examples to demonstrate acceptable/unacceptable face images to help in interpreting the image quality levels such as Blurred, Looking Away, Too Dark/Light, Eyes-Closed, Washed-Out, Hair-Across-Eyes, Mouth-Open, Unnatural Skin Tone. It is worth mentioning that here the concept of image quality no longer necessarily reflects its classic meaning (i.e. only a noisy image presents bad quality) but also will encompass other criteria such as the mouth must be closed. In this sense, several businesses delivering commercial biometrics technology began to release SDKs that serve to auto-verify the compliance of face images with ISO/ICAO standards for the document issuing process.

Over the years, there has been thorough research on image quality assessment which is often an early processing stage for vision-based applications. However, the research reported in the literature is limited in terms of ISO/ICAO requirements. Authors in [5] define 17 quality requirements and discuss basic approaches to assess them. All in all, their work is mostly concerned with the impact of image quality on the facial recognition accuracy, not with ISO/ICAO compliant face analysis. In [6], the authors propose a different set of requirements together with the corresponding evaluation algorithms and present a series of tests on 189 images from people within their organization despite most of the images being incompliant with ISO/ICAO specs. A web-based system built on 28 ISO/ICAO requirements is proposed in [7]. This paper however lacks a complete experimental study. In [8] a potential framework is briefly described to determine the compliance level of each ISO/ICAO requirement by measuring quality scores that are almost always in line with the human perception, according to the authors.

There exist several other papers in the literature that only cover a few specific requirements. For example, the work presented in [9] exploits geometric attributes of the face. Each attribute is characterized by a numeric score and all the individual scores are then merged into a single global score. [18] tackles the constraints associated with lighting, sharpness and head pose by applying Gabor filters and Discrete Cosine Transform. The work in [10] addresses "eyes closed, red eyes and looking away", [11] takes into consideration "unnatural skin tone, shadows across the face and flash reflection on skin" and [12] deals with "pixelation, hair across eyes, veil over face and mouth open".

2 Contribution to Applied Artificial Intelligence Systems

The authorities that issue identity documents such as national ID cards, driving licenses, passports, etc., use printed and/or digital face photos from the citizens. As stated earlier, ICAO compliance guidelines serve as a global reference to be used by these authorities to check photos for quality correctness. Three of these guidelines must always be met, namely, mouth closedness, eyes openness and no veil-over-face. In this paper, we focus on the inspection of these events and attempt to automatically determine if any of them is absent on a face image. For this purpose, we propose a processing pipeline that incorporates multiple modules such as raw face data capturing, face detection, facial landmark extraction, cropping and/or scaling, image quality analysis. This last module is, in fact, the focus of this paper, aiming to verify the three quality attributes mentioned above although we build up and evaluate the entire pipeline to ensure that our testing conditions will closely resemble real-world scenarios. The previous works mostly proceed with such verification by applying classic machine learning methods despite all the size, accuracy and speed constraints of these. We will also propose a classification-based approach but, in our case using deep learning (DL), to solve the multi-classification problem. We define DL network architectures, efficient enough to extract representative features with lighter computations to make fast and accurate predictions on mouth closedness, eyes openness and no veil-over-face. The remainder of the paper is organized as follows: Firstly, an overview of the pipeline is provided. Next, we discuss the DL networks and model specifications for quality analysis; Lastly, we cover the DL relevant parts (e.g. training), and a comprehensive set of experiments is presented to validate the accuracy of the DL models as well as the performance of the overall pipeline based on the results obtained.

3 Quality Analysis Pipeline

We now outline how we approach the problem of face image quality inspection by means of a pipeline designed to perform a complete computer vision workflow. Figure 1 illustrates the structure of our proposed pipeline as a block diagram. An overall description of this pipeline is provided below.

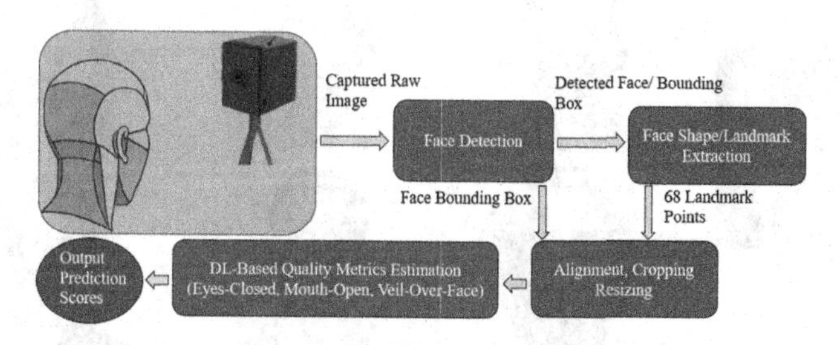

Fig. 1. The sketch of the proposed pipeline.

Our pipeline starts by capturing a person's face through a monocular RGB camera and can flexibly operate in two modes 1- video streaming (i.e. each frame is processed)

2- one single still image at a time. There is no strict restriction to the camera choice, provided that the region tightly spanning the face has a minimum resolution of 100 × 100. The subject being photographed should stand at a range of 0.5 m from the camera lens, with the face being frontal relative to the camera direction. A frame is then recorded and transmitted to the subsequent module in the pipeline. This module is responsible for face detection which involves finding the face in the input image. Face detection was handled in traditional computer vision using classical feature-based techniques such as the cascade classifier [14], however in the past few years the use of deep learning has been preferred, mainly because they achieve improvements in both accuracy and speed when applied on standard benchmark face detection datasets. One of the most popular DL-based face detectors is the Multi-task Cascade Convolutional Neural Network, or MTCNN for short [15]. This network employs a cascade architecture combining three networks: *proposal network* makes candidate proposals of face regions; *refine network* removes false bounding boxes; and the *third network* estimates facial landmarks. Implementing the MTCNN architecture is not easy due to its complexity, but open-source implementations are available for public use and can be used to train a custom DL model of our own on a dataset of face images. The face detection module outputs the coordinates of a bounding box that nicely encloses the face region. The next module deals with the extraction of facial landmarks. For this purpose, we apply the dlib toolkit which is quite popular and widely used in a range of computer vision applications [16]. We select dlib over MTCNN for landmark extraction considering that its face shape, which consists of 68 landmark points, better represents a facial structure and is also estimated with great precision by the toolkit´s shape prediction functionality. All we need to do is to train the dlib shape predictor with the detection output of the MTCNN face detector. You can see the preset shape landmarks in Fig. 2. The face bounding box and the detected landmarks are passed together onto another module as input (Fig. 2 also shows some shape estimates with only the landmarks in use). This module utilizes this information to identify, crop and rescale the regions of interest to be processed by the quality analysis module which is meant to verify the face image quality with respect to mouth-open, eyes-closed and veil-over-face attributes.

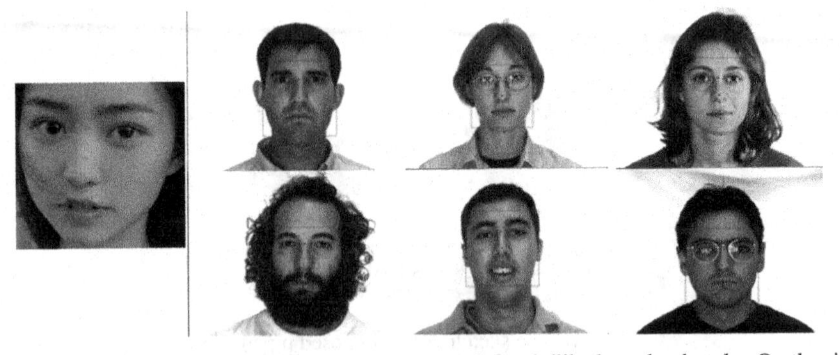

Fig. 2. The single face on the left represents the pre-defined dlib shape landmarks. On the right the pipeline's result is shown i.e. a bounding box and the relevant landmarks.

4 DL-Based Quality Analysis

The quality analysis here is equivalent to one computational metric for each of the 3 attributes. The core algorithm of the metric is implemented as a binary classification. Thus, we will end up with three image classification tasks for eyes-closed, mouth-open and veil-over-face and 3 DL models are derived to extract highly discriminative information depending on the category/object being classified.

4.1 Mouth-Open/Eyes-Closed Classification

Figure 3 shows some example training images for both the categories of mouth-open and eyes-closed. These images illustrate the two possible classes i.e. presence and absence of a category which we call positive and negative samples respectively for simplicity's sake. While the samples may look very similar (as they all contain the mouth or the eyes) subtle differences will arise in texture and pixel-level variations when the mouth or the eyes make the transition from one state to the other. These differences must be precisely captured by the convolutional layers of the deep network we want to construct. VGGNet [17] is particularly common in classification tasks. It makes an improvement over AlexNet [20] by replacing large kernel-sized filters (11 and 5 in the first and second convolutional layer, respectively) with multiple 3×3 kernel-sized filters one after another. Multiple smaller size kernels stacked together do better than one larger size kernel because they lead to an increase in the network´s depth, allowing this network to learn more complex visual features and at a lower computational cost as well. While VGGNet achieves remarkable accuracy it has two major limitations: 1- painfully slow to train; 2- the network weights are quite large in terms of disk/bandwidth; Due to its depth and number of fully-connected nodes, VGG is over 533 MB for VGG16 and 574 MB for VGG19, meaning that deploying VGG is a tedious task. For this reason, smaller network architectures are often preferable such as SqueezeNet which is a lightweight network that was designed as a more compact replacement for AlexNet. It has almost $50\times$ fewer parameters than AlexNet, yet it performs $3\times$ faster. This architecture was proposed in [13] and features a mini-architecture called fire module that is composed of *squeeze* and *expand* layers. A squeeze convolutional layer has only 1×1 filters. These are fed into an expanded layer that has a mix of 1×1 and 3×3 convolution filters. Our aim is to build a network that best matches the specificities of our classification task: a) we are dealing with such small images that the choice of a very deep network like Resnet [18] (or Inception [19]) can't be justified; b) the computer vision pipeline must be capable of being smoothly executed on low-power, resource-constrained devices, and be flexible enough for deployment to such devices without any struggle to get it running at the edge. For this purpose, we need to obtain high-performance models; c) Also the final models must produce relatively precise predictions and so there is a need to make a trade-off between inference speed and prediction accuracy.

As a result of the above, we propose a deep neural network architecture that combines the strengths that the networks VGGNet and SqueezeNet offer. In this sense, we propose to make a major adjustment to the output layers by removing the fully connected layers from VGGNet7 (which is the lightest variant of VGGNet) and instead add a 1×1 convolutional layer and a global average pooling over the 2D feature maps just like in SqueezeNet plus a sigmoid activation. Aside from this, small tweaks will be adopted, for example the application of dropouts across the network. Note: integration of the fire module into other architectures can be considered a potential design strategy to attain better hybrid networks.

4.2 Veil-Over-Face Classification

Veil-over-face category has a somewhat different nature from the other two categories, as an external object (i.e. non-body part) is also part of the positive samples. A veil can be thought of as a form of occlusion given that the face gets partially concealed or at least it is barely visible with a wedding veil for example. Refer to Fig. 3 for some example images. Consequently, veil-over-face classification is analogous to classifying a specific type of occlusion. In this case, we will have a larger region of interest than in the previous classification tasks and there is also a greater data variability in the samples. This somehow forces us to adopt a deeper network and thus we will pick VGGNet16 and follow the same correction we made for eyes-closed and mouth-open classification above. The architecture we will apply here is similar but will have two extra building blocks (i.e. SqueezeVGG). A face mask is also an obvious conflict with a correct ID photo and may be assumed as a sort of veil in some cases. We have developed a tool to generate synthetic masks laid over real faces and can benefit from this at least during the training process by increasing our training samples with synthetic images.

5 Experiments and Validation

The proposed pipeline is implemented as a software package in connection with an RGB camera and can run on an embedded board (Raspberry Pi, for example). Here, we avoid irrelevant details about this package and will concentrate specifically on describing the machine learning models developed and trained for use throughout the pipeline. At first, we trained a DL model for the MTCNN face detector. Next, we trained the dlib shape predictor by using as input the detection bounding boxes predicted by the face detector. Then, we need to train 3 more DL models for the quality analysis module. The specifications of the training process are given in Table 1.

Table 1. Overview of the training specs for the classification tasks: mouth-open, eyes-closed and veil-over-face.

	Mouth-open	Eyes-closed	Veil-over-face
Platform/framework	Python/Keras (Tensorflow backend)	Python/Keras (Tensorflow backend)	Python/Keras (MXNet backend)
Model architecture	SqueezMiniVGG	SqueezeMiniVGG	SqueezeVGG
Dataset	~10000 Pos, ~10000 Neg	~8000 Pos, ~8000 Neg	~20000 Pos, ~20000 Neg
Validation	Yes (0.1 of the dataset)	Yes (0.1 of the dataset)	Yes (0.15 of the dataset)
Input image size	72 × 72	56 × 56	128 × 128
Image type	Grayscale	Grayscale	Grayscale
Channels first	Yes	Yes	Yes
Classification type	Binary decision	Binary decision	Binary decision
Number of epochs	100	100	100
Batch size	32	16	8
Use of augmentation	Yes (Rescale, Rotation, Flip, etc.)	Yes (Rescale, Rotation, Flip, etc.)	Yes (Rescale, Rotation, Flip, etc.)

5.1 Data Pipeline

We collected a sufficiently large number of face images from different sources for each classification task. For our data collection pipeline, we can simply reuse the proposed pipeline after making minor adjustments to it as follows: the input image is loaded from disk rather than using a camera and obviously the quality analysis module must be removed. The remaining part can act as our data collection pipeline, through which the image is passed to obtain cleanly cropped/resized portions with the region of interest. For mouth-open, eyes-closed and veil-over-face, we collected a training dataset of about 20000, 16000 and 40000 images respectively with a balanced distribution between positive and negative samples (see Fig. 3 for sample images). The veil-over-face dataset contains, in addition to the real images, images of real faces with a synthetic mask acquired by a custom tool intended to operate as mask augmenter. We performed model training separately for the 3 classification networks while applying data augmentation and validation set.

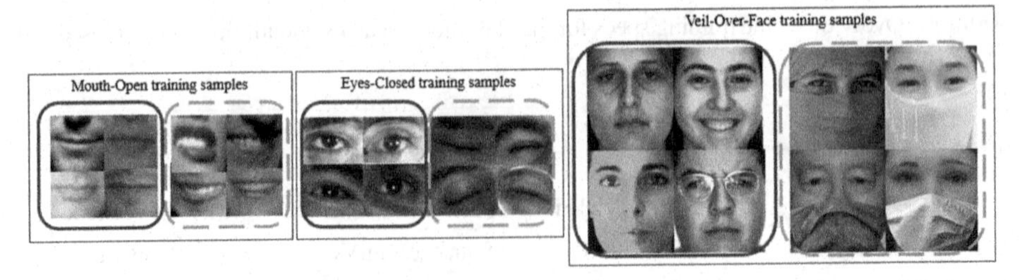

Fig. 3. Examples of the training samples.

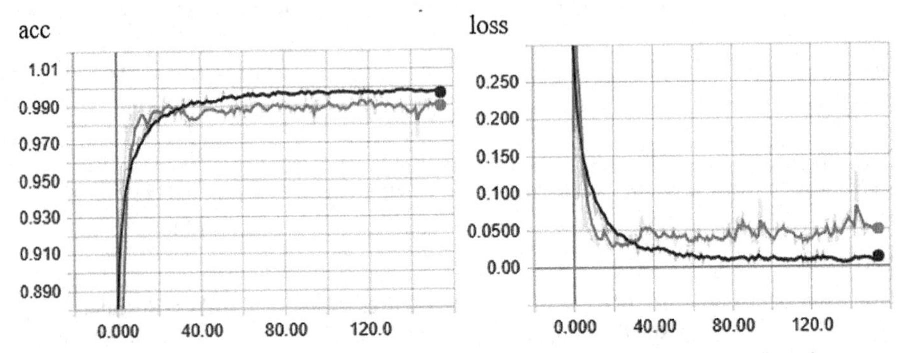

Fig. 4. Accuracy/Loss plots for eyes-closed (Blue curve refers to training and Red curve to validation).

5.2 Training Results

We successfully finished the training process without facing issues like overfitting and the model has shown to generalize well. The Table 2 shows the key measures of the training output, such as final loss, accuracy, Precision and Recall.

Table 2. Presentation of key training measures.

	Mouth-open		Eyes-closed		Veil-over-face	
	Training	Validation	Training	Validation	Training	Validation
Loss	0.003	0.080	0.001	0.050	0.002	0.06
Accuracy	0.965	0.934	0.995	0.990	0.990	0.980
Precision	93%		94%		94%	
Recall	95.5%		97%		97%	

In Fig. 4, we included the training graphs for eyes-closed as an illustration of the training evolution. As you can see in the Accuracy plot, the validation curve smoothly follows the training curve and both curves show a similar behavior, which is an indication of good generalization and no overfitting problem.

5.3 Model Testing and Evaluation Experiments

To assess the performance of the three trained models, we conducted a set of benchmarks on test datasets which are described in Fig. 5. The test images do not overlap with the training datasets. For testing purposes, we execute our entire pipeline after excluding the camera and alternatively, we read stored images from disk. The images go through each module to the next until the three-quality metrics are calculated by performing inference with the models. Then, by running our evaluation framework, we compute all the relevant performance measures (see Fig. 5).

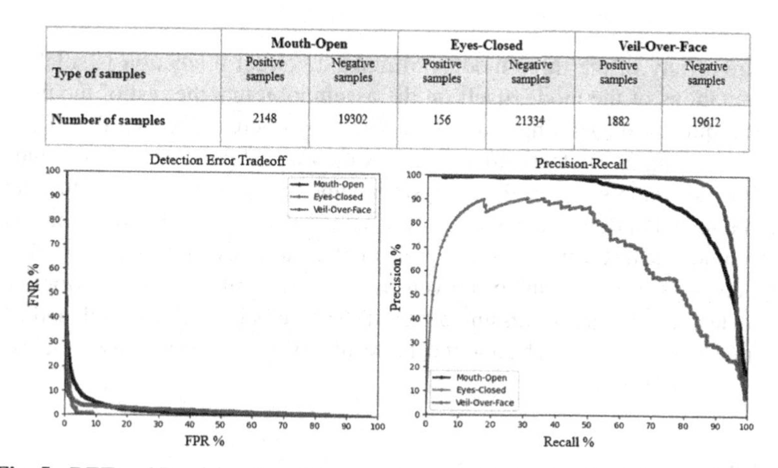

	Mouth-Open		Eyes-Closed		Veil-Over-Face	
Type of samples	Positive samples	Negative samples	Positive samples	Negative samples	Positive samples	Negative samples
Number of samples	2148	19302	156	21334	1882	19612

Fig. 5. DET and Precision-Recall Plots – A table with the distribution of test images

Basically, there is a large proportion of negative samples with respect to positive samples. The prediction scores span the 0–1 range and can be used to generate detection-error-tradeoff (DET) curves which represent the relationship between the false positive rate (FPR) and false negative rate (FNR) as they vary from 0% to 100%. We are mainly concerned with both the lowest FPR and the lowest FNR and the point where we can get both at the same time is referred to as prediction threshold or aka operating point. The lower these rates the better the prediction accuracy will be. The Precision-Recall curves are presented too. Given fewer positive samples than negative samples, having a lower Precision at the operating point totally makes sense. For mouth-open, for an operating point of 0.072 we obtained 5.12% and 5.68% for FNR and FPR along with a Recall of 94.05%, which sounds satisfactory. For eyes-closed, each eye is classified independently of the other and we only select the higher of the two scores. The operating point is estimated to be 0.0213 for an FNR of 2.12%, an FPR of 2.58% and a Recall of 98.08% which again seems good. For veil-over-face, we obtained an FNR of 4.21% and an FPR of 4.68% at the operating point of 0.246 as well as a Recall of 96.25%.

We also compare the prediction accuracy of our models against metric implementations from two major biometrics solution suppliers (Cognitec and Neurotechnology [21]). However, the veil-over-face metric implementation was not available for evaluation. Table 3 shows the comparison details indicating the ability of our models to produce quite competitive results.

Table 3. Comparison of FAR/FRR with off-the-shelf solutions.

	Cognitec		Neurotechnology		Our solution	
	FPR	FNR	FPR	FNR	FPR	FNR
Eyes-closed	1.53	1.52	3.99	3.87	2.58	2.12
Mouth-open	22.60	22.64	14.38	14.14	5.68	5.12

5.4 Pipeline Assessment

The failure of any of the three models to make a correct prediction is solely caused by the limitations of the model itself on the assumption that the rest of the pipeline is performing quite well. An important issue that arises here is the fact that if the other modules, including face detection/landmark extraction, exhibit a malfunction and do not produce the desired results for the analysis module to use, this will introduce an extra error in the model performance, letting us conclude that the misclassification cases are partially influenced by the model input. From our benchmark results, we realized that this situation could be only serious for no veil-over-face classification where, for example, the face detector is at risk of missing a face if the face is heavily covered, and the face missing rate was estimated to be about 0.1% while for mouth-open and eyes-closed this is so negligible (0.005%).

6 Conclusions

In this paper, we presented a real-time computer vision pipeline for inspecting a captured face photo meant for use in ID documents. The automated inspection is aimed at verifying if any of the three attributes *mouth-open*, *eyes-closed*, *veil-over-face* is present on the image or not. This pipeline is functional and can potentially be integrated into any face capturing system. We have particularly focused on the pipeline´s last module which consists of a deep-learning multi-classification approach to the design of three individual metrics for the three attributes in question. Lastly, our benchmark results demonstrated the effectiveness of our proposed approach at dealing with face image quality verification which clearly has yet to be further developed with future improvements.

References

1. Bourlai, T., Ross, A., Jain, A.K.: On matching digital face images against passport photos. In: Proceedings of IEEE International Conference on Biometrics, Identity and Security, Tampa, FL (2009)
2. Bourlai, T., Ross, A., Jain, A.K.: Restoring degraded face images for matching faxed or scanned photos. IEEE Trans. Inf. Forensics Secur. **6**(2), 371–384 (2011)
3. ICAO: Biometric deployment of machine readable travel documents (2003)
4. ISO International Standard ISO/IEC JTC 1/SC 37 N506: Text of FCD 19794–5, biometric data interchange formats—part 5: face image data (2004)

5. Hsu, R.L.V., Shah, J., Martin, B.: Quality assessment of facial images. In: Proceedings of Biometric Consortium Conference, pp. 1–6 (2006)
6. Subasic, M., Loncaric, S., Petkovic, T., Bogunovic, H., Krivec, V.: Face image validation system. In: Proceedings of International Symposium on Image and Signal Processing and Analysis, pp. 30–33 (2005)
7. Gonzalez-Castillo, O.Y., Delac, K.: A web based system to calculate quality metrics for digital passport photographs. In: Proceedings of 8th Mexican International Conference on Current Trends in Computer Science, pp. 105–112 (2007)
8. Ferrara, M., Franco, A., Maio, D., Maltoni, D.: Face image conformance to ISO/ICAO standards in machine readable travel documents. IEEE Trans. Inf. Forensics Secur. **7**(4), 1204–1213 (2012)
9. Han, Q., Gonzalez, Y., Guerrero, J.M., Niu, X.: Evaluating the content-related quality of digital ID images. In: Proceedings of Congress on Image and Signal Processing, pp. 440–444 (2008)
10. Borges, E.V.C.L., et al.: Analysis of the eyes on face images for compliance with ISO/ICAO requirements. In: SIBGRAPI, Sao Paulo, pp. 173–179 (2016)
11. Andrezza, I.L.P., et al.: Facial compliance for travel documents. In: SIBGRAPI, Sao Paulo, pp. 166–172 (2016)
12. Parente, R.L., et al.: Assessing facial image accordance to ISO/ICAO requirements. In: SIBGRAPI, Sao Paulo, pp. 180–187 (2016)
13. Iandola, F., et al.: SqueezeNet: AlexNet-level accuracy with 50× fewer parameters and textless1 MB model size. In: ArXiv (2017)
14. Viola, P., Jones, M.: Rapid object detection using a boosted cascade of simple features. In: Proceedings of CVPR (2001)
15. Zhang, K., Zhang, Z., Li, Z., Qiao, Y.: Joint face detection and alignment using multitask cascaded convolutional networks. IEEE Signal Process. Lett. **23**(10), 1499–1503 (2016)
16. dlib: A toolkit for making real world machine learning and data analysis applications in C++. http://dlib.net/
17. Liu, S., Deng, W.: Very deep convolutional neural network based image classification using small training sample size. In: 3rd IAPR Asian Conference on Pattern Recognition (ACPR), Kuala Lumpur, pp. 730–734 (2015)
18. He, K., Zhang, X., Ren, S., Sun, J.: Deep residual learning for image recognition. In: IEEE Conference on Computer Vision and Pattern Recognition (CVPR), pp. 770–778 (2016)
19. Szegedy, C., Vanhoucke, V., Ioffe, S., Shlens, J., Wojna, Z.: Rethinking the inception architecture for computer vision. In: CVPR, pp. 2818–2826 (2016)
20. Krizhevsky, A., Sutskever, I., Hinton, G.E.: ImageNet classification with deep convolutional neural networks. Adv. Neural. Inf. Process. Syst. **25**, 1097–1105 (2012)
21. Cognitec: https://www.cognitec.com/, neurotechnology. https://www.neurotechnology.com/

Automatic Cognitive Workload Classification Using Biosignals for Distance Learning Applications

Rui Varandas[1,2](✉), Hugo Gamboa[1,2], Inês Silveira[2], Patrícia Gamboa[1,2], and Cláudia Quaresma[2]

[1] PLUX Wireless Biosignals S.A., Lisbon, Portugal
rvarandas@plux.info
[2] LIBPhys-UNL, Departamento de Física, Faculdade de Ciências e Tecnologia, FCT, Universidade Nova de Lisboa, Caparica, Portugal

Abstract. Current e-learning platforms provide recommendations by applying Artificial Intelligence algorithms to model users' preferences based on content, by collaborative filtering, or both, thus, do not consider users' states, such as boredom. Biosignals and Human-Computer Interaction will be used in this study to objectively assess the state of the user during a learning task. Preliminary data was obtained from a small sample of young adults using physiological sensors (e.g., electroencephalogram, EEG, and functional near infrared spectroscopy, fNIRS) and computer interfaces (e.g., mouse and keyboard) during cognitive tasks and a Python tutorial. Using Machine Learning (ML), Cognitive Workload was classified considering EEG and fNIRS. The results show that it is possible to automatically distinguish cognitive states with accuracy around 84%. This procedure will be applied to adjust the difficulty level of learning tasks, model user preferences, and ultimately optimize the distance learning process in real-time, in a future e-learning platform.

Keywords: Distance-learning · Biosignals · Artificial intelligence · Machine learning · Human-computer interaction

1 Introduction

E-learning has seen an increase in popularity in recent years, however, typical systems fail to monitor students' engagement [1]. On e-learning, the absence of a tutor's in-person supervision can lead to students' inattention. Thus, this study will consider the best variables that maximize engagement: attention, cognitive workload (CW), and emotions, which enables the creation of more comfortable and successful learning atmospheres [1–4].

Our investigation proposes cognitive workload and user's emotional state assessment by using a set of sensors: functional Near-Infrared Spectroscopy (fNIRS), Electroencephalography (EEG), Accelerometer to measure the movement of the head, Respiratory

© IFIP International Federation for Information Processing 2021
Published by Springer Nature Switzerland AG 2021
L. M. Camarinha-Matos et al. (Eds.): DoCEIS 2021, IFIP AICT 626, pp. 254–261, 2021.
https://doi.org/10.1007/978-3-030-78288-7_24

Inductive Plethysmography (RIP), Electrocardiogram (ECG) and finally, Electrodermal Activity (EDA).

The PhD that inspires this work focuses on answering the question: How can the internal state of a person be included in e-learning to improve and optimize engagement and, thus, learning? Therefore, the proposed hypothesis is that the enumerated biosignals will allow to access the internal state of the learner and help to build a system tailored to each individual in different moments. Artificial intelligence (AI) algorithms, namely machine learning (ML) and deep learning (DL) models will be used for the classification of the state of the learners.

This work will focus on CW assessment using a low number of channels of fNIRS and EEG sensors to validate their performance, which contrasts with most current approaches that use a high number of channels, such as pointed out in [8] and [10]. Thus, the objectives of the current work are (1) to define an appropriate data acquisition scenario that properly distinguishes rest and task periods, (2) to analyse fNIRS and EEG signals during different states, namely, engagement vs. baseline and finally (3) to use ML algorithms to automatically identify the state of the participants during the data acquisition procedure. If the third objective is met, then this simpler setup, can be used in e-learning to adequate the contents to the instantaneous state of the user, allowing to optimize engagement and the learning experience.

This article is structured as follows: (Sect. 2) description of the relationship between this work and the conference theme; (Sect. 3) state-of-the-art about cognitive monitoring in learning environments; (Sect. 4) methods and materials applied to this study; (Sect. 5) results of our analysis; (Sect. 6) discussion of the results; (Sect. 7) final conclusions and future work.

2 Relationship to Applied Artificial Intelligence Systems

Since tutors are not present to guide the learning process, Recommendation Systems may be applied in e-learning platforms, referred as Intelligent Tutoring Systems (ITS), which can model learners' interests and states through AI and adapt course contents to maximize learning [9]. This work innovation lies on the integration of different biosignals from learners to identify cognitive states' changes and, subsequently, model learners' optimal state (for learning) and adapt e-learning content accordingly, through the application of AI models.

In this preliminary study, we will focus on the analysis of two specific biosignals with low number of channels - EEG and fNIRS - allied with one ML model to validate the possibility of applying them for automatic cognitive state assessment.

3 Literature Review

Attention plays a crucial role in learning performance [1, 2]. The work of [1] aimed at assessing the student's attention levels based on features extracted from γ, β, α and θ waves of EEG signals, achieving an average accuracy rate of 89.52%.

Related to attention, CW can be defined as the relationship between mental processing capabilities and the performed task demands, being inversely related to performance

[5, 6]. From a neurophysiological point of view, CW is directly associated with the variation of the concentration of oxygenated haemoglobin (HbO) and inversely with the concentration of deoxygenated haemoglobin (Hb) - effect of neurovascular coupling [7, 10].

To measure CW, fNIRS has been increasingly used [11] and the prefrontal cortex (PFC) is commonly the area assessed as it encompasses executive functions, i.e. high-order cognitive processes [12].

In [13] fNIRS was used to monitor participants during various psychological tasks, with accuracy results between 62–71% for the discrimination of tasks and baseline. In turn, the study [14] obtained an accuracy of 78% using only N-Back tasks. According to the study, CW induced by a memory task, N-Back, and fNIRS-based evaluation of PFC constitute a realistic method for passive Brain Computer Interface - BCI [14]. In [6], EEG was used, and results suggested that α waves were the most appropriate brain waves for measuring CW in learning-based cognitive tasks and for discriminating different learning states. Furthermore, recent literature has highlighted the significance of emotions in e-learning environments [4]. Some studies advise research on emotions in e-learning to focus on negative activating emotions (e.g. frustration) and on positive activating emotions (e.g. enjoyment) [15, 16]. While most studies on this topic rely on surveys, [3] adds that EDA and ECG might be the future means of accessing emotions.

4 Materials and Methods

4.1 Experimental Setup

According to the literature, EEG and fNIRS are the sensors that better allow to measure cognitive processes while ECG and EDA can be used to infer emotional regulation responses. We used these sensors along with a RIP band around the upper abdominal region and an accelerometer attached to the head of the participants to measure changes in posture and head movements.

EEG and fNIRS sensors were employed using two channels each (reducing the number of channels to create a close to natural learning-environment), positioned around the F7 and F8 positions of the 10–20 system [17]. Electronic devices and noise sources such as WiFi or Bluetooth devices were not near the sensors to avoid noise. The ECG sensor was applied to measure the lead I of the Einthoven system. Lastly, the EDA sensor was placed in the palm of the non-dominant hand, reducing movement constraints during computer interaction.

N-Back (described in [14]) and Mental Subtraction, were employed as standard cognitive tasks using PsychoPy [18]. Rest periods of 60 s were implemented before, between and after the two main tasks and of 20 s between tasks' explanations and procedure to avoid contamination from reading the instructions. Finally, a rest period of 10 s between difficulty levels of N-Back and between subtraction periods was introduced. Regarding the number of trials, the N-Back task consisted of 4 levels with 60 trials each and mental subtraction had 20 subtraction periods of 10 s, in which participants had to continuously subtract a given number from the result of the previous subtraction while a visual cue was shown.

Finally, participants performed a close-to-real learning task that involved the execution of a Python tutorial with theoretical and practical examples. During this part of the acquisition procedure, besides the physiological sensors, human-computer interaction (HCI) was monitored using Latent [19], which monitors mouse movement, keyboard presses, screenshots, audio, and snapshots using the webcam of the computer. A questionnaire was filled in at the end of the tutorial to get a rough individual self-assessment on thoughts regarding the tutorial, which served as ground-truth.

4.2 Data Recording

First, due to the current pandemic situation, all the equipment and room were disinfected at each acquisition, following government guidelines set by a public health entity (*Direção-Geral de Saúde)*. Also, all ethical procedures were guaranteed. Data was collected using two biosignalsplux acquisition devices (from PLUX Wireless Biosignals) at 1000 Hz and 16-bit resolution. Regarding the fNIRS sensor, specifically, the two optodes emitted at 660 nm and 860 nm and the distance between emitters and detector was 2 cm. In this preliminary study, data acquisition was performed on a sample of 8 volunteering subjects (4 females), aged between 20 and 27 years-old ($M = 22.9$, $SD = 2.1$). All participants were right-handed, none reported to suffer from psychological or neurological disorders or taking medication other than contraceptive pills. All provided written informed consent and none objected wearing the sensors.

4.3 Signals Preprocessing and Features Extraction

To remove physiological artifacts (e.g., heart rate) and long period shifts, a 4th order Butterworth filter with cut-off frequencies of 0.01 and 0.2 Hz was first applied to the raw fNIRS signals. Thereafter, to reduce spikes noise of HbO and experimental errors due to optodes' movement and motion artifact, a 3rd order Savitzky-Golay filter, using a window size of 11 s was applied. The raw optical density signals were then converted to the concentration variations of HbO and Hb via modified Beer-Lambert law. Concerning EEG signals, data was filtered using a baseline shift and a bandpass filter with cut-off frequencies of 3 and 30 Hz. Finally, both fNIRS and EEG signals were normalized and segmented into windows of 2 s, thus originating 2583 samples.

Initially, 176 features from the temporal, statistical and spectral domain were extracted from the HbO, Hb and total haemoglobin (HbT) segments, but only the 15 most relevant features were included, by the feature selection method Select K Best, provided by the scikit-learn python library [20]. This method scores the features based on the distance between the means of different classes and variance of each single class [20].

5 Results

The differences in the fNIRS signals in different conditions will be explored (EEG waves will be explored in Sect. 6). For this purpose, the mean wave of the fNIRS signal in the F7 and F8 positions are shown in Fig. 1 in different procedural states, namely during the

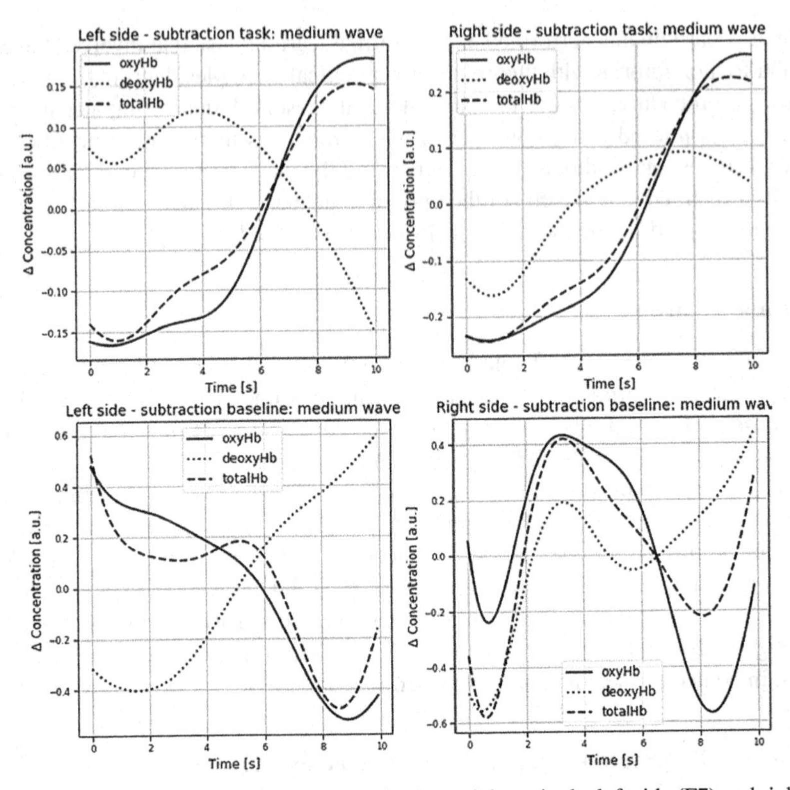

Fig. 1. Mean Waves of fNIRS signals from a single participant in the left side (F7) and right side (F8) of the PFC and during subtraction task and rest.

mental subtraction task and during rest states. These signals (from one participant) are a good example of the neurovascular coupling effect.

The classification performance using Random Forest method will be discussed taking into account the accuracy score, f-score, precision, recall and AUC-ROC. Random Forest consists of a combination of decision trees and uses averaging to improve accuracy and avoid over-fitting [21]. The chosen criterion was entropy and the number of estimators 100. Table 1 shows the results for the classification of the signals of all participants using only the fNIRS signal, only the EEG signals and using both signals. The results displayed correspond to the mean and standard deviation percentage of the 10-Fold cross-validation.

Moreover, to assess if differences in the tasks may influence the classification results, the classification was performed in separate for the N-Back task and the Mental Subtraction task using both sensors and always comparing to the rest state (Table 2).

Table 1. Classification results using Random Forest, considering fNIRS, EEG and both signals after preprocessing and features extraction and selection.

Signal	Accuracy	F-Score	Precision	Recall	AUC-ROC
fNIRS	80.05 ± 1.59	88.33 ± 0.91	80.96 ± 0.98	97.17 ± 0.83	65.70 ± 5.04
EEG	83.55 ± 1.33	90.21 ± 0.81	83.84 ± 1.18	97.66 ± 1.68	82.50 ± 2.16
fNIRS + EEG	83.55 ± 1.33	90.21 ± 0.81	83.84 ± 1.18	97.66 ± 1.68	82.50 ± 2.16

Table 2. Classification results using Random Forest, considering fNIRS and EEG signals after preprocessing and features extraction and selection considering the tasks in separate.

Task	Accuracy	F-Score	Precision	Recall	AUC-ROC
N-Back	76.16 ± 1.99	84.10 ± 1.50	76.92 ± 0.98	92.80 ± 2.76	76.30 ± 3.98
Subtraction	77.24 ± 3.43	82.21 ± 2.48	77.28 ± 3.60	88.00 ± 3.48	83.60 ± 4.82

6 Discussion

Our findings indicate that it is possible to differentiate the cognitive state of the monitored participants while performing a subtraction task and at rest state using a low number of fNIRS channels. The effects of the neurovascular coupling are clearly visible in these signals, expressed by an increase of the variation of the concentration of HbO and a decrease of Hb during task and the inverse for the baseline case. Moreover, PSD analysis of the EEG signals revealed differences during task and at rest states, enabling a distinction between both states. In fact, alpha (α) band power during mental subtraction is 2.92 ± 1.62/3.78 ± 3.12, while at rest this value rises to 3.92 ± 2.48/3.21 ± 1.21, in F7 and F8 positions, respectively. Since α activity is related to a relaxation state and to a decreased amount of attention resources allocated to the task, one would have expected a greater resting α power [1, 2, 22]. Additionally, an increased θ activity means higher mental fatigue and CW [1, 2, 23]. In effect, θ power during mental subtraction was 9.03 ± 8.16/11.41 ± 10.06 and 8.90 ± 7.65/7.78 ± 6.88 during rest, in F7 and F8 positions, respectively. Thus, the task load index, given by the θ/α ratio was 3.09/3.02 during the task and 2.27/2.42 at the resting state, in F7 and F8 positions, respectively [23].

Regarding the third identified objective of this study, ML algorithms could effectively contribute to detect CW changes and, more specifically, differentiate task and rest states. According to Table 1, a hybrid fNIRS + EEG approach resulted in a predictive model as good as the one using only EEG, reaching an accuracy of 83.55 ± 1.33%, while using only fNIRS an accuracy score of 80.05 ± 1.59% was achieved. This happened because the Select K Best algorithm selected the same features in the hybrid dataset as in the dataset consisting only of EEG features. In addition, in line with Table 2, N-Back and subtraction task provided both a successful CW states differentiator, in which accuracies of 76.16 ± 1.99% and 77.24 ± 3.43% were accomplished. The higher accuracy score of the whole dataset is due to the larger number of samples when compared to each task in separate.

7 Conclusions and Future Work

This work proposed a data acquisition scenario that mimics learning in order to develop passive BCI's, that can be used to design better user-adjustable e-learning platforms, which contrast with current solutions. A set of physiological sensors that help to infer attention, CW and emotional states, important in learning processes, was identified. In this preliminary study, only two sensors related to attention and CW, fNIRS and EEG, were analysed and allowed to conclude that brain functioning activity related to learning could in fact be inferred by their signals. Finally, it is possible to conclude that ML algorithms could automatically detect different states, specifically using both fNIRS and EEG signals. Furthermore, N-Back was more adequate to induce mental state changes than the mental subtraction case, based on the results of the ML algorithm.

Notwithstanding the positive results, more participants will be included in future work, allowing to have more data to train the ML classifiers and to increase the statistical relevance of the work, currently limited by the low number of participants.

Next steps of investigation will include the use of other sensors to understand if they can, in fact, expand further the current results. Furthermore, the Python tutorial data, including HCI data should be analysed to understand if the results of the cognitive tasks can be extrapolated to real e-learning scenarios. Finally, the resulting classifiers will be used in an e-learning context, where users will be monitored and the classifiers will infer about learners' cognitive states, allowing for the continuous update of the e-learning content in real-time to optimize engagement and, thus, learning.

Acknowledgements. This work was partly supported by Fundação para a Ciência e Tecnologia, under PhD grants PD/BDE/150304/2019 and PD/BDE/150672/2020 and by PLUX Wireless Biosignals S.A.

References

1. Chen, M.C., Wang, Y.J., Yu, M.C.: Assessing the attention levels on students by using a novel attention aware system based on brainwave signals. Br. J. Edu. Technol. **48**(2), 348–369 (2015). https://doi.org/10.1111/bjet.12359
2. Liu, H.N., Chiang, Y.C., Chu, C.H.: Recognizing the degree of human attention using EEG signals from mobile sensors. Sensors **13**(2), 10273–10386 (2013). https://doi.org/10.3390/s130810273
3. Mayer, E.R.: Searching for the role of emotions in e-learning. Learn. Instr. **70**, 101–213 (2020). https://doi.org/10.1016/j.learninstruc.2019.05.010
4. D'Errico, F., Paciello, M., Cerniglia, L.: When emotions enhance students' engagement in e-learning processes. J. e-Learn. Knowl. Soc. **12**(4), 9–23 (2016). https://doi.org/10.20368/1971-8829/1144
5. Maior, H., Pike, M., Wilson, L.M., Sharples, S.: Continuous detection of workload overload: an fNIRS approach. In: Contemporary Ergonomics and Human Factors, pp. 450–457 (2014)
6. Mazher, M., Aziz, A.A., Malik, S.A., Amin, U.H.: An EEG-based cognitive load assessment in multimedia learning using feature extraction and partial directed coherence. IEEE Access **5**, 14819–14829 (2017). https://doi.org/10.1109/ACCESS.2017.2731784

7. Herold, F., Wiegel, P., Scholkmann, F., Müller, N.G.: Applications of functional near-infrared spectroscopy (fNIRS) neuroimaging in exercise–cognition science: a systematic, methodology-focused review. J. Clin. Med. **7**(12), 466 (2018). https://doi.org/10.3390/jcm7120466
8. Lai, C.Q., Ibrahim, H., Abdullah, M.Z., Abdullah, J.M., Suandi, S.A., Azman, A.: Literature survey: recording set up for electroencephalography (EEG) acquisition. In: ISCAIE 2018 - 2018 IEEE Symposium on Computer Applications & Industrial Electronics, pp. 333–338 (2018). https://doi.org/10.1109/ISCAIE.2018.8405494
9. Kulkarni, S., Rodd, S.F.: Context aware recommendation systems: a review of the state of the art techniques. Comput. Sci. Rev. **37**, 100255 (2020). https://doi.org/10.1016/j.cosrev.2020.100255
10. Bracken, B., Festa, E., Sun, M.H., Leather, C., Strangman, G.: Validation of the fNIRS PioneerTM, a portable, durable, rugged functional near-infrared spectroscopy (fNIRS) device. In: Special Session on Real-World Assessment of Individuals During Everyday Routines, pp. 521–531 (2019). https://doi.org/10.5220/0007471405210531
11. Pinti, P., et al.: The present and future use of functional near-infrared spectroscopy (fNIRS) for cognitive neuroscience. Ann. N.Y. Acad. Sci. **1464**(1), 5 (2018). https://doi.org/10.1111/nyas.13948
12. Moriguchi, Y., Hiraki, K.: Prefrontal cortex and executive function in young children: a review of NIRS studies. Front. Hum. Neurosci. **7**, 867 (2013). https://doi.org/10.3389/fnhum.2013.00867
13. Herff, C., Dominic, H., Felix, P., Johannes, H., Fortmann, O., Schultz, T.: Classification of mental tasks in the prefrontal cortex using fNIRS. In: 35th Annual International Conference of the IEEE EMBS, Japan, pp. 3–7 (2013). https://doi.org/10.1109/EMBC.2013.6609962
14. Herff, C., Heger, D., Fortmann, O., Hennrich, J., Putze, F., Schultz, T.: Mental workload during n-back task—quantified in the prefrontal cortex using fNIRS. Front. Hum. Neurosci. **7**, 935 (2014). https://doi.org/10.3389/fnhum.2013.00935
15. Duffy, M.C., Lajoie, S.P., Pekrun, R., Lachapelle, K.: Emotions in medical education: examining the validity of the medical emotion scale (MES) across authentic medical learning environments. Learn. Instr. **70**, 101150 (2020). https://doi.org/10.1016/j.learninstruc.2018.07.001
16. Harley, J.M., Lajoie, S.P., Tressel, T., Jarrell, A.: Fostering positive emotion and history knowledge with location-based augmented reality and tour-guide prompts. Learn. Instr. **70**, 101163 (2020). https://doi.org/10.1016/j.learninstruc.2018.09.001
17. Acharya, N.J., Hani, A., Cheek, J., Thirumala, P., Tsuchida, N.T.: American clinical neurophysiology society guideline 2: guidelines for standard electrode position nomenclature. J. Clin. Neurophysiol. **33**(4), 308–311 (2016). https://doi.org/10.1097/wnp.0000000000000316
18. Peirce, J.W., et al.: PsychoPy2: experiments in behavior made easy. Behav. Res. Methods (2019). https://doi.org/10.3758/s13428-018-01193-y
19. Cepeda, C.: Latent: a flexible data collection tool to research human behavior in the context of web navigation. IEEE Access **7**, 77659–77673 (2019). https://doi.org/10.1109/ACCESS.2019.2916996
20. Pedregosa, F., et al.: Scikit-learn: machine learning in python. J. Mach. Learn. Res. **12**, 2825–2830 (2011)
21. Breiman, L.: Random forests. Mach. Learn. **45**, 5–32 (2001). https://doi.org/10.1023/A:1010933404324
22. Benedek, M., Schickel, J.R., Jauk, E., Fink, A., Neubauer, C.A.: Alpha power increases in right parietal cortex reflects focused internal attention. Neuropsychologia **56**(100), 393–400 (2014). https://doi.org/10.1016/j.neuropsychologia.2014.02.010
23. Fernadez, R., et al.: Electroencephalographic workload indicators during teleoperation of an unmanned aerial vehicle shepherding a swarm of unmanned ground vehicles in contested environments. Front. Neurosci. **14**, 40 (2020). https://doi.org/10.3389/fnins.2020.00040

Design of an Attention Tool Using HCI and Work-Related Variables

Patricia Gamboa[1,2](✉), Cláudia Quaresma[1], Rui Varandas[1,2], Helena Canhão[3,4], Rute Dinis de Sousa[3,4], Ana Rodrigues[3,4], Sofia Jacinto[3,4,5], João Rodrigues[1], Cátia Cepeda[1], and Hugo Gamboa[1,2]

[1] Departamento de Física, LIBPhys, FCT-Universidade Nova de Lisboa, Almada, Portugal
{pg.neves,r.varandas,c.cepeda}@campus.fct.unl.pt, {q.claudia, jmd.rodrigues,hgamboa}@fct.unl.pt

[2] PLUX Wireless Biosignals S.A., Lisbon, Portugal

[3] Comprehensive Health Research Centre, NOVA Medical School, Lisbon, Portugal
{helena.canhao,sofia.jacintobraga}@nms.unl.pt

[4] EpiDoC Unit, CEDOC, NOVA Medical School, Lisbon, Portugal

[5] ISCTE, CIS, IUL, Lisbon, Portugal

Abstract. The project Prevention of Occupational Disorders in Public Administrations based on Artificial Intelligence (PrevOccupAI) aims to identify and characterize profiles of work-related disorders (WRD) and daily working activities profiles. WRD have major impacts on the well-being and quality of life of individuals, as on productivity and absenteeism. Thus, to increase individuals' quality of life and productivity, a tool focusing on human attention is being developed, integrating the insights of workers of AT (*Autoridade Tributária*) and the literature on attention and time management. By inputting Human-Computer Interaction (HCI) and work-related variables into an Artificial Intelligence (AI) layer, a dashboard system will provide workers' information on causes of loss of focus they may not be aware of. Additionally, another layer will provide Recommendations, such as mindfulness-based tips, to assist in the management of feelings, emotions or work-related concerns, possibly increasing awareness and focus on the present. This manuscript presents the preliminary design of this tool.

Keywords: Artificial intelligence · HCI · Attention · Work-related disorders · Occupational health

1 Introduction

Mental health and musculoskeletal disorders are currently the most prevalent work-related disorders (WRD) [1], impacting the quality of life of workers, and the organizational productivity and absenteeism [2]. Occupational hazards continue to be a cause of disorders, with an effect on mortality worldwide, even with the significant improvements due to technologies and measures introduced over the last decades in workplaces [2]. Presently, cognitive demands of working tasks are high due to constant interruptions,

© IFIP International Federation for Information Processing 2021
Published by Springer Nature Switzerland AG 2021
L. M. Camarinha-Matos et al. (Eds.): DoCEIS 2021, IFIP AICT 626, pp. 262–269, 2021.
https://doi.org/10.1007/978-3-030-78288-7_25

ambient distractions, information overload, etc. [3]. The literature available on these topics has underlined that providing meaningful feedback to workers based on their personal data and delivering recommendations on ways to improve work efficacy and well-being contribute to reducing risk factors of WRD related to mental health difficulties and disorders. To the best of our knowledge, there is a lack of scientifically validated tools able to collect variables related to attention management at office environments, coupled with the delivery of personalised feedback and recommendations.

This work is part of the project Prevention of Occupational Disorders in Public Administrations based on Artificial Intelligence (PrevOccupAI) that aims to identify and characterize profiles of work-related disorders (WRD) and daily working activities profiles of individuals working in the Public Administration, in particular AT (*Autoridade Tributária*). In this project, both ergonomic and mental health risk factors will be assessed by the group of researchers, though solely the latter will be discussed in this manuscript.

The present paper is structured as follows: a brief literature review (Sect. 2) that includes the role of attention and time management and links to work performance and well-being; and the role of feedback and recommendations in the enhancement of those variables; the framing of the current work with AI systems (Sect. 3); the presentation of the concept of an attention promotion tool to assist public office workers and its development roadmap (Sect. 4) through: (i) the selection of measures to gather personal data from office workers and definition of variables; (ii) a *focus group* to explore with the workers, the measures selected so the feedback provided is meaningful and personalised, promoting workers' self-awareness and self-reflection on their work-related tasks; and to explore the display of personalised tips to improve well-being and work performance; (iii) the validation of the tool; (3) a brief conclusion and orientations regarding future work (Sect. 5).

2 Literature Review

2.1 Attention and Time Management at Work

Working implies to rely on executive functions, a set of mental processes that include three core functions: inhibition control, working memory and cognitive flexibility [4]. Selective or focused attention (one of the mechanisms of inhibitory control), in particular, enables individuals to attend to selected stimuli while suppressing attention to other stimuli [4]. Some salient stimuli attract attention in an involuntary way, such as loud noises, while others in a more voluntary way, based on personal goals or intention [4]. In work performance, attention enables individuals to pursue goals without getting distracted by alternative stimuli available in physical and virtual environments [5]. However, constant interruptions, ambient distractions (e.g., doorbell rings in home office, nowadays more common due to the COVID-19 pandemic [6]), and information overload, are factors that contribute to create cognitive straining conditions, impairing task performance and diminishing the well-being at work [3]. Indeed, work stress is at the top of the most commonly reported causes of WRD and loss of work performance [7].

WRD, also named occupational disorders, are caused primarily as a consequence of exposure to risk factors related to a work activity or job [1]. They have multiple causes, with work environment variables (e.g., physical and psychosocial) playing a role, together with other risk factors, such as personal determinants related to demographic variables and medical history [1]. The most prevalent WRD worldwide are musculoskeletal and mental health disorders (e.g., [8]) which, in recent studies [9, 10], accounted for around 30% and 50% of occupational reports, respectively. Moreover, work content, work relationships and work pace represented 40% of the top risks identified [9].

Therefore, it is essential to manage cognitively straining factors and reduce their harmful repercussions for individual workers, organizations, and society [3]. The promotion of a healthy working environment must include temporal, spatial and mental separation of work and private life components [11]. This can be done by implementing time management strategies such as organizing the working time, including breaks and quiet moments [12], and through the creation of an ergonomic workplace and a working environment with reduced distractions [11]. In order to foster attention and time management, solutions such as browser extensions and mobile apps are available. For instance, TogglTrack [13] allows individuals to track the time spent in activities such as emails, websites, etc. and block predefined websites such as social media. Other solutions set limits to websites (e.g., RescueTime [14]) or remind individuals to take breaks (e.g., Time Out [15]). Within the context of our project, these time management strategies will be explored and coupled with feedback and recommendations so that self-knowledge and self-awareness are enhanced in a more comprehensive and personalised manner, providing a novel tool to support office workers.

2.2 Feedback and Recommendations

Enhancing self-knowledge in the work context can be achieved through the use of digital solutions that track personal data, analyse it and provide feedback [16]. In fact, receiving meaningful feedback enhances self-awareness regarding work performance, which also impacts job motivation, as suggested by Hackman and Oldham (1975, cit. by [16]). A recent study with factory workers has combined well-being metrics and work performance-related metrics and presented them to workers via a Worker Feedback Dashboard web application [16]. Moreover, this study highlighted three key-design features feedback applications should provide: meaningful personal overviews, guidelines to act on based on those overviews and consideration for unquantified aspects relevant to work (e.g., social support).

Providing recommendations on how to act on (based on the feedback gathered) is also key to support workers' well-being and productivity [16]. Adopting strategies towards attentional processes such as mindfulness [17] can be included in the recommendations. Mindfulness is beneficial to help workers improving their attention towards working tasks, to disconnect from work when they need to [6] and to assist in the management of work-related concerns, while also enhancing self-awareness and positive emotional states [18]. Other tips that elicit behaviour change can also be useful to promote healthy actions related to work aspects and well-being.

3 Relation to Applied Artificial Intelligence Systems

Work-related disorders are a major concern in working environments and solutions that try to prevent them are limited by the variables that researchers are able to monitor/extract and by the knowledge available (i.e., variables highlighted in the literature review). By embedding AI into our tool, we will understand the variables that are better appropriate to assess attention and the AI models will expand on the previously programmed event detection by learning new sources of inattention/strain that might not have been defined previously. Thus, AI will play a major role in extending the prevention of WRD and in monitoring attention and cognitive constraints in the workplace.

4 Tool Development

4.1 Concept

Our tool aims to combine variables from HCI with work-related variables that can be associated with attention and known to have an effect on work performance and well-being. The variables will be chosen taken into consideration both the literature review and the *focus group* with a group of workers from AT (the number of participants and departments as the protocol for data acquisition is not yet decided). The data collected will be displayed into a Dashboard System and analysed in order to deliver meaningful easy-to-interpret personal outcomes that facilitate self-awareness and self-reflection regarding working aspects. The tool concept, illustrated in Fig. 1, consists of 4 main layers: 1 - interaction; 2 – acquisition; 3 - analysis and 4 – feedback and recommendations. The interactive layer will gather data from the use of tools (HCI) and from questionnaires to deliver data to layer 2. On layer 3, the data gathered will be integrated and analysed (AI models will also be used) and subsequently displayed into a Dashboard System in order to deliver meaningful easy-to-interpret feedback on personal outcomes that facilitate self-awareness and self-reflection regarding working aspects. Additionally, this integration will allow us to introduce recommendations based on sound knowledge regarding the identified factors, promoting targeted actions in working environments.

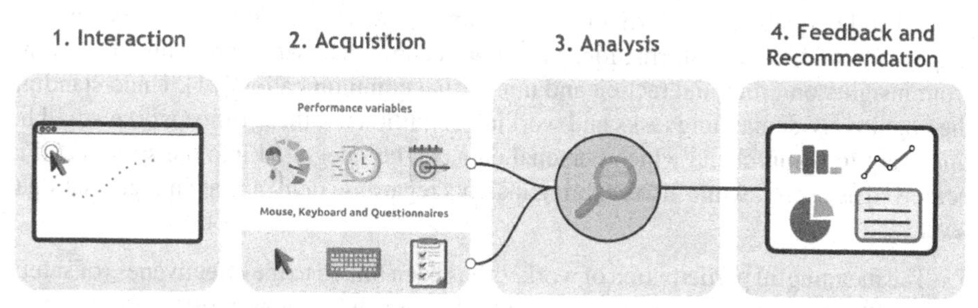

Fig. 1. Overview of the tool concept and its 4 layers - 1. Interaction, 2. Acquisition, 3. Analysis and 4. Feedback and recommendation.

4.2 Development Roadmap

Variables Definition. As office workers have to rely on the use of a computer to perform most of their work, their interaction with it is an important source of information, enabling us to retrieve personal data related to work processes and tasks. In that sense, HCI tools can be used to assess focused attention and human performance by providing variables such as the time and success in task completion, among others [19]. HCI techniques have also been successfully used to measure human behaviour based on their browser activity, namely by means of mouse pointer, keyboard, among other measures. Understanding these variables can provide insights on workers' mental state and task engagement, being therefore relevant to assess focused attention [20]. Variables contributing to cognitive strain and closely related to attention include those that directly disrupt the primary task the worker is attending to, such as: interruptions from colleagues [3], notifications [5] or environmental constraints [6]. Through HCI these interruptions can be collected (e.g., the number of interruptions resulting from chats or notifications). Regarding environmental constraints, this input may be directly introduced by the worker into the dashboard tool, for example.

On the other hand, variables that can promote a balanced working life and attention management, such as quiet working hours [12] and break times [11], can also be tracked through HCI. Though the frequency and duration of breaks is not consensual in the literature, we propose to collect this data in order to have a broad set of variables and to meet this gap in the literature.

For other variables, we will develop specific measures based on questions eliciting qualitative assessments by the workers. Important questions might be related to leisure times during work hours (e.g., activities during breaks and social interactions), cognitive information, overload perception, etc. Portuguese versions of scales for measuring particular aspects of work productivity can also be used.

We will define a list of pertinent variables to track based on the literature available and also use the *Focus group* with the workers to gather information on more pertinent ones to add or remove.

Focus Group. *Focus group* will be used as part of our research tools to capture information that will assist the definition of the work-related variables and HCI to be collected (e.g., detailed qualitative information on disruptions at work). This method favours the acquisition of broader information, in a more economical way, while also benefiting from insights on group interaction and non-verbal communication [21]. Understanding the cognitively demanding tasks and working conditions of these office workers will be important to comprehend which personal data can be integrated into the system and is perceived as useful, while also enabling insights regarding demands at an organisational level.

The meaningful participation of workers has been linked to the effectiveness of safety and health programs and workers are often the ones who know most about potential hazards associated with their jobs [22] so, eliciting their insights is an essential part of creating this tool. Moreover, we will add questions related to user acceptance and experience in order to gather information relevant to consider for the design of the dashboard system.

Validation. We will focus our research efforts on testing: (1) if the tool is able to infer attention focus from the HCI and work-related variables chosen? (2) if the tool is perceived as effective and generating positive impacts? (3) if using the tool produces work performance enhancement? (4) if using the tool has an impact on well-being.

To answer these questions, we will need to operationalise variables, some of which have to take into consideration work-related variables that are not measurable. In such cases, questionnaires with rating scales can be useful tools. To assess the proposed tool, we will develop a user experience questionnaire and gather information on users' adherence (e.g., tool metrics use such as days of use). To operationalize work performance, we will collect input from workers about how their tasks are usually evaluated. This information might also be gathered through *focus group* and interviews with managers. Regarding the well-being assessment we will select, from previously validated measures, the instruments that better capture key variables defined in our project.

5 Conclusion and Future Work

With the rise of prevalence of WRD (e.g., [1])] and highly cognitive demanding environments, particularly office workplaces (e.g., [3]), attention tools that promote workers' well-being and work performance are needed.

The present work focuses on the development of an innovative attention tool for office workers. The proposed concept combines HCI and work-related variables embedded into a dashboard system that, by using AI models, provides feedback on meaningful personal data, enhancing self-awareness and self-reflection towards work performance. Eliciting feedback has been found to impact well-being and work performance, which in turn can lead to enhanced productivity [16]. On top of this, our tool will display personalised recommendations, that will be automatically determined in the AI layer, which has not been combined in other studies [16].

Promoting workers' well-being should be a top priority regarding occupational health promotion since it benefits the worker and the organisation: by increasing workers' health and reducing absenteeism, also enhancing organizational performance [23]. We believe that by integrating different dimensions of the workers' experience and presenting recommendations, such as mindfulness-based tips, we will be able to increase office workers' well-being and work performance.

As highlighted in the previous section, future work on the development of the tool will focus on the selection of variables that will be tracked as well as operationalizing them and establishing how to measure them. The dashboard will be designed taking into account the most relevant variables from both sources, i.e., HCI and work-related parameters, together with workers' insights (since involving them as co-constructors will likely empower them). Finally, the tool will undergo a validation step with evaluation regarding acceptance towards the tool and user experience in order to enhance it, as well as measures pertaining to the validity and reliability of the tool.

Some of the expected limitations of the system relate to the collection of data regarding important constructs to infer when investigating work and attention processes that are not easy to measure using existing metrics or methods, such as motivation and work relationships. This limitation can be overcome by including information retrieved from other sources such as the COPSOQ (Copenhagen Psychosocial Questionnaire) [24], a questionnaire that assesses psychosocial variables and risk factors at workplaces.

Questions regarding privacy concerns and the use of the application will also have to be elicit during the tool development. Furthermore, we need to have a careful approach in defining certain metrics as though users value positive feedback from the application [16] if feedback confronts aspects of the self, such as self-image (e.g., lower work performance measures than expected), feelings of self-competence and self-esteem may decrease (Stiglbauer et al. 2019 cit. by [16]).

The presented concept is still an idea on its early stages of development, but it is our contention that it will allow the collection of relevant data and its integration into a system that has the worker at the core will allow a better understanding of variables playing a role in attentional processes at work and ways to foster occupational health promotion.

Acknowledgments. This work was partly supported by Fundação para a Ciência e Tecnologia, under project PREVOCUPAI (DSAIPA/AI/0105/2019) and PhD grants PD/BDE/142816/2018, PD/BDE/150304/2019, PD/BDE/150672/2020.

References

1. World Health Organization. Occupational and work-related diseases. https://www.who.int/activities/occupational-and-work-related-diseases
2. Rushton, L.: The global burden of occupational disease. Curr. Environ. Health Rep. **4**(3), 340–348 (2017). https://doi.org/10.1007/s40572-017-0151-2
3. Kalakoski, V., Selinheimo, S., Valtonen, T., et al.: Effects of a cognitive ergonomics workplace intervention (CogErg) on cognitive strain and well-being: a cluster-randomized controlled trial. A study protocol. BMC Psychol. **8**, 1 (2020). https://doi.org/10.1186/s40359-019-0349-1
4. Diamond, A.: Executive functions. Annu. Rev. Psychol. **64**(1), 135–168 (2013). https://doi.org/10.1146/annurev-psych-113011-143750
5. Roda, C. (ed.): Human attention and its implications for human-computer interaction. In: Roda, C. (ed.) Human Attention in Digital Environments, pp. 11–62. Cambridge University Press (2011). https://doi.org/10.1017/CBO9780511974519.002
6. Toniolo-Barrios, M., Pitt, L.: Mindfulness and the challenges of working from home in times of crisis. Bus. Horiz. (2020). https://doi.org/10.1016/j.bushor.2020.09.004
7. Page, K.M., Milner, A.J., Martin, A., Turrell, G., Giles-Corti, B., LaMontagne, A.D.: Workplace stress: what is the role of positive mental health? J. Occup. Environ. Med. **56**(8), 814–819 (2014). https://doi.org/10.1097/JOM.0000000000000230
8. Luger, T., Maher, C.G., Rieger, M.A., Steinhilber, B.: Work-break schedules for preventing musculoskeletal symptoms and disorders in healthy workers. Cochrane Database Syst. Rev. **23**, 7 (2019). https://doi.org/10.1002/14651858.CD012886.pub2
9. Netherlands Center for Occupational Diseases. Statistics on Occupational Diseases 2018. https://www.occupationaldiseases.nl/content/statistics-occupational-diseases-2018
10. Health and Safety Executive. Health and safety at work Summary statistics for Great Britain 2020. https://www.hse.gov.uk/statistics/
11. Mojtahedzadeh, N., Rohwer, E., Lengen, J., Harth, V., Mache, S.: Gesundheitsfördernde Arbeitsgestaltung im Homeoffice im Kontext der COVID-19-Pandemie [Health-promoting work design for telework in the context of the COVID-19 pandemic]. Zentralbl Arbeitsmed Arbeitsschutz Ergon. **7**, 1–6 (2021). https://doi.org/10.1007/s40664-020-00419-1

12. König, C.J., Kleinmann, M., Höhmann, W.: A field test of the quiet hour as a time management technique. Eur. Rev. Appl. Psychol. **63**(3), 137–145 (2013). https://doi.org/10.1016/j.erap.2012.12.003
13. TogglTrack. https://toggl.com/
14. RescueTime. https://www.rescuetime.com/
15. Time Out. https://www.dejal.com/timeout/
16. Heikkilä, P., et al.: Quantified factory worker: field study of a web application supporting work well-being and productivity. Cogn. Tech. Work (2021). https://doi.org/10.1007/s10111-021-00671-2
17. Bakker, A.B., Demerouti, E., De Boer, E., Schaufeli, W.B.: Job demands and job resources as predictors of absence duration and frequency. J. Vocat. Behav. **62**, 341–356 (2003). https://doi.org/10.1016/S0001-8791(02)00030-1
18. Brown, K.W., Ryan, R.M.: The benefits of being present: mindfulness and its role in psychological well-being. J. Pers. Soc. Psychol. **84**(4), 822–848 (2003). https://doi.org/10.1037/0022-3514.84.4.822
19. Lazar, J., Feng, J.H., Hochheiser, H.: Research Methods in Human Computer Interaction, 2nd edn. Morgan Kaufmann, San Francisco (2017)
20. Cepeda, C., et al.: Latent: a flexible data collection tool to research human behavior in the context of web navigation. IEEE Access **7**, 77659–77673 (2019). https://doi.org/10.1109/ACCESS.2019.2916996
21. Nagle, B., Williams, N.: Methodology brief: introduction to focus groups. Center for Assessment, Planning and Accountability (n.d.). http://www.mmgconnect.com/projects/userfiles/file/focusgroupbrief.pdf
22. United States Department of Labor. Occupational Safety and Health Administration: Recommended Practices for Safety and Health Programs. https://www.osha.gov/shpguidelines/worker-participation.html
23. Danna, K.D., Griffin, R.W.: Health and well-being in the workplace: a review and synthesis of the literature. J. Manag. **25**, 357–384 (1999). https://doi.org/10.1177/014920639902500305
24. Burr, H., et al.: The third version of the copenhagen psychosocial questionnaire. Saf. Health Work **10**(4), 482–503 (2019). https://doi.org/10.1016/j.shaw.2019.10.002

Smart Healthcare Systems

Assessment of Visuomotor and Visual Perception Skills in Children: A New Proposal Based on a Systematic Review

Ana Isabel Ferreira[1,2,3](✉), Carla Quintão[1,2], and Cláudia Quaresma[1,2]

[1] Departamento de Física, Faculdade de Ciências e Tecnologia da Universidade Nova de Lisboa, Caparica, Portugal
aix.ferreira@campus.fct.unl.pt
[2] LIBPhys - UNL, Faculdade de Ciências e Tecnologia da Universidade Nova de Lisboa, Caparica, Portugal
[3] Departamento de Saúde, Escola Superior de Saúde do Instituto Politécnico de Beja, Beja, Portugal

Abstract. Vision is a dominant sense in humans and its performance is a critical factor in children's development and learning. For health sciences it is essential to identify the tools most used in the last decade to assess visuomotor and visual perception skills in children under 6 years of age. For that reason, systematic research was conducted according to the PRISMA criteria. The research was performed using B-on and Pubmed and were included articles published between 2011 until 2021. Included were 17 articles highlighting 2 different samples: children with typical development and children with abnormal development. The assessment protocol differs between researches. A large diversity of tests were observed, usually involving "paper and pencil" tasks. Surprisingly, the association of neuroimaging or electrophysiological techniques with traditional assessment is not common in clinical settings. This aspect will be fully analyzed and a proposal of change will be presented.

Keywords: Visuomotor skills · Visual perception skills · Assessment · Children

1 Introduction

Vision is the most powerful sense and gives information about our surroundings from the first day of life [1, 2], with the visual skills development occurring during childhood [2, 3]. At 5 to 6 years of age, the relationship between visuomotor performance, handwriting execution and future verbal number skills is evident [4, 5].

Visuomotor integration is the degree to which visual perception and hand finger movements are well coordinated [6]. For many, visual perception can be defined as the interpretation of visual stimuli, the intermediate step between simple visual sensation and the process of cognition [6–9]. In the same way, visual perception could be explained as the ability to extract information from what is seen [10]. The functional use of these

© IFIP International Federation for Information Processing 2021
Published by Springer Nature Switzerland AG 2021
L. M. Camarinha-Matos et al. (Eds.): DoCEIS 2021, IFIP AICT 626, pp. 273–284, 2021.
https://doi.org/10.1007/978-3-030-78288-7_26

skills is fundamental to everyday life and its impact on overall development, social communication and learning has already been reported [11–14]. These skills have been greatly influenced by cerebral components, so they could be an impairment even in children with typical or near–typical visual acuity.

Assessment is a milestone in any (re)habilitation approach and also crucial for the investigation process. In the REHAB – Cycle this is described as a continuous process that involves the identification of individual problems, needs and relates the problems of relevant factors to the person and the environment [15, 16]. Assessment of multiple performance areas is essential in understanding children's strengths and limitations and therefore critical for developing a focused intervention plan to improve performance [17]. In pediatric rehabilitation the evaluation tends to use qualitative and quantitative measures. Both in research and in rehabilitation, a holistic approach is currently recommended to better understand and characterize the phenomena under study.

In the last few decades, a considerable revolution in technology has taken place. This provided the opportunity to introduce new tools in health care. In rehabilitation practice these tools could provide benefit from the youngest to the oldest patients [18–21].

Nowadays is consensual that introduction of technology in health is a strong way to improve the quality of care. The maturation of computing technologies has dramatically altered the face of healthcare. Recent technological developments that can be harnessed to replicate, enhance, or create methods for assessment of functional performance [22]. The implementation of this measures will increase the quantity and diversity of digital data and facilitate artificial intelligence. These newest field of engineering when implementing in health care has the ability to cover areas including prevention, treatment and rehabilitation, following the care continuum [23].

1.1 Motivation

In therapeutic practice, the assessment of visuomotor and visual perception skills has been, up until now, uneven. It seems from clinical and therapeutic practice that the lack of a standard protocol or technological equipment limit health professionals from making a structured assessment. Given this knowledge, the main motivation for performing this systematic review is to better know the most common instruments used in the last 10 years to assess visual visuomotor and visual perception skills. This knowledge will guide your reflection to structure a new proposal of assessment that included technology in the assessment phase.

The first aim of the article is to identify the instruments most used in the last decade to assess the visuomotor and visual perception skills in children up to 6 years of age. The second is to present a new assessment proposal that includes a technological solution and could contribute, in the future, for artificial intelligence application.

2 Contribution to Life Improvement

Health professional's performance is dependent upon knowledge and quality tools that are available for a patient's treatment. In our knowledge this is the first systematic review on the assessment of visuomotor and visual perception skills in children. So, it could be useful to offer a better selection of the tools used in the assessment process of children with visuomotor or visual perception skills impairment. A better assessment is, without a doubt, the basis for better intervention which can contribute to the children's quality of life [17].

Building on the information collected in this systematic review, it is also possible to stimulate the identification of technological solutions that can, in the future, be integrated in the visuomotor and visual perceptive skills assessment. The evidence shows that these two measures are directly related with the increase of professional efficiency and the improvement of the patient's quality of life.

3 Materials and Methods

For this review, the preferred reporting items for systematic reviews and meta-analysis (PRISMA) [24] were followed. As a research strategy two databases were used: Pubmed and ISI Web of Knowledge. In both, the advanced search mode was used. The research was conducted in January 2021, using the following keywords and boolean operators: "visual development" OR "visuomotor" OR "visual perception" AND "assessment".

Some filters were used: articles from last 10 years, humans, full articles available, children until 18 years old. To select the articles the following inclusion criteria were used:

1. Studies that evaluated visual perception and visuomotor skills in the methodology protocol.
2. Research in babies and children of six or less years of age;
3. Original, experimental or observational research published between 2011 and 2021;
4. Published scientific periodical journals with peer reviews;

and the following exclusion criteria as well:

1. Conducted with animal research;
2. The full article is unavailable in the databases used;
3. The paper is in a language other than English or Portuguese.

The temporal window of the last 10 years (2011 until January 2021) was used because the purpose was to collect the most recent methods and techniques used in visuomotor and visual perception assessment in children.

3.1 Selection Method

All the papers that did not follow the inclusion criteria were eliminated. This occurred in the different phases of PRISMA methodology, such as those reported in Fig. 1. At the end of the PRISMA methodology application 17 articles remained to include in the systematic review. It is important to note that some articles included in this review reported investigations that included some children up to six years of age, however, the participants mean age is less than 6 years of age.

3.2 Methodology for Collecting Information

In a systematic review an in-depth, systematic and critical examination is made regarding the object of study. The information is collected and organized to clarify the following aspects: type of study, sample characteristics and assessment protocol used to assess visuomotor and visual perceptive skill.

After the systematic review conclusion, was done the reflection about the introduction of technology in visuomotor and visual perception assessment. This on presented based on literature-based evidence and clinical practice requirements.

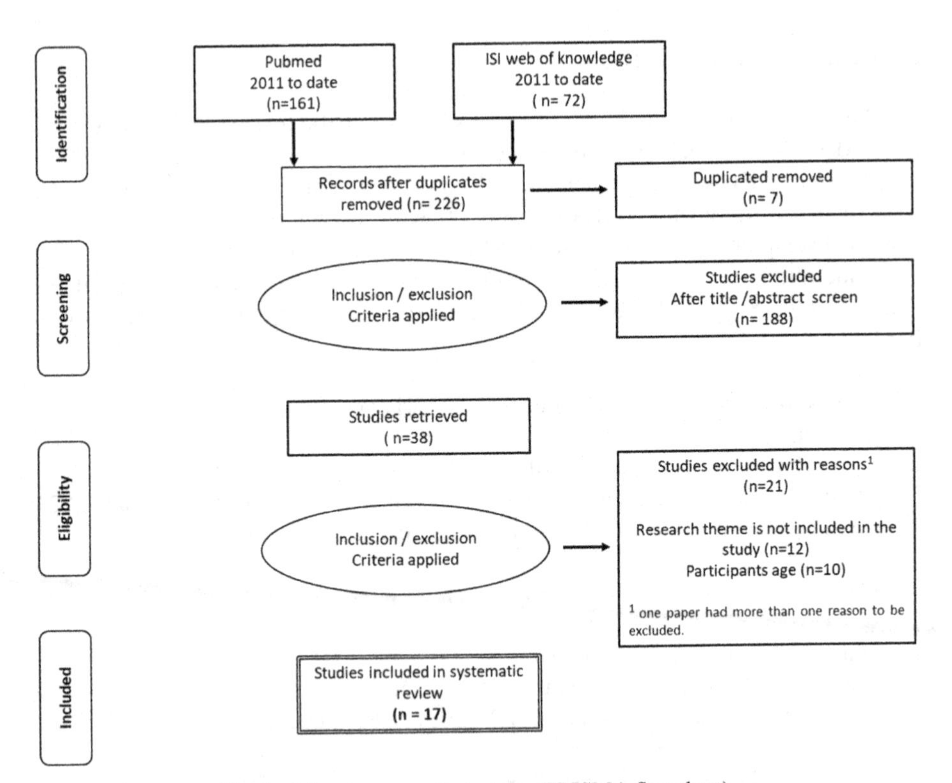

Fig. 1. Literature search strategy (PRISMA flowchart).

4 Results

At the end of the process, 17 articles remain in the inclusion criteria and were enrolled in the analysis (Appendix A). The studies included present mostly a clinical orientation and 12 of them are related to the impact of a specific clinical diagnosis in visuomotor or visual perception skills development/performance. Related to the time perspective to data collected, there was not a clear trend. In this systematic review, 8 transversal studies, 7 longitudinal and 2 case reports were found. The longitudinal researches are particularly rich on data and follows the children clinical situation during a time period.

It is also important to mention that 5 articles report a phase of a tool development, which leads us to reflect about the necessity for new and more efficient ways to assess children that face clinical and/or developmental issues.

Concerning the assessment tools used, the results were found to be relatively diverse. The Beery-Buktenica Developmental Test of Visual Motor Integration (Beery VMI) is the most commonly used to assess the visuomotor and visual perception skills and were used in 10 studies, as appears in Fig. 2.

The next most common type of assessment was the Developmental Test of Visual Perception, which was used in 3 studies. The Rey Complex Figure and PreviAs questionnaire were used once each in two studies. As appears in Fig. 2, more 9 other tools were found, each in their own separate studies.

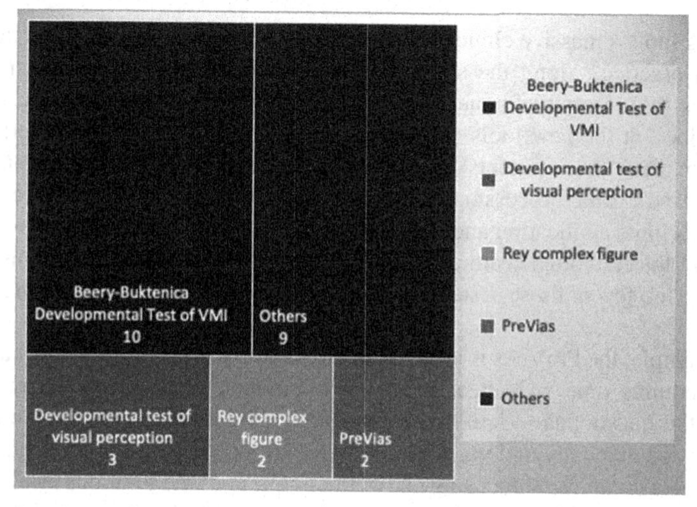

Fig. 2. Tools used for visuomotor and visual perception skills assessment.

The most common situation under study is typical development (n = 8) followed by pre term born (n = 6), as shown on Fig. 3. It is interesting to note that 5 studies have both a clinical group and a control group, which shows us that only 3 studies use subjects with typical development exclusively.

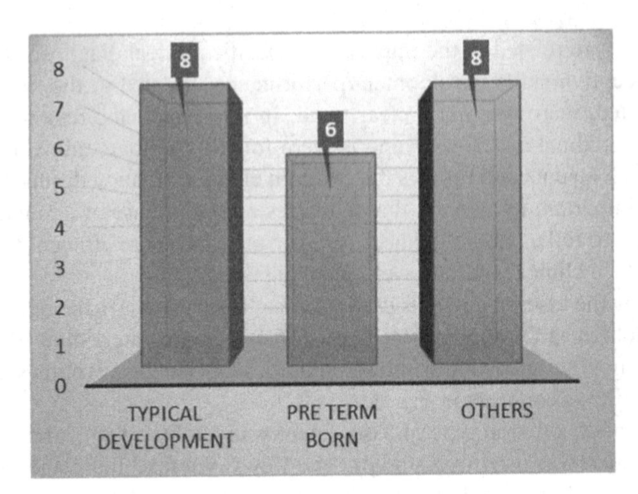

Fig. 3. Development situation under study.

5 Discussion of Results and Critical View

The results show a massive clinical orientation, which highlights the theme importance in clinical practice. Along the same line, the development of new assessment tools emphasizes the necessity for new assessment options in clinical practice. However, when we look at the new tools (Children's Visual Impairment Test, Preverbal Visual Assessment (PreViAs) – parents' questionnaire and Battery for the Evaluation of Visual Perceptual and Spatial processing in children) none of them appears with technological components in its application and/or results analysis. These results are not surprising if we consider that, although healthcare delivery can be improved using health information technology, too few of those systems are implemented and used in developing countries [25].

For example, the PreViAs is a questionnaire delivery to parents on paper and whose analysis requires time and attention. In the same manner, if the health professional reapplies the questionnaire later to reappraise the children's evolution, the data have to be analyzed manually and quick access to the evolution information is not possible. Switching to a digital version, using one of the simple and free solutions available on the market, will facilitate the results analyses and allows an easy follow-up of the patients, monitoring changes quicky and giving information for intervention adaptation.

Surprisingly, among the articles enrolled, no technology was used to accurately conduct the visuomotor and visual perception assessment. Thinking more broadly, increasing technology in diagnosis and treatment will allow big data analyses [26].

As far as the clinical studies are concerned, the Beery VMI clearly appears to be the most frequently used tool. It seems like this instrument is recognized by most of the therapists as the gold standard for visuomotor and visual perception skills assessment. This is a "paper and pencil" tool composed of 3 sub scales: visuomotor integration, visual perception and motor coordination. It takes approximately 30 min to apply and another 30 min to analyze the results [9]. The time necessary to do that in a proper manner is the highest constraint to use on a large scale in a clinical setting. For this reason, we point the development of a technological solution like VMSreport a possible solution in order to speed up the process [18].

Another aspect that this systematic review highlights is the lack of association of neuroimages and electrophysiological data with the traditional "paper and pencil" tools. The use of a portable visual evoked potential device are progressively introduce in the last years [27, 28]. Although these systems are mostly use with screens, so a work to adapt them to instruments like Beery VMI should be done.

The introduction of an eye tracker could be useful to measure the ocular movements during the paper and pencil tests performance. These technological tools are commonly used to assess visuomotor skills in children with cerebral visual impairment [29–31].

The considerable number of longitudinal studies enrolled in this systematic review shows that a large amount of data is available, and that its digitalization should be a priority that can, in the future, improve the analyses and pair the information with artificial intelligence.

6 Conclusion and Further Work

The Beery VMI was the tool most often used to assess visuomotor and visual perception skills in clinical practice. However, it demands a considerable amount of time to score and perform qualitative analyses. For this reason, the development of a tool that automates the process and allows for a longitudinal patient follow-up is recommended. Along these lines, it would be beneficial if all questionnaires were digitalized.

This will allow for quick data collection, without paper and accompanied with the potential benefit of big data analysis. It is also possible to work with other associated technological tools, for example, including the introduction of eye tracker or portable device for electrophysiological signs assessment. The use of portable and/or remote devices is a trend in rehabilitation science and allows the monitoring of patients and their health progression. These generate an extensive quantity of data that could be analysed with different artificial intelligence methods.

Appendix A

See Table 1.

Table 1. Main Characteristics of the studies

Article Author Study type	Population (sample/diagnosis/time assessment)	Instruments used for Visuomotor and Perception Skills assessment
1 Ricci et al., 2014 Longitudinal	n = 5, with Dravet syndrome Participants followed between 1st seizures (±2-4 M old) until 7Y, periodic assessment at 2, 4, 6 and 7y	Atkinson ABCDEFV Battery (2002) - Shape matching (five shape board) - Copying block design The Beery-Buktenica Developmental Test of Visuo-Motor Integration (2000) - Frostig cats' silhouette task Developmental test of visual perception - Form completion and figure ground WISC III (WISC, 2006) - Block design subtest The Rey Complex Figure test - Complex Figure copy
2 Vancleef et al., 2019 Transversal	n = 301, between 3 to 6Y old Typical development	Children's Visual Impairment Test - Object recognition, - Degraded object recognition, - Motion Perception Global–Local Processing
3 Vancleef et al, 2019 Transversal	n = 59, MA = 4y 10Mo Four groups: - typically developing children (MA = 5.1Y) - children with cerebral visual impairment (MA = 4.11 Y) - intellectual impairment (MA=5.0Y) - typical developing but with simulated impaired vision (4.7Y)	The Beery-Buktenica Developmental Test of Visuo-Motor Integration L94 visual perceptual battery
4 Caravale et al., 2011 Longitudinal study	n = 26, MA 4Y 11 Mo PTB without major neurological disabilities n = 23, MA 5Y, TD	The Beery-Buktenica Developmental Test of Visuo-Motor Integration Developmental test of visual perception Block construction (based on paradigm of Stiles et al. 1996)

(*continued*)

Table 1. (*continued*)

Article Author Study type	Population (sample/diagnosis/time assessment)	Instruments used for Visuomotor and Perception Skills assessment
5 Lorenzo et al., 2013 Case control study	n = 43, 40 Mo, NF1 children n = 43, 40 Mo, TD (the sample and data were included in a longitudinal project)	The Beery-Buktenica Developmental Test of Visual-Motor Integration (5th Ed.)
6 Pueyo et al., 2014 Transversal	n = 298, between 0.1 to 24 Mo (MA = 11.2 Mo), TD	Preverbal Visual Assessment (PreViAs) – parents questionnaire: - visual attention - visual communication - visual-motor coordination - visual processing
7 Michel et al., 2016 Longitudinal	n = 48 children with motor coordination impairment, n = 48 TD Describing: n = 18: 4-year-olds n = 57: 5-year-olds n = 21: 6-year-olds	The Gestalt Closure subtest of the FEW-2 Developmental Test of Visual Perception
8 Garfinkle et al., 2020 Longitudinal	n = 221, 4,5 y, PTB	The Beery-Buktenica Developmental Test of Visual-Motor Integration (6th Ed.)
9 Sanchez Joya et al., 2017 Longitudinal	n = 54, assessed between 4 to 5Y: 27 PTB 27 TB	The Rey Complex Figure Test (Rey, 1997)
10 Geldof et al., 2017 Transversal	n = 106 PTB assessed at 5,5 y	The Beery-Buktenica Developmental Test of Visual-Motor Integration
11 Willoughby et al., 2014 Case report	n=1, 4Y 1Mo, with 18 deletion syndrome	The Beery-Buktenica Developmental Test of Visual-Motor Integration
12 Linde et al., 2019 Longitudinal	n=167 PT, assessed at 5 and 11Y	Visuomotor and visuospatial functions: - subtests visuomotor precision - assessing graphomotor speed - accuracy Design copying: assessing motor and visual-perceptual skills associated with the ability to copy two-dimensional geometric figures
13 Schmetz et al., 2017 Transversal	n = 179; 5-14Y TD The subgroup between 5-6 Y n = 19 children	Battery for the Evaluation of Visual Perceptual and Spatial processing in children (BEVPS): - visual perceptual object recognition - basic visual spatial processing

(*continued*)

Table 1. *(continued)*

Article Author Study type	Population (sample/diagnosis/time assessment)	Instruments used for Visuomotor and Perception Skills assessment
14 Verkerk et al. 2014 Longitudinal	n = 117, assessed at 3 ½Y and 5½Y, with VLBW but without CP n = 3 ½ Yo, 41 TD CA	The Beery-Buktenica Developmental Tests of Visual-Motor Integration
15 Garcia – Ormaechea et al., 2014 Transversal	n = 220; questionnaire applied to parents of children under 2Y	Preverbal Visual Assessment (PreViAs) questionnaire, - visual attention - visual communication - visual–motor coordination - visual processing
16 Veen et al., 2019 Transversal study	n = 54 5Y PT; n = 28 TB with TD	The Beery-Buktenica Developmental Test of Visual–Motor Integration (6th ed.) - visual motor integration - visual-perception - motor-coordination
17 Nicola et al., 2016 Transversal study	n = 100 children, from 4 to 14Y, MA = 5,99Y Children with severe specific language impairment	The Beery-Buktenica Developmental Test of Visual–Motor Integration (3rd, 4th and 5th Ed.)

CA - corrected age; MA – Mean age; Mo - Months; PTB - pre term born; TB - Term born; TD-Typical development; VLBW - Very low birth weight; Y – years.

References

1. Zeki, S.: A: Vision of the Brain. Blackwell Scientific Publications, Oxford (1993)
2. Atkinson, J.: The Developing Visual Brain. Oxford Psychology Series, New York (2008)
3. Lueck, A., Dutton, G.: Vision and the Brain – Understanding Cerebral Visual Impairment in Children. American Foundation for the Blind, New York (2015)
4. Bara, F., Gentaz, E.: Haptics in teaching handwriting: the role of perceptual and visuomotor skills. Hum. Mov. Sci. **30**, 745–759 (2011). https://doi.org/10.1016/j.humov.2010.05.015
5. Cornu, V., Schiltz, C., Martin, R., Hornung, C.: Visuo-spatial abilities are key for young children's verbal number skills. J. Exp. Child Psychol. **166**, 604–620 (2018). https://doi.org/10.1016/j.jecp.2017.09.006
6. Beery, K., Beery, N.: The Beery – Buktenica Developmental Test of Visual – Motor Integration, 6th edn. Pearson, Texas (2010)
7. Atkinson, J., Nardini, M.: Visuospatial and visuomotor development. In: Reed, J., Rogers, W. (eds.) Child Neuropsychology, pp. 183–217. Blackwell, Oxford (2008)
8. Ego, A., et al.: Visual – perceptual impairment in children with cerebral palsy: systematic review. Dev. Med. Child Neurology **57**(Suppl. 2), 46–51 (2015). https://doi.org/10.1111/dmcn.12687
9. Williams, C., Northstone, K., Sabates, R., Feinstein, L., Emond, A., Dutton, G.: Visual perceptual difficulties and under – achievement at school in a large community-based sample of children. Plos One **6**(3) (2011). https://doi.org/10.1371/journal.pone.0014772
10. Hard, A., Hellstrom, E.: Subnormal visual perception in school-aged ex-preterm patients in a paediatric eye clinic. Eye **18**, 628–634 (2004)

11. Clark, G.: The relationship between handwriting, reading, fine motor and visual-motor skills in kindergarteners. Iowa State University. Graduate Theses and Dissertations. Paper 11399 (2010). http://lib.dr.iastate.edu/cgi/viewcontent.cgi?article=2432&context=etd
12. Dale, N., Sonksen, P.: Social communicative variation in 1–3 years-old with severe visual impairment. Child Care Health Dev. **40**(2), 158–164 (2013). https://doi.org/10.1111/cch.12065
13. Kaiser, M., Albaret, J., Doudin, P.: Relationship between visual-motor integration, eye-hand coordination, and quality of handwriting. J. Occup. Ther. Sch. Early Interv. **2**, 87–95 (2009). https://doi.org/10.1080/19411240903146228
14. Coallier, M., Rouleau, N., Bara, F., Morin, M.F.: Visual – motor skills performance on the Beery – VMI: a study of Canadian kindergarten children. Open J. Occup. Ther. **2**(2) (2014). https://doi.org/10.15453/2168-6408.1074
15. Steiner, W., Ryser, L., Huber, E., Uebelhart, D., Aeschlimann, A., Stucki, G.: Use of the ICF model as a clinical problem-solving tool in physical therapy and rehabilitation medicine. Phys. Ther. **82**(11), 1098–1107 (2002). https://academic.oup.com/ptj/article/82/11/1098/2857661
16. World health organization: World report on disability (2011). http://www.who.int/disabilities/world_report/2011/en/
17. Case-Smith, J., O'Brien, J.: Occupational Therapy Children Adolescents, 7th edn., pp. 1–26. Elsevier, Canada (2015)
18. Ferreira, A., Quaresma, C., Quintão, C.: VMSReport: an application for visual performance and motor skills evaluation. In: Proceedings of the 12th International Joint Conference on Biomedical Engineering Systems and Technologies, pp. 280–284 (2019)
19. Santos, C., Ferreira, A., Quaresma, C., Quintão, C.: RehabVisual: validation of an application to stimulate visuomotor skills in preterm babies with developmental alterations. In: Proceedings of the 12th International Joint Conference on Biomedical Engineering Systems and Technologies, pp. 248–255 (2019)
20. Ferreira, A., et al.: RehabVisual: application on subjects with stroke. In: Camarinha-Matos, L.M., Farhadi, N., Lopes, F., Pereira, H. (eds.) DoCEIS 2020. IAICT, vol. 577, pp. 355–365. Springer, Cham (2020). https://doi.org/10.1007/978-3-030-45124-0_34
21. Van der Roest, H.G., Wenborn, J., Pastink, C., Dröes, R.M., Orrell, M.: Assistive technology for memory support in dementia. Cochrane Database Syst. Rev. (6) (2017). https://doi.org/10.1002/14651858.CD009627.pub2. Article No. CD009627
22. Cook, D., Schmitter-Edgecombe, M., Jonsson, L., Morant, A.: Technology-enabled assessment of functional health. IEEE Rev. Biomed. Eng. **12**, 319–332 (2018)
23. Kassam, A., Kassam, N.: Artificial intelligence in healthcare: a Canadian context. Healthc. Manage. Forum **33**(1), 5–9 (2020)
24. Moher, D., Liberati, A., Tetzlaff, J., Altman, D.G., PRISMA Group: Preferred reporting items for systematic reviews and meta-analyses: the PRISMA statement. Ann. Intern. Med. **151**(4) (2009). https://doi.org/10.1371/journal.pmed.1000097
25. Ahlan, A., Ahmad, B.: An overview of patient acceptance of Health Information Technology in developing countries: a review and conceptual model. Int. J. Inf. Syst. Proj. Manag. **3**, 29–48 (2015)
26. Davenport, T., Kalakota, R.: The potential for artificial intelligence in healthcare. Future Healthc. J. **6**, 94–98 (2019)
27. Lin, B., Lin, B., Yen, T., Hsu, C., Wang, Y.: Design of Wearable Headset with Steady State Visually Evoked Potential-Based Brain Computer Interface. Micromachines **10**, 681 (2019)
28. Krigolson, O.E., Williams, C.C., Colino, F.L.: Using Portable EEG to Assess Human Visual Attention. In: Schmorrow, D., Fidopiastis, C. (eds.) Augmented Cognition. Neurocognition and Machine Learning. LNCS, vol. 10284, pp. 56–65. Springer, Cham (2017). https://doi.org/10.1007/978-3-319-58628-1_5

29. Koiker, M., Pel, J., Steen-Kant, S., Steen, J.: A method to quantify visual information processing in children using eye tracking. J. Vis. Exp. (113), e54031 (2016). https://doi.org/10.3791/54031
30. Harezlak, K., Kasprowski, P., Dzierzega, M., Kruk, K.: Application of eye tracking for diagnosis and therapy of children with brain disabilities. In: Czarnowski, I., Caballero, A., Howlett, R., Jain, L. (eds.) Intelligent Decision Technologies 2016. Smart Innovation, Systems and Technologies, vol. 57, pp. 323–333. Springer, Cham (2016). https://doi.org/10.1007/978-3-319-39627-9_28
31. Pel, J., Dudink, J., Vouk, M., Plaisier, A., Reiss, I., Steen, J.: Early identification of cerebral visual impairments in infants born extremely preterm. Dev. Med. Child Neurol. **58**, 1030–1035 (2016)

Benefits, Implications and Ethical Concerns of Machine Learning Tools Serving Mental Health Purposes

Patricia Gamboa[1,2](✉), Cláudia Quaresma[1], Rui Varandas[1,2], and Hugo Gamboa[1,2]

[1] Departamento de Física, LIBPhys, FCT - Universidade Nova de Lisboa, Lisbon, Portugal
{pg.neves,r.varandas}@campus.fct.unl.pt, {q.claudia, hgamboa}@fct.unl.pt

[2] PLUX Wireless Biosignals S.A., Lisbon, Portugal

Abstract. In recent years, Healthcare and Mental Health have been in the spotlight for the creation of tools using Artificial Intelligence (AI). Mental Health technologies have proliferated in the last years, from social robotics to self-help tools and internet-based intervention programs. In particular, machine learning algorithms have been embedded into applications, for example, to provide a probability or classification regarding risk behaviours (e.g., suicide prevention tools). This paper reflects on the use of AI applied in mental healthcare tools, to assist clinicians in diagnosis, differential diagnosis and monitoring of patients with brain-related disorders. Benefits regarding the use of these technologies in mental healthcare will be discussed as well as some limitations and ethical concerns.

Keywords: Mental health · Artificial Intelligence · Machine Learning · Healthcare technologies

1 Introduction

Artificial Intelligence (AI) has been a research subject for decades. However, only recent advances in computer processing capabilities enabled a pronounced development of AI systems and technological areas such as Virtual Reality, Robotics and Wearable Sensing, supporting the rise of innovative solutions in Healthcare [1].

Healthcare-related technologies relying on digital and internet communication, i.e., eHealth, increased portability and flexibility in terms of time and location (e.g., teleconsultation) and cost-effectiveness [2], allowing typically out-of-reach patients or communities (e.g., chronically ill patients) to be more engaged in their healthcare [3]. In mental health, these technologies tackled some support seeking barriers (e.g., anonymity concerns) and increased awareness for mental health conditions, psychotherapy and psychiatric treatments [4], empowering patients' participation in therapeutic activities beyond appointment hours (e.g., [5]).

Mental health conditions are increasing worldwide, with a 13% rise in these conditions and substance use disorders reported between 2007–2017 [6]. Depression is a

© IFIP International Federation for Information Processing 2021
Published by Springer Nature Switzerland AG 2021
L. M. Camarinha-Matos et al. (Eds.): DoCEIS 2021, IFIP AICT 626, pp. 285–294, 2021.
https://doi.org/10.1007/978-3-030-78288-7_27

primary cause of disability and suicide is the second leading cause of death among young people [6]. New ways of promoting mental health or conducting interventions may be developed and pushed forward to meet the demand (e.g., remote care videocalls or chats, universally adopted in the COVID-19 pandemic [7]).

Solutions using AI can support patients' healthcare and assist mental health professionals identifying and monitoring mental health disorders (e.g., [8, 9]). Machine Learning (ML), a subtype of AI, enables computers to modify or adapt their actions to become increasingly more accurate (hence the word *learning*) (e.g., [10]). ML algorithms can learn from data and as many health-related tasks involve reading from certain type of data (e.g., numerical as in heart rate or image as in radiography), they can provide a probability or classification of having some disorder or condition.

AI can assist in the creation of solutions to enhance citizens' well-being and assist all stakeholders involved in healthcare. In this paper, we reflect on the use of ML for mental health purposes, highlighting its benefits while also unveiling some limitations and ethical considerations that future studies should contemplate.

2 Artificial Intelligence, Machine Learning and Mental Health

Social robots and mobile applications for various mental health disorders (e.g., [3, 4]) have been emergent technologies, partly due to advancements in different areas of AI such as Natural Language Processing (NLP). The study of human language to create intelligent systems able to comprehend, break down and separate significance from text and speech [11], played a major role in developing emotional chatbots.

Mobile applications present an opportunity to expand the availability and quality of mental health solutions [12] and promote well-being in cost-effective ways [13]. Though they are growing annually, with more than 10000 targeting anxiety, depression, or emotional well-being [14], their efficacy or effectiveness is largely unknown [15] as few undergo rigorous assessments through Randomized Controlled Trials (RCTs) [16]. In a review of psychosocial wellness and stress management apps, amongst the 1009 analysed, only 47 (4.66%) targeted individuals with psychological disorders and 21 (2.08%) had published feasibility and/or efficacy peer-reviewed studies [17]. Another review on apps targeting anxiety and depression, identified efficacy studies for only 10 apps (6.2%) in 162 stating an evidence-based theoretical framework [18]. Limitations to RCTs studies emphasise they should be independently conducted [15], include large samples [15], well-defined control groups [13], report effect sizes [17] and effectiveness over longer time periods [16].

Despite these limitations, mental health apps can support nonclinical populations by adopting a preventive approach [16]. Furthermore, they can be combined with traditional clinical support for psychotherapeutic homework goals (e.g., symptom tracking and skills practicing [13]) or therapeutic progress assessment [16]). They can be categorised based on their function: self-management, symptom tracking, skills-training, cognition improvement, social support, and passive data collection [19]. Recent comprehensive resources (e.g., PsyberGuide [16]) can overcome the lack of quality control standards [17] and assist individuals searching for self-help tools or professionals identifying effective solutions to enhance clinical outcomes.

The following table (Table 1) presents few mental health apps that were developed with mental health professionals and integrate evidence-based principles, mostly Cognitive Behavioural Therapy (CBT) as this framework provides larger effects on multiple outcomes [20]. They seem appropriate when combined with professional support, for particular difficulties or disorders such as stress and anxiety (Woebot, Headspace, MoodKit) or Post-Traumatic Stress Disorder (PTSD Coach, PE Coach[1]).

Table 1. Mobile apps for mental health purposes

	Self-management	In conjunction with professional support	Evidence-based (e.g., CBT)	RCT	Target
Woebot	✓ *	✓	✓	✓ [21]	a, b
Headspace	✓	✓	✓	✓ [22]	a, b, c
MoodKit	✓	✓	✓	✓ [23]	a, b
PTSD Coach	✓	✓	✓	✓ [24, 25]	d
PE Coach		✓	✓		d

CBT – Cognitive-Behavioural Therapy; RCT – Randomized Control Trial.
a) Stress and Anxiety; b) Mood Disorders; c) Sleep; d) Post-Traumatic Stress Disorder.
* Only for those experiencing mild stress or "feeling blue".

Some of these apps, such as the emotional chatbot Woebot, use AI, but specific reference to algorithms or features is not available [21]. Recommendations to improve the design, user experience, validation and efficacy of mental health apps can be found in [16]. Also, expectancy effects and individuals' characteristics that might impact the outcomes should be considered and examined [27].

Other emergent technologies to support clinicians in the diagnosis and monitoring of patients with brain-related disorders [e.g., 9] rely on ML, which focuses on the learning and adaption of AI [10], so their actions are increasingly more accurate.

Machine learning techniques are distinguished in different types but, for the scope of this paper, we will only focus on supervised learning models (SL) and unsupervised learning (UL) models. SL models are built from examples which are labelled and based on a training set, so that the algorithm generalizes to respond correctly to different inputs of the same kind [10]. In other words, these learning algorithms (also known as *classifiers*) learn to identify similarities between inputs that belong to the same class with the purpose of classification [10]. Having this in mind, they are useful tools to enable the screening of large populations for mental health difficulties or disorders, assisting in diagnosis (e.g., [28]), predicting behaviours (e.g., [29]) or facilitating patients' monitoring.

From studies using ML for mental health, conducted in the last 5 years, we highlight research with clinical purposes [8, 9, 29, 30].

[1] This app was developed exclusively for therapy and the study available is not a RCT [26].

In clinical assessment tasks performed by mental health professionals, the analysis and prediction of behaviours is often a complex task. By coupling automated speech analysis with SL techniques, researchers [30] were able to detect alterations in speech data (semantics and syntax) to predict psychosis. ML techniques may be further explored to create new tools for the diagnosis, prognosis and in treatments' decision-making of patients with Schizophrenia [30].

The identification of suicide risk is also a common task in clinical assessment. Using SL models namely decision tree techniques, researchers [29] were able to predict with high levels of accuracy if a patient belongs to a suicide risk group (vs no-risk), with a low number of variables (gathered from a large pool of suicide risk assessment items). These techniques apply if-then rules, mutually exclusive and sequentially applied, in a top-down process [29] which enabled the identification of variables playing a part in the "risk status" [28]. A brief assessment tool to track and detect suicide risk is also feasible, which would benefit the recognition of suicide risk behaviour over time and more timely responses in managing these situations [29].

On the other hand, UL models are developed using unlabelled examples so that these algorithms identify inputs that have something in common and are categorized together [10]. With no information about the correct outputs, the algorithm must discern similarity between different inputs for itself [10] but it needs reasonable amounts of data to learn from, which also increases computational time and storage [10].

Unsupervised algorithms that employed Deep Learning (DL) - namely by applying clustering k-means receiving the features extracted from a Convolutional Neural Network followed by an autoencoder for dimensionality reduction - were used to help diagnose disorders using image-based data as input such as X-rays or histologic samples [31]. These algorithms are able to detect abstract patterns or trends from image data, subsequently allowing generation of predictions on new data [9]. As several psychiatric and neurological symptoms are best explained with network-level analysis of changes in physiological structures, these algorithms are relevant to research neuroimaging correlates of brain-related disorders [9] as they are able to extract discriminative features. Several diagnostic studies reviewed by [9] corroborate the application of DL techniques to data from structural MRIs to detect Alzheimer's Disease (AD) and Mild Cognitive Impairment (MCI) with high levels of accuracy [9] and also in conversion-to-illness studies - from MCI to AD [9]. Taken together, these studies highlight DL techniques as valuable in the diagnostic and prognostic of brain-related diseases using biomarkers or neuroimaging. They may also prove useful in patients' treatment, assisting clinicians in decision-making and improving long-term clinical outcomes of several disorders. Nonetheless, the identification of complex nonlinear relationships from functional brain data, needs larger samples to compensate for the great number of variables to be estimated [9].

3 Contribution to Applied Artificial Intelligence Systems

In the following section we highlight the main advantages of ML techniques applied to mental health solutions. Important aspects regarding the construction of AI systems in this area, namely ethical standards and constrains and limitations that future studies should overcome, are also mentioned.

3.1 Benefits of Machine Learning Tools in Mental Health

AI approaches with ML techniques can increase prevention and intervention in mental health. eHealth allows professionals to reach diverse populations, improve their trust and openness to clinical assistance [3], track relevant parameters or support self-monitoring tasks (e.g., [13, 16]). Exposure of sensitive or potentially stigmatizing information, such as through AI-emotional chatbots, is also facilitated, with patients reporting feeling of less embarrassment than in face-to-face appointments [3].

Tools with ML algorithms allow innovative diagnostic paradigms of brain-related disorders by offering other measures besides self-reported symptoms, enabling better timing in the identification of disorders [8], better distinction between them (e.g., [9]) and prediction of relevant clinical behaviours, such as suicidal [29] or psychotic symptomatology [30]. Compared to traditional techniques (manual approaches of data collection and data analysis), they are also rapid and less expensive, easily adapted to research/clinic environments [28]. Compared to statistical inference, traditionally used to perform data analysis in psychometrics, ML data analysis is model agnostic and primarily focused on prediction (instead inference), enabling generalization/replication of results to unseen data. Therefore, these methods present a complementary approach that can also be used for psychometric purposes pointing to deeper biologically meaningful findings [28].

SL techniques may be particularly well-suited to disentangle the role of personal, situation-specific and sociocultural variables on the onset, development, maintenance and remission of psychopathology [32]. On the other hand, DL techniques applied to large sets of image-based data, in particular, might allow the recognition of biomarkers relevant for identifying conversion-to-illness or discrimination amongst different stages of brain-related disorders [9].

3.2 Limitations and Ethical Considerations of Machine Learning Tools in Mental Health

Despite the positive outcomes these technologies bring to mental health, their misuse or ethical implications need to be taken seriously. The temptation to replace them by clinical services, further exacerbating existing health inequalities, should be prevented [3]. We highlight relevant aspects to take into consideration when developing tools with AI and ML for mental health purposes.

Systems Built by Multidisciplinary Teams and Incorporating Diversity of Views. Collaboration/training between clinicians and developers designing these technologies needs to be strengthened and a common language to describe digital technologies for health should be adopted [33]. Since AI algorithms require human involvement (e.g., defining features, pre-classifying training data, adjusting thresholds and parameters), biases also need to be acknowledged and properly addressed (i.e., the statement that algorithms will classify more 'objectively' should not be taken at face value [34]).

Systems Built on Scientific Evidence. Tools to support mental health should be carefully designed, with evidence-based frameworks and well-planned RCTs (e.g., [3, 16]). Each disorder's symptomatology should be carefully considered. In a study about the psychosis' monitoring, adverse events or symptoms were largely neglected [35]. Algorithms may result in decision-making that lacks precision or damages the patient (e.g., compulsory measures) when data misrepresents the reality. Therefore, rigorous data collection and analysis of data used to train the algorithms is needed to avoid the AI system reproducing that bias [36]. Data embedded into algorithms usually exclude contextual variables important in mental health assessment (e.g., interpersonal, socioeconomic or environmental variables [36]), hence, an effort should also be made to realize how to add this into systems.

Systems Built with Regulations and Ethical Standards. Despite AI being embedded in systems for the last decades, the area is lacking strong ethical and regulatory frameworks [37]. Just as other medical devices, authors (e.g., [3]) advocate they ought to undergo scrutiny through rigorous risk assessment and regulatory oversight, partly due to biased algorithms that can exclude or harm in unintended ways yet contributing to social inequalities. Clear standards on confidentiality, privacy and data security by intelligent agents should be developed. Furthermore, AI in mental health applications should be bounded by the same ethical code of human mental health professionals. Though they seem to be aligned with the *principle of beneficence*, other principles (e.g., *principle of nonmaleficence*) need to be further explored, such as in cases of robots' malfunctions [3]. General guidelines initiatives for research in AI are emerging (e.g., Good AI), still not specifically related to mental health [3]. These are critical since the ethical considerations this area deals with are not transversal to other areas (e.g., compulsory measures, suicidal assessment). Early identification of ethical issues by researchers, and developers should be encouraged in the design and creation of the next generation of AI systems for mental health [3].

Systems with Supervision and Monitoring Mechanisms. Systems should be supervised frequently by humans and mechanisms for rapid identification of bias and errors implemented (e.g., signals of attentive hacking or unauthorized monitoring [3]). Some AI algorithms, namely DL, lack transparency. The output of the algorithm rarely has any concrete sense of how or why a particular classification has been arrived at from inputs [36]. Indeed, the inputs themselves may be entirely unknown or known only partially [9] and so models can have an excellent performance despite using irrelevant features (e.g., orientation of the neuroimage) instead of relevant information. Their lack of an explicit model might also make it difficult to directly relate to existing biological knowledge [28]. Consequently, clarifying the inner process of an algorithm displaying the "*logic trails to show how any conclusion has been reached, so decisions can be scrutinized and challenged*" [38], leading to algorithms' transparency may, in the field of mental health, allow a deeper understanding of brain-related diseases.

Systems Built with all Stakeholders. Despite AI advances in mental health, key stakeholders such as patients, caregivers and families, are still excluded from the discussions about AI in mental health [35]. Indeed, stakeholder participation and social debates [38] are an ethical imperative for AI development. Therefore, including all stakeholders involved in AI solutions for mental health should be encouraged.

4 Conclusions

AI and ML techniques present great advantages for mental health purposes including the possibility to enrich our knowledge on the onset and development of brain-related disorders, the monitoring of clinically relevant symptomatology and the identification of at-risk patients (e.g., suicide or psychotic behaviours). Despite allowing cost-effective and timely solutions, AI systems in mental health should not be an excuse for reducing the provision care by trained mental health professionals [3]. Moreover, these solutions do not come without research challenges, ethical concerns and a general lack of understanding of societal implications (e.g., [39]). In order to overcome some of these challenges, AI systems applied to this sensitive area should be built by multidisciplinary teams and incorporate diversity of views, including all stakeholders in their creation [38]. Moreover, they should take into account scientific evidence, incorporate solid regulatory/ethical standards, be supervised regularly, have mechanisms to signal possible inaccuracies or faults [3].

Further studies on the long-term effects of these technologies on individuals, societies and communities are also required. Ensuring the quality of life and respect for patients should be an essential aspect of innovative technologies applied to mental health. However, there has been a lack in recognizing concerns surrounding trust, privacy, and autonomy. Research on patient acceptance and treatment outcomes of most of disseminated AI applications in mental health fields is also lacking (e.g., [3, 16]). The impact of some of these technologies in human relationships, in human conditions and disorders or attitudes regarding caregiving, is still a grey area (e.g., [39]). For example, patients, specially from vulnerable groups, may become very attached to or dependent on these applications, altering social values and healthcare systems, changes in human communication and social interactions [3].

On the other hand, by possibly narrowing our understanding of disorders with applications tackling some acknowledged determinants but leaving behind the bio-psycho-social factors involved in mental health disorders, the widespread of AI systems in the area can contribute to exacerbate "trends of reductionism", i.e., oversimplification of complex subjects, in mental health [3].

Therefore, it may be argued that while promising, these technologies require further research from a sound core of specialists from both areas - AI and Mental Health - working towards the mitigation of ethical concerns and long-term consequences regarding the integration of AI systems in the area of mental health and in including all stakeholders into the development and enhancement of these systems.

Acknowledgments. This work was partly supported by Fundação para a Ciência e Tecnologia, under PhD grants PD/BDE/150304/2019 and PD/BDE/150672/2020.

References

1. Lovejoy, C., Buch, V., Maruthappu, M.: Technology and mental health: the role of artificial intelligence. Eur. Psychiatry **55**, 1–3 (2019). https://doi.org/10.1016/j.eurpsy.2018.08.004
2. Oh, H., Rizo, C., Enkin, M., Jadad, A.: What is eHealth: a systematic review of published definitions. J. Med. Internet Res. **7**, 1 (2005). https://doi.org/10.2196/jmir.7.1.e1
3. Fiske, A., Henningsen, P., Buyx, A.: Your robot therapist will see you now: ethical implications of embodied artificial intelligence in psychiatry, psychology, and psychotherapy. J. Med. Internet Res. **21**(5), e13216 (2019). https://doi.org/10.2196/13216
4. Aboujaoude, E., Starcevic, V., (eds.): Mental Health in the Digital Age: Grave Dangers, Great Promise. Oxford University Press, Oxford (2015)
5. Taylor, C.B., Luce, K.H.: Computer- and Internet-Based Psychotherapy Interventions. Curr. Dir. Psychol. Sci. **12**(1), 18–22 (2003). https://doi.org/10.1111/1467-8721.01214
6. World Health Organization. https://www.who.int/health-topics/mental-health
7. Vieta, E., Pérez, V., Arango, C.: Psychiatry in the aftermath of COVID-19. Revista de psiquiatria salud mental **13**(2), 105–110 (2020). https://doi.org/10.1016/j.rpsm.2020.04.004
8. Richter, T., Fishbain, B., Markus, A., Richter-Levin, G., Okon-Singer, H.: Using machine learning-based analysis for behavioral differentiation between anxiety and depression. Sci. Rep. Nat. Res. **10** (2020). https://doi.org/10.1038/s41598-020-72289-9
9. Vieira, S., Pinaya, H., Mechelli, A.: Using deep learning to investigate the neuroimaging correlates of psychiatric and neurological disorders: methods and applications. Neurosci. Biobehav. Rev. **74**, 58–75 (2017). https://doi.org/10.1016/j.neubiorev.2017.01.002
10. Marsland, S.: Machine Learning: An Algorithmic Perspective. CRC Press, New York (2015)
11. Clark, K., Althoff, T.: How to help someone feel better: NLP for mental health. The Stanford Language Processing Group (2016). https://nlp.stanford.edu/blog/how-to-help-someone-feel-better-nlp-for-mental-health/
12. Chandrashekar, P.: Do mental health mobile apps work: evidence and recommendations for designing high-efficacy mental health mobile apps. mHealth **4** 3 (2018). https://doi.org/10.21037/mhealth.2018.03.02
13. Neary, M., Schueller, S.M.: State of the field of mental health apps. Cogn. Behav. Pract. **25**(4), 531–537 (2018). https://doi.org/10.1016/j.cbpra.2018.01.002
14. Baumel, A., Muench, F., Edan, S., Kane, J.M.: Objective user engagement with mental health apps: systematic search and panel-based usage analysis. J. Med. Internet Res. **25**, 21 (2019). https://doi.org/10.2196/14567
15. Lui, J.H.L., Marcus, D.K., Barry, C.T.: Evidence-based apps? A review of mental health mobile applications in a psychotherapy context. Prof. Psychol. Res. Pract. (2017). https://doi.org/10.1037/pro0000122
16. Bakker, D., Kazantzis, N., Rickwood, D., Rickard, N.: Mental health smartphone apps: review and evidence-based recommendations for future developments. JMIR Ment. Health **3**(1), e7 (2016). https://doi.org/10.2196/mental.4984
17. Lau, N., O'Daffer, A., Colt, S., et al.: Android and iPhone mobile apps for psychosocial wellness and stress management: systematic search in app stores and literature review. JMIR Mhealth Uhealth 22, 8(5), e17798 (2020). https://doi.org/10.2196/17798.
18. Marshall, J.M., Dunstan, D.A., Bartik, W.: Apps with maps-anxiety and depression mobile apps with evidence-based frameworks: systematic search of major app stores. JMIR Ment. Health **7**(6), e16525 (2020). https://doi.org/10.2196/16525
19. National Institute of Mental Health. Technology and the Future of Mental Health Treatment (2017). https://www.nimh.nih.gov/health/topics/technology-and-the-future-of-mental-health-treatment/

20. Linardon, J., Cuijpers, P., Carlbring, P., Messer, M., Fuller-Tyszkiewicz, M.: The efficacy of app-supported smartphone interventions for mental health problems: a meta-analysis of randomized controlled trials. World Psychiatry **18**, 325–336 (2019). https://doi.org/10.1002/wps.20673
21. Fitzpatrick, K.K., Darcy, A., Vierhile. M.: Delivering cognitive behavior therapy to young adults with symptoms of depression and anxiety using a fully automated conversational agent (Woebot): a randomized controlled trial. JMIR Ment. Health **4**(2), e19 (2017). https://doi.org/10.2196/mental.7785
22. Champion, L., Economides, M., Chandler, C.: The efficacy of a brief app-based mindfulness intervention on psychosocial outcomes in healthy adults: a pilot randomised controlled trial **13**(12), e0209482 (2018).https://doi.org/10.1371/journal.pone.0209482
23. Bakker, D., Kazantzis, N., Rickwood, D., Rickard, N.: A randomized controlled trial of three smartphone apps for enhancing public mental health. Behav. Res. Ther. **109**, 75–83 (2018). https://doi.org/10.1016/j.brat.2018.08.003
24. Possemato, K., et al.: Using PTSD Coach in primary care with and without clinician support: a pilot randomized controlled trial. Gen. Hosp. Psychiatry **38**, 94–98 (2016). https://doi.org/10.1016/j.genhosppsych.2015.09.005
25. Kuhn, E., Kanuri, N., Hoffman, J.E., Garvert, D.W., Ruzek, J.I., Taylor, C.B.: A randomized controlled trial of a smartphone app for posttraumatic stress disorder symptoms. J. Consult. Clin. Psychol. **85**(3), 267–273 (2017). https://doi.org/10.1037/ccp0000163. PMID: 28221061
26. Reger, G.M., Skopp, N.A., Edwards-Stewart, A., Lemus, E.L.: Comparison of prolonged exposure (PE) coach to treatment as usual: a case series with two active duty soldiers. Mil. Psychol. **27**(5), 287–296 (2015). https://doi.org/10.1037/mil0000083
27. Firth, J., Torous, J., Nicholas, J., et al.: The efficacy of smartphone-based mental health interventions for depressive symptoms: a meta-analysis of randomized controlled trials. World Psychiatry **16**(3), 287–298 (2017). https://doi.org/10.1002/wps.20472
28. Orrù, G., Monaro, M., Conversano, C., Gemignani, A., Sartori, G.: Machine learning in psychometrics and psychological research. Front. Psychol. **10**, 2970 (2020). https://doi.org/10.3389/fpsyg.2019.02970
29. Morales, S., Barros, J., Echávarri, O., García, F., Osses, A., et al.: Acute mental discomfort associated with suicide behavior in a clinical sample of patients with affective disorders: ascertaining critical variables using artificial intelligence tools. Front. Psychiatry **8** (2017). https://doi.org/10.3389/fpsyt.2017.00007
30. Corcoran, C.M., Carrillo, F., Fernández-Slezak, D., Bedi, G., Klim, C., et al.: Prediction of psychosis across protocols and risk cohorts using automated language analysis. World Psychiatry **17**(1), 67–75 (2018). https://doi.org/10.1002/wps.20491
31. Xie, J., Liu, R., Luttrell VI, J., Zhang, C.: Deep learning based analysis of histopathological images of breast cancer. Front. Genet. **10** (2019). https://doi.org/10.3389/fgene.2019.00080
32. Coutanche, M.N., Hallion, L.S.: Machine learning for clinical psychology and clinical neuroscience. In Wright, A.G.C., Hallquist, M.N. (eds.) The Cambridge Handbook of Research Methods in Clinical Psychology. Cambridge (2019). https://doi.org/10.31234/osf.io/7zswh
33. World Health Organization Classification of digital health interventions. Geneva: World Health Organization (2018)
34. Burrell, J.: How the machine 'thinks': understanding opacity in machine learning algorithms. Big Data Soc. (2016). https://doi.org/10.1177/2053951715622512
35. Carr, S.: 'AI gone mental': engagement and ethics in data-driven technology for mental health. J. Ment. Health **29**(2), 125–130 (2020). https://doi.org/10.1080/09638237.2020.1714011
36. Zuiderveen Borgesius, F.: Discrimination, artificial intelligence, and algorithmic decision-making. Council of Europe, Directorate General of Democracy (2018)

37. Gamble, A.: Artificial intelligence and mobile apps for mental healthcare: a social informatics perspective. Aslib J. Inf. Manag. **72**(4), 509–523 (2020). https://doi.org/10.1108/AJIM-11-2019-0316
38. EU High-Level Expert Group on AI. Ethics Guidelines for Trustworthy AI. https://ec.europa.eu/digital-single-market/en/news/ethics-guidelines-trustworthy-ai
39. Cresswell, K., Cunningham-Burley, S., Sheikh, A.: Health care robotics: qualitative exploration of key challenges and future directions. J. Med. Internet Res. **20**(7), e10410 (2018). https://doi.org/10.2196/10410

Multi-agent System Architecture for Distributed Home Health Care Information Systems

Filipe Alves[1,2](✉), Ana Maria A. C. Rocha[1], Ana I. Pereira[2], and Paulo Leitão[2]

[1] ALGORITMI Center, University of Minho, 4710-057 Braga, Portugal
arocha@dps.uminho.pt
[2] Research Centre in Digitalization and Intelligent Robotics (CeDRI), Instituto Politécnico de Bragança, Campus de Santa Apolónia, 5300-253 Bragança, Portugal
{filipealves,apereira,pleitao}@ipb.pt

Abstract. In recent years, the aging population has increased. The intervention of Home Health Care (HHC) has been an asset, however, needs technological innovation for the high level of complexity and requirements. Innovation in the HHC system is crucial since management still occurs manually using classical methods, usually centralized and static. The mapping of real HHC problems, enables an application model of a distributed intelligent system, considering the operational planning needs, promoting a digital and sustainable ecosystem. This work aims to specify a flexible architecture for routing and scheduling tasks in distributed HHC. It considers multi-agent systems technology to guarantee the fast response to condition changes in existing planning, merged with optimization algorithms that allow achieving optimal solutions. Collaboratively, the information digitalization for real-time monitoring will coordinate a socialized solution using different tools and techniques, ensuring robustness and responsiveness in a domain with emerging needs.

Keywords: Home Health Care · Multi-agent system · Optimization

1 Introduction

Over the last decade, Home Health Care (HHC) services have significantly increased [9]. In Portugal, for example, many elderly people live alone, isolated, specifically in interior regions. Faced with this scenario, HHC has been a response to the needs of treating, caring, and supporting dependent people, seeking to promote healthy aging and the best possible quality of life in them [6]. Traditional research in elderly care separates HHC from other home care services. Normally, home care offers non-clinical help, while HHC provides professional medical assistance. The position of this work focuses more on HHC, however it allows the collaboration of different care, in the sense that both involve skilled knowledge and the planning of visits routing.

The increasing worldwide needs efficient and effective HHC system, considering the increase in the elderly population, higher exigency, pressure from governments and

© IFIP International Federation for Information Processing 2021
Published by Springer Nature Switzerland AG 2021
L. M. Camarinha-Matos et al. (Eds.): DoCEIS 2021, IFIP AICT 626, pp. 295–303, 2021.
https://doi.org/10.1007/978-3-030-78288-7_28

stakeholders, the development of novel effective approaches for HHC decisions is imperative, such as modernization for more dynamic and optimized solutions. Despite these challenges, applied Artificial Intelligence (AI) holds tremendous promise for transforming the provision of HHC as critical services [14]. In this context, health or social units must perform the respective allocation of the resources, manage the scheduling, and optimize the routes in decision-making processes. However, the planning, strategic and operational management, occur manually and without computational support and especially without monitoring [9]. In this sense, public or private health care providers, generates non-optimized planning, probable waste of financial and human resources, and emergencies that are not covered. From informal to formal HHC, there is a delivery network with several actors [9]. A set of problems will be considered to address three dimensions. The first one deals with the decisions through the planning horizon. The second one disseminates the functions through decisions: routing, and staff management. Finally, the third dimension describes the operation of digitalization. Thus, the use of a system based on information and communications technology (ICT) and ageing research [5], for knowledge-based decisions to improve service quality, becomes urgent.

The main research question arose from "how to provide faster and more dynamic solutions in distributed intelligent systems (when needed) without losing optimum (whenever possible) applied in HHC services?", it is hard and difficult to deal with distributed systems using only centralized methods, such as the classical optimization methods since they have a high response time and do not provide dynamic and learning behavior considering the environment changes. Therefore, multi-agent systems (MAS) offer an alternative way to design and control systems, differing from the conventional approaches due to their inherent intelligent capabilities to cooperate and adapt to unexpected events. However, the use of only MAS, in turn, may not complement the search for optimized solutions provided by optimization models. The research prediction is that, merging the better of these two worlds, will allow a service coordination architecture for innovative solutions ensuring responsiveness and providing intelligent support in autonomous decision-making.

The main motivation of the PhD work is to build an innovative scheduling and routing system, with the application of distributed AI and optimization algorithms, using technology-supported services to generate "optimal" or near optimal solutions, and digitalize, deploy, and monitor the HHC information. The challenge of combining MAS with optimization algorithms will be supported on modern information technology systems, to solve complex procedures, by leveraging an architecture that benefits the interoperability and flexibility of the HHC decision-making. The system decentralization of different decision-makers will allow to maintain high levels of optimized solutions and, reduce the operating costs with fast responses. The assignment decision can be made using a negotiation scheme or optimization methods, trying to converge to the global objective. The idea is to reconstruct decision-making in operational planning, implementing intelligent algorithms, and promoting a better service quality, robust and sustainable. The architecture specification, fully distributed, aims to manage optimized and automated route planning, collaboratively based on swarm concept, to exhibit simple behaviours, and to compromise a socialized solution from different sources, tools, and techniques.

The paper is organized as follows: Sect. 2 overviews the contribution to applied AI systems, and Sect. 3 describes the related literature. Section 4 presents the research contribution and innovation, while Sect. 5 presents the discussion and critical view. Finally, Sect. 6 rounds up the conclusions.

2 Relationship to Applied Artificial Intelligence Systems

Nowadays, it is increasingly urgent to promote smart information and innovate technologically for intelligent systems applied, reconstructing, and modernizing basic health concepts using AI, such as primary health care at home [10].

The traditional HHC system in an all-round way, is still not intelligent, neither computerized and contains several limitations in resource management, unbalanced routes/schedules and even in unexpected events. In this sense, considering the growing need of the elderly people to receive their needs, public or private providers need to specify and implement computational, intelligent and decision support measures, capable of supporting an increasingly accurate distributed service. This service is crucial in the interior regions of Portugal and even in the context of the pandemic COVID 19, allowing due to the ease of care and follow-up of patients. Thus, within the scope of this doctoral work, the design of a prototype with evolutionary algorithms with the ability to optimize the entire operational management of the HHC service appears, merged with MAS, equipped with automated planning and autonomous scheduling [15]. The application of AI systems, carried out using MAS, are included in the area of distributed AI systems [8]. MAS offers a promising and innovative way to model, design, and manage the implementation of distributed systems and essentially distribute the intelligence by different nodes, allowing to divide a complex problem into several simple problems ("divide to win"). MAS paradigm is composed of a society of intelligent, autonomous, and cooperative entities (agents), which interact and coordinate their activities, based on the local knowledge and skills, to achieve their goals and capable of independent or group decision-making [16]. The collaboration of these technologies will be supported by a digitalized tool for management and control, making HHC service more efficient. New research points to the development of collaborative business ecosystems for integrated elderly care systems, to offer a more personalized service and promote intelligent concepts based on collaborative networks [3]. Smart HHC is not just a simple technological advancement, but also an all-round, multi-level change, embodied in the following: decentralized changes in the HHC model and changes in knowledge-based systems to emulate human cognition in the HHC tasks for decision-making and business analysis [10].

This work, aims to explore the concept of distributed HHC, focusing on an intelligent infrastructure to perceive, transmit and process information using cloud computing. Distributed HHC can promote interaction in the entities, facilitating the rational allocation of resources, routes, and health professionals. An impact on smart HHC planning is expected, representing a qualitative and quantitative improvement in the resource's optimization, a reduction in the costs involved and, a reduction in the patients' waiting time. The intelligent real-time support could be crucial in the early detection of events of aggravation or fast response in existing planning by MAS, elimination of non-urgent urgencies in hospitals. The impact of scheduling, monitoring, and decision support tools, characterized by exponential digitalization, will lead to competition, training, and regional strengthening of HHC ecosystems.

3 Related Literature

HHC visions are facing unprecedented pressure because of changing demographics, administrative requirements, resource constraints, workforce shortages, growing needs of the population, and increased demand for HHC innovation.

Operational research today applies algorithms and mathematical models to classic HHC problems, usually in a centralized model that considers only the static problem settings. This optimization problem is complex, where specific requirements must be considered. Exact methods, hybrid methods, or metaheuristics provide "optimal" solutions, mainly in the HHC operations planning or routes timing [2, 9]. Normally, studies in HHC routing and scheduling focus mainly on the traveling issue (VRPs), however, this project will address multiple objectives such as costs, minimize the number of professionals, constraints violations, and continuity of care. Thus, these conventional methods, do not seem sufficient with the urgency of modernizing the HHC logistic, considering dynamic settings and the real-time events that may occur [4]. Considering the traveling issue and the multiple objectives, this project intends to introduce real-life needs to seek efficiency in planning resources, workload balance, experience, and potential online reactions. An additional complexity, only with operational research, will consume a lot of time and have a high effort. Thus, combining intelligent agents (even with worse solutions) with optimization algorithms will enhance cooperation, and responsiveness, allowing task effort distribution that would hardly have an "admissible" solution with the strategies separately. This includes the reactive adjustment of individual schedules for adaptively deal with a dynamic environment while balancing whenever possible, the optimized solutions. Thus, the interaction of different interconnected and even decision-capable smart algorithms, cloud computing, and digital concepts can provide powerful intelligent solutions to challenges not yet addressed to HHC operation [7, 17]. For that reason, AI, and software engineering, highlighted the efficacy and potential of intelligent health applications [12, 15]. This area includes the concept of agents. Hence, since an agent can be for instance a part of an automatic workflow or an individual representative of a real-world person, seems promising to apply MAS, as a sub-discipline of distributed AI [16]. These concepts can support automatic coordination, message communication, and interactions among real-world agents. Several approaches make use of MAS to support operational HHC in terms of allocation and scheduling, dealing with uncertainty cases [1, 11, 13]. In addition to theoretical contributions, the research has some limitations, such as the dynamic information not previously known are generated randomly. Generally, it does not provide outcomes for dynamic procedures in the long-term plan for multiple planning stages.

In general, centralized optimization methods have been widely studied over the years, which despite stability, cost savings, and good solutions, take time and do not support the reactive scheduling in the service runtime. However, restructuring is urgent, where oscillating with the decentralized model is needed, making the HHC problem more critical, scalable, and tolerant to emergencies. In turn, knowing that a single intelligent decentralized system may have more security risks and does not guarantee optimized performance. Thus, the research hypothesis in merging different innovative and technological assets, such as AI, in a distributed computing system, will be challenging, especially to generate robust/flexible settings.

4 Contribution and Innovation

This project aims to contribute to the innovation and modernization of a digital ecosystem for distributed HHC. The idea is to respond to the lack of dynamic and optimized solutions in a single system, able to support the emerging needs of HHC. Smart architecture with an adaptive scheduling approach, and distributed computing, is designed and presented in Fig. 1. It intends to integrate a well-structured system, using ICT concepts to specify in an interface, monitoring, and HHC decision-making.

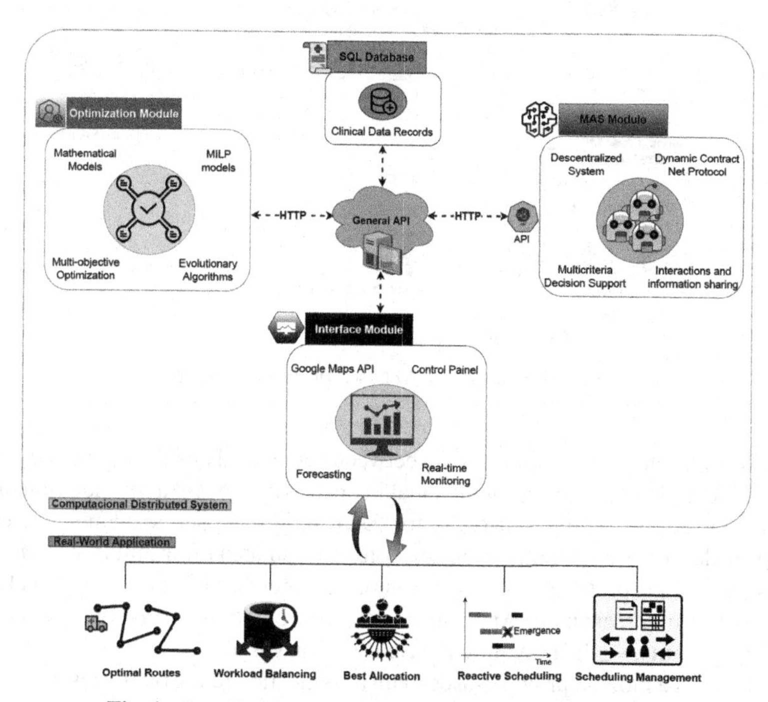

Fig. 1. Specification of the conceptual system architecture.

The wireframes modules are structured with intelligence and optimization skills for the best use of resources of HHC providers. Briefly, the computational distributed system specifies a digitalized infrastructure, which according to a cloud design, can enable reduced costs, scalability, and flexibility between components. With the general application programming interface and, the access to a database with medical records (health units' partnership), the system can acquire, store, and retrieve the data set to manage. The components will contain a RESTful server for displaying micro-services. The optimization module will be able to communicate with the service layer, collaborating in optimized scheduling combinations. This module will feature advanced technologies, such as mathematical models, evolutionary algorithms, integer linear programming, and multi-objective optimization for conflicting goals, when the problem allows to be solved stochastically or deterministically. In turn, the MAS module will be equipped with a smart platform, which will also communicate with the service layer, to support automated planning using distributed AI (Fig. 2).

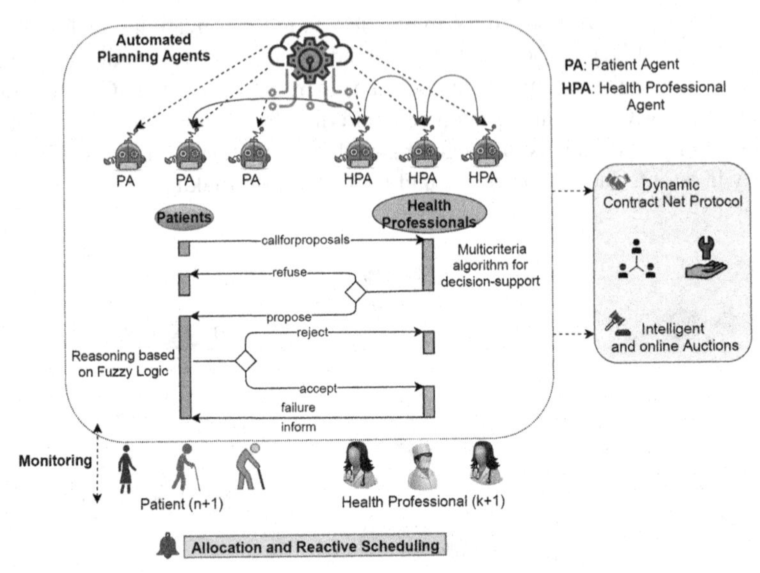

Fig. 2. Distributed AI based on MAS Module.

Interactions and information sharing between agents will enable distributed scheduling and decentralized problem-solving, making it possible to find a new solution through the system itself, efficiently, especially for fast responses in surgical emergencies. The MAS provides a fast evolving, which promotes coordinated effort, multi-criteria strategies using trading protocols among autonomous agents, and adapts their behaviour dynamically using reasoning. Any patient data manipulation will be the responsibility of the health entity, so the system will have no privacy issues.

The interface module provides users with a connection to the platforms using a user-friendly interface, which allows real-time monitoring of the solution state. The Google Maps service will serve as setup engine (maps, routes, and locations). By proposing the interconnection of all these modules, and consider the current gaps, which focus on centralizing the solution or not consider dynamic environments, the system enhances the versatility, essential to digitalize the HHC process.

In conclusion, the proposed disruptive infrastructure to support decision-making for HHC real-world application, promoting operational competitiveness but also strategic planning to ensure efficiency to achieve better routes combination, better resources allocation, workload balancing and consequently scheduling optimization.

5 Discussion and Critical View

HHC information systems, are generally based on operational management of scheduling, routing, and resources allocation. Usually, these health services are complex procedures due to their modelling complexity and are generally performed manually. Some simulations already carried out in real context, using the optimized module, based on deterministic and/or stochastic methods, have benefited in obtaining optimized solutions and significantly improving the profitability of planning. The results of resource allocation and scheduling in a health unit managed to reduce (approximately 30%) the maximum time spent in route to existing plans [2].

Nowadays HHC services are facing an increasing demand, where the digitalization of primary health care and the consequent monitoring is imposed. However, the HHC environment requires a functional balance between static and pre-planned service, as well as alternative responses to dynamic environments, resulting in uncertainties that require real-time actions. Empower service autonomy in the event of an emergency, require a fast and optimized distributed system, to make the HHC more flexible and reduce the patient waiting times. HHC services need AI mechanisms capable of solving large real-world situations in a reasonable time and providing good solutions in a dynamic environment with resource-poor settings. Some preliminary results, with the use of agent-based models in HHC, assisted a distributed architecture in obtaining autonomous and coordinated solutions. Tests with unexpected events in online planning provided a faster and more accurate reaction to the emergency (new patient or new service) by intelligent agents, and a significant improvement in their usefulness [1]. In turn, the combination of these approaches can come to guarantee, task effort distribution and better solutions/planning in real-world HHC management.

6 Conclusions and Further Work

This paper points out and discusses the application of distributed HHC architecture highlighting the benefits of combining it with intelligent procedures, such as MAS, optimization methods, and the process of data digitalization. The development of robust expert systems for HHC modernization is urgently necessary. Sometimes the imprecise information, without coordination, negotiation, or any optimized solution, could be addressed and overcome using AI. Distributed HHC, in a decentralized manner, can be answered by technology-supported services of different smart procedures and components. However, it is necessary to introduce the control layer in the solution, encapsulating an intelligent system that consists of merging agents with optimization methods, powered by a digital application for online monitoring, providing ample opportunities to use AI to improve public health outcomes.

Nowadays, the lack of computational availability in the real-time operational management of HHC services is still evident, namely in the current emergency in combating the pandemic COVID'19. Smart HHC support is urgently needed, freeing health units and hospitals. Thus, if an HHC problem can be solved in a stochastic or deterministic way, the algorithms will provide optimized solutions, however, it is important to enabling the system to respond to condition changes in the planning. The architecture design, specifically the MAS module, allows intelligent coordination to increase efficiency and dealing with the dynamic environments based on AI. The information digitalization will provide transparency, forecasting, reaction, and real-time routes. All modules combined may be relevant to a potentially promising approach to eliminate gaps in technologies used centrally and separately.

In conclusion, the proposed distributed system can explore multidisciplinary technologies with extreme applicability in HHC, a domain with emerging needs.

Acknowledgments. This work has been supported by FCT - Fundação para a Ciência e a Tecnologia within the R&D Units Projects Scope: UIDB/00319/2020 and UIDB/05757/2020 and supported by grant number SFRH/BD/143745/2019.

References

1. Alves, F., Pereira, A.I., Barbosa, J., Leitão, P.: Scheduling of home health care services based on multi-agent systems. In: Bajo, J., et al. (eds.) PAAMS 2018. CCIS, vol. 887, pp. 12–23. Springer, Cham (2018). https://doi.org/10.1007/978-3-319-94779-2_2
2. Alves, F., Pereira, A.I., Fernandes, F.P., Fernandes, A., Leitão, P., Martins, A.: Optimal schedule of home care visits for a health care center. In: Gervasi, O., et al. (eds.) ICCSA 2017. LNCS, vol. 10406, pp. 135–147. Springer, Cham (2017). https://doi.org/10.1007/978-3-319-62398-6_10
3. Baldissera, T.A., Camarinha-Matos, L.M.: Towards a collaborative business ecosystem for elderly care. In: Camarinha, L.M., Falcão, A.J., Vafaei, N., Najdi, S. (eds.) DoCEIS. IAICT, vol. 470, pp. 24–34. Springer, Cham (2016). https://doi.org/10.1007/978-3-319-31165-4_3
4. Becker, C.A., Lorig, F., Timm, I.J.: Multiagent systems to support planning and scheduling in home health care management: a literature review. In: Koch, F., et al. (eds.) AIH 2018. LNCS (LNAI), vol. 11326, pp. 13–28. Springer, Cham (2019). https://doi.org/10.1007/978-3-030-12738-1_2
5. Camarinha-Matos, L.M., Afsarmanesh, H., Ferrada, F., Oliveira, A.I., Rosas, J.: A comprehensive research roadmap for ict and ageing. Stud. Inform. Control **22**(3), 233–254 (2013)
6. Cissé, M., Yalç ındag, S., Kergosien, Y., Sahin, E., Lenté, C., Matta, A.: Or problems related to home health care: a review of relevant routing and scheduling problems. Oper. Res. Health Care **13**, 1–22 (2017)
7. Elhoseny, M., Abdelaziz, A., Salama, A.S., Riad, A., Muhammad, K., Sangaiah, A.K.: A hybrid model of internet of things and cloud computing to manage big data in health services applications. Future Gener. Comput. Syst. **86**, 1383–1394 (2018)
8. Ferber, J., Weiss, G.: Multi-Agent Systems: An Introduction to Distributed Artificial Intelligence, vol. 1. Addison-Wesley, Reading (1999)
9. Fikar, C., Hirsch, P.: Home health care routing and scheduling: a review. Comput. Oper. Res. **77**, 86–95 (2017)
10. Jiang, F., et al.: Artificial intelligence in healthcare: past, present and future. Stroke Vasc. Neurol. **2**(4), 230–243 (2017)
11. Marcon, E., Chaabane, S., Sallez, Y., Bonte, T., Trentesaux, D.: A multi-agent system based on reactive decision rules for solving the caregiver routing problem in home health care. Simul. Model. Pract. Theory **74**, 134–151 (2017)
12. Reddy, S., Fox, J., Purohit, M.P.: Artificial intelligence-enabled healthcare delivery. J. R. Soc. Med. **112**(1), 22–28 (2019)

13. Shakshuki, E., Reid, M.: Multi-agent system applications in healthcare: current technology and future roadmap. Procedia Comput. Sci. **52**, 252–261 (2015)
14. Vinuesa, R., et al.: The role of artificial intelligence in achieving the sustainable development goals. Nat. Commun. **11**(1), 1–10 (2020)
15. Wahl, B., Cossy-Gantner, A., Germann, S., Schwalbe, N.R.: Artificial intelligence (AI) and global health: how can ai contribute to health in resource-poor settings? BMJ Global Health **3**(4) (2018)
16. Wooldridge, M.: An Introduction to Multiagent Systems. Wiley, Hoboken (2009)
17. Yang, Q., Yang, T., Li, W.: Smart Power Distribution Systems: Control, Communication, and Optimization. Elsevier Science (2018)

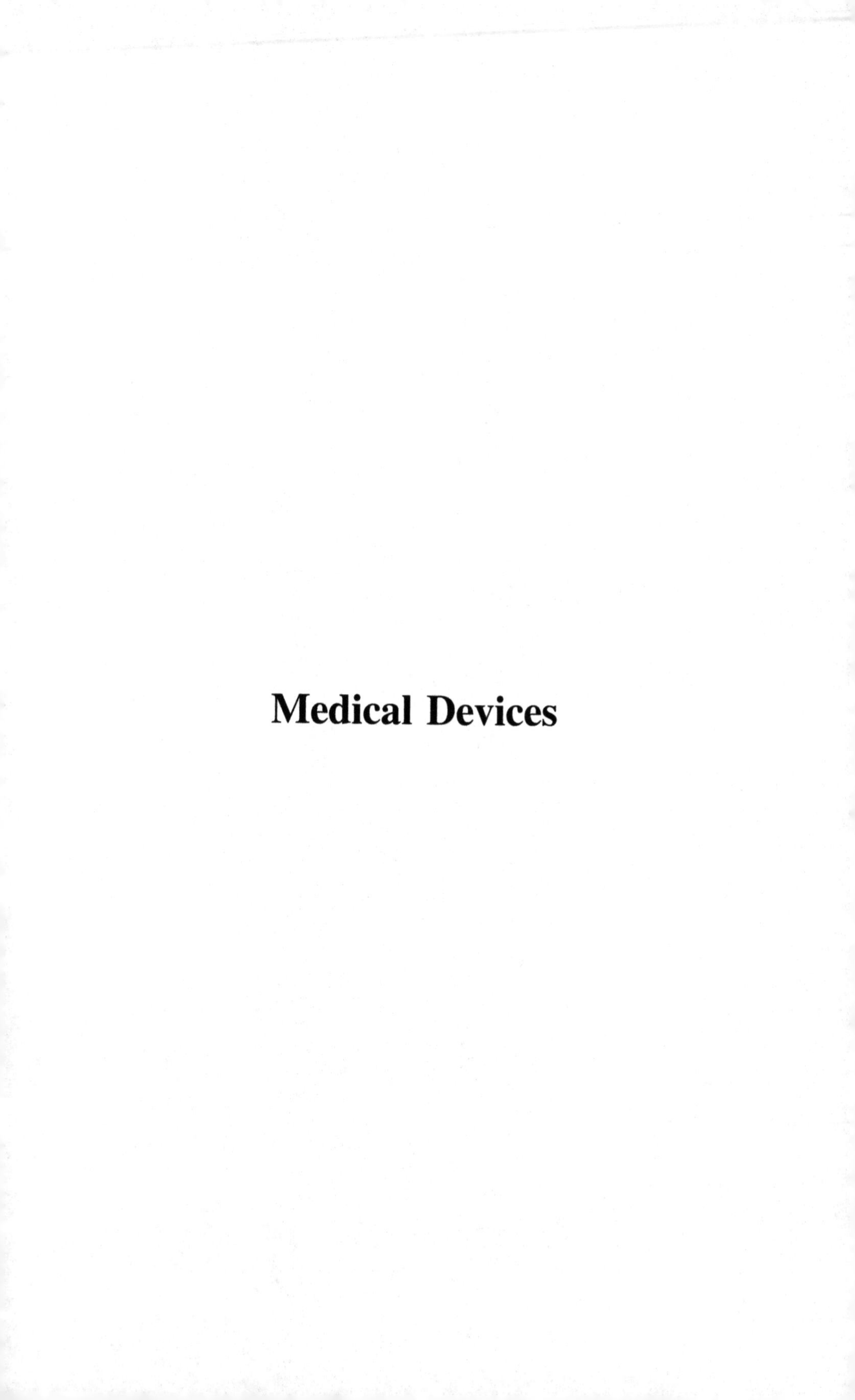

Medical Devices

Analysis of Electromyography Signals for Control Models of Power-Assisted Stroke Rehabilitation Devices of Upper Limb System

Paulo Bonifacio[1,2](✉), Valentina Vassilenko[1,2], Guilherme Marques[1], and Diogo Casal[3]

[1] Laboratory for Instrumentation, Biomedical Engineering and Radiation Physiscs (LibPhys-UNL), NOVA School of Science and Technology, Campus FCT UNL, Caparica, Portugal

[2] NMT, S.A., Edíficio Madan Parque, Rua dos Inventores, Caparica, Portugal
p.bonifacio@nmt.pt

[3] Nova Medical School – Faculdade de Ciências Medicas, NOVA University of Lisbon, Lisbon, Portugal

Abstract. Stroke is a significant affliction that can affect people with varying degrees of severity. One of the most common consequences of stroke is the impairment of the muscular motor function to some degree with two-thirds of the patients being affected by upper-limb paralysis. For those cases, the most effective forms of regaining muscular motor function are through rehabilitation therapy, traditionally this must be done in a clinical environment. Developments in robotics, batteries and electronics have made accessible the prototyping, production, and utilization of exoskeleton type devices technically adapted for personal and residential rehabilitation. This paper presents and discusses the results of EMG signals from upper limb of brachial biceps muscle, obtained from a cohort of healthy volunteers. The methodology for testing is presented and explained, additionally, a preliminary discussion is made on the obtained data. Some control considerations, variables and methods are also presented and discussed.

Keywords: Control · Electromyography EMG · Rehabilitation · Stroke · Signals · Upper-Limb

1 Introduction

Currently, one in four people aged above 25 is expected to have a stroke in their lifetime. Worldwide, over 80 million people are living that have suffered from this affliction [1]. After a stroke has afflicted the patient, the loss of some degree of motor function is common; moreover, more than two-thirds of those have arm paresis [2]. One of the most effective ways of curtailing this loss of mobility comes from technology supported rehabilitation training [3]. Presently, this type of rehabilitation training is typically confined to the clinical environment in hospitals and specialized rehabilitation facilities.

© IFIP International Federation for Information Processing 2021
Published by Springer Nature Switzerland AG 2021
L. M. Camarinha-Matos et al. (Eds.): DoCEIS 2021, IFIP AICT 626, pp. 307–315, 2021.
https://doi.org/10.1007/978-3-030-78288-7_29

Thus, the exercises have a schedule limitation, and the full benefits to the patient can be less than those that could be obtained if the patient had easier access to those kinds of exercises. For this situation to be possible, it is necessary to take these training or assistance aids and move them out of the clinics or rehabilitation centers, inserting them into a domestic environment. On the other side, the rehabilitation device must possess specific characteristics such as being self-contained, compact and allow for a significant degree of user movement freedom. For example, a device-assisted rehabilitation system for the upper limbs (exoskeleton) can be composed of some electromechanical support located at the shoulder, elbow, forearm, and up-to-hand level. Finger mechanical supports are not common due to their inherent complexity and frailty. Those supports are actuated via an electric motor, being linear, stepper or servo types. Whose control is made via an external system, typically, a desktop computer. This type of system is usually found in the classical-clinical environment [4]. In more recent iterations of this kind of device, the control is placed in an integrated microcontroller board (IC board) built into the exoskeleton's frame and combined with a self-contained power pack for increased patient mobility.

For rehabilitation work, the classical approach is usually focused on an objective-driven therapy, where a computer controls the electromechanical device that assists the patient's reach of objective via a human-machine interface display (HMI) and presents cues to guide the patient's upper extremity movement. In general, this approach has proven successful in improving the patient's daily activities, albeit so far, it has not been clear if it helps improve muscle strength [4]. This type of solution is mainly used for training and must be used under supervision in a clinical environment. Advances in the miniaturization and the large-scale dissemination of cost-effective electronics, actuators, and motors, coupled with the ease of access to 3D printing and advanced prototyping venues, have brought forth a time where it is possible to provide custom-made, patient-related motor-assisted rehabilitation aids at a reasonable cost. Nevertheless, this is also possible due to a resurgence of the do-it-yourself (DIY) paradigm. Thus, after some initial assisted training, a system that performs mainly unsupervised (i.e., at the patients' home) is expected. A rugged system controller with a fair degree of tolerance variation to input signals and a learning capacity is recommended. Figure 1 shows the idealized exoskeleton actuator device.

This paper focuses on the characterization of the brachial biceps' myographic signals during the flexion movements to obtain some initial reference rules for posterior application in a possible fuzzy logic controller for a rehabilitation exoskeleton. This work set the basis for one of the authors' master thesis [5] and is a part of an ongoing research project. The remainder of this paper is composed as follows: after the introduction, the aim of this research project is presented, the experimental methods for sampling the signals are described in Sect. 3; in Sect. 4, the results are compiled and analyzed with a controller topology based on those signals being proposed; finally, the conclusions and the future research work are presented.

2 Aim of the Research

The development of a self-contained exoskeleton-type assistance system can be split into 3 focus areas, biomechanics, electronics, and power electronics. Biomechanics is used to model, design, test-fit the rehabilitation frame (i.e., the exoskeleton's frame); electronics are used for signal sampling and the command and control (C&C) system; finally, power electronics are used for the design and selection of actuators, power supply and power and energy needs. In a daily utilization, control input signals should be as natural and as robust as possible, so to select the potential muscular areas of interest, a Neuro-Musculo-Skeletal system model was used. This is a two-joint limb system with two pairs of antagonist muscles connected around two hinge joints. The muscle actuators are the brachial biceps, brachial triceps, posterior deltoid, and anterior deltoid, represented in the right image of Fig. 1. For simplification, a single joint with a single pair of antagonist's muscles is enough for initial parameter configuration [6]. Thus, for system control, the brachial biceps muscle characterization through electromyography (EMC) signals was chosen in the present work. These muscles are easily accessible, and their EMG can be used to collect enough data to allow for a fair degree of signal repeatability. Quantifying those signals is an essential first step to establish baselines for the control algorithms of the system. As the signal characterization and detection of motion artefacts or other such issues could constrain the type of control strategy that can be applied for exoskeleton C&C.

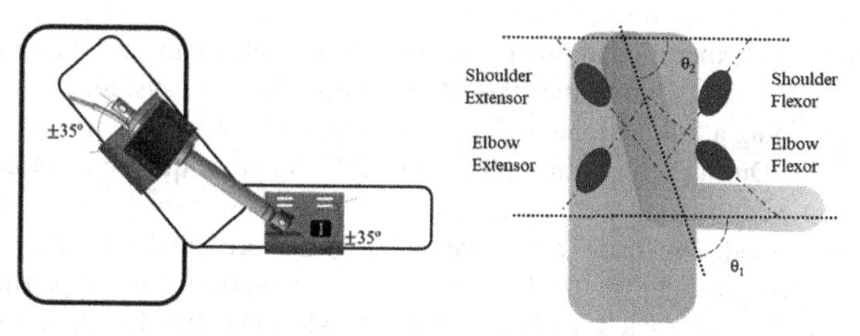

Fig. 1. The proposed 3D printer-ready model with linear actuator (left) [5] Model of Neuro-Musculo-Skeletal two-joint limb system with 2 muscle pairs, (right), adapted from [6].

3 Methods and Basic Assumptions

This research was a preliminary study conducted in the academic environment where the volunteers were mainly healthy, young individuals (i.e., aged <30). Some volunteers with ages above 40 were also used for the reference and posterior analysis. At this first step of the study, the inclusion of stroke-affected volunteers in the test group was not considered. However, it was assumed that presently recorded data will be compared with signals obtained from individuals affected by stroke in future work.

3.1 Study Characterization

The study was conducted with a cohort of 13 volunteers, seven females and six males, aged 17 to 55. The volunteers were generally healthy and presented no physical limitations in the upper extremities that could affect the test procedure (i.e., no limitations at forearm, elbow, or shoulder level that in any form could impair the flexion and extension with the different test loads). Additionally, three volunteers aged 40 were used for comparison, one female and two males aged (44, 43 and 55, respectively). All the volunteers were right dominant arm. Whenever possible, the brachial biceps signals were recorded for biceps of both rights and left arms. For the procedure, volunteers were seated with the elbow supported in a chair armrest and the arm-forearm flexion angle of 130°, approximately. The electrode lead cable was placed so as not to interfere with the natural forearm movement. Each volunteer's experimental measurements were realized in a single session and lasted no more than 40 min. The experimental protocol was composed of 3 main steps, namely:

i. The measurement protocol was explained to each volunteer, and the critical parts of the exercise were showed.
ii. The three disposable electrodes were placed onto the brachial biceps (positive and negative near the muscle insertion) and connected by electrode lead cable to the MP35 unit according to the international EMG guidance protocol [7].
iii. Calibration and recording of the EMG signals of biceps contraction were performed continuously (based on [8], for forearm flexion movement).

During all the experimental procedure of steps ii) and iii), the volunteer was in the supine sitting position. Before the start of each recording, the system was zeroed and calibrated by doing a full flexion movement (i.e., from 0 to 80°) with the maximum test load, i.e., 2 kg. During a forearm flexion, the EMG signal acquisitions of consequent brachial muscle contraction were performed for three different loads: 0.5, 1 and 2 kg on the volunteer's hand. The load's values were chosen as more suitable for this study since the maximum weight to lift by the forearm of the person after stroke impairments were determined as 2 kg. For each load, the EMG signals were sampled in sets of 3, each group consisting of flexing the forearm at three different angles, 45, 60 and 75°. The angle position was measured by the goniometer. This procedure allows assessing the signals of biceps contraction for various amplitude movements and the different loads. Figure 2 shows the schematic layout of the experiment and a picture of a test setup. The signal acquisition starts with the 0.5 kg and flexion angle of 45° and continue for other angles and increasing the load. The measurements were recorded at each angle, for the repeated movement at least 6 times to allow for signal averaging and variability assessment. Each recording flexion exercise was completed, typically, in less than a minute. Finally, after EMG signals recording from the dominant arm, the same experimental procedure was repeated for another arm of the volunteer.

Data acquisition was made via an MP35 acquisition unit datalogger from BIOPAC System, Inc., using the BSL PRO 3.7 software with the following channel configuration: EMG signal; AC coupling; no offset; ×500 gain and bandpass filter configured to 0.05 Hz to 50 Hz. The sample rate was 1000 Hz. After recording, signals were typically noisy, and automatic post-processing filtering in the 20 Hz band was applied using the BIOPAC tools. Muscular movements, even when explosive, can be classified as a slow phenomenon, with a relatively low fundamental frequency, more even if those movements are repetitive, as in this study. Considering a repletion rate of 120 movements per minute, those would produce a movement frequency of 0.5 Hz. Using the sampling

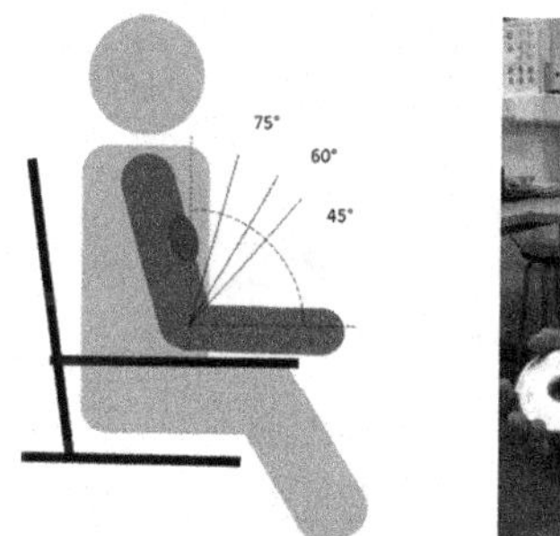

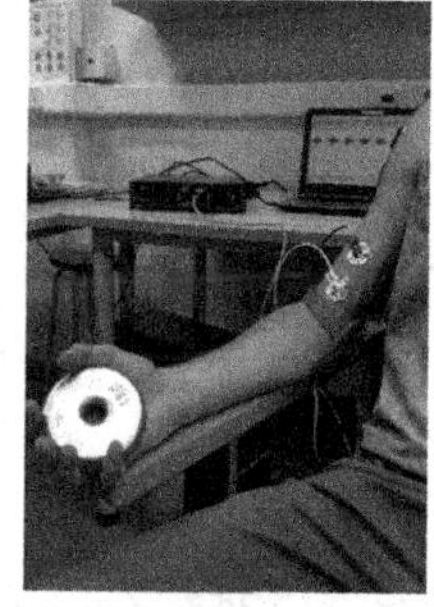

Fig. 2. Subject layout for myographic signal acquisition (left); the placement of the electrodes on the biceps brachial with the weight on the right hand (right image) [5].

(Nyquist) theorem, a frequency above 1.5 Hz would be enough to record this periodic movement and obtain viable data. This is a gross underestimation as the interest is in the movement behaviour and not its pure period characteristic, so the objective was to apply a frequency that allowed to oversample in such a way that enough information could be extracted to characterize and classify different stages on a single movement. Using a sampling frequency higher than 1000 Hz was deemed unnecessary for the purpose of this study as the interest was mainly focused on myographic signal trend for time parameter estimation and not a full signal amplitude-time relation [9]. Bandpass filtering was essential, as, at low frequencies, the low amplitude of the recorded signals is susceptible to external noise from electrical sources and motion artefacts.

4 Results and Discussion

A significant amount of data was collected in the present study: 288 recorded files of total 1728 EMG signals of brachial biceps contraction. Statistical analysis of that raw data led to the creation of data sets for better visualization, based on the average of the 6 recorded signals for each flexion movement and each individual condition pairs (i.e., load and angle). Signals were firstly split between female and male, and then right hand and left hand. Figure 3 shows an averaged full data set for a movement of 45° with all the test weights. The top three graphics present the data collected for what was considered as the start of the foreman lift movement, the 1st 400 ms; the bottom three graphics present the remainder of the lift action; a small pause at the top of the target angle, followed by the downward movement and breaking muscular action to reach rest position.

To establish the movement definition, time phases where change on the signal trend was visible were obtained from the data and grouped as presented in Fig. 4. In the left image, there are two main areas of interest where the myographic signal is such that the muscle recruitment is clear. The time slot between 100 to 150 ms has a pronounced positive slope. Additionally, the signal strength threshold is such as to allow for the signal to be used as an initial setpoint for movement "start phase". Considering the next time slot, going from 300 to 350 ms, here the signal slope as decreased in relation to the previous time slot; this corresponding to a decrease or stabilization in speed/strength of the recruited muscles. Above 400 ms, the movements' "start phase" can be considered

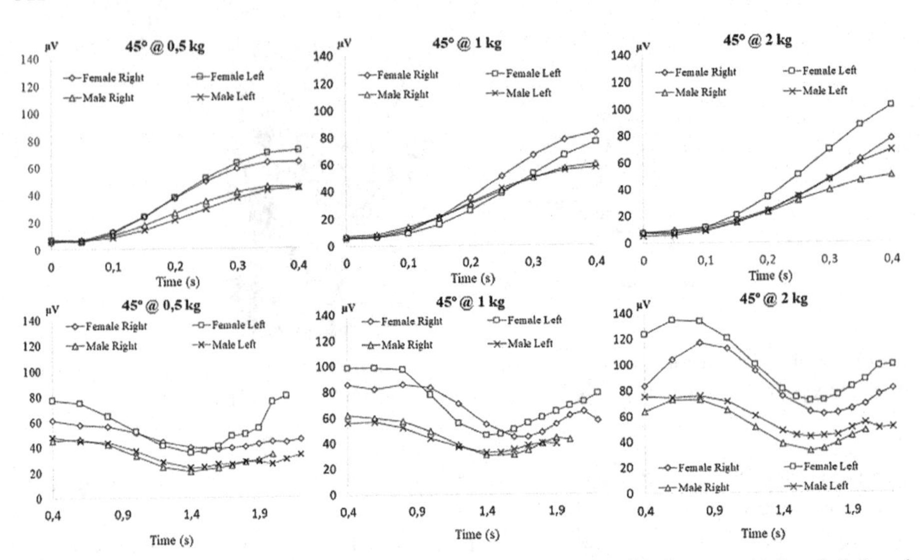

Fig. 3. The full range of averaged male and female data at 45° with the test weights, 0.5, 1 and 2 kg.

as finished, and the intensification of the signal starts to be less significant as the forearm reaches the maxim height of the movement. Applying the same type of experimental analysis for the right image, several stages of the movement can be defined in time: 400–590 ms; 600–750 ms; 800 ms–1.3 s; 1.35–1.65 s; +1.7 s. These later five stages, clearly indicated by the changes on the characteristics of the myographic signal can be use as set points on control system to be implemented for exoskeleton control. From 400–590 ms the signal slope is steadily decreasing as the muscular movement goes from the initial boost to a steady speed and strength until it enters a slowing motion phase as the maximum height is reached. From 600–750 ms occurs the infection on the slope of the signal, corresponding to muscular relaxation for the beginning of the descent movement of the forearm. From 800 ms–1.3 s there is a steady slope corresponding to the descent control of the biceps brachial. From 1.35–1.65 s, signal slope inflection again changes as muscular recruitment again increases when entering the stopping phase of the movement. Finally, after 1.7 s the finalization of the movement occurs. Interestingly, here it can be observed that muscular recruitment varies in duration, becoming dependent of the speed of the movement.

The myographic signal from the brachial biceps presented an inherent amplitude variability with the different loads and angles that, for their contribution, do not allow for the specification of a particular start/stop time for any part of the movement, as can be seen in the signal grouping of Fig. 5. This intrinsic characteristic of the muscular myographic signals, as already been reported in the literature [9, 10] and brings forth a specification for a control system that can adapt and accommodate those changes. Increasing the sampling rate for the myographic signal acquisition device will bring an increase in the amplitude, as previously referred. Still, to the nature and variability of myographic signal, this increase will be noticed at all loads and angles. At this stage of the research, it is not clear that a significant distinction between classes can be achieved to

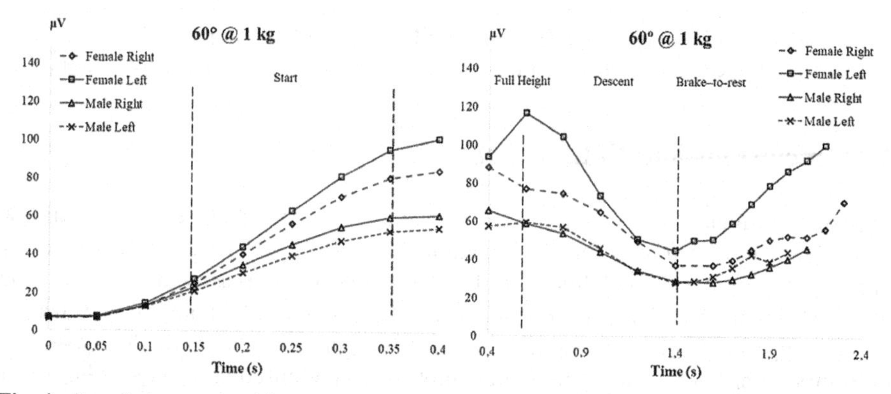

Fig. 4. Sample images used for movement definition phases, full movement for a weight of 1 kg at 60°.

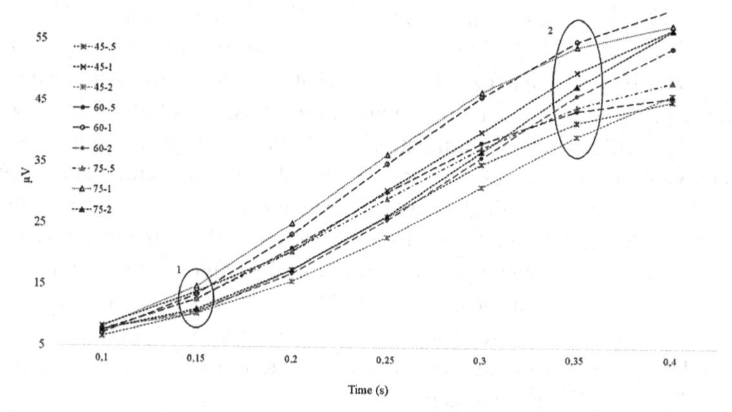

Fig. 5. "Movement start" for the dominant forearm of males for all experimental loads and angles.

allow for a better classification. As an example, considering zone 1 and 2 in Fig. 5; here, the grouping of signals with different loads and at different angles does not allow for clear control rules to be established; at the point considered to be the start of the movement, 100 ms, minimum and maximum values vary meaningfully for each test setup and are contained in a 4 µV difference. An analogous situation can be noticed in the second reference point, at 300 ms, as the slope change indicates the slowing of the movement as the target height is reached. Where the maximum recorded value of the myographic was measured with the 1 kg weight for 60 and 75°, 54 µV; with a full voltage swing of 16 µV for all the recording, the signal grouping, again, does not allow to establish a clear control rule for single signal control. The critical analysis of the data present in this paper, lead the authors to detect a fault in the test setup, "movement speed" of the forearm on the movement was not correctly considered. As each volunteer unknowing or unwillingly moved at his own natural speed, a variable difficult to control, as a result, that "natural speed" must be considered when recording muscular myographic signals. Practically this issue can be solved with very little impact on the system controller's footprint. An accelerometer integrated circuit (IC) mounted on the forearm support (Fig. 1), could provide the necessary signals to complement the biceps brachial myographic signal.

5 Conclusions and Future Work

This study evaluated the viability of the myographic biceps brachial muscle response as a control input variable for rehabilitation device control. The detected variability of the signals in the test conditions lead to the conclusion that using a single variable for exoskeleton control would be challenging if not unfeasible, unless the utilization of some type of Artificial Intelligence (AI), controller could be used. Otherwise, the utilization of accelerometer type IC to complement the muscular signals and/or other control variables (i.e., additional muscular signals) will be necessary to complete the base signals. Future work will refine the experimental procedure, adding acceleration recording and probably, evaluating complementary myographic signals from the forearm and other muscular locations on the upper extremities to complement the muscular base model of [6]. With the collected signals, the review of control topologies and their contrast initially led to the proposal of a fuzzy logic type controller, as the most indicated "classic" control topology to accommodate the signal variabilities, as is further discussed in [5]. Additional work will evaluate the utilization of artificial intelligence on the data to try to obtain an improved set of control rules and gain the ability to accommodate the evolutive changes in the user's physiological conditions as he grows back to total health or as close as possible to it. It is expected that as the user sample signal database grows AI algorithms will be instrumental in establishing clear control rules. AI algorithms for control and data mining will be evaluated in the next phases of this research. The biceps brachial signals, couple with signals from an accelerometer IC and the proposed controller topology, are expected to be used in a first iteration low-cost stand-alone prototype of a self-power exoskeleton for rehabilitation assistance.

Acknowledgments. The authors thank all volunteers for participating in the study; and the support from the combined effort of NOVA School of Science and Technology and NMT, S.A. Partial support comes from Fundação para a Ciência e Tecnologia (FCT, Portugal) through the PhD grant (PD/BDE/130083/2017) of the Doctoral NOVA I4H Program.

References

1. WSO, Global Stroke Fact Sheet. World Stroke Organization, p. 12 (2019)
2. World Health Organization, Cardiovascular diseases (CVDs). https://www.who.int/news-room/factsheets/detail/cardiovascular-diseases-(cvds). Accessed 01 Oct 2019
3. Jørgensen, H.S., Nakayama, H.: Stroke. Neurologic and functional recovery the copenhagen stroke study. Phys. Med. Rehabil. Clin. N. Am. **10**(4), 887–906 (1999)
4. Mehrholz, J., Hädrich, A.: Electromechanical and robot-assisted arm training for improving generic activities of daily living, arm function, and arm muscle strength after stroke. In: Mehrholz, J. (ed.) Cochrane Database of Systematic Reviews. John Wiley & Sons, Ltd, UK (2012)

5. Marques, G.: Desenvolvimento de um protótipo de exosqueleto para reabilitação motora do membro superior, FCT-UNL (2020)
6. Nunes, G., Vassilenko, V., Gil, P., Palma, L.: Bi-dimensional two-joint upper limb model. J. Biomech. **40** (2009)
7. Hermens, H.J., Freriks, B.: Recommendations for sensor locations in arm or hand muscles Muscle. http://www.seniam.org/. Accessed 01 Feb 2020
8. Li, K., Zhang, J., Liu, X., Zhang, M.: Estimation continuous elbow joint movement based on human physiological structure. Biomed. Eng. Online **18**(1), 31 (2019)
9. Ives, J.C., Wigglesworth, J.K.: Sampling rate effects on surface EMG timing and amplitude measures. Clin. Biomech. **18**(6), 543–552 (2003)
10. Reaz, M.B.I., Hussain, M.S., Mohd-Yasin, F.: Techniques of EMG signal analysis: detection, processing, classification and applications. Biol. Proced. Online **8**(1), 11–35 (2006)

AI-Based Classification Algorithm of Infrared Images of Patients with Spinal Disorders

Anna Poplavska[1,2](✉), Valentina Vassilenko[1,2], Oleksandr Poplavskyi[3], and Diogo Casal[4]

[1] Laboratory of Instrumentation, Biomedical Engineering and Radiation Physics (LIBPhys-UNL), NOVA School of Science and Technology - NOVA University of Lisbon, 2829-516 Caparica, Portugal

an.poplavska@campus.fct.unl.pt

[2] NMT, S.A., Edifício Madan Parque, 2825-182 Caparica, Portugal

[3] Kyiv National University of Construction and Architecture, Kyiv 03680, Ukraine

[4] NOVA Medical School|Faculdade de Ciências Médicas, 1169-056 Lisboa, Portugal

Abstract. Infrared thermal imaging is a non-destructive, non-invasive technique that has shown to be effective in the detection and pre-clinical diagnosis of a variety of disorders. Nowadays, some medical applications have already been successfully implemented in pre-clinic diagnostics using thermography based on AI algorithms to support decision-based medical tasks. Though, the massive amount of image types, disease variety, and numerous individual anatomical features of the human body continue to give researchers more challenging jobs that still need to be solved. This paper proposes a novel methodology using a convolutional neural network (CNN) for analyzing with high accuracy infrared thermal images from the spine region for quick screening and disease classification of patients.

Keywords: Biomedical applications · Medical thermography · AI decision making · Convolutional neural network · Spinal disorders

1 Introduction

Medical applications based on AI algorithms have been successfully implemented in monitoring and pre-clinic diagnostics of complex medical data. Advances in AI development will change approach clinical problem-solving and seem to make it possible to address issues like misdiagnosis or detecting disease on the last stage. However, while some AI applications can compete with doctors to solve challenging medical tasks, they still must also be completely incorporated, implemented, and improved to be utilized in daily medical routines. The enormous amount of image types, disease variety, and numerous individual anatomical features of the human body continue to give researchers challenging tasks and undergoing extensive evaluation.

Infrared thermal imaging (IRTI) techniques due to their non-invasive, non-destructive, and painless way have obvious benefits among other diagnostic methods.

© IFIP International Federation for Information Processing 2021
Published by Springer Nature Switzerland AG 2021
L. M. Camarinha-Matos et al. (Eds.): DoCEIS 2021, IFIP AICT 626, pp. 316–323, 2021.
https://doi.org/10.1007/978-3-030-78288-7_30

IRTI in the medical field can give high-quality thermal images for disease monitoring and pre-clinical diagnosis in real-time by displaying thermal anomalies present in the body. Some recent publications discussed the clinical utility of infrared thermography for spinal diseases, as diagnoses and evaluate pain symptoms [1], scoliosis [2, 3], rheumatic diseases [4], spinal disorders [5, 6], etc. But the majority of research methods use manual feature extraction and traditional methods of classification.

In recent years, thermal data starting to be applied by researchers as input features for AI classifiers that tried automatically solve challenging tasks in the medical field. Convolutional neural network (CNN) for detecting Alzheimer's disease [7], Artificial Neural Networks (ANN) for detecting diabetes disease [8], Support Vector Machines (SVM) for breast cancer detection [9], k-Nearest Neighbor (k-NN) to segment hands, aiding in the evaluation of this health problem, Decision Trees (DT) for the detection of the existing rheumatoid arthritis disease for improved diagnosis [10], Fuzzy methods [11], etc. are some examples of this type of learning. Most research works based on the developing AI algorithms for medical thermal images are focusing mainly on breast cancer detection [12–14] through a considerable number of open-access databases. A breast cancer diagnosis is a topic with the highest number of publications for the thermal imaging application with ML algorithms. The latest article focused on the systematic review and analysis of the application of ML classifiers using infrared thermography for biomedical applications published in 2021 identified 719 records through database searching. After proper review and analysis of the eligibility criteria from identified records, the quantitative synthesis was performed only for 34 of the 68 encountered publications [15] and only one article related to the back problems [16]. There were not found publications on implementing the AI analysis for infrared image classification of patients with any spinal disorders. Consequently, the present research study aimed to develop an AI algorithm for the classification of infrared images database of patients with spinal disorders to healthy and unhealthy classes which were not done before.

2 Relationship to Applied AI Systems

Based on the statistical analysis of the global disease database 266 million individuals (3.63%) worldwide have degenerative spine disease, from which 39 million individuals (0.53%) were found to have spondylolisthesis, 403 million (5.5%) individuals with symptomatic disc degeneration, and 103 million (1.41%) individuals with spinal stenosis annually [17]. Spinal disorders significantly limit mobility and agility, increasing the disability and leading to early retirement, lower well-being levels, and reduced ability to participate in society. Degenerative spine conditions (DSC) are characterized by the progressive loss of normal spine structure and function over time, i.e. treatment varying depending on the type and severity of the disorder. [17]. The treatment process began at a later stage leads to a long rehabilitation process or painful operation treatment. Early detection of spinal problems is not only more likely to continue a healthy human lifestyle but is also essential for better care and a lower treatment period.

The development of medical applications based on AI algorithms using infrared image data is a growing and promising research worldwide. These applications have enormous potential in medical imaging technology, treatment process, medical meta-analysis, and diagnostics. The fundamental difference between our research and other works (based on traditional feature selection or classification) is that there is no necessity to define features in the pre-processed dataset since the CNN is responsible for determining which image features belong to which class. A significant contribution of the current research consists of developing of methodology for the classification of our infrared images database of patients with spinal disorders based on a CNN algorithm, which was not done before.

3 Materials and Methods

To build an efficient algorithm, firstly, computer systems must to fed structured data, i.e. each pixel from the image has a label identifiable to the algorithm. After the CNN has been exposed to a sufficient number of data sets and labels, the performance results are dissected to ensure precision. The algorithm typically includes known data, allowing evaluation of the algorithm's capacity to find out the correct answer. Based on the testing results, CNN can be modified or fed more data to improve outcome results.

3.1 Sample Size

The dataset used in this work comprises 480 infrared images of the region of interest of patients with different types of spinal disorders and 220 infrared images of the healthy participants from two different European countries, Portugal and Ukraine, were obtained [4, 5]. The dataset was divided into two groups as healthy or with the spinal disease, as is shown in Fig. 1.

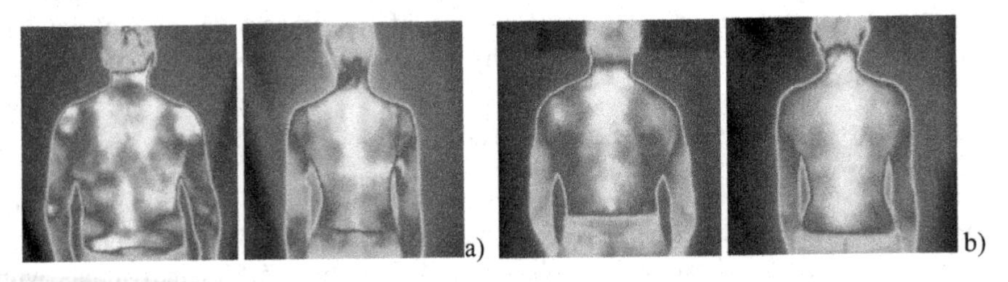

Fig. 1. Example of the spinal thermogram of participant (a) with spinal disease and (b) healthy

Since to use CNN architecture the database is necessary to be balanced, images of the healthy set were increased to 320. CNN classification in our approach was performed using each image of each patient.

3.2 Measurement Protocol

The majority of the measurements were performed under supervising by the medical staff of the Center of Medical Rehabilitation & Sports Medicine, Vinnytsia, Ukraine, hence to the experimental protocol described elsewhere [4, 5, 18]. The infrared (IR) images were obtained in a laboratory room with a maintained temperature of 21 °C and humidity of

50%, approximately, using IR camera FLIR® E6 (320 × 240) with <0.06 °C thermal sensitivity. The emissivity parameter for the skin (0.98) was set in the thermal camera settings. Before the measurements the thermal camera was switched on for 15 min, as well as each volunteer had to stay at the ambient temperature for accommodation. As a backdrop, a black matte curtain was used. Each participant, during the measurements, stood in the same position, the arms down and facing the wall with the head straight ahead.

3.3 Deep Learning Model

The Convolutional Neural Network (CNN) is a class of DL based on the idea that the model function properly fits a local understanding of the image. The main types of learning are: supervised (reference label must be accessible to each image), semi-supervised (reference label have only a subset of all images), and unsupervised learning (reference label is unavailable), as is shown in Fig. 2.

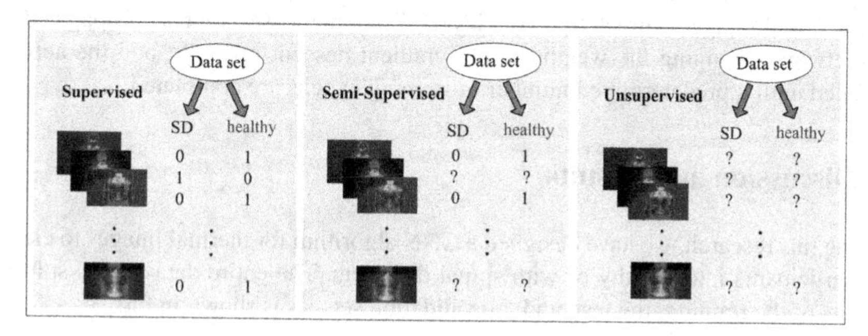

Fig. 2. The main types of learning

CNN is defined as the integral of the product of the two functions after one is reversed and shifted. The integral is evaluated for all values of shift, producing the convolution function [3, 15]. A digital image during image processing can be viewed as a discrete function of a two-dimensional area, marked as f(x,y). Assuming the existence of a two-dimensional convolution function g(x, y), the output image z(x,y), which can be used to extract image features is represented by the following formula:

$$z(x, y) = f(x, y) * g(x, y) \tag{1}$$

Similarly, in deep learning (DL) applications the input image is a multi-dimensional array of 3 × image width × image length when the input is a color image containing RGB three channels and the convolution kernel is defined in the learning algorithm as the accounting. The computational argument is a multi-dimensional array as well. After, when two-dimensional images are fed into the program, the following formula is used to calculate the corresponding convolution operation:

$$z(x, y) = f(x, y) * g(x, y) = \sum_t \sum_h f(t, h) g(x - t, y - h) \tag{2}$$

If a convolution kernel of m × n dimension array is given, the formula is:

$$z(x, y) = f(x, y) * g(x, y) = \sum_{t=0}^{t=m} \sum_{h=0}^{h=n} f(t, h) g(x - t, y - h) \tag{3}$$

where f – the input image G.

CNN architecture consists typically of a convolution layer, a non-linear activation layer, and a max-pooling layer [1, 4, 15]. To create a set of linear activations, the convolution layer operations are executed in parallel. The convolution operation's goal is to extract high-level features from the input image. Then each linear activation is executed through the most used activation functions rectified linear activation function. The pooling layer, like the convolutional layer, is in charge of reducing the spatial size of the convolved feature. Through dimensionality reduction, the computational power required to process the data is reduced. Furthermore, it is useful for extracting dominant features, allowing the model to be successfully trained. The process of training a CNN algorithm is similar to that of a feedforward neural network until a loss function is calculated, each thermal image is directed via the layers. Then the losses are backpropagated into the network, changing the weights using gradient descent methods, and the action is repeated until a predetermined number of training epochs are completed.

4 Discussion and Results

During this research, we have designed a CNN algorithm for thermal images to classify the participants into healthy or with spinal disorders. The entire dataset was split into subsets of the training, the test, and the validation sets, as is shown in Fig. 3.

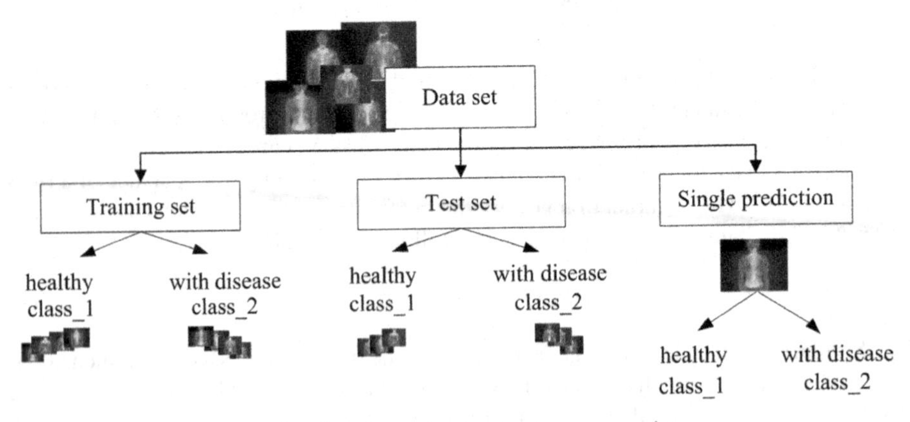

Fig. 3. The schematic of dataset pre-processing

Our dataset composed of 800 IR images was divided into two categories: to estimate a final model 40 test images were used to fit on the training dataset, and 760 training images to fit the model. This proportion was obtained empirically.

Before an AI-based classification algorithm was implemented, all database images were treated by our previously developed algorithm [4]. Using pre-processed infrared images, CNN was trained and tested on selected regions of interest (ROI) of the human body. The main algorithm steps for thermal images classification using a CNN are shown in Fig. 4.

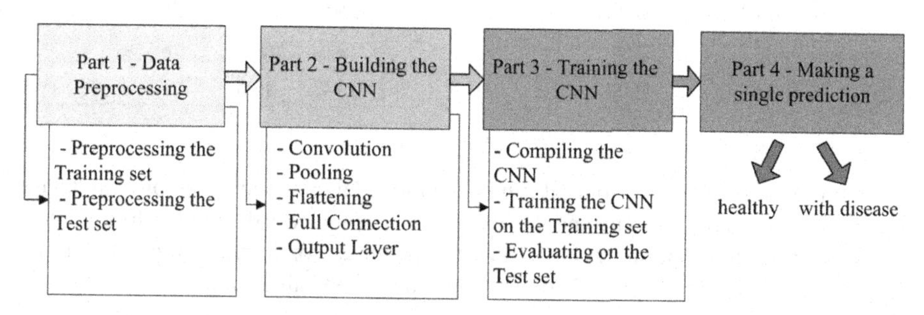

Fig. 4. The algorithm steps for thermal images classification using a CNN

The CNN architecture was constructed with a 0:001 learning rate and a 0:75 dropout rate. Two Convolutional Layers with the values of the 5×5 convolutional kernel and 32 outputs were used in the proposed architecture, followed by two Max Pooling Layers that calculates the maximum value in each patch of each feature map. The ReLU was used to keep the computation needed to operate the neural network from growing exponentially. The output layer divided the database into categories: healthy and with the disease, and is a completely connected layer. Cross-validation ensures that each image in the database is evaluated in train and test sets. To most effectively use our deep learning model an extension to stochastic gradient descent Adam Optimizer was used. As our algorithm has only two label classes (healthy and with the disease), binary cross-entropy class was used to calculate loss between true labels and predicted labels. After training the CNN on the training set and evaluating it on the test set was making a single prediction on a randomly chosen thermal image.

As the database has a small number of images the methodology is composed of a set of 80 experiments based on thermal images, each time randomly mixed of the training set and test set to make a single prediction. Table 1 is shown the results of descriptive statistical analysis of developed methodology for the classification of infrared images database of patients with spinal disorders based on a CNN.

The obtained results showed a good outcome with 95% accuracy and 94% specificity, which is a significant impetus to continue work on the classification of infrared images database of patients with spinal disorders based on a CNN algorithm.

On another side, according to the International Statistical Classification of Diseases and Related Health Problems [19], the study group could be divided into disease classes, as follows: 1) patients with deforming dorsopathies (kyphosis, lordosis, scoliosis, etc.); 2) patients with spondylopathies (osteochondrosis, spondylolisthesis, etc.), and 3) patients with other dorsopathies (torticollis, leg length discrepancy, etc.). However, in that case, the sample set would be small, which in turn has led to the impossibility to train an AI

Table 1. The results after using CNN on our infrared image database

Experim.	Accuracy	Sensibility	Specificity	PPV	NPV	Time (ms/step)
1.	0.96	0.93	0.94	0,93	0,93	89
2.	1	1	1	1	1	169
3.	0.94	0.93	0.94	0.95	0,96	173
..	…	…	…	…	…	…
Mean	0.95	0.94	0.93	0.94	0,95	152

algorithm. So, as a negative point, it can be mentioned a relatively small present dataset of thermal images of the spine and the absence of open-access database information.

Meanwhile, the reported results show the potential for implementing IR thermal imaging of patients with spinal disorders based on a CNN algorithm.

5 Conclusions

Medical applications based on AI algorithms using infrared image data can be successfully used for spinal disease classification. One limitation of the present study was a relatively small quantity of IR images and the absence of an open-access spine thermograms database with the label by types of the diseases. However, the first obtained results allow assuming that our methodology can easily be applied to a much larger set of data, conducting even more precise results.

In subsequent researches, we expect to increase the database of the spine thermograms to classify them not only by two classes (healthy and with the disease) but specify by the type of disease to which it belongs, as well as to use different CNN architectures to compare results.

Acknowledgments. The authors would like to express their deepest gratitude to all volunteers and medical staff from the Center of Medical Rehabilitation & Sports Medicine, Vinnytsia, Ukraine, for participating in the study. Special thanks to Professor Petro F. Kolisnyk and Professor Sergei P. Kolisnyk from National Pirogov Memorial Medical University for assistance, and Professor Dr. Sergei V. Pavlov from Vinnytsia National Technical University for help in research work. This work was financing by Fundação para a Ciência e Tecnologia (FCT, Portugal) and NMT, S.A. as the Ph.D. grant (PD/BDE/142791/2018) of the Doctoral NOVA I4H Program.

References

1. Ring, E.F.J.: History of thermology and thermography: pioneers and progress. Thermal. Int. **22**(3), 3–7 (2012)
2. Kwok, G., et al.: Postural screening for adolescent idiopathic scoliosis with infrared thermography. Sci. Rep. **7**(1), 1–8 (2017). https://doi.org/10.1038/s41598-017-14556-w

3. Lubkowska, A., Gajewska, E.: Temperature distribution of selected body surfaces in scoliosis based on static infrared thermography. Int. J. Environ. Res. Public Health **17**(23), 1–16 (2020). https://doi.org/10.3390/ijerph17238913
4. Poplavska, A.A., Vassilenko, V.B., Poplavskyi, O.A., Pavlov, S.V.: Algorithm for automated segmentation and feature extraction of thermal images. In: Camarinha-Matos, L.M., Farhadi, N., Lopes, F., Pereira, H. (eds.) DoCEIS 2020. IAICT, vol. 577, pp. 378–386. Springer, Cham (2020). https://doi.org/10.1007/978-3-030-45124-0_36
5. Vassilenko, V., et al.: Automated features analysis of patients with spinal diseases using medical thermal images. In: Optical Fibers and Their Applications 2020, vol. 11456, pp. 116–124 (2020). https://doi.org/10.1117/12.2569780
6. John, H.E., Niumsawatt, V., Rozen, W.M., Whitaker, I.S.: Clinical applications of dynamic infrared thermography in plastic surgery: a systematic review. Gland Surg. **5**(2), 122–132 (2016). https://doi.org/10.3978/j.issn.2227-684X.2015.11.07
7. Wen, J., et al.: Overview of classification of Alzheimer's disease. Med. Image Anal. **63** (2020)
8. hirunavukkarasu, U., et al.: Human tongue thermography could be a prognostic tool for prescreening the type II diabetes mellitus. Evid. Based Complement. Altern. Med. **2020** (2020). https://doi.org/10.1155/2020/3186208
9. Francis, S.V., Sasikala, M., Saranya, S.: Detection of breast abnormality from thermograms using curvelet transform based feature extraction. J. Med. Syst. **38**(4), 1–9 (2014). https://doi.org/10.1007/s10916-014-0023-3
10. Frize, M., Ogungbemile, A.: Estimating rheumatoid arthritis activity with infrared image analysis. Stud. Health Technol. Inform. **180**, 594–598 (2012). https://doi.org/10.3233/978-1-61499-101-4-594
11. Kvyetnyy, R.N., et al.: Group decision support system based on Bayesian network. Prz. Elektrotechniczny **96**(9), 123–128 (2020). https://doi.org/10.15199/48.2020.09.26
12. Roslidar, R., et al.: A review on recent progress in thermal imaging and deep learning approaches for breast cancer detection. IEEE Access **8**, 116176–116194 (2020). https://doi.org/10.1109/ACCESS.2020.3004056
13. Vardasca, R., Magalhaes, C., Mendes, J.: Biomedical applications of infrared thermal imaging: current state of machine learning classification. In: Proceedings, vol. 27, no. 1, p. 46 (2019). https://doi.org/10.3390/proceedings2019027046
14. De Freitas Oliveira Baffa, M., Grassano Lattari, L.: Convolutional neural networks for static and dynamic breast infrared imaging classification. In: Proceedings of 31st Conference on Graphics, Patterns and Images (SIBGRAPI 2018), pp. 174–181 (2019). https://doi.org/10.1109/SIBGRAPI.2018.00029
15. Magalhaes, C., Mendes, J., Vardasca, R.: Meta-analysis and systematic review of the application of machine learning classifiers in biomedical applications of infrared thermography. Appl. Sci. **11**(2), 1–18 (2021). https://doi.org/10.3390/app11020842
16. Koprowski, R.: Automatic analysis of the trunk thermal images from healthy subjects and patients with faulty posture. Comput. Biol. Med. **62**, 110–118 (2015). https://doi.org/10.1016/j.compbiomed.2015.04.017
17. Ravindra, V.M., et al.: Degenerative lumbar spine disease: estimating global incidence and worldwide volume. Glob. Spine J. **8**(8), 784–794 (2018). https://doi.org/10.1177/2192568218770769
18. Christiansen, J., Dudley, W.: International Academy of Clinical Thermology Quality Assurance Guidelines Standards and Protocols in Clinical Thermographic Imaging, no. January, pp. 1–35 (2015). https://doi.org/10.13140/RG.2.2.28341.78562
19. Khoury, B., Kogan, C., Daouk, S.: International classification of diseases 11th edition (ICD-11). In: Zeigler-Hill, V., Shackelford, T.K. (eds.) Encyclopedia of Personality and Individual Differences, pp. 1–6. Springer, Cham (2017)

Improvements on Signal Processing Algorithm for the VOPITB Equipment

Filipa E. Cardoso[1,2,3](✉), Valentina Vassilenko[1,2,3], Arnaldo Batista[4], Paulo Bonifácio[1,2], Sergio Rico Martin[3,5], Juan Muñoz-Torrero[3,6], and Manuel Ortigueira[4]

[1] Laboratory of Instrumentation, Biomedical Engineering and Radiation Physics (LIBPhys-UNL), NOVA School of Science and Technology - NOVA University of Lisbon, 2829-516 Caparica, Portugal
feo.cardoso@campus.fct.unl.pt

[2] NMT, S.A., Edifício Madan Parque, 2825-182 Caparica, Portugal

[3] Iberian Network on Arterial Structure, Central Hemodynamics and Neurocognition, Caceres, Spain

[4] UNINOVA CTS, NOVA School of Science and Technology - NOVA University Lisbon, 2829-516 Caparica, Portugal

[5] Department of Nursing, Nursing and Occupational Therapy College, Universidad de Extremadura, Caceres, Spain

[6] Department of Internal Medicine, Hospital San Pedro de Alcantara, Caceres, Spain

Abstract. The pulse signal obtained non-invasively through an oscillometric method can accurately measure the Cardio-Ankle Vascular Index (CAVI) and Pulse Wave Velocity (PWV), two valuable physiological markers of arterial stiffness and cardiovascular health. The VOPITB device is designed to obtain these markers whose accuracy heavily depends on the correctness of feature extraction from pulse wave signals. Typically, a threshold method is obtained, leading to excessive detection success dependency on the established level. To overcome this limitation two signal processing methods are proposed, one based on a modified version of the Pan-Tompkins algorithm and the other centered on a Wavelet approach. A statistical study is presented assessing the accuracy of both methods. The new algorithms are presented as an alternative to the simple thresholding method.

Keywords: CAVI · Signal processing · Pulse wave velocity · Wavelet analysis

1 Introduction

In the last decades, the morbidity and mortality from Cardiovascular Disease (CVD) have been decreasing [1]. Despite this progress, CVD continues to be one of the main causes of death worldwide [2]. Strategies for the early detection of vascular disease may be the key to prevent CVD.

© IFIP International Federation for Information Processing 2021
Published by Springer Nature Switzerland AG 2021
L. M. Camarinha-Matos et al. (Eds.): DoCEIS 2021, IFIP AICT 626, pp. 324–330, 2021.
https://doi.org/10.1007/978-3-030-78288-7_31

Arterial stiffness is an indicator of vascular disease and has been recognized as a crucial component in cardiovascular risk assessment since it precedes hypertension, target organ damage, and has been associated with cardiovascular mortality and morbidity [3]. The arterial stiffness can be evaluated with the Pulse Wave Velocity (PWV) and Cardio-Ankle Vascular Index (CAVI). The PWV is considered the gold standard for measuring arterial stiffness and has been recommended by the European Society of Cardiology and the European Society of Hypertension to evaluate asymptomatic organ damage in hypertensive patients [4]. CAVI is an alternative marker of arterial stiffness that overcomes some of the PWV disadvantages, due to its independence from the blood pressure level and its high reproducibility and sensitivity [5].

The VOPITB equipment (Velocidad de Onda de Pulso Índice Tobillo Brazo – Pulse Wave Velocity Index Ankle-Brachial) [6] has been validated to measure the PWV and CAVI indexes [7, 8]. This device registers the pulse wave by placing cuffs and electrodes on the ankle and arm. The pulse wave is created by the interaction of the cardiac contraction and the distensibility of the arterial walls. The arteries expand due to the increased blood volume caused by the cardiac contraction and when the elastic energy produced throughout the distension is released, the arteries contract. For that reason, the arteries have a regular pulse called the pulse wave [9].

In the analysis of the pulse wave obtained from the VOPITB cuffs, it is crucial to have a correct identification of key points to accurately determine the PWV and CAVI.

Some studies have been published regarding this subject. Jang *et al.* [10] developed a method for pulse peak determination that was tested in Digital Volume Pulse signals. A true detection rate of 97.32% was achieved with a normalized error rate of 0.18%. Vadrevu *et al.* [11] studied three pulse peak methodologies in photopletismogram (PPG) signals. An overall accuracy of 99.43%, 87.45% and 52.89% was achieved for the multiscale sum algorithms, Hilbert transform and pulse waveform delineator, respectively. Argüello-Prada [12] proposed the mountaineer's method for peak detection in PPG signals. Three datasets were analyzed in which the algorithm sensitivity ranged from 97.72% to 99.48% and presented a failed detection rate between 0.86% and 5.92%.

The goal of this work was to overcome the limitations of the previous VOPITB detector by combining a modified Pan-Tompkins algorithm and a wavelet-based detector.

2 Contribution to Life Improvement

One of the main objectives of CVD primary prevention should be the identification of asymptomatic individuals to decrease clinical symptoms and the progression of the disease. The evolution in technology is crucial to the development of new parameters for CVD assessment. The PWV and CAVI are non-invasive markers of arterial stiffness with promising clinical value that can be applied in risk population as well as in asymptomatic patients. The correct determination of these markers relies on the accurate identification of signal peaks.

3 Methods

The CAVI index calculation is given by [13]:

$$CAVI = \frac{2\rho}{\Delta P}\left(ln\frac{Ps}{Pd}\right)PWV^2 \quad (1)$$

where ρ is the blood density, Δ P is the pulse pressure, Ps is the systolic blood pressure and Pd is the diastolic blood pressure. The PWV is given by [13]:

$$PWV = \frac{L}{T}. \quad (2)$$

$$T = t_b + t_{ba}. \quad (3)$$

where L is the length from the origin of the aorta to the ankle, T is the time taken for the pulse wave to propagate from the aortic valve to the ankle, t_b is the time between the rise of the brachial pulse wave and the rise of the ankle pulse wave, and t_{ba} is the time interval between aortic valve closing sound and the notch of brachial pulse wave [13]. The assessment of these parameters is achieved by the analysis of the pulse wave signal.

The Pulse Wave Signal (PWS) shown in Fig. 1 contains the three points necessary to evaluate the PWV and CAVI. Those points are the onset mark, the systolic peak followed by a minimum notch. The accurate detection of these three points, which may be challenged by the natural PWS variations and motion artefacts, is crucial for the CAVI and PWV correct evaluation. Two methods are presented: the modified Pan-Tompkins ECG algorithm [14] and a Wavelet-based detector [15]. The Pan-Tompkins algorithm has been successfully used in the R-waves detection of the ECG and is a de-facto standard method for this task. Adaptations were introduced to address the PWS parameters such as its lower frequency band [16]. The notch point was obtained as the local minimum between two successive systolic points, and the onset point was obtained using a slope

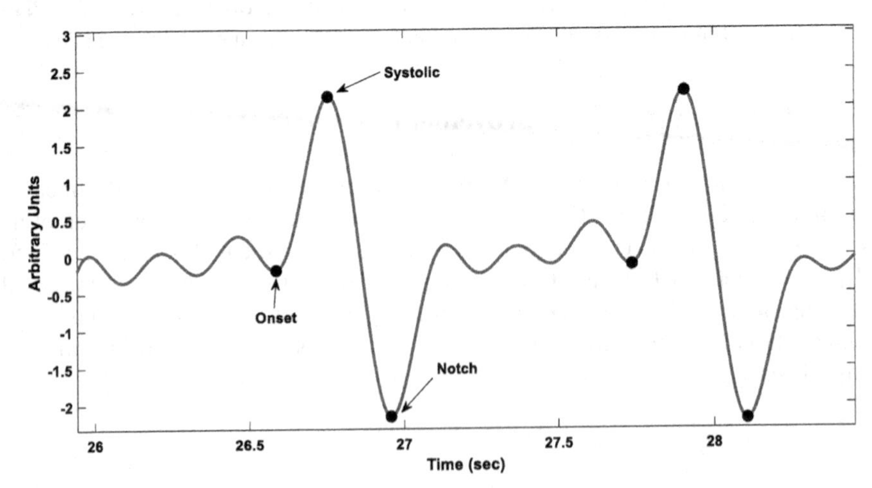

Fig. 1. A PWS showing the three relevant points to be detected: onset, systolic and notch.

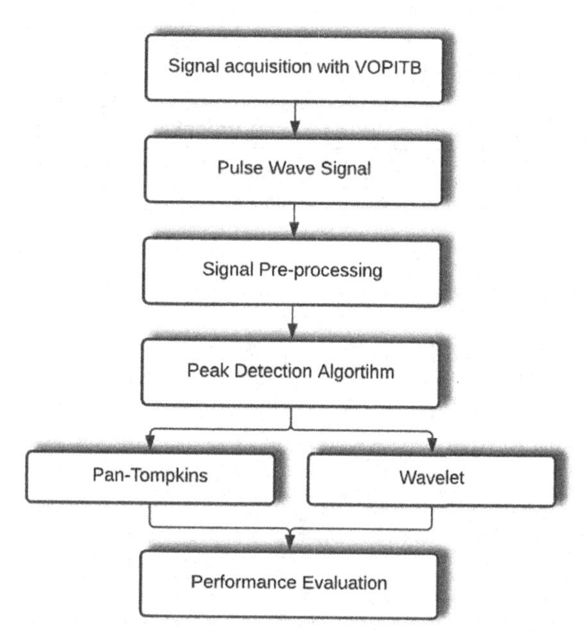

Fig. 2. Methodology description flowchart which includes the modified Pan-Tompkins and wavelet detectors.

detection methodology. Both the notch and the onset points correct localization depends on the detection accuracy of the systolic point. A signal pre-processing step is included with the application of a filter with passband between 0.4 to 4 Hz. A detrending and trimming procedure was then applied. The flowchart of the global process is shown in Fig. 2. The Wavelet detector is based on an adapted version of the R-wave peak detector introduced by Sahambi *et al.* [17]. An adjustment in the calculation of the optimal wavelet level for the algorithm input is made by obtaining the respective wavelet scale using:

$$S = Fc/(Fp \times \Delta). \tag{4}$$

where Fc is the central frequency of the selected wavelet, Δ is the sampling period and Fp the central frequency of the PWS band. Having in consideration that the bandwidth of the PWS extends from 0.4 to 4 Hz a $Fp = 2$ Hz is selected which, with $\Delta = 1/200$ s produces wavelet scale equal to 25 equating to the closest wavelet level of 5. The selected wavelet was the Mexican hat given its similarity with the signal under study. An adaptive thresholding methodology is applied to the wavelet coefficients in level 5 of the transform after which the systolic point is obtained. The process is represented in Fig. 3.

For this study, a total of 39 PWS were analyzed from 30 men and 9 women. The Body Mass Index (BMI) ranged from 25.5 to 32.8, with mean of 29.7. All data were analyzed with MATLAB®.

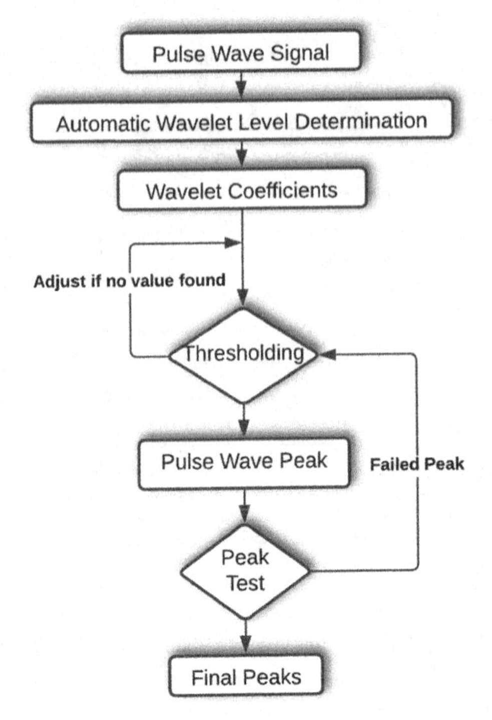

Fig. 3. Wavelet algorithm description flowchart. See text for details.

4 Results

The proposed algorithms were evaluated using the mentioned dataset. The results represented in Table 1 show that the wavelet algorithm outperforms the Pan-Tompkins' in all the detected points. Moreover, as expected, the similarity between the obtained sensitivities in the three studied points is patent since the fiducial systolic point is the key mark for the localization of the two other points. The better results in the wavelet algorithm can be explained by the good correlation between the Mexican hat used wavelet with the PWS and due to the denoising operation implied by the selection of one wavelet level only. Comparatively, the above-mentioned studies present better sensitivity outcomes. However, this comparison should be made with caution since different datasets may produce nonequivalent results due, for instance, different present noise levels. Computationally both algorithms are equivalent as far as complexity is concerned. Regarding computational load the Pan-Tompkins algorithm is roughly 1.5 times faster than the Wavelet algorithm. For an AMD platform, 32 GB and Windows 10 the average processing time for a one minute record is 300 ms. Figure 4 illustrates the detection results for a signal of the used dataset.

Table 1. Evaluation of Pan-Tompkins and the Wavelet-based algorithm performance in the PWS

	Pan-Tompkins sensitivity (%)	Wavelet sensitivity (%)
Systolic	84.06	93.67
Notch	82.89	93.32
Onset	83.15	91.65

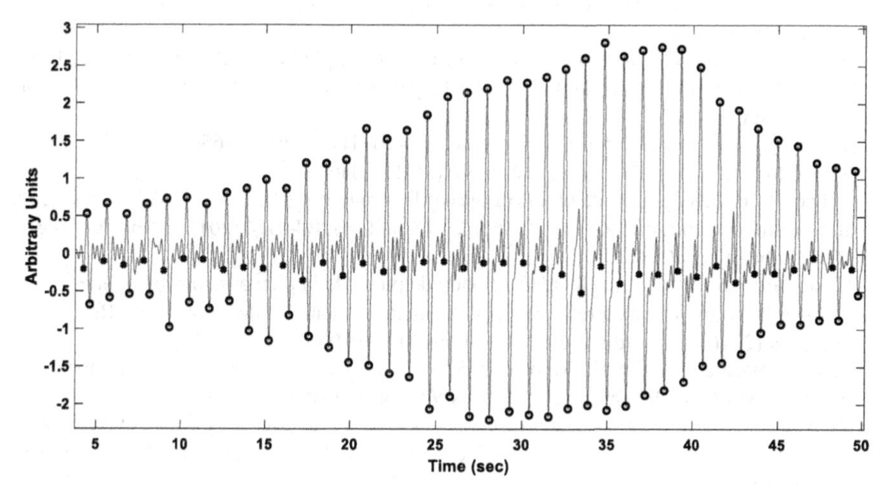

Fig. 4. Example of PWS from the used dataset where all the peaks are correctly identified using the wavelet-based algorithm.

5 Discussion and Conclusion

The calculation of the PWV and the CAVI rely on the accurate localization of three main features in the PWS: the onset, systolic and notch points.

Some studies [11, 12] presented different peak determination algorithms for the PPG signal, such as the mountaineer's method. The accuracy of the systolic peak detection presented in this work (93.67%) is comparable to the Jang *et al.* [10] and Argüello-Prada [11] results, 97.32% and 97.72%, respectively. Despite the similar nature of the PWS and PPG, one must keep in mind that the recording sensor for these signals is different.

Commonly, a challenging thresholding technique is applied for the detection of these points with poor results due to the natural signal variability and amplitude between subjects. Two algorithms for the localization of these points are presented. The wavelet-based method demonstrated to produce more accurate localization points. The algorithm is adaptive by adjusting the detection rules to the signal amplitude and is also computationally light enough to be easily embedded in real-time systems.

The peak detection is essential for feature extraction in the several biomedical signals. In future work, machine learning methods, such as neural networks, could improve the accurate assessment of crucial futures for prevention and early detection of CVD.

Acknowledgments. This work was funded and supported by the Fundação para a Ciência e Tecnologia (FCT, Portugal) and NMT, S.A in the scope of the PhD grant PD/BDE/150312/2019. Partial support also comes from Fundação para a Ciência e Tecnologia through the program UIDB/00066/2020 (CTS- Center of Technology and Systems).

References

1. Mensah, G.A., et al.: Decline in cardiovascular mortality. Circ. Res. **120**(2), 366–380 (2017). https://doi.org/10.1161/CIRCRESAHA.116.309115
2. WHO: The top 10 causes of death (2020). https://www.who.int/news-room/fact-sheets/detail/the-top-10-causes-of-death.
3. Verwoert, G.C., et al.: Does aortic stiffness improve the prediction of coronary heart disease in elderly? The Rotterdam Study. J. Hum. Hypertens. **26**(1), 28–34 (2012). https://doi.org/10.1038/jhh.2010.124
4. Covic, A., Siriopol, D.: Pulse wave velocity ratio. Hypertension **65**(2), 289–290 (2015). https://doi.org/10.1161/HYPERTENSIONAHA.114.04678
5. Asmar, R.: Principles and usefulness of the cardio-ankle vascular index (CAVI): a new global arterial stiffness index. Eur. Heart J. Suppl. **19**(suppl_B), B4–B10 (2017). https://doi.org/10.1093/eurheartj/suw058
6. Rico Martín, S., et al.: La velocidad de onda de pulso de la pierna menos brazo medida con un dispositivo propio se correlaciona con la cuantificación de calcio coronario. Rev. Clínica Española (2016). https://doi.org/10.1016/j.rce.2016.01.006
7. Sánchez Bacaicoa, C., et al.: Velocidad de onda de pulso brazo-tobillo con un dispositivo propio. Rev. Clínica Española (2020). https://doi.org/10.1016/j.rce.2019.12.012
8. Rico Martín, S., et al.: Cardio-ankle vascular index (CAVI) measured by a new device: protocol for a validation study. BMJ Open **10**(10), e038581 (2020). https://doi.org/10.1136/bmjopen-2020-038581
9. Alastruey, J., Parker, K., Sherwin, S.J.: Arterial pulse wave haemodynamics. In: Anderson, S. (ed.) 11th International Conference on Pressure Surges (2012)
10. Jang, D.-G., Farooq, U., Park, S.-H., Hahn, M.: A robust method for pulse peak determination in a digital volume pulse waveform with a wandering baseline. IEEE Trans. Biomed. Circuits Syst. **8**(5), 729–737 (2014). https://doi.org/10.1109/TBCAS.2013.2295102
11. Vadrevu, S., Manikandan, M.S.: A robust pulse onset and peak detection method for automated PPG signal analysis system. IEEE Trans. Instrum. Meas. **68**(3), 807–817 (2019). https://doi.org/10.1109/TIM.2018.2857878
12. Argüello-Prada, E.J.: The mountaineer's method for peak detection in photoplethysmographic signals. Rev. Fac. Ing. Univ. Antioquia (90), 42–50 (2019). https://doi.org/10.17533/udea.redin.n90a06
13. Shirai, K., Saiki, A., Nagayama, D., Tatsuno, I., Shimizu, K., Takahashi, M.: The role of monitoring arterial stiffness with cardio-ankle vascular index in the control of lifestyle-related diseases. Pulse **3**(2), 118–133 (2015). https://doi.org/10.1159/000431235
14. Pan, J., Tompkins, W.J.: A real-time QRS detection algorithm. IEEE Trans. Biomed. Eng. **BME-32**(3), 230–236 (1985). https://doi.org/10.1109/TBME.1985.325532
15. Pinto, I.V., Alves, L.B., Ortigueira, M.D., Batista, A.G.: ECG wave detector and delineation with wavelets, vol. 4 (2005). http://www2.uninova.pt/~mdo/publ_files/D93-ECGWAVEDETECTORANDDELINEATIONWITHWAVELETS.pdf
16. Sedghamiz, H.: Matlab Implementation of Pan Tompkins ECG QRS, pp. 1–3 (2014). https://www.researchgate.net/publication/313673153_Matlab_Implementation_of_Pan_Tompkins_ECG_QRS_detector
17. Sahambi, J.S., Tandon, S.N., Bhatt, R.K.P.: A new approach for on-line ECG characterization. In: Proceedings of the 1996 Fifteenth Southern Biomedical Engineering Conference, pp. 409–411. https://doi.org/10.1109/SBEC.1996.493262

Pilot Study for Validation and Differentiation of Alveolar and Esophageal Air

Paulo Santos[1,2](✉), Valentina Vassilenko[1,2], Carolina Conduto[1], Jorge M. Fernandes[1,2], Pedro C. Moura[1], and Paulo Bonifácio[1,2]

[1] Laboratory of Instrumentation, Biomedical Engineering and Radiation Physiscs (LibPhys-UNL), NOVA School of Science and Technology, Campus FCT UNL, Caparica, Portugal
ph.santos@campus.fct.unl.pt, vv@fct.unl.pt
[2] NMT, S.A., Edíficio Madan Parque, Rua dos Inventores, Caparica, Portugal

Abstract. Breath analysis is an expanding scientific field with great potential for creating personalized and non-invasive health screening and diagnostics techniques. However, the wide range of contradictory results in breath analysis is explained by the lack of an optimal standard procedure for selective breath sampling. Recently we developed novel instrumentation for selective breath sampling, enabling the precise collection of a pre-determined portion of exhaled air using AI (Machine Learning) algorithm. This work presents pilot study results for validation of developed technology by differentiation of alveolar and oesophagal air obtained from the healthy population (n = 31). The samples were analyzed in-situ by Gas Chromatography-Ion Mobility Spectrometry (GC-IMS) apparatus, and obtained spectra were processed with proper multivariate classification tools. The results show a promising performance of proposed AI-based technology for breath sampling adapted to users' age, genre, and physiological conditions.

Keywords: Alveolar air · Selective air acquisition · Breath sampling · Machine learning · Medical instrumentation · Principal Component Analysis

1 Introduction

Molecular analysis of exhaled volatile compounds (breathomics) has been innately attractive, allowing non-invasive, quick, and straightforward observations of multiple biochemical processes of the human body. Indeed, modern technology breakthroughs have placed the analysis of exhaled air metabolites as a reliable non-invasive diagnostic and a prognostic tool for a wide variety of medical conditions to assess different vital organ functions [1]. Recently the non-invasive detection of biomarkers in breath associated with tuberculosis (TB), chronic obstructive pulmonary disease (COPD), asthma and an array of cancers have been reported [2, 3].

In every single human breath, more than one thousand different molecules are exhaled. Volatile Organic Compounds (VOCs) arise in exhaled breath, urine, blood,

© IFIP International Federation for Information Processing 2021
Published by Springer Nature Switzerland AG 2021
L. M. Camarinha-Matos et al. (Eds.): DoCEIS 2021, IFIP AICT 626, pp. 331–338, 2021.
https://doi.org/10.1007/978-3-030-78288-7_32

saliva, and faeces, and are also emitted by skin [4]. VOCs can have an endogenous metabolic origin either related or not to previous exogenous exposures (environment, smoking, medication, food, etc.) [1] or can have a microbial origin (*i.e.,* in the gut or airways) [5, 6]. The concentration of exhaled VOCs is also influenced by the compound-specific blood/gas partition coefficient (*i.e.,* respiratory gas exchange), cardiac output and alveolar minute volume. Therefore, the exhaled air composition also shifts according to its respiratory origin or source. The first exhaled portion of a tidal breath corresponds to oesophagal air, approximately, one third (around 150 ml) of the tidal breath volume (500 ml in an average adult). It is known as physiological dead space and contains molecules from mouth, larynx, trachea, and bronchi. This air type has increased concentrations of exogenous VOCs (mainly linked to room air, environmental exposure, odour, food, *etc.*) The remaining two-thirds of a complete exhalation is composed of end-tidal or alveolar air (*i.e.,* 350 mL) [7]. Alveolar air has been deeply studied due to the direct exchange of breath constituents with systemic blood. Such phenomenon provides an analysis of a higher concentration of endogenous VOCs, offering a metabolic window of the biochemical processes of the body [7].

As alveolar and oesophagal (*i.e.,* dead space air excluding mouth) carry specific clinical information, devices used to collect exhaled VOCs should be intelligent by adapting to patients' breathing characteristics and controlling the sampling procedure when isolating an air portion for further analysis.

Notwithstanding the recent and quick development of breathomics, no robust and repeatable breath-related VOCs' profiling technologies have been clinically validated. The major challenges for the validation of breath sampling technologies are linked to lack of standardized procedures to accurately collect extremely low concentrations of source-dependent exhaled air constituents that can be originated from oral cavity, oesophagus, and alveoli. Unsolved issues related to exhaled breath sampling include correction for ambient inspired volatiles, type of sampling (total versus alveolar breath), sampling duration (single-breath versus fixed-time or fixed-volume breathing), the effect of expiratory flow, breath hold, type of materials, sample pretreatment, the effect of humidity, food/medications, exercise, smoking and co-morbidities [8].

A full control of the breath sampling procedure by assessing the patients' respiratory cycle enables the identification of part of the respiratory tract from which the sample derived from. Presently the most used devices that control breath sampling identify the different phases of the breathing cycle by measuring CO_2 concentration, breathing flow, pressure, temperature, or humidity. However, most of these methods introduce high variability in breath samples due to: (a) the way the air is expelled, (b) the breath frequency, (c) the length and depth of the breath cycle and (d) the mental and physical condition of the patient. The problems remaining to be solved comprise the question of how to achieve accurate, selective, and repeatable sampling, how to ensure easy and safe handling, and maybe most importantly, the issue of sample stability to allow a proper chemical analysis. Therefore, up-to-date research in breath analysis tries to pursue a suitable device and a precise protocol for sampling exhaled air independently of patients: age, gender, metabolic production of CO_2, smoking habits, nutrition, and health conditions; thus, harmonizing the breath collection methods already approached by the scientific community. The research herein presented aims to disclose the benefits of implementing Artificial Intelligence in an advanced breath sampling prototype capable of selectively collecting exhaled air samples according to the user's respiratory source, independently of their metabolic production of carbon dioxide [9].

2 Relationship to Applied Artificial Intelligence Systems

This paper reports the results of the performance of a novel ML-based system for a selective and adaptative sampling of breath, as well as its differentiation, through the experimental measurements by fast, reagent-free, and portable analytical instrumentation of Ion Mobility Spectrometry with Gas-Chromatography pre-separation (GC-IMS) and high sensitivity and selectivity for VOC in ppb_V (parts per billion by volume) or ppt_V (parts per trillion) concentrations range [9, 10].

Most breath samplers comprise some algorithms to analyze the user respiration cycles to detect inspiration and expiration phases and to, consequently, determine the time window for breath sampling. However, and erratic respiratory rhythms that determined the time window for a sample is shorter and brought up multiple issues when obtaining small portions of exhaled air. Only the system patented by Capnia, Inc. (WO2015143384 A1, 2015) is configured to impose a breath frequency to users (young children and non-cognizant patients) to avoid those erratic respiratory episodes. Even so, that imposed frequency does not adapt itself with the user's breathing pace by combining a set of users' characteristics as the proposed system does.

The breath sampling ML-based innovative prototype was developed in our group by researchers from NMT, S.A. and NOVA School of Science and Technology Nova University of Lisbon, Portugal (patent WO/2018/047058, 12 09 2016). It performs continuous real-time breathing flow measurements to collect a pre-determined portion of exhaled air by synchronizing a previously modelled respiratory cycle with the breathing cycle of the user. Through real-time synchronization of breathing cycles, the device detects optimized sampling instants through a machine learning-based algorithm described elsewhere [9, 10]. The system includes two hardware units (communication module and end-user) controlled by intelligent software loaded on a computing device (*e.g.*, desktop, or tablet). The software contains a human-machine interface (HMI) and a sampling algorithm to control and personalize breaths' sampling procedure. Such HMI enables: (a) visual feedback of operations (*i.e.* sensor signal, breathing pacer and sampling status), (b) personalization of breath collection procedure (by defining sampling features and users' characteristics such as age, gender, and physiological state) and (c) the recording real-time flow measurement data.

In turn, the sampling algorithm implemented in the intelligent control software was configured to (i) measure the user's respiratory flow, (ii) distinguish inspiratory and expiratory breath phases, (iii) synchronize the respiratory cycle measured with representative and modelled respiratory cycle and, (iv) to calculate the user's average time of expiration (ATE). The machine learning (ML) algorithm implemented in the software algorithm allows predicting the time of a new exhalation and, consequently, precise prediction of sampling timeframes. This approach enables the ML process to assess the user's respiratory cycle and test it on the modelled respiratory cycle intrinsically contained in the sampling algorithm [10]. Afterwards, and within timeframes predicted, the software communicates with the end-user to channel the sample, either into a collection reservoir or to direct online analysis [9].

On the other side, to validate the performance of this patented technology, a PhD work plan of one of the authors consists of a demonstration of how this AI-based technology works in field measurements and if it is possible to separate the very small portions of breath, *i.e.*, the alveolar and esophageal exhaled air. For this purpose, a series of experimental measurements described in this work was performed. The obtained samples of exhaled air were analyzed on-line by GC-IMS instrumentation. Since each spectrum contains extensive data of analyte information, they were processed with proper for spectral analysis multivariate classification tools: Principal Component Analysis, PCA (Unsupervised Learning Procedure) and Partial Least Square Discriminant Analysis (Supervised Learning Procedure).

3 Methodology for Breath Differentiation

The methodology herein presented was applied during *in-situ* implementation tests that focused mainly on breath volatolome differentiation using the abovementioned our breath sampler prototype. Therefore, the prototype's sampling selectivity (*i.e.*, the ability for sampling and differentiation) was tested through the collection and on-line analysis of esophageal and alveolar air samples obtained from an independent cohort of university students [6]. The 31 healthy non-smokers volunteers, without lung diseases, heart conditions and gastric disorders and not pregnant, aged 20 to 35, participate in the study. Additional pre-conditions were also required: (a) 3–5 h of fasting; (b) no prior consumption of alcohol or leguminous plants; (c) 3 h from the last mouth wash; (d) absence of hygiene products or perfume prior to the measurements and (e) light meal before the test (avoiding products as meat or fish). Within these tests, each volunteer attended two sessions (alveolar and esophageal exhaled air acquisition) occurring on separate days. Although the laboratory environment presents a stable VOC content, as previously reported [1], all participants were exposed to environmental air for the same timeframe (*i.e.*, 30 min) before any breath collection.

3.1 Exhaled Air Sampling and Analysis

In previously reported work [10, 11], have demonstrated that ML algorithm led to improvements in the sampling procedure, reducing standard deviation for average time of exhalation (ATE), the number of cycles and time required to start sampling. Therefore, a similar protocol for breath sampling was applied during breath differentiation tests. Thus, after powering and plugging the advanced prototype into a computing device, the prototype's HMI suggested a breathing rhythm to each user according to its age, gender, and physiological state. Afterwards, each volunteer was asked to breathe until the fraction of exhaled air was sampled by the device. Such process ensured that only a specific fraction of breath was diverted to 5 ml syringes. Breath samples were analyzed by BreathSpec® device (from GAS Dortmund). Such device couples an Ion Mobility Spectrometer (IMS) with Gas Chromatograph (GC), where gas analytes are pre-separated in the chromatographic column [13]. A description of IMS principle and details of its work can be found in a previous publication [14]. However, it is worth mentioning the ability of this instrumentation to deliver results without the need for any chemical reagent or sample pre-processing. Exhaled breath analytes were analyzed for 15 min with a carrier gas flow of 10 mL/min for the first 5 min and 50 mL/min for the remaining time. The constant flux of 150 mL/min for drift gas was used. As a result, the 3D GC-IMS spectra were obtained. The spectra features include the drift time (Dt), retention time (Rt) and intensity (I), as it shown in Fig. 2. Dt (in milliseconds) is relative to the Reactive Ion Peak (RIP), representing the number of ions available to ionize analytes. Rt indicates the time VOCs to travel the GC column, and is expressed in seconds [14].

3.2 Data Analysis

Laboratory Analysis Viewer (LAV) software (version 2.2.1) was used to visually compare spectra and create area-sets for each relative intensity peack. Relative intensities within each area-set were exported for multivariate data analysis (MVA) analysis: Principal Component Analysis (PCA) using IBM SPSS Statistics software (version 23) and Partial Least Square Discriminant Analysis (PLSDA) (Fig. 1).

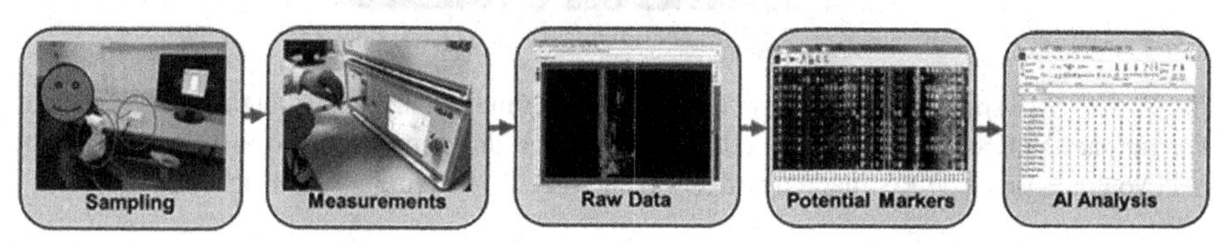

Fig. 1. Workflow of the processes applied throughout the study for breath differentiation. From left to right: breath sampling, measurements, spectra analysis, area-set definition, and AI analysis.

4 Results and Discussion

The analysis of esophageal and alveolar air samples (Fig. 2) revealed 31 and 33 GC-IMS spectral intensity peaks, respectively. A small group of intensity peaks were found to be subject specific (individual variability) while others showed relevant differentiation (regularly or not) for both types of exhaled air. The intensity of GC-IMS spectral peaks correspondent to ethanol (monomer and dimer) was significantly higher ($p < 0.05$) for esophageal air than for alveolar air.

Alveolar and esophageal air specific fingerprints spectra bring forward differences between the two types of air. Besides the fact that most VOCs are simultaneously present in both alveolar and esophageal airs, the pivotal divergences can be seen in compounds' intensity. In Fig. 2, four intensity peaks, are marked in both alveolar and esophageal spectra. Ethanol's monomer (left) and dimer (right) are marked with a solid yellow line, whereas both the red and blue dashed lines point to two still not identified compounds. Although being a very common compound in indoor and outdoor airs [1], ethanol shows a source-dependent behavior for breath samples, exhibited by significant variations in the intensities of the spectra for both types of air. For esophageal air, ethanol's characteristic peaks (solid yellow line) show higher intensity values than for alveolar air samples. This may be related to the influence of the (a) food ingestion path across the esophagus or (b) environmental air nearness. However, the two unidentified compounds exhibit an opposite behavior (higher in alveolar air) and, therefore, can be correlated with metabolic VOCs participating in gas lung exchanges also reflecting concentrations in blood [15].

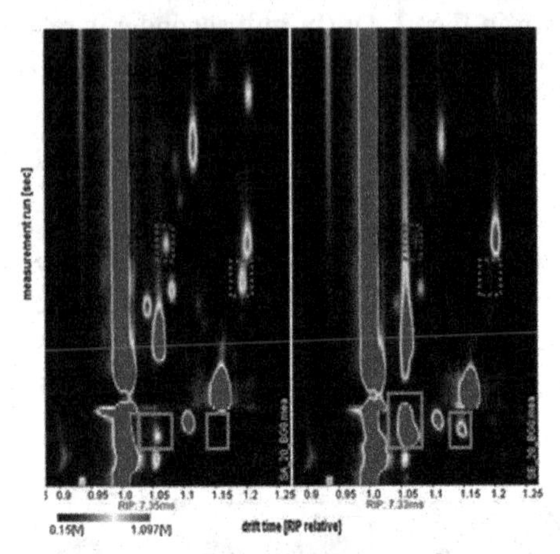

Fig. 2. GC-IMS spectra representative of alveolar (left) and esophageal (right) airs. Most visually discriminant VOCs are highlighted (ethanol (monomer and dimer) marked in yellow solid line and two unidentified VOCs marked with a red and blue dashed line). (Color figure online)

Although visual spectra comparison provides a qualitative assessment of the most concentrated compounds, proper statistical data analysis allows to perceive hidden (or not so visible) evidence and differentiate patterns for each sample type. The application of unsupervised PCA (Fig. 3), highlights the differences between the profile of alveolar (red points) and esophageal (blue points) air samples. Bi-dimensional representation of PC1 and PC3 displays higher visual differences between both clusters.

Principal Components (PC) exhibited 93.7% [PC1], 3.1% [PC2] and 1.1% [PC3] of the total explained variance of the data set for the observations of both types of exhaled air. Some esophageal measurements (53.3% of the esophageal cases) were clustered within the cohort of alveolar air samples that were more correctly grouped (only 6.5% of alveolar cases were wrongly clustered as esophageal). This result indicates the collection of a mixture of exhaled air types (usual phenomenon in breath sampling) that is thought to be caused either by: (a) the increased temperature of the prototype's solenoid valve and working failures posteriorly linked to an arrival to its functioning hysteresis region (hardware drawback); (b) individual variation of esophageal sphincter closure degree when breathing; (c) individual differences in respiratory physiology.

Measured VOCs spectra from exhaled air were also processed by another Multivariate Data Analysis, a Partial Least Square Discriminant Analysis (PLSDA). However, the results for alveolar and esophageal air differentiation obtained by PLSDA were less clear than by PCA ones, thus are not presented.

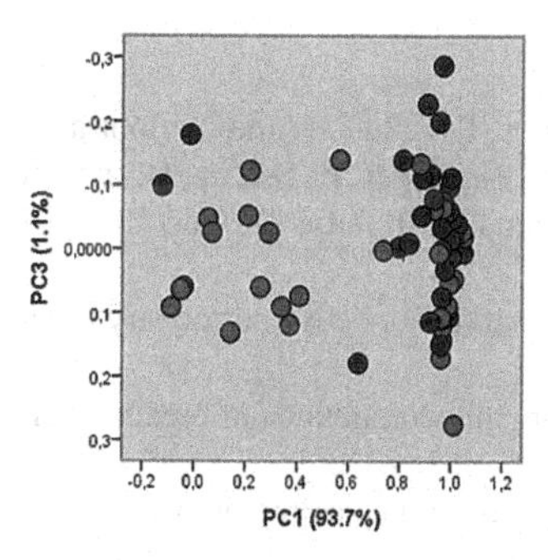

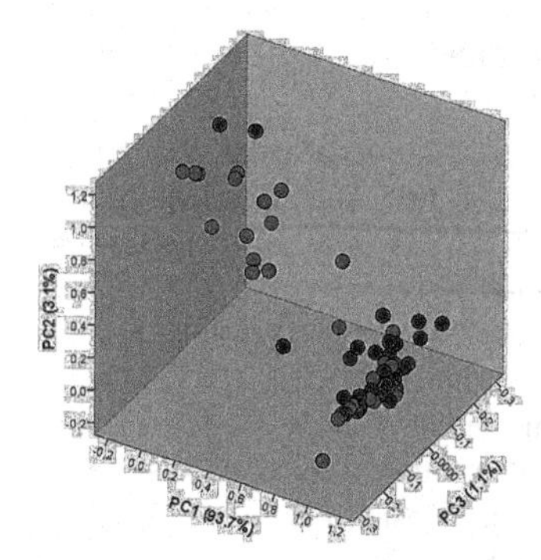

Fig. 3. Representation of alveolar (red) and esophageal (blue) air patterns after PCA (for 2 (left) and for the 3 (right) most relevant principal components - PC). Total variance is also included for each principal component (PC1, PC2 and PC3). (Color figure online)

5 Conclusions and Future Work

In this paper a novel AI-based technology for selectively sampling exhaled air according to subjects' characteristics (*i.e.*, age, gender, metabolic production of CO_2 and physiological state) was presented. Results obtained from breath measurements showed differentiation in exhaled air profiles related to breath source/origin. Two distinguishable VOC patterns were determined, and ethanol (monomer and dimer) was identified as one of the main characteristic compounds of esophageal exhaled air.

In this work, two multivariate classification tools were applied to identify better the unperceived variations between both types of exhaled air samples: Unsupervised Learning Procedure, PCA, and Supervised Learning Procedure, PLSDA. PCA comprised the most suitable approach to differentiate both exhaled air profiles so far, thus revealing the ability of our device to collect breath samples according to the respiratory source/origin. Furthermore, a deeper analysis resorting to alternative classification tools, such as t-SNE t-distributed Stochastic Neighbor Embedding, is planned to evaluate cluster separation.

Our breath sampler and its capability for breath differentiation through AI must be highlighted as the potential of application for clinical screening is increased for several diseases whose VOC biomarkers concentration depend on the source of air to sample. Therefore, the workflow process herein presented can be adopted, and widely used as it proves obvious advantages of implementing AI in breath sampling devices. Thus, this paper paves the way to implement this methodology for clinical purposes by improving the development of standard procedures for selective breath sampling.

Acknowledgments. The authors thank all volunteers for participating in the study. The work benefitted from the continuous support of the combined effort of NOVA School of Science and Technology and NMT, S.A. Partial support came from Fundação para a Ciência e Tecnologia (FCT, Portugal) through the PhD grant (PD/BDE/114550/2016).

References

1. Moura, P.C., Vassilenko, V., Fernandes, J.M., Santos, P.H.: Indoor and outdoor air profiling with GC-IMS. In: Camarinha-Matos, L.M., Farhadi, N., Lopes, F., Pereira, H. (eds.) DoCEIS 2020. IAICT, vol. 577, pp. 437–444. Springer, Cham (2020). https://doi.org/10.1007/978-3-030-45124-0_43
2. Phillips, M., et al.: Point-of-care breath test for biomarkers of active pulmonary tuberculosis. Tuberculosis **92**, 314–320 (2012)
3. Van Berkel, J.J.B.N., et al.: A profile of volatile organic compounds in breath discriminater COPD patients from controls. Respir. Med. **104**, 557–563 (2010)
4. de Lacy Costello, B., et al.: A review of the volatiles from the healthy human body. J. Breath Res. **8**, 014001 (2014)
5. Gonçalves, M., Fernandes, J., Fetter, V., Diniz, M., Vassilenko, V.: Novel methodology for quick detection of bacterial metabolites. In: 2019 IEEE 6th Portuguese Meeting on Bioengineering (ENBENG), Lisbon, Portugal (2019)
6. Conduto, C., Vassilenko, V.: Desenvolvimento do dispositivo para teste não-invasivo da infecção por bactéria H. pylory. Master thesis, NOVA University of Lisbon (2018)
7. Xu, M., Zhentao, T., Yixiang, D., Yong, L.: GC-based techniques for breath analysis: current status, challenges, and prospects. Crit. Rev. Anal. Chem. **46**, 291–304 (2016)
8. Phillips, M.: Method for the collection and assay of volatile organic compounds in breath. Anal. Biochem. **247**, 272–278 (1997)
9. Vassilenko, V., Santos, P.H.C.: System for controlled and selective sampling of exhaled air and corresponding operating procedure. WO/2018/047058 (2016)
10. Santos, P.H.C., Vassilenko, V., Vasconcelos, F., Gil, F.: Implementation of machine learning for breath collection. In : BIODEVICES 2017 - 10th International Conference on Biomedical Electronics and Devices, Proceedings; Part of 10th International Joint Conference on Biomedical Engineering Systems and Technologies, BIOSTEC 2017, Porto, Portugal, pp. 163–170 (2017)
11. Santos, P., Roth, P., Fernandes, J.M., Fetter, V., Vassilenko, V.: Real time mental stress detection through breath analysis. In: Camarinha-Matos, L.M., Farhadi, N., Lopes, F., Pereira, H. (eds.) DoCEIS 2020. IAICT, vol. 577, pp. 403–410. Springer, Cham (2020). https://doi.org/10.1007/978-3-030-45124-0_39
12. Phillips, M., et al.: Detection of an extended human volatome with comprehensive two-dimensional gas chromatography time-of-flight mass spectrometry. PLoS ONE **8**(9), e75274 (2013)
13. Kanu, A., Hill, H., Jr.: Ion mobility spectrometry detection for gas chromatography. J. Chromatogr. A **1177**, 12–27 (2008)
14. Fernandes, J.M., Vassilenko, V., Santos, P.H.: Algorithm for automatic peak detection and quantification for GC-IMS spectra. In: Camarinha-Matos, L.M., Farhadi, N., Lopes, F., Pereira, H. (eds.) DoCEIS 2020. IAICT, vol. 577, pp. 369–377. Springer, Cham (2020). https://doi.org/10.1007/978-3-030-45124-0_35
15. Wondka, D., Bhatnagar, A.: Selection, Segmentation and Analysis of Exhaled Air for Airway Disorders Assessment. US Patent WO/2015/143384 (2015)

Application of Machine Learning Methods to Raman Spectroscopy Technique in Dentistry

Iulian Otel[1,2](✉), J. M. Silveira[1,3], V. Vassilenko[1,2], A. Mata[1,3], and S. Pessanha[1,2]

[1] Laboratory of Instrumentation, Biomedical Engineering and Radiation Physics (LIBPhys-UNL), NOVA School of Science and Technology - NOVA University of Lisbon, 2829-516 Caparica, Portugal

[2] NOVA School of Science and Technology - NOVA University of Lisbon, 2825-149 Caparica, Portugal

[3] Faculty of Dental Medicine - University of Lisbon, 1649-003 Lisbon, Portugal

Abstract. Raman spectroscopy is nowadays regarded as a practical optical method and non-destructive photonic tool, which can be applied in several biomedical fields for analyzing the molecular composition. This technique is considered appropriate for human dental tissues characterization, from caries detection to evaluation of demineralization caused by acidic external agents. Discrimination techniques (linear regression), and classification techniques (neural networks) are often used for spectroscopic data analysis in disease detection and identification. Usually, Raman raw spectra obtained from teeth are **processed** using baseline correction, smoothing, **normalized** for noise, fluorescence, shot noise removal, and subsequently **analysed** using principal component analysis, to reduce the variable dimensionality. Raman chemical images can be constructed with another simple and uncomplicated unsupervised machine learning method – represented by k-means clustering, enabling the identification of similar areas/features, for classifying different acquired spectral data. The Machine Learning methods choice depends always on type and amount of information provided by Raman spectra. In this paper, was applied Principal Component Analysis methods to the analysis and interpretation of several parameters extracted from Raman spectra acquired before and after a simulated acid challenge of human enamel. These parameters and their correlation allow to assess the protective effect of a fluoride-based dental varnish.

1 Research Question and Its Motivation

Raman spectroscopy, an emerging technique based on the functioning principle of vibrational spectroscopy, is presently regarded as a viable, non-destructive and practical optical method for different biomedical applications, which is mainly employed for the analysis of molecular biochemical and structural composition. This method is becoming progressively relevant in scientific biomedical research especially for its main features, such as high biochemical and structural specificity, contactless, non-invasiveness, non-destructiveness, and extremely low water sensitivity, as well as the possibility to be employed in the near-infrared (NIR) region and remotely by using with fiber-optic

© IFIP International Federation for Information Processing 2021
Published by Springer Nature Switzerland AG 2021
L. M. Camarinha-Matos et al. (Eds.): DoCEIS 2021, IFIP AICT 626, pp. 339–348, 2021.
https://doi.org/10.1007/978-3-030-78288-7_33

probes and devices [1, 2]. When light arrives to an examined sample, a small part of it is scattered in several different directions. When these light photons are scattered from a certain molecule or existent crystal, the greatest part of all these photons is elastically dispersed. The largest part of the scattered photons is of the same frequency when compared to the incident photons. Nevertheless, a little fraction of light (which is approximately 1 in 10 million photons) is scattered at optical frequencies distinct, and typically lower, than the frequency of the incident photons. The process causing the described inelastic scatter is mainly known as the Raman scattering. And when a given sample, compound or mixture that is under examination is irradiated or illuminated by a monochromatic light source, such as laser, the obtained spectrum resulting from the scattered light involves a strong main line, called the exciting line, being of the same frequency as the incident light together with weaker lines on each side shifted from the main line [3–7]. A typical Raman spectroscopic measurement usually consists in directing a focused laser beam onto the sample and recording the energy profile of the light that is scattered [8–10]. Raman spectroscopy has shown repeatedly to be an appropriate method for the characterization of dental tissues, from caries detection to the evaluation of demineralization caused by acidic external agents [1, 2, 11]. The sensitivity of this technique for alterations in the symmetric stretching band that is characteristic for the phosphate ions in hydroxyapatite matrix can be used as a powerful tool for early diagnostics, even before signs of demineralization are detected by conventional methods [8, 9]. Human dental enamel represents the highest mineralized, as well as the toughest and hardest tissue in the human body. Its main function consists in covering and protecting

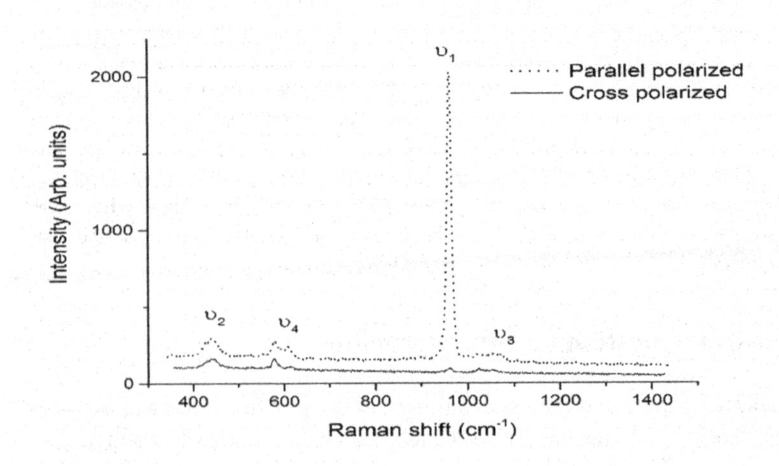

Fig. 1. Representation of two distinct Raman spectra, obtained with parallel and orthogonal polarized configurations of the used spectrometer, acquired from dental sound enamel. Raman peaks ν_2 at approximately 430 cm^{-1}, and ν_4 at 590 cm^{-1}, attributed to PO_4^{-3} groups in symmetric and asymmetric bending vibrations, respectively. Peak ν_1 is assigned to symmetric stretching band of phosphate at ~959 cm^{-1}, while ν_3 corresponds to a band with two distinct peaks at 1042 and 1070 cm^{-1} which is specific for PO_4^{-3} groups in the asymmetric stretching vibration of surface enamel's hydroxyapatite.

the anatomic crown of the tooth. It resists to chewing forces and protects the internal layers, dentin, and pulp [3, 4, 11]. The information and evidence on the tooth's enamel crystalline state is provided by the determining the depolarization ratio (DR) of the *v1* symmetric stretching band of phosphate (located approximately at 959 cm^{-1} wavenumber), while the determination of the DR of phosphate characteristic band is achieved by acquiring and comparing two distinct Raman measurements (Fig. 1) of the same spectral region. These measures are usually obtained with parallel and cross-polarized (orthogonal) configurations of the employed spectrometer [1, 2, 5, 11, 12].

A machine learning (ML) model that combines principal component analysis (PCA) as well as support vector machine (SVM) optimized algorithms can be successfully implemented for an enhanced distinction and classification of spectral data, especially to detect and identify specific characteristics. Raman chemical images can be constructed by using another simple and unsophisticated, however useful unsupervised machine learning algorithm method, known as k-means clustering, that enables the identification of similar areas with the same features, to classify the acquired spectral data based on several Raman peak intensity ratios. The choice of ML methods to apply depends always on the type and amount of information contained in the Raman spectra [5].

2 Raman Spectroscopy Combined with PCA Method

In the last decades, the potential and usefulness of using multivariate techniques (indicated in Fig. 2) for spectroscopic data analysis in disease detection, identification, comparison, as well as classification, has been successfully explored, providing very good results [1–5, 8, 11, 12]. All existent multivariate classification techniques can be mainly separated into unsupervised methods and supervised learning procedures. Data compression method such as principal component analysis (PCA) is often employed to contribute for variability in the investigated data. PCA, considered a projection method, is a preprocessing statistical procedure that transforms several correlated variables into a lesser number of variables that are uncorrelated (called principal components) that still contains most of the information of the primary larger set. Consequently, analysis methods, for instance, hierarchical cluster analysis (HCA), linear discriminant analysis (LDA) and other types, have also been frequently used to create classification algorithms for normal healthy condition and disease differentiation [6, 9]. Machine learning (ML) can include multivariate methods, which encompass several multivariate classification methods (also known as pattern recognition techniques) and multivariate regression. In unsupervised pattern recognition techniques, for example, PCA and cluster analysis (CA), there is not required any prior knowledge about the training set samples (in this case, represented by the acquired Raman spectra). Both referred statistical analysis methods are frequently applied to consider differences and/or similarities between spectra or image areas with the same features. Alternatively, supervised pattern recognition techniques, for instance, artificial neural networks (ANNS) and LDA necessitate minimal previous information from preceding experiences, for instance, undeniably detecting and identifying examined samples from disease or differentiating samples from healthy normal cases. In this manner, supervised learning methods are resulting in a more precise and accurate identification and classification, while unsupervised methods are considered more useful for investigative studies and exploratory analysis of data [9]. Generally, statistical methods applied to spectroscopic techniques, such as PCA, are based on the analysis of an entire given spectrum (comprising characteristic bands known as fingerprints) that is under examination. However, this approach does not provide valuable interpretations or explanations into the origins of the detected/identified changes. Additionally, statistical analysis methods usually presume a linear relationship between the components belonging to a certain Raman spectrum. Therefore, an adequate selection of quantitative information about the source of the Raman specific spectral peak data can be often problematic because due to the disorganized or, sometimes, unclear tissue type identification/classification or interference/overlay between different classes or varieties of spectroscopic characteristics (such as fluorescence, scattering, and absorption effects). Consequently, there is a tremendous need for developing quantitative models and quantifiable approaches that consider the investigated optical, structural, and biochemical properties of the examined tissue [6, 9].

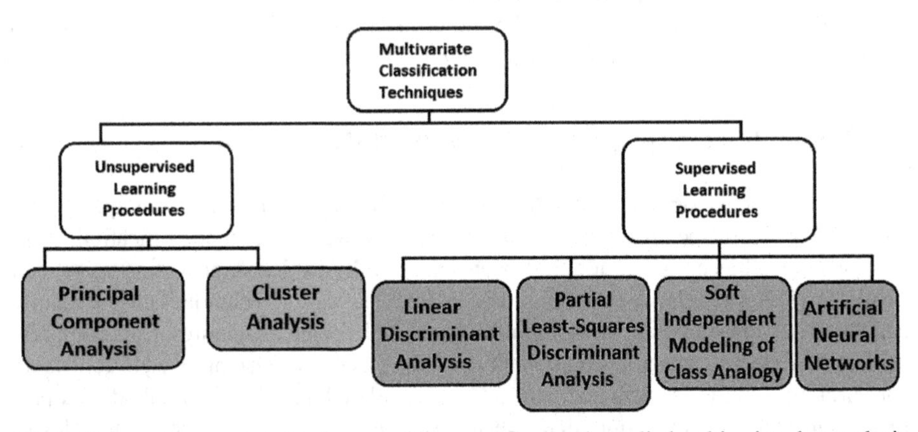

Fig. 2. Schematic representation for some of the most frequently applied multivariate data analysis (MVA) methods to spectroscopic techniques and spectral data processing and analysis [6].

So far, the principal component analysis method represents the unsupervised multivariate statistical tool most extensively used, which is widely applied especially when vast spectral data must be transformed into a smaller number of independent variations known as principal components (PCs), while contributions of these components are known as scores, which are extensively used as parameters for classification. PCA algorithms are frequently applied directly to collected (Raman) spectra within a certain data set to reduce the original dimensionality into a linear combination of orthogonal basis spectra known as principal components (PCs), resulting afterwards in derived loading plots represented as plots of first three PCs as function of the wave number. Generally, the first PC is the most important and accounts for the spectral features with highest variation, while subsequent secondary and tertiary PCs represent features with progressively lower variance. PCA method is typically used to characterize and distinguish the Raman spectra of a specific "calibration set" of samples that contain at least two distinct features/chemical components, as determined by pathology under study. As already described, in the case of Raman measurements, PCs represent an orthogonal set of spectral data (with varying spectral parameters), a linear numerical combination of which can accurately provide valuable insights on each of the existent spectra in the sample set. By correlating the mentioned fitting coefficients "scores" of the analyzed spectra in the data set with their established classifications, an accurate diagnostic algorithm can be easily obtained. However, its main disadvantage lies on the fact that PCs are pure mathematical concepts, without any direct physical significance or meaning [6, 9].

3 State of the Art - MVA Applied to Raman Spectral Data Acquired from Dental Samples

According to several previous research studies [3–5, 11–22], Raman spectroscopy can be employed to obtain precise results, showing a very good sensitivity and specificity. When this spectroscopic technique is used in combination with PCA [12, 15–19, 21] or other MVA [9, 18–21] methods, it allows us to obtain unique spectral characteristics extracted from raw acquired spectra, which can be used for identification of similar areas, specific features, or certain types of samples, along with differentiation and classification of different sample or tissue condition, according to the case. Gonzalez-Solis et al. [15] demonstrated that Raman spectroscopic technique and PCA method can be used simultaneously to discriminate healthy tooth with sound enamel from severe dental fluorosis samples with high levels of sensitivity and specificity. Furthermore, the Raman data of affected enamel by fluorosis "allowed to identify the molecule of calcium fluoride and the vibrational modes of phosphate and carbonate ions" [15]. Another research group – Barrera – Ortega [16] performed a study showing also that Raman-PCA combination can be used to differentiate sound from demineralized enamel, as well as identify and assess enamel remineralization level by using different fluoride solutions. The authors stated that Raman-PCA technique represent "an excellent non-invasive method to demonstrate qualitatively the early detection and monitoring of incipient lesions due to caries". In a study performed by Mihaly et al. [17] FT-Raman spectroscopy-PCA methods were also used for the analysis of enamel surfaces of healthy unaffected, affected (cavitated), and highly affected tooth samples. This work revealed the existence of a susceptibility and tendency in teeth to caries that can be directly correlated with the structural/compositional enamel alterations that occur mainly in the principal c-axis of hydroxyapatite crystals. Thus, MVA unsupervised methods, such as PCA, applied to Raman technique have a great utility for data analysis in several relevant fields of dentistry diagnostics and research, as follows: (1) early detection and recognition of carious lesions; (2) identification and differentiation between normal and affected samples (by tooth decay, hypo-mineralization, fluorosis, Amelogenesis Imperfecta); (3) bleaching products performance; (4) assessment of dental pharmaceutical products; (5) demineralizing attack from acidic challenges, foods, and beverages; (6) proteomic differences between different types of human teeth; (7) remineralization agents and other related treatments. Raman raw spectra obtained from dental samples are usually processed by carrying out initially a baseline correction, smoothing, and normalization for noise, fluorescence, and/or shot noise removal, and then analysed using PCA, to reduce the variable dimensionality, to facilitate and simplify the data processing and differentiation [12]. The

Raman spectral changes are mainly due to demineralization-induced and decay alterations of enamel crystallite morphology, structure, and orientation. Any small change in the enamel tissue that is produced by caries could end in a higher value of depolarization ratio of ν_1 symmetric stretch band, while the other bands of regions ν_3, ν_2 and ν_4 do not show significant alterations [3, 21].

4 Research Contribution and Innovation - Evaluation of Protective Effect of Dental Varnish using Raman Microscopy and PCA Approach

4.1 Dental Samples

Two experimental groups of human dental enamel samples, control (C) and treatment (T), each containing 10 tooth samples, were subjected to an acid challenge, in order to test the erosion effect of the acid on the enamel. Previously to the acid attack, the T group was cleaned with Couto toothpaste and treated with a commercial dental fluorinated varnish - VOCO Profluoride, while group C was only cleaned with Couto toothpaste.

4.2 Research Design and Methodology

Both sets of samples were analysed using Raman during three distinct stages: 1 - before any treatment, 2 - after application of dental varnish and/or toothpaste and 3 – after acid challenge. Raman spectra were acquired using a Horiba XploRA Raman Confocal Microscope employing a NIR laser diode source operating at a wavelength of 785 nm, using a 1200 lines/mm grating, with a spectral range between 300 cm^{-1} and 1800 cm^{-1}, resulting in a spectral resolution of 4 cm^{-1}. An entrance slit of 200 μm together with a confocal hole of 300 μm were used to disperse the scattered radiation collected by an 100x objective (N. A. = 0.9) onto the air-cooled CCD array of an Andor iDus detector. It was also employed a 50% neutral density filter resulting in an incident power on the dental sample of 5.0 ± 0.4 mW (lasercheck®, Edmund optics). For each enamel specimen, an average of 20 measurements (10 different points with parallel polarization, always followed by other 10 with orthogonal polarization) were performed, with an exposure time for each measurement of 20 s with 4 accumulations. The following parameters were obtained and compared in each step of the study: depolarization ratio (DR), anisotropy, band position and full width at half maximum (FWHM) of the symmetric stretching band of phosphate (~959 cm^{-1}), according to Pessanha et al. [22]. PCA was performed using the mean values of all spectral parameters for each sample.

4.3 Results and Discussion

In this work, the first three principal components were extracted from the spectral parameters of all enamel samples and were used to identify, distinguish, and categorize two small clusters: control and varnish treated sample groups (Fig. 3) and to show likewise the correlation degree between these 4 different peak spectral features, namely the depolarization ratio, anisotropy, peak position, and FWHM, which yield useful structural

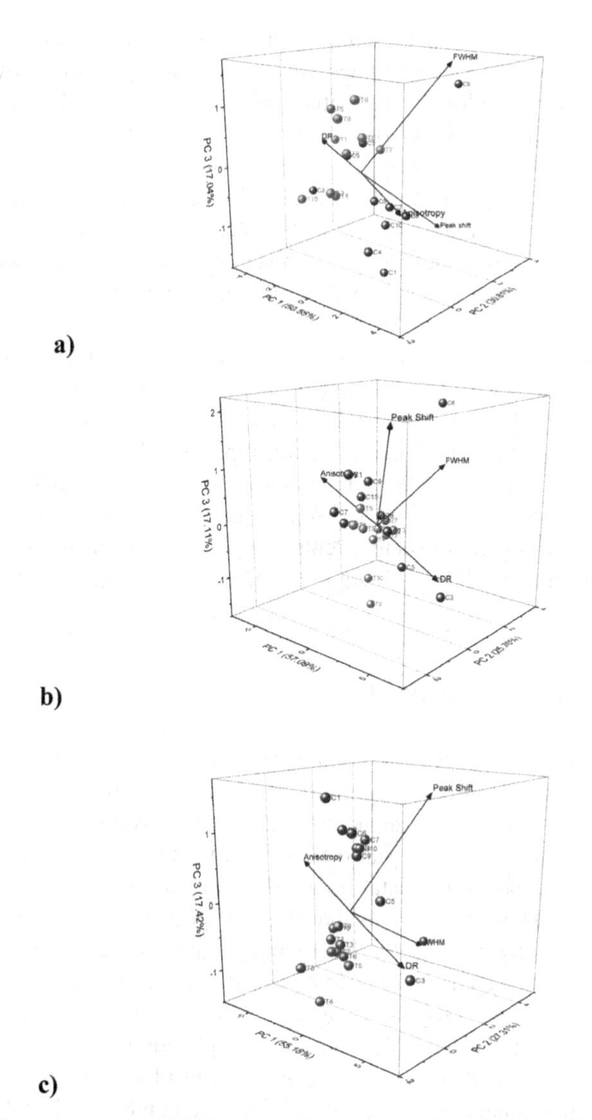

Fig. 3. 3D representation of PCA-correlation scatter biplots of analysed Raman parameter vectors (blue) and differentiation between examined control (black) and dental varnish treated (green) sample groups, corresponding to the following study phases: **a)** 1st – before any treatment; **b)** 2nd – after dental products application; **c)** 3rd – after acid exposure. (Color figure online)

and chemical information. PC1 scores account for the majority of variance within all analysed data sets, with proportions of 50.55%, 57.09%, and 55.18% for 1st, 2nd, and 3rd treatment stage, respectively. As can be seen in Fig. 3, after 1st treatment stage the samples are randomly dispersed, revealing that there is no significant difference between the samples' overall condition within and between groups initially. After the 2nd stage, the treated samples tend to form a group in the centre, starting to separate from control samples that continue dispersed. After the 3rd stage, there is a clear separation between the two groups, with the treated samples getting spatially very close to each other, indicating that most of the varnish treated samples (8 out of 10) share almost the same biochemical characteristics, mineral content, and structural arrangement after undergoing the treatment and acid challenges, remaining equally affected. The key meaning of these biplots representing the sample distribution is that all analysed spectral parameters, especially band position and DR, are strongly influenced by the chemical environment, which has a great impact on hydroxyapatite chemical bonds, and inter- and intramolecular forces of outer enamel layers.

The exposed results show that PCA can distinguish and separate two different sample groups, according to the main three PC scores extracted from spectral parameter analysis, with the 1st PC score accounting the most. In this study, were chosen the first three most representative components since their summed scores represent all together the greatest majority, varying between 98% and 99,9%, maintaining the most important information at a significant level. The exposed results confirm that the combination of Raman-PCA methods has a strong capability to early detect dental incipient caries, and to monitor their evolution by performing an overall assessment of the demineralization/remineralization processes.

5 Conclusions and Further Work

The results obtained during this study show that after erosive acidic procedure, all dental enamel samples were strongly affected by the demineralization erosive process. The mineral loss was more obvious in the samples from the control group, meaning that the acid attack has a greater impact on the samples washed/treated only with toothpaste, opposite to the treated samples with dental fluorinated varnish (with surface adherent remineralizing capacity). This study proves that Raman spectroscopy technique combined with PCA have a strong potential to differentiate healthy sound enamel samples from demineralized ones, as well as control from treated samples with good sensitivity and specificity levels. Raman-PCA technique can be certainly employed to monitor evolution of dental samples during different dental product application and acid challenges, providing objective, precise, real-time, accurate and fast results, significantly diminishing the subjectivity to human error. In future research the number of dental samples should be increased for a higher statistical significance. Moreover, PCA method could be applied directly to acquired Raman spectra to improve the extraction of the parameters to be evaluated. This way, a more precise examination of enamel de- and remineralization processes could be obtained.

Acknowledgements. The present research study is included in I4H Doctoral Program and financially supported by the Foundation of Science and Technology, identified with the Research Grant PD/BDE/143107/2018. Authors would also like to mention the contribution of the following professors: M. L. Carvalho and J. P. Santos.

References

1. Ko, A.C.-T., Hewko, M., Sowa, M.G., Dong, C.S., Cleghorn, B., Choo-Smith, L.: Early dental caries detection using a fibre-optic coupled polarization-resolved raman spectroscopic system. Opt. Express **16**(9), 6274–6284 (2008)
2. Vargas-Koudriavtsev, T., et al.: Effect of tooth-bleaching agents on phosphate concentration in dental enamel by means of Raman spectroscopy. Rev. Odontol. Mex. **19**(4), 228–235 (2015)
3. Ramakrishnaiah, R., et al.: Applications of raman spectroscopy in dentistry: analysis of tooth structure. Appl. Spectrosc. Rev. **50**(4), 332–350 (2015)
4. Buchwald, T., Okulus, Z., Szybowicz, M.: Raman spectroscopy as a tool of early dental caries detection–new insights. J. Raman Spectrosc. **48**(8), 1094–1102 (2017)
5. Lussier, F., Thibault, V., Charron, B., Wallace, G.Q., Masson, J.-F.: Deep learning and artificial intelligence methods for Raman and surface-enhanced Raman scattering. TrAC Trends Anal. Chem. **124**, 115796 (2020)
6. Nunes, A., Magalhaes, S.: Raman spectroscopy applied to health sciences. IntechOpen **13**, 275–291 (2018)
7. Vandenabeele, P.: Practical Raman Spectroscopy – An Introduction, John Wiley & Sons, Ltd, New Jersey. Raman spectroscopy–Study and teaching (2013). ISBN 978-0-470-68319-4
8. Ferraro, J.R., Nakamoto, K., Brown, C.W.: Introductory Raman Spectroscopy. Elsevier, Amsterdam. Second Edition (2003). ISBN: 978-0-12-254105-6
9. Vo-Dinh, T.: Biomedical Photonics Handbook. CRC Press, Boca Raton (2003)
10. Matousek, P., Morris, M.: Emerging Raman Applications and Techniques in Biomedical and Pharmaceutical Fields (2010)
11. Monteiro, M., Chasqueira, F., Pessanha, S.: Raman spectroscopy in the characterisation of carious dental tissues. Spectrosc. Eur. **30**(3), 11–14 (2018)
12. Kekkonen, J., Finnila, M.A.J., Heikkila, J., Anttonen, V., Nissinen, I.: Chemical imaging of human teeth by a time-resolved Raman spectrometer based on a CMOS single-photon avalanche diode line sensor. Analyst **144**, 6089 (2019)
13. Akkus, A., Akkus, O., Roperto, R., Lang, L.: Investigation of intra-and inter-individual, variations of mineralisation in healthy permanent human enamel by Raman spectroscopy. Oral Health Preventative Dent. **14**(4), 321–327 (2016)
14. Castro, J., Godinho, J., Mata, A., Silveira, J.M., Pessanha, S.: Study of the effects of unsupervised over-the counter whitening products on dental enamel using μ-Raman and μ-EDXRF spectroscopies. J. Raman Spectrosc. **47**(4), 444–448 (2015)
15. Gonzalez-Solis, J.L., Martinez-Cano, E., Magana-Lopez, Y.: Early detection of dental fluorosis using Raman spectroscopy and principal component analysis (2014)
16. Barrera-Ortega, C.C., Vazquez-Olmos, A.R., Sato-Berru, R.Y., Araiza-Tellez, M.A.: Study of demineralized dental enamel treated with different fluorinated compounds by Raman spectroscopy. J. Biomed. Phys. Eng. **10**(5), 635–644 (2020)
17. Mihály, J., Gombás, V., Afishah, A., Mink, J.: FT-Raman investigation of human dental enamel surfaces. J. Raman Spectrosc. Int. J. Original Work Aspects Raman Spectrosc. Including High. Order Process. Brillouin Rayleigh Scattering **40**(8), 898–902 (2009)
18. Bērziņš, K., Sutton, J.J., Loch, C., et al.: Application of low-wavenumber Raman spectroscopy to the analysis of human teeth. J. Raman Spectrosc. **50**(10), 1–13 (2019)
19. Sharma, V., et al.: Mapping the inorganic and proteomic differences among different types of human teeth: a preliminary compositional insight. Biomolecules **10**(11), 1540 (2020)
20. Das Gupta, S., et al.: Mineralization of dental tissues and caries lesions detailed with Raman microspectroscopic imaging. Analyst **146**(4), 1705–1713 (2021)

21. Natarajan, A.K., Fraser, S.J., Swain, M.V., Drummond, B.K., Gordon, K.C.: Raman spectroscopic characterisation of resin-infiltrated hypomineralised enamel. Anal. Bioanal. Chem. **407**(19), 5661–5671 (2015)
22. Pessanha, S., et al.: Evaluation of the effect of fluorinated tooth bleaching products using polarized Raman microscopy and particle induced gamma-ray emission. Spectrochim. Acta Part A: Biomol. Spectrosc. **236**, 118378 (2020)

Gas Chromatography-Ion Mobility Spectrometry Instrument for Medical Applications: A Calibration Protocol for ppb and ppt Concentration Range

Jorge M. Fernandes[1,2](✉), Valentina Vassilenko[1,2], Pedro C. Moura[1], and Viktor Fetter[3]

[1] Laboratory of Instrumentation, Biomedical Engineering and Radiation Physics (LIBPhys-UNL), Department of Physics, NOVA School of Science and Technology, NOVA University of Lisbon, 2829-516 Caparica, Portugal
j.manuel@campus.fct.unl.pt
[2] NMT, S.A., Edifício Madan Parque, Rua dos Inventores, 2825-182 Caparica, Portugal
[3] Airbus Defence and Space GmbH - Space Systems, Department of TESXS Science Engineering, 88046 Friedrichshafen, Germany

Abstract. Medical diagnosis research is driven into the development of non-invasive diagnosis devices centered in fast and precise analytical tools and instrumentation. This led to Volatile Organic Compounds (VOCs) being identified as metabolomics biomarkers for several diseases, including respiratory infections, cancer and even COVID 19 non-invasive test. While VOCs give a direct access to physiological states, their applicability requires detections at low concentration ranges (ppb_V-ppt_V). However, its clinical success is strongly dependent on precise and robust calibration methods. In this work we describe a calibration protocol of volatile organic compounds in low concentration range (ppbv-pptv) for analytical GC-IMS technology which offer a quick in-situ results in medical diagnosis. The calibration is based on permeation tubes which are monitored using thermogravimetric methods to estimate mass loss ratio over time establishing emitted concentrations. Notwithstanding future improvements, herein calibration methodology results are a promising step forward in medical diagnosis and applications.

Keywords: Metabolomics · Volatile organic compounds · Medical diagnosis · Analytical techniques · Calibration · Automated systems · Artificial intelligence

1 Introduction

Modern medicine relies on innovative technology breakthroughs that enable to identify different diseases and physiological states rapidly, accurately, and effortlessly. Thus, research appears to be shifting its route towards techniques that permit rapid analysis of biological samples at low-cost, with reliable results and, mainly, non-invasively.

© IFIP International Federation for Information Processing 2021
Published by Springer Nature Switzerland AG 2021
L. M. Camarinha-Matos et al. (Eds.): DoCEIS 2021, IFIP AICT 626, pp. 349–357, 2021.
https://doi.org/10.1007/978-3-030-78288-7_34

Consequently, systems of identification and quantification of compounds described as pathological biomarkers are increasingly desired.

Ion Mobility Spectrometry (IMS) has been asserting itself as one of the most promising and adequate analytical technologies to fulfil the contemporary necessities of medicine [1]. The excellent reputation IMS has been gaining in latest years is due to its extraordinary detection limits of volatile organic compounds (VOC), specifically, in low ppb_V (parts per billion by volume) or ng/l (nanograms per litre) of concentration ranges or even in ppt_V (parts per trillion by volume) or pg/l (picograms per litre) [2]. Similarly, its analytical flexibility, real-time monitoring and low-cost, as well as, its high selectivity and sensitivity when coupled with Gas Chromatography (GC) technique, contribute to affirm GC-IMS as one of the most important and useful portable analytical instrumentation for health applications [3, 4]. GC-IMS operates by creating ions from any volatile organic compound generally ionised by a Tritium radiation source, which pass through the IMS drift tube due to a weak but homogenous electric field after having been pre-separated inside a chromatographic column [5, 6]. A more detailed description of the IMS principle is given elsewhere [7].

IMS outstanding sensitivity combining with its selectivity and ability to deliver results promptly facilitates the rapid characterization of biological samples and detection of biomarkers [8]. A biomarker is an indicator of, not only, physiological states, but also, pathological conditions. The blood stream has dozens of distinct volatile organic compounds resulting from these endogenous activities and once emitted, analysed, and identified, they represent a non-invasive, rapid, painless, and economic door to human being's health assessment [9, 10]. The emission can occur via skin [11], fluids, and even exhaled breath [12]. A considerable number of diseases was already been correlated to specific biomarkers, and they belong to an extensive spectrum that includes conditions, such as, smoking-habits identification [13], asthma and diabetes [14], and even concerning conditions like lung or breast cancer [15]. Nevertheless, endogenous volatile compounds can still function as a biomarker for unnormal situations accordingly with their concentrations (low ppb_V). Even if a compound is frequently found in a regular basis, its distinct concentration from ordinary levels, may indicate physiological alterations or abnormality. Hence, not solely identification, but also VOC quantification have an extreme relevance in defining a biomarker, however, scientific research for precise VOC quantification and efficient calibration method are scarce and often incomplete. Therefore, developing an efficient and precise calibration method for GC-IMS calibration would be a big step for both IMS and medical diagnosis.

Herein we propose a calibration methodology of a GC-IMS devices based on permeation tubes to generate low VOC concentrations (ppb_V) by a thermogravimetric approach. The generation of gas standards from pure substances requires the creation of precise and repeatable concentrations and many methods have been developed for gas generation, which are divided into two categories: static and dynamic [16–18]. Static methods include gravimetric, partial pressure and volumetric approaches, and flexible, single and multiple rigid chamber, whilst dynamic methods include six types: injection, permeation, diffusion, evaporation, electrolytic and chemical [16, 17].

Permeation tubes are a dynamic method with an advantage over other diffusive and static techniques, they can generate low concentrations more stable over time. The basic design of a permeation tube or source is a liquid or gas-filled tube of PTFE or other semi-inert permeable material which is temperature-controlled (Fig. 1) [18]. Inside a permeation tube, a chemical can permeates through its walls at a constant rate for a given temperature; then its vapor mixes and is carried by a diluent, or a make-up flow into an analyser [16–18].

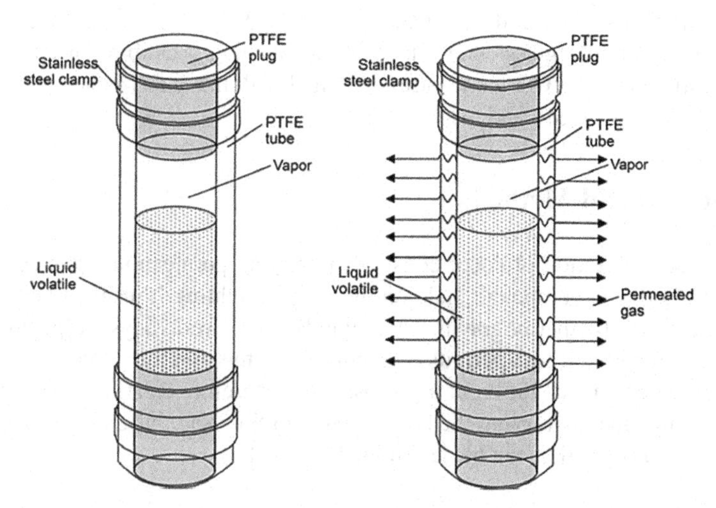

Fig. 1. A generalize schematic of permeation tubes including its components [18].

2 Relationship to Applied Artificial Intelligence Systems

The calibration protocol presented here combined with a previously published work on the development of an algorithm for automatic peak detection and quantification of GC-IMS Spectra, establishes a project to develop an automated tool for qualitative and quantitative identification of VOCs in low concentration (ppb_V/ppt_V) [7]. Such tools aim to improve the applications and results from GC-IMS analysis in air quality, space exploration and human health. As such, it is crucial to develop and implement an intelligent algorithm alongside with the GC-IMS technology, which is capable of identify and, more importantly, assess the concentration levels of organic compounds.

Our development of a precise and effective calibration protocol not only improves the current position of IMS calibration methodologies but is also, the next phase in the development and improvement of our previously mentioned algorithm. This algorithm was qualified to identify and quantify VOC compound signals in GC-IMS spectra. However, it lacked the ability to establish its relationship with a concentration value, which is crucial for some clinical applications. With the development of a calibration protocol this issue can be addressed and solved, therefore, improving the algorithm and enable it to evaluate potential risks by its own means. This relies not only on our calibration protocol already established but also on a large and diversified dataset of samples and a big compound library which are currently both currently being built.

Using neuronal networks, the current algorithm abilities can be enhanced in relation to compound identification, risk assessment and in establishing disease biomarkers. Also, several IMS data processing methods, as denoising (e.g., wavelets), scaling (min-max scaling), baseline correction, supervised (e.g., genetic algorithm) or unsupervised analysis, such as Principal component analysis (PCA) or cluster analysis, can benefit from machine learning and artificial intelligence implementation. Moreover, machine learning can improve collected information from GC-IMS data, as well as the modulated linear or logarithmic regression involved in establishing a calibration curve and the resulting estimation of VOCs concentration, which will inevitably benefit both medical instruments related to IMS and medical diagnosis.

3 Materials and Methods

Our proposed calibration protocol consists in creating permeation tubes containing a pure volatile organic compound and continuously weighting it inside a hoven at constant temperatures by thermogravimetry methods over several days. Adjusting a linear regression to tube mass loss permits to estimate an emission rate from its slope. Each temperature will generate different mass loss ratios therefore creating different concentration by simultaneous varying the hoven make-up flow and thus, after applying Eq. 1 the pure gas concentration can be determined [16, 19].

$$C = \left(q_d \times {}^{22.4}/_{M}\right)/Q \tag{1}$$

In Eq. 1, C is the concentration in ppm, q_d the permeation ration ng/min, M the compound's molecular weight in g/mol, and Q the flow ratio in mL/min.

3.1 Instrumentation and Selected Compound

A BreathSpec® device from GAS Dortmund was used for the developed calibration method. This instrumentation consists of an Ion Mobility spectrometer coupled with Gas Chromatography (GC-IMS) which used an MXT-200 column, of 30 m length and 0,53 mm internal diameter coated with a 1 μm thickness mid-polar stationary phase of trifluoropropylmethyl polysiloxane. Whereas this IMS instrumentation uses a Tritium, 3H (β-radiation: 300 MBq) ionisation source, a drift tube length of 98 mm with a 5-kV switchable polarity and an electric filed strength of 500 V/cm. Purified air was used as a carrier and drift gas which was filtered by a device coupled with the GC-IMS, named Circular Gas Flow Unit (CGFU) from GAS Dortmund.

A LABSYS evo TGA 1150® device from Setaram instrumentation was employed for thermogravimetric analysis of four permeation tubes, which has a temperature range from room temperature to 1150 °C, a weighing precision of 0.01% with a resolution of 0.2 μg; 0.02 μg and uses purified air as its flow gas.

The selected compound was 2-hexanone, purchased from Sigma-Aldrich with + 99% purity and utilized to assemble four permeation tubes generating several standard gas concentrations.

3.2 Calibration Systems and Procedure

Four permeation tubes were made by depositing 0.2 mL of 2-hexanone in a ¼" PTFE tubing with a length of 2 cm. Tube extremities were sealed with 5 mm PTFE end caps of 0.5 cm length which were lock in place with 0.5 cm length mild steel end crimps pressed by a crimping vise (Fig. 1). Tube effective length, or the distance between the two interior end plug surfaces, was 1 cm. Materials for the permeation tube were fabricated by Owlstone Inc. and are available as a Permeation Tube Manufacturing Kit.

The calibration systems were comprised of a CGFU couple with GC-IMS connected in its sample inlet to the TGA device by a Teflon tube of approximately 40 centimetres. The CGFU was responsible for purifying the drift and carrier gas into the GC-IMS. The GC-IMS is a gas analyser and the device to be calibrated. Whilst the TGA device provided accurate mass loss ratio from the permeation tubes, temperature control and flow into the sample inlet. Temperature values used for creating accurate concentration were 40, 60 and 85 °C and the flow values included 25, 50, 100, 150 and 200 mL/min. Measurements were taken each 15 min after a stable mass loss ratio was achieved, and for each concentration value 5 replicates were made, while each gas flow change was interspersed by 15 min before any measurement was performed.

4 Results and Discussion

Several conditions and parameters were examined and analyzed leading to the creation of a calibration protocol and characterization of a calibration curve (Fig. 2). Our proposed calibration protocol is defined by three main phases: (i) permeation tube construction and filling; (ii) estimating emission rate of the permeation tube by thermogravimetry analysis; (iii) generating several concentrations from each tube emission by changing flow rate. In phase one, during the construction of the tube, it was important to keep their dimensions as similar as possible and strongly crimping their extremities to avoid any liquid leakage.

Once constructed and filled, the tubes were left to stabilize for 24 h. Afterwards a tube was placed inside the TGA device's hoven and set at a desired temperature for approximately 5 days, considering the amount permeating a tube is relative to the compound inside it and the hoven temperature. The thermogravimetric device would control temperature and weigh constantly the tube's mass, producing a decreasing graphic with a linear behavior. When a stable emission was achieved a linear regression was adjusted to this graph estimating its slope. Afterwards, GC-IM measurements were analyzed, calculating an intensity value for 2-hexanone from its two occurring peaks. Finally, a plot was constructed with concentrations and respective intensities to which a logarithmic function was adjusted. Hence, results provided an expression to determine peak intensity from concentration values, known as a calibration curve (Fig. 2).

Table 1 shows concentration, values mean intensities and standard deviations used to develop our presented calibration curve (Fig. 2). Generally low standard deviations were observed from measurements indicating an elevated stability and reputability from the GC-IMS. The lowest concentration created was 46 ppb, however when estimating the GC-IMS limit of detection (LOD), a value of 26 ppb was observed.

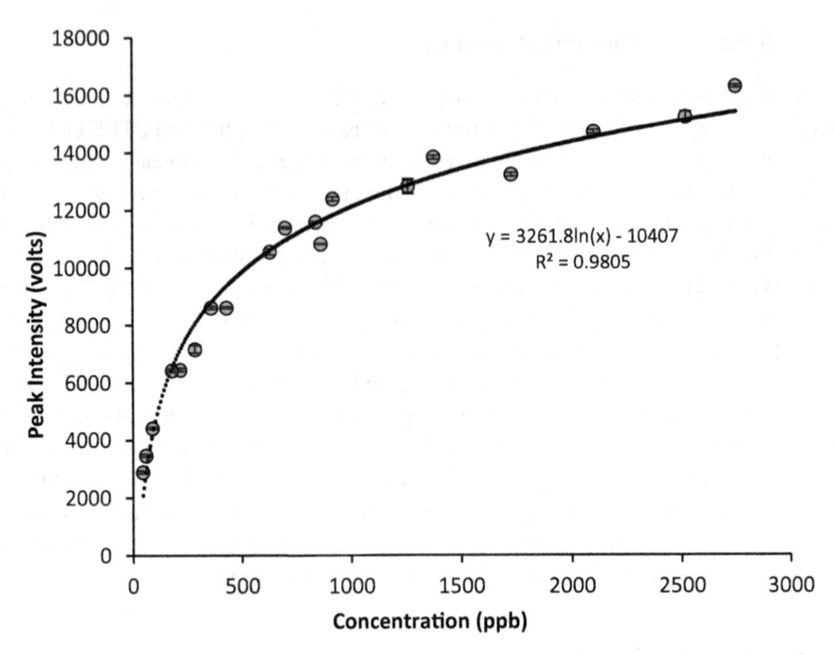

Fig. 2. Logarithmic regression for peak intensity (volts) per concentration (ppb).

Table 1. Intensity and standard deviations of four permeation tubes and estimated concentration

Concentration [ppb]	Mean intensity (volts)	Standard deviation
Permeation tube 1	–	–
2753	16309,60	47,94
1376	13840,21	70,28
918	12403,41	70,42
702	11394,99	33,99
Permeation tube 2	–	–
1727	13241,45	69,39
864	10837,40	21,90
432	8611,60	28,27
288	7168,54	133,17
220	6458,79	58,55
Permeation tube 3	–	–
2521	15247,31	177,88
2101	14727,63	67,01

(*continued*)

Table 1. (*continued*)

Concentration [ppb]	Mean intensity (volts)	Standard deviation
1260	12832,12	250,80
840	11598,73	18,36
630	10557,16	107,10
Permeation tube 4	–	–
362	8607,41	46,32
181	6428,60	48,64
91	4424,19	45,90
60	3473,57	47,66
46	2888,47	49,69

Emission rates from tube 1, 2, and 3 are 615, 193, 564 and 126 ng/min respectively and the calibration curve is expressed by Eq. 2 having an R^2 of 0.98.

$$y = 3261,8 \times \log(x) + 12125 \tag{2}$$

5 Conclusions and Future Work

A calibration protocol was established using the dynamic method of permeation tubes by controlled temperature and carrier flow with a thermogravimetry device. Three main phases were defined in the protocol which allowed to create a concentration range from 2700 to 46 ppb. Using the developed protocol, it was possible to calibrate a GC-IMS device for 2-hexanone attaining a logarithmic calibration curve, $y = 3261{,}8 \times \log(x) + 12125$, with an R^2 of 0.98.and an estimated LOD of 26 ppb.

During protocol development it became evident certain parameters and conditions were crucial for developing an accurate calibration curve. Temperature control was essential in the calculation of an accurate emission rate, whilst this emission rate should be conducted in a period of 4–5 days or more. Whereas for IMS measurements it was essential to allow an interval between flow changes and their respective samples. Nonetheless, if the proper conditions are established, calibration is a straightforward procedure which can be improved and automated by implementing machine learning or artificial intelligence to processing thermogravimetry and GC-IMS spectra data. Moreover, this same protocol can be used for the calibration of VOCs in ppb and ppt ranges of concentration. Calibration of GC-IMS devices in low ppb is a crucial point in implementing it in medical diagnosis or medical devices, and its improvement by automated tools further expands its potential and applicability in the field of medicine.

Acknowledgments. The authors would like to thank the Fundação para a Ciência e Tecnologia (FCT, Portugal) for co-financing of the PhD grants PD/BDE/130204/2017 and PD/BDE/150627/2020 from the Doctoral NOVA I4H Program as well as NMT, S.A. and Volkswagen Autoeuropa Lda respectively. Likewise, acknowledgements are due to The Laboratório de Análises organization and a support lab of the Associated Laboratory for Green Chemistry REQUIMTE of FCT-UNL.

References

1. Ruszkiewicz, D., et al.: Diagnosis od COVID-19 by analysis of breath with gas chromatography-ion mobility spectrometry - a feasibility study. E Clin. Med. **29**, 5019–5540 (2020)
2. Kirk, A., Allers, M., Cochems, P., Langejuergen, J., Zimmermann, S.: A compact high resolution ion mobility spectrometry for fast trace gas analysis. Analyst **138**, 5159–5504 (2013)
3. Borsdorf, H., Eiceman, G.: Ion mobility spectrometry: principles and applications. Appl. Spectrosc. Rev. **41**(4), 323–375 (2006)
4. Creaser, C.S., Griffiths, J.R., Bramwell, C.J., Noreen, S., Hill, C.A., Paul Thomas, C.L.: Ion mobility spectrometry: a review. Part 1. Structural analysis by mobility measurement. R. Soc. Chem. **129**, 984–994 (2004)
5. Kanu, A., Hill Jr., H.: Ion mobility spectrometry detection for gas chromatography. J. Chromatogr. A **1177**(1), 12–27 (2008)
6. Moura, P., Vassilenko, V., Fernandes, J., Santos, P.: Indoor and outdoor air profiling with GC-IMS. In: Technological Innovation for Life Improvement. DoCEIS 2020. IFIP Advances in Information and Communication Technology, vol. 577, pp. 437–444. Costa de Caparica, Portugal (2020)
7. Fernandes, J., Vassilenko, V., Santos, P.: Algorithm for automatic peak detection and quantification for GC-IMS Spectra. In: Technological Innovation for Life Improvement. DoCEIS 2020. IFIP Advances in Information and Communication Technology, vol. 577, pp. 369–377. Costa da Caparica, Portugal (2020)
8. Costello, B.D.L., et al.: A review of the volatiles from the healthy human body. J. Breath Res. **8**, 014001 (2014)
9. Montero-Montoya, R., López-Vargas, R., Arellano-Aguilar, O.: Volatile organic compounds in air: sources, distribution, exposure and associated illness in children. Ann. Glob. Health **84**(2), 225–238 (2018)
10. Santos, P., Roth, P., Fernandes, J., Fetter, V., Vassilenko, V.: Real time mental stress detection through breath analysis. In: Technological Innovation for Life Improvement. DoCEIS 2020. IFIP Advances in Information and Communication Technology, vol. 577, pp. 403–410. Caparica, Portugal (2020)
11. Ruzsanyi, V., et al.: Ion mobility spectrometry for detection of skin volatiles. J. Chromatogr. B **911**, 84–92 (2012)
12. Vassilenko, V., Bragança, A.M., Ruzsanyi, V., Sielemann, S.: Potential and suitability of Ion Mobility Spectrometry (IMS) for breath analysis. In: 6th International Conference on Technology and Medical Sciences (TMSi), pp. 317–318. Porto, Portugal (2010)
13. Pilon, P., Dion, D., Binette, M.-J.: The detection of nicotine in e-liquids using ion mobility spectrometry. Int. J. Ion Mobility Spectrom. **19**, 113–119 (2016)
14. Smith, D., Spanel, P., Fryer, A., Hanna, F., Ferns, G.: Can volatile compounds in exhaled breath be used to monitor control in diabetes mellitus? J. Breath Res. **5**, 1752–1759 (2011)

15. Sutinen, M., et al.: Identification of breast tumors from diathermy smoke by differential ion mobility spectrometry. Eur. J. Surg. Oncol. **45**, 141–146 (2019)
16. Nelson, G.: Gas Mixtures: Preparation and Control. CRC Press, Boca Raton, Florida (1992)
17. Barratt, R.: The preparation of standard gas mixtures. A Rev. Anal. **106**(1265), 817–849 (1981)
18. Spinhirne, J.: Generation and calibration of standard gas mixtures for volatile fatty acids using permeation tubes and solid phase microextraction. Air Poll. Agric. Oper. III **46**(6), 1639–1646 (2003)
19. Boyle, B.: Generating Explosive Calibration Standards with OVG-4 and Permeation Tubes. Owlstone Inc

Correction to: Characteristics of Adaptable Control of Production Systems and the Role of Self-organization Towards Smart Manufacturing

Luis Alberto Estrada-Jimenez, Sanaz Nikghadam-Hojjati, and Jose Barata

Correction to:
Chapter "Characteristics of Adaptable Control of Production Systems and the Role of Self-organization Towards Smart Manufacturing" in: L. M. Camarinha-Matos et al. (Eds.): *Technological Innovation for Applied AI Systems*, IFIP AICT 626, https://doi.org/10.1007/978-3-030-78288-7_4

Chapter "Characteristics of Adaptable Control of Production Systems and the Role of Self-organization Towards Smart Manufacturing" was previously published non-open access. It has now been changed to open access under a CC BY 4.0 license and the copyright holder updated to 'The Author(s)'. The book has also been updated with this change.

The updated version of this chapter can be found at
https://doi.org/10.1007/978-3-030-78288-7_4

© The Author(s) 2022
L. M. Camarinha-Matos et al. (Eds.): DoCEIS 2021, IFIP AICT 626, p. C1, 2022.
https://doi.org/10.1007/978-3-030-78288-7_35

Correction to: Predictive Manufacturing: Enabling Technologies, Frameworks and Applications

Terrin Pulikottil, Luis Alberto Estrada-Jimenez,
Sanaz Nikghadam-Hojjati, and Jose Barata

Correction to:
Chapter "Predictive Manufacturing: Enabling Technologies, Frameworks and Applications" in: L. M. Camarinha-Matos et al. (Eds.): *Technological Innovation for Applied AI Systems*, IFIP AICT 626, https://doi.org/10.1007/978-3-030-78288-7_5

Chapter "Predictive Manufacturing: Enabling Technologies, Frameworks and Applications" was previously published non-open access. It has now been changed to open access under a CC BY 4.0 license and the copyright holder updated to 'The Author(s)'. The book has also been updated with this change.

The updated version of this chapter can be found at
https://doi.org/10.1007/978-3-030-78288-7_5

© The Author(s) 2022
L. M. Camarinha-Matos et al. (Eds.): DoCEIS 2021, IFIP AICT 626, p. C2, 2022.
https://doi.org/10.1007/978-3-030-78288-7_36

Author Index

Printed in the United States
by Baker & Taylor Publisher Services

Printed in the United States
by Baker & Taylor Publisher Services